The 36th Infantry
United States Colored
Troops in the Civil War

# The 36th Infantry United States Colored Troops in the Civil War

*A History and Roster*

JAMES K. BRYANT, II

McFarland & Company, Inc., Publishers
*Jefferson, North Carolina, and London*

LIBRARY OF CONGRESS CATALOGUING-IN-PUBLICATION DATA

Bryant, James K.
The 36th Infantry United States Colored Troops in the Civil War : a history and roster / James K. Bryant, II.
p. cm.
Includes bibliographical references and index.

ISBN 978-0-7864-6878-2
softcover : acid free paper ∞

1. United States. Army. Colored Infantry Regiment, 36th (1864–1866) 2. United States. Army. North Carolina Colored Infantry Regiment, 2nd (1863–1864) 3. United States — History — Civil War, 1861–1865 — Participation, African American. 4. North Carolina — History — Civil War, 1861–1865 — Participation, African American. 5. United States — History — Civil War, 1861–1865 — Regimental histories. 6. North Carolina — History — Civil War, 1861–1865 — Regimental histories. 7. African American soldiers — North Carolina — Registers. 8. United States — History — Civil War, 1861–1865 — Registers. I. Title.
E492.94 36th.B79 2012      973.7'415 — dc23      2012024859

BRITISH LIBRARY CATALOGUING DATA ARE AVAILABLE

©2012 James K. Bryant, II. All rights reserved

*No part of this book may be reproduced or transmitted in any form or by any means, electronic or mechanical, including photocopying or recording, or by any information storage and retrieval system, without permission in writing from the publisher.*

On the cover: Workers in the Dutch Gap canal on the James River in Virginia, 1864 (Library of Congress)

Front cover design by Bernadette Skok (bskok@ptd.net)

Manufactured in the United States of America

*McFarland & Company, Inc., Publishers
Box 611, Jefferson, North Carolina 28640
www.mcfarlandpub.com*

For Ms. Amy

# Table of Contents

| | |
|---|---|
| *List of Abbreviations* | viii |
| *Preface* | 1 |
| *Introduction: The Resurrection of Peter Wilson, Company C, 36th USCT* | 3 |

### Part One: "A Model Regiment"

| | |
|---|---|
| 1. I Belonged to a Man | 10 |
| 2. Noble Men and Patriots | 24 |
| 3. They Are Most Reliable Soldiers | 39 |
| 4. Selected from the Most Intelligent Among Them | 57 |
| 5. De Bottom Rail on Top | 80 |
| 6. First and Foremost of Them All | 101 |
| Conclusion: "Pure Patriotic Principles" | 125 |

### Part Two: Unit Roster

| | |
|---|---|
| 36th Infantry, United States Colored Troops (formerly 2nd North Carolina Colored Volunteers), 1863–1866 | 132 |
| *Appendix 1. Composition of a Regiment of Infantry* | 195 |
| *Appendix 2. U.S. Army Ranks* | 197 |
| *Appendix 3. Unit Organization in the Union Army* | 198 |
| *Appendix 4. Colonel Alonzo G. Draper's Report of Knott's Island, N.C., the Arrest of Nancy White, and the Altercation with Lieutenant Colonel Fredrick F. Wead, 98th New York Volunteers* | 199 |
| *Appendix 5. Letter of Sergeant Major Henry N. Adkins, 36th USCT, Requesting an Appointment as a Second Lieutenant, with Endorsements and Reply* | 203 |
| *Chapter Notes* | 207 |
| *Bibliography* | 229 |
| *Index* | 243 |

# List of Abbreviations

| | |
|---|---|
| *AMA* | *American Missionary Association Manuscripts*, Dillard University, New Orleans, Louisiana |
| CMSR | Compiled Military Service Records |
| Co./Cos. | Company/Companies |
| DU | Rare Book, Manuscript, & Special Collections Library, Duke University, Durham, North Carolina |
| F&S | Field and Staff |
| GPO | Government Printing Office |
| LPL | Lynn Public Library, Lynn, Massachusetts |
| MA | Massachusetts Archives, Boston, Massachusetts |
| *MSSMCW* | *Massachusetts Soldiers, Sailors, and Marines in the Civil War* |
| MHS | Massachusetts Historical Society, Boston, Massachusetts |
| NARA | National Archives and Records Administration, Washington, D.C. |
| NCSA | North Carolina State Archives, Raleigh, North Carolina |
| NHHS | New Hampshire Historical Society, Concord, New Hampshire |
| *NMSUS* | *The Negro in the Military Service of the United States*, Washington, D.C. |
| NOR | *Official Records of the Union and Confederate Navies in the War of the Rebellion.* |
| OR | *War of the Rebellion: A Compilation of the Official Records of the Union and Confederate Armies* |
| OR Supp. | *Supplement to the Official Records of the Union and Confederate Armies.* |
| pt. | part |
| RG 15 | Record Group 15: Records of the Veterans' Administration |
| RG 94 | Record Group 94: Records of the Adjutant General's Office, 1780s-1917 |
| RG 105 | Record Group 105: Records of the Bureau of Refugees, Freedmen, and Abandoned Lands |
| RG 393 | Record Group 393: Records of the United States Army Continental Commands, 1821–1920 |
| ser. | series |
| USAMHI | United States Army Military History Institute, Carlisle, Pennsylvania |
| USCC | United States Colored Cavalry |
| USCLA | United States Colored Light Artillery |
| USCT | United States Colored Troops (usually designated for Infantry) |
| vol./vols. | volume/volumes |
| VTHS | Vermont Historical Society, Montpelier, Vermont |

# Preface

I begin this preface 148 years to the day Colonel Alonzo Draper took command of what was then the 2nd North Carolina Colored Volunteer Infantry at New Bern, North Carolina, and marvel at how far the United States has come since that time. The Civil War has always captured my interest since the day when, living in Alabama, I heard my fourth grade classmate relate how one of his great-grandfathers had been shot in the leg at Gettysburg, decided he had enough of war and returned to Alabama on foot to start his family. More intrigued by the reasons that would compel someone to go so far away to fight in a war than by the fact that had this Confederate soldier continued in the army my classmate might never have been born, I began a life-long fascination with this war.

At the age of 13 during a visit to my birth state of North Carolina, my father presented me with the gift of John G. Barrett's *North Carolina in the Civil War* to see if it would be useful. I read and reread the chapter on Edward A. Wild's "African Brigade" and its raid into the northeastern counties of North Carolina until the pages frayed. During the last year of my undergraduate education, I began one of my careers as a seasonal park ranger at the Fredericksburg and Spotsylvania National Military Park in Fredericksburg, Virginia. One of my first self-initiated projects was researching the five African American Civil War soldiers buried in the Fredericksburg National Cemetery. One of them was Peter Wilson of the 36th USCT. When I discovered that the 36th USCT had been the 2nd North Carolina Colored Volunteers, I was further intrigued in finding out how a member of this unit went from North Carolina and ended up in Fredericksburg, Virginia.

This present work has been 18 years in the making, seeing its first incarnation as a master's thesis in 1996 ("'A Model Regiment': The 36th U.S. Colored Infantry in the Civil War") and a second incarnation as a doctoral dissertation in 2001 ("The Model 36th Regiments: The Contribution of Black Soldiers and Their Families to the Union War Effort, 1861–1866"). It is flattering to see these two efforts of a procrastinating graduate student referenced in footnotes or included in bibliographies of works on black Union soldiers. Most recently, Professor Richard M. Reid has written *Freedom for Themselves: North Carolina's Black Soldiers in the Civil War Era*, a wonderful addition to the broader scholarship on southern black soldiers fighting for the Union. His concise and comprehensive work on four black regiments initially organized in North Carolina is the logical extension of his expertise and interest in General Edward A. Wild's efforts of turning former slaves into soldiers literally in the Confederacy's backyard. The 36th USCT receives its due coverage along with the other two units (the 35th and 37th USCT) he raised as part of his African Brigade.

Although the 36th USCT is rooted in Edward A. Wild and his African Brigade, the story of this "model regiment" can stand on its own as a medium in the transition from slavery to freedom. The soldiers were not alone in this transformation as they not only carried their family members and fellow slaves into this period of vast change, but also brought along their white officers and others who worked on their behalf in this change. Just as important, almost 43 percent of the soldiers in the regiment claimed their place of birth in the counties and localities of Virginia. Thus, the 36th USCT is just as much a Virginia unit as it is a North Carolina one, giving it a broader reach in the history of the highly contested regions of the South during the Civil War.

My long journey has involved numerous people including family, friends, and colleagues for whose moral support and encouragement I am eternally grateful. Several institutions and repositories, including universities, historical societies, as well as state and federal agencies, continue to have my sincerest gratitude for resources, documents, images, and sound advice kindly provided me over the years in the preparation of this work. I hope that this latest effort does justice to the help I have received.

Ultimately, I am solely responsible for the conclusions drawn in this work and claim responsibility for any and all mistakes contained therein. It is my sincerest hope that the 36th USCT as a "model regiment" illuminates what President Abraham Lincoln posed as the meaning of the Civil War in 1863, that the nation "shall have a new birth of freedom." On a smaller but no less important scope, it might help answer the question of an at-risk African American youth visiting the Fredericksburg and Spotsylvania National Military Park more than a decade ago—"What did *we* do in the war?" Peter Wilson, residing in the Fredericksburg National Cemetery, may provide a small part of the answer to this question.

# Introduction

## *The Resurrection of Peter Wilson, Company C, 36th USCT*

If one visits Grave #814 in the Fredericksburg National Cemetery in Fredericksburg, Virginia, she will see etched in the government-issue headstone "Peter Wilson U.S.C.T." A search through the cemetery records of the Fredericksburg and Spotsylvania National Military Park would reveal that Wilson died on June 16, 1864, and that his body was taken some time after the war from a place known as Pierson's Farm in Richmond County. This particular county with several others located between the Rappahannock and Potomac Rivers forms Virginia's Northern Neck region. A search through the *Official Records of the War of the Rebellion* yields a report by Colonel Alonzo G. Draper commanding an expedition of African American soldiers of the 36th USCT in an engagement with Confederate home guard units at Pierson's Farm.[1]

The "USCT" designation stood for United States Colored Troops, a bureau created by the U.S. War Department in May 1863 to administer the affairs of black soldiers serving in the Union army. Wilson's compiled military service record in the 36th Infantry, United States Colored Troops (USCT) confirms his June death; he was killed in a "skirmish with guerrillas."[2]

A more thorough search through pension records reveals that Peter Wilson was born a slave near the town of Windsor in Bertie County, North Carolina, on September 15, 1829, according to an 1867 affidavit of his former owner, Dr. Turner Wilson, of the same locale. Dr. Wilson had owned 32 slaves and 2,500 acres of land in 1860. Nearby was the farm of Patrick Henry Winston, Sr., who was a prominent jurist and state legislator. Before the war, Peter married "according to custom" Judge Winston's house servant Barbery. Their union ended shortly before the war when Barbery allegedly "took up" with another slave of Judge Winston. Post-war testimony from some of Dr. Wilson's former slaves indicated that his owner had always been wary of Peter's marriage to Barbery and had encouraged him to leave her as a result of her apparent infidelity.[3]

As the Civil War was well underway by the spring of 1863, Union forces had already captured key positions in eastern North Carolina, launching frequent expeditions near Windsor. Dr. Wilson, considered a staunch secessionist, had been arrested by Union military authorities and his property (including slaves) confiscated. That summer, Peter Wilson would be among the numerous fugitive slaves seeking refuge at Union-held Plymouth, North Carolina, where he enlisted in the 2nd North Carolina Colored Volunteers. Wilson's enlisting officer, Captain Charles A. Jones of the 1st North Carolina Colored Volunteers, recorded his place of birth as Bertie County, North Carolina. His complexion, eyes, and hair were black and he stood five feet, five inches. Rather than listing "slave" as Wilson's pre-war occupation, Captain Jones recorded "farmer," which was the primary function of slaves throughout the antebellum South as agricultural laborers. Although Wilson's military service and pension records indicated that he was 37 years old at the time of his enlistment, it might very well be possible that Wilson told Jones that he was 34 years old, which would be consistent with his birth year. Poor handwriting initially on the part of Captain Jones in recording the enlistment information and subsequent copying of this information into descriptive books and muster rolls by others during the war could have easily transformed "34 into "37." If the month and date of Wilson's birth is correct, he would have been just 33 years old at the time of his enlistment.[4]

Once enlisted, Private Wilson was sent to the town of New Bern situated between the Trent and Neuse Rivers where his company and regiment were stationed. In August, the 2nd North Carolina transferred to Portsmouth, Virginia, and stationed with other black regiments in the Union-occupied region of southeastern Virginia. Here Wilson met and soon after married his "second wife" Anna Lipscomb in a church ceremony in nearby Norfolk.[5]

Wilson's "Company C" did not participate in the large expedition into the northeastern counties of North Carolina that December liberating his brethren from the shackles of slavery. It was the lot of his company to perform duty at Camp Hamilton in Hampton, Virginia, during these months "to make a parade and attract recruits" for the regiment. But instead of attracting recruits for their infantry regiment, most black recruits in Hampton, enamored by the prospect of savoring the glamour of being cavalrymen, enlisted into the 1st and 2nd U.S. Colored Cavalry regiments instead.[6]

In late February 1864, Wilson and the 2nd North Carolina (now designated the 36th USCT) transferred to St. Mary's, Maryland, where they guarded Confederate prisoners at Point Lookout and made occasional expeditions against Confederate militia and home guard units in Virginia's Northern Neck counties just across the Chesapeake Bay.[7]

Wilson participated in one such expedition into Richmond County in June 1864 and met his demise at the hands of Confederate "guerrillas" in an engagement known as Pierson's Farm. Upon official notification of Wilson's death, his wife Anna, back in Portsmouth, continued to receive rations as the spouse of a Union soldier killed in action. After the war, she received a widow's pension from the U.S. government for several years. At one point, the Bureau of Pensions stopped her monthly payments after allegations that she "had taken up" with another former soldier whom she did not marry were brought to their attention. Her widow's pension was later reinstated as a result of affidavits from her minister, neighbors, and Wilson's former comrades living in Virginia attesting to her good moral character and her destitution without the pension. After a few years, Anna Wilson's widow's pension was suspended again due to an investigation conducted by pension examiners of Wilson's "first wife," Barbery, in North Carolina who claimed that she was his true and only widow. Going by the name of Barbery Bateman, Wilson's first wife had unsuccessfully sought a pension as his widow since the end of the war when some of his North Carolina comrades returned home and related his death. Among the numerous affidavits supporting Barbery's claim included these former soldiers, a son from a previous union before Wilson, and the nephew of Wilson's owner who had served in the Confederate army.[8]

To complicate things further, a woman in North Carolina claiming to be Peter's mother sought a pension as a destitute dependent. Other affidavits from at least five individuals claiming to be Peter's siblings either supported Barbery's pension claim or that of his supposed mother, Phyillis Wilson, who stated that her son never had a wife while a slave. These multiple investigations lasted into the first years of the 20th century with little evidence from the records of a final resolution. Wilson had no children in his "marriages" to either Barbery or Anna.[9] The ironic fact is that Peter Wilson's "life" is only revealed in his death through the testimonies of numerous individuals black and white, former slaves and former masters, soldiers and civilians without Wilson ever writing or uttering a single word. His life continued 45 years after his death in the quest of satisfying pension claims of others and serves as the point of departure for telling the story of the 36th USCT — a regiment composed of mostly former slaves during the Civil War.

The 36th USCT, mustered into federal service on October 28, 1863, participated in one of the earliest large-scale expeditions conducted almost exclusively by black soldiers in the Eastern Theater of the war. It was one of the first black military units assigned to guard duty at one of the war's largest military prisons. As part of an assault by several black regiments, the 36th USCT successfully captured a Confederate defensive position manned by veterans of the "Texas Brigade" serving under Confederate General Robert E. Lee at the Battle of New Market Heights near Richmond, Virginia, in the fall of 1864. The regiment crowned its military achievements by becoming one of the first Union regiments to reach the city limits of the abandoned Confederate capital on April 3, 1865, before being halted by higher authority. The men of the 36th USCT made the transformation from slaves to soldiers inspiring African American war correspondent Thomas Morris Chester to write in 1864, "The 36th is a model regiment and wherever it has operated, it has been distinguished by the undaunted bravery of the men and gallantry of its officers."[10]

The regiment was not only a "model" for southern black soldiers; it also symbolized a hopeful future for African Americans, the vast majority of whom had been slaves before the war. While the soldiers of the 36th USCT went through their military development, their family and kin also made their own transition from slaves into free citizens. Family members left behind in government refugee settlements maintained family ties and kinship networks in the hopes of forging their place in an American society transformed by the war and what President Abraham Lincoln would call the world's "last best hope."

Peter Wilson was one of the 178,975 African Americans serving as Union soldiers during the Civil War and among the 36,847 African American soldiers who lost their lives while in the service of the United States.[11] Wilson also accounted for the more than three-fourths of African Americans who claimed their birthplaces in the nation's slaveholding states that made up the South. This is consistent with the fact that almost 90 percent of the entire black population in the United States in 1860 resided in these particular states and that just fewer than 94 percent of this majority were slaves. Although black southerners served in larger numbers in the Union Army than black northerners, the latter group held the monopoly of having their wartime contributions preserved for historical memory. About 75 percent of the total population of free black male northerners between the ages of 18 and 45 served in the Union Army. These 34,745 soldiers within the northern black population, freed from the restrictions imposed by slavery, enlisted into the army in greater proportion to their regional population than their southern counterparts.[12]

The black soldiers' contribution to the Union war effort had already been committed to the written record by the war's conclusion. Among the earliest accounts was William Wells Brown's *The Negro in the American Rebellion* (1867). Brown, a former slave, sought to glorify the military service of black soldiers justifying the equal treatment they expected to receive. In addition to Brown, three black Union army veterans published general histories of black participation in the Civil War during the latter half of the nineteenth century. They were Joseph T. Wilson, *The Black Phalanx: African American Soldiers in the War of Independence, the War of 1812, and the Civil War* (1887), George Washington Williams, *History of the Negro Troops in the War of the Rebellion, 1861–1865* (1888), and Christian A. Fleetwood, *The Negro as a Soldier* (1895). These veterans had been free men before the war and wrote from the experience of free men and often reflected the point of view of black northerners.

Southern slaves were the central issue of the Civil War for both the Union and Confederate armies. The Confederacy hoped to utilize enslaved black families as they had before the war to sustain their agricultural productivity. Moreover, able-bodied black men, slave and free, were to be used as military laborers. This they did in the first year of the war. By the second year, Union forces had gained footholds in the South. The Union army would be forced, through large numbers of fugitive slaves seeking refuge in Union lines, to recognize the importance of southern black families to the Union war effort.[13]

Peter Wilson (1829–1864), born a slave in Bertie County, North Carolina, served a month short of a year in the 2nd North Carolina Colored Volunteers (36th USCT) before he met his demise at the hands of Confederate "guerrillas." His apparent act of courage in attempting to rescue a fugitive slave while on an expedition into Richmond County, Virginia, earned him his final resting place in the Fredericksburg National Cemetery in spite of the squabbles of his family members in seeking survivor benefits (James K. Bryant, II).

Civil War scholarship during the first half of the 20th century has rarely addressed slavery during the war except as a peripheral issue that would soon become extinguished and treated as an inevitable forgone conclusion. Bell Irvin Wiley, in his classic study of black southerners during the war, wrote in 1938, "Studies of the slave era usually end with the outbreak of the war...those which deal with the period since emancipation usually begin with 1865, or treat the war years in sketchy fashion." Slavery did not immediately end when the war began on April 12, 1861, with the Confederate firing on Fort Sumter, South Carolina. While the start of the war arguably signaled the dismantling of slavery, it hardly suggested the eventual outcome of this "peculiar institution." Recent scholarship from the final decade of the 20th century into the 21st focusing on African Americans in the Civil War has emphasized the fact that their fate lay at the heart of this struggle between North and South intricately linking the Civil War and slavery.[14] This important link had a significant impact on nearly four million African Americans.

Very few regimental histories of black units composed of former slaves have been produced examining their military contributions during the war. Edward G. Longacre's *A Regiment of Slaves*, a study of the 4th USCT during the war, is one of these few. This regiment, recruited in the slave "border state" of Maryland, provides a microcosm of what Longacre terms "an intriguing mix of free blacks and fugitive and liberated chattel."[15] Although a slave state, Maryland remained in the Union during the war. It was the birth state of two of antebellum America's most famous fugitive slaves: Frederick Douglass and Harriett Tubman. Moreover, the 4th USCT was the unit that the aforementioned chronicler of black soldiers in the war, Christian A. Fleetwood, a free black man from Baltimore and Congressional Medal of Honor winner in the war, served as regimental sergeant major.

Most recently, Richard M. Reid's *Freedom for Themselves: North Carolina's Black Soldiers in the Civil War Era* examines the four black Union regiments recruited in North Carolina (to include the 36th USCT) providing a much needed treatment on the subject. Although three of these units initially formed Edward A. Wild's original "African Brigade," they were soon reassigned to different commands and did not serve together by the end of 1863. In the specific case of the 36th USCT, no more than 51 percent of the black soldiers claimed their place of birth in North Carolina. The fact that almost 43 percent claimed their place of birth in Virginia gives the "Old Dominion" as much pride as does the "Old North State" in making contributions to the Union war effort.[16]

Many southern black soldiers were illiterate and had lived in states that outlawed their access to education before the war. Therefore, very few published autobiographies or letters written by them have been available when compared to published letters, newspaper correspondence, autobiographies, and speeches of black northern soldiers. The family and kin of these former slaves who freed themselves or were freed by the Union military still receive moderate attention despite the wealth of general scholarship on wartime Reconstruction efforts.[17] These former slaves and their families placed themselves at a greater risk than their northern comrades because once the former slave joined the Union ranks, the concern over his own status and that of his family increased.

Black Union soldiers, North and South, generally fought for the emancipation of their race. But, northern black freemen often held slightly different motives for going to war than southern freedmen. Although nominally free, black northerners often lacked equality under the laws of the states in which they lived. It was a foregone conclusion in southern states that all black southerners were slaves and part of the racial and patriarchal hierarchy of southern society. Black men born free and residing in northern states fought explicitly to prove themselves equal to their white countrymen. Freed slaves, if not implicitly seeking equality, sought the immediate and practical gains of emancipation and employment for the benefit of themselves, their families, and their communities that had emerged through slavery.

Equality under the laws of the United States would be the result of the former slaves determining the course of the war for both the Union and Confederacy. Former slaves helped the Union government and military create policies on their behalf regardless if such policies had not been the Union's initial intention in prosecuting the war. Union army regiments composed of black men, particularly from the South, demonstrated tangible efforts on their part in elevating their own status while serving the cause of the Union and freedom. The southern black soldier and his family and kin were the primary contributors to these ends. Any military history of southern black soldiers must co-exist with the social history of their antebellum and wartime relationships with their families and fellow slaves. Not only has this necessary link between military and social history been ignored in scholarship dealing with the role of African Americans in the Civil War, but nineteenth-century social history itself has been neglected in general Civil War scholarship. Viewing the Civil War as a catalogue of bloody battles, military strategy and tactics, and brave heroes charging in front of a line of cannon misses the point of why this is a defining period in the American nation. As Maris A. Vinovskis writes, "The study of wars cannot be left only to military historians but must also be undertaken by other scholars, so that we can better appreciate the costs and meanings of warfare in our past as well as today."[18]

In war, things change. The soldiers of the 36th USCT had every reason to believe that their participation and sacrifice in the Union war effort earned them their freedom and guaranteed them equal opportunity under the law in the pursuit of their livelihoods. The regiment not only symbolized a "model regiment" strictly in a military sense, but also functioned as a "model" for the slaves' transition to freedom. It was the Union army that facilitated the military and social development of black Union soldiers and their families in preparation for their new roles as free American citizens.[19] Their participation in the Civil War was a continuing tradition in their struggle for freedom.

The United States originally emerged from such a revolutionary struggle for freedom against imperialist tyranny. African Americans helped to create, internalize, and perpetuate this tradition in spite of the presence of slaves within the former thirteen British colonies of North America. Sylvia Frey, in her work on African American resistance during the American Revolution, concludes that the Revolutionary War created the development of autonomous resistance among African Americans (slave and free) against slavery and racism. "The majority of African Americans," she writes, "whose spirit was no less revolutionary, resorted to cultural assertiveness."[20] This cultural assertiveness emerging from the late 18th century was carried into the new century as slavery took a firmer hold in the American South. This assertiveness took the form of the slave community that sustained generations of black southerners before and during the Civil War. It was this slave community composed of family and kin that contributed to the Union war effort that paved the way toward freedom. African Americans realized the best atmosphere in which to enact legal changes in their status was their participation in a military crisis in which their efforts were needed and valued. As Mary F. Berry suggests, "It was through military service that these adjustments in status could be negotiated."[21]

Although free black northerners never wavered in their calls for active black participation in the military, Union authorities ignored their direct appeals early in the war. It was southern slave families entering Union lines that forced a reluctant United States government to make policies eventually leading to the enlistment of all black soldiers. The southern black solider would offer himself and his family on the "altar of freedom" in throwing off the shackles of slavery forever.

In death, Private Peter Wilson, Company C, 36th USCT, a former slave from Bertie County, North Carolina, speaks volumes about his past without uttering a single recorded word. Yet to his former fellow slaves, comrades-in-arms, and relatives, he becomes the focal point of a broader history seeking to find membership in the great American drama.

# Part One
# "A Model Regiment"

CHAPTER 1

# I Belonged to a Man

*Reconstructing Lives in
Slavery and Secession*

"I heard my father's name was Isaac Bishop and he belonged to Billy Bishop," Civil War veteran Saunders Norfleet told his pension examiners in 1902. Norfleet, born near Britton Cross Roads in Bertie County, North Carolina, confessed that he "[c]an't give year of my birth ... [and] was born a slave to a man named Stephen Norfleet." Saunders appeared on an 1844 inventory of his master's slaves indicating that he had been born in 1834. His master, Stephen Andrews Norfleet, ranked as the third largest cotton producer and seventh largest property owner in the county with 3,952 acres of land valued at $40,000 in 1860. He also fell into the 2.2 percent of North Carolina slaveholders owning 100 slaves or more with 115 slaves contributing to his considerable wealth. "My mother's name was Jennie [or Jinny] Norfleet as she belonged to my master," Saunders also told the examiners. "I derived my name from [my] master."[1]

Saunders, at age 30, enlisted as a private into Company D, 36th USCT, on January 5, 1864, after being "stripped and given a thorough physical examination." His occupation was given as a farmer and he stood 5 feet, 5 inches tall and possessed a black complexion, black eyes, and black hair. Private Norfleet served with his company and regiment in camp at Norfolk and Portsmouth in Virginia. Within two months, his regiment would be sent to Point Lookout, Maryland, serving as guards over Confederate prisoners. By the late summer of 1864, Private Norfleet would serve in the trenches before the Confederate capital of Richmond, Virginia, and received his baptism of fire on September 29, 1864, at New Market Heights (near Richmond, Virginia), popularly known as Deep Bottom by his comrades. Surviving this combat experience, Norfleet was sent to the hospital at City Point in March 1865 for treatment of rheumatism. He was discharged for medical disability on December 12, 1865, at Fort Monroe, Virginia.[2]

Receiving his back pay of $200 after his discharge and his promised $300 enlistment bounty by 1867, Saunders Norfleet married the former Aggie Parker of Gatesville, North Carolina, in 1866. "She is still living with me," the aged Norfleet reported, "I have no children under 16 years of age. I never had a slave wife." Aggie Norfleet had been married previously to a Joseph Parker who died around 1897. They had a number of children and Saunders pointed out to the examiners that "[s]he left him [Joseph Parker] so she said before the war but never got a divorce from him."[3]

Saunders Norfleet disappears from the record after 1907 where his last pension increase was recorded. It is possible that he may have lived well into his 90s or that his death date was not officially recorded in government records. Norfleet represented 52 percent of the

36th's soldiers claiming their birthplaces in the northeastern counties of North Carolina.[4] The 1,076 soldiers who served in the regiment represented only a minute fraction of close to four million slaves living in the South on the eve of the war. The fact that the majority of them were slaves cannot be ignored. Their antebellum life and experiences as human property influenced their decisions to support the Union war effort in exchange for freedom and citizenship.[5]

These future soldiers, more often than not, resided on land holdings with 20 slaves or more. This confirmed the preponderance of small numbers of slaveholders owning the larger portions of the slave population.[6] The plantation and farming regions in northeastern North Carolina and southeastern Virginia were mostly rural. Slaveholders tended to be resident planters and often saw their slaves on a daily basis. Even larger slaveholders owning more than 75 slaves maintained their holdings on smaller units spread among two or more plantations or larger farms within a day's ride from the others.[7] Such large numbers of slaves to small numbers of slaveholders helped foster unique and dynamic slave communities.

Richard G. Cooper of Murfreesboro, Hertford County, North Carolina, owned Romulous Cooper as well as his sisters, Lucy and Elizabeth. Cooper's plantation was valued at $60,000 in 1860, took up 5,600 acres, and included 66 additional slaves. Allen Cooper was also a Cooper slave on the same plantation but not related to Romulous and his sisters. Both Romulous and Allen joined the 36th USCT in late 1863.[8]

Other antebellum slave communities within and between plantations in the region contributed black men who would later serve in the 36th USCT. "I belonged to a man by the name of Hodges Gallop at Currituck [North Carolina] before the war and worked on a farm," recalled Spencer Gallop. Hodges Gallop's "farm" and other holdings in the North Banks District of the county consisted of 1,000 acres valued at $2,000 and 56 slaves. Among these slaves included Spencer's older brother, Malachi, and Malachi's wife, Eliza.[9] Nearby were fellow slaves and future comrades-in-arms John Lee and Hannibal Wheadbee. "I knew him [Malachi Gallop] before the war," Lee recalled years later in a pension affidavit on behalf of Malachi. "He belonged to Hodges Gallop and I to Edward Lee of Perquimans County, N.C. their farms adjoined and we knew each other well." Wheadbee, a slave of H.B. Wheadbee, remembered that he had also "lived very near [Malachi Gallop] and knew him well."[10]

A second set of siblings owned by Hodges Gallop, who also retained their master's surname, were George, Richard, and Nancy. Apparently George and Richard were both romantically involved with another Gallop slave named Ann. According to Nancy Gallop, her brother George "tried to court Ann, who would have nothing to do with him." His sister further asserted that prior to running away and marrying another man in 1863, Ann cohabited for a time with George's brother Richard, a union that produced a daughter. Ann, in her own claim for a widow's pension, maintained that she and George had been formally married in September 1857 and that their marital union produced two children before the war. Two of George's pre-war slave neighbors who were brothers and comrades in the 36th USCT, Thomas and John Blango, supported Ann's claim of being George's legal wife and mother of their two children. Another Gallop slave, James, had married a slave woman named Mabel owned by Caleb T. Sawyer, a small farmer who lived at Powell's Point in Currituck County with his 7 slaves.[11]

Brothers Frank and James Cornick served in Company K while their brother Peter served in Company E. Frank and Peter had been born in Princess Anne County, Virginia. James had been born in neighboring Norfolk County. "I was a slave and John [Gornto] was my owner," Frank recalled after the war. Gornto owned 28 slaves in 1860. John Cornick of

Company I was a slave of James Gornto who owned only 6 slaves in 1860.[12] While the familial relationship between the Cornicks as slaves and the Gorntos as owners is not clear, the complexities of the "peculiar institution" often involved members of the same families whether as slaves or as masters.

Isaac Kellum, who joined Company B, 1st U.S. Colored Cavalry, recalled that he and Samuel Kellum, Company K, 36th USCT, "had been both raised together" in Accomack County on Virginia's Eastern Shore. Samuel was one of 16 soldiers in the 36th claiming their birthplace in Virginia's two Eastern Shore counties.[13] Although Samuel and Isaac served in different units during the war, their regiments served in the same locations with the Army of the James by the fall of 1864. Familial and kinship ties before the war also extended between regiments as well as within a regiment.

Regardless of possible blood relations with their fellow slaves or white masters, these soldiers often kept the surnames of their owners during and after the war like the Jaycox slaves. "I was a brother of Thomas Jaycox," asserted Sawney Jaycox who lived in neighboring Perquimans County, "we were raised in North Carolina about 30 miles below Elizabeth City. When I was partly grown my master took us from Windsor to Franklin Co. N.C. I was always with my brother from children up to the time he died [in 1897]." Jesse C. Jaycox owned the Jaycox brothers. A possible half-brother of Thomas and Sawney, Henry Jaycox had received wages of up to $8 a month for work performed on their master's plantation. Henry used these funds for purchasing food and clothing for his mother, Celia, living on the plantation of Jonathan Jaycox. All three would serve in the 36th USCT by 1864. Another set of siblings owned by Jesse Jaycox was Cicero Jaycox and his half-brother, Richard, who also kept their owners' name while soldiers during the war. John Buck of Company D told his pension examiners several years after the war that he "was born and raised in Pitt Co. N.C ... and was owned by one John Buck, after whom I took my name."[14]

Of course not all members of the 36th USCT used or kept the names of their owners. David Henderson of Petersburg, Virginia, changed his name to David H. Allen prior to running away from his master and enlisting in the regiment. He feared his master, Dr. Epps of City Point, would find him. His parents used Henderson for their surname, which may have been the name of a previous owner or one of the family's own choosing. Perhaps in deference to his own father, who apparently served in another black regiment under the name Henderson and maybe to prevent confusion, the younger Henderson kept the name Allen for the duration of his service in the 36th and changed it back at war's end. Frederick Henry Harris, who lived near Warsaw in Richmond County, Virginia, dropped his father's surname, Harris, when he enlisted in Company G. He added it back after the war. John Bufort of Currituck County, North Carolina, who joined Company D in January 1864, gave the name of his parents as Leon and Charity Ashby when he married his second wife in 1880. More than likely, his surname was one of his own choosing or that of his last owner if it was different from his parents.[15] Nevertheless, Bufort knew the names of his parents despite differences in their surnames revealing the general acknowledgement of familial ties among slaves and recognition of such relationships even if their surnames did not match or they had different owners.

This also provided insight into how slaves identified themselves. Slave-naming practices served the slaves' own purposes rather than those of their white masters. Since male slaves were more likely to be sold than female slaves, males were often given the names of male relatives (fathers, brothers, grandfathers, or uncles) as a way of maintaining familial links with blood kin.[16] Frank Cornick claimed that "I never had any name other than Frank Cornick. My Fathers name was Frank Cornick. My mother Nancy Cornick." James Cornick of Company I (no sibling relation to Frank, but possibly related to John Cornick of the same company), who had been born near the courthouse in Princess Anne County, Virginia, recalled, "My father's name was James Cornick ... my mother's name was Betsy Cornick.... I don't know how my father got the name Cornick but I took my name from him."[17]

Many soldiers of the 36th USCT went by their antebellum names since their masters and other white southerners had acknowledged them. Unsure of their treatment within the Union ranks under white officers, black soldiers continued using these names while in the army. However, if a name were to be changed, the soldiers preferred changing their surname instead of their first names as suggested by post-war pension applications.[18]

If slaves could determine their identity through naming practices, they had little accurate knowledge of their ages and birth dates. Many of the soldiers of the 36th and their families shared the same problem before the war as former slave-turned-abolitionist editor Frederick Douglass did. "By far the large part of the slaves know as little of their ages as horses know theirs," Douglass sarcastically proclaimed from his own slave experiences in Maryland, "and it is the wish of most masters within my knowledge to keep their slaves thus ignorant." Sometimes, slaveholders provided their former slaves with this information. More often than not, slaves resorted to identifying significant events such as births, marriages, and deaths based upon coinciding events of the day. Events for agricultural laborers in particular included natural occurrences such as blizzards, floods, and drought. In one instance, Private Harrison Gordon of Richmond County, Virginia, recalled that he had lived in neighboring King George County "at the time of the hanging of John Brown" before returning to his birthplace. Gordon would enlist in Company G during the spring of 1864. In another instance, Ann Maria Brown recalled several years after the war that she and her husband, Private Moses Brown of Company H, had been married on "the very day Cape Hatteras, N.C. fell [August 29, 1861]."[19]

Slaves knew, as former slave Booker T. Washington asserted in his 1901 autobiography *Up from Slavery*, they "must have been born somewhere at some time." Typical was Private Noah C. Cherry of Bertie County, North Carolina, who remembered, "I was born in slavery and have but slight knowledge of my age, or the circumstances surrounding my birth, but as near as I can say I was born on the eighth day of August, 1830."[20] Forty-two years after the war, Spencer Gallop presented his pension examiners with a family Bible printed in 1845. It listed the name of his parents (both using "Gallop" as their surname) and his birth date as March 16, 1837, and his brother Malachi with a birth date of March 27, 1827. Spencer admitted to his examiners that the entries had been made in 1869 as "he had no Bible before the Civil War and consequently had no record." Therefore, when he enlisted into the 36th he gave his age "to the best of his judgment" which was 19 in 1863.[21] Quite possibly the Gallop veterans received their birth dates and ages from their former owners as their comrade James H. Samuel had. Samuel, a "farmhand" owned by Seth Rockwell of Richmond County, Virginia, gave his birth date as August 10, 1843. "I remember [this] date as given [to] me by my former owners," he recalled.[22]

In 1917, Victoria Broward Cornick, widow of Private Henry Cornick of Company A, testified on her age in support of her application to receive a widow's pension. She stated:

> I have no record of the date of my birth, and have to guess at my age. I cannot tell you how old I was when the Civil War closed. I cannot tell you how old I was when I first got married. I was born July 16 but do not know the year. I think I will be fully 69 years old next July. I believe I am older than that but will say I will be 69 to be on the safe side.[23]

Mrs. Cornick had been one of former President John Tyler's 43 slaves on his Charles City County, Virginia, farm where she had remained during the war. She married Henry Cornick in 1910.[24]

The average age of the soldiers in the 36th USCT was 26. Anthony Collins, a farmer from Norfolk, Virginia, became the oldest member of the regiment at age 52 when he

1844 slave list. Private Saunders Norfleet, Company D, 36th USCT is the 13th name listed on this inventory of slaves owned by Stephen A. Norfleet of Bertie County, North Carolina. "My mother's name was Jennie Norfleet as she belonged to my master," he related years after the war. "I derived my name from [my] master." "Jinny's" name (the second one) can be seen to the right of Saunders'. Lists such as these give a stark reality to those who could claim "I belonged to a man." This was the history of the majority men of the 36th USCT (Norfleet Papers, Southern Historical Collection, Wilson Library, University of North Carolina at Chapel Hill).

enlisted in Company E on August 13, 1863. He was discharged on June 1, 1865. Zachariah Taylor, at age 14, became the youngest member of the regiment when he enlisted in Company I on September 13, 1863. This native of Blackwater in Princess Anne County, Virginia, had been a waiter before the war and was mustered out with the regiment in 1866.[25] Assuming that the typical antebellum male slave reached his peak labor performance between the ages of 16 and 26, it is no wonder southern planters as well as Confederate military authorities dreaded the prospect of their slaves escaping to Union lines. These particular slaves were the South's primary source of agricultural and military labor.[26] Moreover, male slaves successfully bringing family and kin with them into Union lines decreased the South's manpower in supporting the Confederate war effort. The role of the family would take on even greater importance within the community that slaves had made for themselves.

Slave marriages were major ties, both real and symbolic, in creating and strengthening the slave family within the larger community. It is difficult to determine the exact number of soldiers in the 36th who had married as slaves before the war. Company G was the only company listing the marital status of soldiers in its records. There were 13 married soldiers and 38 single soldiers in this particular company. Since the average age for the black soldiers in the regiment was 26, soldiers in their mid-20s and older seemed to have had already married and had children at the start of the war.[27] Miles James and his wife, Sarah Brock, residing near Norfolk, Virginia, had married sometime in June 1850 and "being slaves were not married by a minister." The couple had two children born to them during the war: John in 1861 and Ella Frances in 1862. James, at age 34, joined Company B in 1863.[28]

Marriage ceremonies varied from the simple consent of the master to formal ceremonies performed by slave owners or by members of the slave community. An example of the first case was Paul and Lucy Wiggins of Gates County, North Carolina, who had been married sometime in 1855. "We were not married by any ceremony," Lucy recalled, "just by the 'master's mouth.' Paul asked him for me and he said 'if you want her you can have her.'" Paul later enlisted into the 36th in 1864.[29] An example of the second case involved John Critcher of Westmoreland County, Virginia, who married his slave, Susan Johnson, to future 36th soldier, James H. Johnson. "Whilst my slave," Critcher wrote, "she was married by me out of the Episcopalian Prayer Book, in my parlour, according to the most approved form of that day."[30] Ann and George Gallop's contested marriage in 1857 "consisted in obtaining the consent of their owners and then laying their hands on the bible and promising to live together as man and wife: a colored man (acting as minister of the gospel but having no license) married them."[31]

The power of white slaveholders to separate slave couples prevailed despite their general attempts to maintain stable marital unions among their slaves. John Cornick of Company I had been married to a slave woman named Mary ten years before the war. She was sold away by his master Horatio Cornick of Princess Anne County, Virginia. Marrying again in 1855, Cornick suffered the sale of his second wife shortly thereafter. In 1863, he married Mary Cannon whose sisters lived a few houses away from them on their master's plantation.[32]

Since the majority of African Americans resided in the South as slaves in 1860, most soldiers of the 36th had been slaves prior to the time of the firing on Fort Sumter, South Carolina, on April 12, 1861.[33] Only Companies C, F, and H listed whether soldiers had been free on or before the firing on Fort Sumter, South Carolina. At least 3.8 percent of the regiment's soldiers had been free before the war although there were probably more soldiers from the other companies whose true status went unrecorded. Six soldiers claimed their birthplaces in northern non-slaveholding states. They were: Henry N. Adkins, Company E, a gardener from New York City; Samuel Guy, Company I, a coachman from Camden, New Jersey; Daniel Parker, Company I, a servant from Chambersburg, Pennsylvania; John A. Brown, Company K, a barber from New Castle, Maine; and George E. Pool, Company K, a sailor from New York City. One soldier, Charles H. Williams, worked as a waiter before joining Company H and gave his birthplace as Bermuda.[34]

Three soldiers from Company H, Rigdon Mosley of Craven County, North Carolina, Riley Moore of Washington, North Carolina, and John Stewart of Bertie County, North Carolina, indicated that they had been "born free." All three were listed as farmers. These free men probably worked as tenant farmers, farm laborers, or worked their own lands in the North Carolina plantation counties of Beaufort, Bertie, Currituck, and Pasquotank as well as Norfolk and Nansemond Counties in Virginia.[35] Freeborn Moses Brown of Hamilton, Martin County, North Carolina, married his free wife, Ann Maria, before going to Union lines and enlisting into Company H. A friend of the couple recalled that they had been married in 1861 "at my home by ... .a Justice of the Peace." Brown's occupation had been listed as a fireman possibly on the railroad before the war and he had been "free on or before April 19, 1861."[36]

Richard Etheridge, born a slave but apparently free before the war, had been living with the white family of John B. Etheridge on Roanoke Island. He would join Company F and later promoted to the rank of Commissary Sergeant. Although Etheridge's mother, Rachel Dough, was a slave owned by another family, speculation remains that his father was possibly the Outer Banks' wealthy entrepreneur John B. Etheridge. Richard Etheridge would gain local notoriety after the war as the "Keeper" (or chief) of the African American crew at Pea Island for the United States Life Saving Service stationed along North Carolina's Outer Banks.[37]

The bulk of the 36th's soldiers were listed as farmers for their occupation when enlisting since agricultural labor was the primary work they performed as slaves. The 760 men identified as farmers made up about 71 percent of the regiment.[38] The regiment also included 119 laborers, 34 servants, 25 waiters, 19 carpenters, 11 fishermen, 11 teamsters, 5 sailors, 5 blacksmiths, 5 masons or bricklayers, 4 shinglers or shingle makers, 3 hostlers, 3 oysterman, 2 coopers, 3 cooks, and 3 employed by the government (probably as laborers).[39] These skilled individuals may have been employed by Union forces in their talents when they entered Union lines. It was not unusual for former slaves to become personal servants to white Union officers or cooks and waiters for a Union general's headquarters. Some of the youngest members of the regiment with ages ranging from 14 to 16 served as servants, waiters, errand boys, and drummers.[40]

Pre-war occupations have to be examined carefully and are not be taken immediately at face value. Anson Farrier of Kennansville, Duplin County, North Carolina, was listed as an engineer for his pre-war occupation. His pension information provided no indication that he practiced this learned profession before the war, and he worked as a laborer following the war. Perhaps the recruiting officer recorded this particular occupation at the time of Private Farrier's enlistment since he probably worked as a general laborer for the army's engineer department. March and George Ferebee, both of Currituck County, North Carolina, and serving in Company E, were also listed as engineers. In a similar way, soldiers listed as teamsters for their pre-war occupation often had transported military supplies for the ordnance and quartermaster departments before their enlistment. Recruiting officers often had great difficulty in getting officials in the army's engineering, ordnance, and quartermaster departments to release black laborers who had enlisted into the USCTs but were still employed by these departments on detached service or on special labor details.[41]

Other pre-war occupations not necessarily held in abundance by black southerners generally or the 36th's soldiers in particular were those of James T. Johnson, a brakeman from Suffolk, Virginia (Company B); Simon Gaylord, a merchant from Washington, North Carolina (Company F); William Watts, a butcher from Hampton, Virginia (Company H); and Solon Green, a miner from Smithfield, Virginia (Company K). It is not clear if these soldiers were independently employed, apprentices (free or slave), or slaves hiring themselves out.[42] Nevertheless, some of these soldiers might have held positions of prestige and responsibility while slaves. Isaiah Dickson of Company D, who had been a slave of Mrs. Betsey Walke of Norfolk, Virginia, had been "sort of a preacher" before the war according to one of his former comrades and confirmed by the company descriptive book. John Buck of Martin County, North Carolina, had been a slave, but was listed as a clerk in his company's descriptive book.[43]

Although most of the future soldiers who served in the 36th USCT resided in rural areas, a significant number of its members lived and worked in the urban areas of Norfolk and Portsmouth in southeastern Virginia. Norfolk County, Virginia, with 112 soldiers in the 36th claiming it as their place of birth, held the single highest number for a birthplace in the regiment. Approximately 96.5 percent of the slaveholders in the county owned between 1 and 19 slaves.[44] Slaves in this county had more opportunities to acquire skilled occupations and trades, hire themselves out, and become part of a larger African American community consisting of both slaves and free persons.

Agricultural labor was the primary support slaves gave to the Confederacy as white southerners marched off to battle. It is clear that several future soldiers of the 36th USCT soldiers were previously employed as farm laborers supplying the Confederacy with food, military laborers on fortifications, teamsters transporting essential supplies, or personal servants to Confederate officers or units before going to Union lines. A Union officer stationed at Fort Monroe near Hampton in 1862 understood the value of fugitive slaves who had been connected with the Confederate Army. He wrote:

> Although we had a secret spy service of white men we never really got any information of value through it. The only information which proved of notable assistance to us we got from the fugitive negroes. These negroes all passed through the rebel lines in escaping to our protection. Many of them had been servants of officers in the rebel army, and we got much information from them.[45]

Prior to their enlistment, these men provided Union forces with useful information concerning activities of white inhabitants in northeastern North Carolina and southeastern Virginia. This often involved citizens in these occupied areas who supposedly declared their loyalty to the United States, but covertly aided Confederate partisan guerrilla forces or who were guerrillas themselves. Andrew Messner of Company F, native of Camden County, North Carolina, told his white officers that Mrs. Patsey Grandy was the wife of guerrilla captain Cyrus Grandy and that he had lived with them for 21 years as their slave. He reported that Mrs. Grandy "furnished the guerrillas with bacon, [and] lard ... she also sends bacon across the lines to sell to the Rebel Army." Erastus Furby of Company A who had been born in Norfolk County, Virginia, but raised across the state line near Sligo in Currituck County, North Carolina, reported to Union military officials that William Sussden of Currituck County had been a Confederate "guerrilla." This information earned Furby the position as a scout for Union cavalry patrols in pursuit of Sussden.[46]

According to the joint testimony of Peter Furby and Bristow Foreman, Edmund Simmons of Currituck County, North Carolina, "used to send provisions to the rebels at Roanoke Island" before its capture by Union forces in early 1862. Furby, a native of Currituck County, and Foreman, a native of neighboring Princess Anne County, Virginia, joined Company A and both rose to the rank of sergeant. Simmons did not escape the notice of his own slave Robert Frost who reported "he used to feed ... Rebel Cavalry without pay, from sympathy." Frost later joined Company A and rose to the rank of corporal. Bristow Foreman also reported to Union authorities that E.W. Albertson of Pasquotank County, North Carolina, a suspected guerrilla, "was a rank secessionist" and had served with Confederate forces early in the war. Foreman claimed to have known Albertson well since he, himself, had "been working in rebel fortifications" and saw Albertson in the army.[47]

Instead of succumbing to harsher measures and surrendering their own humanity under the infant Confederacy, slaves accumulated resources created in antebellum days through the slave community and prepared for "an unprecedented struggle for freedom." For the moment, they would watch and wait to ascertain their best course of action. W.E.B. Du Bois, the preeminent African American scholar, aptly expressed the views of the general slave population at the beginning of the war. "There was no use in seeking refuge in an army which was not an army of freedom; and there was no sense in revolting against armed masters who were conquering the world," he wrote.[48] The soldiers of the 36th USCT and their families bided their time to see what direction the war would take. As soon as Union forces began capturing key strategic areas of eastern North Carolina by early 1862, the general slave population in the region cautiously evaluated whether to stay put or seek refuge in Union lines.

Evidence during the war years supports the idea that the decision of slaves to cast their lot either with the Union or Confederacy was a slave community decision. Runaway slaves during antebellum days tended to be young men escaping alone; however, the Civil War changed the faces of runaway slaves once the fighting commenced.[49] More slave families escaped to Union lines as opportunities presented themselves even if other family or community members were left behind.

The legacy of the antebellum runaway slave loomed large in the minds of slaves on the eve of the Civil War. The influence of these runaway slaves before the war had undermined the arguments of white southerners that slavery benefited both slave and master. Even Elizabeth Curtis Wallace, the wife of a Norfolk County, Virginia, slaveholder, wrote sometime before the war that "if masters of slaves were uniformly kind, considerate, and forebearing towards them, treating them well, and making them comfortable in all respects there would in my opinion never had been any runaways — or any underground railroad." Mrs. Wallace resided at the Glencoe Plantation in the same county that many of the 36th's soldiers and their families had resided as slaves and would later conduct military operations during the war.[50]

Captain Charles B. Wilder, a white Union officer in charge of supervising black refugees in and around Fort Monroe, Virginia, in May 1863 testified before an investigating committee on the condition of 10,000 former slaves under his supervision. "They come here from all about, from Richmond and 200 miles off in North Carolina," he stated. Having been a missionary among these freedmen early in the war before receiving his army commission, Wilder elaborated further:

> When I got at the feelings of these people I found they were not afraid of the slaveholders. They said there was nobody on the plantations but women and they were not afraid of them.... One woman came through 200 miles in Men's clothes. I found hundreds who had left their wives and

families behind. I asked them "Why did you come away and leave them there?" and I found they had heard these stories [about being sold in slavery to Cuba], and wanted to come see how it was. "I am going back again after my wife" some of them have said "When I have earned a little money." ... I have had them come to me to borrow money, or to get their pay, if they earned a months wages, and to get passes. "I am going for my family" they say. "Are you not afraid to risk it?" "No I know the Way." ... Colored men will help colored men and they will work along by paths and get through.[51]

Fugitive slaves, usually men, would often venture out to ascertain conditions within Union lines before returning with their families. For some slave families, conditions may have been relatively better on a plantation with the white master and overseer away in the Confederate army. Heavy reliance and responsibility would be placed on the slave families for continued plantation operations. For other slave families, true freedom meant physical removal from the place of their enslavement. The Union army could render needed sanctuary. Moreover, working on behalf of the Union war effort made their perceptions of freedom real.

Malachi and Spencer Gallop left the Currituck County, North Carolina, plantation of their master Hodges Gallop for nearby Roanoke Island held by Union forces during the fall of 1863. Their fellow slaves, John Lee and Hannibal Whitby, also left with them. "I cut wood and helped to build forts for the Yankees," Spencer Gallop remembered on his service as a laborer on Roanoke Island. At least seven of the Gallop slaves enlisted into the 2nd North Carolina Colored Volunteers (36th USCT) in the late summer of 1863. Romulous Cooper's sister Lucy recalled, "We all stayed with our owners until Newberne N.C. was captured then we left our owners and came to Newberne N.C. I think my brother ... came to Newberne fore [sic] we all did." One of Jesse C. Jaycox's slaves, Soney Jaycox, escaped with his wife, Hannah, and eight month old son, Madison, from their owner's Perquimans County plantation to Roanoke Island sometime in December 1862.[52] An illustrative example of the general exodus of slaves to Union lines once they captured important towns and points in eastern North Carolina were the 40 slaves owned by the Grimes family of Pitt County, North Carolina, "that went to the Yankees in Washington, N.C." in 1862. Twenty-one of the group were female with all but three under the age of 16. The oldest in the group was a 64-year-old man. Pitt County had 45 soldiers serving in the 36th USCT.[53] One slaveholder in southeastern Virginia complained to a Confederate legislator in August 1861 "in the last twenty days, some forty (40) or fifty (50) [slaves] have thus escaped" from the lower portion of the Nansemond River near Newport News.[54] Escape was indeed a group decision that included men, women, and children as well as young and old alike.

Lucy Wiggins remembered that she and her husband Paul left their Gates County master and "came through the [Union] lines together," with their daughter Adeline, where they worked on the confiscated Baker Farm near Norfolk prior to Paul's enlistment into the 36th. Sixteen-year-old David H. Allen somehow managed to elude his City Point, Virginia, master and find his way to Union-held southeastern Virginia by 1863. It is possible he may have escaped to Union regiments serving in the Army of the Potomac and followed a transferred unit to Fort Monroe near Hampton. He may have also served as a servant or errand boy to Union soldiers before enlisting as the bugler for Company A due to his young age.[55]

It is not clear how many slaves voluntarily left North Carolina and Virginia farms for Union lines. Recent scholarship has suggested that most North Carolina slaves entering Union lines arrived within the first two years of the war, since most slaves in the state resided in these captured areas. By 1863 approximately 37,706 Virginia slaves eluded capture by wartime slave patrols, home guard units, and Confederate forces in seeking their freedom. This number was slightly over 10 percent of Virginia's estimated slave population at that time.[56] Slaves in these areas were definitely supporting the Union cause by the actions of their feet.

One impetus for slave families to seek refuge in Union lines was the mass removal of slaves from eastern North Carolina into the interior by their masters as Union forces began occupying key areas along the coastal regions. Slaveholders hoped that by transplanting their slaves on landholdings further inland or hiring out their slaves to trusted colleagues in the Piedmont region, they could protect their human property. Often this involved the breakup of families. Many North Carolina slaves escaped to keep their families intact, thereby reconciling themselves to casting their lot with Union military forces whether or not they were destined to bring freedom.[57]

Straddling the North Carolina and Virginia border mere miles from the Atlantic Coast was the Great Dismal Swamp that provided another source of motivation and an escape avenue for soldiers, their families, and kin associated with the 36th USCT. This one thousand square mile swamp dominated the line between Elizabeth City, North Carolina, and Norfolk, Virginia. Many of the future soldiers in the 36th USCT who hailed from Camden, Chowan, Currituck, Gates, Pasquotank, and Perquimans Counties in North Carolina, as well as Isle of Wight Nansemond, Norfolk, and Princess Anne Counties in Virginia, were quite familiar with the mysterious significance this region held before the war. This region would figure prominently in the 36th USCT's early military operations in late 1863.[58]

Perhaps one of the most notable "maroon" communities of significance in the antebellum United States, the Great Dismal Swamp claimed an estimated population of 2,000 fugitive slaves, free blacks, and those of Indian ancestry residing within its borders at any given time. Constant fear of slave insurrection in the areas of northeastern North Carolina and southeastern Virginia plagued white residents in the area in the years following Nat Turner's slave rebellion in 1831 in nearby Southampton County, Virginia. The specter of the Great Dismal Swamp only reinforced this white fear.

Most importantly for antebellum slaves, the Great Dismal Swamp symbolized potential freedom through the folklore and culture of the maroon community. As a practical measure, fugitive slaves from the region before the war sought refuge in the Swamp where most white "paddyrollers" dared not venture. They understood white fears of slave insurrection and isolated communities that threatened the widely scattered farms and plantations of white slaveholders and non-slaveholders alike. Nevertheless, the community emerging from the Swamp maintained its existence for several decades. While most slaves in the antebellum South did not run away (or failed in the attempt), many slaves had genuine sympathy and hidden admiration for those who did successfully escape and defy the peculiar institution of slavery. In some instances, the Swamp maroons ventured out among slaves on nearby farms and plantations, perhaps making contact with their actual family members. For slaves living near the Great Dismal Swamp, the knowledge of and potential communication with escaped family members currently residing in the Swamp elicited an emotional mixture of anxiety, relief, and pride.[59]

Scottish-born James Redpath — "The Roving Editor" and contemporary chronicler of John Brown's antislavery exploits in "Bleeding Kansas" — visited the Great Dismal Swamp in 1857, dubbing the region "Canada in the United States" in its connection with fugitive slaves. Redpath related in his description of the region the second-hand narrative of Charley who had escaped his master into the Swamp some years before and later found his way to the real Canada. Charley, who had been given up for dead, discovered that his master had forced his wife to marry another man who he deemed a poor choice for a mate. How Charley was able to discover this information about his wife neither he nor Redpath revealed. The "grapevine" communication line between "Swampers" and surrounding slave community continued to transmit information while being concealed from white residents.[60]

"Dar is families growed up in dat ar Dismal Swamp dat never seed a white man, an' would be skeered most to def to see one," Charley stated as Redpath reprinted his transcribed narrative, "Dreadful scenes, I tell ye, 'sprerienced in de Dismal Swamp, sometimes, when de masters comes dar. Dey shoot down runaways, and tink no more sendin' a ball t'rough dar hearts and sendin' dar hearts into 'Ternity dan jist nothin' at all. But de balls will be seen in 'Ternity, when de master gets dar 'spectin' to stay; 'spect dey'll get dispinted a heap!" Charley believed that it was safer to leave the Dismal Swamp after such experiences as white slave patrols grew more aggressive in their pursuit of fugitive slaves even into the Great Dismal Swamp. This prompted Charley to conclude "'Spect I better not tell de way I comed: for dar's lots more boys comin' same way I did."[61]

Frederick Douglass seconded Charley's adherence to a code of secrecy among runaway slaves in the antebellum South. Douglass believed that the revelation of such escape routes and locations along the Underground Railroad would "most undoubtedly induce greater vigilance on the part of the slaveholders ... and thereby run the hazard of closing the slightest avenue by which a brother slave might clear himself of the chains and fetters of slavery." Joseph Church, a slave hired out as a lumberman in the Dismal Swamp, told Frederick Law Olmsted touring the Great Dismal Swamp in 1853 that not only children of fugitive slaves had been born and bred in the Swamp, but the skeletons of those fugitives shot by their masters later described by Charley could still be seen. Church had buried the bodies of some of these executed fugitives. "'But some on 'em would rather be shot than be took, sir,'" Church informed Olmstead.[62]

Fears of slave rebellion did not hinder continued trade (albeit illegal) between escaped slaves residing in the Swamp and white southerners (mostly of the poorer class) living along its borders. The importance of the broader region to the economic and transportation development of the area would have significant impact on the maroon community. Between 1816 and 1861, the Dismal Swamp Land Company produced close to 1.5 million shingles a year from the swamp's native juniper trees. Free black men, hired slaves, and runaways were actively employed in shingle production. The 36th USCT had at least four shinglers or shingle makers before the war as well as three lumbermen from the surrounding region. Additionally, the swamp canal, completed in 1805, enabled goods and produce to travel between points along North Carolina's Albermarle Sound and Virginia's Chesapeake Bay. Olmsted in 1853 noted that the hired slave lumberman "lives measurably as a free man; hunts, fishes, eats, drinks, smokes and sleeps, plays and works, each when and as much as he pleases." Moreover, the Great Dismal Swamp became a literary haven for the likes of Harriet Beecher Stowe through her 1856 novel *Dred: A Tale of the Dismal Swamp* and Henry Wadsworth Longfellow through his poem "The Slave in the Dismal Swamp."[63]

Since maroon communities in the southern United States were a rarity when compared to those in the Caribbean and South America, slaves in eastern North Carolina and southeastern Virginia to include the soldiers who would serve in the 36th USCT strengthened their own slave communities in admiration of the independence of the Swamp maroons. The folklore derived from the Great Dismal Swamp, including the socio-religious position of "conjurers" and "root doctors," may have maintained a sense of hope and communal inclusiveness for many slaves. Such attributes enabled many to strike out for freedom with their families when war finally came.

The fact that large numbers of slaves in the South did not participate in massive large-scale uprisings against their masters at the time of John Brown's ill-fated raid on Harpers Ferry, Virginia (now West Virginia), in 1859 or during the Civil War confounded both white northerners and southerners. Black southerners, both free and enslaved, knew they stood to lose what little they possessed by participating in such uprisings that had high probabilities of failure. They were very much aware of the control masters held over slaves and how very little they could manipulate things within their society to their own advantage. All they could do for the moment was protect themselves, their families, and communities from any consequences that could result from the slightest hint of a slave rebellion or insurrection against their masters. As the Civil War got underway, the slave society and its inherent power moved into a state of flux and slaves began to seize the initiative for their own benefit.

Although constantly in a state of change and adaptation from slavery itself, the antebellum slave community sustained familial and kinship ties through mutual cooperation and support during the war. Frederick Douglass recalled his own experience among his fellow slaves while hired out in 1835. Douglass wrote:

> For the ease with which I passed the year, I was, however, somewhat indebted to the society of my fellow-slaves. They were noble souls; they not only possessed loving hearts, but brave ones. We were linked and interlinked with each other. I loved them with a love stronger than any thing I have experienced since. It is sometimes said that we slaves do not love and confide in each other. In answer to this assertion, I can say, I never loved any or confided in any people more than my fellow-slaves, and especially those with whom I lived at Mr. Freeland's. I believe we would have died for each other. We never undertook to do any thing, of any importance, without a mutual consultation. We never moved separately. We were one; and as much so by our tempers and dispositions, as by the mutual hardships to which we were necessarily subjected by our condition as slaves.[64]

The soldiers who joined the 36th USCT came from similar slave communities before the war. Echoing Douglass, these soldiers and their families "were one" and would act with "mutual consultation" on the course of their future as the war got underway.

The former slaves carried a reverence for familial bonds and kinship as they escaped to Union-controlled territories in eastern North Carolina and southeastern Virginia. No longer would any of them belong to any man. They would seek to assert their own rights as free people and citizens once they entered Union lines. Their aspirations would help dictate Union policy in their favor as the war progressed.[65] The southern slave was the primary catalyst in gaining eventual freedom for African Americans through the Civil War. These former slaves who enlisted into black regiments like the 36th USCT were the symbolic agents for carrying this mission out on the battlefields, while their families continued supporting them and the general war effort within Union lines.

Like white northerners and southerners who went to war in 1861, the black southerners who would join the 36th USCT and their families had lives before the war. Their lives were as simple or as complicated as most white Americans during the mid-nineteenth century. What made their lives significantly different from other Americans was the fact that they were the property of others because of the color of their skin. Within the restrictive boundaries of antebellum southern society, black southerners shaped their individual lives, familial relationships, and community actions in coping under an unjust institution. Black southerners, like those connected to the 36th USCT during the Civil War, would not be passive bystanders on the road to preserve the Union, but would set the stage of becoming active participants in an unprecedented struggle for freedom. This would not only forever change their own lives and status, but also change the lives of every American citizen within the span of four years.

CHAPTER 2

# Noble Men and Patriots

*Forming the 2nd North Carolina Colored Volunteers, August–November, 1863*

"I spent the night and Saturday in the camp of the 2nd N.C. Col Reg of Vol. where I was treated with great kindness by Col. [Alonzo G.] Draper, Lieuts. [Joseph J. Hatlinger], and [Sidney W.] Phillips," the Reverend H.S. Beals, an American Missionary Association (AMA) agent, reported to his superiors at Union-occupied New Bern, North Carolina, in August 1863, "These officers are noble men, as well as patriots. Never a word of profanity did I hear among them and they seemed to have an almost fatherly care of their men as well as the qualities of good soldiers." The clergyman's paternalistic impression of the black soldiers' camp quickly gave way to the "voice of prayer & praise" on that first evening that inspired "the spirit of earnest devotion in every heart."[1]

The next morning, Beals visited the nearby camp of 1,200 black men, women, and children "gathered from inland portions of the state." At the entrance gate, he encountered a black man preaching to his neighbors that included about 200 black soldiers.[2] "The preacher had no church connection," Beals wrote, "had preached seven years along the borders of Dismal Swamp, called himself a prophet, [he] had other strange ideas." The black soldiers of Colonel Draper's infant regiment were probably familiar with this "prophet." Many of them had been born and labored as slaves in the northeastern counties of North Carolina bordering the Great Dismal Swamp. After their "prophet" finished, Beals offered his own sermon by permission of the black worshipers. Beals described the effect his sermon had on the freedmen. He wrote:

> Their hope rested in their own efforts for Freedom. I can never forget the tears that glistened in the eyes of those noble colored soldiers, when I reminded them that God, and all just men were on their side. That, the prayers of millions of Christians, would follow them to the conflict; prayers that God would cover their heads in the day of slaughter, protect their wives and children, many of whom might be yet with the enemy who had robbed them of their manhood, and that they might return triumphant from fields of battle, to enjoy Freedom & Justice for themselves & then to generations yet unborn.[3]

Witnessing the stern determination in the eyes of the soldiers of the 2nd North Carolina Colored Volunteers, Beals expressed confidence in their earnest desire to fight, their willingness to endure the harsh conditions of soldiers, and risk death for the freedom of the "long oppressed millions of their race."[4]

Later that day, Beals visited freedmen at a church built by their own hands for services. "There were gathered four or five hundred, listening to a sermon from a devoutly pious negro," he wrote, "He was a Baptist & had no regular license, though he had that morning baptized several persons, prepatory to their admission to the church." Readily granted permission for the second time that day to address the freedmen, Beals "did not intend to stir the excitable elements of their nature." But, the rudely constructed church, the "wild appearance" of his surroundings, and the "unlettered preaching," contrasted, in Beals' mind, with visions of freedom and civilization that were opening up for the many dark faces in his audience and inspired him with enthusiasm as he preached for a half an hour.[5]

At another religious gathering of black Methodists, Beals encountered an aged woman, who had been a slave "bearing the marks of sorrows, endured long years beneath the demons' iron heel." This woman, grabbing his hand, asked in Beals' version of black dialect, "'Is all dese tings true; which you has told us? Is we to have schoolhouses, & churches, & books and ministers, and Jesus neber more to be shut up to us?'" Beals found the same interest in freedom and thirst for knowledge among these Methodists as he had in the Baptist service. He noted that the black regiments at New Bern, mainly the 2nd North Carolina, needed chaplains as soon as possible. David Stevens, appointed chaplain of the 2nd North Carolina, had not yet arrived to assume his duties. Stevens, an African Methodist Episcopalian minister and native of Harrisburg, Pennsylvania, would be considered the only black officer to serve in the regiment in his ordained capacity. Beals believed that the regimental chaplain in black regiments "could teach portions of every day when the reg. was not in active service; could do much to help ... in the camp, act ... for those who have no means of communicating with their families, follow them to the field of battle and whisper words of counsel & comfort to their sick, and administer for them the rites of Christian burial." To most white northern missionaries, the freedmen's religious expressions were both a curiosity and somewhat an embarrassment to their established modes of worship. It would be the duty of AMA missionaries to provide freedmen with proper religious training. Most importantly, Beals wanted "to mould, by clear exhibitions of divine truth their crude faith, and soften & soothe their exciting mode of worship."[6]

Besides interest in the freedmen's religious development, Beals concerned himself also with the progress of their education. Observing a black man "just able to read" teaching 600 children at New Bern without a Sabbath or day school, Beals reported that the superintendent in charge of the freedmen "would gladly welcome a faithful teacher and afford all the assistance in his power." The fact that freedmen were already placing the responsibility of educating their children into their own hands without white supervision demonstrated the initiative of the freedmen's community in the transition from slavery to freedom.[7]

Visiting the contraband school at Roanoke Island, Beals found the 16 students having few books available for instruction. The school at nearby Plymouth, with 80 children including some adult freedmen, taught its pupils for an hour and a half a day with the assistance of off-duty white Union soldiers stationed in the area. Beals even found his own son who had recently been a soldier in the Union army "spending his leisure hours teaching these colored children how to write." Beals insisted to his AMA superiors that the schools needed faithful teachers and books.[8]

Clearly, the foundations of the 2nd North Carolina Colored Volunteers (afterwards 36th USCT) were laid as soon as Union military forces occupied eastern North Carolina in early 1862. Large numbers of slave men, women, and children escaping to Union lines became underlying components of these foundations. This influx of black families gradually pushed the cautious administration of U.S. President Abraham Lincoln into developing policies utilizing fugitive slaves as laborers, officer servants, and spies on behalf of the Union war effort. Although the majority of Union military authorities justified such employment of fugitive slaves as a practical war measure against the Confederacy, a small minority of influential army officers used this practical military policy to bring about a broader change in the war's primary aims. Thus, the objective of preserving the Union would serve as a stepping stone in turning the war into a moral crusade for destroying slavery and proclaiming new-found freedom. This would be done through the recruitment and organization of former slaves into the Union armies. This effort would be further accomplished with the help of the families and kin of these soldiers under Union protection. The 36th USCT beginning its service as the 2nd North Carolina Colored Volunteers was one of three black regiments initially composed of former slaves from North Carolina eventually making up the "African Brigade" organized by Brigadier General Edward A. Wild.

After the first shots of the Civil War were exchanged at Fort Sumter, South Carolina, on April 12, 1861, Lincoln's policy of preserving the Union was top priority. Slavery could be maintained where it had already existed in the remaining loyal slave states (border states). Some Federal military commanders in these border states generally enforced the Fugitive Slave Act of 1850, which required the return of runaway slaves to owners who petitioned for their return and claimed loyalty to the United States. But, not all Federal commanders acted in unison. Those possessing "abolitionist tendencies" believed that the war presented opportunities for full emancipation of slaves. Lincoln reversed such early decisions of his generals on at least two occasions. In late August 1861, Major General John C. Frémont, commanding Federal forces in Missouri, declared martial law for the entire state, emancipating all slaves owned by citizens actively aiding the Confederacy and also for those failing to take an oath of allegiance to the United States whether or not they aided the Confederacy. Fearful of losing Missouri to the Confederacy, Lincoln revoked Fremont's order, concluding that the general's actions "will alarm our Southern Union friends and turn them against us."

Similarly in May 1862, Major General David Hunter — commanding Federal forces occupying the coastal areas of South Carolina, Georgia and Florida and declaring "[s]lavery and martial law in a free country are altogether incompatible"— ordered the emancipation of slaves in these states. Lincoln rescinded Hunter's order, noting that such questions he reserved for himself as commander in chief and that he "cannot feel justified in leaving to the decision of commanders in the field."[9] Lincoln could not afford to lose Missouri, Kentucky and Maryland, states with divided loyalties to the Confederacy. Moreover, he deemed it crucial to maintain property rights, including slaves, in areas of the South under Union control.

Major General Benjamin F. Butler presented the earliest policy concerning fugitive slaves for the Union at Fort Monroe, Virginia, in May 1861. As the most unlikely candidate to act on behalf of fugitive slaves, Butler had gained notoriety as a successful trial attorney, wealthy businessman, and Massachusetts state legislator. As a staunch Democrat before the war, he believed that slavery was not the paramount issue of the day and supported federal measures protecting slaveholder rights that allowed them to settle with their slaves into the unorganized territories of the United States. In 1860, Butler nominated then–Senator Jefferson Davis of Mississippi (later president of the Confederacy) for president at the contentious Democratic Party Convention initially held at Charleston, South Carolina, as he believed that he was the only individual of national stature to unite the fracturing nation. When Davis resigned his senate seat upon Mississippi's secession from the Union, Butler threw his support behind southern Democrat John C. Breckinridge of Kentucky, the outgoing vice president. Once the war commenced, Butler offered his services to his native

Massachusetts, and commanded a brigade of that state's volunteers. He was among Lincoln's first "political generals" in the attempt to maintain bipartisan support of the Union war effort. Butler's first command was the defense of Washington, D.C., and shortly after, the occupation of Maryland to keep it in the Union. Maryland, a slave state, had significant numbers of Confederate sympathizers. A violent mob in Baltimore had attacked one of Butler's regiments—portions of the 6th Massachusetts—passing through on its way to Washington. Nevertheless, Butler offered to put down any attempts of slave insurrections and assisted in the capture of Maryland's fugitive slaves to be returned to their owners who remained loyal to the Union. But his views were soon to change when he was reassigned to command Fort Monroe, Virginia, in mid–May 1861.[10]

Fort Monroe had been a haven for fugitive slaves even before Butler's arrival according to *New York Tribune* correspondent Charles D. Brigham who had been assigned to cover the post. Ironically, it was regular members of the U.S. Army who fostered the early policies regarding fugitive slaves. As soon as Butler took command, he was approached by Lieutenant Grier Tallmadge the post's chief quartermaster.[11] Tallmadge, as Brigham later recalled, had already been harboring and feeding a group of fugitive slaves who had sought Union protection from their masters and wanted Butler's approval of his actions. On a prior occasion, Tallmadge, in an insubordinate gesture toward a senior officer, had upbraided Commodore Garrett J. Pendergrast of the U.S. Navy for returning fugitive slaves to their owners who had sought protection on board his ships at nearby Norfolk.

Tallmadge expressed his own views to Butler concerning fugitive slaves in the presence of Commodore Pendergrast and *Tribune* correspondent Brigham. Looking over the fort's ramparts, he pointed towards nearby Hampton and told Butler:

> General, it is a question you will have to decide and that, too, very soon; for in less than twenty-four hours, deserting slaves will commence swarming to your lines. The Rebels are employing their slaves in thousands in constructing batteries around us. And, in my judgment, in view of this fact, not only slaves who take within our lines are "contrabands," but I hold it as much our duty to seize and capture those employed, or intended to be employed in constructing batteries, as it is to destroy the arsenals or any other war-making element of the Rebels, or to capture and destroy the batteries themselves.

Then turning to Pendergrast, Tallmadge declared, "It is my opinion Mr. Flag Officer that you greatly erred the other day when you sent back under the fugitive slave law the slave who sought the flagship of freedom. [Those] who defy the laws of the country and propose to destroy the Government are not entitled to any benefit under the fugitive slave law." That same evening fugitive slaves, Shepard Mallory, Frank Baker, and James Townsend, escaped to the fort. Their owner, Charles K. Mallory, commanded the 115th Virginia Militia at Hampton.[12]

The next day Major John B. Cary, on Colonel Mallory's behalf, petitioned Butler under a flag of truce for the return of the three fugitives and cited the Fugitive Slave Act of 1850 as the legal basis for his request. Butler refused to comply with Cary's petition on the grounds that Virginia had recently passed its ordinance to secede from the Union and considered itself a political entity outside the boundaries of the United States. Therefore, the Fugitive Slave Act could not apply to a foreign power.[13] Moreover the fugitive slaves in question had reported to Butler that they had been employed by their owners in the construction of fortifications and gun emplacements in Hampton arrayed against Fort Monroe. They faced the possibility of leaving behind their wives and children to accompany Confederate forces moving out of the area. They also reported that their refusal to comply would cause their families to be sold farther South. This was their only incentive to continue laboring for the Confederacy. Butler suggested that if Mallory formally declared his allegiance to the United States, his slaves would be returned to him; otherwise, they were to be considered "contrabands of war" duly confiscated from the enemy. These "first" contrabands were immediately put to work in constructing additional buildings around the fort.[14]

News of Butler's actions spread throughout the African American communities, both slave and free, in the surrounding localities of Hampton, Newport News, Yorktown, and Williamsburg. "Such is the mysterious spiritual telegraph which runs though the slave population," reported Edward L. Pierce, then a Union soldier stationed at Fort Monroe. Pierce had studied law under Salmon P. Chase, Lincoln's treasury secretary, and was a friend of both Senator Charles Sumner of Massachusetts and famed abolitionist Wendell Phillips. Pierce witnessed scores of black families seeking refuge at "de freedom fort."[15] Lacking the necessary labor to improve the fort's defenses, Butler placed Pierce in charge of organizing and supervising black laborers for this endeavor. Pierce, a fervent abolitionist in his own

The Flagship of Freedom. Fort Monroe, Virginia, became a haven for fugitive slaves early in the war prompting General Benjamin F. Butler to declare them "contrabands of war" after discovering that his officers had already been harboring some of them when he took command in May 1861. Men, women, and children flocked to "de freedom fort" when the opportunity presented itself making their desires known by the actions of their feet. The fort remained in Union hands during the war (Library of Congress).

right, handled the general affairs of the arriving black families in the following months.[16] This was one of the earliest organized attempts in the war to utilize black labor for the Union war effort. Butler could not ignore the presence of women and children entering his lines with this new labor source of black men. "As a political question and a question of humanity can I receive the services of a Father and a Mother and not take the children?" he inquired of his military superiors. "Of the humanitarian aspect I have no doubt. Of the political one I have no right to judge." Butler soon received approval from the U.S. War Department to accept all members of black families of disloyal owners.[17]

Butler's contraband policy influenced subsequent Union polices concerning the status of fugitive slaves. On August 6, 1861, the U.S. Congress passed a Confiscation Act declaring slave owners in open insurrection against the United States forfeited their claim to slave ownership (and implied slave confiscation by the federal government) but not giving slaves the status of freed people. Many northern conservatives hoped that this act went far enough to nullify any further attempts of abolitionist-minded military commanders from taking matters into their own hands in promoting full emancipation inconsistent with the Lincoln Administration's policy of preserv-

Benjamin Franklin Butler (1818–1893), one of President Lincoln's "political generals," established fugitive slaves seeking refuge with the Union Army as "contrabands of war" while commanding Fort Monroe, Virginia, in 1861. After a controversial stint as military governor of New Orleans, Butler took command of Federal forces in eastern North Carolina and southeastern Virginia in 1863 as a strong supporter of Wild's efforts in raising black regiments and providing for their families (Library of Congress).

ing the Union as the primary war aim. Northern abolitionists and sympathetic antislavery politicians believed this Confiscation Act would encourage more policies benefiting fugitive slaves.[18]

Although Butler received popular northern support from both factions, his subsequent policies at Fort Monroe providing work and provisions for slaves not proven to have been laboring specifically for the Confederate war effort, particularly women and children, did not sit well with some high officials. Large numbers of free blacks and fugitive families from outside the immediate region of Fort Monroe also sought protection, provisions, and work, creating more perplexing problems for the Union army unprepared for its newly acquired mission.[19] Some of the very fugitives who had benefited from Butler's early contraband policy in 1861 enlisted into the 36th USCT and other black regiments at Fort Monroe, eventually serving under his command at the end of 1863.

Butler briefly commanded the Union military expedition that captured Hatteras Island off the North Carolina coast in late August 1861 before his reassignment as military governor of recently captured New Orleans. His success at Hatteras set the stage for the larger expedition commanded by Major General Ambrose E. Burnside in early 1862, which gained a firmer Union foothold into eastern North Carolina. Burnside, although instructed by his military superiors not to implement any specific policies regarding fugitive slaves in the region, immediately confronted large numbers of them arriving daily at his headquarters at New Bern. Burnside refused to return fugitive slaves to owners who had not proven their loyalty to the United States as outlined by the Confiscation Act. "They [North Carolina citizens] have been taught that the institution of slavery, which their leaders have made them believe is a great element of strength, is in fact an element of weakness," he wrote to Secretary of War Edwin M. Stanton. "This is just what we want," commented one of Burnside's soldiers serving in the 8th Connecticut Infantry, "let commanders of Divisions look out for traitors, and the slaves will take care of themselves, to be cared for by their friends."[20]

By mid–1862, fugitive slaves were employed in and around New Bern, Roanoke Island, and other locations captured in Burnside's North Carolina expedition. This continued presence and use of these slaves by military authorities in several Union-occupied areas of the South prompted the U.S. Congress yet again to pass a series of bills on July 17, 1862. One included provisions that not only freed all slaves captured by Federal forces or slaves of disloyal owners escaping on their own accord, but also allowed for the employment with Union forces suitable persons of African descent "under such regulations, not inconsistent with the Constitution and laws, as the President may prescribe." In part, this legislation enabled Lincoln to order military commanders to enlist the use of former slaves in the construction of entrenchments, performance of general camp duties, general labor, or any military or naval service for which they were found to be competent. This also included the organization of armed black men into units protecting black refugee settlements where many families were kept. Pay for these military laborers was set at $10 per month ($3 of which was for clothing) and one standard ration of food and supplies.[21]

Lincoln issued a Preliminary Emancipation Proclamation on September 22, 1862, following the Battle of Antietam, Maryland. Although not a resounding Union victory, the retreat of the Confederate Army of Northern Virginia under General Robert E. Lee back into Virginia set the stage for the emancipation of slaves in the rebelling states. This Preliminary Emancipation gave notice to the states in rebellion that if they did not return to the Union by the first day of January 1863, slaves in these states would be free. Lincoln hoped that the rebellious states would accept his overtures of compensated emancipation plans following the example of Washington, D.C., in April 1862 when Congress emancipated the slaves in the District of Columbia and appropriated government funds offering up to $300 in compensation to loyal slaveholders for each slave freed by this measure.[22]

The Emancipation Proclamation enacted on January 1, 1863, outlawed slavery in the states that were in rebellion, but not in areas of the South under Union control. The failure of early Union military campaigns in the East, high numbers of casualties already incurred, and decrease in enlistments of white volunteers prompted Lincoln to assert in the Emancipation that freeing the slaves and incorporating them into the war effort was a "fit and necessary war measure." If the Confederacy had maintained a psychological edge over the Union fighting for its own independence earlier in the war, then the arming of former slaves to fight against their former masters canceled this advantage.[23] The Confederacy would lose its early "backbone" of support with the Union's use of black soldiers and laborers. Assisting in the emergence of black soldiers would be those military leaders with abolitionist backgrounds who desired to destroy slavery and elevate the freedmen to full citizenship.

Five black regiments had been raised prior to the Emancipation Proclamation and portions of others had been recruiting in several northern states since the beginning of the war in spite of the War Department's reluctance to accept them into federal service. In early 1863, Massachusetts Governor John A. Andrew received authorization to raise the 54th and 55th Massachusetts (Colored) regiments. George L. Stearns, a wealthy businessman and prominent Massachusetts abolitionist, became a recruiting officer for these two regiments and recruited black men from the New England and the "Old Northwest" states. Stearns had been a member of the "Secret Six" who had clandestinely funded John Brown's ill-fated raid on Harpers Ferry, Virginia, in 1859.[24]

One of Stearns's co-conspirators in the "Secret Six" was Thomas W. Higginson, a Unitarian minister, nineteenth century literary critic, and militant abolitionist who would be soon sent to South Carolina to command the 1st South Carolina Colored Volunteers from among the abandoned slaves on South Carolina's coastal islands. The families of these particular soldiers received assistance from the efforts of the Port Royal Experiment — a massive and ambitious humanitarian effort where numbers of teachers, ministers, and social reformers relocated to the Sea Islands off the coasts of South Carolina, Georgia, and Florida. The base of operations centered on the South Carolina town of Port Royal where the rudiments of education and improved agricultural techniques were taught to the freedmen. In return, the freedmen were the active labor force keeping cotton production viable to the joy of U.S. Treasury Department agents eager to fund the war effort. Equally as important was the continued food crop production that supplied Union forces in the region with much needed commissary stores.[25] It was not by coincidence that Stearns had thoughts of organizing units of former slaves in Union-occupied areas of eastern North Carolina and had a more than sympathetic colleague, Edward A. Wild, in mind to head such a task.

Wild, a Harvard-educated physician, had traveled the world as a military adventurer and humanitarian. He had witnessed the revolutionary struggles in Northern Italy as well as offered his services to the Ottoman Turks during the Crimean War. Wild began the war as a captain commanding Company A, 1st Massachusetts Infantry Regiment. His right hand was permanently

Edward Augustus Wild (1825–1891), former Captain of Company A, 1st Massachusetts and Colonel of the 35th Massachusetts, was appointed a brigadier general of volunteers in 1863 with the specific purpose of recruiting and organizing up to four regiments of former slaves in Union occupied areas of eastern North Carolina for the United States. The 2nd North Carolina Colored Volunteers (renamed the 36th USCT) was one of three regiments Wild ultimately created. He was responsible for selecting the initial officers of the regiment and commanded a large expedition composed of almost 2,000 black soldiers into the northeastern counties of North Carolina in December 1863 (Library of Congress).

crippled from artillery shrapnel at the Battle of White Oak Swamp, Virginia, in early 1862. Later that year, Wild was appointed a colonel commanding the 35th Massachusetts Infantry until the loss of his left arm at the Battle of South Mountain, Maryland, in the fall of 1862. He had been recuperating at his home in Brookline, Massachusetts, when Stearns asked for his help in recruiting black soldiers for the 54th Massachusetts.[26]

In April 1863, Lincoln appointed Wild a brigadier general with authority to raise an "African Brigade" from among able-bodied black men in Major General John G. Foster's Department of North Carolina. Foster had succeeded Burnside in command of Union-occupied North Carolina. Wild arrived at departmental headquarters at New Bern in June to begin his work. Through the influence of Governor Andrew, Wild was given additional authority in the selection and appointment of white officers for his four (later three) proposed black regiments who were to come from the commissioned and enlisted ranks of white Union regiments.[27]

Colonel Robert G. Shaw, commanding the 54th Massachusetts (Colored) Infantry, believed Wild to be "an excellent man," but doubted that he would remain in active service for long on account of his debilitating wounds, "though he is determined to try it." Governor Andrew had hoped that former slaves in North Carolina and Virginia could fill the ranks of the 54th Massachusetts if it was sent to New Bern. Shaw protested (threatening to resign his commission) on the grounds that if his half-filled and partially trained regiment were sent to North Carolina and brigaded with Wild's "contrabands," the moral effect upon the Massachusetts population would be lost. However, high enlistments among black northerners in Shaw's regiment as well as its sister regiment, the 55th Massachusetts, caused Andrew to press for the continued enlistment of a separate "African Brigade" among former slaves in North Carolina and later Virginia.[28]

Wild embarked upon recruiting the 1st, 2nd, and 3rd North Carolina Colored Volunteers for his brigade as Union-occupied areas of eastern North Carolina and southeastern Virginia were consolidated into the Department of Virginia and North Carolina in July 1863. General Foster, upon assuming command of this new organization, moved his headquarters to Fort Monroe. Wild's brigade and the remaining white troops in North Carolina were designated the 18th Army Corps.[29]

Preoccupied with reinforcing Union forces arrayed against the Confederates under General Robert E. Lee in northern and central Virginia, the U.S. War Department encouraged Foster to continue his use of black labor to strengthen defenses in and around Fort Monroe, Norfolk, and Portsmouth. In addition to manpower shortages for military and labor duties, Confederate guerrillas raiding small Union depots plagued Foster in several parts of his extended command. Not only were Union soldiers spread thin throughout the command, but several of Wild's recruiting officers were sent up to Fort Monroe from North Carolina "to induce them [black men] to enter his brigade" at the suggestion of Secretary Stanton. Foster hoped that Wild's brigade could be soon put into active service in the counties north of the Albemarle Sound in North Carolina where "many negroes may be obtained and the guerillas at the same time punished." By June 25, 1863, the 1st North Carolina Colored Volunteers under Colonel James C. Beecher had been organized. The 2nd North Carolina had begun recruiting its first soldiers 12 days before.[30]

In addition to using black soldiers for military operations in North Carolina that would drive a Union wedge between that state and Virginia, Wild envisioned Roanoke Island as an ideal place where families of the soldiers in his command could seek refuge from their former masters and begin building their lives as free citizens. Joseph E. Williams, a black recruiting agent, reported Wild's future plans for black families to his colleagues of Philadelphia's *Christian Recorder*. He wrote:

> General E.A. Wild has surveyed and examined Roanoke Island, and established a colony there for the support of the wives of the soldiers in his brigade, and also homes for the old and young and those not fit for service. He will establish and erect churches and schoolhouses for the use of the colony; and also a number of vessels of all sizes, such as schooners and small sail boats that are lying along the island, which have been captured from the rebels, will be turned over for the use of the colony.[31]

Wild's plans for a massive expedition into the interior of North Carolina were dashed when he was ordered to take command of black units in and around Charleston, South Carolina. By the end of July, Wild would arrive at Folly Island, South Carolina, with the 1st North Carolina, the 55th Massachusetts (Colored) Infantry that had just arrived at New Bern, and Company H of the 2nd North Carolina under Captain B.F. Oakes to augment the sick soldiers of the 1st North Carolina. One supporter of Wild's African Brigade expressed to recruiter George Stearns his disapproval of Wild's transfer. "I very much doubt if the government has profited by this new arrangement," he wrote. "I had hoped that the experiment of using a large body of [black] troops under the particular lead of Gen. [Wild] might have been fairly tested:— and I do hope it may be yet, for I have great confidence in his skill and valor." Shortly after Wild's departure, Colonel Alonzo G. Draper arrived at New Bern to take command of the infant 2nd North Carolina and other elements of the African Brigade.[32]

At New Bern, Draper found only 140 men of the 2nd North Carolina present for duty. "These one hundred and forty were almost to a man, without uniforms, arms or equipments," he reported to Governor Andrew of Massachusetts. "To aid me in organizing, clothing, equipping, arming, and disciplining, and drilling them, there are only two officers left me." Draper also had detachments of the 1st North Carolina and 55th Massachusetts under his command.[33]

Draper spent his first week at New Bern issuing uniforms, weapons, and equipment as well as finding a temporary surgeon and the appropriate medicines to treat sick soldiers. White officers assigned to Draper's companies were immediately sent away for recruiting duty in North Carolina and Virginia. Recruiting stations for the 2nd North Carolina in North Carolina were located at New Bern (the regimental headquarters), Washington, Plymouth, Beaufort, and Roanoke Island. The recruiting stations in Virginia were located at Fort Monroe, Hampton, Yorktown, Portsmouth, and Norfolk. In addition to the initial lack of available officers, the 2nd North Carolina continued suffering from the lack of supplies as a result of indifference or refusal to support the use of black troops in the Union army. Draper's acting quartermaster had difficulty in procuring supplies for the black soldiers since the regiment had not been officially mustered into the federal service and not recognized as a part of the New Bern command according to the post commander, Brigadier General Innis N. Palmer. Palmer had instructed his quartermasters and commissary officers not to issue any rations to the 2nd North Carolina "unless ration returns agree with the consolidated morning reports." Since a portion of the 2nd North Carolina was in South Carolina, the regiment's actual strength at New Bern was not enough to be considered officially part of Palmer's command.[34]

Despite having very little time for military training and drill, Draper made repeated requests to Major General John L. Peck, commanding the District of North Carolina, for permission to conduct recruiting raids in the vicinity. But when Draper finally "had just obtained permission from Gen. Peck to make a raid with my own men and the detachments from the Brigade, in all about three hundred men, into Onslow County, in quest of recruits ... we were ordered to Fortress Monroe." Within two hours of receiving their orders, at least 258 of the soldiers of the 2nd North Carolina left New Bern on August 29 bound for Fort Monroe, Virginia. The regiment, at this time, numbered no more than 438 men with 180 still on duty in South Carolina according to Draper's own tabulations.[35] The soldiers were leaving behind family and friends on Roanoke Island and at New Bern.

Once in Virginia, Draper ran into more difficulties in recruiting troops for the 2nd North Carolina. General Foster, commanding the Department of Virginia and North Carolina, used the black soldiers for building fortifications and digging trenches, which was a far cry from his previous sentiments to Secretary of War Stanton for using them against Confederate guerrillas. This may have been as a result of more explicit orders from the War Department to compel as many able-bodied black men in Virginia to work in the quartermaster's department as laborers freeing up white Union soldiers for combat duty against Confederate forces under General Robert E. Lee. Draper attributed Foster's change in position to his being "surrounded by a Copper head staff at Fortress Monroe." Draper argued that Foster had only "some passive sympathy" for Wild's efforts at recruiting an effective military unit of former slaves, but influential officers were thwarting these plans.[36]

Draper singled out Brigadier General Henry M. Naglee, commanding the District of Virginia with headquarters at Norfolk, and Captain George H. Johnston, Naglee's chief of staff, as the leading culprits within the Union command hindering his own recruiting efforts. Foster had earlier issued orders sanctioning the enlistment of black men employed as laborers in the various military departments and that such men be paid immediately for their work before releasing them to their regiments. But Naglee, according to Draper, "who is openly and bitterly hostile" to using black soldiers in combat pointed out certain irregularities in Foster's orders as a personal snub to his superior.[37]

Captain Henry F.H. Miller, one of Draper's recruiting officers at Fort Monroe and future commander of Company K, 2nd North Carolina, attempted to enlist Jerome Johnson into the regiment in early September. "He had been in the employ of the government for some nine days," Miller reported, "but had made no agreement for any length of time whatever." Miller enlisted Johnson and procured a pass for his travel from Fort Monroe to Portsmouth where the regiment was camped. Once Miller and Johnson boarded the transport boat, Lieutenant Colonel C.W. Thomas, the department's quartermaster, demanded Johnson's return and halted them. Miller replied that "Jerome Johnson was a free man and consequently chose for himself and that he had enlisted." Thomas, unsatisfied with Miller's reply, stormed away but returned with Foster's chief of staff Brigadier General George Potter. "I showed the general my papers, and said to him that the man was free and was anxious to fight his countries [sic] battles and that in my opinion there was no power on earth to stop him from leaving," Miller recounted.[38]

Johnson was taken away against his will "with tears in his eyes," and Miller was forbidden to enlist any more black men employed by the government. Miller asked Draper for assistance in obtaining Johnson and any other persons who wished to enlist as "others wanted to go but were stopped in the beginning." But Foster, that same day, had forbidden the enlistment of black soldiers specifically from the quartermaster's department at Fort Monroe.[39]

Following this incident, Lieutenant James N. North of the 1st North Carolina, detailed as one of Draper's recruiting officers, reported that he had enlisted Braxton Sanders, Livian

Adams, and Robert Thomas into the 2nd North Carolina. Foster telegraphed Naglee to discharge the three black men from the engineering department. Naglee pointed out U.S. Army regulations that stated:

> No enlisted man shall be discharged before the expiration of his term of enlistment without authority of the War Department, except by sentence of a general court-martial, or by the commander of the Department or of an army in the field, on certificate of disability, or on application of the soldier after twenty years' service.[40]

Foster decided that the three men could enlist, but would be detailed for temporary duty in the engineering department denying North and the 2nd North Carolina three valuable recruits. Draper countered Foster's rationale by quoting another army regulation that "recruits are not to be put to any labor or work which would interfere with their instruction, nor are they to be employed otherwise than as soldiers, in the regular duties of garrison and camp."[41]

Foster and Naglee, in accepting the first regulation, acknowledged the three black men as soldiers rather than military laborers under the Second Confiscation Act of July 1862. Since they were not soldiers until they enlisted into a military unit, this regulation as written did not apply to them if they were to be used exclusively as laborers. Foster seemed to have been aware of this and took the further step in allowing their enlistment then detailing them for temporary duty in their previous work. Draper correctly pointed out to Governor Andrew that these men "are not mechanics, but simply day laborers, and as such been employed in the Engineer Department." Very little could be done when Foster shortly thereafter issued orders restricting the enlistment of black soldiers working as laborers in the quartermaster's, ordnance, and engineering departments of his command without the consent of the respective department heads. Moreover, all unemployed black men were impressed for labor in the trenches. "We are thus cut off from three-fourths of our sources of enlistment," Draper reported. In spite of such obstacles, Lieutenant North had still recruited 30 men that week.[42]

Service as soldiers competed with employment as military laborers. Civilian employment in the quartermaster's, ordnance, and engineering departments at New Bern before Wild's departure for South Carolina attracted more black men than joining a military unit. Common laborers were paid $10 a month which was the same for black soldiers by mid–1863, and they did not have to face death, separation from families, and the deliberate pay discrimination that black soldiers had to endure. Skilled laborers could earn more.[43] Draper, in Virginia, noted that the three soldiers who had been returned to the engineering department acknowledged that they "had been receiving eighty or ninety cents a day," therefore earning between $24 and $27 a month. This pay was over twice as much being offered to soldiers and general laborers. Black soldiers usually had $3 dollars taken for clothing and equipment leaving a net gain of $7 a month. But many of them were willing to give up these financial advantages to be soldiers.[44] Draper, like Wild, was convinced that fair recruitment of black soldiers was the proper course despite incentives for black men to remain government laborers.

Draper's recruiting practices did not necessarily trickle down to some of his junior officers. One example involved Second Lieutenant Aaron Parker of the 2nd North Carolina and recruiting officer at Yorktown. Parker had recently recruited 14 men for the regiment. Brigadier General Isaac J. Wistar, commanding Union forces at Yorktown, refused to supply the recruits with rations "on the grounds that the men were not entitled to rations until they were mustered into the U.S. Service." These men were apparently lost for enlistment due to this lack of supplies.[45] The fact that the 2nd North Carolina had not been accepted into federal service by late September was a legitimate concern for Draper. Without proper supplies, the men could not be maintained and trained, but without being mustered into the service they could not be paid, and technically could not receive such supplies and rations. Draper believed that Wistar wanted to use black soldiers for his own purposes as laborers for his Yorktown command. Wistar had reported to General Naglee, his immediate superior, that Lieutenant Parker had no recruits for the 2nd North Carolina and recommended that he be removed from recruiting. Furthermore, Wistar had requested of Foster permission to execute his own plans to recruit black soldiers. Captain Johnston showed Draper documents concerning Wistar's contradictory actions whose own views of black soldiers Draper did not trust.[46]

Immediately, Draper sent "my ablest Capt. [Miller]" to relieve Parker as recruiting officer at Yorktown. When he reported to Wistar, Miller asked for the general's influence in making his recruiting efforts successful. Wistar informed him that he had just sent 400 black men to Washington, D.C., and had no more than 50 left in his command. Miller soon found out from other Union officers at Yorktown that at least 180 black men were available for recruitment. But to Miller's dismay, these same officers told him that they "thought Lieut. Parker had given the death blow to recruiting in the vicinity and that he had taken some Cavalrymen to the contraband camp and took some fourteen of them by force and that since then the colored men had lost all confidence." Wistar, apparently angered by Parker's actions, told him that he believed in enlisting black soldiers but that they were to be enlisted voluntarily as other men, not impressed into military service.[47]

Miller enlisted 20 men within the first 24 hours of his arrival at Yorktown and promised 100 more from the engineer's department, but these recruits were soon taken away as a result of Foster's orders forbidding such recruitments. It is not clear if Draper's other recruiting officers forced or threatened black men to enlist into the regiment as Parker was allegedly accused of doing, but it may have been more than likely the case than acknowledged. Lucy Wiggins recalled that while employed on the confiscated Baker Farm near Norfolk that her husband, Paul, was drafted into the 2nd North Carolina. She stated, "Some white man told him he had to go in the army and took him away." Nevertheless, 162 soldiers enlisted into the regiment for the month of September, which was the second highest for the 2nd North Carolina in any given month. Whether through the voluntary decisions of able-bodied black men or coercion by recruiting officers, these recent enlistees brought the regiment up to 600 men.[48]

Draper's efforts at training and drilling the 2nd North Carolina were superseded by frequent orders for fatigue duty in the trenches often requiring three-fourths of the regiment. But Draper made sure that the remaining troops were drilled on a rotating basis for six hours a day "as they were wholly uninstructed in the duties of a soldier." Draper further reduced his guard posts to allow more men to participate in drill and evening parades. He was more concerned with the military precision of his command than "ornamenting the camp."[49] This may have led to criticism of the 2nd North Carolina's camp two months later.

In November, Dr. N.P. Rice, an army medical inspector, visited the 2nd North Carolina's camp and reported that the "command still continues in a most miserable state ... [and] shows strong evidences of want and care of discipline." Rice noted soldiers' tents improperly stockaded for permanent habitation and that no regimental hospital existed as previously ordered. Draper, strongly believing that Rice's unfavorable report did a "great injustice" to his command, sent a rebuttal report to departmental headquarters to refute these findings. Draper cited the lack of men, unavailable stockading supplies, and the absence of animal teams to complete the stockading of the camp and the building of the regimental hospital. Affidavits and testimonies were submitted on behalf of the regiment that previous orders implied the preference for hospital tents over log hospitals. A previous inspection report was also submitted indicating a favorable recommendation of the regiment's camp by the departmental assistant inspector general who reported that the black soldiers' cleanliness in arms and clothing and proficiency in drill "reflects the greatest credit on the officers."[50] Wild, who had returned from South Carolina to take command of black troops in southeastern Virginia at this time, inspected Draper's camp. In his estimation, Draper's complaints over the lack of stockading equipment were slightly exaggerated as he observed, "Every company in the command was engaged in the process of building." But the regiment's equipment, particularly the tents, was of second-rate quality and worthless, which would have made any camp look poorly.[51]

Prior to Wild's return to Virginia, Draper attempted to conduct recruiting raids into Norfolk and Princess Anne Counties in Virginia and Currituck County in North Carolina composed of "a recruiting officer with a small squad of men for his protection" from guerrillas. Foster refused to grant Draper's request on the grounds that the "colored regiments are required either in fatigue duty on the new fort or in drilling the discipline and drill should be quite perfect before sending the party through a section of country where opportunities for plundering often occurs."[52] Ironically, fatigue duty was keeping a good portion of Draper's men from perfecting the military drill needed to participate in such recruiting expeditions.

Foster's star began to fade quickly in Draper's estimation. He confided to Governor Andrew that he believed "no general has a right to restrain men from enlisting, or to limit the field of our operations." The stars of the black men in the 2nd North Carolina, however, looked bright to Draper. He wrote:

> Nothing can exceed the devotion and patriotism of these freedmen; they leave their corn in the field, their horses at the

Alonzo Granville Draper (1835–1865) was a labor leader, temperance advocate, and committed abolitionist from Lynn, Massachusetts. He took command of the 2nd North Carolina Colored Volunteers (36th USCT) as its colonel on August 1, 1863, at New Bern, North Carolina. "They make the best soldiers in the world," Draper wrote of the regiment the majority of whom had been slaves. He held regimental command for just under eight months before assuming higher command responsibilities. Draper was appointed a Brevet Brigadier General of Volunteers on October 28, 1864, for gallantry (Massachusetts Commandery Military Order of the Loyal Legion and the U.S. Army Military History Institute).

plough, and their families helpless and defenseless, to fight for their country at seven dollars a month. They make the best soldiers in the world; learn the drill faster than white men, are obedient and well disciplined from the moment they set foot in camp; they are also free from most of the vices of white men. During the seven weeks that I have been in command, not a case of infraction has occurred in the Regiment among the enlisted men; not a fight has occurred in my Regiment, and not a single case of venereal disease has been detected by the surgeons, and this I am sure, cannot be said of any white regiment in service.[53]

Draper hoped that with the return of his men on duty with Wild in South Carolina, the 2nd North Carolina would be mustered into service. The men could receive their pay and have a better opportunity to participate in active military operations. Additionally, Draper hoped that with Wild's return, the 2nd North Carolina would be permitted to conduct recruiting raids where at least two thousand recruits from the surrounding area could be found completing the regiment's organization and filling up the 3rd North Carolina. The 2nd North Carolina finally mustered into federal service on October 28, 1863, at Fort Monroe.[54] The second regiment of Wild's African Brigade was now organized, but serving in Virginia while the rest of the brigade, namely the 1st North Carolina, was in South Carolina with Wild. More than geographical distances would soon separate Draper and Wild.

Draper had one brief interview with Wild following his appointment as commander of the 2nd North Carolina "and never had over two hours conversation with him in my life." He believed that Wild and Foster were of similar mind with regard to the use of black soldiers, but his recent experiences in Virginia with Foster and his subordinates made him think otherwise. Draper stated to Governor Andrew that he would have gone straight to the War Department with his complaints if he did not have "a desire to avoid any interferences with the policy which Gen. Wild may have marked out for himself ... I am therefore groping in the dark, so far as regards his purposes, and am further embarrassed by the belief that he has confidence in Gen. Foster's disposition towards this movement." He explained to the Massachusetts governor how the commander of the 10th USCT went directly to the War Department because he found "too many obstacles in his way" and obtained permission to recruit soldiers on Virginia's Eastern Shore. The 10th USCT's colonel apparently enlisted 700 men in one night. Although Draper believed that he "not be too squeamish about channels," he wanted to allow Wild ample opportunity to get the African Brigade, including his own regiment, into action.[55]

In early November it looked as if Draper would get his wish. Wild had been assigned to command all black regiments at Norfolk and Portsmouth, and Brigadier General James N. Barnes, who was a strong supporter of using black soldiers, replaced Naglee as commander of the District of Virginia. The reassignment of General Benjamin F. Butler to Fort Monroe prompted Draper to proclaim to Governor Andrew that "without doubt, the presence of Gens. Butler, Wild and Barnes will greatly stimulate enlistment of Colored Troops. It looks as if Time and Your excellency, were doing something to help us."[56] It remained to be seen how Draper's 2nd North Carolina would perform under this new arrangement.

CHAPTER 3

# They Are Most Reliable Soldiers
*Liberation in Virginia and North Carolina,
November–December, 1863*

Captain Charles Herbert Frye quipped in his report that he was the "officer of geese." He had earned this sobriquet by taking a dozen or so men of the 2nd North Carolina Colored Volunteers to the Edwards homestead in Princess Anne County, Virginia, where 23 turkeys were killed and several geese and ducks confiscated. Frye remembered that it had been a "saving sight" when the black servants of Mrs. Edwards, whose husband was away in the Confederate army, first saw the black men in uniform arriving on her property that November day in 1863.

This joyous scene of liberation of slaves by former slaves-turned-soldiers in U.S. Army blue was short-lived upon the approach of white Union troops under the command of Lieutenant Colonel Frederick F. Wead of the 98th New York Infantry. Wead demanded Frye explain under whose authority gave him the right to confiscate property and conduct searches in an area that was under his jurisdiction. Frye, who at age 23 had probably seen more than enough of war in his short life, may have felt that he did not owe any explanation to the superior officer since he was only a part of a larger expedition led by a full colonel and sanctioned by a brigadier general commanding the colored troops at nearby Norfolk and Portsmouth.

A clerk from Salem, Massachusetts, Frye had already served in two white Massachusetts units before receiving his commission in the 2nd North Carolina. He was a seasoned combat veteran and the dull pain in his left thigh as a result of a shell shrapnel wound from Fredericksburg a year before may have reminded Frye of his larger purpose, which was not to get into an altercation with a higher ranking officer. Frye recommended Wead file a complaint through the proper military channels as he had his orders and would continue to carry them out. It could not have been lost on the young captain that the New York colonel was almost removed from command as a result of a petition generated from among his own subordinate officers almost six months before. Moreover, the presence of black soldiers in combating Confederate "guerillas" within Wead's geographical area of responsibility where his own 98th New York was tasked in the same mission may have led him to perceive a want of confidence in his abilities by higher authorities.[1] This would cause any officer in this circumstance to challenge any and all threats, real or imagined, that would upset the established order. Wead had been barely able to retain his own command now he was facing an armed force of former slaves led by highly motivated white officers bent on disrupting the status quo in his jurisdiction in the name of liberation. It was all the more imperative that the officers and men in the 2nd North Carolina Colored Volunteers understood that threats to their own safety and those whom they liberated not only came from Confederate guerrillas or white residents in sympathy with them, but potentially from white Union soldiers as well.

The return of Major General Benjamin F. Butler to Virginia on November 11, 1863, renewed hope of the 2nd North Carolina proving itself in battle. The Lincoln Administration believed that Butler's assignment would allow the furor over his highly controversial tenure commanding Union-occupied New Orleans to subside. Moreover, the Department of Virginia and North Carolina was a large enough command for Lincoln to give Butler in order to keep the support of other "War Democrats." The War Department, however, considered the command to be a "backwater region" and intended to keep him preoccupied with peripheral operations instead of participating in major military operations in Virginia.[2]

Benjamin Butler was unlike his by-the-book predecessor. He sought to turn his new command into a major theater of operations by unconventional means. One such method was the use of black soldiers as an essential component in accomplishing his military and personal aims. Butler believed that black men, especially former slaves, could and should be made into fighting soldiers under the proper leadership of white officers. Although only a recent convert to the enlistment of black soldiers, Butler had reluctantly accepted their use in New Orleans and even allowed the Louisiana Native Guards, an antebellum all-black militia unit, to retain their black officers once they declared their loyalty to the United States. Now returned to Virginia, Butler knew that he would not receive any additional white troops for his command.[3]

Eager to prove that Edward Wild's brigade of black regiments at Norfolk and Portsmouth were as good as white soldiers, Butler authorized expeditions of black troops into the outer fringes of his command. Such expeditions would create nuisances for the main Confederate forces in Virginia and North Carolina by destroying supply depots, stemming the tide of guerrilla activity, and encouraging the recruitment of more black men to increase the department's manpower while reducing the Confederacy's noncombatant strength. The military success of black regiments, such as Alonzo Draper's 2nd North Carolina, could also redeem Butler's fledgling military qualities and open a larger realm of political opportunities for him. Butler hoped Wild would prove useful in leading black regiments in his command. The first test of the 2nd North Carolina would be in politically sensitive Princess Anne County, Virginia.[4]

Princess Anne County had been under Union occupation since May 1862 when Confederate forces abandoned nearby Norfolk and the Gosport Naval Yard at Portsmouth to meet the Union military threat near Richmond. This area was exempted from Lincoln's Emancipation Proclamation, as were other selected areas of the South under Union control. Draper's expedition, although insuring protection of property of loyal white inhabitants in the enforcement of the Emancipation Proclamation, was also designed to demonstrate an armed presence and forceful posture to make it difficult for supposedly loyal slave owners to restrain their slaves from voluntarily leaving their plantations without fear or threat. This was in keeping with Lincoln's desire of compensating loyal slave owners for the loss of their slaves on an individual basis. However, Draper, Wild, and Butler were skeptical of the loyalty of the white inhabitants of Princess Anne.

Wild ordered Draper, with 100 men of the 2nd North Carolina, to conduct an expedition into Princess Anne County on November 17, 1863. Draper's orders specified three goals: the recruitment of black soldiers, armed protection of black families returning with the expedition, and pursuit of Confederate guerrillas.[5] It was this last goal that held the most interest for Draper as it promised to be the 2nd North Carolina's first opportunity to engage in combat.

As revealed during the early months of the war, black refugees entering Union lines were among the best sources of information on guerrilla activity and on the location of Confederate sympathizers who aided the guerrillas. As winter approached, guerrillas often disbanded and returned to their homes until the spring. Draper had already targeted two guerrilla leaders operating in Princess Anne who were known to be at their homes at this time: Major Edgar Burroughs and Captain John T. Caffee.

A Methodist minister, Burroughs had been defeated by former Virginia governor Henry A. Wise as a delegate to the secession convention in 1861 representing the Norfolk area. He owned 12 slaves in 1860. Burroughs later served as a major in the 15th Virginia Cavalry until his resignation in the fall of 1862 due to ill health and "family afflictions." His personal initiative and influential leadership among the men of his former regiment enabled him to obtain permission from Confederate authorities to raise a battalion of "partisan rangers" and operate against Union forces in the region by 1863.[6] Caffee, a Princess Anne neighbor of Burroughs and considered a man of "substance and energy," was the owner of 11 slaves in 1860. Caffee commanded the "Pungo Rangers," a company of mounted guerrillas organized for local defense and special services within the county in early August 1863. Burroughs hoped that Caffee's company, along with several "home guard" com-

John Ware Fletcher (1824–1905) had served as a lieutenant in the 43rd Massachusetts Infantry (9 months service) and in the U.S. Signal Corps before accepting a commission as a captain in the 2nd North Carolina Colored Volunteers (36th USCT). He commanded Company A from September 10, 1863, to his resignation on May 14, 1864. His company was among the first in the regiment to conduct raids of liberation in portions of southeastern Virginia in November 1863. After the war, Fletcher served in the Massachusetts state legislature and had a brief term as mayor of his hometown of Chelsea, Massachusetts (Massachusetts Commandery Military Order of the Loyal Legion and the U.S. Army Military History Institute).

panies of the 68th North Carolina operating in nearby Camden, Currituck, and Pasquotank Counties across the state line, could mount an effective defense against Union forces in the region.[7]

Draper's expedition of six officers and 112 men left Portsmouth on the same day their orders were issued armed with second-class Enfield rifled muskets instead of their usual weapons of picks, shovels, and axes for military labor. The expedition stopped on the first night after covering ten miles, recruiting black men for the regiment well into the night. Draper reported "collecting at the same time such colored men, women, and children, as chose to join our part."[8] The expedition carefully canvassed crossroads and plantations for more recruits and their families near the county courthouse the next day. After two days, Draper received information from slaves that a large force of guerrillas commanded by Captain Caffee was gathering at the lower end of the county. Draper's column headed toward Caffee's residence. Nearing the residence, Draper learned that Caffee and about 40 men had just left heading farther up the road. Short on rations, Draper decided to forgo a pursuit of Caffee's guerrillas and resupplied his depleted rations at Caffee's home. Reports came back that Caffee, enraged by the confiscation of his property, provisions, and slaves, would soon give Draper's "black soldiers hell." Burroughs planned to join forces with Caffee to drive Draper's expedition out of the county. In addition to requesting Caffee's cooperation, Burroughs called for reinforcements from nearby Currituck County, North Carolina.[9]

Suspecting that Burroughs would make an attempt to visit his family, Draper sent a portion of his troops back towards the courthouse deceiving some of Burroughs' scouts into thinking the black soldiers were returning to Portsmouth. Shortly thereafter, with the help of a "colored guide," the entire expedition united, doubled back, and occupied the Burroughs' farm located on a small island between North Bay and Back Bay. Sentinels were posted in all directions to warn of Burroughs' possible approach, and the occupants of the only other homestead on the island were arrested to prevent information being passed to Burroughs.[10]

At Burroughs' residence, the house was carefully searched and the women of the house were confined to a lower room to keep them from signaling for help. "They assured us that the Major was a man of too much sense to come to the house," Draper wrote of the Burroughs women. But their servants assured him that Burroughs would indeed return home to carry his slaves away from the clutches of the Union military. Draper was also informed that a Ms. Crutchfield, who lived six miles away, had been passing information on the movements of the black soldiers to Burroughs earlier that morning and a detachment was sent to her residence to arrest the family.[11]

Believing that Burroughs and any force he might have would attempt to land by water at the southern end of the island rather than the usual landing at the house, Draper posted his men in a nearby barn "with strict orders not to speak above a whisper" in preparation to receive the enemy "according to their own custom, with an ambuscade." Draper's men waited through the night and the next morning. As the noon hour approached, sentinels signaled the appearance of a boat on the river heading for the southern landing. Ordering his men at the double-quick to the landing, Draper soon was hampered by a thicket covering about a quarter mile immediately obscuring the view of the boat and its party. Reports came back to Draper that two men had disembarked from the boat with weapons drawn. As soon as Draper's men negotiated the thicket, Major Burroughs and one of his men were back in the boat and shoving off into the river. When the leading elements of Draper's men arrived at the landing, Burroughs was already several yards away when they opened fire on the boat. When Draper arrived on the scene, he shouted for the boat's occupants to surrender. Refusing the request, Burroughs and company threw themselves to the bottom of the boat. Continued firing by the black soldiers striking the boat convinced Burroughs to throw up his cap "in token submission." Nine of Burrough's slaves were taken under Draper's protection. While Burroughs was in Draper's custody, Caffee apparently escaped into North Carolina.[12]

The nine-day expedition brought back between 450 and 475 black refugees. In addition to Burroughs, three Confederate cavalrymen on furlough and several citizens suspected of being Confederate sympathizers were taken prisoner. The black soldiers confiscated 104 wagons and carts, 3 carriages, 120 horses and mules, and 1 yoke of oxen. Draper believed that the black population in Princess Anne was loyal to the Union, but "nineteen twentieths" of the white population was openly disloyal according to his own personal observations. Most of Draper's information concerning the guerrillas came from slaves, while many supposedly loyal white inhabitants attempted to keep Burroughs and Caffee appraised of Draper's operations. The expedition confirmed Draper's skepticism of the professed loyalty to the Union of Princess Anne inhabitants. Some of the refugees, who Draper and his men went through great efforts to protect, later enlisted as soldiers in the 2nd North Carolina.[13]

Lucy Chase, a white teacher who volunteered through the Boston Education Commission to work among the freed people along with her sister Sarah, wrote to her folks in Worcester, Massachusetts, on the result of the 2nd North Carolina's successful expedition, "Two or three days ago, 4 hundred negroes followed on the heels of a force sent out from Norfolk in search of guerillas and now we find them at our doors. Not to spend the winter, not to tarry but a night, but with their faces firmly turned forever and a day from their homes?" The Chase sisters appreciated the "cordial invitation" the black soldiers extended to the floods of black refugees. They had hoped that this exodus of freedmen would continue throughout the winter.[14]

Edgar Burroughs, on his way to Norfolk as a prisoner and denying that he headed a band of guerrillas, maintained that he commanded a legitimate battalion of partisan rangers sanctioned by the Confederate government. Draper further ascertained from other reports that Burroughs had been implicated in the capture of a Union vessel, destruction of a local bridge, and the capture of a Union army surgeon. Additionally, Draper believed that Caffee's company in Princess Anne consisted of no more than 70 men and Burroughs' entire command did not exceed 300 men. Burroughs would be tried as a guerrilla by a military tribunal the following month and sentenced to death. While being treated at a Portsmouth hospital for smallpox, Burroughs would make an escape attempt on January 26, 1864, only to be shot dead by black soldiers guarding him.[15]

The armed presence of the 2nd North Carolina tempered much of the overt resentment of many Confederate sympathizers in Princess Anne where the white inhabitants still held the legal right to maintain slavery under the Emancipation Proclamation provided that they were deemed loyal to the United States. Nevertheless, Princess Anne's white citizens would find it increasingly difficult to maintain the peculiar institution. As long as Union forces were in close proximity, slave emancipation would be a reality, if not always officially sanctioned.

Not surprisingly, Draper's expedition was not without its critics, and interestingly enough, several complaints came from white inhabitants with the endorsement of white Union officers. Captain John Ebbs of the 3rd New York Cavalry reported to his immediate superior, Lieutenant Colonel Frederick W. Wead of the 98th New York Infantry, that there had been numerous instances of violations committed against the white citizens of Princess

Anne County by Draper's expedition. Wead, commanding the post at Pungo Point Bridge in the county, submitted specific complaints to departmental headquarters that Draper's men had "committed the grossest outrages."[16] These "outrages" ranged from the confiscation of property including wagons, carts, horses, mules, and slaves to the use of profanity and insulting language by black soldiers to the white inhabitants, particularly women.

When Ebbs' report with the alleged complaints and Wead's endorsement reached Draper, he requested detailed statements from the officers on the expedition to answer the specific allegations of depredations committed upon the inhabitants they had visited. Draper argued to his superiors that his written orders from Wild implicitly authorized his confiscation of property, farming implements, and other supplies from disloyal residents when his own supplies were exhausted and for the black families brought under his protection. "Whenever a house was to be searched for arms or to be visited for any purpose," Draper wrote, "an officer was invariably sent in command of the detachment with strict orders to permit no plundering by the men and to protect the citizens from insult, and not permit the men to reply where insulted by citizens, as they frequently were.... I reminded the men that plundering would be met with severity."[17]

Captain Frye had already reported his adventure at the Edwards homestead and his encounter with Wead. He was not alone in providing detailed reports of his operations and the conduct of those under his command. Lieutenant Leonard T. Gaskill of the 2nd North Carolina encountered a typical accusation of theft and insulting language toward white women during his visit to the home of Mr. Andrew Smith: "I took ... about 50 head of poultry, 2 Hogs, and a horse which I was informed he had purchased for his son in the Conf. Army." Gaskill further reported that his soldiers had uttered no insulting language to any females present. Captain Daniel Foster, on loan from the 3rd North Carolina Colored Volunteers and accompanying the expedition, had taken 12 of Draper's soldiers to the home of Mary Healy who had also complained of abusive language leveled at her. She had a husband reportedly in the Confederate Army. "At her house ... I carried out your orders and prevented the men from all pillage," Foster maintained. "I allowed no one but myself to enter her house.... I permitted no abusive language at her house or at any other on the part of the soldiers."[18] But, Draper's officers could also report the reception received by liberated slaves amidst their alleged theft of property and insulting language toward white civilians.

Lieutenant Benjamin F. Kinsley of the 2nd North Carolina reported that he and his men had taken a horse and cart from Mr. and Mrs. Bell. They both protested over the confiscation of their property "and used very insulting language to Mr. Hodges (our guide—not a soldier)." Hodges, a black man and possibly a former slave of the Bells, inquired after some of his relatives who had lived with the Bells. Kinsley remembered that Mr. Bell called Hodges a "damned lying nigger." Hodges had informed Kinsley that Bell had been in the habit of "bucking" his slaves and had allegedly killed seven of Hodges' relatives. "I had to put a stop to the talk and sent Mr. Hodges out of the yard," Kinsley reported. "All the soldiers with me behaved orderly and had not talked with Mr. Bell."[19]

A particularly noteworthy charge made specifically by Captain Ebbs involved Lieutenant Oren A. Hendrick, another officer on loan from the 3rd North Carolina Colored Volunteers accompanying Draper's expedition. Hendrick reported that he and a squad of men had visited the home of Solomon W. Caffrey. According to Ebbs, Caffrey alleged that the black soldiers "pointed their bayonets at him, and threatened to 'stick him if he opened his mouth.'" As they searched the house, Caffrey's daughter protested against them disturbing her room where one of the black soldiers allegedly "told her that if she did not keep still, that he would take her into her bed room, and use her." This alleged disrespect of white women by black soldiers was a sensitive issue for white southerners. In defense of the soldiers as well as himself, Hendrick wrote in his later report:

> Upon arriving near the house I posted three or four men around the buildings, giving them orders to allow no one to leave the place during the search. While this was being done Mr. Caffrey came out of the house, and coming towards me had to pass one of the sentinels, who halted him and Mr. Caffrey not halting the sentinel presented his bayonet. I immediately ordered the sentinel to let him pass. Which order he obeyed. I heard no such threat as the soldier is reported to have made and as I stood within a few feet from him should have heard the remark if one had been made. I then informed Mr. Caffrey that I had orders to search his house for arms. He seemed very indignant at the idea of having his house searched by Officers or soldiers of a Negro regiment, and said "if they were white soldiers he would not care so much." He then told me that "his house had already been searched, and that I should find nothing." There he also told me that he "had been confined in Fort Norfolk for sometime, and had lately been released" stating that "the Federal Authorities could not find sufficient evidence against him to warrant his being kept in confinement." I then told him I would be as civil as possible, and requested him to show me around the house, which he did. I took only one soldier with me, posting him at the door of each room, as I searched that room. When I came to his daughter's room, she protested against my searching that, but as I had no orders to omit any rooms in my search, of course I could not comply with her request, but merely looked in. The soldier made no such insulting remark as is stated in Capt. Ebbs report, but all of the soldiers at the house behaved like gentlemen, although the women were very insulting to them. The two servants went with us of their own accord as recruits for the 2nd N.C.C. Vols. The horse, and cart, I had orders to take for the transportation of Contrabands.[20]

Such allegations of inappropriate behavior, rape, and attempted rape of white women would continue to follow the black soldiers of the 2nd North Carolina as well as black soldiers serving in the Union army for the duration of the war.

Hendrick and his squad later visited the home of Judith M. Dyer, a widow who alleged that the soldiers discarded the keys to her premises, destroyed locks to her out-buildings, and took six of her slaves into custody in addition to confiscating her horse, cart, and some eggs. While searching Mrs. Dyer's house, Hendrick "found there a pistol, which by your order, I turned over to [the] ordnance officer. No locks were broken, or anything taken by any of the soldiers. Six servants (a mother, and her children) came away with us, of their own accord, taking the horse, and cart for the transportation, of their things to Norfolk, and the eggs were taken by them for their subsistence." The soldiers discovered no keys, but Hendrick suspected that one of the servants might have inadvertently taken them in the hurry to leave.[21]

Answering the charges that slaves were taken against their will, Hendrick replied that he witnessed "nothing that could be construed into unwillingness to leave on the part of any servants, with the exception, that two of the smallest children were crying when they left, but I judged they were tears of joy, rather than of sorrow."[22] Not only was Mrs. Dyer typical of slaveholders who expressed shock and surprise over the voluntary departure of their slaves during the war, but her concern over her lost keys may reflect her own individual loss of power over her farm.[23] The act of the black mother leaving with her children to go with Hendrick and the black soldiers further displayed Mrs. Dyer's depleted power.

Actual theft by Union soldiers did occur during the expedition, but not at the hands of the 2nd North Carolina. Dr. Myles McSweeney, acting assistant surgeon of the 2nd North Carolina, had taken a squad of men to the home of Mrs. Messner where they found two white Union soldiers each confiscating her chickens. The soldiers were believed to have been from either the 3rd New York Cavalry or 98th New York Infantry. The only item taken from Mrs. Messner by the 2nd North Carolina was a glass of milk for Dr. McSweeney, which she readily gave to him.[24]

Draper personally encountered similar theft committed by Union soldiers not connected to the 2nd North Carolina during the expedition. "After reinforcements had joined me [from the 5th USCT]," Draper reported, "I learned that two widows had been robbed during the night of a considerable poultry." He discovered that several men of the 5th USCT were connected with the robbery and for punishment had them "traced up by the thumbs." Draper also found "one man of the 5th [USCT] attempting to rob a hen roost. I cut at him with my saber but by leaping a fence and falling to the ground he escaped the cut, receiving the flat of the saber on his rump." Another soldier, presumably of the 5th, attempted to steal sweet potatoes. Draper fired his revolver at him "about ten inches behind his back — after this I heard of no men plundering." Draper ordered Captain Gustave Fahrion, commanding Company C, 5th USCT, to take up a collection from the men of his regiment accused of stealing to compensate the residents for their losses. Draper contributed seven dollars from his own pocket to this fund. Unfortunately, Fahrion failed to give the residents the collected funds prompting Draper to later comment that Fahrion's moral theory was far greater than his practice.[25]

Draper's indictment of soldiers in the 5th USCT, a black regiment recruited from Ohio, was severe and did not smooth relations between black free men and freed men. Although the 5th had mostly free men, former slaves were recruited to augment the regiment's strength once it arrived in southeastern Virginia. No doubt the members of the 5th would have attributed such behavior to their comrades who had been recently enlisted into the regiment fresh off the plantation. Moreover, Draper's relations with white Union soldiers under Colonel Wead would further deteriorate as future events unfolded. Draper developed more trust in the assistance and support of black inhabitants while white inhabitants continued to place obstacles in the path of his soldiers. Although criticized by some, the 2nd North Carolina indeed had its supporters.

A *New York Tribune* correspondent concluded that Draper's Princess Anne expedition was so well managed "that it was not known that he had gone at all until news was received here [Norfolk, Virginia] of his success and of his being on his return.... Col. Draper's regiment is a credit to the service."[26] Another correspondent for the *New York Times*, known as "Tewksbury," summarized the importance of the 2nd North Carolina's recent expedition. He wrote:

> The success which crowned the late expedition of Col. Draper of the Second North Carolina (colored) regiment, to Princess Anne County, resulting in the large enlistment of a large number of recruits, the release from bondage of hundreds of slaves, the discomfiture of the guerrillas and the capture of their chief, induced Gen. Wild, the commander of the colored troops in this department, with approbation of Maj.-Gen. Butler, to plan a raid of a similar character but on a much more extensive scale, beyond our lines into North Carolina. This plan was in one respect entirely original. The success of a raid is usually made to depend upon the secrecy with which it is executed — a dash into the enemy's country, rest nowhere, and a hasty return. But Gen. Wild resolved to be absent a month, to occupy and evacuate towns at his leisure, relying upon a novel species of strategy and the bayonets of his sable braves to recross our lines in safety when his work should be accomplished.[27]

The stage was now set for a much larger demonstration using the soldiers of the 2nd North Carolina Colored Volunteers in the cause of freedom.

Brigadier General Edward A. Wild's raid into North Carolina reinforced Major General Benjamin F. Butler's desire to rid the "no man's land" between Norfolk, Virginia, and Elizabeth City, North Carolina, of large bodies of Confederate guerrillas. Several Confederate guerrilla camps were situated in remote areas of the Great Dismal Swamp from where they staged raids against Union outposts and harassed loyal inhabitants of northeastern North Carolina.[28]

Butler further backed Wild's raid by issuing General Orders No. 46 designed to encourage the enlistment of fugitive slaves Wild would bring in by providing a measure of protection for their families. Through this military order, Butler reaffirmed his "contraband of war" theory that by providing an appealing environment for black refugees, the capacity of the Confederacy to wage war against the United States would diminish. Butler's order consolidated efforts in handling freedmen's affairs in his command into a unified Bureau of Negro Affairs, which would be a forerunner of the Freedman's Bureau as well as an early foundation for post-war Civil Rights legislation for freedmen.[29]

Wild's 20-day expedition into North Carolina in December 1863, a subject of recent interest to historians, was the largest military operation up to that time conducted almost exclusively by black soldiers. According to the Emancipation Proclamation, all of North Carolina was still under a state of rebellion. Wild held wide discretion as to how he conducted military operations and handled confiscated property including slaves of the local inhabitants.[30] A successful expedition by the black soldiers that included the 2nd North Carolina would not only establish a visible military presence in the Union-occupied areas of North Carolina, but would allow southern black soldiers the opportunity to rescue families and fellow slaves bringing them under Union protection.

Having high expectations and heavy responsibilities, the expedition started out on December 5 traveling in two columns. The first column, composed of soldiers from the camps outside Portsmouth, included 400 men of the 2nd North Carolina under Lieutenant Colonel Benjamin F. Pratt and 700 men of the 1st USCT under Colonel John H. Holman. Wild personally led this column from Portsmouth into North Carolina by way of Deep Creek Village and the Dismal Swamp Canal. The second column, composed of 530 men of the 5th USCT under Colonel James W. Conine and a consolidated force of 100 men from both the 1st North Carolina Colored Volunteers and 55th Massachusetts under Captain Charles A. Jones of the 1st North Carolina, left its entrenched camps northeast of Norfolk and traveled through the villages of Kempsville, Great Bridge, and Northwest Landing into North Carolina. Elizabeth Curtis Wallace, the mistress of Glencoe Plantation, made an entry in her diary on December 6 as Wild's men passed through her property. "Two negro regiments passed on their way to Carolina," she wrote. "Their white officers declare they will picket every cross road till they catch the Guerrillas."[31]

On December 7, the two columns rendezvoused at South Mills, North Carolina. It was here that the expedition learned that its supply steamers had traveled down the wrong canal and Wild ordered them to continue on to Elizabeth City without them. His force, augmented by 120 men of the 5th and 11th Pennsylvania Cavalry regiments and a section of artillery from the 7th New York Independent Artillery Battery, lived liberally off the land until they arrived at Elizabeth City four days later. This support detachment of white cavalry and artillery were to accompany Wild's men only "at a distance," but still keep watch over the black soldiers.[32] Draper, meanwhile, had been left behind at Fort Monroe to serve on the military court martial trying and convicting his Princess Anne County nemesis Major Edgar Burroughs, whom he had recently captured, as a guerrilla. Later, accompanied by *New York Times* correspondent "Tewksbury," Draper traveled from Fort Monroe to Elizabeth City catching up with the expedition sometime on the evening of December 11.[33]

Elizabeth City, the seat of Pasquotank County and once thriving community, appeared virtually deserted with "its stores closed and streets grown over by grass," Tewksbury noted. The doors to the bank stood open, guerrillas having looted it upon the approach of Union forces. Wild made temporary headquarters at the "fine residence" of Dr. William G. Pool. Pool's farmyard and outbuildings served as a temporary camp for his troops, large numbers of refugees, and confiscated property.[34] Using Elizabeth City as a base from which to conduct operations, Wild sent out several detachments of his command to recruit soldiers, pursue guerrillas, and forage for supplies. Transport steamers loaded down with black refugees, horses, and confiscated property were sent to Roanoke Island and Norfolk. A naval gunboat was also at Wild's disposal and periodically fired its guns to scare off hostile forces.[35]

Wild continued to make his presence known in the region by issuing official proclamations to the inhabitants of Currituck, Pasquotank, Perquimans, Gates, and Chowan counties. "General Butler intends to exterminate all guerillas east of [the] Chowan River," he bluntly stated, "and will use any means to do so." Rating the guerrillas who styled themselves as "home guard militias" as no better than pirates, Wild asserted that neither the Confederate government nor the state of North Carolina could legally sanction the type of warfare they practiced. Therefore, ordinary measures in dealing with guerrillas were useless in his estimation and "a more rigorous style of warfare" would be adopted. This entailed the destruction of homes and other property of disloyal citizens, confiscation of livestock and crops, and taking hostages from among the family members of suspected guerrillas. The names of loyal residents in the region were published so that Wild's subordinate commanders would leave them undisturbed. Most importantly, Wild provided loyal white inhabitants two ways of protecting black families. He declared that black families were welcomed to accompany his command as they swept through the region or stay where they were without coercion on the part of white citizens. He suggested to white inhabitants that by assisting slaves with food and transportation, those loyal to the Union would eliminate the "necessity of visitations from the colored troops." Butler had previously warned a Norfolk resident concerned by the presence of black troops that "if you do not die until the negroes hurt you, if you behave yourself, you will live forever."[36]

Wild's tenure at Elizabeth City was not without its own controversy. A detachment composed of elements of the 1st and 5th USCT led by Colonel Holman captured the wives of two members of a guerrilla company they were pursuing. These women were held as hostages to insure the safe return of a black soldier captured by guerrillas. A suspected guerrilla, Daniel Bright, was arrested and charged with "carrying on robbery and pillage in the peaceable counties of Camden and Pasquotank." After a brief "drum-head" court-martial proceeding, Bright was executed near Hinton's Crossroads in the presence of several local citizens. Afterwards, a placard was placed on Bright's body that read: "This guerilla hanged by order of Brigadier-General Wild. Daniel Bright of Pasquotank County."[37]

Believing he had obtained as many refugees and property as he could, Wild left Elizabeth City on December 17 and divided his command into three columns. The first column of 250 men, under Captain Frye of the 2nd North Carolina, ferried by steamboat 23 miles down the Pasquotank River to Powell's Point and marched northward toward Currituck Courthouse. The second column, consisting of 400 men of the 1st and 2nd North Carolina and 5th USCT under Draper, ferried directly across the Pasquotank River to Camden Court

House. Wild led the third column of 1,200 men, including the accompanying artillery, cavalry, and baggage, back toward South Mills.[38]

Draper's detachment spent the night at Shiloh, a village five miles to the southeast of Camden Court House. Pickets were secretly placed at various points maintaining campfires "to amuse the guerillas." During the night, about 70 Confederate guerrillas made a strong attack against the detachment of black soldiers driving in the pickets and pouring heavy volleys upon the campfires. Returning fire, Draper's pickets drove away the attackers before the rest of the command could be assembled. The next afternoon, near Sandy Hook, a force estimated about 200 men attacked Draper's troops. Ordering his men to lie prone, Draper directed the bulk of his men to concentrate their fire on the hiding enemy to hold them in place. Captain John M. Smith, commanding Company I, 2nd North Carolina, with 50 men maneuvered around to the left of the enemy's position. Simultaneously, Lieutenant Joseph G. Longley commanding Company F, 2nd North Carolina, moved with 50 men to the right of the enemy and charged the position with fixed bayonets.[39] Whether by meeting stiff enemy resistance or poor maneuvering, both flanking detachments failed to envelop the guerrillas.

Draper, frustrated by this failure, ordered Captain George B. Cock, commanding Company G, 5th USCT, to reinforce Longley's position with his own men and resume the assault on the enemy's right. Cock's successful charge compelled the guerrillas to flee.[40] In this fight, Draper's detachment had 11 casualties killed and wounded. The loss in killed for the guerrillas was estimated at 13. Among the first combat deaths for the 2nd North Carolina were Private Joseph Mullen, Company I, a laborer from Norfolk, Virginia, and Private John Preston, Company F, a teamster from Fort Monroe, Virginia. Sergeant Miles Sheppard, a laborer from Portsmouth, Virginia, and Private Joseph Sarr, a farmer from Hampton, Virginia, both of Company I were wounded. Sarr would die of consumption three months later. The 5th USCT lost four soldiers as casualties. Later that day, Draper resumed his march to the village of Indiantown where guerrillas attacked the rearguard of his command.[41]

Meanwhile, Wild reached South Mills where he sent the 1st USCT, the detachment of cavalry and artillery, and confiscated property to Norfolk. With the remaining companies of the 5th USCT, he resumed his march to Indiantown and met Draper's column on December 19 at the plantation of a Dr. McIntosh. Their combined column pursued a guerrilla force into a "swamp citadel." Although the guerrillas escaped, the black soldiers confiscated rifles, ammunition, miscellaneous provisions, and partial rosters of the guerrillas' military organization from their secluded camp. After burning neighboring houses of Confederate sympathizers, Wild moved toward Currituck Court House where he met up with Captain Frye's column along with the canal steamer and gunboat.[42]

Transferring additional refugees and confiscated property on the steamer bound for Roanoke Island, Wild sent Draper with 170 men to nearby Crab's Island in pursuit of another guerrilla company. Finding another empty camp consisting of elaborate log huts with bunks enough for 75 men, Draper's men confiscated guns, equipment, and gray uniforms before burning the camp to the ground. The detachment also arrested Major Gregory, a 73-year-old Confederate sympathizer, in retaliation for the capture of an unidentified black soldier of the 2nd North Carolina.[43]

On December 21, Wild sent Draper and 250 men by transport steamer to Knott's Island where they would march back to Portsmouth, sweeping in refugees and destroying guerrilla encampments along their way. Wild remained at Currituck Court House supervising

Liberation in North Carolina. Originally appearing in the January 23, 1864, issue of *Harpers Weekly*, this drawing depicts a column of black soldiers and their white officers liberating North Carolina slaves from a plantation on the route from Elizabeth City to Camden County. They were part of the larger expedition into North Carolina led by Brigadier General Edward A. Wild. The 2nd North Carolina Volunteers (36th USCT) participated in this expedition along with the 1st and 5th USCTs and detachments of the 1st North Carolina Colored Volunteers (35th USCT) and the 55th Massachusetts (Colored) Infantry (courtesy North Carolina Office of Archives and History, Division of Historical Resources, Raleigh, North Carolina).

the transfer of his sick and wounded on steamers bound for Norfolk. Draper believed the guerrillas he was pursuing were part of Captain John Caffee's Pungo Rangers who escaped from him in Princess Anne County only a month before. The success of this previous expedition compelled some of Caffee's men to seek refuge across the state line at Knott's Island. This included Henry White and his brother Caleb, suspected as Caffee's senior lieutenant and first sergeant respectively. Their property on Knott's Island would be Draper's primary targets. Upon giving orders for his men to set fire to Henry White's home and dependencies, White's wife Susan reportedly proclaimed "'If you burn my house, there will be no houses left standing on this Island.'" As Wild later related, Draper perceived Susan White's statement as a retaliatory threat that her family members in Caffee's organization would burn the homes of the loyal Union residents of the island. In an effort to guard against this possibility, Draper placed Mrs. White under arrest. The immediate problem was that she was due to deliver a child at any time. The available alternative was the Whites' 23-year-old daughter Nancy who still resided with them. When Nancy White did not immediately give Draper an answer of consent, he decided that she would have to go in her mother's place. She was allowed to accompany the expedition with a trunk containing her clothing after she witnessed the burning of both her parents' home and the nearby home of her Uncle Caleb.[44]

Wild, still at Currituck on the following day, received reports from Union cavalry that a strong force of Confederates was on its way to intercept his expedition. Having only 400 troops and encumbered by 73 confiscated animal teams as well as numerous refugees, Wild loaded them onto all available transports and made a hasty march toward Northwest Landing just across the Virginia line, sending word to the various Union outposts to inform Draper of the recent developments. As Wild left North Carolina, *New York Times* correspondent Tewksbury observed from the direction of Knott's Island that "smoke was seen rising from several points ... showing that Col. Draper was carrying out the order of the General. 'to burn pretty freely.'"[45]

News of the Confederate threat against Wild's column reached Draper through Lieutenant Colonel Wead commanding Union forces at Pungo Point Bridge, Virginia. Knott's Island, North Carolina, as well as the lower end of Princess Anne County, Virginia, fell under Wead's jurisdiction. Wead deemed "it not improper" to inform Draper that the white inhabitants in the region had taken the oath of allegiance to the United States "almost without exception." Many of them believed that Wild's expedition had committed, or soon would commit, depredations upon their property and sought protection of white Union soldiers from black Union soldiers. "In this [I] am directed to protect private property & especially that of persons who have taken the oath of allegiance, against violence of whatever nature," Wead declared. He then offered Draper's men two army wagons for their use that had accompanied his messenger and further subsistence should Draper need it. Shortly, another dispatch from Wead advised Draper's command to march immediately to his headquarters to obtain supplies to reinforce Wild. Wead planned to reinforce the 81st New York Infantry at nearby Northwest Landing, and he also intended to make sure Draper's black soldiers did not overstep their bounds in his district as they had less than a month before. As far as Wead was concerned, the sooner Draper resupplied and left to reinforce Wild, the better.[46]

Draper's men marched to Wead's headquarters at the Northwest River and resupplied themselves at the boat landing. The subsequent chain of events that occurred at Pungo Point Bridge on December 22, 1863, has continued to remain subject to debate. According to Draper's version of the historical record, he sought out Wead for further information on the Confederate threat. Hearing that Draper's soldiers had taken Nancy White hostage, Wead sent a direct order to Draper's subordinates to bring her to his headquarters. Lieutenant George W.S. Conant of Company G, 2nd North Carolina, escorted Miss White to Wead's headquarters under the mistaken belief that the order had come from Draper himself. When Conant and Miss White arrived, Wead informed Draper that the hostage could not leave his jurisdiction. Draper maintained that the arrest was made in accordance with the orders of his immediate superior General Wild. Draper also reminded Wead that he outranked him as a full colonel. As he needed to get his command underway, Draper suggested that Wead file a protest through the proper military channels and ordered Conant to escort Miss White back to the command. Wead blocked Conant from the doorway and physically pushed him back. Attempting to find another exit, Conant quickly discovered all other doors had been locked. Draper rushed to the couch where he had placed his sword as Wead drew his revolver. Conant attempting to leave Wead's headquarters with Miss White through the only accessible doorway discovered the entire building surrounded by the 98th New York Infantry.[47]

Grabbing Wead by the shoulder, Draper swung him away as Conant made another attempt to leave the building with Miss White. Perceiving Wead's revolver aimed at his chest, Draper grabbed the barrel with his left hand, and dragged Wead outside. There, Draper and Conant were "choked and roughly handled" by Wead's white soldiers until someone answered Draper's plea to assemble his command located 50 to 60 rods away. Hatless and with a bent sword, Draper escaped to meet his approaching black soldiers. The 98th New York meanwhile formed a line of battle ready to receive the black soldiers of the 2nd North Carolina. A cavalry detachment joined Wead's men giving him a numerical advantage.[48]

A cooler head prevailed in the person of Colonel Edgar M. Cullen commanding the 96th New York Infantry, who quelled the potential armed clash between black and white Union soldiers. Approaching Draper first, Cullen convinced him to restrain his men until he conferred with Wead. After some delay, an impatient Draper resumed his march toward Wead's command and halted within 30 yards from his position at Cullen's command. Two proposals were presented. The first required Draper to turn Miss White over to Wead. In return, Draper would receive a certificate stating that Wead had commandeered the prisoner under his own authority by force and would accept whatever consequences higher military authority dictated for such action against a superior officer. Wead reminded Draper that he was outnumbered almost two to one. Enraged by the haughty tone of an officer junior in rank, Draper replied "with perhaps too little courtesy, that I did not care a damn if he had ten thousand, as my orders had no reference to numbers." Wead immediately apologized for his remarks; however, Draper was not satisfied.

The second proposal would enable Draper, under his own guard, to personally escort Miss White to Wead's immediate superior, General James H. Ledlie headquartered at Great Bridge, Virginia. Draper could not consent to this as he was not part of Ledlie's command and therefore not subject to his orders. Instead, Draper offered his own proposal. He would deliver Miss White to General James Barnes commanding the District of Virginia, who was an ally of both Draper and Wild concerning the use of black soldiers. Moreover, Barnes was the immediate superior of both Wild and Ledlie. Cullen agreed with Draper's solution, but suggested that Draper and Miss White report to Ledlie with a written explanation from Wead and then report to Barnes to await further orders concerning the disposition of Miss White. Both Draper and Wead agreed. Draper's command marched to Ledlie's headquarters where it was met by Wild. Learning of the situation that had occurred between Draper and Wead, Wild filed a formal complaint against Wead who had attempted to take Draper's hostage *vi et armis*. Draper completed a report of the events that transpired at Knotts Island and Pungo Point Bridges some time on the evening of December 22 (see Appendix 5). Due to Ledlie's absence, Wild personally escorted Miss White to General Barnes at Norfolk along with a portion of his command on December 23. Draper marched with the expedition's remaining troops to Portsmouth on the following day.[49]

Frederick Wead's version of events at Pungo Point Bridge differed a great deal from Alonzo Draper's. Learning that the homes of Henry and Caleb White were burned by Draper's men, Wead probably felt a combination of rage and guilt. This rage stemmed from Draper's second incursion into Wead's jurisdiction usurping his command authority. The guilt emerged from the simple fact that he was unable to protect the property of the residents in his geographical area of responsibility even if they possessed questionable loyalty.

Filing his own report to Ledlie's headquarters on the same day as his adversary, Wead maintained that when Draper and his men arrived with Miss White, he extended every courtesy to assist them. Draper, on his own accord, brought Nancy White to Wead rather than Wead concocting an elaborate ruse to send orders directly to Draper's subordinate officers. Wead asserted that the basis of their argument centered on Draper's actions in arresting Nancy White without authority that he deemed a "violation of the laws of War and humanity." What the two men did agree on was that Wead would not allow Nancy White to remain with Draper's command and would take her into his own custody. It came as no surprise that Wead charged Draper with instigating their physical scuffle and calling for his soldiers to attack the Pungo Point Bridge garrison. Wead preferred nine charges against Draper that included malicious destruction of property of U.S. citizens, disobeying orders, conduct unbecoming an officer and gentleman, and conduct prejudicial to good order and military discipline. Both Wead's report and charges were endorsed by General Ledlie and Ledlie's superior General George W. Getty.[50]

Wead, in the effort defend himself, believed that his problems with Draper originated the previous month during the 2nd North Carolina's expedition into Princess Anne County where he believed the reports of white inhabitants that the black soldiers conducted themselves poorly. This had already formed the basis of negative opinions that Draper and Wild had of him. Wead pointed to conversations heard secondhand that Wild had referred to him as a "copperhead" hostile to the recruitment of black troops and implying that his support for the Union war effort was half-hearted. Wead further maintained the he was consistently antislavery and supported black military recruitment. Moreover, he argued if the incident had involved white troops his actions would have been the same and concluded that the resulting events would be similar.

Draper pointed out in his own December 22, 1863, report that during the Princess Anne expedition, "Lt. Col. Wead had informed me that had he not seen my written orders, he should have been obliged to fight me."[51] Wead almost made good on this promise a month later. One would find it very difficult to find in the annals of Civil War history an instance where two units of white Union soldiers were drawn up to clash with the force of arms over an issue as simple as command jurisdiction. The central issue went deeper. Although on the surface Draper's and Wead's dispute was over jurisdiction and rank, it was evident that Wead did not relish the idea of black soldiers holding any white woman hostage. This demonstration of power of black men over helpless white women remained an anathema for white northern and southern soldiers alike.

It was no wonder that Wild did not just view the white inhabitants and armed guerrillas of northeastern North Carolina as the only hostile forces facing his black soldiers. While at Elizabeth City, Wild had sent a dispatch to General Barnes at Norfolk filing a complaint against Colonel John E. Ward, commanding the 8th Connecticut Infantry, who allegedly sent out Union cavalry patrols to warn white residences in the vicinity of Elizabeth City that the "nigger stealers" were on their way. Such actions hampered the recruitment of black soldiers and hindered Wild's overall mission. Wild's charges against Ward for warning the residents of his approach during the expedition and also his vigorous defense of Draper against Wead prompted Butler to report to his superiors in Washington that "a considerable degree of prejudice against colored troops" existed among the white soldiers in his command.[52]

General Butler being apprised of Wead's charges against Draper and the pending trial, removed Wead from command of the 98th New York. Meanwhile, Nancy White was now being held as a witness for the upcoming trial rather than as a hostage or prisoner. Wild did not wish to have her "tampered with by Lt. Col. Wead and his gang." Residing at the Norfolk quarters of Captain James N. Croft and his wife, Nancy White had a fairly pleasant experience under the circumstances while in the custody of Union authorities. While details of the trial proceedings and witness testimonies remain elusive in the written record, Draper was exonerated and Wead reprimanded for exceeding the boundaries of his authority by attempting to release Miss White by force from Draper's custody as well as ordered to make an apology to Draper. Within a day, Butler restored Wead to his command in an effort to ease tension. White was released the day after expressing her gratitude to Wild for being "treated very kindly" by Captain and Mrs. Croft during her "imprisonment." Perhaps following Butler's lead in promoting goodwill, Wild had Nancy White escorted to Wead's headquarters. "I take the liberty of consigning her to your care," Wild wrote Wead, "trusting that you will forward her to Knott's Island, and believing also, that it will give you pleasure to do so." Two days later, Wild received a reply from Wead indicating that she had been restored to her family at the site of her former home and that Wild had been correct that his gesture "affords me great pleasure to return this lady to her friends ... [and] see a wrong redressed." While the matter seemed settled, the affair at Pungo Point Bridge would revisit Alonzo Draper, this time having major implications affecting his relationship with some of his subordinate officers.[53]

Draper's altercation with Wead did not deter the ultimate success gained during Wild's expedition into North Carolina. The black soldiers of the 2nd North Carolina could claim credit in participating in the release of about 2,500 of their brethren from bondage and relocating them on Roanoke Island and Norfolk. Boats and trains filled with confiscated horses, wagons, carts, weapons, and other properties accompanied the expedition. Dozens of homesteads of disloyal inhabitants, 2 distilleries, and 4 guerrilla camps were destroyed. Six Confederate soldiers on furlough and 4 civilians as hostages were taken prisoner for captured black soldiers. However, this success did come with a price. Wild's expedition suffered a loss of 7 soldiers killed, 9 wounded, and 2 taken prisoner. Nine soldiers were incapacitated by smallpox and several others contracted mumps. The 2nd North Carolina, in particular, suffered 2 killed, 2 wounded, and 1 captured who later escaped.[54]

"The men marched wonderfully," Wild commented, when evaluating the black soldiers under his command, "never grumbled, were watchful on picket, and always ready for a fight. They are most reliable soldiers." Butler endorsed Wild's assessment of the soldiers' performance in the recent expedition. "I think we are much indebted to General Wild and his negro troops for what they have done," Butler reported to the Secretary of War, "and it is but fair to record that while some complaints are made of the action authorized by General Wild against the inhabitants and their property ... the negro soldiers ... conducted themselves with propriety."[55]

Wild's harsh views of Confederate guerrillas did not escape the wrath of Confederate authorities. In January 1864, Colonel Joel R. Griffin, Confederate commander at Franklin, Virginia, located 20 miles southwest of Norfolk, sent a note to Butler about one of the captured black soldiers, Private Samuel Jordan, Company D, 5th USCT. Jordan had been executed in retaliation for Wild's execution of Daniel Bright. Butler had previously received a letter from a group of loyal citizens from Pasquotank County who claimed to have found Jordan's body dangling at the end of a rope. They anxiously asked Butler not to "attach blame to any of the citizens of this neighborhood," as they were entirely ignorant of the circumstances in which they discovered the body. Apparently Jordan had been executed across the Chowan River at Hintonsville, North Carolina, and his body brought to hang at the Turnpike Gate outside of South Mills.[56]

Griffin further requested that Butler release the wives of two guerrillas captured during the expedition in exchange for captured black soldiers currently held in irons. Butler replied that the women would be released as soon as their husbands reported to him and take their place. Griffin probably expressed the general sentiments of local whites toward Wild and the black soldiers in the wake of the expedition. He stated:

> Your stay, though short, was marked by crimes and enormities. You burned houses over the heads of defenseless women and children, carried off private property of every description, arrested noncombatants, and carried off ladies in irons, who you confined with negro men.... Your negro troops fired on confederates after they had surrendered, and they were only saved by the exertions of the more humane of your white officers.[57]

Colonel J. Wilson Shaffer, Butler's chief of staff and self-appointed political advisor, believed Wild was becoming a liability to his superior's future military and political advancement and urged that he be removed from command.[58] Yet, Butler kept Wild in the department for the time being. His success in leading black soldiers in a major raid into Confederate territory elevated Butler's own stature among northern abolitionists and Radical Republican politicians. Also realizing the need for the cooperation of loyal white inhabitants within his command and to maintain his show of strength, Butler would make sure Wild had limited authority and control in the future. "General Wild ... appears to have done his work with great thoroughness, but perhaps with too much stringency," Butler surmised.[59] The 2nd North Carolina had every reason to be proud to have taken a part in Wild's expedition. Shortly after Wild left Elizabeth City, North Carolina, a mounted force of 200 men of the normally scattered companies of the 68th North Carolina under Colonel James W. Hinton occupied the town. The Confederate Government hoped that this force would help alleviate the sad state of affairs in the Dismal Swamp region.[60]

In January 1864, the Confederate House of Representatives conducted an investigation into Wild's expedition "To Inquire Into Certain Outrages of the Enemy." The five-member special committee condemned Wild and the black soldiers under his command for hanging Daniel Bright, arresting the wives of two suspected guerrillas, burning the homes of suspected guerrillas, and hastening the death of a released prisoner. Bright, according to the committee's report, had been discharged from the 62nd Georgia Cavalry to return to his native Pasquotank County, North Carolina, farm and raise a local defense company authorized by the Governor of North Carolina. Finding few recruits, Bright "had retired to his farm, and was there seized, carried off and executed." Moreover, the wives of the suspected Confederate guerrillas, "two most respectable ladies," had been made prisoner. It was charged that one had been arrested in the presence "of her three children, of whom the oldest was ten years of age." The women, confined together in the same room, their every moments, including "necessary duty" were under watchful eyes of the black soldiers guarding them. Major Gregory, the old man arrested by Draper's men, had been recently released from Fort Norfolk; but upon returning home found his home destroyed, and he soon died "from a paralysis with which he was stricken while a prisoner in the enemy's hands."[61]

A correspondent of the *Richmond Enquirer* reported that in addition to the recent expedition, "Wild now commands the negro troops at Norfolk and Portsmouth, under Beast Butler; and the defenseless [sic] women and children of those lamented cities, whose inhabitants ... 'are thoroughly peeled' and trodden under foot, are subjected to ignominious insult by day and night, in their houses and upon the streets, from the loathsome negro guards." Such descriptions of severe depredations by many white citizens encountering black soldiers would be made throughout the war and specifically of the 2nd North Carolina. No doubt fear had spread through the communities in northeastern North Carolina that former slaves were out for retribution and would retaliate for countless years of enslavement. But the black soldiers under Draper's command were more concerned over liberating their family members and fellow slaves from bondage and leading them to the relative safety of Union-held places such as Roanoke Island and Norfolk.

In spite of negative views from Confederate authorities and the inhabitants of northeastern North Carolina, Tewksbury of the *New York Times* proclaimed:

> Colonel Draper testifies to their [2nd North Carolina] behavior under fire, and declares that he could wish to lead no better men into battle; that he feels perfectly secure with them, and can depend upon them at a critical moment with as much confidence as upon white troops less accustomed to obey commands of superiors.... When the rebellion shall have subsided into partisan warfare, so far from lasting [forever] as Jeff Davis threatens our colored troops will take care that its end is soon reached.[62]

The 2nd North Carolina Colored Volunteers participated in a full dress military parade and review at Fort Monroe on January 1, 1864, in commemoration of the first full year of emancipation for many of the soldiers' family members. General Butler witnessed the presentation of the 2nd North Carolina's regimental flag made by the "colored ladies" of Washington, North Carolina.[63] These soldiers endured conflict from white citizens in some of the very regions they had lived and labored in bondage. They fought armed guerrilla parties in the field and fought white racism within the Union army while at the same time opening the way of freedom and opportunity for their fellow slaves and families. Their work was just beginning.

CHAPTER 4

# Selected from the Most Intelligent Among Them
*Leadership, Discipline and Discrimination*

Captain Henry F.H. Miller of the 2nd North Carolina Colored Volunteers under orders from Brigadier General Edward A. Wild conducted a small expedition (possibly composed of Companies E and K) from Portsmouth, Virginia, to nearby Camden County, North Carolina, in the final days of January 1864. After pursuing retreating bands of Confederate guerrillas to Camden Court House, Miller's troops came upon the homestead of Colonel Henry M. Shaw, commander of the 8th North Carolina (Confederate) Infantry. The black soldiers began confiscating his property and slaves. Without provocation, Shaw's wife attempted to strike Sergeant William Davis over the head with her cane. Davis replied, "Madam you do not think to strike." "Are you not ashamed to be the leader of a gang of negroes?" she asked Captain Miller. He responded, "It seems you were not ashamed to hold these men, women, and children in bondage and why do you tell me should I be ashamed to lead them to sweet liberty." Even Mrs. Shaw's threat of a massacre by her husband's regiment that "would soon manure this land of mine with your Negro troops" did not deter Miller in his mission. Such threats were only a part of his military and moral mission. In speaking of the slaves that joined his expedition on the journey back to Portsmouth, Miller remarked, "The rejoicing of the contrabands was indeed great, all night they were praying and praising God for their deliverances, I felt I was indeed well payed [sic] for my exposure; for God was truly smiling upon us with his blessing."[1]

Captain Miller had been regimental chaplain of the 35th Massachusetts Infantry under then-Colonel Edward A. Wild earlier in the war. Born in Germany in 1832, Miller had been a Baptist minister in Norton, Massachusetts, until his appointment to the 35th in 1862. Maintaining "steadfast ways," Miller grew extremely frustrated by not converting the "unsanctified" white soldiers. One soldier in the 35th believed that Miller's inability to promote religion made his influence over the men an instrument "for evil rather than for good." In addition to his duties as regimental chaplain, he served as regimental postmaster, which some of the soldiers later observed "was also unpleasant to him," as it was his job to convey news of soldiers' deaths to families at home. Active service in command of former slaves seemed to have been the remedy to his frustrations. He resigned as chaplain in March 1863.[2]

Miller proved to be a dependable officer and capable leader while in command of Company K. Balancing military efficiency with a solid moral foundation in leading black soldiers, Miller would have a longer tenure in command of the same company than any other captain in the regiment. He would only relinquish command when his enlistment expired in August 1866.[3] Captain Miller would not have fulfilled his mission without the cooperation of black noncommissioned officers in the regiment like Sergeant Davis. Davis, a 27-year-old "farmer" from Halifax, North Carolina, would later earn promotion to first sergeant leading Company E into battle (due to the shortages of officers) at New Market Heights near Richmond, Virginia, on September 29, 1864. This episode at the Shaw homestead served as a prime example of the alliance between black soldiers and their white officers that was "forged in battle" during the Civil War.[4]

Officers and enlisted men in white regiments in both Union and Confederate armies often knew each other before the war. In a sense, northern and southern white soldiers serving in companies and regiments composed of men from the same communities created surrogate homes in the armies. Fellow comrades were often neighbors and commanding officers were often their community leaders.[5]

Southern black Union soldiers often served in the same companies and regiments with family, kin, and fellow slaves from the same plantations, as did the black soldiers in the 2nd North Carolina. However, they had no prior knowledge of their white officers nor could they expect that their home communities mainly on southern plantations and farms would remain intact through the course of the war. At least 35 percent of the black soldiers in the regiment served as noncommissioned officers during their military service. It would be these intermediary leaders who attempted to bridge the racial and cultural gaps between black soldiers and their white officers.[6]

In general, white officers and black noncommissioned officers had to make sure that they understood the distinctions between being a slave and being a soldier when it came to training and disciplining black units. Black soldiers were to be treated as soldiers and men regardless of their previous condition of servitude. Punishment handed down by officers perceived to resemble those meted out by overseers on the plantation could adversely affect military morale and discipline.[7]

In spite of their best intentions, white commanders held complex and often contradictory views of former slaves and their ability to make good soldiers. Major General Benjamin F. Butler, while military governor of New Orleans in 1862, concluded that former slaves would make good soldiers because "they are all disciplined ... they have learned a thing we can never learn — at least, not until after three or four years, and then very imperfectly — and that is, to do as they are told." Colonel Thomas W. Higginson, commanding the 1st South Carolina Colored Volunteers, argued that former slaves "will depend more upon their white officers than white troops and be more influenced by their conduct."[8]

Free black soldiers in black units recruited in the North were particularly sensitive to any perception of unfair treatment in the ranks for the simple fact that while they had suffered discrimination at the hands of white northerners, they had little or no experience being under the master's lash. Less than 4 percent of the men serving in the 2nd North Carolina claimed to have been free before the war, therefore the majority of noncommissioned officers would eventually be chosen from among former slaves giving them leadership experience and official authority to exercise leadership sanctioned by the Union military establishment rather than at the pleasure of individual slaveholders.[9]

It was of crucial importance that black soldiers did not view their black noncommissioned officers simply as "slave drivers" for white commissioned officers. Antebellum slaves often held negative views of black slave drivers because of the power they had held over them. More often than not, slave drivers had walked the narrow line between enforcing the plantation rules established by masters and overseers while advocating the interests of their fellow slaves.[10]

Ironically, the qualifications for slave drivers on larger southern plantations were similar to the qualifications of noncommissioned officers in the Union army. Antebellum slave drivers, regardless of their power or how much they might have held their master's confidence, were still part of the slave community. Similarly, noncommissioned officers, although holding rank and privileges above privates, were still enlisted men like privates. Slaveholders had sought drivers to assist white overseers and who were honest, industrious, not openly opinionated or too talkative, good workers in their own right, and faithful in carrying out their assigned tasks. It was the model slave driver who could best articulate and relay the master's or overseer's wishes and impulses.[11]

Likewise, noncommissioned officers were the buffers between commissioned officers and enlisted men. They transmitted and translated the orders of the regimental and company commanders to the men while exercising their authority through personal leadership and moral character. It was the company commander who nominated the first sergeant, sergeants, and corporals for his particular company subject to the approval of the regimental commander. The regimental commander chose the regimental noncommissioned officers.[12]

These "men in between" commissioned officers and privates enforced discipline and good order in the regiment. Black "non-coms," however, carried a special burden. On the one hand, as noncommissioned officers they could not freely fraternize with privates. On the other, the fact that they were noncommissioned officers did not mitigate the racism they received from soldiers in white regiments or pay that was less than what was due them at their respective ranks.[13] Nevertheless, the black noncommissioned officers in the 2nd North Carolina often served in these positions within their own companies longer than many of their white commissioned officers. Under these circumstances, high morale, strict discipline, and good military performance were often maintained by these black "non-coms."

The U.S. War Department gave Brigadier General Edward A. Wild wide authority in the selection of white officers for his African Brigade in April 1863. Wild picked junior officers and enlisted men who had served in white regiments with combat experience and were on duty in areas where many of the black recruits had lived as slaves. Moreover and most importantly, Wild sought officers who shared his abolitionist beliefs and desire to aid the black race.[14]

The first officers for the 2nd North Carolina Colored Volunteers (36th USCT) selected in July 1863 came mostly from Massachusetts regiments. It was clear that the "Old Bay State" desired to have her native sons leading the black ranks in destroying the Confederacy. Only six had been officers in white regiments, one had been a regimental chaplain, two had been noncommissioned officers on regimental staffs, six had been sergeants, seven had been corporals, ten had been privates, and two had been civilians. Therefore, these newly appointed white officers as well as the black recruits would be learning their new roles on the job.[15]

The nucleus of the 36th's officers came from Wild's former command, the 35th Massachusetts Infantry, and from the 25th Massachusetts Infantry which had been a part of General Ambrose Burnside's North Carolina Expedition in 1862 and had been stationed near New Bern ever since. Captains Benjamin Franklin Pratt and Daniel Johnson Preston, commanding Companies H and F respectively in the 35th Massachusetts, held two of the three ranking field officer positions in the 36th USCT. Pratt, a 39-year-old shoe manufacturer from North Weymouth, Massachusetts, became lieutenant colonel. Preston, a 46-year-old shoe cutter who became major, hailed from Danvers, Massachusetts.[16]

Wild did not stop with officer appointments just from among his wartime acquaintances in the 35th Massachusetts. George Washington Smith Conant, who had served as a private in Company A, 1st Massachusetts Infantry, which Wild commanded as a captain in 1861 and 1862, was appointed a second lieutenant in Company G, 36th USCT. Conant, a butcher from Boston, had received a gunshot wound in his left arm at the Battle of Seven Pines (Fair Oaks), Virginia, in June 1862. His wound had been severe enough for him to be discharged for disability. Conant was already receiving an invalid's pension when Wild sought him out in September 1863. No doubt Wild persuaded the 20-year-old veteran to become an officer in the 36th USCT by referring to his own wounds received in battle and his own perseverance to ameliorate the condition of the black race by organizing a brigade of former slaves.

Another veteran comrade of Conant's, also in Company A, 1st Massachusetts, was Private Charles D. Griggs who subsequently served in the 2nd Massachusetts Cavalry attaining the rank of first sergeant. Griggs was appointed first lieutenant and regimental adjutant for the 36th USCT. Much of the early orders and other communications for the 2nd North Carolina Colored Volunteers (36th USCT) would be transmitted through Griggs. Private Hiram W. Allen of Company E, 1st Massachusetts, was appointed a first lieutenant in the 36th and served as one of Wild's staff officers for the greater part of the war. Wild also appointed his younger brother, Walter, as a captain in the 36th, and retained him as a staff officer as well. Walter had just received a commission as a first lieutenant in Colonel Robert G. Shaw's 54th Massachusetts (Colored) Infantry.[17]

Four additional enlisted men from the 35th Massachusetts were commissioned as lieutenants in the 36th USCT in early 1864. Corporal Francis A. Bicknell, Company H, 35th Massachusetts, was 20 years old when he became a second lieutenant in the 36th. Serving under Pratt in the 35th, Bicknell worked as a shoe cutter before the war. Private William M. Titcomb left his comrades in Company I, 35th Massachusetts, and accepted his commission as a second lieutenant in the 36th USCT with the hope of his comrades that "success and prosperity attend him." Sergeant Frank W. Rhoades and Private Amory O. Balch, both of Company K, 35th Massachusetts, accepted commissions as first and second lieutenants respectively in the 36th USCT.[18]

These white veterans of the 35th Massachusetts had considerable combat experience early in the war while serving under then Colonel Wild in the Army of the Potomac. Lieutenant Colonel Pratt, as a captain, had been wounded at the Battle of South Mountain, Maryland, in the fall of 1862. Due to the regiment's heavy losses at the Battle of Fredericksburg, Virginia, in December 1862, Pratt temporarily served as acting lieutenant colonel well into the new year further honing his leadership and administrative skills at higher command levels. Another veteran of Fredericksburg was Sergeant Charles H. Frye of Company F, 21st Massachusetts, who was appointed the rank of captain and commanding officer of Company B, 36th USCT.[19]

The transfer of the 35th Massachusetts to the border state of Kentucky and its brief service there may have been the catalyst that encouraged some of the men to leave their white comrades and command former slaves. Kentucky had declared its neutrality at the start of the war and maintained slavery within its borders. A Confederate invasion in 1862 forced this reluctant slave state to remain in the Union. President Lincoln, recognizing the delicate situation in his birth state and wishing to keep it in the Union, left it exempt from the Emancipation Proclamation as if had it never been issued. Perhaps one of the most unpleasant and ironic tasks that the 35th Massachusetts had to perform was guard duty at a slave auction.

## 4. Selected from the Most Intelligent Among Them

Another incident that might have proven to be an epiphany for some of the men involved a young runaway slave boy named Mace. Mace had gained asylum with the 35th Massachusetts and held the affections of the entire regiment for several weeks before being returned to his master. One of the regiment's lieutenants had refused to return the young boy, but had to relinquish him since the owner declared his loyalty to the United States. Such incidents affected these future officers in the 36th USCT making their decision to serve as officers in a regiment of former slaves easier.[20]

The 25th Massachusetts Infantry contributed seven enlisted soldiers as officers to the 36th USCT. All of them had been either privates or corporals. These soldiers had participated in combat at Roanoke Island and New Bern and had considerable knowledge of the conditions many of the soldiers they were to command had been under. Moreover, the prestige and pay of commissioned officers were also strong incentives for these enlisted men. Private Edwin Collins Gaskill, Company B, 25th Massachusetts, followed in his brother Leonard's footsteps as an officer in the 36th USCT. Leonard Taft Gaskill, formerly a corporal in the 25th Massachusetts, had been one of the original appointments Wild made to the regiment as a second lieutenant. Edwin would be appointed a second lieutenant in early 1864. The Gaskill brothers had been farmers from Mendon, Massachusetts, before the war.[21]

Wild's most important appointment to the 36th USCT in the spring of 1863 was Alonzo Granville Draper as colonel commanding the regiment. Draper came from a Massachusetts regiment outside of Wild's sphere of influence. Draper shared similar views with Wild on the arming of former slaves to fight the Confederacy. Draper would be the driving force in making the 36th USCT the symbolic model for former slaves and the American public in the destruction of slavery toward the elevation of the black race. Although succeeding to higher levels of command as the war progressed, Draper continued to keep his "model regiment" within his sphere of influence and control. His own life before and during the war would have significant effects on the black soldiers and white officers under his command.

Born in Brattleboro, Vermont, on September 6, 1835, young Draper had been

Benjamin Franklin Pratt (1824–1890) was a shoe manufacturer from North Weymouth, Massachusetts. Early in the war, he served as a captain in the 35th Massachusetts Infantry, leading his company through the brutal battles of South Mountain and Fredericksburg. Pratt took his place as Lieutenant Colonel of the 2nd North Carolina Colored Volunteers (36th USCT) on September 5, 1863, and would be the acting regimental commander from its service at Point Lookout, Maryland, to the fall of Richmond, Virginia. In this photograph, Pratt is wearing the uniform of a brigadier general that he earned by brevet on March 13, 1865 (Massachusetts Commandery Military Order of the Loyal Legion and the U.S. Army Military History Institute).

already identified as something of a child genius. The second child and eldest son of Alonzo and Hannah Draper, young Alonzo grew inquisitive over the meaning of words and numerous subjects brought up in adult conversations that caused many to dub him "a lawyer in embryo." He also possessed a photographic memory. His father, a music teacher specializing in piano and wind instruments, composed a book of military marches and fife melodies that was well known throughout New England. In 1843, the Drapers moved to Boston where young Alonzo attended the Otis High School, graduating in 1850. It was during this time that he became involved in the temperance movement and gave his first public lecture at age 15 in Boxwood, Massachusetts. Shortly after this, Draper helped organize a temperance society in Boston with the specific goal of attracting younger members as well as senior citizens. He was responsible for drafting this organization's constitution and bylaws. He maintained his commitment to temperance as a member of the cadets of temperance for eight years and later, as an adult, in the Sons of Temperance.[22]

In 1854, Draper graduated as first scholar from Boston's English High School, winning two Franklin medals and three other academic prizes. At the commencement ceremony, he delivered an address entitled "Compromises with Slavery." According to Draper, his address "was so radical that the Principal, Thomas Sherwin, a thorough abolitionist, felt compelled to modify it, to avoid giving offences to Mayor Smith, Chairman of the School Committee." Mayor Jerome Van Crowninshield Smith had just sanctioned the legal return of fugitive slave Anthony Burns back into slavery under the Fugitive Slave Act of 1850. This was Draper's earliest known recorded commitment to abolitionism.[23]

Daniel Johnson Preston (1817–1886), a leading citizen of Danvers, Massachusetts, and a veteran captain of the 35th Massachusetts Infantry, joined the 2nd North Carolina Colored Volunteers (36th USCT) as its major on December 6, 1863. It was hoped that the combined combat experience of both Preston and Pratt would provide Colonel Draper ample expertise in shaping the 36th USCT into a "model regiment" (Massachusetts Commandery Military Order of the Loyal Legion and the U.S. Army Military History Institute).

Unable to afford college, Draper hoped to read and study law as a legal apprentice and moved to Lynn, Massachusetts, sometime in 1855. Since Lynn was a major nineteenth-century shoe-manufacturing town, Draper learned the shoemaker's trade within three weeks and earned good wages. He also taught himself to play the harp and made occasional money performing at various balls and other formal functions around the city. He also taught private classes in French and mathematics to supplement his earnings. In 1856, he married the daughter of the local justice of the peace with the consent of his own father, since he was under 21 at the time. It was probably best since his first daughter, Sarah, would arrive in less than eight months.[24]

By 1859, Draper had become

actively involved in the emerging labor movement advocating the interests of journeyman shoemakers. An overstocked market causing a decline in prices and the beginning rise in shoe-making factories threatening the existence of individual shoemakers led to the creation of the Lynn Mechanics Association. In March 1859, Draper became editor of the short-lived *New England Mechanic* as the public vehicle for this association addressing the shoemakers' interests and concerns. By 1860, the journeyman shoemakers went on a series of large strikes causing tensions between the striking workers and local law enforcement officials. Nevertheless, striking workers received support among non-shoemakers in Lynn and sympathetic populations outside New England.[25]

Draper, as a major strike leader, canvassed New England and New York State on behalf of Lynn's shoemakers. His fluent extemporaneous speaking to churches and local benevolence organizations helped gain moral support for the shoemakers and raise funds on behalf of striking workers' families. The *Lynn* (Massachusetts) *Weekly Reporter* assessed Draper as a strike leader, "a man of ability, and a conservative leader, invariably counseling moderation and deprecating, at all times, any resort to violence." The organizational success of the striking shoemakers led to political success in the Lynn municipal elections in December 1860. Candidates backed by labor organizations involved in the strike swept into office. Draper became an assistant city marshal taking control of the police force. He fired the police chief and replaced him with someone from the ranks of the journeyman shoemakers.[26]

The beginning of the Civil War in April 1861 interrupted Draper's preparation to enter the legal profession and he organized a local militia company composed of primarily shoemakers. "At this time," he recalled, "I was totally ignorant of military tactics, but in six days, I had enlisted a company to the maximum, committed to memory Casey's Tactics, and began to instruct my men, and in two days more, passed a successful examination before the board" to become a captain. Three months later this company, the "Mechanics Phalanx of Lynn," would be assigned to the 14th Massachusetts Infantry as Company C.[27]

The 14th Massachusetts (later the 1st Massachusetts Heavy Artillery) spent the early part of the war as garrison troops in and around Washington, D.C., with a brief stint of duty at Harper's Ferry, Virginia. Draper continued to drill his company as infantry and heavy artillery. In August 1862, Draper's brigade commander ordered him to instruct the 17th New York Infantry in both infantry and artillery tactics, reflecting favorably upon his abilities as a military instructor and disciplinarian. On January 16, 1863, he was promoted to major and held command of Fort Albany, and later Fort Craig, which were part of the Washington defenses. While performing his military duties, Draper also found time to become involved in the Masonic Order, which provided him influential military and political connections as the war progressed.[28]

As the search for officers to command black troops was in full swing, Draper's name was among the many that had crossed the desk of Massachusetts Governor John A. Andrew, who had successfully organized the 54th and 55th Massachusetts (Colored) Infantry regiments. As "an anti-slavery man, and friend of the negro race," Draper believed commanding a black regiment of former slaves was the proper pursuit in which his talents could be utilized and his ambitions realized. He wrote Andrew in April 1863:

> I am but twenty-seven years old and am anxious after nearly two years of garrison duty to distinguish myself in the field, by a fruitful devotion to duty, and, aside from my selfish motives, I have a sincere desire to assist in ameliorating the condition of the colored race, and in their enfranchisement from that social depression to which an ignorant popular prejudice has consigned them. This sentiment is not a novel one to me, but is consistent with the whole course of my life.[29]

Draper's commanding officer, Colonel Thomas R. Tannatt, believed that Draper was "a too severe disciplinarian" to command black troops despite his ability to train and lead white troops. Expressing stereotypical but paternalistically sympathetic views of former slaves similar to many northern abolitionists and missionaries, Draper responded to his former regimental commander's remarks:

> The Negro, while he is docile, immature, and easily taught[,] is more ambitious of approbation, than he is fearful of punishment, and that he should be governed by a kind yet steady and firm discipline; and I should no more think of applying to recruits the discipline suitable for old soldiers, than I should of feeding an infant on diet proper for an adult.[30]

Draper believed that the military service of former slaves was the best means of elevating them to free citizens. His concerns for black soldiers' families who had been in slavery stemmed from his concerns over shoemakers' families before the war trapped under an economic slavery. The extensive efforts Draper made on behalf of the workingmen of Lynn, Massachusetts, were equally displayed on the former slaves serving under his command. Draper, undoubtedly, was ambitious and possibly hoped for political office at the war's conclusion.

Major General Benjamin F. Butler, upon his return to Virginia in 1863, took Draper under his wing. Although Draper and Wild enthusiastically supported the military recruitment of former slaves, providing care and protection for their families, they often held different views in commanding black soldiers and the type of white officers leading them. After Wild's December 1863 expedition into North Carolina, Butler realized that Wild was more extreme in his methods than he himself was willing to go at that time. Butler, although supporting black recruitment and soldiers' families, was still undergoing his own transformation from viewing former slaves simply as practical war necessities to active participants in righting the moral wrongs of slavery.

It is possible that Butler had viewed Wild as a member of the exclusive higher social circles of Massachusetts. Butler continued to remain an outsider in these circles in spite of his rise to wealth and prominence before the war, and this may have caused a social distance between the two men. Butler probably saw a younger version of himself in Draper. Both were New England transplants to Massachusetts (Butler born in Maine, Draper born in Vermont). They sought to realize their ambitions in Massachusetts. Butler had viewed his own life as a "rags-to-riches" story like Draper and had championed the rights of factory workers as a Massachusetts state legislator.[31] Butler probably believed that Wild was too set in his ways to be influenced by him since they were both in their early 40s. However, Draper was still in his late 20s with a promising future and could be cultivated as one of Butler's many protégés in the Union army. The 36th's assignment to Point Lookout, Maryland, in February 1864 may have been in part due to Butler's desire to keep Wild from influencing Draper and creating problems from interfering with his own plans with regard to the black soldiers in his command. This new assignment might have also been an attempt to shield Draper from continued furor over his activities during Wild's 1863 expedition into northeastern North Carolina.

When Draper took command of the 36th USCT, when it was still known as the 2nd North Carolina, he was not immediately impressed with the officers Wild had appointed for the regiment. "I have ten line officers now with the Regiment," he wrote in September 1863, "most of them novices in drill, and in the knowledge of Company books and papers. They are with few exceptions capable, and will make good officers. But they have generally been unaccustomed to military discipline; in the sense in which I have understood it." Draper placed his companies under the command of black noncommissioned officers "selected from the most intelligent among them" until many of his white officers returned from recruiting service. This shortage of white officers was similar in the other regiments of Wild's African Brigade. It was such leadership shortages and practical necessities rather than sweeping changes in military policy from the War Department that dictated the emergence of black noncommissioned officers. Although black enlisted men held the noncommissioned ranks from first sergeant down to corporal, white soldiers who were later commissioned as junior officers when vacancies in the regiment opened held the initial noncommissioned staff positions in the regiment.[32]

Black Union regiments, recruited among northern freemen, were allowed to have black noncommissioned officers serving as first sergeants, sergeants, corporals, and on the regimental noncommissioned staff. Regiments composed of former slaves were to have a white noncommissioned staff, including sergeant major, quartermaster sergeant, and commissary sergeant, as well as white company first sergeants. It was believed that white supervision was required over former slaves at almost every level of command within these particular regiments. In the 36th USCT, John Owen, Jr., a white Harvard student from Cambridge, Massachusetts, served as regimental sergeant major from January 23 to April 26, 1864, when he was commissioned a second lieutenant. Eugene J. Courtney, a clerk born in Killarney, Ireland, residing in Boston, served as regimental quartermaster sergeant from September 24, 1863, to November 23, 1864, when he was commissioned a second lieutenant. Daniel J. Courtney, a clerk from Wales, served as regimental commissary sergeant from December 26, 1863, to November 25, 1864, when he replaced Eugene Courtney as quartermaster sergeant and served in that position until his commission as a second lieutenant on March 25, 1865. Charles F. Bly, who eventually served as a first lieutenant in the 36th USCT, had been the white sergeant major of the 37th USCT.[33]

Sometimes white officers commanding regiments of former slaves sought free educated black enlistees to serve in the higher noncommissioned ranks. Doing so would allow former slaves to interact with those of their race. Henry N. Adkins, a freeborn black gardener from New York, replaced Owen as sergeant major on May 1, 1864. He had enlisted in Company E on September 1, 1863, as a sergeant, and was appointed company first sergeant five days later. On February 13, 1864, Adkins was demoted to private for an unspecified reason a few months before his promotion to sergeant major. His promotion was a big leap in the enlisted ranks.[34]

Adkins, as sergeant major, in theory, outranked the white quartermaster and commissary sergeants until their commissions as junior officers in the regiment. But these two particular noncommissioned ranks normally took their orders from the regimental quartermaster, usually a first lieutenant, and not from the sergeant major. With few exceptions, the sergeant major was the highest rank that black soldiers, regardless of qualifications and previous condition, attained during the war.[35]

The sergeant major functioned as the regimental commander's liaison to the enlisted men. Literacy and free status before the war seem to have been the early prerequisites for black noncommissioned officers. Nevertheless, personal leadership and respect of fellow soldiers as well as the respect of white officers soon became the major qualifications for black noncommissioned officers. Leadership experiences on the battlefield would shatter previous stereotypes of former slaves turned soldiers. It probably did not hurt matters at the regimental headquarters that Adkins was described as "light" in complexion rather than having a "dark" or "black" one. Adkins' ability to read and write was an asset to the regiment as well as to himself in the estimation of his white officers. While the regiment served in the Petersburg trenches in November 1864, Brigadier General Charles J. Paine, commanding the 3rd Division, 18th Army Corps, Army of the James, requested nominations for literate black privates from the regiments in his command to fill the position of clerk at higher headquarters. Major William H. Hart, reporting for the 36th USCT, replied that Adkins was the only individual in the regiment qualified, but could not be detailed for this duty, as he was greatly needed in the regiment. White officers in other black regiments reported very few or no qualified privates except for their sergeant majors and first sergeants to fill these positions and that they too were needed in their regiments.[36] By the end of the war, all the 36th's noncommissioned officers, including those on the regimental staff, were black. During the late spring of 1865 after the fall of Richmond, the 36th USCT gained clerical assistance from a literate black draftee on loan from one of the USCTs organized in Pennsylvania named Alonzo (or Lorenzo) Gould, who was briefly attached to the regiment from mid–April 1865 to the first few months it was stationed in Texas.[37]

The black soldiers of the 36th USCT early on viewed Draper as their advocate and judged him a fair but firm individual. Colonel Tannatt, Draper's former commander in the Washington defenses, still concerned that his former subordinate would be harsh on his new regiment, had opened the possibility for Draper to become a colonel in a white regiment suited for his type of discipline and thoroughness. Draper replied to Andrew that "it is not the blacks who try my patience, it is white officers." Draper, later commanding the 36th, informed Andrew, "I am making arrangements to establish a regular evening school in my Regiment, for the instruction of the enlisted men. The difficulty is to find teachers enough for the number who desire to learn, my officers being fully employed in learning their own duties, and in reciting tactics."[38]

By May 1864, while the regiment served in St. Mary's County, Maryland, several weekly sessions for the military instruction of noncommissioned officers were conducted by their company officers. One session was devoted to black noncommissioned officers who could read and write well, in preparation for them to serve as teachers among the freedmen on nearby confiscated farms.[39]

The regimental chaplains in black units, particularly if they themselves were black, served as educators of the men in addition to being spiritual advisors. Article 24, *Revised Regulations for the Army, 1861*, allowed for each colonel of a regiment to appoint chaplains on the nomination of company commanders. "None but regularly ordained ministers of some Christian denomination, however, shall be eligible to appointment," according to the regulations. Full consideration was given to the soldiers in the regiment for their own preference and support for particular candidates for chaplain.[40] Since black soldiers and white officers had not shared similar community experiences before the war, General Wild appointed a black chaplain for the regiment who he believed held the best interest of the soldiers in the 36th. This was Chaplain David Stevens.

Stevens, an African Methodist Episcopalian minister from Harrisburg, Pennsylvania, served as the regiment's chaplain for much of its Civil War service. Appointed in July 1863, Stevens was the only black officer in a technical sense to serve in the regiment. Claiming to have been a drummer boy in the War of 1812, he was well over 60 years old when he assumed his duties. In April 1864, while the regiment was on duty at Point Lookout, Maryland, Stevens submitted his resignation to the War Department citing his advanced age and ill health. Butler's personal endorsement rejecting his resignation stated that Stevens "is certainly but six months older than when he took his commission.... If ever he were fit for his position, he is as fit now as ever." Chaplain Stevens continued on in his position until his resignation was accepted finally on June 6, 1865. He counted as one of only 14 black chaplains to serve with black regiments in the Civil War.[41]

Black chaplains commissioned in 1863 had initially received $10 a month, the same as black laborers. In addition to pay discrimination, black chaplains were often the victims of racial slights and insults like black soldiers. By June 1864, they received their proper pay of $100 a month, equivalent to a major of cavalry. Thomas Scott Johnson, formerly the white chaplain of the 127th USCT, replaced Stevens on September 12, 1865, while the regiment was stationed at Brazos Santiago, Texas.[42] Despite the presence of black chaplains and surgeons, control over the organization of black regiments in the Union army remained a "white man's affair."

The Bureau of Colored Troops, created by General Order No. 143 on May 22, 1863, assumed responsibility in handling all affairs concerning black regiments and selecting and examining white officers in black units. As an agency of the Adjutant General's Office in the War Department, the Bureau of Colored Troops was responsible for renaming the 2nd North Carolina Colored Volunteers to the 36th Infantry, United States Colored Troops, in late February 1864.[43]

The change in the unit's name reflected two developments. First, it established the U.S. government with the chief responsibility of managing the affairs of freedmen as outlined initially in the Emancipation Proclamation. Second, in a more subtle way, it implied the supremacy of national allegiance over state allegiance at a time when the status of persons of color in the United States remained uncertain. While some of the black units raised in northern states (54th and 55th Massachusetts, 29th Connecticut, and 5th Massachusetts Cavalry) kept their original unit designations, most black units received USCT designations regardless of where they were raised.

The War Department had made it clear that white officers would command black soldiers as soon as U.S. policy sanctioned the recruitment of black soldiers. General Wild as well as Governor Andrew had hoped that qualified black commissioned officers would be accepted into the 54th and 55th Massachusetts and subsequent black regiments. When this did not occur, Wild appointed his share of qualified black professionals as chaplains (like David Stevens), surgeons, and assistant surgeons for his North Carolina African Brigade before the Bureau of Colored Troops took over officer selections. While these positions were not command (or line officer) positions, those serving in them expected to receive the pay, prestige, and military courtesy of commissioned officers.[44] Butler, commanding the Department of Virginia and North Carolina in December 1863, inquired of the Bureau of Colored Troops if he had authority to commission black officers. Secretary of War Edwin M. Stanton informed him, "You are authorized to make such appointments as you saw proper, provisionally, subject to the approval of the President, and that upon reporting them to this Department, they would be commissioned by him." President Lincoln had struggled to convince the Union military and northern public to accept the use of black soldiers. He was not ready as of yet to take a step further to approve large numbers of black commissioned officers.[45]

On March 18, 1865, Sergeant Major Henry N. Adkins submitted a request to the Bureau of Colored Troops to be commissioned a second lieutenant in the regiment. He was about 21 years old at the time he made his request. Lieutenant Colonel Benjamin F. Pratt, commanding the regiment at the time, endorsed Adkins' request and added that he "has had a good education ... has always been a faithful and good soldier, always done his duty, whether in camp, on the march, or in Battle." Pratt forwarded the request to Alonzo Draper, at this time brigade commander and brevet brigadier general, who added that if it was the policy to commission black officers, "Sergt. Major Adkins has all the required qualifications." Adkins' request followed up through to the division commander, Brigadier General Edward A. Wild, who earnestly approved, and corps commander, Major General Godfrey Weitzel, who disapproved the request.[46] The Bureau of Colored Troops in its reply to General Weitzel formally disapproved Adkins' request for a commission on the grounds that "there is no authority under which colored men can be commissioned as officers.... It is considered highly inexpedient to introduce dissension into the colored corps by such recommendations."[47] Adkins' unsuccessful attempt for an officer's commission was the only one known to have been made by a black soldier in the 36th USCT.

As early as September 1863, Draper began weeding out the officers in his regiment appointed by Wild and replacing them with some of his own former comrades and associates. Most of Wild's appointments, in his estimation, possessed too little military experience and moral aptitude to command black soldiers who had been slaves. Draper believed that his officers should be devoted to their military duties and set good examples for the men at all times. As a result, consumption of alcohol was prohibited and the use of profanity was discouraged. Moreover, the good nature of the enlisted men should not be taken advantage of by their officers who knew how to behave. Draper would have numerous problems in enforcing such rules of appropriate behavior.[48] His strict adherence to measures such as these would cause friction among some of his subordinate officers.

While at Portsmouth, Virginia, Draper suspected that some of his officers on recruiting duty spent more time "on the streets" than recruiting soldiers. This was the case when he disapproved Captain George Bradbury's request for a 30-day leave. Bradbury commanded Company G and had been on recruiting duty at nearby Hampton and Newport News.[49]

Another problem Draper confronted involved his officers committing offenses against their men. Since many white officers believed that black soldiers would rely heavily on them due to their apparent docile nature, particular care had to be exercised on the part of officers when interacting with them. This was not always the case. First Lieutenant Joseph G. Longley of Company F had allegedly consumed some of his men's food rations in addition to other items purchased for their own use. Draper filed a complaint to Wild against Longley. Longley made an unsuccessful attempt at vindicating his actions to Wild. Refusing to grant his request for a second interview, Wild charged that Longley owed the men in his company at least $10 to replace the rations and anything further he had to say would not help his situation.[50] Wild further noted that while "the specific injuries inflicted on any of the men are trivial in degree ... [Longley's] whole tone and manner toward them as illy adapted to the treatment of African troops, and must be corrected in the future. If Lt. Longley protests against this decision he must be referred to a Court Martial or Court of Inquiry." Longley made numerous unsuccessful attempts to get a medical discharge from the 36th and was finally successful on June 29, 1864.[51]

It should be noted that Longley's motives for serving as an officer in a regiment of former slaves seemed sincere as extant records show. Born in Hawley, Massachusetts, Longley attended Oberlin College in Ohio one of the first interracial and co-educational institutions of higher learning in the nation as well as a well-spring of antebellum abolitionist activity. Employed as a teacher in Westborough, Massachusetts, he enlisted as a private in Company C, 51st Massachusetts, at the start of the war. His company commander happened to be the radical abolitionist Thomas W. Higginson, who had secretly funded support for John Brown's ill-fated raid on Harpers Ferry, Virginia, in 1859 and who would soon take command as colonel of the 1st South Carolina Colored Volunteers (33rd USCT). It was because of his early associations that Wild selected Longley among his initial list of officers to serve under Draper. Longley, at 40, was one of the older company officers in the regiment, and Wild may have hoped that he would prove to be a reliable and experienced voice of reason for the younger Draper.

Ill health plagued Longley during his military tenure with the 36th USCT and may have accounted for his reliance on consuming additional rations from his own men as well as the negative behavior he was charged with displaying toward them. His appeals for a medical discharged may not have been taken seriously at a time when Draper, as a new commander, wanted to establish his command presence with his subordinate officers by holding fast to rigid policies.

After his discharge, Longley was appointed by the American Missionary Association as superintendent of freedmen schools in North Carolina's Lower Cape Fear region, demonstrating his continued desire and commitment to assist former slaves. At war's end, Longley attended a theological seminary in Auburn, New York, where he graduated in the hopes of becoming a Congregational minister. Death cancelled his pastoral plans in 1871.[52]

Longley's alleged offense was not unusual. The taking of money by white officers from black soldiers was one of the more common and unfortunate offenses committed, but not exclusively peculiar to black regiments. Draper, as a major in the 14th Massachusetts, had dealt with a lieutenant who was indebted to the white soldiers of the regiment in the amount of $1,000. This same lieutenant had previously asked for an appointment in a black regiment, and Draper later revoked his letter of recommendation on his behalf.[53] The little money the black soldiers were paid would be needed for their families and Draper went to great lengths to safeguard their finances.

In the fall of 1864, Draper, commanding a brigade that included the 36th USCT near Petersburg, Virginia, ordered the regimental sutlers of his three black regiments to close their operations. These "civilian stores" accompanying regiments throughout the war offered numerous items for soldiers to purchase. Draper's sutlers were expelled due to "their repeated violations of express orders in practising [sic] a system of uniform extortion upon the soldiers," observed black news correspondent Thomas Morris Chester. One historian of the 5th USCT, a black regiment in Draper's brigade, wrote that his action, while temporarily depriving the men of comforts provided by sutlers, demonstrated his care for the men. "Colonel Draper ... inspired the men by proving that they fought in a common cause," he concluded.[54]

Moreover, in October 1864 Butler authorized the establishment of a freedmen's savings bank in Norfolk, Virginia, for the benefit of all black soldiers in his department. An officer from each regiment, usually the chaplain, made regular deposits into the bank on behalf of the soldiers. Care was taken to send separate descriptive rolls accurately recording the amount of money deposited in individual accounts. Although former slaves were by no means ignorant of the value of money and savings, this freedmen's bank allowed many of them to actively participate in their own personal financial management and future investment.[55]

Besides finances, Draper remained concerned over the moral development of his black soldiers. Therefore, temperance remained a major requirement for Draper's white officers as well as the men. "My habits are strictly temperate," Draper had informed Governor Andrew in March 1863 while seeking command of a black regiment. Citing himself as a member of the Sons of Temperance, Draper "used no liquor until my illness three months ago, and then only in small quantities, and strictly according to the Surgeon's prescriptions, and according to the terms of my temperance pledge." In October 1863, Captain George W. Ives, commanding Company F, had his officer's commission revoked by Wild, admitting to drunkenness while on duty. Ives had been appointed by Wild from the 46th Massachusetts Infantry where he had served as a sergeant. Given the opportunity to tender his resignation, Ives wrote, "In good faith I accepted an appointment in the 2nd N.C. Cold. Vols. I find that my habits which are intemperate, render my usefulness of no effect."[56] To Draper's chagrin, this left Lieutenant Longley in command of Company F for the time being.

By March 1864, Draper began replacing the 36th's white officers with many members from his old command, the 14th Massachusetts (now 1st Massachusetts Heavy Artillery). It was at this time that the regiment had been assigned to the District of St. Mary's, Maryland, where they guarded Confederate prisoners at Point Lookout. The district commander, Brigadier General Edward W. Hinks, issued orders concerning the interaction between officers and enlisted men that included the 36th USCT and the other white regiments on duty there.

While much of his order covered specific procedures regarding guard duty at the prison, Hinks noted that officers under his command allegedly set bad examples for their men through unmilitary habits in manner and dress. "It is useless," Hinks reasoned, "to expect valuable service from men commanded by slovenly officers." It was extremely important for soldiers to show personal deference and respect to superior officers by refraining from loud talking, profanity, and boisterous conduct in their presence. However, soldiers could not be expected to have the respect of an officer "loafing about in his shirt sleeves" among the troops.[57]

Draper took further measures to insure his officers were accountable for their actions and carrying out their responsibilities as commissioned officers. He ordered that no special rules for the discipline of the men by individual company commanders were enacted that did not apply to the entire regiment. All disciplinary actions had to receive his full endorsement. Additionally, Draper required company commanders to be present in the company streets at "taps" each night to make sure lights were out for the evening and quiet restored among the men. Reviving his pre-war temperance pledge and crusade, Draper prohibited all commissioned officers in the regiment from keeping "intoxicating liquors" in their tents at any time.[58]

Frustrated over stifled independence of command and authority over their men by Draper, eleven officers of the 36th USCT submitted their resignations at various times in early 1864. Nine resignations were collectively forwarded to Butler's headquarters at Fort Monroe in April 1864. Six officers had served in the 25th Massachusetts Infantry, and one officer each had served in the 24th Massachusetts Infantry, the 34th Massachusetts Infantry, and the 24th New York Artillery Battery. All had been appointed by Wild. The officers collectively cited the aforementioned directives recently made by Draper, other unmilitary orders, and a want of confidence in him as a commanding officer as just grounds for their resignations.[59] Individual officers held more specific grievances against Draper. For example, Captain George F. Allen, commanding Company D, stated that Draper had personally insulted him by reporting to General Hinks that he thought Allen's education was insufficient for commanding a company in the 36th USCT.[60]

Draper's particular lack of confidence in Captain Allen's educational capacity for a company command seemed puzzling. Allen, a 34-year-old carpenter from Worcester, Massachusetts, had been a private in the 25th Massachusetts Infantry. Prior to his commission as a first lieutenant in the 36th USCT, Allen had been detailed for special duty at New Bern as part of a detachment pursuing Confederate guerrillas. Shortly thereafter he was in command of a "sappers and miners camp and was in charge of detailed men from other Regiments and away from his own regiment," according to one of his comrades in the 25th.[61] Allen would have had possessed exceptional organizational, technical, and military skills to lead a unit that would be forerunners to demolition units in the modern military while still holding the rank of a private. Moreover, he was among the older officers in the 36th USCT and former comrades in the 25th Massachusetts, giving him the maturity necessary to take on the responsibilities of a company officer. On paper, Allen's military experience alone would have made him a capable officer in Draper's regiment.

Butler personally interviewed the officers at Fort Monroe in the presence of General Wild despite Draper's written endorsement that "the good of the service will be promoted if their resignations are accepted," and Hinks' blunt comment that these officers "be dismissed the Service as worthless officers." Butler wished to "fully hear their statements of the grievances which caused the resignations of so many officers, at the same time, in the face of the enemy, thus tending to bring their Regiment into a state of inefficiency." He was amused at the additional complaint made by the officers that Draper "had issued orders, making it the duty of every officer in command of a company to see that his men had been vaccinated as a prevention of small pox."[62]

At the interview, the officers admitted to Butler that they had fully understood Draper's orders regarding strict temperance when they received their commissions. Furthermore, the "oppressive" order for them to be in the company streets in the evening to police the conduct of their men caused Butler to conclude that since "taps" was sounded at 10 in the evening, and "the officers were obliged to rise at shortly passed five o'clock in the morning they would therefore have seven hours sleep in the night." As far as Butler was concerned, these officers got more sleep than he or any other officer in his command ever received.[63]

Butler failed to see "anything objectionable in either of these orders of Colonel Draper which should give cause to any right-minded, patriotic officer to resign." The officers agreed that Draper had treated them with respect, with the exception of Captain Allen. Butler concluded that "the alleged causes for these resignations were wholly groundless and frivolous, and that such a number of officers, resigning at the same time and for the same frivolous reasons was evidence of a combination to force some action upon their Colonel, and was a very grave breach of contract."[64]

These grievances had been apparent for several months, but Butler observed that they were not sufficient enough to bring forward "until the winter had passed, in comparative ease, and the Spring campaign was about to open." Since the officers had not been issued commissions but simply mustered into the service as officers upon the sole recommendation of Wild, Butler ordered that their musters and provisional appointments in the 36th be revoked and they were ordered to return to their former regiments at their previous ranks to serve out their enlistments; or as a news correspondent reported, they had been reduced to "high privates."[65] Wild had agreed with Butler's decision while in his presence, but it must have been a personal setback to his goals of creating and leading effective black regiments in combat. These were some of the very officers he had handpicked for the regiments of his African Brigade and in whom he trusted in carrying out his mission. This may have been the beginning of resentment between Wild and Draper that would worsen as the war progressed.

On April 26, 1864, a short time after Butler's interview, the six officers who had served in the 25th Massachusetts before their appointments as officers in the 36th refused to return to the 25th "unless they were given their former rank held in the 36th U.S.C.T." George B. Proctor, George F. Allen, George L. Seagrave, Edward Townsend, and Leonard T. Gaskill considered Butler's order for their dismissal "annulled and cancelled." An order was issued for their immediate arrest, and they were taken into custody for violating a direct order from a commanding general.[66]

Captain George B. Proctor and Second Lieutenant Henry M. Field, who had been ordered to return to his former 34th Massachusetts Infantry, attempted to send a message to Supreme Court Associate Justice Stephen D. Field, who was the uncle of the latter officer. They had hoped the Associate Justice would appeal to President Lincoln on behalf of the dismissed officers. Draper apparently charged them with treason for doing this. Later, letters from officers in the 25th Massachusetts were sent to several Massachusetts congressmen attesting to the honorable conduct of the dismissed officers.[67]

On May 3, 1864, the commanding officer of the 25th Massachusetts forwarded a letter to the War Department and certified that the dismissed officers who had been in his regiment were "men of the highest principles and character, always having done their duty promptly, bravely, and faithfully.... Since their promotion I have always heard them well spoken of. I believe them to be gentlemen, as well as soldiers of upright and honorable motives."[68]

John W. Fletcher, who had commanded Company A, 36th USCT, but recently discharged, visited Massachusetts Congressman John D. Baldwin in Washington seeking a fair hearing for his fellow officers in the 36th. Fletcher had served as a lieutenant in the 43rd Massachusetts and the U.S. Signal Corps before his appointment by Wild. He had a note of introduction from Governor Andrew who believed Fletcher "is perfectly familiar with the whole matter out of which grew the disgrace of the young officers concerning whom I wrote the enclosing the papers of their case a few days ago." Andrew, too, had hoped that a fair hearing could be obtained for the dismissed officers.[69]

Lieutenant Colonel Benjamin F. Pratt and Major Daniel J. Preston of the 36th USCT submitted a co-authored letter on May 9, 1864, indicating that they supported the sentiments expressed by the 25th Massachusetts commander concerning his former soldiers. "Judging by their conduct while connected with this regiment as Captains and Lieutenants, we believe them fully entitled to the character set forth in his [25th Massachusetts commander's] certificate of May 3rd.... We say, that during their connection with this regiment as officers, up to the time they tendered their resignations, covering a period of about eight months, they were considered as good, reliable, faithful officers, always ready to do their duty, brave and fearless at all times."[70]

While there is no evidence that Draper ever had any personal disagreements with Pratt or Preston, his second- and third-in-command, it is possible that these former captains of Wild's 35th Massachusetts believed that their old commander was losing influence in Butler's command. They may have resented the fact that Draper was quickly gaining considerable influence and prestige at the expense of someone they had been seen as a pioneer in the recruitment of black troops. There had been a general dislike of Butler by many white soldiers when he took command of the Department of Virginia and North Carolina, and this dislike may have also been directed at officers, like Draper, who were influenced by him. The common element that Pratt, Preston, and Fletcher seemed to rally around in defense of the dismissed officers was Butler's implication that their grievances against Draper were attempts to conceal their own cowardice and lack of desire to confront the enemy. In

### 4. Selected from the Most Intelligent Among Them

this instance, any officer acquainted with them would have been quick to refute any direct or implied statements of a similar nature. One's honor was important to northern-born men, as it was for southerners.

It is also possible that Pratt and Preston believed that the tension between their colonel and his company officers was simply a test of conflicting wills that would soon dissipate either with the dismissal of Draper or the collective group of officers. Neither Pratt nor Preston had anything to fear as they were considered leading citizens in their respective hometowns and had earned their status as brave and experienced veterans on the battlefield before their commissions in the 36th USCT.

Not mentioned as part of the collective grievances presented to Butler was a serious charge leveled at Draper by at least one of the dismissed officers. Captain George B. Proctor of Company F had tendered his resignation as a result of the dispute Draper had with Lieutenant Colonel Frederick F. Wead of the 98th New York Infantry during Wild's North Carolina expedition in December 1863. Draper's arrest of the young white woman, Nancy White, as a hostage for the return of captured black soldiers on the expedition sparked a jurisdictional argument with Wead, who forcefully took the hostage from Draper. Proctor, in a May 3, 1864, letter to Massachusetts Governor Andrew, alleged that Draper had ordered the black soldiers to attack the white soldiers of the 98th New York. His instructions to Lieutenant James B. Backup of Company I was to have his men concentrate their fire on Colonel Wead in an effort to kill him. As Draper's men marched towards the New York camp, Proctor wrote that Draper rode along the line of his regiment and made use of vulgar and profane language in directing what should be done demonstrating the unfitness for command.[71]

If Proctor's account is accurate, then Draper displayed an egregious lapse of judgment in this particular instance. During his early tenure in command of the 36th USCT, Draper suffered from speaking before thinking when frustrated or angered. This he had admitted to a certain extent in his version of events that took place the previous December (see Appendix 5). Realistically, Draper had only 250 men arrayed against a full regiment.

George B. Proctor (1841–1932), had served as a corporal in the 25th Massachusetts Infantry, before his appointment as a first lieutenant in the 2nd North Carolina Colored Volunteers. Promoted to captain and given command of Company F in early 1864, Proctor believed Colonel Draper's volatile temper and unbalanced demeanor made him unfit for command. Submitting his resignation along with several other officers in early April 1864, he was discharged from the service as a corporal by General Butler. The U.S. War Department later revoked Butler's orders and honorably discharged him from the service as a captain (J. Waldo Denny, *Wearing the Blue in the Twenty-fifth Massachusetts Volunteer Infantry with Burnside's Coast Division, 18th Army Corps, and Army of the James* [Worcester, MA: Putnam and Davis, 1879] after p. 258).

Even if Wead was killed in a volley directed by Lieutenant Backup's men, the black soldiers would have been massacred by twice the muskets supported by a cavalry detachment, dashing Drapers own ambitions of leading his troops in major combat against the Confederate foe. The two junior officers connected directly to this confrontation, James Backup and George Conant, who had charge of Nancy White,remain silent in the available written records.

Although it might make sense to order troops to defend fellow officers from being targets of hostile action, it is unlikely that even a junior officer such as Backup would have obeyed an unlawful order to deliberately fire at a particular individual serving on the same side. Backup continued to serve in the 36th USCT, displaying meritorious service and attaining the rank of captain before his discharge in March 1865 for disability. Conant was discharged from the service in mid–May 1864 presumably for disability.

It is not clear if Proctor had been present with the detachment at Pungo Point Bridge, since he was at the time first lieutenant of Company G where Conant served as second lieutenant. Proctor was promoted to captain and took command of Company F in the first days of March 1864; that had to have Draper's approval. Therefore, it remains a mystery as to what created the animosity between these two men.[72]

The case of the nine officers dismissed from the 36th USCT eventually reached President Lincoln. He asked the army's Judge Advocate General Joseph Holt for his views in the matter. "Here are several officers who have resigned, no matter whether the reasons were sufficient or not," Lincoln wrote to Holt. "General Butler thinks they are not, and he issues an order revoking their musters-out and musters-in and orders them back to the ranks from which they were promoted. Now, had General Butler any right to so revoke their musters or do as he has, without a trial by court-martial." Holt responded that commissioned officers could not be reduced to the ranks except for desertion, and only after a trial or court martial sentence. The War Department issued Special Orders No. 287 that revoked Butler's orders dismissing the officers and honorably discharging them from the service in the commissioned ranks they held in the 36th USCT.[73]

Most of these officers left the military completely, but two remained in the army. Benjamin Oakes subsequently served in the 4th Massachusetts Cavalry, reenlisting as a private and ending the war as a second lieutenant. Henry Field more than likely used his family connections to be reinstated a second lieutenant back into the 36th USCT in early March 1865.[74]

New vacancies allowed for new opportunities more to Draper's satisfaction. Ten enlisted men from Draper's former regiment had been appointed officers in the 36th USCT by early 1864. Draper's brother-in-law, Richard F. Andrews, a shoemaker who had been a sergeant in his old company, was appointed a second lieutenant on March 21, 1864. Andrews shortly received a promotion to first lieutenant and served several months on the regimental staff as adjutant responsible for the regiment's correspondence, personnel information, and orders. In February 1865, he became a captain commanding Company I. Another member of Draper's old command, his younger brother, Algernon, received his appointment as a second lieutenant on March 12, 1864. Algernon had been a laborer in Boston and ended the war as a captain commanding Company D.[75]

William H. Hart, a shoemaker and cordwainer who had been a sergeant and briefly a second lieutenant in Draper's former regiment, was appointed captain commanding Company H on May 11, 1864. In September 1864, Lieutenant Colonel Pratt commanding the 36th, recommended Hart to replace Preston as major who had been discharged from the service. "Since Capt. Hart has been connected with this Regt, he has always performed his duties promptly, and faithfully," Pratt wrote. "He is an able tactician, no line officers in the Regt. excel him, he is reliable, energetic, and efficient, and better qualified to fill the office of Major, than any other connected with the Regt." Pratt also pointed out that Hart was not the senior captain in the 36th USCT. "Of those who rank him, the senior, Capt. [Henry F.H.] Miller is at present sick in M.S. General Hospital ... Capt. [Charles H.] Frye ... has tendered his resignation on Surgeon's certificate of Disability ... Capt. [Walter H.] Wild is on duty with Genl. Wild on recruiting service.... He has never been on duty with the Regt." Hart stood ready to be examined by a promotion board at any time. The remaining captains who outranked Hart, Joseph J. Hatlinger and Joseph Wall, were simply mentioned by Pratt.[76]

Draper had never been impressed with Hatlinger's performance as an officer in the 36th USCT. Hatlinger, a 28-year-old medical student born in Hungary, had served as the sergeant major of the 5th Rhode Island Infantry before joining the 36th as a first lieutenant in early 1864. Draper believed Captain Hatlinger an "inefficient officer," particularly during the regiment's expeditions from Point Lookout, Maryland, to Virginia's Northern Neck region in the Spring of 1864, despite Hatlinger's suitable military background and experience. He would resign from the regiment on March 19, 1865.[77] Wall, formerly of Draper's old regiment, may not have risen to his colonel's expectations as well. Pratt's request for Hart's promotion traveled to higher headquarters. It received the favorable endorsement of General Paine, commanding the 3rd Division, 18th Army Corps, who admitted that Hart had been the most efficient company officer he had seen, "but if an equally good officer can be found elsewhere, I think it would be better to appoint him than to promote [Hart] over so many ranking officers." Hart's promotion to major over him was the "final straw" prompting Captain Wall's resignation from the regiment on November 15, 1864.[78]

Perhaps the most disgraceful officer to serve in the 36th USCT was Second Lieutenant Samuel S. Simmons, Company C, 36th USCT. Simmons earned Draper's scorn in his official report on the Battle of New Market Heights in September 1864. Serving as an aide-de-camp on Draper's brigade staff, Simmons "abandoned me shamefully at the ravine, and went to Deep Bottom without my knowledge." Simmons, whose real name was apparently DeForest, had been a soldier in the 5th New Hampshire Infantry that had been stationed at Point Lookout, Maryland, along with the 36th USCT in early 1864. Draper recommended that Simmons "be dismissed for cowardice." Simmons, failing to appear before a scheduled military commission, was dismissed from the service on January 23, 1865. Newspaper correspondent Thomas Morris Chester reported in the aftermath that "no officer will retain a place in [Draper's] command unless he conducts himself within the bounds of discipline."[79]

Another short-term officer came in the form of Second Lieutenant John O'Brien. Apparently O'Brien was a Philadelphia, Pennsylvania, native when the war found him working as a laborer in Union-occupied New Orleans. He enlisted into Company B, 14th Maine Infantry, in 1862 stationed in "The Crescent City." His appointment as a lieutenant in the 36th USCT came from General Butler whose command he had been under in New Orleans. In less than two weeks of his arrival at Point Lookout, O'Brien participated in his first mission as a commissioned officer accompanying the 36th USCT on an expedition into Westmoreland County, Virginia in June 1864. Draper commented that in spite of a single violation of one of his orders that he might give allowances to a new officer, O'Brien otherwise "performed his duties in a very acceptable manner."[80]

O'Brien seemed to have caused numerous problems for Draper and Pratt during his two-month tenure in the regiment. In August 1864, while the 36th was on duty with the Army of the James in the Petersburg trenches, O'Brien was brought up on charges for disobedience of orders, drunkenness on duty, conduct unbecoming of an officer, and breach of arrest. Personally interviewed by General Paine, his division commander, for repeated "drunkenness and gross offenses," O'Brien was recommended to be dismissed from the service. Paine ordered Draper, who was acting brigade commander, to forward charges against O'Brien to Butler. Draper wrote Butler that O'Brien "was grossly intoxicated in the presence of his men on duty; he also disobeyed the order of Lt. Col. Pratt, and left his regiment after being placed in arrest, and went half a mile from camp."

Sometime later, O'Brien, in the presence of some of the officers and men of the 36th, declared that Pratt had been responsible for preferring false charges against him and that he planned to desert to the enemy. He "did not care a damn for Col. Draper or Col. Pratt or any of the staff, and they might all go to Hell." Butler wasted no time in dismissing O'Brien from the service on August 9, 1864, causing him to forfeit all entitlement to payment and allowances.[81]

Perhaps ambitious to a fault and not known as a tactful individual in certain situations, Draper consistently worked to make sure that the reputation of his black soldiers and white officers as well as his own personal reputation was above reproach. Throughout the war, Draper surrounded himself with news correspondents sympathetic to the plight of freedmen and supporters of black military recruitment. This tactic of boosting favorable public opinion through the press served him well in his days as a labor leader in Lynn, Massachusetts. "Tewksbury" of the *New York Times*, as well as the correspondent of the *New York Tribune* during the 36th USCT's tenure in southeastern Virginia, gave Draper and his black soldiers favorable press on their expeditions into Princess Anne County, Virginia, and eastern North Carolina. "Physic," correspondent of Baltimore's *American and Commercial Advertiser* accompanied the 36th USCT on its frequent expeditions into Virginia's "Northern Neck" counties while stationed as guards over Confederate prisoners at Point Lookout, Maryland. While the regiment was a part of Butler's Army of the James in the trenches before Richmond and Petersburg, Thomas Morris Chester of the Philadelphia *Press* attached himself to Draper's brigade during much of 1864–1865.[82]

Chester, a freeborn African American from Harrisburg, Pennsylvania, had been educated in Vermont and spent several years before the war as a teacher and minor government official in Liberia. Hired as a correspondent for the *Press* in August 1864, Chester sent dispatches from the Virginia Front under the pseudonym "Rollin."[83]

Although Draper had frequent conflicts with his own officers as well as his military superiors, he had many supporters inside and outside the military establishment. Chester, painted a favorable picture of Draper's relationship with his officers in March 1865. On this occasion he wrote:

> One of those nice little ceremonies which illustrate the cordiality, respect, and confidence which exist between officers and their superior occurred an evening or two ago at the headquarters of Brevet Brig. Gen. Alonzo G. Draper. The members of his staff, after his amiable adjutant general, Lieut. W.H. Rock, had enticed him from his quarters, passed in unobserved and pleasantly seated themselves. The moment the General entered the door, and before he had time to recover from the surprise which the scene occasioned, Lieut. G.C. Prichard began to address him in a very impressive manner — to assure him of the respect which members of the staff possessed for him as a gentleman, and the confidence which they reposed in him as a soldier — that such expressions were not the adulations of a flatterer, but the sentiments of the gentlemen by who he was surrounded, whose opportunities were unlimited for acquainting themselves with the attributes of his character. After many other good things well spoken by the Lieutenant, he presented to the general, in the name of the staff, a splendid sword, elaborately gotten up, a magnificent sash, and

superb belt. The whole affair being a perfect surprise, General Draper, being unprepared for such a mark of respect and affection, found considerable difficulty in recovering his usual composure. He appropriately thanked the staff for their assurances, and accepted the articles in the same spirit in which they were given.[84]

Draper held the confidence of his brigade staff officers and a large number of officers in the black regiments he commanded including the 36th USCT. Chester's description of the presentation of the sword to Draper illustrated this. As Draper's position within the military hierarchy increased, his influence and ability to appoint officers whose views were compatible with his own also increased. It is clear through such descriptions of Draper that he could be a cordial and charming individual that few could ever forget. Despite such favorable opinions of Draper, some believed that as his reputation and authority grew so did his ego. Lieutenant Stephen F. Hathaway, who would join the 36th in early 1865 and had served as an enlisted man in Draper's old regiment, wrote to his cousin when he heard Draper had visited their hometown of Lynn, Massachusetts, while on furlough at the end of the war. "I suppose that General Draper looked gay while at home," Hathaway wrote, "he would like to be somebody if he could."[85]

General Wild, who would become a fellow brigade commander with his former subordinate by the close of the war, believed that Draper played favorites among his subordinate white officers and often allowed "private soldiers to go to him w/grievances against their sergeants or their Co. officers" skipping the proper chain of command for such grievances.[86] Since the dismissal of the nine officers of the 36th at Point Lookout, Maryland, in April 1864, the relationship between Draper and Wild continued to be strained for the duration of the war.

Like the white officers who had been dismissed from the regiment, there were instances of noncommissioned officers who defied the authority of their officers on behalf of their men in the 36th USCT. On August 22, 1864, Dr. Mortimer Lampson, assistant regimental surgeon for the 36th, sent a message that traveled to 18th Army Corps headquarters that Lieutenant Colonel Pratt and other line officers of the regiment reported considerable Confederate movement in their front indicating a possible offensive.[87]

Shortly after this, while the regiment labored in the stressful surroundings of the Petersburg trenches anticipating a possible attack, Private Silas Holly, Company G, 36th USCT, was shot by First Lieutenant Francis A. Bicknell. Holly was not killed. Bicknell believed that his brand of summary justice was justified for Holly's "alleged stubbornness, disobedience of orders, and manifesting a mutinous spirit."[88] Several of the men resented this shooting and began exhibiting resistance to authority thereafter. For many who had been slaves before joining the regiment, such immediate deadly punishment against them by white officers without a hearing only imitated the legal authority their former masters had held over them. Since being in the military service, many former slaves learned how the system of justice was supposed to work.[89] Holly's shooting did not seem to have had been carried out according to the proper justice they had come to expect.

This particular incident immediately resonated throughout the Union command at Petersburg when a staff officer reported to General Adelbert Ames commanding a white division in the 18th Army Corps that "the Thirty-sixth Regiment Colored Troops seem unsteady and unreliable." Portions of the 4th Massachusetts Cavalry were ordered to the regiment "to be stationed among the men and restore confidence by their presence and by keeping down the enemy fire."[90] The presence of white troops did nothing to lessen the resentment of the black soldiers in the 36th.

On August 25, 1864, Sergeant Thomas Artis, Company G, 36th USCT, angered over the shooting of Private Holly by Lieutenant Bicknell, refused to obey the orders of Second Lieutenant José A.A. Robinson of Company A. Robinson had ordered Artis to disperse a group of noisy soldiers and make sure that there were no further disruptions in the camp. Artis reportedly told Robinson, "Oh! Let the men go to hell — I'll have nothing more to do with them." Artis allegedly added, "I cannot stand by and see the men shot down like dogs by anybody." Corporal Alexander Gregory of Company A, 36th USCT, allegedly added fuel to this disturbing situation when he said of Lieutenant Bicknell, "The son of a bitch! He had better be careful how he shoots our men; he may get shot himself when he goes into a fight."[91]

Lieutenant Edwin C. Gaskill, commanding the Reserve Camp composed of elements from Companies A and G of the regiment, attempted to quell any mutinous action led by Artis and Gregory but was blocked by Private Edward Roby of Company A. Repeatedly ordering the 36-year-old Roby to go to his quarters without success, Gaskill drew his pistol, whereupon Roby replied, "Shoot and be damned." Roby went to the nearby stack of arms and returned aiming his rifled musket at Gaskill. Soon the black soldier and white officer got into a scuffle each attempting to disarm the other. Lieutenant Robinson stepped in on Gaskill's behalf to subdue the enraged Private Roby. In the aftermath, Artis was reduced to the ranks and, along with Roby, sentenced to one year of hard labor at Fort Norfolk with a ball and chain attached to their right legs. Corporal Gregory was given only a severe reprimand as it was found that he had not been given an opportunity of pleading to the charges and specifications against him.[92]

More often than not black noncommissioned officers in the 36th sought to protect their men and maintain the overall morale of the command at the expense of unruly individual soldiers. On September 19, 1864, Private John Wesley of Company I, confined for disorderly conduct, told his first sergeant, Miles Sheppard, that "if I ever get out of here, there are two men in Company I that I will kill. If I had been in the company all the time, I would have killed them before." The names of the two individuals were not recorded, but First Sergeant Sheppard reported Wesley's death threat to the regiment's Officer of the Day who happened to be Lieutenant Gaskill. In attempting to interview Private Wesley based upon Sheppard's report, Gaskill and Wesley ended up in a brief physical struggle. Wesley was court-martialed for physically assaulting a superior officer. Sentenced to hard labor at Fort Norfolk, Wesley had a ball and chain attached to his right leg.[93]

In addition to the tensions between the black soldiers and white officers in the 36th USCT, there were other conflicts among black Union soldiers based upon their previous condition of servitude. While conflicts between black soldiers who had been born free recruited in the North and those who had been former slaves recruited in the South has not received adequate attention in Civil War scholarship, it was nevertheless an important issue within the larger African American community. Since black men in the North were recruited into the Union army in greater proportions to their population than those recruited in the South, most of the wartime views expressed by black Union soldiers often came from the perspective of free black men living in the North. This takes for granted the former slave, who by joining the Union army had to trust the welfare of his family to the Union military authorities in contraband and refugee camps often located very close to major battlefronts. Class differences between free men and freed men of color in the Union army added another dimension to how African Americans viewed their roles during the Civil War.[94] Nevertheless, these subtle tensions among black soldiers did not overshadow racial discrimination within and outside the Union army.

As early as November 1863, tensions had grown between the 36th USCT and black units recruited from the North serving in southeastern Virginia. Believing that his soldiers were assigned menial tasks due to their previous status as slaves, Draper expressed his thoughts to departmental headquarters. "The position of my regiment is peculiar," he wrote, "instead of recruiting and organizing in some Northern state, with two or three months drill and preparation, it has had its birth in actual service, laboring in the trenches, parading in review on common time and performing all the duties of any regiment in the field." While Draper lamented over the apparent unfair treatment his own soldiers received because they had been slaves, the 5th USCT from Ohio often believed that the "contraband" regiments received more favorable treatment because of Butler's specific concern over former slaves and their families. The white commander of the 5th, Colonel James W. Conine, thought Draper used his influence with Butler to gain more favorable military assignments than his own regiment.[95] The 5th USCT served in the same brigade with the 36th USCT and 38th USCT, commanded by Draper, in the fall of 1864 in the Petersburg trenches. The 38th had been recruited from among former slaves in Virginia. Lieutenant Colonel Giles W. Shurtleff, commanding the 5th at this time, considered the other two regiments of the brigade "undisciplined regiments of contrabands" and resented Butler's decision to place supposedly weaker regiments like the 36th and 38th with veteran regiments like the 5th.[96]

If northern black families suffered from the unequal pay of their male relatives serving as Union soldiers, the families of former slaves serving in the Union army not only suffered financially, but were closer to battle fronts in Union-occupied areas throughout the South. Southern black families often suffered from abuse by white civilians as well as unsympathetic Union military officials. This did not even begin to cover those family members left on plantations and farms behind Confederate lines.

In June 1864, the U.S. Congress authorized black soldiers to receive the same pay as white soldiers with back pay dating from January 1, 1864. Black soldiers who had been free on or before April 19, 1861, received back pay if they had enlisted in late 1862 and 1863. The majority of the men in the 5th USCT who had come from Ohio benefited from this act. Their brigade comrades in the 36th USCT did not fare as well, since most had been slaves before April 19, 1861. The equal pay issue would not be resolved until March 1865 when Congress enacted legislation equalizing all soldier pay.[97]

While black regiments of free men protested the government's unequal pay scale by refusing to accept pay, black regiments recruited from occupied areas of the South and Border States composed of "freedmen," like the 36th USCT, accepted their unequal pay to support their families. These former slaves accepted their pay and highlighted the irony Butler pointed out in 1863 that the "colored man fills an equal space in the ranks while he lives [and] an equal grave when he falls."[98]

CHAPTER 5

# De Bottom Rail on Top

*Point Lookout, Maryland and Virginia's "Northern Neck," February–July 1864*

The correspondent of the Baltimore *American and Commercial Advertiser*, known as "Physic," observed the arrival of nine companies of the 36th United States Colored Infantry at Point Lookout, Maryland, in late February 1864. He reported:

> On last Tuesday evening, the 28th, the North Carolina (Colored) arrived at the wharf and marched to the sound of most excellent music to their quarters, near the Brick House. They are over 1,000 strong, and came here in transport, via Washington and Long Branch, from Fortress Monroe. They presented a fine appearance and kept most excellent time and a glance along the lines while marching showed every foot raised to a step as regular as clock-work. Various rumors were afloat in regard to the object in sending them here. These rumors were quieted in the morning at guard mounting by seeing them take their turn at guard duty around the prisoners' camp. There was a good deal of jeering but the majority of the prisoners took a sensible view of the matter and remained quiet, attending quietly to their own business, and the negro sentinels to their orders. They were somewhat a curiosity, as a great many had never seen a negro soldier before.... All the balance of the officers are white, and from the drilling I witnessed I am satisfied they are posted in military tactics.[1]

Private John W. Stevens, Company K, 5th Texas Infantry, and Confederate prisoner of war, held a different observation of the arrival of the 36th USCT at Point Lookout. He recalled:

> I think it was on the 18th day of February, '64, that at guard mounting in the morning, about four companies of negroes, ex-slaves from North Carolina, were marched into prison. The colonel commanding was a Roman nose Yankee from Massachusetts, and all the officers ... were splinters from the same stick. As they marched in at the big gate every officer drew his pistol and cocked it and the negroes had their guns at carry arms, with bayonets fixed. They evidently expected some hostile demonstrations from the prisoners. To say that they gave every evidence of being scared is not over-drawing the picture, for 12,000 or 14,000 men could have rushed upon them and disarmed and captured them in five minutes, but the universal feeling of the entire body was just the opposite. It was a feeling of the most inexpressible contempt for the government which had lowered the dignity of the United States soldiery by placing its uniform, escutcheon and arms in the hands of pressed slaves. That was the sentiment of every thinking man in the prison. As to our feeling toward the negro, it was more a feeling of sympathy than anything else. Of course we knew the poor negro was not blamable, because all through the south he was faithful to the charge we had left in his hands while we were in the army. There he was true to his instincts as a servant, faithfully protecting the women and children at home.... The soldiery of any country should represent the highest type of her manhood, and when the United States government — the grandest government to day on earth — places our flag uniform and weapons of war in the hands of the

negro, she reverses the order of things. It's a shame.... The bulk of them were young, black, slick looking fellows, and were doubtless highly inflated with the idea that they were U.S. soldiers, had guns and were guarding white men. Prompted, doubtless, by their officers, they soon became overbearing and very insulting.[2]

These two versions of the 36th USCT's arrival at Point Lookout characterized their tenure as prison guards. It is interesting to note that the Confederate prisoner believed that it was beneath any respected government to employ black soldiers in its military, but these same soldiers, while as slaves, were worthy enough and expected to protect southern women, children, and homesteads, which most Confederate soldiers placed great value upon. This was the typical view held by most Confederate soldiers and southern sympathizers. On the Union side, it did not hurt white commanders of black units, like Draper, to have sympathetic observers making favorable reports to the northern public of the great virtues of the black soldiers and the white officers who commanded them in the effort to crush the Confederacy and unite the nation. Sympathetic as well as hostile whites presumed "to know" and speak on behalf of these former slaves.

The 36th USCT was one of the first black Union regiments to be assigned guard duty at a major prisoner-of-war facility. Point Lookout, located on the peninsula between the Chesapeake Bay and the St. Mary's River, held at one time during the Civil War over 20,000 Confederate prisoners. Brigadier General Gilman Marston had commanded the district since July 1863, which was transferred from the Department of Washington to Butler's Department of Virginia and North Carolina in December 1863. The district consisted of three white infantry regiments and a battery of artillery when the 36th arrived.[3] This would be the regiment's first and only assignment with white Union regiments during the war.

The presence of the 36th was a humiliating experience for the prisoners, which made their "Southern blood boil." It had only been a short time that the black soldiers themselves had been prisoners within the institution of slavery. Resentment by prisoners was directed more at white officers commanding black soldiers rather than the soldiers themselves. In the minds of many white southerners (as well as some white northerners), the natural inferiority of the black race exonerated them from taking up arms against their former masters. The only logic that could be provided by the prisoners was that these soldiers enlisted into the Union army through the coercion of white army officers.

Nevertheless, this way of thinking did not keep the prisoners from taunting or provoking the men of the 36th directly. There is little doubt that these black soldiers were guarding their former masters. Several guards and prisoners had lived in the same places of eastern North Carolina and southeastern Virginia before the war. One black soldier recognized his former master, gave him $10, and befriended him during his stay. More often Confederate prisoners held at Point Lookout in their post-war accounts wrote about the arrogance and cruelty of their black guards. They often repeated a remark of black soldiers that "de bottom rail is on top."[4]

Life at Point Lookout ran on a regular routine. Every 24 hours, a different infantry regiment provided soldiers to guard the Confederate prisoners on a rotating basis. The prisoners' camp took up about ten acres of land in a rectangular shape. A board fence about 14 feet high surrounded the prison pen or "bull-pen," as coined by the prisoners. It contained at least 10,000 prisoners in early 1864. The prisoners were divided into 10 numbered "divisions" which were subdivided into lettered companies. Some lived 12 to 16 men in Sibley tents while most lived five men each in "A-tents." Each day prisoners were formed in a line, answered roll calls, and their persons and tents searched. On the inside of the pen below

**Point Lookout, Maryland, was the location of a prisoner of war camp that contained close to 14,000 Confederate prisoners by early 1864. The 36th USCT was assigned as guards arriving on February 28, 1864, where they remained until July 3, 1864 (Library of Congress).**

the top of the fence was a three-foot wide platform where some of the armed sentinels on duty paced back and forth. From this vantage point they could overlook the entire pen, since most of the ground was perfectly level. Captured Confederate officers had been separated from the enlisted men into a smaller camp and usually sent to Fort Delaware prison at a later time.[5]

"The nigs feel their responsibility & glory in guarding their old masters," Sergeant Major John Owen wrote home. "Gen. Marston in command here praises the 36th very much." Owen would soon have his commission as a second lieutenant. Dining with an old acquaintance who served as a captain in the 5th New Hampshire also stationed at Point Lookout, Owen was told by this officer that he had no doubts that some of his own white soldiers had sold arms and civilian clothes to the Confederate prisoners. Deserters from the white Union regiments seemed to cause more trouble than the prisoners. Owen further revealed that "these Rebs have a regular organization in their camp & murder & rob their own men even." Two boats built by prisoners and hidden away for the right moment of escape had been discovered filled each with a week's worth of rations and supplies. This prompted everyone in the camp to keep their eyes open.[6]

Corporal James E. Hall of the 31st Virginia Infantry recalled that shortly after the 36th's arrival, "a prisoner laughed at the awkwardness of one of the negroes, when an officer drew his revolver and snapped twice at him, and then cut him dangerously over the hand with his saber. All this done for laughing at a negro!"[7] The prisoners often poked fun at this supposed awkwardness and imbecility of the black soldiers. This was the case when Private John Green, Company I, 36th USCT, was accidentally shot on April 29, 1864. It is not clear whether Green shot himself or a fellow comrade while practicing the manual of arms shot him. Green, a 19-year-old hostler, hailed from Petersburg, Virginia. While the regimental books of the 36th and some of the prisoners reported that Green had shot himself, news correspondent "Physic" and other prisoners reported that another soldier of the regiment had shot him. Nevertheless, prisoner John W. Stevens of Texas remembered that he and his fellow prisoners "laughed heartily" as Green apparently fell dead with a broken neck.[8] Such was the contempt prisoners held for the black soldiers of the 36th.

About a month into the 36th's assignment at Point Lookout, a group of Confederate officers, who had been a part of Confederate General John Hunt Morgan's raiding party that had reached as far north as Ohio, arrived as prisoners. Captain Lawrence W. Peyton of the 10th Kentucky (Confederate) Cavalry asked Sergeant Edwin Young of Company A, 2nd New Hampshire Infantry, who was assisting the provost marshal in assigning them prison tents, to get him alcohol, as the sergeant seemed to "look like a damned old whisky head." Young refused the prisoner's request. Puzzled by the black soldiers on guard duty, Peyton pointed to one of the 36th's soldiers and asked Young, "Which would make the best soldiers, you or the negroes?" Young replied that the black soldiers made better guards than white soldiers, suggesting the innate instinct of obedience among former slaves. "Yes, I suppose the negroes are superior," Peyton allegedly responded. Young informed him that he could talk to some men that way, but not to him while on duty. After a further exchange of words between the two men and Peyton's dare for Young to shoot him, Young drew his revolver shooting Peyton dead.[9]

A board of inquiry at Point Lookout found Sergeant Young justified in shooting Peyton. Colonel William Hoffman, Commissary-General of Prisoners, whose office was located in Washington, approved the board's decision. Hoffman forwarded the board's findings to his immediate superior, Brigadier General Edward R.S. Canby, acting assistant adjutant general at the War Department, who was not satisfied with the board's findings, believed that Peyton's shooting was "entirely unjustifiable," and that Young should be put on trial for murder. General Marston, as commander at Point Lookout, forwarded the board's transcripts to General Butler at Fort Monroe as a matter of courtesy, since the prison fell within his department. Butler immediately fired off a polite complaint to Hoffman, calling his attention to the fact that the composition of the investigating board and the board's finding had been sent directly to Marston without going through his headquarters.

Butler also believed that if departmental commanders selected board members for such inquiries, the outcomes would be more satisfactory rather than those of biased boards favoring the guards. "But it seems to me that in a very delicate matter of inquiring into the taking of the life of a man, especially a prisoner of war," Butler reasoned concerning Peyton's shooting, "which may be misrepresented to our rebel enemies and lead to retaliation, it should appear that the facts were found by the board which, like Caesar's wife, should be beyond suspicion." Hoffman apologized for the apparent slight to Butler, but maintained that as Commissary-General of Prisoners he had been in the habit of communicating directly with prison commandants and only dealt with departmental commanders under special circumstances, since going through several levels of command often led to embarrassing delays. Such boards convened by him were informal and only used to gather information to determine if formal investigations and charges needed to be pursued. President Abraham Lincoln had previously appointed Butler a commissioner of prisoner exchange. Periodically, Butler conferred and arranged with his Confederate counterparts the exchange and release of Union and Confederate prisoners.[10] Incidents such as these with speedy exonerations could delay the release of Union prisoners of war held in southern prisons. Apparently, no further action seems to have been taken against Young. Nevertheless, it was a negative remark made to a white Union soldier comparing him to a black Union soldier that resulted in the violent death of a Confederate prisoner.

The 36th USCT was not only the target of prisoners, but of white Union soldiers and civilians as well. On April 17, 1864, Corporal Granville Williams, Privates Allen Wiggins, Smith Cornick, Irving Williams, and Dick Richmond, all of Company D, 36th USCT, were returning to camp when they were ordered out of the road by three mounted soldiers of the 2nd New Hampshire Infantry accompanied by a civilian. The riders made several attempts to charge the soldiers and forced one of the black soldiers on his knees as they rode around him making thrusts and cuts at him. Two days later, Drummer Larry Griffin, Company H, 36th USCT, was returning to camp with a group of his comrades when a local white resident, Frank Smith, galloped toward him and kicked him in the stomach. "Get out of my way, you damned black sons of a bitch!" Smith was reported as shouting as he rode off. Draper ordered Smith's arrest with a speedy trial and punishment if found guilty.[11] "Physic," the pro-36th USCT correspondent for Baltimore's *American and Commercial Advertiser*, reported the outcome of Smith's trial:

> Mr. Frank Smith, a young Southern blood in feelings and actions, residing in this county, was arrested lately for riding with a horse over a negro soldier, the soldier being without arms. He was tried by a military court, and sentenced by Gen. Butler to sixty days' confinement in the guard-house — a just sentence, and we hope his experience may be a lesson to others of this class. The antipathy of this gentleman to negroes is proverbial and well known, and it is hoped the above lesson will be an example that will learn him that Uncle Sam in accepting the services of negro soldiers also knows how to protect them.[12]

Such incidents and subsequent actions taken by the black soldiers in retaliation and self-protection may have prompted Lieutenant Colonel Benjamin F. Pratt to issue two unique orders to the regiment on May 9, 1864. The first dealt with soldiers' possession of personal side arms. Company commanders were responsible for confiscating any pistols found on their men immediately after dress parades. Captured pistols were to be labeled with the owner's name and retained until further orders were issued.[13]

Pratt's second order arose from complaints by local farmers of unspecified "depredations" allegedly committed by the men of the 36th. "All such conduct is a disgrace to a soldier of the United States," Pratt declared, "and any man found guilty of insulting citizens of committing any depredations on their property will receive the severest punishment such conduct deserves."[14] It is interesting to note that the only punishment given to soldiers violating the first order was the confiscation of their pistols indefinitely. Perhaps Pratt understood the complex situation and pressure his men were under as prison guards. Nevertheless, his second order confirmed that under no circumstances would his soldiers retaliate against white civilians.

While white Union soldiers and local civilians had the ability to move about the area and could inflict armed violence on the black soldiers, the unarmed Confederate prisoners seemed less of a physical threat. Nevertheless, deliberate provocation of black guards by the prisoners led to several unfortunate shooting incidents. On the evening of April 18, guards of the 36th allegedly wounded Private Paul Thoroughgood of the 4th North Carolina Cavalry and a prisoner of war. The camp surgeon reported that Thoroughgood received a rifle "mini-ball" that entered his right side just below the shoulder. The projectile ricocheted off the rib cage and exited approximately eight inches on the same side so that the "cavity of thorax [was] not opened and no bone injured." The second ball was a superficial wound to the flesh.[15]

Three evenings later, Private Mark Lisk, 60th Tennessee Infantry, was shot in the right foot by a guard of the 36th while attempting to relieve himself in an unauthorized area after hours. Lisk later died of his injury. Sergeant Major William H. Laird, a Confederate prisoner and spokesperson for the prisoners, submitted a statement the next day to Captain W.A. Crafts, assistant provost marshal, detailing previous incidents in which guards of the 36th committed malicious acts of abuse upon them to "satisfy their past grievances, whether real or imaginary."[16]

Laird recalled two incidents prior to Lisk's shooting in which the black guards allegedly ordered prisoners out of their tents during the night for making supposedly harmless comments. The prisoners were threatened with being shot for disobedience of orders by their guards. In one instance, a prisoner "was made to double-quick from the center ditch to the bay fence and back." In another instance, a prisoner received a ball that slightly grazed his foot for not responding to the guard's orders promptly.[17]

Colonel Hoffman, Commissary-General of Prisoners, visited Point Lookout on May 20 "to examine into the condition of the force placed here in charge of the prisoners of war, the measures into their security, and all other matters in this connection."[18] Colonel Draper at this time had been made acting district commander. Hoffman believed that the command at its present strength was sufficient to guard prisoners, but he suggested to the War Department that if an additional 5,000 prisoners were brought into the camp, a regiment of veteran troops or two regiments of state militia should complement the guard.[19] It was not only important that Draper's military strength was sufficient to guard prisoners, but also to resist any raids by Confederates wishing to free prisoners or detach Union forces into Virginia's Northern Neck as needed to discourage the enemy's peripheral supply sources.

Two gunboats stationed at the depot on the Potomac River side were at Draper's disposal. One was a sailing vessel, the other steam-driven. Draper explained to Hoffman that the U.S. Navy's Potomac Flotilla often called the steam vessel away on its frequent naval expeditions leaving Point Lookout with the slower moving sailing vessel. "I would therefore recommend," Hoffman later reported in response to Draper's concerns, "that application to the Navy Department for a steam gun-boat to be stationed permanently at the depot to guard against a descent of the enemy from the Virginia shore and overawe the prisoners."[20]

Hoffman further recommended that some of the Confederate prisoners already employed as laborers around the camp continue their work under the supervision of the post quartermaster to make up for the lack of civilian laborers. "This arrangement is of great convenience to the service and very economical, and there seems to be no objection to it, provided the prisoners employed are carefully guarded," he concluded. The employed prisoners would still be paid a daily rate of nine cents in tobacco for general work, policing and improving the grounds, and building camp roads. The partition separating officers and enlisted men in the prison was recommended to be removed to allow more room to accommodate additional prisoners. The officers confined in the prison camp simply had too much unnecessary room. The sick were in hospital tents which were "well arranged and in good condition." However, Hoffman suggested that sheds be constructed for the hospital buildings "as a matter of economy."[21]

Three days after Hoffman's inspection tour, Private Miles Holloway, Company F, 36th USCT, allegedly shot Private William Jones of the 2nd Virginia Cavalry. This latest shooting prompted Draper to convene a board of inquiry to investigate and report on both the Lisk and Jones shootings. Beginning on May 24, the board conducted interviews with the officers and enlisted men involved in the Lisk shooting. The members of this board of inquiry were Colonel Charles E. Hapgood (5th New Hampshire Infantry), Major H. George O. Weymouth (1st United States Veteran Volunteers), and Captain Henry F.H. Miller (36th USCT). Captain William H. Hart, 36th USCT, soon replaced Colonel Hapgood on the board on account of ill health. Hearings were held at the regimental headquarters of the 5th New Hampshire with Major Weymouth as board president and Captain Hart as official recorder of the proceedings.[22]

Lieutenant Edwin C. Gaskill, 36th USCT and junior officer of the guard, on April 21 reported that he had hurried from the guardhouse to the scene of the shooting as soon as the shot was heard. He encountered Private Irving Williams, Company D, 36th USCT, who told him "he had shot one of the prisoners for refusing to obey the orders which he was instructed to enforce, which was to allow no nuisance to be committed except in the tubs." White Union soldiers had assaulted Williams, a 19-year-old farmer from Greenville, North Carolina, recently, and it was not clear if he had overreacted in the discharge of his duties.[23] Gaskill and the enlisted men on guard duty had been instructed by Lieutenant William M. Titcomb, 36th USCT, senior officer of the guard that evening, "to allow no men to cluster around the cook-houses except at meal times, and to allow none of the men at night to do their business anywhere on the grounds except at the portable sinks built for that purpose." Gaskill further testified that the guards and sentinels were required to allow three verbal warnings for the prisoners who refused to comply with their orders. After these verbal warnings, the guards had just cause to shoot them. Lisk had been carried away before Gaskill arrived five minutes after the shooting. Since it was not determined how far Private Williams was from the sentinel walking the next beat, there was no way to ascertain if anyone else "could have heard the orders that [Williams] gave the prisoner."[24]

Williams testified shortly after Gaskill and plainly admitted, "I am the man who shot the prisoner." His orders, as were told to him by Lieutenant Titcomb, were "to allow no collections at the kitchen doors, nor to allow any of the prisoners to do their business in the ditch or on the grounds, only at the sinks." According to Williams, Private Lisk had gone to the side of the kitchen "to do his business," which prisoners were prohibited from doing. Ordering Lisk to get up, Williams received the reply that he would "do his business first." Lisk got up and went between his tent and the officers' tent "to do his business." Williams, for the second time, ordered Lisk to leave the area. Lisk, again, replied that he would "do his business first." Williams ordered Lisk to get up for the third time or "I would help him up." Lisk was shot in the foot and "hallooed until they came and pulled him into the tent."[25]

Williams recalled that the time of the shooting was just before daylight. However, Gaskill and other subsequent testimonies agreed that the time of the shooting was closer to two o'clock in the morning. Williams' time discrepancy may have been due to the excitement at the scene of the shooting, nervousness in appearing before the board, or a misunderstanding by the board members his description of the time of day.[26]

Titcomb, unable to appear due to illness, reported in a written statement that he was away inspecting the guards posted at the nearby contraband camp and was not informed of the shooting until 45 minutes after it occurred. Titcomb, along with the officer of the day and four soldiers, went to the place where Lisk had been shot "but saw no tub there" as reported by the Confederate prisoners. The group went to the prison hospital, but did not speak to Lisk and returned to the guardhouse. Titcomb reiterated to the board his orders for the guards that day "to allow no one to ease himself except at the sinks. First, to order them away three times, and if then they did not go, to shoot them." These were the instructions Titcomb had received from the officer of the day.[27]

The board also received a written statement from Corporal Miles James, Company B, 36th USCT. James was on detached duty at Piney Point, Maryland, with 22 soldiers of the 36th when the hearings convened. He had been corporal of the guard and Private Williams' immediate superior on the evening Lisk was shot. James, a future Congressional Medal of Honor winner, stated:

> The prisoner sat down to ease himself [at the] side of a house, which was against orders; the sentinel ordered him to leave from there. The prisoner got up, but when the sentinel's back was turned sat down again for the same purpose. The sentinel this time asked him what he was going to do there. The prisoner replied, "I am going to ease myself." The sentinel told him to get up or he would shoot him; the prisoner not obeying him, the sentinel shot at him and wounded him, of which wound he afterward died. I went to the sentinel's beat to see why the gun was fired, and got there about four minutes after the discharge of the gun. It is my opinion that that some of the prisoners must have put a tub at the place where the man was shot, between that time and morning, as I am confident that there was no tub there at the time the shooting took place.[28]

After conducting these interviews, the board visited the prison camp to obtain information from the prisoners themselves. Unfortunately, no evidence or testimony could be obtained from them that had any bearing on the case, according to the examiners. Perhaps the Confederate prisoners believed that there was no use in assisting the board in their investigation since the prevailing sentiment was that they would continue to be "tantalized" by their "insolent and brutal" black captors.[29] It probably did not help matters for the prisoners that two of the three board members were officers in the 36th USCT. The remaining member commanded an experimental regiment of "galvanized Yankees" made up of former Confederate prisoners who had agreed to enlist into the U.S. service after taking the oath of allegiance.

Draper forwarded the transcripts of the board's proceedings to Colonel Hoffman with the opinion that, based upon the evidence presented, Private Williams was justified in shooting Lisk. The case against Private Holloway in the Jones shooting "was discontinued by direction of Major-General [Silas] Casey, who was specially authorized to investigate it." Casey commanded the Department of Washington. No further action seemed to have been taken against Holloway.[30]

After the Lisk and Jones shootings were put to rest, Colonel Hoffman made a report to the War Department on May 24. He wrote:

> Four hundred and ninety-four prisoners of war arrived from Belle Plain last evening. Yesterday afternoon as the prisoners were going from dinner a sentinel of the Thirty-sixth Colored Regiment, without justification, fired at one of them, wounding him mortally, of which he died last night, wounding another seriously and two others slightly. I respectfully recommend that a court of inquiry of officers not belonging to the post be ordered to investigate the affair.[31]

On that same day, Draper issued General Orders No. 25 at Hoffman's suggestion. This order attempted to maintain prisoners without resorting to unnecessary violence. Guards were ordered to take prisoners into custody for violations of established prisoner rules, unless they violently resist "and if the prisoner attempts to run away the sentinel will fire upon him, always being careful, if possible, not to shoot in the direction of other prisoners." Prisoners were forbidden to assemble outside their tents or pass from tent to tent after dark except for the purposes of going to the night sinks. Any problems with prisoners encountered by sentinels should be brought to the attention of the guard if possible before action was taken. A sentinel should report minor offenses committed by prisoners to the guard "and will not resort to violent measures to enforce this order except where violence is attempted on himself, when he will do whatever may be necessary in self-defense." Finally, "in any case of the shooting of a prisoner of war by one of the guard," Draper reiterated, "the fact will be immediately reported to the officer of the day" who would immediately go to the scene to ascertain the circumstances of the shooting.[32]

Prison guard duty did not keep the black soldiers of the 36th from conducting expeditions into Virginia. As a deterrent to attempts by Confederate forces to launch an expedition to free their imprisoned comrades, Union forces launched their own expeditions into enemy territory spearheaded by the 36th USCT. The regiment participated in at least three major expeditions in cooperation with the U.S. Navy. The black soldiers generally received praise from their white officers and sympathetic supporters while earning the scorn of southern inhabitants.[33]

Brigadier General Edward W. Hinks, a former Massachusetts state legislator and protégé of Butler, succeeded Marston as commander of the District of St. Mary's on April 3, 1864. Hinks conducted the first of three expeditions into Virginia's Northern Neck region that involved the 36th USCT. Preparations were made on the evening of April 12, as Hinks with 300 men of the 36th under Draper and 50 men of the 2nd and 5th U.S. Cavalry embarked upon the army transport *Long Branch* "in search of contraband goods and to break up blockading establishments." By the following morning, the expedition met up with a detachment of naval gunboats under Lieutenant Commander T.H. Eastman. Eastman, fleet captain and second-in-command of the Potomac Flotilla, were under orders to assist Hink's expedition with the gunboats *Resolute* and *Yankee* to be joined by the gunboats *Fuchsia*, *Teaser*, and *Anacostia* shortly thereafter.[34]

Disembarking at Raggy Point (known locally as Cole's Point) on the right bank of the Lower Machodoc Creek, Draper led the landing force on its mission "to scour the peninsula between it and the Nomini River." Four armed crews from the *Teaser* and *Anacostia* added to the military strength of the land forces. The landing went uncontested as the initial group of 30 to 40 Confederate horsemen seen at the landing earlier had retired from their position.[35] The significance of this particular area could not have been lost on Draper. This peninsula, located on the lower end of Westmoreland County, Virginia, was less than 7 miles southeast of Stratford Hall, the birthplace of the Union army's primary foe, Confederate General Robert E. Lee. About 7 miles to the northwest was Wakefield Plantation along Pope's Creek, which was the birthplace of George Washington.

Draper's command seized from Joseph H. Maddox 177 boxes of high quality tobacco estimated at $40,000 in U.S. currency at his residence near the landing site. Maddox, taken prisoner and sent immediately to Hinks for questioning, insisted that he was a loyal "emissary of the Federal Government," but it was later revealed he had been previously arrested as a blockade-runner and had bribed U.S. officials to clear him of the charges.[36]

Later in the evening, Captain James W. Lawrence, Hinks' chief of staff, with 150 men of the 36th and the cavalry detachment, discovered a small body of Confederate cavalry near Coles Point on the opposite bank of the Machodoc. The Confederate forces sought cover near several houses. The small force of Union troops "immediately advanced to attack them, when they [Confederate cavalry] fell back to a hill about 6 miles from the place of our landing," Hinks later reported. The attacking black soldiers charged at the Confederates "in good order," observed news Baltimore *Commercial and Advertiser* correspondent Physic. A pursuit of the fleeing enemy in the direction of Hague was made, but soon abandoned. Some of the buildings from which the enemy fired upon the soldiers of the 36th were burned to the ground.[37]

A correspondent for the pro-Confederate *Richmond* (Virginia) *Daily Enquirer* bearing the sobriquet of "Scout" reported this same skirmish with Union forces led by Captain Lawrence, who "having encountered a few of our soldiers, returned to the infantry from which they did not venture again during their stay." He added, further revealing the Southern contempt for the presence of the 36th USCT in the region,

> But, on the line of their travels, they endeavored to gratify their wicked propensities for devastating and destroying by setting fire to the dwelling of Mr. R.S. Lawrence, and the barn and corn house of the Hon. W. Newton. They forced the servants away from two farms, though the poor creatures implored them, with tears, to allow them to remain with their masters. A few servants went off with them of their own accord. The barn which was destroyed contained several hundred barrels of corn, and a large quantity of wheat, upon which many families were relying for bread. In several instances the negro soldiers were insulting in their conduct *even* to ladies. The negroes said previous to their departure, that they were about to leave for Meade's Army [Army of the Potomac]— spoke boastingly of going "to the front." When the clash of arms is heard again upon the Rapidan [River], and Southern soldiers are required to meet these sable *heroes* in arms, may they remember the wrongs they have so often done our helpless friends, exposed to their raids, of which this visit is but one instance in an hundred.[38]

Despite this allegation that black servants left their masters against their will, Scout had to acknowledge that some of the slaves did leave on their own volition. Perhaps the black soldiers of the 36th remembered the "wrongs" committed upon them and their families under slavery by white southerners like those encountered in Westmoreland County. The *Enquirer*, in a subsequent issue, reported that the farming implements of the Honorable Willoughby Newton, mentioned in Scout's report, were confiscated from him with "the negroes saying they would have farms in Maryland and would need them."[39]

Hinks had this idea in mind when the expedition returned to Point Lookout on the evening of April 14 with 50 rescued back refugees, large quantities of high-grade tobacco, and a suspected blockade-runner in the person of Joseph Maddox, who was soon sent to General Butler's headquarters at Fort Monroe "without any loss of men and material."[40] Utilizing confiscated resources taken on expeditions could be used get the abandoned farms and plantations in St. Mary's back into production. Hinks expressed his views to Butler concerning such abandoned lands and the employment of fugitive slaves on them. Three farms in particular caught Hinks' attention. The Thomas Farm along the Patuxent River was the best site in his estimation to employ at least 100 black refugees. However, the owner, residing in Baltimore, had a life interest and a right of dowager to the property, despite the fact that three of her sons were Confederate soldiers. Hinks had on one occasion sent his provost marshal, Major H. George Weymouth, to investigate the overseer on this farm who had allegedly abused slaves remaining on the property. The second property, the Forrest Estate, had "no pretended loyal owner," but was devoid of adequate buildings necessary for agricultural endeavors. It was possible that the third farm, owned by John H. Sothoron, could be made available, but the property was reported occupied by soldiers under Brigadier General William Birney recruiting black soldiers for the Union army. Butler provided Hinks with his approved procedures in confiscating abandoned farms of disloyal owners in slave states, like Maryland, still in the Union and not subject to the Emancipation Proclamation. Hinks' would not have the opportunity to put his plans into motion when he was ordered to a combat command with the Army of the James.[41]

When Draper assumed command of the District of St. Mary's on April 20, 1864, as "acting brigadier general," he continued his predecessor's focus on the abandoned farms along the Patuxent River. "I have seized over 7,000 acres of land belonging to the Rebels," he reported to his superiors. This seizure included both the Forrest and Sothoron farms that were destitute of "stocks and tools." In order to get these farms back into a productive mode, Draper requested permission to continue conducting expeditions into Virginia to procure much needed supplies, equipment, and black refugees. Butler, confident in Draper's ability, allowed him "to make raids when he sees fit" and "whenever it appears necessary."[42]

On the evening of May 11, Draper led the 36th's second foray into Virginia with 300 men from the regiment and 13 men from a U.S. cavalry detachment. Draper's expedition was a part of a larger mission conducted by the 1st Division of the Potomac Flotilla under the command of Acting Volunteer Lieutenant Edward N. Hooker, U.S. Navy. By the next morning, Hooker's five naval gunboats escorted Draper's army transports *Star* and *Commodore Foote* to the mouth of Mill Creek in Middlesex County, Virginia. Acting Master William Tell Street, commanding the gunboat *Fuschia*, landed with 100 armed sailors and marines and took possession of the beach near the farm of R.C. Garland known as "a notorious Rebel." This landing was followed shortly by an advance guard of the 36th USCT under Captain Charles H. Frye that confiscated Garland's property and took him prisoner.[43]

Two lines of torpedoes (land mines) were discovered nearby, of which three were detonated and two removed. Once an 8-pound howitzer battery crew of 35 sailors from the gunboat *Yankee* joined the landing party, Draper and Street marched their forces two miles inland to the home of Henry D. Barrick, a former Confederate officer, whose mill was set ablaze. It was here that the expedition learned that 60 Confederates including marines were encamped close by, but a quick reconnaissance discovered that they had already left. The farm of R.C. Taylor, a Confederate army officer, was diligently searched yielding numerous pistols and sabers. It was here that the expedition split into two columns. Street, with the navy component, took the Saluda Road to destroy a gristmill and confiscate corn and wheat reported to be stored in the vicinity. Draper, with the army component, marched along the road that ran southeast across the portion of the county between the Rappahannock and Piankatank Rivers. Near Stingray Point, Draper's column discovered four more torpedoes concealed in the woods. A close examination of the devices showed that they were constructed with tin cases and each containing 50 pounds of powder.[44]

Suspecting the presence of the enemy in the area, Draper threw out skirmishers in advance of his column as it proceeded down the peninsula and extended three miles. The skirmishers had a difficult time negotiating the broken terrain of thick woods and undergrowth, often separating the men of the 36th into smaller clusters. One such cluster of six soldiers ran into a group of nine Confederate cavalrymen and marines. Isolated and outnumbered, the black soldiers resolved to attack their enemy and began firing. Soon other groups from Draper's skirmishers joined in the fray. Private David Berry, Company F, 36th USCT, although wounded with a shattered arm by enemy fire, pursued the fleeing forces with his rifle in his good hand and captured one of them. In the end, the black soldiers killed or captured the entire group except one. "This little affair was conducted wholly by the black men," Draper reported, "as no officers arrived until after the fight." Draper credited Sergeant Sylvester Price, Company H, 36th USCT, for restraining the rest of the men from executing their prisoners on sight. The black soldiers' success came at the price of losing Private Thaddeus Baxter, Company A, 36th USCT, who was killed during the skirmishing.

Historian Joseph T. Glatthaar has suggested that this particular skirmish under the exclusive leadership of black noncommissioned officers demonstrated that these soldiers "had good reason to clamor for the promotion of noncommissioned officers into commissioned ranks."[45]

Among those captured was Acting Master Bennett G. Burley of the Confederate Navy, who had been a Confederate spy. Draper's men found documents on him from the Confederate Secretary of War that contained a pass describing him as "a citizen of Great Britain, to pass beyond the limits of the Confederate States." Burley's accomplice, Acting Master John Maxwell, a former U.S. Navy officer, was among the Confederates killed. He was shot while attempting to escape his captors by swimming the Piankatank River. These men were apparently responsible for the theft of the Union vessel *Titan* several weeks before.[46]

After spending a night at Stingray Point, Draper and his men embarked on their transports and crossed the Piankatank River to Milford Haven the next morning. The column marched the eight miles to Mathews Court House. A Confederate sergeant and corporal were captured along with 33 head of cattle and 22 serviceable horses and mules. These confiscated animals along with captured wagons and carts would be useful to black refugee families on the farms along the Patuxent River. The expedition returned to Point Lookout on May 14 from another successful mission.[47]

News correspondent Physic, accompanying the expedition, recalled that there had been no serious reports of depredations against the local white citizens by the black soldiers of the 36th USCT. "On the march of the negro troops through the country," he wrote, "it was observed that they were easier to manage and did less mischief than white troops." However "small acts of piracy" in the form of the taking of individual chickens, turkeys, and geese occurred. In one instance, an officer of the 36th asked a black soldier why he had a duck under his shirt. The soldier replied that he "could not tell, unless it was because when marching it being so warm he opened his shirt, when the duck flew in."[48] Nevertheless, successful raids by the 36th USCT like these would continue to strike effective blows against the Confederate military machine and force many Confederate soldiers to return home to protect their families and property.

Draper feared that the war would be over without his regiment having taken part in the developing spring offensive in Virginia where General Butler's Army of the James would play a major role. Several black regiments had already served briefly as prison guards at Point Lookout that spring before heading for the Virginia Front with the Army of the James.[49]

Lieutenant General Ulysses S. Grant, appointed general-in-chief of all Union forces in the field in March 1864, had already begun an offensive movement in Virginia against Confederate forces under General Robert E. Lee on May 4, 1864. The Army of the Potomac under Major General George G. Meade was to vigorously pursue Lee's forces from the north while Butler's Army of the James would simultaneously advance from the southeast to cut Lee's rail and supply lines to the Confederate capital at Richmond.

On June 10, 1864, Butler asked the War Department as well as General Grant to have the 36th USCT assigned to the Army of the James. The District of St. Mary's was scheduled to become a part of the Department of Washington at the end of the month. Butler was eager to have Draper, "as he is a valuable officer," and the 36th under his command before Point Lookout fell from his authority.[50] The time for the men of the 36th USCT to prove themselves in combat had arrived.

After two months, Grant's forces appeared no closer to defeating Lee's Confederates or capturing Richmond than he had been when he started his campaign. After capturing

Bermuda Hundred and City Point, the Army of the James had gotten itself "bottled up" along the peninsula at the confluence of the James and Appomattox Rivers by a hastily gathered force of Confederate troops from Petersburg. At the time of Butler's request for the 36th, portions of his command, including several black regiments, had made an unsuccessful assault on Petersburg. This began the ten-month siege of Petersburg, the important transportation and supply center for Lee's forces in Virginia. Grant reasoned that once Petersburg fell, Richmond would soon follow. Butler needed as many troops as he could gather for the Army of the James to help break this siege.[51]

Despite Butler's need for the 36th, the War Department denied his request for the regiment's transfer. As more Confederate prisoners arrived at Point Lookout from the Virginia Front, security at the prison tightened. Secretary of War Edwin M. Stanton directly ordered Draper, still in temporary command of the District of St. Mary's, to capture and detain deserters from Union regiments stopping through the district on their way to reinforce Union forces in Virginia. Butler had earlier instructed Draper to make sure that news correspondent Physic limit the information about Confederate prisoners arriving at Point Lookout and identifying Union regiments on their way to Virginia. "Caution him against giving any more movements of troops," he wrote, "or else shut him up in the rebel prison."[52]

Draper shielded his disappointment at not being sent to a combat assignment by requesting permission to lead a third expedition into Virginia. On the evening of June 11, Draper left Point Lookout with 475 men of the 36th and 49 men of the 2nd and 5th U.S. Cavalry under First Lieutenant Jeremiah C. Denney on board the army transports *Georgia*, *Charleston*, *Long Branch*, and *Favorite*. Lieutenant Hooker of the U.S. Navy accompanied the expedition with five gunboats. The water-born caravan headed toward Pope's Creek, Virginia, off the Potomac River for "the purpose of procuring horses for the quartermaster's department, and farming implements, transportation, &c., for the contraband settlement on the Patuxent River."[53]

Landing at Pope's Creek in Westmoreland County, Virginia, 50 miles above the mouth of the Potomac River, Draper divided his command. Captain William H. Hart, Company H, 36th USCT, marched his column of 300 men to the town of Warsaw, county seat of Richmond County. Draper and the remaining army component, accompanied by Acting Master Street and 100 armed sailors and marines, headed for Montross, the county seat of Westmoreland County. The two columns planned to rendezvous at Warsaw the next evening.[54]

The next morning, Draper's column captured a mounted Confederate horseman two miles outside of Warsaw who turned out to be the enrolling officer for the Richmond County home guard militia. Continuing on to Warsaw, the column captured large quantities of Confederate uniforms, tobacco, whisky, and "other blockade goods." Later that evening, Hart's column joined the rest of the expedition near Durettsville having confiscated horses and cattle. His column had a brief skirmish with Confederate guerrillas. One of the white Union cavalrymen accompanying his column was captured. His captors threatened that "they had a piece of rope awaiting for him" and that he would be hung at sunset. But when the black soldiers charged the enemy position, the guerrillas retreated and the cavalryman made his escape, thanks to the 36th USCT. Captain Hart's detachment had also been busy burning several grain and flour mills.[55]

Later that evening, Draper, with a cavalry escort, rode along the Rappahannock River opposite the town of Tappahannock and conferred with Lieutenant Hooker and his flotilla of gunboats. The naval officers reported an abundance of horses at Occupacia Creek and

Layton's Wharf on the south side of the river. "Finding horses scarce and poor on the Northern neck, between the Potomac and Rappahannock," Draper reported, "I resolved to transfer the field of operations to the south bank of the Rappahannock."[56]

Most of June 13 was spent directing troops to concentrate at Durettsville and sending some of the army transports back to Point Lookout loaded with confiscated property. By the next day all of the smaller detachments sent out to canvass the area for removable property arrived except Company E, 36th USCT, under Captain Joseph J. Hatlinger. Described by Draper as "an inefficient officer," Hatlinger's company had taken a wrong turn but arrived later that evening. Although Hatlinger was senior to Hart, Draper had more confidence and placed more responsibility on the latter officer. They were both from Lynn, Massachusetts, and Hart had served under Draper in the 14th Massachusetts Infantry earlier in the war. The next morning, the command marched to Union Wharf on the Rappahannock River where it was met by Lieutenant Hooker's gunboats and the remaining army transports. Much of the day was spent rebuilding the wharf that had been burned some time before during a raid of Union cavalry under Brigadier General Judson H. Kilpatrick.[57]

On June 16, the enemy appeared in the rear of the expedition and Draper ordered the cavalry detachment forward while Captain Hatlinger with 150 men of the 36th USCT was held in readiness to support them. Draper took command of 40 cavalrymen as a result of Lieutenant Denney being unable to take the field. Draper dispatched three cavalrymen as an advance guard to ascertain the enemy's strength. The cavalrymen initially reported about 200 Confederate cavalry in the distance, but this number was found to be much smaller. At a suitable distance, Draper ordered the cavalry to charge, whereupon the enemy opened fire. Draper best explained what occurred next. He reported:

> After riding to within sixty yards of the rebel position, I found myself almost alone, only my assistant adjutant-general and a few faithful orderlies remaining by me. I turned and ordered the cavalry to close up; whereupon the rebels set up their customary yell, and my escort turned their horses' heads to the rear and ran for their lives, seeing the rebels immediately charged upon us. I tried in vain to rally my men, calling upon them a dozen times to halt and face the enemy. In this attempt I was seconded by Captain Gibbs, of the Fourth Rhode Island Volunteers, my acting assistant adjutant-general, by a few men among the cavalry who repeated my orders to halt. I remained on the ground until my orderly and one other man had been captured by my side, and another dismounted man had time to run to the rear, get over the fence, and escape. Finally, finding myself enveloped in the dust of the rebel pursuit and entirely alone, I followed the crowd.[58]

Hatlinger's detachment, which had been slow to support Draper's initial charge, came on the scene. Draper ordered the infantry into action as the Confederate guerrillas fell back in retreat.[59]

During this time, Second Lieutenant John O'Brien, Company D, 36th USCT, had permitted three black soldiers from Company C to leave the column against Draper's explicit orders. The soldiers approached a house located a mile from where the command was skirmishing and were fired upon by a group of mounted guerrillas. According to news correspondent Physic, "The Rebels ran down a negro soldier and a contraband, both of whom were murdered in cold blood, the men seeing them shot at after they fell, and their bodies were [later] found riddled with balls." The murdered soldier was Private Peter Wilson. One of Wilson's comrades, Private Henry Lee, was "wounded and probably killed, as he crawled into the woods and could not afterwards be found," Draper later reported. The third unidentified soldier apparently escaped from harm and returned to the command.[60]

Draper meanwhile posted Hatlinger with 75 men at the edge of a wooded area while he personally led another 75 men through the woods in the attempt to get behind the guerrillas while keeping his own movements concealed. Several unexpected "bays of open plain" forced Draper to make a seven-mile circuit through thorny underbrush. As darkness approached, he could make out the campfires of the guerrillas 600 yards in front of him. Hoping to catch the enemy while it was bivouacked for the evening, Draper prepared his men for the attack when an accidental discharge of one of the men's rifles gave notice of their approach. Draper's soldiers emerged from the woods only to find the enemy campsite deserted.[61]

The next morning, June 17, the anniversary of the Battle of Bunker Hill, Draper was determined "to make one more attempt to wipe out the disgrace the cavalry had brought upon the expedition." Leaving 300 men to load the transports at Union Wharf, Draper marched 200 men of the 36th USCT and 36 cavalry troopers along the road near the location of the previous day's engagement. Draper had received word the night before that the guerrillas had received reinforcements and would block his way. "This intelligence was communicated, as usual, by the plantation negroes," Physic reported.[62]

According to Draper's report, his column encountered 150 cavalrymen, presumably of the 9th Virginia Cavalry, but in reality mounted local militia, supported by 450 men made up of home guard units under the overall command of Meriwether Lewis. Lewis was a former lieutenant colonel in the 9th Virginia Cavalry earlier in the war. Draper posted his cavalry at a bend in the road backed by 50 men of the 36th concealed in the woods "to rake the roads" in case the cavalry should again be repulsed. This position was about 1,000 yards in front of the enemy position. Orders were given for the cavalry to charge the position whenever the bugler sounded the call. Draper formed the remaining 150 men into a battle line along the edge of the woods behind a ditch within 500 yards of the enemy's position. Twenty men from this group moved to the rear as a reserve. Captain Hart recalled encountering the body of a black soldier, presumably Private Peter Wilson, "lying by the roadside ... with bullet holes through both feet."[63]

The enemy "worked like ants" completing a barricade across the road and placed their mounted forced in front of Draper's cavalry. Expecting a combined charge of Union cavalry and infantry, the Confederates reserved their fire with the intent of opening up on Draper's men at close range, thereby preserving their ammunition and making every shot count. "I ordered my men to fix their sights at 500 yards, and directed company commanders to pass along the line to see that every sight was properly raised," Draper reported. Further cautioning them to aim steadily at the bottom of the fences used as the enemy's barricade, Draper rode out of the woods from the right of his command's position to observe the effect of fire.[64]

Reserving his own firepower to better determine the enemy's strength and detect any attempts of the enemy to flank his position, Draper ordered his men to fire by the ranks. The first volley took the enemy by surprise since it was expecting a charge. Several Confederates fell screaming, although they returned fire. The men of the 36th kept up a rapid succession of volleys and "soon threw the rebels into great confusion." As the Confederates broke through the woods in retreat, the commands of their officers ordering the retreating men out from the woods and their curses of cowardice could be heard above the din of battle.[65]

Draper's cavalry was able to maneuver through a breach in the series of barricades and formed for a charge upon the "Fleet-Footed Virginians." However, the fifth volley from the black infantry dispersed the Confederates. As Draper's force advanced to take the enemy works, the position was completely abandoned. Draper lost no men during this engagement known as Pierson's Farm. He would not be able to determine the casualties his black soldiers inflicted upon the enemy until later. "The gallantry of the colored troops on this occasion could not be excelled," Draper declared. "They were as steady under fire and as accurate in their movements as if they were on drill." The men of the 36th in the abandoned works gave nine rousing cheers. The soldiers returned to Union Wharf and boarded their transports with their captured property. As the expedition pulled away from the wharf, the Confederates appeared on the beach where the navy gunboat *Commodore Read* opened fire and sent them some "grape and shell," which scattered the enemy, but destroyed the wharf that had been recently rebuilt.[66]

Disembarking at Lloyds Landing in Essex County, Virginia, Draper marched his men eight miles towards Lloyds, capturing horses, mules, and cattle as they moved. A large gristmill owned by Robert M.T. Hunter, a former U.S. senator and current Confederate senator, was set ablaze. However, the Union soldiers distributed a good deal of stored flour, intended for use by Confederate forces, among "the poor families connected with these extensive estates." Hunter's mansion was visited by the expedition, bringing a large number of his slaves to be taken back to Point Lookout as refugees. Draper's operations were soon overlapping with those of the main Union forces fighting in Virginia. Information had been received that Major General Philip H. Sheridan, with portions of Union cavalry from the Army of the Potomac, had passed through nearby Newtown on a raid the night before with Confederate General Wade Hampton's cavalry in pursuit. Some of Hampton's men were reported as being as close as five miles away from Draper's position and carefully observing his movements.[67]

Finding it prudent to return to his transports, Draper and his men spent the night at Layton's Wharf, where the refugees, captured animals, and other confiscated property were loaded on board the transports. As more reports of a Confederate build-up of troops around the town of Tappahannock reached Draper, his cavalry fanned out in all directions to detect the movements of this force. The 36th was sent up the river by transports to reinforce a portion of the cavalry skirmishing with Confederates at Tappahannock. While the black soldiers held the town, the cavalry continued bringing in captured items from the surrounding area. On the afternoon of June 19, the enemy had driven Draper's advanced scouts and pickets. Soon dust clouds heralded the approach of a sizable enemy force. The soldiers of the 36th USCT immediately took up arms and began singing "John Brown's Body" for a solid ten minutes.[68] This particular moment for Draper and his black soldiers appeared to symbolize the pinnacle of their very existence. Like Brown, if these former slaves-turned-soldiers died at the hands of Confederate troops whose government supported slavery, then they too would be hailed as martyrs for the cause of freedom.

Fortunately, the climatic moment for the 36th USCT would be postponed for another year. As the dust cleared, it was found that Draper's own cavalry had been the cause of the commotion after briefly skirmishing with the enemy before returning to the command. The expedition returned to Point Lookout on June 21. Approximately 335 head of cattle, 160 horses and mules, 600 black refugees (including 60 to 70 recruits for the army and navy), and a large number of plows, harvesters, cultivators, wheat drills, corn-shellers, harnesses, carts, and carriages were obtained for the contraband settlements near the prison and along the Patuxent River. A few days after the expedition's return, portions of the Potomac Flotilla returned to Union Wharf where it was learned that the Confederate loss at Pierson's Farm was two wounded and from three to five killed. "A colored woman reported that she saw 4 corpses, besides 1 covered up in a cart, and that the 'chief captain' was wounded," Acting Master Street of the U.S. Navy reported through Draper. Two members of the Union cavalry detachment had been taken prisoner during the expedition. The bodies of Private Peter Wilson and the unidentified contraband, "who it appears was attempting to get within our lines with the negro soldier," were located and buried near the scene of the skirmish.[69]

The 36th USCT enlisted 63 soldiers between April and June 1864. Most of these new enlistees had been slaves born in the "Northern Neck" counties of Essex, Westmoreland, Middlesex, King and Queen, Richmond, and Lancaster. The addition of more fugitive slaves in the District of St. Mary's demonstrated the black soldiers' success in rescuing their brethren from bondage and relocating them on abandoned plantations and farms in support of the Union war effort. This also strengthened the resolve of the general community of freed people to contribute toward the Union war effort.[70]

Despite the expedition's success, several exaggerated reports were received at the U.S. War Department suggesting that Draper had undertaken this latest raid into Virginia without proper authority or that he had greatly exceeded his orders. However, nothing came from these reports. Although Draper appreciated and praised Lieutenant Hooker and his sailors for their "cheerful cooperation" during the expedition, higher naval authority was not so content. Commander Foxhall A. Parker, Jr., commanding the Potomac Flotilla, had ordered Hooker not to allow any more naval personnel or howitzer crews to be used as ground forces after June 17, since he apparently had a want of confidence in Acting Master Street and that his own choice for the naval ground commander was disregarded and this officer was left behind on board the *Commodore Read*. Additionally, Parker had not been entirely clear on Draper's objectives for the expedition and could not have his sailors engaged "in enterprises of which I know not the nature." In future expeditions, the Potomac Flotilla would render any assistance to Draper that it could from the river, but he would need to get his own army reinforcements "from Point Lookout should he need them."[71]

Government authorities in the Confederate capital were already receiving preliminary reports from the Northern Neck inhabitants of Draper's expedition into Westmoreland and Richmond Counties prompting Secretary of War James A. Seddon to write General Robert E. Lee on June 24. "The larger portion of these marauders are negroes," Seddon explained, "and they are allowed, and in not a few cases encouraged, by their officers to commit deeds of spoliation, destruction, and infamy unexampled even among the many atrocities heretofore practiced by them in this war." Mindful that Virginia's Northern Neck region lacked effective local militia, Seddon appealed to Lee to send a small "nucleus" of trained troops that able-bodied men "may rally." He further suggested that Lieutenant Colonel John S. Mosby, the partisan leader and "Grey Ghost of the Confederacy," be sent from eastern fringes of the Shenandoah Valley to the Northern Neck "giving countenance to the people capable of arms in organizing, and with them punishing the marauders who may venture into any part of the Neck."[72]

Lee responded two days later frankly admitting that while the reports were extremely distressing, the atrocities committed "are more to be deplored because they cannot be prevented." He could not send troops to the area, as they could not be spared from the entrenchments in and around Petersburg. If he could send a small force from his army, "they could do nothing against the bands landed from boats, who could avoid them on every occasion and be thoroughly informed of their movements by traitors and negroes in the country whom they have in their employ." Seddon's suggestion of Mosby's command being assigned to the Northern Neck would be an unsafe move, "as his retreat could be easily cut off and his presence there would certainly be betrayed." Additionally, Mosby was actively working in tandem with Major General Jubal A. Early and a portion of Lee's army in an offensive campaign in the Shenandoah Valley to relieve the pressure Union forces under General Ulysses S. Grant were bringing to bear on Petersburg and Richmond.

Harboring a bit of resentment over the residents in the region of his birth, Lee related to Seddon, "I have always heard there were a great many men in that country who should have been in the army, but who could not be got." In his estimation, the best way that the region could repel future raids was to find strength within themselves to organize, turn out and defend their homes. "I think it would be far better and more advantageous if a citizen of the Northern Neck and one of the counties south of the Rappahannock would organize the men in their respective districts and operate against the enemy as Mosby has done in the Piedmont country," Lee concluded.[73]

The residents of Northumberland County, one of the few Northern Neck counties spared from Draper's recent expedition, sent Confederate President Jefferson Davis a resolution soon after the Union troops left the region. Providing an account of the events that transpired in the neighboring counties of Westmoreland and Richmond, the Northumberland residents considered the confiscation of livestock, crops, and slaves as well as the destruction of property "of minor importance" when compared to "the insults and outrages heaped on an unoffending community by these beastly savages."

The black soldiers of the 36th USCT they claimed were allowed to roam uncontrolled throughout the countryside heaping insults at white female inhabitants when they were encountered. "The most disgusting proposals were made to some, others were subjected to indecent familiarities or rude and revolting embraces," the resolution charged. "Twelve or fifteen escaped almost miraculously from successful violence, and four at least became unfortunate victims of brutal list." Fearful of future visits from the "brutal negroes," the resolution requested that the Confederate government exempt Northumberland County from the present conscription laws provided that the able-bodied men in the county eligible for conscription would instead join the local militia for defense in addition to arms and ammunition.[74]

Davis forwarded the resolution to Secretary Seddon recommending that the county use non-conscript men for their local defense. He reasoned that Lee could not detach regular troops from his own army. Additionally, "[t]he veteran regiments of Virginia are entitled to and sorely need recruits" from among eligible conscripts. Instructing Seddon to reply to the Northumberland County representatives "of my deep sympathy and of the sorrow I feel at my inability to give them ample protection." Seddon responded to his chief, "A better reply cannot be given than to transmit the above indorsement (sic)." He further recommended that Davis acknowledge receipt of the resolution and that it had been referred to the Secretary of War, who was doing all in his "power to organize reserves and supply arms ... for home defense."[75]

Lucy A. Bramham of Tappahannock, who had "been a great sufferer by our ruthless enemies, and have lost what all the wealth of the world could not have purchased," had a letter published within an article in the July 5, 1864, issue of the *Richmond Enquirer*. In the letter she described for the readers how her property was confiscated, her home ransacked by the black soldiers, and servants taken away against their will.[76] In the general article describing the "atrocities" and "outrages" of the June expedition, the *Enquirer* also reported that six black soldiers of the 36th USCT "violated the person of Mrs. G eleven times, she being the wife of a brave soldier of the Ninth Virginia cavalry, being also sick at the time, with an infant six weeks old at her breast." They were also accused of other similar violations on at least 25 other white women in the area.[77]

On the same day the *Enquirer* article appeared, Captain John S. Braxton, a Richmond County native and Confederate staff officer in the Department of Richmond (responsible for the Confederate capital's defense), wrote his immediate superior Major Theodore O. Chestney a report on the June raid by black soldiers. He related the incident in Westmoreland County the *Enquirer* had described:

About the 14th ultimo, at a place called Hutt's Store, near the center of Westmoreland County, some of the negro troops went to the house of Private George, of Ninth Virginia Cavalry, and committed a rape upon his wife, who had just been confined with a babe only six weeks old. She is now almost a maniac, and begs that some one will kill her. This atrocious crime can be verified by a number of witnesses who are personally cognizant of the fact. In Warsaw, Richmond County, the negro troops attempted to ravish white ladies but were foiled by the assistance of the female slaves of the households. In the case of Mrs. Belfield, she escaped by flight to the woods.

Braxton stated that Lieutenant Colonel Lewis, formerly of the 9th Virginia Cavalry, had improvised a force of 40 mounted men and a few infantry from among the furloughed soldiers in the area and local residents. They "attacked the enemy in open field and drove them back, capturing two, wounding several others, among whom was the colonel badly injured, and killing four negroes." Braxton's account, likely from second-hand information, contained several erroneous details. His description of the engagement at Pierson's Farm near Union Wharf was only the initial skirmish of Draper's advance guard that withdrew as the main infantry force advanced. Moreover, Draper emerged from the conflict without a scratch. Reiterating the call of the Northumberland County residents to exempt those eligible for conscription, Braxton believed this would prevent future incursions in order "to protect the honor of our mothers, wives, and daughters."[78]

Braxton's report was forward to Lieutenant General Richard S. Ewell, commanding the Department of Richmond, who repeated previous recommendations of sending a small force under an experience officer to the Northern Neck to help organize the local residents. "I was told at the War Department," Ewell wrote, "that this matter rests with General Lee." Lee, upon receiving Braxton's report, insisted that he could not detach any troops. "If the people will do nothing to defend themselves against such outrages," he declared, "I can see no remedy for them."[79]

Reports of the outrages on Draper's June raid continued to reach Union commanders. Commander Parker of the Potomac Flotilla asked Lieutenant Commander Eastman to investigate the involvement of naval personnel who had accompanied Draper's expedition. Eastman inquired of Lieutenant Hooker commanding the naval contingent of the expedition for any particulars "with regard to the entering of houses during the last raid under Colonel Draper and yourself." His main concern was if any naval officers or sailors under his command "behaved improperly toward unarmed or unprotected women" or if anything had been stolen from them by his sailors. Hooker replied on September 1, 1864, that he could find no evidence that his sailors were guilty of such conduct. "I am aware that such things were done by the negro soldiers," he reported, "and some of them were severely punished by Colonel Draper for it."[80]

These were the most serious accusations leveled at the regiment during its service. No clear basis had been established if these allegations against the black soldiers held any truth. The soldiers of the 36th USCT certainly had ample opportunity to commit such crimes, given the isolated areas of the region, the absence of armed military forces to oppose them, and the vulnerability of the remaining inhabitants. Richard Reid has argued that there may have been truth to the allegations, citing an undated letter of Captain George B. Proctor to an unnamed recipient. Proctor, who had been dismissed from the service two months before the expedition and no longer at Point Lookout, wrote that Draper, "while in command of an expedition, some of the men committed *rape* & Col. D never endevored (sic) to ferret out the person." Draper certainly possessed the resources and the ability to cast his men in a favorable light, going as far as to potentially cover up any such crimes that may have been committed by his men. Yet given Draper's past history, he would have been more likely to openly punish (via execution) his soldiers found guilty of rape to serve as an example to the rest of the men and to protect the future existence of the 36th USCT.

Executions of foreign-born and black soldiers in the Union army accounted for slightly more than 54 percent of all wartime executions. The proportion of black soldiers executed was 21 percent larger than the entire population of executed Union soldiers. Union authorities, as Ervin Jordan has argued on these same allegations against the 36th USCT, were more than likely to execute black soldiers for raping white women than any other violation. It may be that Draper's men heaped insults on the inhabitants, made threats, and perhaps physically removed them in a forceful manner from their premises, but that these threats turned into rumors and exaggerations that for the inhabitants of the region and Confederate authorities became actual heinous crimes.

Lieutenant Hooker assured his superiors in the Navy that Draper had punished his soldiers for violations committed by them on the expedition. If the rape of white women by black soldiers was punishable by death, the severe punishment supposedly meted out by Draper and his white officers fell short of this. There was no indication in the regimental records during this period indicating convictions of soldiers for rape or punishments resulting in death.[81]

On June 20, 1864, while the 36th USCT was on its expedition through the Northern Neck, a black soldier in the 23rd USCT named William Johnson was executed on Jordan's Farm just outside the Union trenches near Petersburg. He had deserted after raping a white woman and was later captured. Admitting to his crime during his trial, Johnson was convicted and sentenced to death. In view of the Confederate trenches, Union officials hoped that this scene would prove to their adversaries that black Union soldiers convicted of rape would be punished. It was later reported that Confederates paraded their black laborers in view of Johnson's swinging body, persuading them that the Yankees hanged runaways. Johnson's photographic image immediately after his execution, frozen in time, served as a stark reminder to black Union soldiers their delicate and still precarious situation by serving in the Union army. Their actions would be scrutinized more so than white soldiers.[82]

Garland H. White, black chaplain of the 28th USCT recruited from among Indiana's free black population, believed slavery had kept black southerners in such ignorance that there had been no choice for the Union but to force them into military service for the use of their labor and care for their families. Those who had been born free or had escaped slavery and lived North before the war had gained broader opportunities and developed admirable aims in life. "I am sorry to say that while white & colored men from the north are breathing out their last breath upon the Battle field in freeing these stupit [sic] creatures, they are left Idle to rove over the country like ox that feed the army," he wrote.[83]

Chaplain White served as the spiritual advisor of another condemned black soldier that same summer. The soldier had been a former slave and was to be executed by firing squad. "He was charged with having attempted to kill his captain and insubordination," White wrote after the execution. "He was a Virginian, and had never lived North. His regiment was raised in Virginia, and has a white chaplain, who was not here at present." White had hoped that this black soldier's execution would also serve as a warning to other black soldiers, particularly former slaves who became Union soldiers. Ironically, White himself had been a Virginia slave before running away.[84]

The concept of "de bottom rail on top" may have been a double-edged sword for the soldiers in the 36th USCT. Former slaves being placed as guards over their former masters certainly upset the southern social in the extreme. This may have embolden their attitudes

**The hanging of Private William Johnson, 23rd USCT, served as a stark reminder what the punishment for the rape of a white woman would be to black soldiers if convicted of the offense. Accusations of "outrages" committed against defenseless white women by soldiers of the 36th USCT during Draper's expedition into Princess Anne County, Virginia, in November 1863 and on another in Westmoreland County, Virginia, in June 1864 would plague the regiment throughout its war service whether such charges were real or imagined (Library of Congress)**

toward Confederate civilians while participating in three expeditions into Virginia's Northern Neck. In spite of negative views by both Union and Confederate authorities, the 36th USCT continued to prove their worth, strengthening Draper's conviction that his black soldiers could handle themselves upon any field of battle. They continued to liberate black families, as they had before, who would aid the Union war effort as laborers on confiscated farms. Their lot was cast with the Union army. "We hear fearful accounts of the barbarity of the rebels at Plymouth [N.C.] and Fort Pillow [TN] towards the colored troops," Lieutenant John Owen of Company H, 36th USCT, reflected in May 1864. "I think our boys will either come off successful or fight to the death — Better to be killed fighting to the last than tortured to death after surrendering."[85]

CHAPTER 6

# First and Foremost of Them All
*From New Market Heights to the Frontiers of Mexico, 1864–1866*

Brevet Brigadier General Alonzo G. Draper, the original commander of the 36th USCT, commanding a brigade in the Army of the James that included the 36th. remarked in 1864, "I would not exchange my command for any troops in the world." A year of leading black soldiers convinced him that they "have all the qualities of a good soldier, bravery, subordination, endurance, sobriety, contentment and ... all the élan of the French soldier, with all the stubborn courage of the British."[1] Moreover, being a part of the Army of the James in the war's last year and a half increased the 36th's importance in the military legacy of the Civil War. The actions of the soldiers on the battlefield and the conditions they experienced as part of a major military campaign would affect their family, kin, and brethren.

The Army of the James, commanded by Major General Benjamin F. Butler, held unique characteristics that set it apart from most other major Union army commands during the war. Its participation in the battles at the Virginia front around Petersburg and Richmond enabled the former slaves serving in the 36th USCT to prove themselves in battle. Created as the military field force of Butler's Department of Virginia and North Carolina in April 1864, the Army of the James would have an ambiguous military record but influenced the role African Americans would play as soldiers. It held between 35,000 to 40,000 officers and men at any given time during its service. The 146 infantry, cavalry regiments and the artillery batteries that served in the Army of the James came from primarily the New England states, New York, New Jersey, and Pennsylvania. The majority of the men came from small cities, towns, and villages rather than larger cities. The army's strength included at least 8,000 former slaves serving in black Union regiments like the 36th USCT.[2]

The Army of the James was a command that had the highest percentage of non–West Point trained general officers. From General Butler, as army commander, to the brigadier generals commanding brigades, many of the ranking officers had little to no pre-war military experience. Many of them had been local and state-level politicians before the war. Moreover, Butler's army consisted of men who by 1864 adhered to either the Republican Party or held strong Union loyalties. It did not hurt matters that Butler, as the highest-ranking Union general officer appointed from civilian life and an ambitious politician, filled his ranks with men who shared his similar political views making it a "quintessential Yankee command." Men like Alonzo Draper certainly found an organization where their own personal ambitions might be realized.[3]

The Army of the James also held the distinction of having 40 percent of its numbers made up of black soldiers that included the 36th USCT. This was largest contingent of black soldiers concentrated in any Union army command. Additionally, Butler had deliberately planned to use USCTs to spearhead his spring offensive.[4] When Butler embarked from Fort Monroe with the Army of the James on May 4, 1864, on what would be known as the Bermuda Hundred Campaign, the first troops to be put into action were black regiments under Brigadier General Edward A. Wild that seized the strategic points of Wilson's Wharf (or Fort Pocahontas) and Fort Powhatan along the James River. Another brigade of black regiments seized City Point at the junction of the James and Appomattox Rivers that would later serve as Grant's field and supply headquarters for the duration of the war.[5] The Army of the James demonstrated that the war had in fact changed from the preservation of the Union to ending slavery through the full participation of black soldiers fighting for their freedom. Butler insured that the black soldiers would play a major role in the military campaign to end the war.

Butler's army held the distinction of being the only Union field army whose primary mission involved some demonstration against the Confederate capital at Richmond, Virginia. Controversy continues as to what Butler's actual orders were for Lieutenant General Ulysses S. Grant's Virginia Campaign beginning in May 1864. This military operation involved the Army of the Potomac under Major General George G. Meade pursuing the Confederate Army of Northern Virginia under General Robert E. Lee from the north while keeping Washington, D.C., protected. Simultaneously, the Army of the James would proceed up the James River from southeastern Virginia toward Richmond, cutting Lee off from his rail lines and making an attack on the Confederate capital itself. Butler understood his orders as securing bases along the James and Appomattox Rivers below Richmond from which to launch joint assaults in cooperation with the Army of the Potomac against the Confederate capital.[6]

As early as January 1865, Butler expressed how he had understood his orders for Grant's Virginia Campaign. He told an audience in his hometown of Lowell, Massachusetts,

> The intention with which that army [Army of the Potomac] set out upon its march was to move round the north side of Richmond, above Mechanicsville, strike the James River above the city of Richmond, and there forming a junction with the Army of the James, which was to move up toward Richmond on the south side of the James River, get around the city on the south side, and thus cut it off.[7]

Such a junction by the two armies would not only cut Lee off from Richmond, but would occupy the Confederate capital with sheer military strength alone. Nevertheless, as it turned out, neither the Army of the James nor the Army of the Potomac was able to achieve its military objectives by the end of June 1864.

At that time the Army of the James was entrenched in front of Confederate defenses between Petersburg and Richmond. Butler would need all the help he could get in additional troops to break the stalemate. Colonel J. Wilson Shaffer, Butler's chief of staff, suggested to his commander a reorganization of the black regiments in the Army of the James, to be placed under the command of Brigadier General Charles J. Paine. Draper and Colonel Samuel A. Duncan, commander of the 4th USCT, would lead the two proposed brigades of Paine's division. In order to move toward the realization of this plan, the 5th Massachusetts (Colored) Cavalry relieved the 36th USCT of prison guard duty at Point Lookout, Maryland, on July 1, 1864. The regiment embarked on transports bound for Bermuda Hundred, Virginia, where the Army of the James had concentrated and immediately went into Camp of Instruction for training and drilling in preparation for duty in the Petersburg trenches.[8]

By the end of August, the 36th was assigned to the 2nd Brigade, 3rd Division, 18th

Army Corps. Draper, as senior colonel and acting brigade commander for the 2nd Brigade, commanded the 5th, 36th, and 38th USCT. Lieutenant Colonel Benjamin Pratt retained command of the 36th for the greater part of the year. General Paine, the division commander, was an untested Massachusetts attorney. The 18th Army Corps at this time fell under the command of Major General Edward O.C. Ord, a career army officer possessing marked indifference toward the use of black soldiers.[9]

Life for the soldiers on both sides was stressful as the siege around Petersburg dragged on. The common routine of digging, improving, and building up entrenchments all along the battle lines in dirt and mud was augmented only by random shots taken at soldiers who were not shielded by the earthen fortifications. Lieutenant John Owen, Jr. of Company H, 36th USCT, described to his mother how the entrenchments were constructed:

> The trenches so called are breastworks of earth & timber thrown up to the height of the neck so that the troops behind them can easily fire from between sandbags place on the top, at the enemies line of breastworks or on the foe when advancing.... Beyond the breastworks is a row of abattis [sic] (shar[p] stakes & old brush stick in the ground with the points towards the enemy —) in most cases there is a line of skirmishers in front of the breastworks and abattis [sic] i.e. 6 or 8 men in a large hole-that has earth thrown round the top thus making a small breastwork — the skirmish holes are some 4 or 5 feet apart-the rebs have a line similar close to ours.... When practicable holes are dug in the ground with small openings & covered with logs & earth — these are bomb-proofs & are usually used as protections from pieces of shell more than the shell itself-which will break through any moderate barrier — these bomb proofs are often built — out of the trenches under the brow of a hill....[10]

Leaving the protection of the trenches was often a dangerous enterprise to soldiers on both sides who exposed themselves to the fire of well-placed sharpshooters. At least four of the 36th's soldiers received fatal gunshot wounds to the head or neck during their first month in the trenches and an additional four soldiers were killed by sporadic shell firing from the Confederate lines. Additionally, seven soldiers had received gunshot wounds ranging from slight to severe injuries during this time period. It was clear that the regiment had a great deal to learn about survival in the siege lines. "There is not a day but what some brave black defender of the Union is made to bite to the dust by a rebel sharpshooter or picket," observed black war correspondent Thomas Morris Chester, "but his place is immediately and cheerfully filled by another."[11] On one occasion occurring on November 25, 1864, a Confederate artillery shell ripped through a house serving as a picket post on the Union line. Two USCT soldiers on duty were killed instantly and a third wounded. One of them, Private Andrew Newberne of Company G, 36th USCT, was "blown all to pieces" scattered in every direction for sixty yards.[12]

In the midst of the death and destruction between the trenches of the opposing armies, Lieutenant Owen noted aspects of life that remained constant while writing to his mother from Deep Bottom, Virginia, on September 10, 1864:

> I just heard the cowing of a cow — close by — think of that for the front — here are 2 women, wives of the men in the Regt. that have necessitated in following us — through shot & shell — i.e. not now but while we were before [Petersburg] — They do not seem to be afraid — one is our cook.[13]

The presence of women in the camps of the Union army was not all that unusual. Many of the wives of the 36th's soldiers had been employed as company laundresses to wash the clothing of the men. By 1864 laundresses were paid $10 a month. This was among the highest pay black women received in government employment than in any other capacity.

Initially, women were prohibited from being in the enlisted men's quarters while the regiment was stationed at Portsmouth, Virginia, and later at Point Lookout, Maryland. However, the presence of sizeable black populations nearby contraband camp and the fact that many soldiers were marrying in spite of the ongoing war prompted Draper and Pratt to gradually modify their orders by having soldiers obtain permission from them to have women in camp. Later, the wives of enlisted men were generally welcomed in camp daily until 5 P.M.[14]

Periodically throughout the fall of 1864, the 36th was placed on duty, as were several other black regiments, digging a canal at Dutch Gap that was located at the neck of a large bend in the James River 15 miles below Richmond. The bend itself, five miles in length, could become as short as 500 feet once the canal was dug. Confederate forces had placed obstructions in the area to hinder the canal's construction and frequently shelled the working parties of Union troops. Butler hoped that the canal would enable Union gunboats and monitors to have a shorter route along the James River to shell Richmond. Danger, nevertheless, prevailed as the soldiers labored under constant shelling of Confederate artillery.[15]

On November 12, 1864, as a detachment of the 36th USCT were at their turn on detail digging the canal, a shell exploded in their midst killing Sergeant Spencer Beasley of Company C. Corporal John Buck of Company D was knocked unconscious. Private Paul Wiggins, a comrade in Buck's company, remembered that Sergeant Beasley's clothes had caught on fire when he was struck and that he himself "was scared almost to death" in the confusion afterward. Beasley's body was carried out of the ditch and taken back to the regiment.

Dutch Gap Canal was Butler's "brain child" of building a canal at the neck of a five-mile peninsular bend in the James River. This enabled Union gunboats a shorter route for shelling Richmond without Confederate obstructions. The USCTs were the primary labor force in the canal's construction often braving Confederate shell fire in the process. The men of the 36th USCT took their turn as canal builders in November 1864. One wonders if this might be an actual glimpse of some the regiment's members along with one of their white officers (Library of Congress).

Meanwhile, according to Corporal Buck, Sergeant Samuel Gilchrist of Company K and Private Alfred Bray of Company C had also been wounded just as pieces of the shell struck the crowbar he had been using to operate the steam engine used to dig the ditch. Buck, himself, had to be carried into a bombproof where he "staid all night" without treatment for two days. Although correspondent Chester hailed these soldiers as a "powerful element" in suppressing the rebellion, labor on the canal continued to be a hazardous duty for them.[16]

Opportunity for a military victory that could end the war and display the effectiveness of black soldiers presented itself to Butler in late September. After two failed attempts by the Army of the Potomac to break the outer defenses of Richmond, Grant decided to allow Butler's Army of the James to try. Butler divided his command into two columns. His left column under the command of General Ord was to storm the exterior lines near Chaffin's Farm, with the capture of the Confederate-held Fort Harrison as the primary objective. Four miles to the east, the right column under the command of Major General David B. Birney with 14,000 troops was to advance from its base at Deep Bottom and capture the Confederate works on a rise of ground running parallel behind the New Market Road known as New Market Heights. Once these works were captured, Birney's column was to swing to the west along the New Market Road where it would join Ord's column making a general advance upon Richmond.[17]

Butler wrote detailed orders for this operation. The promise of extra pay, promotion, and furlough was the incentive for the first Union troops to enter Richmond. Accurately determining the diminished strength of Confederate forces holding the outer works around Richmond, Butler urged swift and immediate action by his troops. It was his intention to catch the enemy by surprise and give the black soldiers of Paine's 3rd Division the honor of leading the assault to capture the Confederate positions on the heights along the New Market Road.[18]

In the early morning hours of September 29, Ord's column crossed the James River at Aiken's Landing while Birney's column, which included Paine's Division, crossed the river at Deep Bottom. Paine had three brigades that composed his division. The 1st Brigade, which consisted of the 1st, 22nd, and 37th USCT, was under the command of Colonel John Holman. Draper commanded the 2nd Brigade, which included the 5th, 36th, and 38th USCT. Finally, Colonel Samuel A. Duncan commanded the 3rd Brigade, consisting of the 4th and 6th USCT. These eight black regiments amounted to approximately 3,000 men. The 36th probably had at least 450 soldiers participating in this assault.[19]

Paine's black division formed up on a plain "shelved by the river" where they were out of sight from the enemy on New Market Heights. At four o'clock that morning, Butler rode among these troops to give them encouraging words in preparation for the assault. "I told them that this was an attack where I expected them to go over and take a work which would be before them after they got over the hill," Butler recalled. "They must take it at all hazards." Butler further reminded his black soldiers that their cry should be "Remember Fort Pillow," in honor of the black soldiers who had been brutally slain in Tennessee by the men of Confederate cavalryman Nathan Bedford Forrest after their garrison had formerly surrendered on April 12, 1864.[20]

At 4:30 A.M., Paine led his division from Deep Bottom toward the Confederate works followed by the two white divisions of Birney's column. The Confederate fortifications on New Market Heights formed the extreme left of the outer defenses of Richmond and was garrisoned by 1,800 men consisting of the famed "Texas Brigade" on loan from Lee's veteran Army of Northern Virginia and augmented by inexperienced troops of the Richmond local

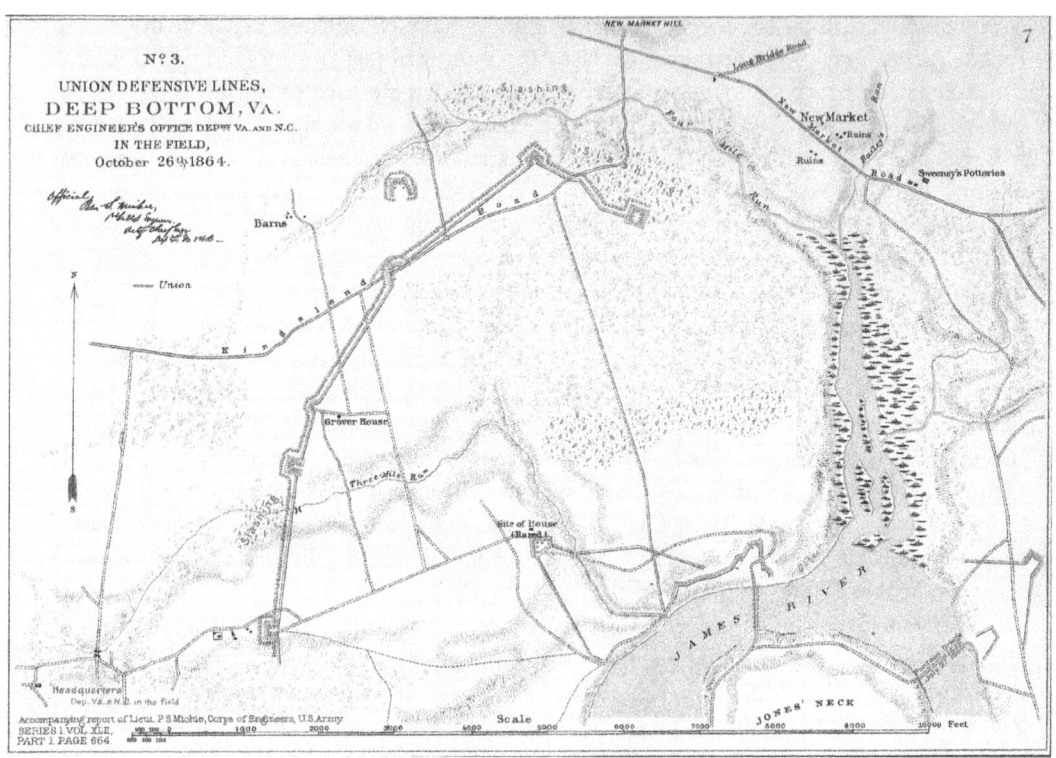

**New Market Heights Battlefield.** This map from the *Official Records* shows a portion of the New Market Heights battlefield in Union possession that had occurred the month before. The 36th USCT, as part of Draper's brigade, crossed the Kingsland Road toward the "slashing" terrain at the top center of the map where they captured the high ground marked "New Market Hill" emerging almost out of view at the top of the map (*Atlas to Accompany the Official Records of the Union and Confederate Armies* [Washington, DC: GPO, 1891–1895], plate 67, map 7).

defense forces. Butler hoped his troops could march around to the right of the Confederate position to cut it off from Richmond.[21]

Chester observed Draper's 2nd Brigade as it formed up in a wooded area in anticipation of the operations that were about to begin:

> Every man looked like a soldier, while inflexible determination was depicted upon every countenance. The officers as they went along the line, were impressed with an unwavering confidence by the martial bearing of the troops. The fears which generally precede the preparation for a desperate conflict soon gave place to hope, and, as the eye ran down the line, the unconquerable purpose manifested in the brightened eyes of redeemed freedmen inspired the officers in command with a settled conviction of victory.[22]

The ground sloped down into a marshy ravine complete with brush and thickets, forcing the black soldiers to shift to the left toward the center of the enemy line. Skirmishers from Duncan's brigade were successful in forcing Confederate pickets at the edge of a wooded area off the Kingsland Road (which ran parallel to the New Market Road) and back to the safety of the fortifications of New Market Heights.[23]

Colonel Duncan's 3rd Brigade shortly went into two lines of battle along the Kingsland Road and began its advance at 5:30 A.M. Under the cover of a dense fog, Duncan's two regiments plunged into the marshy swamp where the Four Mile Creek drained. About thirty yards ahead of the swamp was the first line of abatis or obstacles placed by the Confederate troops. Some of the soldiers, armed with axes, immediately went to work clearing these obstacles away. As the main portion of the charge emerged out of the marsh and up the slope, the Confederates opened fire with small arms and artillery. Duncan's brigade, now stalled in the tangle of obstacles, suffered heavy casualties at the hands of the experienced veterans of the 1st Texas Infantry in their front and the 24th Virginia Cavalry hitting them with enfilading fire on their right. These "battle-tested" Confederates, although under strength, vowed to fight under any circumstances and put up a stout resistance against the assault of black men in blue uniforms.[24]

Draper's brigade, lying in wait about a mile and half from where Duncan began his attack, watched the "slaughter pen" in which their comrades found themselves. Of the estimated 700 men of Duncan's brigade participating in the assault, 400 became casualties in less than 40 minutes. Duncan was severely wounded in the assault and command fell onto the shoulders of Colonel John W. Ames of the 6th USCT. Ames successfully brought what remained of the brigade off the field of battle with a loss of 365 men. This was slightly over 50 percent of its effective strength.[25]

A lull in the bloody contest soon followed as small numbers of Confederate troops ventured out from their entrenchments to confiscate items from the casualties of Duncan's unsuccessful assault. "Muskets had been gathered up, shoes taken from the dead men's feet, pockets turned inside out, and cartridge boxes and haversacks carried away," observed an officer of the 6th USCT. This same officer would later report seeing many of the fallen soldiers being stripped of their clothing.[26]

At about 7:30 A.M., Paine sent the order for Draper to move his brigade to the right of Duncan's position as "we were getting the worst of it here." The 2nd Brigade moved out into a ravine where it was subjected to artillery fire from atop New Market Heights. After waiting for a half hour, Draper led his brigade of 1,300 men in the second assault on New Market Heights. Portions of the 22nd USCT of Holman's 1st Brigade were dispatched as skirmishers to the left of Draper's position.[27]

Draper's men advanced under fire about 300 yards to an open area just to the right of the marsh. The men were prohibited from placing the percussion caps on their rifles as it would tempt them to shoot at the enemy and would easily make them open targets for Lee's Texans. The attack would be made at the point of the bayonet in a swift maneuver. Despite every possible preparation taken, Draper's plans were soon to unravel before him. About 800 yards from the main line of the enemy's works in open ground, some of Draper's men paused to take aim. Unfortunately, they did not have the cover of fog as Duncan's men had had.[28]

The 2nd Brigade, without support from friendly troops, surged forward "with loud cheering" under a severe fire. Soon, the marshy swamp that Duncan could not himself avoid in the first assault impeded their progress. "The firing here was terrible," reported Chester. "The enemy's sharpshooters with unerring aim picked off many officers and men, their balls passing in almost every instance through the head." The Texans were determined to shatter Draper's brigade as they had previously done to Duncan's. Men were "falling by scores" as Draper rode along his lines to instruct his three regimental commanders to rally the troops behind their colors for another charge. Meanwhile, soldiers armed with axes proceeded to hack away at the abatis the brigade encountered. Still, many of the men continued to fire their loaded weapons against orders. Chester observed that it looked as if it was impossible for any of the troops to advance upon the works since the Confederates held the advantage. Yet the black troops were "equally as stubborn in their resolution not to retreat."[29]

"After half an hour of terrible suspense," Draper reported, "by starting the yell among a few, we succeeded in getting them in motion." By this time, Draper, amid a shower of bullets, had dismounted from his horse and was observed by Captain William H. Hart of the 36th "standing on a slight eminence, sword in hand" encouraging the soldiers forward. The grand assault of the Second Brigade was again underway. The 5th USCT, under Lieutenant Colonel Giles W. Shurtleff, led the revitalized charge, followed closely by the 36th under Lieutenant Colonel Pratt.[30]

There were several instances of gallantry displayed by the officers of the 36th as they continued the advance upon the enemy works. Lieutenant Edwin C. Gaskill, in front of the regiment, urged it forward as he waved his sword. As the regiment encountered a second set of abatis, Gaskill fell with a severe wound to the arm just twenty yards from the enemy's works. Lieutenant Richard F. Andrews, who had been excused from duty with a fever, disobeyed orders and accompanied his men into battle. Dismounted from his horse, Andrews led a charge through the swamp but was shot through the leg before reaching the enemy's main line. Another officer of the 36th who had also violated orders to participate in the charge was Lieutenant James B. Backup, who had been excused for lameness as a result of one leg being partially shrunk. Only able to walk for short distances, Backup was shot through the hip just short of the swamp. Several soldiers, including Private James Cornick of Company I, had given up Backup for dead even several years after the war. Backup, although severely wounded, would survive the battle and the war.

Lieutenant Hiram W. Allen was another officer whose reported death on the battlefield like Backup was premature. Allen had served on General Edward Wild's staff for the better part of a year, but rejoined the regiment only three weeks before the assault. He, too, survived the battle and war. Lieutenants Francis A. Bicknell and Isaac W. Thurlow were also wounded in the assault.[31]

The examples of undaunted courage and unselfish bravery displayed by these particular officers had a positive impact on the men of the 36th. Since the regiment was short on officers, several companies were under the command of the black first sergeants when the final charge to take the works commenced. First Sergeants Jeremiah Gray of Company C, William Davis of Company E, Miles Sheppard of Company I, and Samuel Gilchrist of Company K all functioned as company commanders during the remainder of the assault. Sergeant Major Henry N. Adkins, the highest ranking enlisted soldier in the 36th, "was among the most conspicuous in rallying his regiment, and furnished an exhibition of gallant bearing which would rank with the brightest individual records of that day's glory," according to Chester.[32]

One of the first soldiers into the works was Private James Gardner of Company I. Gardner, far ahead of the regiment, rushed forward to the enemy works when a Confederate officer stepped up on a parapet and encouraged his men, "Give it to them, my brave boys!" At this instant, Gardner emitted a loud yell, shot and bayoneted up to the muzzle the enemy officer as the rest of the 36th piled over the entrenchments. Corporal Miles James of Company B had his left arm severely mutilated by artillery shrapnel during this assault. Ignoring his excruciating pain and remaining calm under heavy fire, James continued to load and discharge his weapon with his good arm while encouraging his comrades forward. Private Henry Cornick of Company A was shot through the left upper arm, which the bullet passed into his chest breaking several of his ribs as he charged toward the enemy works.[33]

A Confederate soldier in the Texas Brigade told a "southern" version of Paine's assault against New Market Heights. He recalled:

> A Federal officer shouted in stentorian voice, "Charge, men — Charge!" But only by the negroes immediately in front of the First Texas was the order obeyed by a rush forward that carried a regiment of the poor wretches up to, and in one or more places, across the breastworks, and right in among the First Texans.... In front of the other regiments the darkey charge lasted but a second or two, and covered not more than five paces. It was, in fact, simply a spasmodic response to the order. Then the black line halted, and for a moment stood motionless, obviously deliberating whether the more danger was to be apprehended from the Southern men in front, or the Northern men in the rear. Apparently, they decided on a compromise, for the half of those that survived the terrible fire poured into their ranks, threw down their guns, and wheeling, fled to the rear, and the other half dropped flat on the ground, and lay there until they were led away as captives. In effect, it was a massacre. Not a dozen shots in all were fired by the blacks, not a man in the Texas Brigade received a wound, and save in the First Texas, not a man was for a second in danger.

Another soldier of the 1st Texas likened the black division's charge against the Texas Brigade to "flaunting a red flag before a mad bull."³⁴ Receiving word that Ord's column had captured Fort Harrison, the Confederate forces withdrew from New Market Heights toward Richmond. Draper's brigade then halted to regroup. It had lost 450 men killed, wounded, missing, and captured in this assault. The 36th lost 21 soldiers killed and 87 wounded (including 5 officers). Butler himself surveyed the scene in the aftermath as he "rode across the brook and up towards the fort ... there lay in my path five hundred and forty-three dead and wounded of my colored comrades." Corporal James and Private Gardner received the Congressional Medal of Honor for their bravery at New Market Heights, as did twelve other black soldiers from the other participating regiments during this assault. Butler also issued self-designed medals of valor for all of the black soldiers participating in the assault at New Market Heights.³⁵

The 36th's soldiers, themselves, had to count their losses on a personal level. Corporal John Blango and his brother Thomas Blango of Company A witnessed their company comrade, Thomas Jaycox,

James Gardner (ca. 1844–1905) was born in Gloucester County, Virginia, and worked as an oysterman before enlisting into Company I, 2nd North Carolina Colored Volunteers (36th USCT) on September 15, 1863. At New Market Heights on September 29, 1864, Gardner was among the first to enter the Confederate defensive works and bayoneted a Confederate officer attempting to rally his troops. His actions that day earned him the Medal of Honor. This photograph of Gardner was taken around 1900 as part of an exhibit spearheaded by Dr. W.E.B. Du Bois for the Paris Exposition of 1900 (Library of Congress).

struck down by an enemy bullet. At the same time, their brother, Private Abram Blango of Company H, had been killed in the charge. Both Jaycox and Blango had to be "left on the field."[36] A company comrade of the fallen Thomas Jaycox was much luckier. Private Wilson Burroughs of Company A, who had barely recovered from a smallpox infection while at Point Lookout, Maryland, and still suffering from its damaging effects to his eyes, fell into an exposed rifle pit during the charge of New Market Heights where he "wrenched his right ankle and knee out of place." The effects of disease and physical injury would plague Burroughs for the rest of his life.[37]

Lieutenant Algernon Draper, commanding a detachment of the 36th at work in the Dutch Gap Canal, rode to the regiment's main camp at Deep Bottom the day after the battle. Draper shared the battlefield news with fellow officer John Owen upon his return to the detachment. Owen related the information in a letter to his mother. "They say that the "36th" fought well—& Here I am away from my company or most of it—in the regts first fight," he lamented.[38]

Butler, later in life, explained his rationale for choosing the black division to lead the assault against New Market Heights:

> But in the attack on Newmarket Heights I did deliberately expose my men to the loss of greater numbers than I really believed the capture of the redoubt was worth; for if the enemy's lines at Fort Harrison were captured, as they were, then Newmarket Heights would have been evacuated without loss, for I do not know that they were ever reoccupied by either side afterwards during the war. Now comes the inquiry in the minds of reflecting men: "Why make the attack?" Because it was to be done by my negro troops. "Are we to understand that you would sacrifice your negro troops where you would not your white troops?" No; except for a great purpose in behalf of their race and in behalf of the Union. If I have tried to make anything apparent up to this time in what I have written, it is that from prejudice and ignorance of their good qualities it was not really believed in and out of the army by military men, with a very few exceptions, that the negroes would fight. My white regiments were always nervous when standing in line flanked by colored troops, lest the colored regiments should give way and they [white soldiers] be flanked. This fear was a deep-seated one and spread far and wide, and the negro had had no sufficient opportunity to demonstrate his valor and his staying qualities as a soldier. And the further cry was that the negroes never struck a good blow for their

Thomas Morris Chester (1834–1892), was the only African American war correspondent attached to a major newspaper, *Philadelphia Press*, writing under the pseudonym "Rollin." He reported on the activities of the black units in Butler's Army of the James on the Petersburg and Richmond Fronts. It was Chester who called the 36th USCT "a model regiment" in 1864 (Photographs and Prints Division, Schomburg Center for Research in Black Culture, The New York Public Library, Astor, Lenox and Tilden Foundations).

own freedom. Therefore, I determined to put them in position to demonstrate the fact of the value of the negro as a soldier, *coute qui coute*, and that the experiment should be one of which no man should doubt, if it attained success. Hence the attack by the negro column on New Market Heights.[39]

Summing up the assault of the black regiments at New Market Heights, a staff officer under Paine commented that "this engagement was the severest test of the fighting qualities of colored troops to which the 3rd Division was subjected, and it is believed to be within the bounds of truth to say that no other command of colored troops ever experienced a more trying ordeal."[40] These were the extraordinary lengths Union commanders believed they had to go to convince a skeptical nation that former slaves would and could successfully fight for their own freedom.

On the afternoon of October 27, 1864, the 36th would have a limited role in the action known as Fair Oaks. In an attempt to turn the entrenched Confederate left flank situated between the Darbytown and Newmarket Roads, General Godfrey Weitzel led a mobile column of the 18th Corps that included the USCT brigades of Colonels Holman and Draper. Pushing his white brigades along the Williamsburg Road to "feel out" the enemy, Weitzel sent Holman's brigade to the north along the Nine Mile Road toward the Confederate line and held Draper's brigade (and the 36th) as reserves.[41]

Holman's black soldiers launched an unsuccessful attack on the Confederate position that ended a confusing retreat as enemy reinforcements arrived. Nevertheless the officers and men of the 1st, 22nd, and 37th USCT were praised for individual actions of bravery and particular episodes of exemplary performances in this action. Weitzel ordered a general withdrawal under the cover of darkness later that evening. Draper later reported:

> In the action of the 27th, the Second Brigade of this division performed a subordinate part, lying in line of battle in a dense thicket on the extreme left of our second line. This brigade, at that time under my command, at the same time escaped the dangers and lost the honors of the assault. The losses in the Second Brigade were 1 officer and 6 men wounded and 7 men missing. The missing men are expected to return, as they were probably passed to the rear on the marc by the brigade surgeon.

It was during this withdrawal that Private John Bufort of Company D, 36th USCT, recalled having fallen into a rifle pit knocking his right hip "Completely out of Joint" that had to be put back into its socket by the regimental surgeon. Private Bufort would not be fit for duty for six weeks.[42] The 36th would have its share of minor engagements and skirmishes in the aftermath of New Market Heights and Fair Oaks, but things would remain relative quiet for the remainder of 1864.

Battle deaths were not the primary causes of depletion in the ranks of the 36th USCT. Of the 200 deaths that occurred in the 36th while in active service, slightly more than 70 percent of these deaths occurred from illness and disease. Company B, with 31 deaths, had the highest number among the regiment's companies with 24 of these a result of illness and disease. The 10 deaths to occur in Company D were all related to sickness and disease.[43] Battle deaths on the field accounted for only 14 percent of deaths and 8.5 percent died from battle-related wounds. Company F had the highest number of soldiers killed in action at 6 with an additional 7 later succumbing to their battlefield wounds.[44]

In the larger sense, black Union soldiers would die of disease at a greater rate than their white comrades-in-arms. Two white Union soldiers died of disease for everyone who died in battle while ten black Union soldiers died of disease for each death in battle. More-

Henry Hedge Mitchell (1839–1880), a graduate of Jefferson Medical College in Philadelphia, Pennsylvania, had served as an assistant surgeon in the 39th Massachusetts Infantry prior to his appointment as surgeon for the 2nd North Carolina (36th USCT). It was Dr. Mitchell and the regimental medical staff who maintained strict guidelines for cleanliness in camp to reduce incidences of illness and improve the health of the men (Massachusetts Commandery Military Order of the Loyal Legion and the U.S. Army Military History Institute).

over, one in 12 white soldiers died of disease in the Union army while one in five black soldiers died of disease. Black soldiers, in the Army of the James during the closing months of the war, were four times more likely than white soldiers to be struck with illness. They were also seven times more likely to die from disease and illness than white soldiers. Black recruits, especially former slaves, had entered the military service with more health problems than white recruits.[45] The high death rates of disease among black soldiers, particularly of the 36th USCT, resulted from poor pre-war physical condition, excessive fatigue duty in constructing trenches and other military fortifications, and poor medical care. All of these factors resulted from the general racism these soldiers experienced in the Union army.

Battle wounds often became severe enough to cause disease leading to death or, if the soldier was lucky, a medical discharge from the army. In one instance in the 36th USCT, neither option applied. Corporal Miles James, who had bravely continued firing his weapon after having his left arm mutilated at New Market Heights that earned him the Medal of Honor and a promotion to sergeant, wrote Draper from the U.S. General Hospital at Fort Monroe asking his help to remain in the army. Draper asked his superiors for permission to keep James in the army. "He is one of the bravest men I ever saw," Draper stated, "and is in every respect a model soldier. He is worth more with his single arm, than a half a dozen ordinary men." Offering to place James on his brigade staff, Draper received approval of his request on April 18, 1865.[46]

Numerous pension records of the 36th's veterans claimed that the soldiers had been "sound men" before entering the Union army. Examination of former slaves enlisting into the Union ranks by military surgeons revealed shocking signs of physical abuse received in slavery including scars from whips, burns, and mutilation. More often than not, these soldiers were enlisted despite physical disabilities due to the need for military recruits and the fact that accepting former slave into the military service secured freedom for himself and his family.[47]

Sergeant Smith Pratt of Company K had enlisted in September 1863 and was discharged for physical disability in February 1865. According to one of the regiment's surgeons, James Clark Stockton, Pratt had suffered "injuries received by being run over by a loaded cart, in the month of July 1861, whereby several of his ribs were dislocated, from the effects of which he has never recovered." Despite these injuries, Pratt enlisted and suffered from swollen and blistered feet and legs while enroute from Point Lookout, Maryland, to the Virginia battlefields near Richmond and Petersburg in the summer of 1864. Returning to the hospital at Point Lookout for treatment, Pratt was further injured during a storm where "the building was blown down ... and I was severely injured in left arm, right side & hip & leg by heavy plank falling on me."[48]

Moreover, manual labor and fatigue duty were just as hazardous to the black soldiers as combat. Private Allen Cooper of Company C suffered an "umbilical hernia of considerable magnitude" while erecting fortifications near Point-of-Rocks, Virginia, shortly after the Battle of Newmarket Heights. Treated and returned to duty, Cooper ruptured his abdomen for a second time while on fatigue duty and was discharged from the service in October 1865. Private Malachi Gallop of Company G injured his left foot while cutting wood for the regimental headquarters in February 1864.[49]

Black Union regiments generally suffered from the lack of qualified medical officials. The small number of black doctors commissioned in the Union army served in the general hospitals in Washington, D.C., away from fighting black regiments in the field. Moreover, white medical doctors often refused to serve in black units or refused to treat black soldiers at the front. This left incompetent medical officers treating the soldiers in black regiments. Often regimental hospital stewards (who were equivalent to modern battlefield medics or corpsmen) were made acting assistant surgeons due to shortages in medical staffs. Such limited medical knowledge and skill did not bode well for black soldiers.[50]

The medical staff of the 36th USCT had qualified professionals. Henry Hedge Mitchell, a native of East Bridgewater, Massachusetts, and graduate of Jefferson Medical College in Philadelphia, was appointed as surgeon for the regiment in October 1863. Formerly an assistant surgeon in the 39th Massachusetts Infantry, Mitchell did not arrive to assume his duties until December 1863.[51]

In addition to his medical duties, Mitchell insured that the regimental camp was kept clean and in good sanitary condition. In April 1864 while the 36th was in Maryland, Mitchell made suggestions in the improvement of camp cleanliness. Soldiers were to police the camp daily to discard waste and filth. Tents were to be cleaned every Saturday afternoon and all straw and pine needles removed from the floors. Soldiers' underclothing was to be changed each Sunday morning and company commanders were held accountable to make sure this occurred. Washing clothes in company cookhouses was prohibited and only cooks were allowed in them. Moreover, latrines were to be filled with sand as well as emptied on a daily basis. Moreover, Mitchell or one of his assistant surgeons would make daily inspections of camp.[52]

James Clark Stockton and Mortimer Lampson served as Mitchell's assistant surgeons. Stockton, appointed from civilian life, became regimental surgeon in July 1864 upon Mitchell's resignation. Lampson, appointed from the pool of army medical cadets, resigned in March 1865. Stockton ran the regimental hospital alone for four months until the appointment of Joshua P. Arthur and Theodore Wild as his assistant surgeons in July 1865. John Bryant Fisher, a student and a native of Massachusetts, served as the hospital steward. Fisher, on furlough in early 1865, passed through Cambridge with a letter from Lieutenant Owen of the 36th he promised to deliver to his family.[53] Owen wrote of Fisher to his family, "We enlisted & and came on together over a year ago & we have been firm friends ever since."[54]

Many of the 36th's wounded, particularly those wounded at New Market Heights, were sent to the U.S. General Hospital at Fort Monroe. As hospitals were needed to treat soldiers with wounds received in battle, so were they needed to treat soldiers stricken by disease and illness who often made up the majority of patients. Often teachers sponsored by the American Missionary Association taught wounded black soldiers to read and write while they recuperated.[55] Former slaves may have concealed preexisting medical problems because they may have believed that rejection from military service would deny them their opportunity to earn their freedom. Freedom and the continuation of the war to a Union victory would be the issue of the 1864 presidential election.

"If our elections go off well & Pres. Lincoln is reelected," wrote Lieutenant Owen to his mother less than two months before the election, "the Confeds. States will have to back down."[56] Lincoln's reelection in November secured his position as chief executive for another four years. The Commander in Chief could continue the Union war effort without necessarily relying on numerous political considerations with regards to support from Northern or "Copperhead" Democrats who wanted to make peace with the Confederacy. Moreover, the 1864 national election was a referendum of the Union citizenry to keep fighting the war until victory was won. Lincoln now prepared to conquer the Confederacy and bring them back into the Union as swiftly and as easily as possible.

Lincoln's ultimate victory came from Union soldiers voting in the field. Union soldiers, for the first time in American History, were allowed to vote in the field. The majority of Union soldiers voted for Lincoln over his opponent George B. McClellan, one of his former army commanders. The Army of the James contributed greatly to the course of the war through their votes as much as their battlefield performance.[57]

Lincoln's reelection also enabled Butler's political enemies and military detractors to take advantage of his military shortcomings since the Lincoln Administration was now secured and his political influence weakened. Butler's control of the Army of the James would also be weakened. On December 3, 1864, all of the white regiments in the 10th and 18th Corps of the Army of the James were merged into the new 24th Army Corps. The black regiments in the 10th and 18th Corps of the Army of the James and the black regiments serving in the 9th Army Corps in the Army of the Potomac were consolidated into the 25th Army Corps. This particular corps, the first and largest U.S. military unit composed of entirely black soldiers, fell under the command of Major General Godfrey Weitzel, who was a West Point graduate and Butler protégé. General Ord took command of the 24th Corps. The 36th USCT became part of the 1st Brigade (commanded by Draper), 3rd Division, 25th Army Corps. Butler remained in command of the Army of the James.[58]

Black newspaper correspondent Thomas M. Chester praised this new reorganization of the black regiments on the Virginia front. He believed that it "never exhibited such fine promise of success." But this consolidation of black soldiers would present a detrimental impact on Butler's future as well as the black soldiers in the 25th Army Corps, including the 36th USCT. This move enabled one of Butler's main enemies in the Union army, Major General Henry W. Halleck, Grant's chief of staff in Washington, to control the future destinies of all black soldiers in Virginia.[59] This potentially meant that the 25th Army Corps could be excluded in its entirety from combat assignments in the eastern theater.

In the midst of military activity, the Union armies on the Virginia Front enjoyed a relatively peaceful Thanksgiving Day on November 25, 1864. Chester reported on the festive singing of patriotic songs and sentimental melodies provided by an improvised string band composed of members of the 5th USCT. Among the more notable holiday feasts was the one hosted by Major William H. Hart, who was at present commanding the 36th USCT due to Pratt's sick leave. General Wild's presence made the dinner all the more distinguished in Chester's estimation as was the presence of the regimental chaplain David Stevens, "a gentlemen of color ... from which I would infer that the guests were not at all afraid of his color rubbing off by association."[60]

The 36th USCT remained in front of Richmond and Petersburg for the rest of 1864. Meanwhile, Butler embarked upon the unsuccessful attempt to capture the last remaining Confederate seaport at Wilmington, North Carolina, in late December 1864. Approximately 4,000 black solders participated in Butler's 10,000-man expedition with the assistance of the U.S. Navy under Rear Admiral David D. Porter. Butler's controversial failure prompted Grant to relieve him of command in early January 1865. A second expedition under Major General Alfred Terry later that month successfully captured Wilmington. The black soldiers did not take Butler's removal from command lightly. General Ord succeeded Butler to Army command.[61]

The 36th USCT remained in front of Richmond. In March 1865, it became part of the 1st Brigade, 1st Division, 25th Army Corps. Lieutenant Colonel Pratt retained command of the regiment while Draper commanded the brigade. On the evening of April 2, 1865,

Union forces had broken General Robert E. Lee's lines at Petersburg, and he immediately sent word to the Confederate government to evacuate Richmond. That evening Confederate troops destroyed stockpiles of military equipment and set ablaze supplies contributing to their war effort, so they would not fall intact into Union hands. General Weitzel, commanding the 25th Army Corps, held responsibility of occupying the abandoned Confederate capital.[62]

Leading Weitzel's advance into Richmond was Draper's brigade along the Osborn Road that connected to the main streets of the city. Upon reaching the outskirts of the city, Draper was halted by a white brigade from the 24th Army Corps that was to constitute the provost marshal guard. What ensued next, according to correspondent Chester, was a "grand, but sublime" scene. Officers and men on both sides "mingled with every kind of expression of delight." Black inhabitants out from Richmond greeted the conquering heroes.[63]

Draper ordered the drum corps of the 36th USCT to play "Yankee Doodle" and "Shouting the Battle Cry of Freedom" amid the cheers of civilian onlookers and white soldiers as they marched past. The white soldiers had been given orders to proceed into Richmond once Draper's brigade allowed them to pass, and then Draper ordered his men on the double-quick through the fields toward Richmond. Chester wrote:

> General Draper obeyed the order, and took the left of the road in order to let the troops of Devin go by, but at the same time ordered his brigade on a double quick, well knowing that his men would not likely be over taken on the road by any soldiers in the army. For marching or fighting Draper's 1st Brigade, 1st Division, 25th Corps, is not to be surpassed in the service, and the General honors it with a pride and a consciousness which inspire him to undertake cheerfully whatever may be committed to his execution. It was his brigade that nipped the flower of the Southern army, the Texas Brigade, under [Gregg], which never before last September knew defeat. There may be others who may claim the distinction of being the first to enter the city, but as I was ahead of every part of the force but the cavalry, which of necessity must lead the advance, I know whereof I affirm when I announce that General Draper's brigade was the first organization to enter the city limits. According to custom, it should constitute the provost guard of Richmond.[64]

Companies A and K under Captains Francis A. Bicknell and Henry H.F. Miller were the first elements of the 36th USCT to enter the city limits of Richmond. Draper's former superior, General Wild, commanding the 2nd Brigade, 1st Division, 25th Corps, later complained to higher headquarters that Draper "started his whole Brigade for Richmond without any baggage whatever.... He haste to be first.... He ran his staff through the midst of my advance guard to break them up and set the 36th [USCT] there first."[65]

Draper later wrote to the well-known Washington correspondent for the *Boston Globe*, Benjamin Perley Poore, since there had been "considerable dispute as to what troops first entered Richmond." He acknowledged that the first regiment of the brigade to enter the city limits was his own 36th USCT. Elements of about 50 skirmishers of the 24th Army Corps, who had marched along with the 36th and properly belonged in front of heavy infantry, were "allowed to remain there without competition." Once the 36th USCT entered the city limits with the 22nd and 38th USCT close behind, Draper received orders to halt and file around some nearby fortifications to allow a white brigade of the 24th Corps under General Edward Ripley to continue into the city as the provost guard. "It was at least ten or fifteen minutes before a single white regiment came in sight," Draper recalled, "and when they did pass, the black troops cheered them lustily, but elicited no response. Every officer and soldier of the white Brigade will recollect this circumstance, for some of the officers swore heartily at the presumption of the negroes in outmarching them and entering the city first."[66] Draper further maintained that his brigade was originally two to three miles behind the white brigade and acknowledged their claim of right away into Richmond. "We gave them all the room they needed by taking the double quick step," he boasted, "and maintaining it all the way to Richmond."[67]

The officers of the 36th USCT were not hesitant in heralding the triumphant entrance of their black soldiers into Richmond. "Several regiments were in advance of this regiment when we started," wrote Major William H. Hart to a Lynn, Massachusetts, newspaper, "but the boys of the 36th were found to get to Richmond first ... and planted our colors on the sacred soil of Richmond first and foremost of them all." Lieutenant Colonel Benjamin Pratt later in the month explained in a Boston newspaper that "statements ... have been made in such a way as to lead the public to believe that Draper's brigade was not the first in the city; whereas the truth is, the 36th Regt. U.S.C. Infantry ... was with its colors within the city limits before any other regiment; and the other regiments of the brigade before any other brigade, whether of colored or white troops." Captain Richard F. Andrews remarked in the Union-confiscated *Richmond* (Virginia) *Daily Whig*, that while Ripley's white brigade may have had the honor of performing provost duty in Richmond, "it was not the first to enter the city limits.... The Thirty-sixth United States colored infantry, Lieutenant Colonel B.F. Pratt, led the advance at a 'double quick' until within the city limits." Lieutenant William H. Rock stated, "I do not wish to contend that Gen. Draper's Brigade was the first to enter the main part of the city, but I do contend that it was the first in the Corporation of the city of Richmond." Lieutenant Stephen F. Hathaway simply wrote his cousin, "My Regt. was the first to unfurl the Stars and Stripes within the limits of the city of Richmond."[68]

Controversy continues as to what Union troops entered the abandoned Confederate capital first. The 36th USCT held the strongest claim of being among the first units to enter the Richmond city limits. Other black regiments, including the 29th Connecticut (Colored) Infantry and 5th Massachusetts (Colored) Cavalry, have also made such claims.[69]

The fact that soldiers of African descent held the honor of reaching the Richmond city limits before white troops was imprinted on the minds on the nation. "We shall long remember that the first troops to enter Richmond were niggers of Weitzel's corps," wrote prominent New York diarist George Templeton Strong on April 3. "It is a most suggestive fact." *New York Tribune* founder and future presidential candidate, Horace Greeley, acknowledged that Draper's brigade had been in the advance upon Richmond.[70]

It is quite clear that racism on the part of white Union troops still prevailed from the highest levels of command down to the common soldier. If black troops would be kept from taking formal possession of the Confederate capital, the symbolic act of their entering Richmond first provided a fitting epitaph to the mission of the martyred John Brown six years before.

The 36th USCT, along with the other black regiments of Draper's brigade, assisted in policing the former Confederate capital. They rounded up troublemakers, extinguished fires that had been set by the fleeing Confederates, and distributed rations and supplies with the jubilant but destitute black population. Ironically, the black soldiers were charged for a brief time with the protection of white women and children left behind without receiving any major complaints as they had earlier in their service.[71]

On one occasion Emma Mordecai, a young white woman residing at the Rosewood Plantation near Richmond, had a horse and saddle seized by black mounted soldiers. Seeking redress, Miss Mordecai, accompanied by two black servant girls, visited Draper, who was commanding black occupation troops at nearby Camp Lee. A Union officer who had escorted her to Draper advised her before entering that he sympathized with her plight, "but please hide them in talking to General Draper.... He is not a member of the regular army, and is something of a fanatic." The young woman described the former commander of the 36th USCT as a "sleek, dapper, unmilitary looking man." Nevertheless, Draper kept his manners by offering her the only chair in his headquarters tent.[72] Assuring her that the manner in which the black soldiers seized her property was against regulations, he suggested that she see the commander of the 5th Massachusetts (Colored) Cavalry, as he believed that the soldiers came from that regiment. Draper gave her pass into Richmond to seek out the 5th Massachusetts' commander as well as the Provost Marshal without being subjected to further rude behavior. Miss Mordecai had never felt so "majestically and proudly defiant" as she moved through the camp with its "black and blue" soldiers.[73]

A grand jubilee meeting was held at Richmond's African Church, one of the largest buildings in the city and that had hosted major addresses by the now-fugitive Confederate President Jefferson Davis during the war. War correspondent Thomas M. Chester presided over the meeting, noting that inside the church was standing room only and crowds of hundreds were surrounding the building outside unable to enter. Once Chester opened the meeting, Chaplain David Stevens of the 36th USCT gave "an able speech" from the pulpit. Chester observed "that no colored man had ever in that church, though belonging to that oppressed people, dared to speak to the people from the pulpit." Since its organization in 1841, the African Church always had a white Baptist minister as its head pastor. "Chaplain Stevens was the first to ascend," Chester continued. "Negro ministers were permitted to speak from the altar, but no higher." The 36th USCT continued to make "firsts" during the war.[74]

Despite past allegations of brutality and atrocities committed upon white citizens leveled at the 36th's soldiers during their 1863 North Carolina expedition, their expeditions in Virginia's Northern Neck region, and their duty as prison guards at Point Lookout, the 36th USCT performed its duties as a professional military unit during their brief occupation of Richmond. However, the fragile peace between the races did not last long. The subsequent surrender of General Lee and the Army of Northern Virginia at Appomattox, Virginia, and the assassination of President Lincoln shortly thereafter brought confusion and added responsibility to the Union military as to the future course of reconstructing the conquered South as well as the future disposition of the freed slaves. As defeated Confederate soldiers returned to their homes, increased allegations of misconduct on the part of black soldiers were brought to the attention of Union military authorities. General Weitzel quickly defended the character of the black soldiers in his corps, dismissing such allegations as "racist exaggerations." Weitzel's superior, General Ord, known to have expressed the meanest opinions of black soldiers, provided a lukewarm endorsement on their behalf when he stated, "I do not consider the behavior of the colored corps ... to have been bad, considering the novelty of their position.... In the city of Richmond their conduct is spoken of as very good." Weitzel, before the Congressional Committee on the Conduct of War, later testified that when Ord ordered him to take the 25th Army Corps out of Richmond, he marched them through the heart of Richmond and down to Petersburg. "One of my colored regiments, at the request of a rebel officer, sang the John Brown song as they marched along," Weitzel stated.[75]

Overreacting to such exaggerated reports concerning the behavior of black soldiers and because the war was over, Secretary of War Stanton suspended the recruitment of new black regiments on June 1, 1865. General Halleck, one of Butler's nemeses who arrived from Washington to take overall command of Union occupation troops in Virginia, received approval from the War Department to transfer all black soldiers in the 25th Army Corps whose enlistments had not yet expired to Texas. On May 31, 1865, the 36th USCT, as part of the 1st Division, 25th Corps, embarked for Brazos Santiago, Texas, in support of a U.S. expedition under Major General Phillip H. Sheridan to protect the border with Mexico as a result of French occupation.[76] Despite the triumphant entrance of these black veterans into the Confederate capital, their symbolic victory was short-lived.

Butler continued to praise the Union government for allowing him to undertake the efforts to organize the freedmen and their families through General Orders No. 46 even after his removal from command by Grant. The soldiers of the 36th USCT and their families were beneficiaries of his policies. In a speech given in his hometown of Lowell, Massachusetts, in January 1865, Butler boasted of his own role in this endeavor:

> I established system, order, and organization of labor, so that the freedmen who would work could work; and those who would not work might find means whereby they should work; and so that every freedmen, woman, and child should have what, thank God, we always have had in Massachusetts for all, food and raiment, and protection from the inclemency of the weather.... Aided by your fellow-citizens.... I applied myself to this work, and presently order and industry arose out of chaos in the affairs of the freedmen of North Carolina and Virginia.[77]

Butler's departure from active military command was just the beginning in the removal of several of Butler's subordinate commanders who had led black soldiers in the war. "After you left," one USCT commander wrote Butler, "it was understood to be a 'Butler man' was to be doomed, and that the term included every man who had too much generosity not to kick a lion supposed to be dead."[78]

Lucy Wiggins continued laboring on the Union-confiscated Baker Farm near Norfolk, Virginia, while her husband, Paul, served in Company D, 36th USCT. She had only seen her husband three times on his furloughs during the war and had to care for the new addition to their family: a son named Augustine. Periodically Paul had someone write letters to his wife and send her money. Lucy was not alone in her surroundings as "the government had out a lot of colored people" on the farm. She lived with Mary Wiggins, who had come from the same Gates County, North Carolina, plantation she and her husband had worked as slaves. "The Government taken care of me," Lucy recalled, "gave me rations & a house to live in on Baker farm, while [Paul] was in the army."[79]

Several of the wives of soldiers serving in the 36th USCT (as well as other black regiments) worked as agricultural laborers and received rations on confiscated farms in southeastern Virginia. These included Mariah (Ferebee) Bufort, wife of Private John Bufort, Company D; Betsey Williams, wife of Private Thomas Williams, Company, A; and Betsey Price, wife of Sergeant Sylvester Price, Company H. These particular women worked on parcels of land that were part of the confiscated Baxter Farm in Norfolk County, Virginia.[80] The Baxter Farm consisted of 3,000 acres employing 70 freedmen by late 1863. Francis W. Bird, a northern abolitionist, testified before the American Freedmen Inquiry's Commission that in spite of shortages in able-bodied men, the Baxter Farm harvested 5,090 bushels of corn on 300 hundred acres of cultivable lands. The farm had a black overseer. Comparing this farm with a nearby farm under a white overseer, Bird stated that the latter farm "would have done very much better, if they had one intelligent negroe [sic] for their overseer instead of him."[81]

Once the U.S. Congress in 1865 passed legislation equalizing pay for all U.S. soldiers without regard to race, government and military officials believed black soldiers, regardless of previous condition of servitude, could now provide for their families without further government assistance. Unfortunately for black units composed of former slaves, like the 36th USCT, their family and kin had been left behind to fend for themselves in government camps in North Carolina and Virginia as well as on plantations and farms in the South.[82]

Butler's hopes for special consideration for the black soldiers and their families he had expressed in General Orders No. 46 was soon a thing of the past in future polices concerning the disposition of black families who had once been slaves. General Lorenzo Thomas, Adjutant General of the U.S. Army and early organizer of black Union troops in the Upper Mississippi Valley region, believed that the government supported black soldiers' families out of necessity since their pay was so low. "But now," he wrote to Secretary of War Stanton, "when their pay is equal to that of the white soldier, they are abundantly able to provide for their families." Thomas further argued that continued support of these families would produce idleness and they would be less inclined to help themselves.[83] Captain Orlando Brown, as a newly appointed assistant commissioner of the Freedmen's Bureau in Virginia received orders from his military superiors to discontinue issuing rations to black families. "I do not consider the United States Government through its agent, Maj. Genl. Butler, bound by the contract of Dec. 5, 1863, since the pay of colored soldier was raised," Brown's superior wrote. "None of the families will receive rations after the tenth of this month unless they are such as, in Northern towns, would be admitted to the county poor house."[84]

The soldiers of the 36th USCT grew concerned over reports from family members and wounded comrades on living conditions at Roanoke Island, North Carolina. Butler's General Orders No. 46 had assured these soldiers that the government would provide for their families so long as they remained in the military service and behaved well. But the calls by their loved ones for the soldiers to do something to correct the corrupt mismanagement of affairs of black families on Roanoke Island could not be ignores. Reports of women and children having their rations reduced for no reason, being refused admittance to the commissary stores for supplies, having payment for labor cease, and having their personal safety threatened at the hands of white Union soldiers prompted Sergeant Richard Etheridge of the 36th USCT and William Benson (presumably of another USCT) to petition Major General Oliver O. Howard, commissioner of the Freedmen's Bureau "to alter Affairs at Roanoke Island."[85] The soldiers singled out Mr. Holland Streeter, one of Captain Horace James' assistant supervisors on Roanoke Island, as a "througher Cooper head [Copperhead] a man who says that he is no part a Abolitionist. takes no care of the colored people and has not Simpathy with the colored people." Captain James was also accused of not properly paying wages to black laborers for their work on Roanoke Island during the past year. Although they did not seek James' removal from his position, the soldiers did wish for Streeter's departure.[86]

Another 36th USCT soldier, Private Frank James, petitioned his commander and former colonel, Alonzo Draper, to have the rations issued to his family at Roanoke Island, recently stopped by the government, continued. Private James stated that "when I inlisted in the united states Service the Government made Promis for to have them Taken Care off [sic]." Draper forwarded and endorsed this letter to the assistant commissioner of the Freedmen's Bureau in North Carolina. "The colored soldiers recruited in this Department under Maj. Gen. Butler had the pledge of the government that their families should receive rations," he added. Bureau officials reassured Draper and the men of the 36th USCT that their families would continue to receive their allotted rations and paid their proper wages until further notice.[87]

These black veterans were keenly aware of the changes taking place within the Union military and its effect on the policies concerning their families. Their recognition of the term "copperhead" for Streeter demonstrated their understanding of northern politics. Copperheads were typically applied to northern Democrats who tended to be sympathetic to the Confederacy and had desired a peaceful settlement with the rebellious states. The fact that the soldiers fell short of asking for Captain James' removal from his position as superintendent of Negro Affairs in North Carolina suggested their recognition of his connection to Benjamin Butler, whose own removal they did not take lightly, and they needed continued support of anyone who had gained his favor on their behalf.

As Butler, Wild, and other Union commanders in the Army of the James who had actively supported the participation of black soldiers in the Union war effort were either retired, transferred, or dismissed from military service, control of the Union army fell under more "conservative" leadership.[88] Nevertheless, the regiment continued to perform its duties, despite combating disease, poor supplies, harsh climate, and short tempers among both officers and men while in Texas.

As demobilization of white soldiers and northern black soldiers in the Union army rapidly proceeded,

William Henry Hart (1836–1897), commissioned a captain commanding Company H, 36th USCT, succeeded Daniel J. Preston as major of the 36th USCT in the fall of 1864. Hart would become acting regimental commander from the regiment's departure from Virginia and during its entire stay in Texas. He held command slightly longer than either Draper or Pratt. He finally attained the rank of Lieutenant Colonel on March 15, 1866 (John Clark Rand, ed., *One of a Thousand: A Series of Biographical Sketches of One Thousand Representative Men, 1888–1889* [Boston, MA: First National Publishing Company, 1890], 286).

black regiments composed former slaves whose terms of muster had not expired finished their service as occupation troops in Texas. The 36th USCT had one year and four months in the United States service before it could be discharged. Individual soldiers in the regiment who had enlisted as early as June 1863 (before the entire regiment had been mustered into federal service on October 28, 1863) could look forward to a discharge by June 1866 due to the expiration of their three year enlistment obligation, if not earlier due to medical disability. Sixty-six soldiers were discharged from the regiment at this time as a result of expired enlistments, and no more would be joining.[89]

The removal of black soldiers from occupation duty in the South enabled the U.S. government to maintain control over black soldiers without adding fuel to southern white hostility. Military planners, maintaining paternalistic views held by many white officers of black soldiers, and civilian missionaries working among their families believed that keeping former slaves-turned-soldiers in the army would help them become incorporated into American society. The army experience would provide food, shelter, clothing, and wages for these former slaves and build the necessary discipline, character, and skills for their future prosperity and that of their families in freedom. This was the positive view of sending black soldiers to Texas. On the other hand, the Union military leadership at the war's conclusion could not conceive long-term authority legally exercised by black soldiers over white citizens regardless of their allegiance during the war.[90] Freedom was one thing, equality was another.

Rumors had circulated throughout the Army of the James concerning the final disposition of black units, including the 36th USCT. One white officer in the 8th USCT speculated over the future of the black soldiers. To his family he wrote:

> They [black regiments] will not be discharged till Congress has made some provision to incorporate a portion of them into the regular army. The men are to be re-enlisted, those who choose to do so, and the officer are to pass a far more rigid examination and receive commissions in the regular army. There are to be no more "U.S.C.T." but "U.S.A." Twenty-four regiments of two thousand men are to be organized — so says General [Silas] Casey.[91]

The black soldiers would remain in the 25th Army Corps and be transferred to Texas along the border with Mexico. The final decision of incorporating black soldiers permanently into the regular army would be postponed until later.

The 36th USCT left their camp at City Point, Virginia, and boarded the larger transport steamer *Western Metropolis* on May 30. They arrived at Fort Monroe "giving the officers a chance to visit Norfolk & get our pay," Lieutenant John Owen reported. The 36th left Fort Monroe on June 5, 1865, and headed for the Gulf of Mexico. Owen reported, "The sea has been very calm — & our only drawback has been the heat which is very oppressive. We sleep on deck at night — & even then find it quite warm." On board with Owen were the 36th and 22nd USCT, the division headquarters staff and the brigade staff all making "quite a jolly time of it."[92]

The 36th arrived at Brazos Santiago, Texas, on June 6 after making

Henry N. Thorburn (1842–1867), an Orange County, New York, native, had served as a sergeant in the 125th New York Infantry and as a second lieutenant in the 9th USCT. Commissioned as a first lieutenant in the 36th USCT, Thorburn served with the regiment in its final year in Virginia and at Brazos Santiago, Texas. He remained in Texas after the war as a U.S. customs official until he succumbed to the effects of yellow fever in the fall of 1867 (Ezra D. Simons, *A Regimental History: The One Hundred and Twenty Fifth New York Volunteers* [New York: Ezra D. Simons, 1888], 177).

stops at Mobile, Alabama, and New Orleans, Louisiana. They bivouacked on this sandy island for two days before marching to White's Ranch along the Rio Grande for four days. On July 1, the 36th marched into Brownsville where it remained for a month. Shortly after, the regiment made the 35-mile return trip to Brazos Santiago and would remain there for the duration of its service "doing guard and fatigue duty."[93] Lieutenant Stephen F. Hathaway of the 36th described his early experience in Texas. He wrote in July 1865:

> We are way down in Texas almost into Mexico. we have been where we could look into the latter place. some of the Officers went over to Matamoras but I did not get a chance to go. We are in a splendid place on a barren sandy island where there is not the first sign of vegetation. all we can see is sand and salt water and that is what we have to live on. eat the sand and drink the water.... It is called a very healthy place that is if we can only get a plenty of fresh provisions, vegetables which I do not see any prospect of our doing so. In addition to poor conditions, boredom and idleness would take up most of the blacks soldiers' time in Texas.

The harsh conditions of the Texas climate took its toll on the 36th's soldiers. Cholera, pneumonia, and scurvy claimed the lives of 46 of the soldiers while in Texas.[94]

The black soldiers of the 36th USCT could still expect efforts in obtaining equality to continue on their behalf through their own efforts in the military service and those who had led them in battle. General Butler, after his removal from command of the Army of the James, continued to make public speeches on behalf of the Union war effort and extolled the virtues of the black soldiers under his command. Very soon, Butler, the staunch Democrat who had once nominated Jefferson Davis for President of the United States and had advocated the extension of slaveholders' rights in the territories, would become a "Radical Republican" Congressman supporting equal rights for former slaves for the duration of his political career.

Moreover, Alonzo G. Draper, nominal colonel of the 36th USCT and Brevet Brigadier General, was viewed as a future political leader among the "Radical Republicans." Prior to following his soldiers to Texas, Draper had written Butler. "I look forward with anxiety for any changes in the cabinet," he asserted. "I trust that in three years more it will be my privilege to take the stump in favor of Gen. Butler's election to the Presidency." Draper hinting at his own future ambitions concluded, "If my humble abilities can be made serviceable to you in any way, you may command them."[95]

Draper commanded the 1st Brigade,

John Sargent Mansur (1833–1904) hailed from Houlton, Maine. After service with the 1st Maine Cavalry as a bugler, Mansur served with the 9th USCT as a lieutenant. He was commissioned a first lieutenant in the 36th USCT in early 1865. After the war, Mansur settled in Brownsville, Texas, making his living as a U.S. customs inspector and publishing a local newspaper (Edward P. Tobie, *History of the First Maine Cavalry, 1861–1865* [Boston, MA: Emery and Hughes, 1887], after 526).

1st Division, 25th Army Corps that included the 36th USCT during its initial assignment at Brazos Santiago, Texas. Shortly thereafter, he briefly commanded the post of Indianola, Texas, and later the 3rd Division, 25th Army Corps. The 36th would later become part of this division. On August 30, 1865, while riding through the camps of his command at Brazos Santiago, Draper was struck by a musket ball that lodged into his spine. The orderly accompanying him reported that no musket sound was heard when Draper suddenly fell from his horse and suspected that it may had come from a stray shot from some considerable distance, as soldiers were continuously firing on the island. An investigation was launched to ascertain whether Draper's shooting was intentional or accidental. No conclusive evidence could be made, but the assumption remained that it was an accidental shot carelessly fired.[96]

Critically wounded, Draper was carried to the post hospital where he lingered on in painful agony for several days. Upon being informed by the surgeons he had little time left to live, Draper reportedly responded, "Gentleman, I am not afraid to die." On September 3, 1865, Alonzo Granville Draper died of his wound just three days before his 30th birthday. His wife and mother on their way to Texas to care for him received word of his death at New Orleans and returned home. His younger brother and brother-in-law, both captains in the 36th, received orders to escort his body back to Lynn, Massachusetts.[97]

Draper's funeral was an elaborate affair having a city council meeting devoted to its planning. Among the pallbearers was Brigadier General Edward W. Hinks, who had been Draper's superior at Point Lookout and briefly in the Army of the James. Reverend C.W. Biddle preached the funeral sermon. The *Lynn* (Massachusetts) *Weekly Reporter* eulogized, "The name of General Draper will occupy a prominent place among those who served their country faithfully and well, and by their death bore testimony to their fidelity to the cause of human liberty and a free united country."[98] In the camps of the 36th USCT as well as the black regiments in the 1st and 3rd Divisions of the 25th Army Corps in Texas, flags were draped and displayed at half-mast for 30 days in memory of Draper. "By his death," wrote a staff officer of the 25th Army Corps, "the Corps has lost one of its bravest, most earnest and conscientious officers, and the colored race one of its most sensible and sincere friends."[99]

The 36th USCT mustered out of federal service on October 28, 1866, at Brazos Santiago, Texas. Post-war Reconstruction was underway. The former slave, emancipated and full-fledged citizen of the United States as a result of the Thirteenth Amendment to the Constitution, sought ways to incorporate himself and his family into active participation in American society. The lack of experience within the established political and economic institutions of the United States as a result of slavery led to former slaves being unjustly branded as "lazy" and "worthless." African Americans believed that their labors had been exploited for the benefit of their former masters. They did not seek to escape from participation in the labor force nor did they attempt to dismiss their civic responsibilities. Confident they had come to the end of "unrequited toil," African Americans sought to forge better lives for themselves, their families, and their future generations on their own terms.[100]

Ten of the regiment's enlisted men and three of its white officers continued to serve in the peacetime army. These black veterans of the 36th USCT joined the 39th United States Infantry, and a few from this number eventually served in the 25th United States Infantry when the 39th and 40th Infantries were consolidated by the War Department in 1869. The 25th would be one of the two black infantry regiments in the army during the latter half of the nineteenth century. The military legacy of the 36th USCT would continue beyond the Civil War.[101]

# Conclusion
## *"Pure Patriotic Principles"*

When Private Frederick Henry of Company G, 36th USCT, sought an invalid's pension in 1885 for wounds received in battle, he appealed to one of his former white officers, George W.S. Conant, for help in locating other officers of the regiment who might collaborate his wounding near Richmond in 1864. "I will do it cheerfully," the former lieutenant responded, "for I know the great difficulties that the colored soldiers labor under in regard to securing evidence of their disability in service." It is not known whether Conant was successful in assisting one of his former soldiers.[1] Many soldiers often relied on their former comrades for affidavits proving their identity, military service, and nature of disability or illness incurred during the Civil War. Such support demonstrated the continuation of the black community.

Any discussion on the role African Americans played in the Civil War has to acknowledge the overriding presence of slavery. Moreover, the majority of black southerners had been slaves on the eve of the war. Black Union soldiers from the southern slave states made up more than 75 percent of total black enlistments, although they were only a small part of the southern black population. It was this particular population made up of slaves that was inseparably linked to the former-slave-turned soldier.

Many black veterans returned to their antebellum communities in eastern North Carolina and southeastern Virginia. They often relocated themselves and their families in areas with large black populations such as Norfolk and Portsmouth in Virginia, and in the areas of the former contraband camps around New Bern in North Carolina. The collection of families, former fellow slaves, and 36th USCT comrades created new communities for the new American citizens.

The former refugee settlements at New Bern later became James City, in honor of the Captain Horace James, superintendent of Negro Affairs in North Carolina. Until 1900, James City would be an autonomous black community in the post-war years. Many of the 36th USCT's veterans lived in the community along with veterans of the 35th USCT until their deaths.[2]

Cities such as Norfolk, Virginia, that had a significant free black population before the war, quickly became the new homes of freed slaves. Frank Cornick of Company K had returned to the Norfolk area after losing his right arm at the shoulder in battle at New Market Heights. While he never married, Frank related to his pension examiners in 1901 the postwar fate of his two brothers and their spouses. His brother Peter who had served in Company E, 36th USCT and his wife, Mary, resided in Norfolk County near Indian Bridge. Frank's brother James who had served with him in the same company had died sometime during this period; his widow also died. Sergeant Miles James, Medal of Honor winner and disabled veteran, returned to his wife, Sarah, and their children in October 1865. Sergeant James and his family continued to reside in Norfolk until complications from his amputated arm and the contraction of smallpox hastened his death in August 1867.[3]

Other veterans who had been former slaves ventured out of the South. Private David H. Allen of Company A changed his name to his father's, which was David H.A. Henderson. Moving to Bridgeport, Connecticut, Henderson married Hattie Brooks who had been born in Virginia. The Hendersons returned to Virginia, residing in Hampton near David's brother. The couple raised five children and lived in Hampton until David's death in 1898. Hattie moved to New York City. Freeborn Henry N. Adkins, the veteran sergeant major of the 36th USCT, returned to New York City where he changed his name to Henry E. Nepean, married Margaret Berry in 1867, and eventually moved to Red Bank, New Jersey. He died in 1889.[4]

Numerous pension applications filed by the regiment's veterans and their dependents indicated the economic decline of African Americans in the late 19th and early 20th centuries and their need for compensation for aged and disabled veterans. Moreover, their application for pensions demonstrated their belief that they had contributed, with their lives and the safety of their families, to the Union war effort and the cause of freedom. They had as much right to compensation as white Union soldiers.

The preservation of family and community, as well as the destruction of slavery, remained the paramount motivation for the black soldiers of the 36th United States Colored Infantry. Black southerners, like those connected with the 36th during the Civil War, were not passive bystanders on the road to preserve the Union, but active participants in the struggle for freedom that would not only forever change their own lives and status but change the lives of every American citizen within the span of four years. The very fact that slaves did not stage massive revolts against their masters immediately before and during the war only attested to their desire to keep as much of their families and communities intact as the uncertainties of war loomed large.

It is important to understand that the lives of the black soldiers of the 36th USCT did not begin when the regiment mustered into the service of the United States. The regiment was a converging point for a particular group of black southerners, mostly former slaves, representing almost 140,000 southern black soldiers serving in the Union army. Since the majority of these soldiers had been slaves at the war's beginning, they reflected their desire for freedom by eventually fighting on their own behalf. Moreover, they fought on the behalf of their families and communities that had been enslaved and who were still enslaved.

The 36th USCT, as a military unit, emerged from the pool of fugitive slaves, countless numbers having labored for the Confederate war effort (and many continuing to do so, directly and indirectly, during the course of the war). Once the slave-turned-military-laborer-turned-soldier received official sanction in the ranks of the Union military establishment, he had to be assured that his family was taken care of if brought with him into Union lines.

Despite difficulties of recruiting, training, and supplying the regiment, the black soldiers conducted successful operations in southeastern Virginia and in northeastern North Carolina during the last months of 1863. The liberation of family members and fellow slaves in these areas demonstrated the importance the family and community had for them. Additionally, the 36th USCT reinforced, on a small scale, the provisions of the Emancipation

Proclamation in some areas, eventually serving as a symbolic reinterpretation of earlier policies on behalf of former slaves. The presence of the 36th USCT discouraged the preservation of slavery.

The relationships between black soldiers of the 36th USCT and their white officers were important bonds that mutually reinforced each other through their success on the battlefield and in their various military assignments. Moreover, the frequent absence of many of the white officers enabled the emergence of strong leadership from among the cadre of black noncommissioned officers. In several instances these black leaders took the place of their white officers. Their leadership experience as well as the military discipline all black soldiers underwent would be needed during the postwar Reconstruction within the African American community.

Such leadership also challenged the prevailing racism within the Union ranks. The issue of equal pay served as a prime example where black soldiers led protests against such discriminatory practices. Black families (as well as white Union soldiers) relied on the soldiers' pay for their support. For southern black Union soldiers, receiving less pay than their white counterparts when they were under the same conditions on the battlefield only heightened the effects of the crushing blow of racism. Some of the war's most well-known instances of mutiny involved black soldiers, under the leadership of black noncommissioned officers, refusing to bear arms until they were given equal pay and equal consideration in the ranks.

The 36th USCT's tenure at Point Lookout prison in Maryland gave former slaves the responsibility of guarding their former masters as Confederate prisoners of war. Moreover, their continued expeditions of liberating their fellow slaves across the bay in Virginia's Northern Neck region reinforced their cause for freedom. However, the regiment's presence as prison guards and successful expeditions into Confederate territory roused the sentiments and feelings of white southerners attempting to make sense over the decaying institution of slavery and the fact that some of their former slaves were fighting against their cause. Some of these exaggerated sentiments were often contradictory and extreme. White southerners had to justify slavery by arguing that the institution had enabled their former slaves to work in their fields and care for their families, giving them a level of civilization that they had never experienced. Once these slaves became Union soldiers, under the control of white officers from the North, they were no longer under the paternalistic guidance of their masters, allowing their innate brutal natures to be unleashed on defenseless white southerners. Unfortunately, the allegations of rape, specifically in Richmond County, Virginia, in June 1864, that may have been committed (but not proven) by a small number of black soldiers in the 36th USCT would have the bulk of the blame placed unfairly on the entire regiment, all black Union soldiers, and the race as a whole.

Moreover, stereotypical views of white southerners and northerners toward freedmen cannot be understated in the context of nineteenth century racial thinking. The majority of Northern missionaries and educators providing the families of these black soldiers with the tools for religious, educational, and economic uplift were sincere in their efforts. Unfortunately, these benevolent workers often ridiculed the religious and cultural practices of many of the 36th's soldiers, families, and kin. Misunderstood by white northerners, these antebellum practices of the freedmen had strengthened and supported their families and communities under slavery.

Military policy implemented by the controversial, but astute General Benjamin F. Butler, began the process by which the former slave, his family, and community would benefit the Union war effort and set the beginning of the long historical process of social welfare legislation on behalf of African American families. The immediate impact of Butler's General Orders No. 46 on black soldiers' families acknowledged and attempted to maintain the existence of the communities the freed people had carried into Union lines with them. Butler's efforts not only guaranteed protection for soldiers' families but also consolidated and coordinated the various relief efforts of benevolent organizations, like the AMA, to greater efficiency.

In the trenches before Petersburg and Richmond, the 36th USCT served alongside its sister black regiments composed of slaves and free men. The large presence of black soldiers in General Butler's Army of the James and their willingness to fight for their freedom influenced the northern population, particularly white Union soldiers, to cast their ballots for the reelection of President Abraham Lincoln in 1864 as a referendum to see the war to its final conclusion with an end to slavery. The 36th's triumphant entrance into the city limits of the abandoned Confederate capital symbolized the realization of John Brown's efforts to lead a rebellion of slaves. Characteristic of the history of race relations of the United States, the regiment's symbolic victory was short-lived, as white Union troops were given the honor to serve as provost marshal troops for the city, thus denying the 36th USCT the honor of basking in the glory of entering Richmond first.

The bonds that held black soldiers and white officers together during the war gradually split as former slaves discharged from the Union army returned to their families to start life anew and their officers returned to resume their lives interrupted by war. This was evident during the late 19th and early 20th centuries when the 36th's black veterans applied for pensions.

Interest in the role of African Americans in the Civil War as well as black families under slavery has increased over the past decade. The Civil War in the slave states of the Upper South, like North Carolina and Virginia, was indeed a "brother's war" among former slaves who joined the Union Army. The military and social history of the 36th USCT bear this out in discussions of the soldiers, their families, and kin before the war. Historian Harold T. Pinkett, in a study of four of his ancestors who were brothers and former slaves from Maryland who joined the Union army serving in both the 7th and 9th

Joseph G. Longley (1823–1871) was born in Hawley, Massachusetts, and attended Oberlin College. Joining the 51st Massachusetts at the beginning of the war, Longley served under Captain Thomas W. Higginson, who had been part of the group that secretly funded John Brown's 1859 raid on Harpers Ferry, Virginia. He was among the early officer appointments General Wild made for the 2nd North Carolina Colored Volunteers, but did not earn the confidence of Colonel Draper. Resigning his commission for disability, Longley became the superintendent for freedmen schools in Wilmington, North Carolina, by war's end (Charles F. Pierce, *Souvenir of Army Life, 1862–1863: Company C, 51st Massachusetts Regiment* [Gardner, MA: Allen, 1885].

USCTs, writes, "Their contributions to the preservation of the Union helped to establish a firm basis for the claims of their race to the benefits of American citizenship."[5] Moreover, the service of the Pinkett brothers along with the Gallops, Jaycoxs, Blangos, Coopers, Cornicks, and Cherrys who served in the 36th USCT also established the survival and continuation of the African American family amidst the Civil War.

This study is also a study of the masses rather than just a look at a few exceptional individuals. It also taps into the larger mindset of a people whose freedom of expression had been either curtailed under slavery or forced to be hidden from the view of their masters and, unfortunately, in many instances away from recorded documentation. The southern black Union soldier could not operate alone, especially if he had been a slave, but operated within a community shaped by the nature of slavery and shaped by the slaves themselves. To discuss the motivations of the former-slave-turned soldier is to discuss his family, kin, and plantation networks. W.E.B. Du Bois, in his 1909 biography of John Brown, wrote:

> To be sure, the freedmen did not, as the philanthropists of the sixties apparently expected, step in forty years after slavery to nineteenth century civilization. Neither, on the other hand, did they, as the ex-masters confidently predicted, retrograde and die. Contrary to both these views, they chose a third and apparently quite unawaited way. From the great, sluggish, almost imperceptibly moving mass, they sent off larger and larger numbers of faithful workmen and artisans, some merchants and professional men, and even men of educational ability and discernment. They developed no world geniuses, no millionaires, no great captains of industry, no artists of the first rank; but they did in forty years get rid of the greater part of their total illiteracy, accumulate a half-billion dollars of property in small homesteads, and gain now and then respectful attention in the world's ears and eyes. It has been argued that this progress of the black man in America is due to the exceptional men among them and does not measure the ability of the mass. Such an admission is, however, fatal to the whole argument. If the doomed races of men are going to develop exceptions to the rule of inferiority, then no rule, scientific or moral, should or can proscribe the race as such.

Du Bois suggests that former slaves recently turned free citizens would not necessarily in a generation begin to perform great feats on par with the white Americans. This was the same prediction Edward L. Pierce, one of the earliest organizers of benevolent assistance to freedmen first at Fort Monroe and later at Port Royal, had predicted in 1861. Nevertheless, as Du Bois points out, to measure the success of a particular race's progress based upon the progress of a few individuals is to not understand the race at all.[6]

None of the 36th's black veterans became nationally known public figures after the war, except within their own post-war communities. There were no authors from among these former slaves to pen regimental histories of their military exploits. No political figures of stature on the state or national level during the Reconstruction Era emerged from the ranks of the members of the 36th USCT. The majority of veterans returned with their families to places familiar to them. They worked as farmers and common laborers. Some gained local notoriety, as in the case of Commissary Sergeant Richard Etheridge, who was the founder of an all-black life saving unit on North Carolina's Outer Banks in the decades following the war, but would only do so in recent years through the writings of persistent scholars in search of how the Civil War military experience enriched the lives of these former slaves.[7] More needs to continue toward these efforts. These newly acknowledged citizens of the United States raised their children in the hopes that the next generation would gain inspiration from their contributions to the Union war effort, both on and off the battlefield.

The black soldiers of the 36th overcame extreme obstacles that uplifted them to execute their duties as soldiers on behalf of the United States, a nation that had not previously recognized their legal existence as citizens. Not only had the race been uplifted, the image among whites of their worthiness had been uplifted during the war. Unfortunately, more obstacles had to be overcome by African Americans before general acceptance of this view prevailed. The 36th United States Colored Infantry was a part of the larger struggle and sacrifice undertaken by African Americans to achieve freedom and equality in the United States. "The story of the part taken by the colored soldier in the war which resulted in establishing the freedom of his race," wrote a Union army staff officer in 1864, "will at the hands of some future historian form a romantic chapter in the history of the progress of the Republic."[8]

Major William H. Hart, commanding the 36th USCT at Brazos Santiago, Texas, wrote to division headquarters on behalf of Musician William Holmes of Company I. Holmes had been sentenced two months before by a general court martial for an undisclosed violation "to have his head shaved and be drummed out of the service in the presence of his Brigade to which his regiment belongs." He would also forfeit his pay and allowance due him. Hart explained that this had been Holmes's first offense and that it was committed "under aggravating circumstances." Because Holmes had been in confinement since June 5, 1865, and he suffered "much lost in mind and body," Hart asked that his sentence be revoked and Homes restored to duty.

Hart was not making his appeal on simple humanitarian motives, but on what he believed was an unjust action taken against an ideal soldier. Hart made his case in defense of Holmes:

> He is and has always been, with the exception of this offence a "model soldier." When his regt. Lay momentary expectation of a desperate engagement with the enemy before Richmond he was afforded an honorable discharge from the United States service which he declined from—pure patriotic principles, and continued to do his duty with an honest upright heart where hundreds of men would have faltered and "gone to the rear."

Holmes, a native of Essex County, Virginia, was a "model soldier" in a "model regiment." Restored to duty, Holmes was mustered out of the regiment on September 20, 1866. An even better title for a member of the 36th USCT was the simple notation found in the remarks section of the entry for Corporal James Gallop of Company G—"A Good Soldier." It is quite possible that Captain Benjamin F. Kinsley thought that much of the Currituck County, North Carolina, native to leave such a lasting description.[9]

Private Peter Wilson of Company C, killed in action at Pierson's Farm, Richmond County, Virginia, on June 16, 1864, continues to rest in Grave #814 in the Fredericksburg National Cemetery in Virginia. Peter, the escaped slave of Dr. Turner Wilson of Bertie County, North Carolina, leaves a permanent mark on the physical and emotional landscape of the Civil War. His death resulted from the apparent attempt to assist a fugitive slave to freedom. He represents the 200,000 soldiers and sailors who supported the Union war effort and is one of among the almost 4 million persons held in bondage at the war's beginning. He continues to serve as a prime representative of the "Model Regiment" that Thomas Morris Chester observed at the trenches before Petersburg, Virginia.

# PART TWO
# Unit Roster

# 36th Infantry, United States Colored Troops (formerly 2nd North Carolina Colored Volunteers), 1863–1866

The 36th Infantry, United States Colored Troops (36th USCT) began its enlistment in June 1863 with recruiting officers stationed in several Union-occupied towns in eastern North Carolina. Recruitment continued in southeastern Virginia when the regiment was transferred to Portsmouth, Virginia. It was mustered into the service of the United States on October 28, 1863, at Fort Monroe, Virginia. Soldiers who had enlisted before October 28, 1863, were obligated to three years of service from the time of their actual enlistment. This did not include those enlistees who were discharged for medical disability. Those enlisting after the regiment's date of muster were mustered out with the regiment on October 28, 1866.

This roster was compiled from the regimental descriptive book as well as the individual company descriptive books. Additionally, the pension index rolls for the 36th USCT were used providing information on death dates for some of the veterans. Information found in selected pension files, the regimental letter book, and miscellaneous unbound regimental papers provided some clarification in some instances.[1]

It should be noted that this unit roster is unique for a regiment composed of former slaves recruited from two states that had joined the Confederacy (North Carolina and Virginia). USCTs recruited from northern states, most notably Connecticut, Massachusetts, Ohio, and Pennsylvania have available published unit rosters. Maryland, a slave state that remained in the Union, also has available published unit rosters for USCTs composed of former slaves.[2]

The 36th USCT experienced a continual shortage of officers during its existence. This was due to several officers being on detached duty for long periods of time serving on staffs at higher headquarters or in one of the specialized departments, as well as recruiting assignments. Colonel Draper's "purge" of nine officers in April 1864 contributed to the officer shortage as well. Additionally, several officers who had prior service in white regiments earlier in the war submitted their resignations when a medical professional certified them unfit for further military service and they were discharged from the service for disability. Unlike the majority of the enlisted men who served in the same companies where they had originally enlisted, the officers were often shifted between companies on a temporary basis due to the aforementioned shortages.

The information contained in the individual company books was often erroneous and incomplete given the high turnover of officers and without any consistent method of maintaining vital information. Therefore, the present roster also has discrepancies (particularly service dates) in company officer assignments and noncommissioned officer assignments on the regimental staff. Draper's early complaints to General Wild about his new officers, many of whom had served as privates and corporals in white units, having very little experience in properly maintaining company records may have been an accurate assessment.

The roster follows a similar format to other Civil War era regimental histories. It is divided into eight categories: (1) Name, (2) Rank, (3) Age, (4) Birthplace or Residence, (5) Occupation, (6) Date of Enlistment or Muster in, (7) Date of Muster out or Discharge, (8) Remarks. These are explained below.

*Name*: This category would seem self-explanatory. In the case of the white officers of the 36th USCT, this was not an issue. Only in one instance (Samuel S. Simmons) was there an alias used, and in a few instances spelling was an issue for officer names as noted in the "Remarks" sections. The black soldiers usually enlisted under names that white people recognized (whether their former masters or Union officers) as well as used aliases to keep from being discovered by their former masters in order to protect family members still living with them. After the war, black veterans used their "second" or "real names," especially when applying for pensions. Such second names appear in parenthesis after the names under which they enlisted.

*Rank*: This listed the military rank of the officer and enlisted man. In the case of enlisted men serving as noncommissioned officers, they were often promoted at the same rate as they were "reduced to ranks" for infractions they may have incurred. Nevertheless, company noncommissioned officers tended to have a longer tenure than the white commissioned officers assigned to their company.

*Age*: The age for the enlisted men given at the time of their enlistment is listed on the present roster since very few were transferred between companies (in some instances where an actual birth date of an enlisted man is known it is reflected in the roster). Those enlisted men promoted and transferred to the noncommissioned staff often have an approximate age provided. The actual birth dates of 32 of the 75 white officers serving in the 36th USCT are known. In each of their assignments within the regiment, their correct age is shown on the roster. Approximate ages for most of the remaining officers are provided based upon their ages given in the units they served before their commissions into the 36th USCT (noted by "c" before the approximate age).

*Birthplace or Residence*: The birthplaces of the enlisted men were given at the time of their actual enlistments. In a majority of cases, they were born where they had lived at the time of the war. Spelling becomes a great issue under this category and adjustments were made to this section where the birthplace of the enlisted men seemed likely (for example "Cummins County, NC," or "Curiumans County, NC," in the company books are presented in the present roster as "Perquimans County, NC," or "Allywhite, VA, " listed as "Isle of Wight County, VA"). Additionally, the distinction between counties and localities with the same names become problematic. (i.e., Beaufort County, NC, vs. Beaufort, NC,—a town in Carteret County, NC; Washington County, NC, vs. Washington, NC,—a town in Beaufort County, NC; Hertford County, NC, vs. Hertford, NC,—a town in Perquimans County, NC). In these several instances, the roster listed the ambiguous birthplace locality as it is actually listed in the rosters.

Several officers were born in places other than their place of residence at the time of their first enlistments into the Union Army. When two localities are listed for officers, the first is their birthplace and the second their residence at the time of the war. If one locality is listed on the roster, this usually reflected that the officer resided in the locality where he was born or that this was his residence at the time of the war.

***Occupation:*** This reflected the occupations held by the regiment's officers prior to their earliest enlistment into the Union army. The majority of the enlisted men had been slaves prior to the beginning of the war, therefore it seemed to have been agreed upon among the regiment's recruiting officers to list their occupations as "Farmers" rather than as "Slaves." This gave them some level of dignity. Some occupations listed for enlisted men, such as "Laborers" and "Teamsters," may have reflected jobs performed by them as civilians in the Union army prior to their enlistment. In the case of Anson Farrier of Company B (and possibly the case for March and George Ferebee both of Company E), he is listed as an "Engineer" for serving as a laborer in the army's engineer department, but identified as a "Farmer" in has pension file.

***Date of Enlistment or Muster in:*** The key date for enlisted men was the date of their original enlistment as reflected in the individual company books. This enlistment date, and not the muster date of the regiment (October 28, 1863) or later individual muster in dates, determined their discharge dates.

The officer dates have presented the greatest problems. Typically, Civil War officers dealt with three important dates: (1) their date of commission (or appointment), (2) their date of accepting their commission (or appointment), and (3) their date of mustering into the service at their commissioned rank (or date of reporting for duty). The present roster reflects a combination of commission (or appointment dates) and the dates officers mustered into the regiment. In some individual company books, the appointment date is often the only date listed when the officer in fact may have taken a 20-day leave of absence after being discharged from his old unit and reporting for duty in the 36th USCT a month later (in some instances two months later).

***Date of Muster out or Discharged:*** This is generally self-explanatory for both officers and enlisted men. This date reflected discharges due to disability, resignations, and dismissals. It also reflected the mustering out of officers and men due to the expiration of their three year term of enlistment or the mustering out of the regiment on October 28, 1866.

***Remarks:*** This section provides miscellaneous information to include promotions, transfers, and discharges for both officers and men. It also lists information such as wounding in action as well as deaths due to combat or illness. When available, it lists the post war military service as well as post-war death dates.

## COMMISSIONED OFFICERS LIST

*Colonel:* Alonzo Granville Draper[3]
*Lieutenant Colonels:* Benjamin Franklin Pratt[4], William Henry Hart[5]
*Majors:* Daniel Preston Johnson[6], Oren Alonzo Hendrick[7]
*Captains:* Henry F.H. Miller[8], Walter Henry Wild[9], John Ware Fletcher[10], Charles Herbert Frye[11], George W. Ives[12], Benjamin F. Oakes[13], George F. Allen[14], George Bradbury[15], John M. Smith[16], Joseph J. Hatlinger[17], George B. Proctor[18], Benjamin F. Kinsley[19], Sidney W. Phillips[20], Hiram W. Allen[21], Richard F. Andrews[22], James B. Backup[23], Francis A. Bicknell[24], Algernon Draper[25], Edwin Collins Gaskill[26], George H. Lamprey[27], John Wadsworth Owen, Jr.[28], Joseph Wall[29]
*First Lieutenants:* Charles D. Griggs[30], Francis Henry Scudder[31], Frank H. Graves[32], Frank

W. Rhoades[33], George Leonard Seagrave[34], Edward Townsend[35], Leonard Taft Gaskill[36], Aaron Parker[37], Joseph G. Longley[38], William M. Titcomb[39], Henry Martyn Field[40], Thomas Jackson Cate[41], José A.A. Robinson[42], Charles Haskell[43], John Curry[44], Warren Pierce[45], Henry N. Thorburn[46], John Sargent Mansur[47], James W. Bacon[48], Elijah Harvey Wheeler[49], Stephen F. Hathaway[50], Eugene J. Courtney[51], William H. Rock[52], Charles F. Bly[53], Daniel J. Courtney[54], Priestly Young[55]

*Second Lieutenants:* Jerry McClair[56], Amory O. Balch[57], George Washington Smith Conant[58], Waldo F. Hayward[59], Michael Sullivan[60], Isaac W. Thurlow[61], John O'Brien[62], Samuel S. Simmons[63], William E. Leonard[64], Edward H. Davis[65], Weston Jenkins[66], Hiram Bixby[67], Alexander Elliott Wakefield[68], James Downing[69], George Emerson Albee[70]

*Surgeons:* Henry Hedge Mitchell[71]; James Clark Stockton[72]

*Assistant Surgeons:* Mortimer Lampson[73], Theodore Wild[74], Joshua P. Arthur[75]

*Chaplains:* David Stevens[76], Thomas Scott Johnson[77]

## Noncommissioned Officers List

### Regimental Staff

*Sergeant Majors*: John Wadsworth Owen, Jr. (white); Henry N. Adkins (black); William H. Overton (black); Jacob Spradley (black)

*Quartermaster Sergeants*: Eugene J. Courtney (white); Daniel J. Courtney (white); William H. Palmer (black)

*Commissary Sergeant*: Daniel J. Courtney (white); William Pierce (black); Richard Etheridge (black); William H. Talbot (black)

*Hospital Steward*: John Bryant Fisher (white); John Smith (black); Washington Whitish (black)

*Principal Musicians*: Larry Griffin (black); Phillip Herbert (black); Adolphus Redding (black); William H. Crocker (black)

### Company A

*First Sergeants*: Charles Brock

*Sergeants*: Peter Furby; Willard Johnson; Brister Foreman, Casear Odin; Jacob Pinor; Peter Sutton; James H. Hunt; Albert Jourdan; Cicero Jaycox; Major Hart; Thomas Jaycox

*Corporals*: William Harvey; Henry Brooks; James H. Hunt; Alexander Gregory; Albert Jourdan; Robert Frost; Jacob Brousbery; John G. Blango; Charles B. Mullen; Peter Sutton; Cicero Jaycox; Charles Brock; George Cooper; Moses Liverman; Erastus Furbey

*Musicians*: David H. Allen (bugler)

### Company B

*First Sergeants*: Gilbert Mezzell; Littleton Cooper; Ransom Coy

*Sergeants*: Peter Herbert; Peter Norfleet; Cornelius Reddick; Franklin Blunt; Edward Beasley; John Pinor; Miles James; Cicero Gustus; Littleton Cooper; Ransom Coy; Abram Bell; Henry Perdy; Henderson Cooper; Noah Sheppard; Edward Bright; James E. Porter; Bailey Phillips

*Corporals*: Edward Beasley; Abram Bell; Edward Griffin; Littleton Cooper; Anthony McCleese; John Pinor; Miles James; Cain Chason; Cicero Gustus; Henry Perdy; Ransom Coy; Noah Sheppard; Henderson Cooper; Edward Bright; James E. Porter; Jacob Gatlin; Charles Fidget; Bailey Phillips; George Moore; Edward Luntsworth; George Beckett; Ezra Wilkins

*Musicians*:

### Company C

*First Sergeants*: Jackson Watson; Frederick Jones; Alfred Sessions; Jeremiah Gray; Frank James

*Sergeants*: Frederick Jones; Isaiah Johnson; Jackson Watson; Walter Washington; Alfred Sessions; Jeremiah Gray; Solomon Beasley; Solomon Moore; Frank James; Friley James; John Jefferson; Thomas Van; Miles Britt; Edward Garrett; John H. Burris; Jacob Fidget; Richard Peterson

*Corporals*: Jeremiah Gray; John Jefferson; Friley James; Rufus Mayo; Solomon Beasley; Sawney Jaycox; Charles Hill; Thomas Van; Henry Van; David G. White; Solomon Moore; Frank James; Hezekiah Blunt; Miles Britt; Edward Garrett; Isaiah Johnson; John H. Burris; James Rolack; Rush Brooks; John Norcum; Calvin McClenney; Grantson Sessions; Moses Ben; Daniel Blunt; Harvey Young William H. Talbot; Jacob Fidget; Richard Peterson

*Musicians*: James Ellison (drummer); James Grantly (drummer)

## Company D

*First Sergeants*: David Pierce; Friley James; Calvin Roundtree; Martin Smith

*Sergeants*: Lewis Pollard; Tilmon F. Hardy; John Drury; Richard Richmond; Calvin Roundtree; David Pierce; Martin Smith; Duke Williams; Smith Cornick; Isaac Pritchett; Henry Morgan

*Corporals*: John Buck; Henry Scott; Duke Williams; Granville Williams; John R. Adams; Henry Hurt; Jacob Whitfield; Martin Smith; Everett Hicks; Smith Cornick; David Pierce; Irving Williams; Amos Fields; Alexander Brown; Joseph Waller; Peter Hardy; Riley Jenkins; Reuben Reddick; Alfred Fletcher; Otis Oliver; Daniel Halstead; Peter Sowell; Mina Brown; John Burfort; William P. Corbin

*Musicians*:

## Company E

*First Sergeants*: Henry N. Adkins; William Davis

*Sergeants*: William Davis; William H. Burton; Oliver Young; Thomas Davis; Gilbert Joiner; Joseph Hone; Sandy Sykes; Miles Fentress; Enoch Wilson

*Corporals*: Spencer Laws; Joseph Hone; Sandy Sykes; Miles Fentress; George Ferebee; William Henry; Africa Ives; Robert Taylor; John Whitest; Enoch Wilson; Sandy Williams; Spencer Laws; George Haynes; Richard Cornick; Shadrick Land

*Musicians*: Richard Still

## Company F

*First Sergeants*: William H. Johnson; Walter Milton; Robinson Tyne; William H. Overton; Lindsey Babley

*Sergeants*: Robinson Tyne; Nicholas Langley; Richard Etheridge; Robert Smith; Hannibal Whitby; Henry Martin; George Williams; Jacob Spradley; Miles Holloway; William H. Overton; Joseph Reed, 2nd; Lindsey Babley

*Corporals*: Lawrence Midget; Hannibal Whitby; Fields Midget; Stewart Bell; Walter Milton; John James; Aaron Mitchell; George Williams; Isaac Overton; Joseph Reed, 1st; Henry Martin; Lewis Curtis; William H. Crocker; Jacob Spradley; Miles Holloway; Lindsey Babley; William H. Overton; Joseph Reed, 2nd; Nixon Keaton; Albert Banks; John Cromwell; Charles Grey; David Cartwright

*Musicians*: Henry F. Willis (drummer); Charles Brown (drummer); Leroy Smith (drummer)

## Company G

*First Sergeants*: Anthony Pool; Merritt Pool; Wilson Stokely

*Sergeants*: Thomas Artis; Richard Piner; Merritt Pool; Elijah Booker; Peter Moore; Isaac Kinney; William Walker; Wilson Stokely; Albert Sawyer; Robert White; George Taylor; Benjamin Robinson

*Corporals*: Peter Moore; William Walker; James Gallop; Wilson Stokely; Robert White; Michilin Smith; Isaac Kinney; Wilson Griffin;

Henry Simmons; George Wilson, Albert Sawyer; Mark Morris; Charles Shield; Ezekiel Nottingham; Benjamin Robinson; George Taylor; Oscar Yerbey; Warren Barnes; Joshua Dudley; Charles Flora; Benjamin Mann; Samuel Dyes; Edward Diggs; Solon Green; Cudjoe Woodhouse
*Musicians*: Henry F. Willis (drummer)

### Company H

*First Sergeants*: Allen Oden
*Sergeants*: Abraham Armstead; Sylvester Price; William Turner; John Brown; William Etheridge; David Rogers; James Keyes
*Corporals*: William Etheridge; Henry Wiggins; William Piner; Charles Cadwell; James Keyes; David Rogers; George Baysmore; Shadrach Keyes; Benjamin Keyes; Robert Greene; Casear Hodges; David Gibbs; William Groves; George Hodges
*Musicians*: Larry Griffine (drummer); Toney Wilson (drummer); Adolphus Redding (fifer)

### Company I

*First Sergeants*: Miles Sheppard; Livian Adams
*Sergeants*: Livian Adams; Harrison Sneed; Philip Bright; Wesley Artise; James Gardner; James Roach; Miles Sheppard; Samuel Fuller; Lamb Lovett
*Corporals*: John Veal; James Roach; Robert Thomas; William H. Palmer; Alexander W. Palmer; Lamb Lovett; Tully Walk; Albert Wilson; Willis Skinner; Nelson Booker; James Bowden; Samuel Fuller; John Brown; Solomon Moore; Marin Van Buren
*Musicians*:

### Company K

*First Sergeants*: Cornelius Crowley; Samuel Gilchrist; John A. Brown
*Sergeants*: Major Meekins; Andrew Nelson; James N. Mitchell; Orange Redmon; Moses Cornick
*Corporals*: Miles Simmons; William H. Nichols; Samuel Crofts; Nelson Jenkins; John A. Brown; Moses Cornick; Jacob Smith; Thomas Jefferson; Henry Case; Smith Pratt; Milton Murray; James N. Mitchell
*Musicians*: David Johnson (fifer); James H. Jefferson (drummer)

*Regimental field and staff and non-commissioned officers appear in order of rank. Men in company rosters are listed alphabetically (to include all commissioned officers and enlisted men). Birthplace and/or residence is listed immediately after age. Dates are enlistment and discharge.*

## FIELD AND STAFF

### Commissioned Officers

Alonzo G. Draper   Colonel; 27; Brattleboro, VT; Lynn, MA; Labor Leader, City Official; August 1, 1863–September 3, 1865; Formerly Major, F&S, 14th MA Inf. (1st MA Hvy Arty); Brevet Brigadier General, USV, Oct.28, 1864; Died Sept. 3, 1865 from accidental gunshot wound at Brazos Santiago, TX.

Benjamin F. Pratt   Lieutenant Colonel; 38; North Weymouth, MA; Weymouth, MA; Shoe Manufacturer; September 5, 1863–October 27, 1865; Formerly Captain, Co. H, 35th MA Inf.; Brevet Brigadier General, USV, Mar. 13, 1865; Absent sick since May 30, 1865; Honorably discharged for disability, Oct. 27, 1865; Died July 29, 1890 at Worcester, MA.

William H. Hart   Lieutenant Colonel; 29; Lynn, MA; Shoemaker; March 15, 1866–October 28, 1866; Promoted Major from Captain, Co. H, Sept. 25, 1864; Brevet Colonel, USV, Mar. 13, 1865; Promoted Lieutenant

Colonel, Mar. 15, 1866; Mustered out with the regiment; Died April 16, 1897.

Daniel J. Preston   Major; 46; Danvers, MA; Shoecutter; December 7, 1863–August 29, 1864; Formerly Captain, Co. E, 35th MA Inf.; Honorably discharged, Aug. 29, 1864; Died Dec. 24, 1886 at Danvers, MA.

Oren A. Hendrick   Major; 28; Agawam, MA; East Long Meadow, MA; Jeweler/Gold China Maker; July 19, 1866–October 28, 1866; Promoted Major from Captain Co. F, July 19, 1866; Mustered out with regiment; Died in 1890.

Charles D. Griggs   Adjutant; 21; Cambridge, MA; Clerk; July 8, 1863–July 19, 1864; Formerly First Sergeant, Co. D, 2nd MA Cav.; Discharged July 19, 1864; Died June 11, 1877 at St. Louis, MO.

Richard F. Andrews   Adjutant; c 27; Lynn, MA; Shoemaker; May 30, 1864–October 21, 1864; Appointed from Co. D; Wounded in action at New Market Heights, VA, Sept. 29, 1864; Promoted Captain, Co. D, Oct. 21, 1864.

Warren Pierce   Adjutant; 24; Tyngsboro, MA; Medical Student; November 6, 1864–March 6, 1865; Appointed from Co. I, Nov. 6, 1864; Transferred to Co. I, Mar. 6, 1865.

James W. Bacon   Adjutant; c 23; Walpole, MA; Painter; March 29, 1865–October 28, 1866; Appointed from Co. B, Mar. 29, 1865; Mustered out with regiment.

Francis H. Scudder (Frank H. Scudder)   Quartermaster; 21; Brookline, MA; September 14, 1863–November 30, 1864; Formerly QM Sergeant, F&S, 88th IL Inf.; Promoted Captain, Commissary of Subsistence, USA, Oct. 24, 1864; Mustered out of regiment Aug. 25, 1865.

Eugene J. Courtney   Quartermaster; c 22; Killarney, Ireland; Boston, MA; Student Clerk; January 31, 1865–October 14, 1865; Appointed Acting Quartermaster from Co. A, as Second Lieutenant until promotion to First Lieutenant, Jan. 27, 1865; Discharged, Oct. 14, 1865.

Charles Haskell   Quartermaster; c 25; Ipswich, MA; Tinman; October 21, 1865–October 28, 1866; Appointed from Co. C, Oct. 21, 1865; Mustered out with regiment.

Henry H. Mitchell   Surgeon (Major); 26; Belfast, ME; East Bridgewater, MA; Physician; November 1, 1863–June 15, 1864; Formerly Asst. Surgeon (First Lieutenant), F&S, 39th MA Inf.; Died in 1880.

James C. Stockton   Surgeon; 28; Pittsburgh, PA; Physician; July 19, 1864–October 28, 1866; Appointed Assistant Surgeon from civil life, Mar. 27, 1864; Promoted Surgeon, Jul. 19, 1864; Brevet Lieutenant Colonel, USV, Sept. 11, 1866; Mustered out with regiment.

Mortimer Lampson   Assistant Surgeon; 21; Medical Cadet; July 30, 1864–March 21, 1865; Formerly Medical Cadet, Balfour U.S. General Hospital, Portsmouth, VA; Honorably discharged, Mar. 21, 1865; Died Aug. 25, 1924 at Jersey City, NJ.

Theodore Wild   Assistant Surgeon; 30; Gusezenhausen, Bavaria, Germany; Medical Student/ Druggist; July 6, 1865–October 28, 1866; Formerly Assistant Surgeon, F&S, 24th IL Inf; Mustered out with the regiment; Died Dec. 13, 1926 at Chicago, IL.

Joshua P. Arthur   Assistant Surgeon; 24; PA; Physician; July 29, 1865–October 28, 1866; Appointed from Acting Assistant Surgeon, USA, Jul. 29, 1865; Mustered out with the regiment; Received M.D. from University of Pennsylvania in 1868; Died Aug. 19, 1898 in Laredo, TX.

David Steven (black)   Chaplain (AME); 61; Harrisburg, PA; Minister; September 1, 1863–June 6, 1865; Honorably discharged, June 6, 1865.

Thomas S. Johnson (white)   Chaplain (Presbyt.); 26; Greenville, NY; Oxford, WI; Seminary Student; September 29, 1865–October 28, 1866; Formerly Chaplain, F&S, 127th USCT; Mustered out with the regiment; Died Feb. 11, 1927 at Beaver Dam. WI.

## *Noncommissioned Staff*

John W. Owen, Jr. (white)   Sergeant Major; 21; Cambridge, MA; Student (Harvard); January 22, 1864–April 29, 1864; Promoted Second Lieutenant, Co. H, Apr. 29, 1864.

Henry N. Adkins (Henry E. Nepean) (black)   Sergeant Major; 20; New York City, NY; Gardner; May 1, 1864–September 1, 1866; Promoted from Private, Co. E, May 1, 1864; Unsuccessful attempt to gain Second Lieutenant's commission, Mar. 18–Mar. 25, 1865;

Mustered out at expiration of service, Sept. 1, 1866; Died June 29, 1899 at Red Bank, NJ.

Jacob Spradley (black)   Sergeant Major; c 35; Surry County, VA; Farmer; September 1, 1866–October 3, 1866; Promoted from Sergeant, Co. F, 36th USCT, Sept. 1, 1866; Mustered out at expiration of enlistment, Oct. 3, 1866.

Eugene J. Courtney (white)   Quartermaster Sergeant; 19; Killarney, Ireland; Boston, MA; Student Clerk; October 28, 1863–November 25, 1864; Promoted Second Lieutenant and transferred to Co. A, 36th USCT, Nov. 25, 1864.

Daniel J. Courtney (white)   Quartermaster Sergeant; c22; Newport, Wales; Brookline, MA; Clerk; November 25, 1864–March 24, 1865; Promoted Second Lieutenant, Co. K, 36th USCT, Mar. 24, 1865.

William H. Palmer (black)   Quartermaster Sergeant; c 20; Accomack County, VA; Laborer; May 1, 1865–October 22, 1866; Promoted from Corporal, Co. I, 36th USCT; Mustered out at expiration of enlistment, Oct. 22, 1866; Died Oct. 30, 1887 at Norfolk, VA.

Daniel J. Courtney (white)   Commissary Sergeant; 22; Newport, Wales; Brookline, MA; Clerk; January 4, 1864–November 24, 1864; Promoted Quartermaster Sergeant, F&S, 36th USCT, Nov. 24, 1864.

William Pierce (black)   Commissary Sergeant; 30; Martin County, NC; Farmer Mechanic; November 25, 1864–July 13, 1866; Transferred from Co. A, 36th USCT, Nov. 25, 1864; Mustered out at expiration of enlistment, July 13, 1866.

Richard Etheridge (black)   Commissary Sergeant; c 23; Roanoke Island, NC; Farmer; July 20, 1866–September 2, 1866; Promoted from Sergeant, Co. F, 36th USCT, July 20, 1866; Mustered out at expiration of enlistment, Sept. 2, 1866; Died May 8, 1900 at Pea Island, NC.

William H. Talbot (black)   Commissary Sergeant; c 21; Plymouth, NC; Farmer; September 2, 1866–October 28, 1866; Promoted from Corporal, Co. C, 36th USCT, Sept. 2, 1866; Mustered out with regiment.

John B. Fisher (white)   Hospital Steward; 23; East Bridgewater, MA; Law Student; January 23, 1864–July 28, 1865; Also served as Sergeant, Co. K, 3rd MA Inf (9 mos.), Sept. 23, 1862–Jun. 26, 1863; Discharged, July 28, 1865.

John Smith (black)   Hospital Steward; c 27; Gloucester County, VA; Farmer; September 24, 1865–June 15, 1866; Promoted from Private, Co. B; Mustered out at expiration of enlistment, June 15, 1866; Died Nov. 9, 1912.

Washington Whitish (Washington White) (black)   Hospital Steward; c 21; Yorktown, VA; Farmer; July 1, 1866–September 20, 1866; Promoted from Private, Jul. 1, 1866; Mustered out at expiration of enlistment, Sept. 20, 1866; Died Aug. 29, 1919 at Method, NC.

Larry Griffin   Principal Musician; c 17; Martin County, NC; Farmer; January 1, 1865–July 12, 1865, July 24, 1865–October 7, 1865, May 1, 1866–July 5, 1866; Promoted from Drummer, Co. H, Jan. 1, 1865; Reduced to ranks for insubordination, Jul. 12, 1865; Promoted Principal Musician, Jul. 25, 1865; Reduced to ranks for disobedience of order, Oct. 7, 1865; Promoted Principal Musician, May 1, 1866; Mustered out at expiration of enlistment, Jul. 5, 1866.

Phillip Herbert   Principal Musician; c 20; Charles City County, VA; Laborer; February 26, 1865–; Promoted from Co. I, Feb. 26, 1865; Reduced to ranks.

Adolphus Redding   Principal Musician; c 25; Martin County, NC; Farmer; October 21, 1865–; Promoted from Fifer, Co. H, Oct. 21, 1865.

William H. Crocker   Principal Musician; c 25; Petersburg, VA; Farmer; July 8, 1866–August 13, 1866; Promoted from Private, Co. F, Jul. 8, 1866; Mustered out at expiration of enlistment, Aug. 13, 1866; Died Feb. 20, 1915 at Holland, VA.

## Company A

David H. Allen (David H.A. Henderson)   Private/Bugler; 16; Petersburg, VA; Farmer; July 15, 1863–July 15, 1866; Mustered out at expiration of enlistment, July 15, 1866; Died Aug. 12, 1898 at Hampton, VA.

Benjamin Banks   Private; 21; Alligator, NC;

Farmer; July 13, 1863–July 13, 1866; Mustered out at expiration of enlistment, July 13, 1866.

Thaddeus Baxter  Private; 18; Currituck County, NC; June 28, 1863–May 11, 1864; Killed in action on the Rappahannock River, VA on May 11, 1864.

Hiram Bixby  Second Lieutenant; c 23; July 29, 1865–October 28, 1866; Formerly First Sergeant, Co. E, 1st Battalion, 14th U.S. Inf.; Appointed Second Lieutenant, Jul. 29, 1865; Mustered out with the regiment.

Wilson Blanchard  Private; 25; Perquimans County, NC; Farmer; August 1863–February 11, 1864; Died in Hospital of Pulmonary Consumption, Feb. 11, 1864.

John Blango  Corporal; 22; Little Washington, NC; June 13, 1863–June 13, 1866; Died Jun. 22, 1921 in James City, NC.

John G. Blango  Private Corporal; 26; Blounts Creek, NC; Farmer; June 13, 1863–June 13, 1866; Died May 2, 1914 in Washington, NC.

Thomas Blango  Private; 28; Little Washington, NC; Farmer; June 13, 1863–June 13, 1866; Mustered out at expiration of enlistment, July 13, 1866.

Alexander Bond  Private; 25; Bertie County, NC; Farmer; July 13, 1863–July 13, 1866; Died Jan. 20, 1911 at National Soldier's Home, VA.

Henry Boyd  Private; 40; Pitt County, NC; Farmer; November 12, 1863–January 18, 1866; Discharged on Surgeon's Certificate of Disability at Brazos Santiago, TX, Jan. 18, 1866.

Charles Brock  Private, Corporal, First Sergeant; 34; Princess Anne County, VA; Cobbler; November 27, 1863–October 28, 1866; Promoted Corporal July 1, 1866; Promoted First Sergeant Sept. 1, 1866; Mustered out with regiment.

Loudon Brockett  Private; 38; Currituck County, NC; Shingler; November 27, 1863–October 28, 1866; Wounded at New Market Heights, Sept. 29, 1864; Mustered out with regiment.

Henry Brooks  Corporal; 21; Little Greenville, NC; Porter; July 22, 1863–July 22, 1866; Mustered out at expiration of enlistment, July 22, 1866; Died Aug. 8, 1919 in Norfolk, VA.

Jacob Brousbery (Jacob Brumsey)  Corporal; 21; Currituck County, NC; Farmer; June 22, 1863–June 22, 1866; Mustered out at expiration of enlistment, July 22, 1866.

Major Brousbery (Major Brumsey)  Private; 25; Currituck County, NC; Farmer; June 22, 1863–June 22, 1866; Mustered out at expiration of enlistment, July 22, 1866.

Andrew Brown  Private; 24; Blackwater, NC; Farmer; November 27, 1863–October 28, 1866; Mustered out with regiment.

William Bryan  Private; 20; Beaufort County, NC; Farmer; June 18, 1863–June 18, 1866; Mustered out at expiration of enlistment, July 18, 1866.

Wilson Burroughs (Wilson Burruss)  Private; 48; Princess Anne County, VA; November 22, 1863–October 28, 1866; Absent sick in Hospital at time of Muster out of the company.

Dorsett Carter  Private; 38; Woodville, NC; Farmer; July 13, 1863–June 14, 1865; Discharged from the Service per order of the War Department June 14, 1865.

Henry Clay  Private; 37; Martin County, NC; Farmer; July 13, 1863–June 13, 1866; Mustered out at expiration of enlistment, July 13, 1866.

George Cooper  Private, Corporal; 27; Hertford County, NC; Farmer; July 13, 1863–July 13, 1866; Promoted Corporal July 1, 1866; Mustered out at expiration of enlistment, July 13, 1866.

Romulous Cooper  Private; 25; Hertford County, NC; Farmer; July 13, 1866–December 22, 1865; Wounded at New Market Heights Sept. 29, 1864; Discharged on Surgeon's Certificate of Disability, Dec. 22, 1864; Died Mar. 27, 1899 at James City, NC.

Henry Cornick  Private; 18; Princess Anne County, VA; Farmer; December 2, 1863–October 28, 1866; Mustered out with the regiment.

Eugene J. Courtney  Second Lieutenant; c20; Killarney, Ireland; Boston, MA; Student Clerk; November 25,1864–January 31, 1865; Promoted from Quartermaster Sergeant, Nov. 25, 1864; Promoted First Lieutenant and appointed Quartermaster, Jan. 31, 1865.

Toney Ellis  Private; 25; Stantonburg, NC; Farmer; June 13, 1863–June 13, 1866; Mustered out at expiration of enlistment, July 13, 1866; Died Aug. 11, 1910 at Little Creek, VA.

Joshua Ellison  Private; 20; Bertie County, VA; Farmer; August 3, 1863–August 3, 1866; Mustered out at expiration of enlistment, Aug. 3, 1866.

Henry Everton  Private; 21; Elizabeth City, NC; Farmer; June 13, 1863–June 13, 1866; Mustered out at expiration of enlistment, July 13, 1866.

Henry M. Field   Second Lieutenant; c 22; Southwick, MA; Farmer Student; March 26, 1865–May 25, 1865; Commission in the 36th USCT restored, Mar. 26, 1865; Transferred to Co. B, May 25, 1865.

John W. Fletcher   Captain; 39; Norridgewock, ME; Chelsea, MA; Merchant; September 10, 1863–May 14, 1864; Formerly Second Lieutenant, Co. K, 43rd MA Inf. (9 mos.); Appointed Captain, Sept. 10, 1863; Honorably discharged on resignation from the service, May 14, 1864: Died Apr. 27, 1905 at Boston, MA.

Brister Foreman (Bristow Foreman)   Sergeant, First Sergeant; 40; Northwest Bridge, VA; Lumberer; July 13, 1863–July 13, 1866; Mustered out at expiration of enlistment, July 13, 1866.

Isaac Freeman (George Clark)   Private; 20; Bertie County, NC; Farmer; July 30, 1863–July 30, 1866; Mustered out at expiration of enlistment, July 30, 1866; Died Feb. 17, 1920 at Powellsville, NC.

Robert Frost   Private, Corporal; 22; Currituck County, NC; Farmer; June 22, 1863–June 22, 1866; Mustered out at expiration of enlistment, June 22, 1866; Died Apr. 11, 1914 in Dare County, NC.

Erastus Furby (Erastus Furbey)   Private, Corporal; 26; Norfolk County, VA; Farmer; December 7, 1863–October 12, 1866; Promoted Corporal July 1, 1866.

Norris Furby   Private; October 4, 1865; Died of chronic diarrhea at Corps D'Afrique Gen, Hospital New Orleans, Oct. 4, 1865.

Peter Furby (Peter Furbey)   First Sergeant; 28; Currituck County, NC; Farmer; June 22, 1863–June 22, 1866; Mustered out at expiration of enlistment, June 22, 1866.

George Gallop   Private; 32; Currituck County, NC; Caulker; June 22, 1863–September 26, 1865; Died of chronic diarrhea at Corps D'Afrique General Hospital, USA, New Orleans, LA, Sept. 26, 1865.

Spencer Gallop   Private; 19; North Banks, NC; Farmer; June 22, 1863–June 22, 1866; Mustered out at expiration of enlistment, June 22, 1866; Died Apr. 11, 1917 at Hertford, NC.

Winsor Garrett   Private; 45; Washington County, NC; Farmer; June 22, 1863–; Absent sick at time of Muster out of the company.

Edwin C. Gaskill   Captain; 20; Mendon, MA; Farmer; October 22, 1864–October, 28, 1866; Promoted from First Lieutenant, Co. C, Oct. 22, 1864; Mustered out with regiment; Postwar military service as First Lieutenant, Co. B, 43rd U.S. Inf.; Assigned to Freedmen's Bureau in Washington, D.C., 1868; Retired as a Captain, Dec. 15, 1870; Died June 17, 1889; Buried at Fort Mackinac, MI Post Cemetery.

Benjamin Gatlin   Private; 20; Hertford County, NC; Farmer; July 13, 1863–July 13, 1866; Mustered out at expiration of enlistment, July 13, 1866.

Primus Gilliam   Private; 24; Bertie County, NC; Farmer; July 13, 1863–July 13, 1866; Mustered out at expiration of enlistment, July 13, 1866.

Alexander Gregory   Corporal; 19; Camden County, NC; Farmer; June 22, 1863–June 22, 1866; Mustered out at expiration of enlistment, June 22, 1866.

George Griffin   Private; 31; Pasquotank County, NC; Farmer; Never Mustered; Claimed to have enlisted in regiment, but no enlistment papers nor officer who enlisted him could be found; No officer named to muster him nor any surgeon accept him on account of physical disability; Commanding officer of regiment dropped him from the company rolls.

Homer Hammond (Homer Hammons)   Private; 37; Beaufort County, NC; Farmer; June 17, 1863–September 15, 1865; Died at Camp 36th USCT, Brazos Santiago, TX on Sept. 15, 1865 (Apoplexy).

Joseph Harrison   Private; 51; Pitt County, NC; Farmer; November 11, 1863–October 28, 1866; Mustered out with the regiment.

Major Hart   Private, Sergeant; 18; Elizabeth City, NC; Farmer; June 30, 1864–September 1, 1866; Promoted Sergeant July 1, 1866 from Private; Died of cholera at Brazos Santiago, TX on Sept. 1, 1866.

William Harvey   Corporal; 40; Elizabeth City, NC; Farmer; June 22, 1863–June 22, 1866; Reduced to ranks per General Court Martial Sentence.

John Hathaway   Private; 23; Edenton, NC; Farmer; July 13, 1863–July 13, 1866; Mustered out at expiration of enlistment, July 13, 1866; Died Oct. 24, 1918 at Edenton, NC.

Waldo F. Hayward   Second Lieutenant; c 31; Walpole, NH; December 5, 1863–August 2, 1864; Appointed Second Lieutenant from civil life, Dec. 5, 1863; Serving on staff of General Wild since first muster into 36th USCT; Promoted to First Lieutenant and transferred to 37th USCT, Aug. 2, 1864.

Richard Henry (Henry Clarke)  Private/Musician; 19; Bertie County, NC; Farmer; July 13, 1863–July 13, 1866; Mustered out at expiration of enlistment, July 13, 1866.

James H. Hunt  Corporal, Sergeant, First Sergeant; 25; Hertford County, NC; Farmer; August 3, 1863–August 3, 1866; Promoted Sergeant July 1, 1866 from Corporal Mustered out at expiration of enlistment, Aug. 3, 1866.

Cicero Jaycox (Cicero Jacocks)  Private, Corporal, Sergeant; 25; Perquimans County, NC; Farmer; July 13, 1863–July 13, 1866; Promoted Corporal Oct. 8, 1865; Promoted Sergeant July 1, 1866; Mustered out at expiration of enlistment, July 13, 1866.

Henry Jaycox  Private; 20; Perquimans County, NC; Farmer; July 14, 1863–; Absent sick in Hospital at time of Muster out of the regiment.

Thomas Jaycox  Corporal, Sergeant; 19; Perquimans County, NC; Farmer; July 14, 1863–July 14, 1866; Promoted Sergeant July 1, 1866 from Corporal; Mustered out at expiration of enlistment, July 14, 1866.

Isaac Johnson  Private; 24; Pasquotank County, NC; Farmer; June 22, 1863–August 18, 1865; Died of pneumonia at Brazos Santiago, TX, Aug. 18, 1865.

Willard Johnson  Sergeant, Private; 23; Perquimans County, NC; Farmer; June 18, 1863–June 18, 1866; Reduced to ranks Nov. 1, 1865; Mustered out at expiration of enlistment, June 18, 1866; Died Jan. 12, 1927 at Norfolk, VA.

Ephraim Jones  Private; 33; Perquimans County, NC; Farmer; June 22, 1863–June 22, 1866; Mustered out at expiration of enlistment, June 22, 1866.

Albert Jourdan (Albert Jordan)  Corporal, Sergeant; 28; Perquimans County, NC; Farmer; June 22, 1863–June 22, 1866; Promoted Corporal Nov. 1, 1864; Promoted Sergeant Nov. 1, 1865; Mustered out at expiration of enlistment, June 22, 1866.

Benjamin F. Kinsley  First Lieutenant; 22; Salem, MA; Clerk; August 1, 1863–January 18, 1864; Formerly Corporal, Co. F, 25th MA Inf.; Appointed First Lieutenant, Aug. 1, 1863; Transferred to Co. F, Jan. 18, 1864.

Joseph G. Longley  First Lieutenant; 40; Hawley, MA; Westborough, MA; Teacher; January 18, 1864–June 27, 1864; Transferred from Co. F, Jan. 18, 1864; Discharged, June 27, 1864; After discharge from the service became superintendent of AMA-sponsored freedmen schools in Wilmington, NC; Died May 4, 1871 at Greenville, IL.

Nelson Lumner  Private; 18; Princess Anne County, VA; Farmer; November 27, 1863–August 28, 1865; Died of pneumonia at Hospital at New Orleans, LA, Aug. 28, 1865.

Isaac Liverman (Isaac Porter)  Private; 24; Hertford County, NC; Farmer; August 3, 1863–August 3, 1866; Mustered out at expiration of enlistment, Aug. 3, 1866; Died at National Soldier's Home, VA, Sept. 29, 1918.

Moses Liverman  Private, Corporal; 23; Hertford County, NC; Farmer; August 3, 1863–August 3, 1866; Promoted Corporal, July 1, 1866; Mustered out at expiration of enlistment, Aug. 3, 1866; Died Oct. 7, 1916 at Winton, NC.

Newsome Long (Ransome Rogers)  Private; 21; Northampton County, NC; Farmer; August 3, 1863–August 3, 1866; Mustered out at expiration of enlistment, Aug. 3, 1866; Died June 13, 1924 at Newark, NJ.

Henry Malburne  Private; 20; Princess Anne County, VA; Farmer; November 27, 1863–October 28, 1866; Mustered out with the regiment; Died Feb. 6, 1929 at Norfolk, VA.

David McRae  Private; 40; Plymouth, NC; Teamster; July 13, 1863–July 13, 1866; Mustered out at expiration of enlistment, July 13, 1866;

Samuel Midgett  Private; 35; Hyde County, NC; Fisherman; June 22, 1863–August 23, 1865; Died of chronic diarrhea at Post Hospital Brazos Santiago, TX, Aug. 23, 1865.

Clairborne Miller (Clayborne Miller)  Private; 21; Hertford County, NC; Farmer; August 3, 1863–September 29, 1864; Killed at New Market Heights, VA, Sept. 29, 1864.

Ezra Moore  Private; 27; Beaufort County, NC; Farmer; June 13, 1863–June 13, 1866; Mustered out at expiration of enlistment, June 13, 1866.

William Moore  Private; 29; Washington County, NC; Farmer; July 13, 1863–; Absent sick in Hospital at time of Muster out of the company.

Charles Mullen  Private, Corporal; 20; Hertford County, NC; Farmer; June 22, 1863–June 22, 1866; Wounded at New Market Heights, Sept. 29, 1864: Promoted Corporal, Nov. 1, 1864; Mustered out at expiration of enlistment, June 22, 1866.

Caesar Oden (Caesar Odin)  Sergeant; 24; Beaufort County, NC; Farmer; July 7, 1863–June 22, 1866; Discharged June 22, 1866.

Miles Perketts  Private; 35; Beaufort County, NC; Farmer; November 18, 1863–October 28, 1866; Mustered out with the regiment.

Edmund Perkins  Private; 24; Camden County, NC; Farmer; December 1, 1863–May 4, 1864; Died of dysentery at U.S. General Hospital Fort Monroe, VA, May 4, 1864; Buried Hampton National Cemetery, VA (Grave No. 18-D-6 as "Edward Perkins").

Warren Pierce  Second Lieutenant; c 23; Tyngsboro, MA; Medical Student; July 1864–September 1864; Transferred from Co. I, July 1864; Transferred to Co. I, Sept. 1864.

William Pierce  Private; 30; Martin County, NC; Farmer Mechanic; July 13, 1863–November 23, 1865; Promoted Commissary Sergeant and transferred to non-commissioned staff, Nov. 23, 1865.

Jacob Pinor (Jacob Poyner)  Sergeant; 33; Currituck County, NC; Farmer; June 22, 1863–June 22, 1866; Mustered out at expiration of enlistment, June 22, 1866.

Henry Poole  Private; 21; Pasquotank County, NC; Barber; July 13, 1863–July 13, 1866; Mustered out at expiration of enlistment, July 13, 1866.

George Potter  Private; 51; Beaufort County, NC; Laborer Cooper; November 12, 1863–June 14, 1866; Mustered out at Fort Monroe, VA, Jun. 14, 1866.

Edward Rabey (Ned Rabey/Roby)  Private; 36; Bertie County, NC; November 20, 1863–; Absent in confinement at the time of Muster out of company.

Edmund Reddick  Private; 22; Nansemond County, VA; Servant; July 6, 1863–July 6, 1866; Mustered out at expiration of enlistment, July 6, 1866; Died June 18, 1926 at Portsmouth, VA.

José A.A. Robinson  First Lieutenant; c18; NY; January 1, 1866–October 28, 1866; Appointed Second Lieutenant, Jul. 23, 1864; Transferred to Co. E, Nov. 4, 1864; Promoted First Lieutenant, Co. A, Jan. 1, 1866; Mustered out with the regiment; Post-war military service as Second Lieutenant, 17th U.S. Inf.; Second Lieutenant, 1st U.S. Arty.; Second Lieutenant, 24th U.S. Inf.; Resigned, July 27, 1871.

David Robuck  Private; 20; Bertie County, NC; Farmer; July 13, 1863–June 30, 1864; Died at Regimental Hospital at Point Lookout, MD, Jun. 30, 1864.

Anthony Rodgers (Anthony Rogers)  Private; 20; Martin County, NC; Farmer; July 13, 1863–July 22, 1866; Mustered out July 22, 1866 detained in service over term of enlistment on account of being on detached service at New Orleans, LA: Died 1891 or 1892 at Williamston, NC.

Lewis Rodgers (Lewis Rogers)  Private; 21; Martin County, NC; Farmer; July 14, 1863–July 14, 1866; Mustered out at expiration of enlistment, July 14, 1866.

Ransom Rodgers  Private; 19; Martin County, NC; Servant; July 14, 1863–July 14, 1866; Mustered out at expiration of enlistment, July 14, 1866.

David Simmons  Private; 49; Camden County, NC; Farmer; December 22, 1863–October 28, 1866; Mustered out with the regiment.

Elijah Simmons  Private; 47; Camden County, NC; Farmer; November 29, 1863–October 28, 1866; Mustered out with the regiment.

Nathaniel (Nat) Simmons  Private; 30; December 28, 1863–May 21, 1864; Died of pulmonary consumption at Point Lookout, MD, May 21, 1864.

George Sutton  Private; 24; Perquimans County, NC; Farmer; June 22, 1863–June 22, 1866; Mustered out at expiration of enlistment, June 22, 1866.

Peter Sutton  Private, Corporal, Sergeant; 19; Perquimans County, NC; Farmer; June 22, 1863–June 22, 1866; Promoted Corporal Feb. 1, 1864; Promoted Sergeant Sept. 11, 1865; Mustered out at expiration of enlistment, June 22, 1866.

Owen Sykes  Private; 21; Princess Anne County, VA; Farmer; November 27, 1863–October 28, 1866; Mustered out with the regiment.

Dorset Taylor (Dorsey Taylor)  Private; 21; Bertie County, NC; Farmer; June 23, 1863–December 26, 1865; Died of chronic diarrhea at Hospital, Point of Rocks, VA on Dec. 26, 1865.

Julius Taylor (Julius G. Taylor) Private; 19; Bertie County, NC; Farmer; July 13, 1863–June 18, 1865; Wounded at New Market Heights Sept. 29, 1864; Discharged June 18, 1865; Died May 7, 1920 at Arthington, Liberia.

William Thoroughgood Private; 28; Princess Anne County, VA; Farmer; December 2, 1863–October 28, 1866; Mustered out with regiment; Died June 15, 1914 at Norfolk, VA.

William M. Titcomb First Lieutenant; c19; Dedham, MA; Student; May 17, 1864–September 18, 1864; Transferred from Co. H, May 17, 1864; Transferred to 38th USCT, Sept. 18, 1864; Died May 5, 1875 at Iowa City, IA.

Thomas Vaughn Private; 33; Hertford County, NC; Farmer; July 13, 1863–July 13, 1866; Mustered out at expiration of enlistment, July 13, 1866.

Isaac Walson Private; 21; Camden County, NC; Farmer; August 3, 1863–September 30, 1864; Killed from accidental musket discharge at Jones Landing, Deep Bottom, James River, VA Sept. 30, 1864.

Britton West Private; 25; Bertie County, NC; Farmer; July 14, 1863–July 14, 1866; Mustered out at expiration of enlistment, July 14, 1866.

George White Private; 27; Bertie County, NC; Farmer; June 24, 1863–June 24, 1866; Mustered out at expiration of enlistment, June 24, 1866.

Frank Whitus (Frank Whitehurst) Private/Musician; 18; Norfolk County, VA; Farmer; October 1, 1863–October 17, 1866; Mustered out, Oct. 17, 1866.

Alexander Wiggins (Aleck Wiggins) Private; 42; Martin County, NC; Farmer; July 14, 1863–December 14, 1865; Wounded at New Market Heights, Sept. 29, 1864; Discharged at Fort Monroe, VA, Dec. 14, 1865.

Frank Williams, 1st Private; 19; Murfreesboro, NC; Farmer; July 30, 1863–; Died at Portsmouth, VA. Never mustered.

Frank Williams, 2nd Private; 22; Murfreesboro, NC; Servant; August 3, 1863–September 20, 1865; Died of pneumonia at Hospital at New Orleans, LA, Sept. 20, 1865.

Harley Williams Private; 35; Dallas, NC; Cooper; November 20, 1863–October 28, 1866; Mustered out with the regiment.

John Williams Private; 19; Princess Anne County, VA; Farmer; November 27, 1863–October 28, 1866; Mustered out with the regiment.

Thomas Williams Private; 32; Princess Anne County, VA; Farmer; November 27, 1863–May 3, 1865; Discharged at Portsmouth, VA, May 3, 1865.

Thomas Williford Private; 43; Bertie County, NC; Farmer; July 14, 1863–June 14, 1866; Discharged at Fort Monroe, VA, June 14, 1866.

Frank Wilson Private; 18; Camden County, NC; Farmer; June 22, 1863–June 22, 1866; Mustered out at expiration of enlistment, June 22, 1866; Died Aug. 15, 1916 at Norfolk, VA.

Jonah Wilson Private; 22; Bertie County, NC; Farmer; August 3, 1863–December 22, 1865; Wounded at New Market Heights, Sept. 29, 1864; Discharged at Hospital New Orleans, LA, Dec. 22, 1865.

Lewis Wilson Private; 29; Bertie County, NC; Farmer; August 3, 1863–; Absent sick at time of Muster out of regiment.;

Robert Wilson Private; 21; Bertie County, NC; Farmer; August 3, 1863–August 3, 1866; Mustered out at expiration of enlistment, Aug. 3, 1866: Died Apr. 2, 1919 at Portsmouth, VA.

Josephus Wise Private; 23; Murfreesboro, NC; Farmer; August 3, 1863–November 22, 1865; Wounded at New Market Heights, Sept. 29, 1864; Mustered out on Nov. 22, 1865 at Hicks U.S. General Hospital, MD.

## Company B

George E. Albee Second Lieutenant; 20; Lisbon, NH; October 23, 1865–October 28, 1866; Transferred from Co. G, Oct. 23, 1865; Mustered out with regiment; Post war service as Second Lieutenant, 41st U.S. Inf.; First Lieutenant, 41st U.S. Inf.; First Lieutenant, 24th U.S. Inf.: Brevet Captain, USA; Medal of Honor Winner, 1869.

James Albert   Private; 19; Suffolk, VA; Laborer; November 19, 1863–; Absent in confinement Gen. Court Martial at time of Muster out of regiment.

Dean Alexander   Private; 25; Essex County, VA; Farmer; June 20, 1864–June 15, 1865; Mustered out of service at Norfolk, VA, June 15, 1865.

Hiram W. Allen   First Lieutenant; c 26; Chelsea, MA; Clerk; May 2, 1864–July 23, 1864; Transferred from Co. I, May 2, 1864; Serving on staff of General Wild since first muster into 36th USCT; Transferred to Co. K, July 23, 1864.

Samuel Allen   Private; 40; Beaufort County, NC; Farmer; September 1, 1863–January 17, 1866; Discharged on Surgeon's Certificate of disability at Hicks U.S. Gen. Hospital, Baltimore, MD, Jan. 17, 1866.

James W. Bacon   First Lieutenant; c 22; Portsmouth, NH; Walpole, MA; Painter; March 6, 1865–March 29, 1865; Transferred from Co. I, Mar. 6, 1865; Appointed Adjutant, Mar. 29, 1865.

Amory O. Balch   Second Lieutenant; 18; Roxbury, MA; Clerk; December 7, 1863–April 25, 1864; Formerly Private, Co. K, 35th MA Inf.; Appointed Second Lieutenant, Dec. 7, 1863; Transferred to Co. D, Apr. 25, 1864.

George Bass   Private; 24; Elizabeth City, NC; Farmer; July 11, 1863–July 11, 1866; Mustered out on expiration of enlistment, July 11, 1866.

Edmund Beasley (Edward Beasley)   Corporal; 22; Plymouth, NC; Laborer; July 13, 1863–July 13, 1866; Appointed Corporal Sept. 1, 1863; Mustered out on expiration of enlistment, July 13, 1866; Died March 11, 1910 at Sumter, SC.

George Beckett   Private, Corporal; 19; Northampton County, VA; Farmer; November 15, 1863–October 12, 1866; Appointed Corporal Sept. 10, 1866; Mustered out at Galveston, TX, Oct. 12, 1866.

Gaston Beckton (Gaston Becton)   Private; 18; Plymouth, NC; Farmer; June 29, 1863–June 29, 1866; Mustered out on expiration of enlistment, June 29, 1866; Died July 20, 1905 at Jones County, NC.

Abram Bell   Corporal Sergeant; 23; Plymouth, NC; Laborer; July 13, 1863–July 13, 1866; Appointed Corporal Sept. 1, 1863; Promoted Sergeant, Jul. 2, 1866; Mustered out on expiration of enlistment, July 13, 1866; Died July 10, 1913 at Kenner, LA.

Francis A. Bicknell   Captain; 19; Weymouth, MA; Shoecutter; October 22, 1864–October 28, 1866; Promoted from First Lieutenant, Co. G, Oct. 22, 1864; Brevet Major, USV, Mar. 13, 1865; Mustered out with the regiment.

Jacob Biner   Private; 18; Plymouth, NC; Farmer; October 22, 1863–June 2, 1866; Died in Post Hospital at Brazos Santiago, TX, Jun. 2, 1866.

John Bird   Private; 20; Granville County, NC; Farmer; July 8, 1863–February 20, 1864; Died of small pox at Portsmouth, VA, Feb. 20, 1864.

Franklin Blunt   Sergeant, Corporal; 21; Beaufort County, NC; Teamster; July 22, 1863–July 22, 1866; Appointed Sergeant Jan. 15, 1864; Reduced to Corporal Aug. 15, 1864; Promoted Sergeant, Jul 14, 1866; Mustered out on expiration of enlistment, July 22, 1866..

Benjamin Boston   Private; 35; Washington County, NC; Farmer; July 2, 1863–February 29, 1864; Died of small pox at Portsmouth, VA, Feb. 29, 1864.

Calvin Bowe   Private; 20; Pasquotank County, NC; Farmer; June 13, 1863–September 18, 1863; Transferred to Co. C, Sept. 18, 1863.

Arthur Bowen (Arthur Bowins)   Private; 19; Essex County, VA; Farmer; June 19, 1864–October 12, 1866; Mustered out at Galveston, TX, Oct. 12, 1866.

David Boyd   Private; 17; Pitt County, NC; Farmer; August 4, 1863–August 4, 1866; Mustered out on expiration of enlistment, Aug. 4, 1866; Died at Lynnhaven, VA, Aug. 3, 1931.

William Braxton (William Broxton)   Private; 29; King and Queen County, VA; Farmer; June 21, 1864–October 12, 1866; Dishonorably discharged the service per Gen. Court Martial, Oct. 12, 1866.

Robert Brickus   Private; 18; Bertie County, NC; Farmer; July 4, 1863–July 4, 1866; Mustered out on expiration of enlistment, July 4, 1866.

Edward Bright   Private, Corporal, Sergeant; 18; Princess Anne County, VA; Farmer; October 20, 1863–October 20, 1866; Appointed Corporal Mar. 7, 1866; Promoted Sergeant Aug. 5, 1866; Mustered out on expiration of enlistment, Oct. 20, 1866.

Allen Brown   Private; 19; Plymouth, NC; Farmer; July 13, 1863–September 11, 1863; Never Mustered. Died of fever at Portsmouth, VA, Sept. 11, 1863 (Buried near entrenched camp near railroad).

Joseph Bunch   Private, Musician; 17; Plymouth, NC; Servant; July 13, 1863–July 13, 1866; Mustered out on expiration of enlistment, July 13, 1866.

John W. Butt (John W. Butts)   Private; 33; Norfolk County, VA; Laborer; October 22, 1863–; Wounded at New Market Heights, VA, Sept. 29, 1864.

Reddick Carr   Private; 22; Duplin County, NC; Farmer; July 8, 1863–June 5, 1865; Wounded before Petersburg, VA, Aug. 23, 1864; Mustered out of service at Fort Monroe, VA Jun. 5, 1865.

Cain Chason (Cain Chasen)   Private, Corporal; 20; Duplin County, NC; Farmer; July 8, 1863–January 19, 1865; Appointed Corporal Apr. 26, 1864; Died of typhoid fever at Point of Rocks Hospital, VA Jan. 19, 1865; Buried at City Point National Cemetery (Grave No. 3501 as "C. Chasen").

Henry Clay   Private; 21; Richmond County, VA; Farmer; June 19, 1864–October 28, 1866; Mustered out with regiment.

George W.S. Conant   Second Lieutenant; 21; South Royalton, VT; Boston, MA; Butcher; April 29, 1864–May 11, 1864; Transferred from Co. G, Apr. 29, 1864; Returned to Co. G, May 11, 1864.

Henderson Cooper   Private, Corporal, Sergeant; 25; Murfreesboro, NC; Farmer; August 3, 1863–August 3, 1866; Appointed Corporal Jul. 27, 1865; Promoted Sergeant Jul. 14, 1866; Mustered out on expiration of enlistment, Aug. 3, 1866; Died May 16, 1917 near Arkansas City, AK.

Littleton Cooper   Corporal, Sergeant, First Sergeant; 20; Winton, NC; Farmer; August 3, 1863–August 3, 1866; Appointed Corporal Nov. 15, 1863; Promoted Sergeant Aug. 19, 1865; Promoted First Sergeant Jul. 14, 1866; Mustered out on expiration of enlistment, Aug. 3, 1866; Died Nov. 21, 1900.

John Cornick   Private; 35; Princess Anne County, VA; Servant; October 22, 1863–October 22, 1866; Mustered out on expiration of enlistment, Oct. 22, 1866.

Daniel J. Courtney   Second Lieutenant; c 24; Newport, Wales; Brookline, MA; Student Clerk; March 25, 1865–May 25, 1865; Formerly Quartermaster Sergeant, Mar. 25, 1865; Transferred to Co. K, May 25, 1865.

Ransom Coy   Private, Corporal, Sergeant, First Sergeant; 23; Great Bridge, VA; Laborer; October 16, 1863–October 17, 1866; Appointed Corporal Aug. 16, 1864; Promoted Sergeant Mar. 1866; Promoted First Sergeant Aug. 4, 1866; . Mustered out on expiration of enlistment, Oct. 17, 1866.

Nathaniel Davis   Private; 26; Edenton, NC; Laborer; October 22, 1863–October 22, 1866; Wounded before Petersburg, VA, Aug. 20, 1864; Wounded at New Market Heights, VA, Sept. 29, 1864; Mustered out at expiration of enlistment, Oct. 22, 1866.

Elber Dean   Private; 20; Norfolk County, VA; Farmer; November 18, 1863–January 18, 1865; Died of chronic diarrhea at Balfour U.S. Gen. Hospital Jan. 18, 1865 (Buried in Hampton National Cemetery Sec. E, 91).

Tony Dickinson (Tony Dickenson)   Private; 19; Pitt County, NC; Farmer; July 7, 1863–July 7, 1866; Mustered out on expiration of enlistment, July 7, 1866.

Joseph Dobson   Private; 26; Duplin County, NC; Farmer; July 8, 1863–January 5, 1865; Wounded before Petersburg, VA, Aug. 13, 1864; Discharged the service on Surgeon's certificate of disability at U.S. Gen. Hospital David's Island, NY, Jan. 5, 1865.

Anson Farrier   Private; 26; Kennansville, NC; Engineer; July 15, 1863–March 9, 1865; Discharged from service per Surgeon's certification of disability Mar. 9, 1865; Died Sept. 17, 1906 at Barboursview, Norfolk County, VA.

Charles Fidget (Charles Fitchett)   Private, Corporal; 18; Accomack County, VA; Farmer; November 15, 1863–October 28, 1866; Appointed Corporal Jul. 14, 1866; Mustered out with regiment.

Leverson Fidget   Private; 19; Northampton County, VA; Farmer; November 15, 1863–October 28, 1866; Mustered out with regiment.

Oswell Fidget   Private; 19; Accomack County, VA; Farmer; November 15, 1863–October 14, 1864; Died of disease at Lovell Gen. Hospital Oct. 14, 1864.

Henry M. Field   Second Lieutenant; c 22;

Southwick, MA; Farmer Student; May 25, 1865–September 4, 1865; Transferred from Co. A, May 25, 1865; Promoted to First Lieutenant and transferred to Co. F, Sept. 15, 1865.

Charles H. Frye   Captain; 22; Salem, MA; Clerk; September 8, 1863–September 24, 1864; Formerly Sergeant, Co. F, 21st MA Inf.; Appointed Captain, Sept. 8, 1863; Died Apr. 12, 1915 at Salem, MA.

Joseph Furby   Private; 19; Elizabeth City, NC; Farmer; July 3, 1863–March 9, 1865; Discharged the service per Surgeon's certificate of disability Mar. 9, 1865.

Jacob Gatlin (Jacob Gatling)   Private, Corporal; 30; Murfreesboro, NC; Farmer; August 3, 1863–August 3, 1866; Appointed Corporal Jul. 14, 1866: Mustered out on expiration of enlistment, Aug. 3, 1866.

Henry Gaylor   Private; 18; Plymouth, NC; Farmer; July 13, 1863–March 16, 1864; Died of small pox at Portsmouth, VA Mar. 16, 1864.

John M. Graham   Private; 18; Raleigh, NC; Servant; July 15, 1863–August 13, 1865; Died of diarrhea at Post Hospital Brazos Santiago, TX Aug. 15, 1865.

Frank H. Graves   Second Lieutenant; 19; July 22, 1864–February 24, 1865; Appointed Second Lieutenant from civil life, Jul. 22, 1864; Serving on staff of Gen. Paine since July 22, 1864; Promoted First Lieutenant and transferred to Co. K, Feb. 24, 1865.

Lucius Graves   Private; James City County, VA; Servant; October 19, 1863–October 19, 1866; Wounded at New Market Heights, VA, Sept. 29, 1864; Mustered out on expiration of enlistment, Oct. 19, 1866.

Edward Griffin   Corporal, Private; 33; Pasquotank County, NC; Steward; August 17, 1863–August 23, 1864; Appointed Corporal Nov. 15, 1864; Reduced to ranks for neglect of duty Jun. 5, 1864; Killed (shot in neck) before Petersburg, VA, Aug. 23, 1864.

Miles Grimes   Private; 24; Pitt County, NC; Farmer; September 21, 1863–September 21, 1866; Wounded at New Market Heights, VA, Sept. 29, 1864; Mustered out on expiration of enlistment, Sept. 21, 1866; Died May 26, 1910.

Cicero Gustus (Augustus Wilkerson)   Private, Corporal; 21; Washington, NC; Farmer; July 2, 1863–July 2, 1866; Appointed Corporal Apr. 26, 1864; Mustered out on expiration of enlistment, July 2, 1866.

Alfred Hart   Private; 40; Nansemond County, VA; Farmer; November 21, 1863–June 14, 1865; Mustered out of the service Jun. 14, 1865.

Samuel Hart   Private; 18; Franklin County, NC; Farmer; July 15, 1863–; Absent in confinement per Gen. Court Martial sentence at muster out of regiment.

Charles Haskell   First Lieutenant; c 24; Ipswich, MA; Tinman; January 3, 1865–February 24, 1865; Transferred from Co. K, Jan. 3, 1865; Transferred to Co. C, Feb. 24, 1865.

Robert Hawkins   Private; 25; Richmond County, VA; Cooper; June 19, 1864–August 5, 1864; Killed (shot in head) before Petersburg, VA, Aug. 5, 1864.

Peter Herbert (Peter Hubbard)   Sergeant, Private; 28; Plymouth, NC; Servant; July 13, 1863–July 13, 1866; Appointed Sergeant Oct. 1, 1863: Reduced to ranks Aug. 15, 1864; Mustered out on expiration of enlistment, July 13, 1866.

Early W. James   Private; 22; Norfolk County, VA; Farmer; November 28, 1863–October 31, 1865; Discharged per Surgeon's certificate of disability at U.S. Gen. Hospital, New Orleans, LA, Oct. 31, 1865; Died Mar. 4, 1919 at Norfolk, VA.

George James   Private; 18; Norfolk County, VA; Farmer; November 28, 1863–; Wounded at New Market Heights, VA, Sept. 29, 1864; Absent sick at final Muster out of regiment (Never heard from after being taken to field hospital from the field of battle).

Horatio James   Private; 20; Princess Anne County, VA; Farmer; November 28, 1863–October 1866

Miles James   Corporal, Sergeant; 34; Princess Anne County, VA; Farmer; November 16, 1863–October 13, 1865; Appointed Corporal Feb. 15, 1864; Wounded Sept. 29, 1864 at New Market Heights; Promoted Sergeant Apr. 14, 1865; Awarded Medal of Honor; Discharged per Surgeon's certificate of disability at Brazos Santiago, TX, Oct. 13, 1865.

Napoleon James   Private; 44; Northampton County, VA; Farmer; November 15, 1863–May 20, 1865; Discharged per Surgeon's certificate of disability from Balfour Gen. Hospital, Portsmouth, VA, May 20, 1865.

Wesley James   Private; 23; Halifax County, NC; Laborer; November 16, 1863–June 29,

1865; Mustered out of service at Fort Monroe, VA Jun. 29, 1865.

Arthur Johnson  Private; 19; Westmoreland County, VA; Farmer; June 21, 1864–October 28, 1866; Mustered out with the regiment; Died Oct. 11, 1910.

James H. Johnson  Private; 30; Westmoreland County, VA; Farmer; June 20, 1864–October 28, 1866; Mustered out with the regiment.

James T. Johnson  Private; 23; Suffolk, VA; Brakeman; August 13, 1863–June 15, 1865; Wounded at New Market Heights, VA, Sept. 29, 1864; Mustered out of service Jun. 15, 1865.

Lewis Johnson  Private; 18; Norfolk, VA; Servant; October 22, 1863–August 29, 1864; Died of wounds received before Petersburg, VA, Aug. 29, 1864 (Buried at City Point National Cemetery, Grave No. 3720).

Peter Jones  Private; 33; Halifax County, NC; Servant; July 10, 1863–July 18, 1865; Wounded at New Market Heights, VA, Sept. 29, 1864; Died of chronic diarrhea at Fort Monroe, VA Jul. 18, 1865.

Richard Jones  Private; 19; Hertford County, NC; Farmer; August 16, 1863–June 14, 1865; Mustered out of service at Fort Monroe, VA Jun. 14, 1865; Died Jan. 3, 1914.

John Lang (William J. Lang)  Private; 18; Winton, NC; Farmer; August 3, 1863–April 1, 1864; Died of small pox at Point Lookout, MD Apr. 1, 1864.

James Little  Private; 44; Hyde County, NC; Farmer; October 2, 1863–October 2, 1866; Mustered out on expiration of enlistment, Oct. 3, 1866; Died Sept. 9, 1883 at James City, NC.

Edward Luntsworth (Edward Lunford)  Private, Corporal; 22; Great Bridge, VA; Farmer; October 17, 1863–October 17, 1866; Appointed Corporal Sept. 1, 1866; Mustered out on expiration of enlistment, Oct. 17, 1866.

Jesse Maltby  Private; 20; Princess Anne County, VA; Farmer; November 28, 1863–October 28, 1866; Mustered out with regiment; Died Oct. 19, 1910.

John McCabe  Private; 29; Beaufort County, NC; Farmer; June 8, 1863–September 19, 1866; Absent on detached service as the reason for not being mustered out at the expiration of term of service.

Anthony McCleese  Corporal; 26; Tyrrell County, NC; Farmer; September 30, 1863–March 26, 1864; Appointed Corporal Nov. 15, 1863; Died of small pox at Portsmouth, VA, Mar. 26, 1864 (Buried in Hampton National Cemetery, VA, Grave No. Sec. 10, 1893 as "A. MacLeese").

Gilbert Mezell (Gilbert Mezzell)  First Sergeant; 27; Plymouth, NC; Laborer; July 13, 1863–July 13, 1866; Appointed First Sergeant Sept. 23, 1863; Mustered out on expiration of enlistment, July 13, 1866.

Nathan Mitchell  Never mustered into service; Died of measles at New Bern, NC, Aug. 26, 1863.

Daniel Moore  Private; 30; Princess Anne County, VA; Farmer; November 28, 1863–June 17, 1864; Died of dysentery at Point Lookout, MD, Jun. 17, 1864.

George Moore  Private, Corporal; 38; Currituck County, NC; Farmer; August 30, 1863–August 31, 1866; Appointed Corporal Aug. 5, 1866; Mustered out on expiration of enlistment, Aug. 31, 1866.

Henderson Moore  Private; 36; Beaufort County, NC; Farmer; June 15, 1863–May 23, 1865; Discharged per Surgeon's certificate of disability, May 23, 1865.

Peter Moore  Private; 20; Pasquotank County, NC; Farmer; November 16, 1863–October 12, 1866; Discharged Oct. 12, 1866; Died Jan. 29, 1914 at Elizabeth City, NC.

Bryan Moye  Private; 19; Pitt County, NC; Farmer; October 1, 1863–February 27, 1864; Discharged on Surgeon's certificate of disability at Portsmouth, VA, Feb. 27, 1864.

Washington Newby  Private; 30; Plymouth, NC; Laborer; July 13, 1863–June 14, 1865; Discharged June 14, 1865.

William Newsom (William Newsome)  Private; 18; Hertford County, NC; Farmer; August 3, 1863–August 3, 1866; Mustered out on expiration of enlistment, Aug. 3, 1866; Died Oct. 28, 1915 at Cofield, NC.

Peter Norfleet  Sergeant; 22; Edgecombe County, NC; Carpenter; August 29, 1863–August 29, 1865; Appointed Sergeant Dec. 1, 1863; Died of chronic diarrhea at U.S. Gen. Hospital New Orleans, LA Aug. 29, 1865.

Robert Norfleet  Private; 18; Edgecombe County, NC; Farmer; July 22, 1863–June 20, 1865; Died of intermittent fever at U.S. Gen. Hospital New Orleans, LA Jun. 20, 1865.

Henry Parker   Private; 19; Pitt County, NC; Farmer; July 15, 1863–September 23, 1863; Transferred to Co. D, Sept. 23, 1863.

Rochus Parker   Private; 19; Murfreesboro, NC; Farmer; August 3, 1863–February 24, 1865; Died of scrofula at U.S. Gen. Hospital at Point of Rocks, VA Feb. 24, 1865.

Henry Perdy (Henry Purdy)   Private, Corporal, Sergeant; 31; Murfreesboro, NC; Farmer; August 3, 1863–August 21, 1866; Appointed Corporal Aug. 16, 1864; Promoted Sergeant Jul. 14, 1866; Mustered out on expiration of enlistment, Aug. 21, 1866.

Bailey Phillips (Bailor Phillips)   Private, Corporal, Sergeant; 23; King and Queen County, VA; Farmer; June 19, 1864–October 28, 1866; Appointed Corporal Aug. 5, 1866; Promoted Sergeant Sept. 19, 1866; Mustered out with regiment.

Warren Pierce   First Lieutenant; c 24; Tyngsboro, MA; Medical Student; September 1865–October 28, 1866; Transferred from Co. I, Sept. 1865; Mustered out with the regiment.

John Piner (John Poyner)   Corporal, Sergeant; 23; Currituck County, NC; Farmer; June 21, 1863–June 21, 1866; Appointed Corporal Nov. 15, 1863; Promoted Sergeant, Aug. 16, 1864; Mustered out on expiration of enlistment, June 21, 1866.

Hamilton Pitman   Private; 27; Edgecombe County, NC; Farmer; September 15, 1863–November 15, 1864; Died of wounds received in action Sept. 29, 1864 (New Market Heights) at Balfour U.S. Gen. Hospital, Portsmouth, VA. Nov. 15, 1864 (Buried in Hampton National Cemetery, VA, Grave Sec. E, 173 as "H. Piedman").

James E. Porter   Private, Corporal, Sergeant; 18; Suffolk, VA; Servant; October 21, 1863–September 9, 1866; Appointed Corporal Jul. 14, 1866; Promoted Sergeant Aug. 5, 1866; Died of cholera at Brazos Santiago, TX, Sept. 9, 1866.

Cornelius Reddick   Sergeant, Private; 23; Suffolk, VA; Servant; October 16, 1863–October 17, 1866; Appointed Sergeant Dec. 25, 1864; Reduced to ranks Apr. 14, 1865; Mustered out on expiration of enlistment, Oct. 17, 1866.

Frank W. Rhoades   First Lieutenant; c 23; Roxbury, MA; Clerk; July 15, 1864–October 1, 1864; Transferred from Co. K, July 15, 1864; Resigned Oct. 1, 1864; Died June 17, 1910 at Hendersonville, NC.

James Robinson   Private; 25; Norfolk, VA; Servant; November 20, 1863–May 2, 1864; Died of fever at Point Lookout, MD, May 2, 1864.

John Rodgers   Private; 19; Martin County, NC; Farmer; August 13, 1863–December 19, 1865; Discharged for disability at U.S. Gen. Hospital New Orleans, LA Dec. 19, 1865.

William Saunders   Private; 19; Essex County, VA; Farmer; June 21, 1864–September 6, 18__; Died of cholera at Post Hospital Brazos Santiago, TX, Sept. 6, 18__

Charles Sheppard   Private; 19; Pitt County, NC; Farmer; October 10, 1863–February 10, 1864; Discharged on Surgeon's certificate of disability at Portsmouth, VA, Feb. 10, 1864.

Noah Sheppard   Private, Corporal, Sergeant; 22; Pitt County, NC; Farmer; September 28, 1863–September 28, 1866; Appointed Corporal Apr. 25, 1865; Promoted Sergeant Jul. 24, 1866; Mustered out on expiration of enlistment, Sept. 28, 1866; Died July 4, 1911 at Tarket Creek, NC.

Charles M. Smith   Private; 22; Pitt County, NC; Carpenter; August 28, 1863–August 28, 1863; Mustered out on expiration of enlistment, Aug. 28, 1866.

John Smith   Private; 25; Gloucester County, VA; Farmer; June 15, 1863–September 24, 1865; Appointed Hospital Steward, Sept. 24, 1865.

Washington Smith   Private; 18; Norfolk County, VA; Farmer; November 23, 1863–October 28, 1866; Mustered out with regiment.

Zachariah Smith   Private; 22; Norfolk County, VA; Farmer; November 23, 1863–October 28, 1866; Mustered out with regiment.

James Stewart   Private; 19; Westmoreland County, VA; Farmer; June 19, 1864–October 28, 1866; Mustered out with regiment.

Frank Swift   Private; 30; Plymouth, NC; Laborer; July 3, 1863–July 3, 1866; Mustered out on expiration of enlistment, July 3, 1866.

William Taylor   Private; 19; Caroline County, VA; Farmer; October 15, 1863–; Wounded at New Market Heights, VA, Sept. 29, 1864; Absent in confinement serving Gen. Court Martial Sentence at Muster out of the regiment.

Winfield Taylor   Private; 27; Prince George County, VA; Wagoner; November 19, 1863–

October 28, 1866; Mustered out with regiment.

Amos Thornton   Private; 18; New Hanover County, NC; Farmer; August 12, 1863–September 5, 1865; Died of disease enroute to New Orleans, LA, Sept. 5, 1865.

Caesar Tollson   Private; 22; Swift Creek, NC; Farmer; August 12, 1863–June 13, 1864; Died of consumption at Point Lookout, MD, Jun. 13, 1864.

Edward Townsend   First Lieutenant; 18; Spencer, MA; Boot Packer; July 24, 1863–April 19, 1864 (–August 31, 1864); Formerly Corporal, Co. C, 25th MA Inf. Appointed First Lieutenant, Jul. 24, 1863; Discharged Apr. 19, 1864 (Aug. 31, 1864).

Mack Vail   Private; 20; Beaufort County, NC; Farmer; June 15, 1863–June 5, 1865; Mustered out of the service at Norfolk, VA, Jun. 5, 1865.

Jasper White   Private; 18; Norfolk, VA; Laborer; November 16, 1863–October 28, 1866; Mustered out with regiment.

George Whitehead   Private; 18; Pitt County, NC; Farmer; October 2, 1863–September 12, 1865; Died of chronic diarrhea at New Orleans, LA Sept. 12, 1865.

Richard Whitehead   Private; 20; Pitt County, NC; Farmer; August 28, 1863–April 13, 1864; Died of small pox at Point Lookout, MD, Apr. 13, 1864.

Ezra Wilkins   Private, Corporal; 23; Norfolk County, VA; Farmer; October 21, 1863–October 21, 1866; Appointed Corporal Oct. 4, 1866; Mustered out on expiration of enlistment, Oct. 21, 1866.

James Wilkins   Private; 41; Norfolk County, VA; Laborer; November 21, 1863–October 28, 1866; Mustered out with regiment.

James Williams   Private; 23; Nashville, TN; Laborer; October 17, 1863–February 14, 1864; Died of fever at Portsmouth, VA, Feb. 14, 1864.

John Williams   Private; 19; Norfolk, VA; Servant; October 21, 1863–October 21, 1866; Mustered out on expiration of enlistment, Oct. 21, 1866.

Isaac Willis   Private; 35; Essex County, VA; Farmer; June 21, 1864–June 5, 1865; Mustered out of the service at Norfolk, VA, Jun. 5, 1865.

Aaron Wright   Private; 22; Elm Grove, VA; Laborer; October 17, 1863–October 31, 1865; Discharged per Surgeon's certificate of disability at U.S. Gen. Hospital, New Orleans, LA, Oct. 31, 1865.

Cornelius Wright   Private; 26; Beaufort County, NC; Farmer; July 13, 1863–October 28, 1863; Discharged by order of the mustering officer, Oct. 28, 1863

Daniel Wright   Private; 18; Norfolk County, VA; Farmer; November 16, 1863–February 16, 1864; Died of pneumonia at Portsmouth, VA, Feb. 16, 1864.

William Wright   Private; 23; Essex County, VA; Farmer; June 21, 1864–; Absent in confinement serving sentence of Gen. Court Martial at the time of Muster of the regiment.

John Young   Private; 19; Norfolk County, VA; Farmer; November 18, 1863–September 29, 1864; Killed in action near Deep Bottom (New Market Heights), VA, Sept. 29, 1864.

## Company C

George F. Allen   Captain; 33; Ashby, MA; Worcester, MA; Carpenter; July 17, 1863–October 27, 1863; Formerly Private, Co. D, 25th MA Inf.; Appointed Captain, Jul. 17, 1863; Transferred to Co. D, Oct. 27, 1863.

Richard F. Andrews   Second Lieutenant; 27; Lynn, MA; Shoemaker; March 21, 1864–April 26, 1864; Formerly Sergeant, Co. C, 14th MA Inf (1st MA Hvy Arty).; Appointed Second Lieutenant, Mar. 21, 1864; Promoted First Lieutenant and transferred to Co. D.

Richard Barritt   Private; 34; Pitt County, NC; Farmer; September 1, 1863–May 27, 1864; Discharged from service on Surgeon's Certificate of disability at Point Lookout, MD, May 27, 1864.

Solomon Beasley   Corporal, Sergeant; 30; Plymouth, NC; Laborer; July 13, 1863–July 13, 1866; Mustered in as Corporal, Oct. 28, 1863; Promoted Sergeant, Feb. 6, 1864; Mustered out on expiration of enlistment, July 13, 1866.

Spencer Beasley   Private; 35; Plymouth, NC;

Laborer; July 13, 1863–November 16, 1864; Killed in the canal at Dutch Gap by a shell from the Rebel Mortar Battery, Nov. 16, 1864.

Ivory Beckton   Private; 19; Duplin County, NC; Farmer; July 8, 1863–July 8, 1866; Free on or before April 19, 1861; Mustered out on expiration of enlistment, July 8, 1866.

Moses Ben   Private, Corporal; 23; Northampton County, NC; Farmer; August 1, 1863–August 1, 1866; Promoted Corporal, July 14, 1866; Mustered out on expiration of enlistment, Aug. 1, 1866.

Daniel Blunt   Private, Corporal; 18; Edenton, NC; Farmer; September 22, 1863–September 22, 1866; Promoted Corporal July 14, 1866; Mustered out on expiration of enlistment, Sept. 22, 1866.

Hezekiah Blunt   Private, Corporal; 25; Halifax, NC; Farmer; July 13, 1863–July 13, 1866; Promoted Corporal, July 27, 1865; Mustered out on expiration of enlistment, July 13, 1866 .

George Boston   Private; 18; Plymouth, NC; Farmer; July 13, 1863–September 30, 1865; Free on or before April 19, 1861; Died of dysentery at Post Hospital, Brazos Santiago, TX, Sept. 30, 1865; Effects claimed by his brother David Pierce, Co. D.

Calvin Bowe   Private; 20; Pasquotank County, NC; Farmer; September 18, 1863–June 13, 1866; Free on or before April 19, 1861; Transferred from Co. B by order of Col. Draper, Sept. 18, 1863.

Alfred Bray   Private; 40; Norfolk, VA; Farmer; October 29, 1863–June 1, 1865; Deserted at Fort Monroe, VA, June 1, 1865.

William Briggs   Private; 23; Henrico County, VA; Laborer; April 15, 1865–October 28, 1866; Mustered out with regiment; Died Oct. 24, 1919.

Miles Britt   Private, Corporal, Sergeant; 35; Portsmouth, VA; Farmer; November 3, 1863–September 18, 1866; Promoted Corporal, Oct. 4, 1865; Promoted Sergeant, July 14, 1866; Died of cholera at Brazos Santiago, TX, Sept. 18, 1866.

Rush Brooks (Rush B. Garrett)   Private, Corporal; 28; Washington, NC; Farmer; September 23, 1863–September 23,1866; Promoted Corporal, July 14, 1866; Mustered out on expiration of enlistment, Sept. 23, 1866.

Willis Brown   Private; 20; Pitt County, NC; Farmer; September 13, 1863–September 13, 1866; Mustered out on expiration of enlistment, Sept. 13, 1866; Died Apr. 10. 1917.

John Bunyan   Private; 18; Plymouth, NC; Farmer; July 13, 1863–September 29, 1864; Killed at New Market Heights, VA, Sept. 29, 1864.

John H. Burris (Henry MacRae)   Private, Corporal, Sergeant; 29; Plymouth, NC; Farmer; September 22, 1863–September 22, 1866; Promoted Corporal, Feb. 10, 1866; Promoted Sergeant, July 14, 1866; Mustered out on expiration of enlistment, Sept. 22, 1866; Died July 20, 1910 at Blount's Creek, NC.

David Cherry   Private; 37; Bertie County, NC; Farmer; July 15, 1863–July 15, 1866; Mustered out on expiration of enlistment, July 15, 1866; Died Dec. 2, 1908.

Richard Cherry   Private; 40; Edgecombe County, NC; Farmer; September 7, 1863–October 10/11, 1864; Died from wounds received New Market Heights, VA (Sept. 29, 1864), Oct. 10/11, 1864.

Henry Clay   Private; 20; Whitford, NC; Farmer; October 31, 1863–October 28, 1866; Wounded at New Market Heights, Sept. 29, 1864; Wounded (and crippled for life) in the hand on Oct. 2, 1864 at Fort Harrison or Chaffin's Farm, VA while on duty throwing up a fort; Mustered out with regiment; Died Jan. 1, 1915 at Portsmouth, VA.

Allen Cooper   Private; 43; Murfreesboro, NC; Farmer; July 13, 1863–November 15, 1865; Discharged the service at Brazos Santiago, TX on Surgeon's certificate of disability with full set of arms and equipments $6.00 per Gen. Orders War Dept, Nov. 15, 1865.

Allen Crawford   Private; 19; Pitt County, NC; Teamster; September 18, 1863–September 18, 1866; Mustered out on expiration of enlistment, Sept. 18, 1866.

George Crayton (George W. Clayton)   Private; 18; Edenton, NC; Farmer; July 13, 1863–; Absent sick at hospital, Fort Monroe, VA since Apr. 24, 1865.

John Curry   First Lieutenant; 30; NY; November 18, 1864–February 23, 1865; Formerly First Sergeant, Co. E, 47th NY Inf.; Appointed First Lieutenant, Nov. 18, 1864; Honorably discharged Feb. 23, 1865.

John Custis   Private; 25; New Bern, NC; Farmer; November 13, 1863–June 13, 1865; Discharged the service at Fort Monroe, VA on Surgeon's certificate of disability, June 13, 1865.

Edward Davis   Private; 34; Richmond, VA; Laborer; April 15, 1865–October 28, 1866; Mustered out with regiment.

Nathan Dempsey   Private; 25; Elizabeth City, NC; Farmer; November 10, 1863–October 28, 1866; Mustered out with regiment; Died 1873 at Suffolk, VA.

Willis Dempsey   Private; 22; Elizabeth City, NC; Farmer; December 11, 1863–June 1, 1865; Wounded at New Market Heights (Sept. 29, 1864); Discharged the service at Balfour Gen. Hospital, Portsmouth, VA on Surgeon's certificate of disability, June 1, 1865.

Peter Downing   Private; 41; Lees Mills, NC; Farmer; July 13, 1863–February 10, 1865; Wounded at New Market Heights, Sept. 29, 1864; Discharged the service at U.S. Gen. Hospital at Philadelphia, PA on Surgeon's certificate of disability, Feb. 10, 1865; Died Jan. 4, 1910.

Joseph Eason   Private; 18; Perquimans County, NC; Farmer; June 28, 1863–January 10, 1866; Discharged the service from Hicks Gen. Hospital, Baltimore, MD on Surgeon's certificate of disability, Jan. 10, 1866; Died June 5, 1928.

James Ellison   Drummer, Private; 16; Martin County, NC; Mason; July 24, 1863–July 24, 1866; Mustered out on expiration of enlistment, July 24, 1866.

George T. Eskey (George L. Eskey/Robert DeWitt)   Private; 31; Bertie County, NC; Farmer; July 16, 1863–; Deserted from Fort Monroe Hospital when discharged and ordered to report to his regiment for duty, Dec. 24, 1865; Possibly served in U.S. Navy under the name 'Robert DeWitt.

Abner Farnshaw   Private; 21; Princess Anne County, VA; Farmer; October 31, 1863–October 28, 1866; Wounded at New Market Heights, VA, Sept. 29, 1864; Mustered out with regiment.

Alexander Fason   Private; 40; Northampton County, NC; Farmer; July 13, 1863–July 13, 1866; Mustered out on expiration of enlistment, July 13, 1866.

Jacob Fidget   Private; 26; Eastern Shore, VA; Laborer; November 5, 1863–October 28, 1866; Mustered out with regiment.

Edward Garrett   Private, Corporal, Sergeant; 32; Roanoke Island, NC; Sailor (U.S. Navy); September 22, 1863–September 22, 1866; Prior service in U.S. Navy; Promoted Corporal, Nov. 5, 1865; Promoted Sergeant, July 14, 1866; Mustered out on expiration of enlistment, Sept. 22, 1866. .

Edwin C. Gaskill   First Lieutenant; Mendon, MA; Farmer; June 19, 1864–October 22, 1864; Formerly Private, Co. B, 25th MA Inf.; Appointed Second Lieutenant, May 17, 1864; Promoted First Lieutenant and transferred to Co. H, July 11, 1864; Returned to Co. C, Jun. 19, 1864; Wounded at New Market Heights, Sept. 29, 1864; Promoted Captain and transferred to Co. A, Oct. 22, 1864.

Leonard T. Gaskill   First Lieutenant; 21; Mendon, MA; Farmer; March 4, 1864–April 19, 1864 (–August 31, 1864); Formerly Corporal, Co. B, 25th MA Inf.; Appointed Second Lieutenant, Aug. 6, 1863; Promoted First Lieutenant, Mar. 4, 1864; Discharged Apr. 19, 1864 (Aug. 31, 1864).

Daniel Goffigan   Private; 19; Eastern Shore, VA; Laborer; November 2, 1863–October 28, 1866; Detached with Paine's Division to Fort Fisher, Dec. 21, 1864; Mustered out with regiment.

James Grantly   Drummer, Private; 16; Elizabeth City, NC; Drummer; July 13, 1863–July 13, 1866; Mustered out on expiration of enlistment, July 13, 1866.

Jeremiah Gray (Jeremiah Walker)   Corporal, Sergeant, First Sergeant; 19; Martin County, NC; Farmer; July 13, 1863–July 13, 1866; Mustered in as Corporal; Promoted Sergeant, Nov. 15, 1863; Promoted First Sergeant, Mar. 20, 1864; Mustered out on expiration of enlistment, July 13, 1866; Died Apr. 24, 1905.

Robert Harris   Private; 28; Norfolk, VA; Farmer; November 5, 1863–October 28, 1866; Mustered out with regiment.

Charles Haskell   First Lieutenant; c 24; Ipswich, MA; Tinman; February 24, 1865–October 21, 1865; Transferred from Co. B, Feb. 24, 1865; Appointed Quartermaster, Oct. 21, 1865.

James Hassal   Private; 28; Williamston, NC; Laborer; July 13, 1863–July 13, 1866; Mustered out on expiration of enlistment, July 13, 1866.

Jasper Hassal (Jasper Hassell)   Private; 40; Plymouth, NC; Laborer; July 14, 1863–July 14, 1866; Mustered out on expiration of enlistment, July 14, 1866.

Belford Herring   Private; 23; Duplin County, NC; Teamster; July 8, 1863–February 13, 1865; Died of typhoid fever at Point of Rocks Hospital, VA, Feb. 13, 1865.

Charles Hill   Private, Corporal; 22; Plymouth, NC; Laborer; July 13, 1863–July 13, 1866; Promoted Corporal, Dec. 14, 1863; Reduced to ranks, Oct. 4, 1865; Mustered out on expiration of enlistment, July 13, 1866.

William Hoggard   Private; 23; Bertie County, NC; Sailor; July 13, 1863–July 13, 1866; Free on or before April 19, 1861; Mustered out on expiration of enlistment, July 13, 1866; Died Mar. 6, 1923.

Charles M. Horton   Private; 18; Edenton, NC; Waiter; October 10, 1863–December 4, 1863; Died of disease at Portsmouth, VA, Dec. 4, 1863.

Frank James   Private, Corporal, Sergeant, First Sergeant; 33; Martin County, NC; Waiter; September 22, 1863–September 22, 1866; Promoted Corporal, July 26, 1865; Promoted Sergeant, Nov. 5, 1865; Promoted First Sergeant, July 14, 1866; Mustered out on expiration of enlistment, Sept. 22, 1866.

Friley James   Corporal, Sergeant; 32; Plymouth, NC; Carpenter; July 13, 1863–May 1, 1866; Mustered in as Corporal; Promoted Sergeant, Apr. 6, 1866; Transferred to Co. D as First Sergeant, May 1, 1866.

John Jaycox   Private; 31; Plymouth, NC; Farmer; July 13, 1863–July 13, 1866; Engaged in the siege of Charleston, SC; Mustered out on expiration of enlistment, July 13, 1866.

Sawney Jaycox (Sawney Jacocks)   Corporal, Private; 25; Plymouth, NC; Laborer; July 13, 1863–July 13, 1866; Mustered in as Corporal; Reduced to ranks, Feb. 9, 1866; Promoted to Corporal June 28, 1866; Mustered out on expiration of enlistment, July 13, 1866.

John Jefferson   Corporal, Sergeant; 26; Bertie County, NC; Servant; July 13, 1863–July 13, 1866; Mustered in as Corporal; Promoted Sergeant, May 24, 1866; Mustered out on expiration of enlistment, July 13, 1866.

Weston Jenkins   Second Lieutenant; c 19; April 2, 1865–October 28, 1866; Appointed Second Lieutenant from civilian life; Reported for duty Apr. 2, 1865; Mustered out with regiment.

William H. Jenkins   Private; 18; Edgecombe County, NC; Farmer; July 25, 1863–July 25, 1866; Mustered out on expiration of enlistment, July 25, 1866.

Isaiah Johnson   Sergeant, Private, Corporal; 19; Elizabeth City, NC; Servant; June 28, 1863–June 28, 1866; Mustered in as Sergeant; Reduced to ranks, Apr. 6, 1866; Promoted Corporal, Apr. 10, 1866; Mustered out on expiration of enlistment, June 28, 1866.

Leonidas Johnson   Private; 42; Washington, NC; Farmer; July 13, 1863–June 13, 1865; Discharged the service at Fort Monroe Hospital, VA on Surgeon's certificate of disability, June 13, 1865.

Richard Joiner   Private; 30; Pitt County, NC; Farmer; September 1, 1863–September 20, 1864; Died of malaria at Base Hospital No. 18 at Point of Rocks, VA, Sept. 20, 1864.

Frederick Jones (Horace Jones)   First Sergeant, Private; 21; Jones County, NC; Farmer; July 13, 1863–July 13, 1866; Mustered in as First Sergeant; Reduced to ranks per Regimental Court Martial, Nov. 4, 1863; Mustered out on expiration of enlistment, July 13, 1866; Died Sept. 29, 1921 at Ennis, TX.

America Lann   Private; 21; Princess Anne County, VA; Farmer; October 26, 1863–March 21, 1864; Died of small pox at Point Lookout, MD, Mar. 21, 1864.

Henry Lee   Private; 20; Norfolk, VA; Laborer; November 5, 1863–June 16, 1864; Killed in action by guerrillas at Union Wharf (Richmond County), Rappahannock River, VA, Jun. 16, 1864.

James Linton   Private; 18; Hyde County, NC; Servant; October 10, 1863–October 17, 1866; Mustered out on expiration of enlistment, Oct. 17, 1866; Died in 1888 at Vandamere, NC.

John S. Mansur   First Lieutenant; c31; Monroe, ME; Houlton, ME; May 22, 1866–October 28, 1866; Transferred from Co. E, May 22, 1886; Mustered out with regiment; Died on Mar. 6, 1904 at Brooklyn, NY.

Rufus Mayo   Corporal; 29; Plymouth, NC; Laborer; July 13, 1863–July 13, 1866; Mustered in as Corporal; Wounded at New Market Heights, Sept. 29, 1864; Mustered out on expiration of enlistment, July 13, 1866; Also served in U.S. Navy; Died Dec. 1909.

Calvin McClenney   Private Corporal; 32; Nansemond County, VA; Cook; October 7, 1863–October 7, 1866; Free on or before Apr.

19, 1861; Wounded and crippled at New Market Heights, VA (Sept. 29, 1864); Promoted Corporal July 14, 1866; Mustered out on expiration of enlistment, Oct. 7, 1866; Died Feb. 12, 1911.

Joseph Mercer   Private; 18; Currituck County, NC; Farmer; November 2, 1863–October 28, 1866; Mustered out with regiment; Died Mar. 6, 1927 at Fentress, VA.

Henry Mills   Private; 18; Beaufort County, NC; Servant; August 10, 1863–February 2, 1864; Died of disease at Portsmouth, VA, Feb. 2, 1864.

Edward Mingo   Private; 35; Norfolk, VA; Farmer; October 29, 1863–October 28, 1866; Free on or before April 19, 1861; Mustered out with regiment.

Solomon Moore   Corporal, Sergeant; 30; Martin County, NC; Farmer; July 13, 1863–July 13, 1866; Promoted Corporal, Mar. 1, 1864; Promoted Sergeant, July 26, 1865; Mustered out on expiration of enlistment, July 13, 1866.

James Morse   Private; 29; Princess Anne County, VA; Farmer; July 13, 1863–July 13, 1866; Mustered out on expiration of enlistment, July 13, 1866.

Matthew Moye   Private; 31; Pitt County, NC; Farmer; October 1, 1863–October 1, 1866; Mustered out on expiration of enlistment, Oct. 1, 1866; Died Nov. 11, 1916 at Pactolus, NC.

John Norcum   Private, Corporal; 20; Chowan County, NC; Farmer; September 23, 1863–September 23, 1866; Promoted Corporal, July 14, 1866; Mustered out on expiration of enlistment, Sept. 23, 1866.

William H. Parker   Private; 25; Norfolk, VA; Farmer; November 5, 1863–October 28, 1866; Free on or before April 19, 1861; Mistakenly reported killed at New Market Heights, VA, Sept. 29, 1864; Mustered out with regiment.

Jacob Parris   Private; 30; Norfolk, VA; Farmer; November 5, 1863–October 28, 1866; Free on or before April 19, 1861; Mustered out with regiment.

Richard Peterson   Private; 21; Norfolk, VA; Farmer; November 5, 1863–October 28, 1866; Free on or before April 19, 1861; Mustered out with regiment.

Edward Phelps   Private; 19; Washington, NC; Servant; July 13, 1863–June 18, 1865; Wounded at New Market Heights, Sept. 29, 1864; Discharged at Fort Monroe Hospital, VA, June 18, 1865.

Sidney W. Phillips   First Lieutenant; c 24; Worcester, MA; Clerk; July 18, 1863–March 4, 1864; Formerly Corporal, Co. A, 25th MA Inf.; Appointed First Lieutenant, Jul. 18, 1863; Appointed Acting Quartermaster, Aug. 1863; Transferred to Co. F, Mar. 4, 1864.

Thomas Pitman   Private; 18; Orange County?, NC; Servant; September 15, 1863–September 15, 1866; Free on or before April 19, 1861; Mustered out on expiration of enlistment, Sept. 15, 1866.

William Powell   Private; 33; Bertie County, NC; Farmer; July 13, 1863–July 13, 1866; Free on or before April 19, 1861; Mustered out on expiration of enlistment, July 13, 1866; Also served in U.S. Navy on board *USS Crusader*; Died Dec. 15, 1915 at Philadelphia, PA.

John Pree (John Dupree)   Private; 20; Pitt County, NC; Farmer; May 1, 1866–July 20, 1866; Transferred from Co. D, May 1, 1866; Mustered out with regiment.

Andrew Pryor   Private; 21; Goochland County, VA; Laborer; April 15, 1865–October 28, 1866; Mustered out with regiment.

Isaac Robertson (Isaac Robinson)   Private; 18; Norfolk, VA; Drummer; July 14, 1863–July 14, 1866; Free on or before April 19, 1861; Mustered out on expiration of enlistment, July 14, 1866.

Ebenezer Rogers (Ebenezer Rodgers)   Private; 18; Plymouth, NC; Laborer; July 16, 1863–July 16, 1866; Mustered out on expiration of enlistment, July 16, 1866.

Moses Rogers (Moses Rodgers)   Private; 18; Plymouth, NC; Farmer; July 14, 1863–July 14, 1866; Mustered out on expiration of enlistment, July 14, 1866

James Rolack   Private, Corporal; 25; Plymouth, NC; Farmer; September 22, 1863–September 22, 1866; Promoted Corporal, May 24, 1866; Mustered out on expiration of enlistment, Sept. 22, 1866.

Joseph Rolack (Joseph Rollax)   Private; 25; Plymouth, NC; Farmer; July 13, 1863–July 13, 1866; Mustered out on expiration of enlistment, July 13, 1866; Died August 19, 1916 at Melville, LA.

Alfred Sessions   Private, First Sergeant, Sergeant; 20; Hertford County, NC; Farmer;

August 2, 1863–July 20, 1865; Promoted First Sergeant, Nov. 10, 1863; Reduced to Sergeant, Mar. 20, 1864; Died of phthisis pulmonalis at Gen, Hospital Fort Monroe, VA, July 20, 1865.

Grantson Sessions   Private, Corporal; 20; Hertford County, NC; Farmer; August 2, 1863–August 2, 1866; Promoted Corporal, July 14, 1866; Mustered out on expiration of enlistment, Aug. 2, 1866; Nephew of Alfred Sessions (above), address at Bethel, Hertford County, NC.

Aaron Shark   Private; 40; Plymouth, NC; Carpenter; July 13, 1863–May 27, 1864; Discharged from service at Point Lookout, MD on Surgeon's certificate of disability, May 27, 1864.

Samuel S. Simmons (DeForest)   Second Lieutenant; c 26; Buffalo, NY; August 4, 1864–January 23, 1865; Formerly Sergeant, Co. C, 5th NH Inf.; Appointed Second Lieutenant, Aug. 4, 1864; Serving on Brevet Brig. Draper's staff; Charged with desertion; Dismissed, January 23, 1865 (Real name believed to be "DeForest).

David Smith   Private; 29; New Bern, NC; Farmer; October 23, 1863–October 28, 1866; Paid at Fort Monroe Hospital for May & June, 1865 ($32.00); Mustered out with the regiment.

Stephen Sparrow   Private; 21; Princess Anne County, VA; Servant; October 31, 1863–October 28, 1866; Free on or before April 19, 1861; Mustered out with regiment

Simon Stewart   Private; 30; Plymouth, NC; Servant; July 13, 1863–July 13, 1866; Mustered out on expiration of enlistment, July 13, 1866; Died Jan. 30, 1908 at Plymouth, NC.

Isaac Tadlock   Private; 29; Bertie County, NC; Farmer; July 13, 1863–July 13, 1866; Mustered out on expiration of enlistment, July 13, 1866.

William H. Talbot   Private, Corporal; 19; Plymouth, NC; Farmer; November 13, 1863–September 2, 1866; Promoted Corporal, Aug. 5, 1866; Promoted to Commissary Sergeant and transferred to noncommissioned staff, Sept. 2, 1866.

Shadrick Tripp   Private; 18; Bertie County, NC; Farmer; July 14, 1863–July 14, 1866; Mustered out on expiration of enlistment, July 14, 1866; Died March 13, 1914 at James City, NC.

Henry Van   Private, Corporal; 21; Hertford County, NC; Farmer; July 13, 1863–June 24, 1865; Promoted Corporal, Feb. 20, 1864; Reduced to ranks; Discharged the service at Fort Monroe Hospital on Surgeon's certificate of disability, June 24, 1865.

Thomas Van   Private, Corporal, Sergeant; 33; Hertford County, NC; Farmer; August 11, 1863–August 11, 1866; Promoted Corporal, Feb. 6, 1864; Promoted Sergeant, July 14, 1866; Mustered out on expiration of enlistment, Aug. 11, 1866.

Prince Walker   Private; 30; Plymouth, NC; Laborer; July 13, 1863–May 27, 1864; Discharged from the service at Point Lookout, MD on Surgeon's certificate of disability, May 27, 1864.

Walter Washington   Sergeant; 25; Washington County, MD; Servant; July 13, 1863–October 22, 1865; Mustered in as Sergeant; Discharged the service at Brazos Santiago, TX on Surgeon's certificate of disability-with full set of arms & equipment ($6.00). Oct. 22, 1865.

Jackson Watson   Sergeant, Private; 35; Plymouth, NC; Laborer; July 13, 1863–January 4, 1865; Mustered in as Sergeant; Accidently shot, Jan. 30, 1864; Reduced to ranks, Feb. 6, 1864; Discharged from the service at Willets Point Gen. Hospital, NY on Surgeon's certificate — address (care of George Webb) at Elizabeth, NJ, Jan. 4, 1865.

Joseph Watson   Private; 28; Bertie County, NC; Farmer; August 1, 1863–September 18, 1865; Died of chronic diarrhea at Corps d'Afrique Hospital, New Orleans, LA, Sept. 18, 1865.

Rhodan Watson   Private; 38; Bertie County, NC; Farmer; July 13, 1863–June 13, 1865; Discharged the service at Fort Monroe Hospital, VA on Surgeon's certificate of disability, Jun. 13, 1865; Died Sept. 21, 1917 at Windsor, NC.

David G. White   Private, Corporal; 29; Plymouth, NC; Servant; July 13, 1863–March 18, 1864; Promoted Corporal, Feb. 20, 1864; Died of small pox at Norfolk, VA, Mar. 18, 1864.

Walter H. Wild   Captain; 27; Brookline, MA; March 11, 1864–August 14, 1866; Transferred from Co. E, Mar. 11, 1864; Serving on staff of Gen. E.A. Wild since May 1863; Mustered out the service on expiration of enlistment, Aug. 14, 1866; Died June 11, 1922 at Andover, MA.

Thomas Wilkinson   Private; 18; Washington, NC; Servant; July 20, 1863–March 6, 1865; Deserted from U.S. Gen. Hospital Summit House, Philadelphia, PA when laying there from wounds received at New Market Heights-(Sept. 29, 1864), Mar. 6, 1865.

Alexander Wilson   Private; 32; Plymouth, NC; Laborer; July 13, 1863–October 28, 1866; Wounded at New Market Heights, VA, Sept. 29, 1864; Mustered out with regiment; Died Nov. 14, 1919 at National Military Home, OH.

Peter Wilson   Private; 34; Bertie County, NC; Farmer; July 13, 1863–June 16, 1864; Killed in action by guerrillas at Union Wharf (Richmond County), Rappahannock River, VA, Jun. 16, 1864.

Bryant Winn   Private; 26; Bertie County, NC; Farmer; August 3, 1863–August 3, 1866; Mustered out on expiration of enlistment, Aug. 3, 1866.

Rolack Winn   Private; 18; Bertie County, NC; Farmer; August 3, 1863–August 3, 1866; Mustered out on expiration of enlistment, Aug. 3, 1866.

Johnson Wood   Private; 19; Fort Monroe, VA; Farmer; November 7, 1863–October 28, 1866; Free on or before April 19, 1861; Mustered out with regiment.

Harvey Young   Private, Corporal; 20; Fort Monroe, VA; Farmer; November 11, 1863–October 28, 1866; Promoted Corporal, July 14, 1866; Reduced to ranks, Aug. 14, 1866; Mustered out with regiment.

## Company D

John R. Adams   Private, Corporal; 25; Essex County, VA; Teamster; June 21, 1864–October 28, 1866; Promoted Corporal, Feb. 15, 1865; Mustered out with regiment.

George F. Allen   Captain; 33; Ashby, MA; Worcester, MA; Carpenter; October 27, 1863–April 19, 1864; Transferred from Co. C, Oct. 27, 1863; Discharged, Apr. 19, 1864; Died Apr. 16, 1915 at Rochester, MN.

Richard F. Andrews   Captain; c 28; Lynn, MA; Shoemaker; February 1, 1865–March 1, 1865; Promoted First Lieutenant from Second Lieutenant, Co. C, Apr. 26, 1864; Appointed Adjutant, May 30, 1864. Promoted Captain, Feb. 1, 1865; Transferred to Co. I, Mar. 1, 1865.

James B. Backup   First Lieutenant; 20; Roxbury, MA; Clerk; May 1, 1864–May, 30, 1864; Transferred from Co. I; Transferred to Co. F.

Amory O. Balch   Second Lieutenant; c 18; Roxbury, MA; Clerk; April 25, 1864–May 18, 1864; Transferred from Co. B, Apr. 25, 1864; Transferred to Co. K, May 18, 1864.

Alfred Battle   Private; 26; Tarboro, NC; Farmer; July 26, 1863–June 4, 1865; Discharged from the service by order of Secretary of War, Jun. 4, 1865.

Charles F. Bly   Second Lieutenant; 19; East Abington, MA; Cordwainer; November 27, 1864–March 18, 1865; Formerly Private, Co. A, 43rd MA (9 mos.); First Sergeant (white), Co. B, 37th USCT; Sergeant Major (white), F&S, 37th USCT; Appointed Second Lieutenant, Nov. 27, 1864; Transferred to Co. E, Mar. 18, 1865.

Alexander Brown   Private, Corporal; 22; Greene County, NC; Farmer; July 26, 1863–July 26, 1866; Promoted Corporal, Jul. 1, 1866; Mustered out on expiration of enlistment, July 26, 1866.

John Brown   Private; 21; Camden County, NC; Farmer; January 2, 1864–October 28, 1866; Mustered out with regiment.

Mina Brown   Private, Corporal; 24; Surry County, NC; Farmer; January 2, 1864–October 28, 1866; Promoted Corporal, Jul. 28, 1866; Mustered out with regiment.

John Buck   Private, Corporal; 23; Greenville, NC; Clerk; September 29, 1863–September 29, 1866; Promoted Corporal, Jan. 1, 1864; Mustered out on expiration of enlistment, Sept. 29, 1866.

John Bufort   Private, Corporal; 27; Currituck County, NC; Farmer; January 12, 1864–October 28, 1866; Promoted Corporal, Jul. 28, 1866; Mustered out with regiment.

Joseph Butts   Private; 25; Princess Anne County, VA; Farmer; January 12, 1864–October 28, 1866; Mustered out with regiment.

William Caffee   Private; 38; Norfolk, VA;

Farmer; August 15, 1863–April 11, 1865; Died of disease at Point of Rocks, VA, Apr. 11, 1865.

Asa Carr   Private; 25; Edgecombe, NC; Farmer; July 26, 1863–May 21, 1864; Died of diarrhea at U.S. Hospital, Alexandria, VA, May 21, 1864.

Glascoe Carr   Private, Corporal?; 24; Greene County, NC; Farmer; July 2, 1863–September 29, 1864; Died of wounds received in action at New Market Heights, VA, Sept. 29, 1864.

John W. Cherry   Private; 21; Bertie County, NC; Farmer; July 13, 1863–July 13, 1866; Mustered out on expiration of enlistment, July 13, 1866.

George Columbus (George C. Jones)   21; Charles City County, VA; Farmer; April 10, 1865–October 28, 1866; Mustered out with regiment.

William P. Corbin   Private, Corporal; 18; Essex County, VA; Waiter; June 2, 1864–September 17, 1866; Promoted Corporal, Jul. 28, 1866; Died of cholera at Brazos Santiago, TX, Sept. 17, 1866.

Smith Cornick   Private, Corporal, Sergeant; 23; Princess Anne County, VA; Farmer; January 12, 1864–September 5, 1866; Promoted Corporal, Dec. 10, 1865; Promoted Sergeant, Jul. 28, 1866; Died of cholera at Brazos Santiago, TX, Sept. 5, 1866.

Ander Dixon   Private; 21; Tarboro, NC; Laborer; July 26, 1863–July 26, 1866; Mustered out on expiration of enlistment, July 26, 1866.

Isaiah Dixon   Private; 24; Norfolk, VA; Preacher; January 2, 1864–October 28, 1866; Mustered out with regiment.

Algernon Draper   Captain; 19; Boston, MA; Laborer; March 1, 1865–October 28, 1866; Transferred as First Lieutenant from Co. F, May 30, 1864; Commanding Co. D since June 1, 1864; Promoted Captain, Co. D, Mar. 1, 1865. Mustered out with regiment; Died Mar. 14, 1874.

John Drury   Private, Sergeant; 47; Norfolk, VA; Carpenter; January 12, 1864–December 16, 1865; Promoted Sergeant, Feb. 6, 1864; Discharged the service at New Orleans, LA by reason of disability, Dec. 16, 1865.

John Eden   Private; 30; Norfolk, VA; Farmer; October 13, 1863–October 17, 1866; Mustered out on expiration of enlistment, Oct. 17, 1866.

Amos Fields   Private, Corporal; 26; New Bern, NC; Carpenter; July 26, 1863–July 26, 1866; Promoted Corporal, Jan. 23, 1866; Mustered out on expiration of enlistment, July 26, 1866.

Pleasant Fleming   Private; 19; Goochland County, VA; Farmer; April 10, 1865–May 30, 1865; Died of diarrhea at City Point, VA, May 30, 1865.

Alfred Fletcher   Private, Corporal; 25; Elizabeth City, NC; Farmer; October 17, 1863–October 17, 1866; Promoted Corporal, Jul. 28, 1866; Mustered out on expiration of enlistment, Oct. 17, 1866; Died Jan. 20, 1919 at Whitakers, NC.

Silas Foreman   Private; 19; Tarboro, NC; Waiter; July 26, 1863–July 26, 1866; Mustered out on expiration of enlistment, July 26, 1866; Died Apr. 18, 1926 at Jacksonville, FL.

Amos Franks   Private; 19; New Bern, NC; Blacksmith; July 26, 1863–June 17, 1865; Wounded at New Market Heights, VA, Sept, 29, 1864; Discharged the service by reason of disability, Jun. 17, 1865; Died May 15, 1917 at New York City, NY.

Franklin Frizzle (Frank Brown)   Private; 21; Greene County, NC; Farmer; July 26, 1863–July 26, 1866; Mustered out on expiration of enlistment, July 26, 1866.

James Futel   Private; 23; Northampton County, NC; Farmer; July 26, 1863–July 26, 1866; Mustered out on expiration of enlistment, July 26, 1866.

John Haddock (John Wilson)   Private; 19; Pitt County, NC; Farmer; October 18, 1863–October 17, 1866; Mustered out on expiration of enlistment, Oct. 17, 1866; Died Mar. 29, 1917 at Greenville, NC.

Frederick Hall   Private; 25; Norfolk, VA; Laborer; January 12, 1864–October 28, 1866; Mustered out with regiment.

Daniel Halstead   Private, Corporal; 18; Norfolk County, VA; Farmer; November 16, 1863–October 28, 1866; Promoted Corporal, Jul. 28, 1866; Mustered out with regiment.

Joseph Hanton (Joseph Harrington)   Private; 19; Pitt County, NC; Farmer; July 26, 1863–July 26, 1866; Mustered out on expiration of enlistment, July 26, 1866.

Nelson Hardy   Private; 26; Beaufort County, NC; Farmer; July 26, 1863–July 26, 1866; Mustered out on expiration of enlistment, July 26, 1866.

Peter Hardy   Private, Corporal; 18; Beaufort County, NC; Farmer; July 26, 1863–July 26,

1866; Promoted Corporal, Jul. 15, 1866; Mustered out on expiration of enlistment, July 26, 1866.

Tillman F. Hardy   Sergeant, Private; 25; Pitt County, NC; Farmer; July 26, 1863–July 26, 1866; Promoted Sergeant, Jan. 1, 1864; Reduced to ranks for disobedience of orders, Apr. 11, 1865; Promoted Sergeant, Jul. 15, 1866; Mustered out on expiration of enlistment, July 26, 1866.

Alfred Hart   Private; 19; July 26, 1863–; Absent sick in hospital since July 1, 1864.

Miles Hart   Private; 19; Greene County, NC; Farmer; July 26, 1863–July 26, 1866; Mustered out on expiration of enlistment, July 26, 1866.

Overton Harris   Private; 41; Essex County, VA; Farmer; July 21, 1864–March 25, 1865; Discharged from the service by reason of disability, Mar. 25, 1865.

Washington Hendley (Washington Henly)   Private; 20; Goochland County, VA; Farmer; April 10, 1865–October 28, 1866; Mustered out with regiment; Died Jan. 12, 1916 at Goochland, VA.

Abraham Hentz (Abram Hence)   Private; 18; Essex County, VA; Waiter; June 21, 1864–October 28, 1866; Mustered out with regiment; Died May 11, 1924.

John Herring   Private; 17; Norfolk, VA; Farmer; October 13, 1863–October 17, 1866; Mustered out on expiration of enlistment, Oct. 17, 1866; Died Feb. 26, 1916 at Norfolk, VA.

Everett Hicks   Private, Corporal; 18; Jones County, NC; Farmer; June 30, 1863–June 30, 1866; Mustered out on expiration of enlistment, June 30, 1866; Promoted Corporal, Aug. 1, 1865.

Charles Hodges (Charles Hagers)   Private; 18; Suffolk, VA; Farmer; November 21, 1863–October 28, 1866; Mustered out with regiment.

James Holliday   Private; 30; Pitt County, NC; Laborer; June 1, 1863–June 1, 1866; Mustered out on expiration of enlistment, June 1, 1866.

Henry Hurt   Private, Corporal; 20; Pitt County, NC; Farmer; July 26, 1863–June 23, 1865; Promoted Corporal, Feb. 15, 1865; Mustered out of service at Fort Monroe, VA, Jun. 23, 1865; Died Jun. 3, 1915 at National Soldiers Home, VA.

Friley James   First Sergeant; 32; Plymouth, NC; Carpenter; May 1, 1866–July 15, 1866; Transferred from Co. C, May 1, 1866; Discharged, July 15, 1866.

James Jenkins   Private; 22; Nashville, NC; Farmer; July 26, 1863–June 5, 1865; Wounded at New Market Heights, VA, Sept, 29, 1864; Mustered out of service at Norfolk, VA by order of Secretary of War, Jun. 5, 1865; Died Nov. 26, 1912 at Gatesville, NC.

Riley Jenkins   Private, Corporal; 21; Greene County, NC; Farmer; July 26, 1863–July 26, 1866; Promoted Corporal, Jul. 15, 1866; Mustered out on expiration of enlistment, July 26, 1866.

Moses Langley   Private; 30; Edgecombe County, NC; Farmer; July 26, 1863–November 5, 1865; Discharged on Surgeon's certificate of Disability at Brazos Santiago, TX, Nov. 5, 1865; Died Dec. 25, 1887.

Thomas Latney   Private; 22; Essex County, VA; Teamster; June 21, 1864–January 31, 1866; Discharged at Baltimore, MD for disability, Jan. 31, 1866; Died Jan. 11, 1917 at Tappahannock, VA.

Rubin Lee (Reuben Lee)   Private; 24; Gates County, NC; Farmer; January 5, 1864–October 28, 1866; Mustered out with regiment; Died Oct. 5, 1910.

Enoch Lewis   Private; 39; Halifax County, NC; Carpenter; July 26, 1863–July 23, 1865; Died of chronic diarrhea at U.S. Gen. Hospital at Fort Monroe, VA, July 23, 1865.

Patrick Lewis   Private; 20; Henrico County, VA; Farmer; April 11, 1865–October 28, 1866; Mustered out with regiment; Died May 26, 1932 at Ashland, VA.

Richard Lewis   Private; 20; New Bern, NC; Farmer; December 25, 1863–October 28, 1866; Mustered out with regiment.

George Middleton (George Griffin)   Private; 18; New Bern, NC; Waiter; August 1, 1863–August 1, 1866; Mustered out on expiration of enlistment, Aug. 1, 1866; Died May 16, 1903 at Goldsboro, NC.

Henry Middleton   Private; 21; Greene County, NC; Waiter; July 13, 1863–July 13, 1866; Mustered out on expiration of enlistment, July 13, 1866.

Henry Morgan   Private, Sergeant; 23; Raleigh, NC; Farmer; January 5, 1864–October 28, 1866; Promoted Sergeant, Jul. 28, 1866; Mustered out with regiment.

Moses Moore   Private; 45; Princess Anne

County, VA; Farmer; January 2, 1864–June 11, 1865; Mustered out of the service at Fort Monroe, VA by order of Secretary of War, Jun. 11, 1865

Alfred Northcut (Alfred Perry)   Private; 23; Bertie County, NC; Farmer; July 26, 1863–July 26, 1866; Mustered out on expiration of enlistment, July 26, 1866.

Saunders Norfleet   Private; 30; Bertie County, NC; Farmer; January 5, 1864–December 12, 1865; Wounded at New Market Heights, VA, Sept, 29, 1864; Mustered out of the service at Fort Monroe, VA, Dec. 12, 1865.

John O'Brien   Second Lieutenant; 30; Philadelphia, PA; New Orleans, LA; Laborer; June 7, 1864–August 13, 1864; Formerly Private, Co. B, 14th ME Inf.; Appointed Second Lieutenant, June. 7, 1864; Dismissed, Aug. 13, 1864.

Otis Oliver (Osea Wilson)   Private, Corporal; 18; Norfolk, VA; Farmer; November 25, 1863–October 28, 1866; Wounded at New Market Heights, VA, Sept, 29, 1864; Promoted Corporal, Jul. 28, 1866; Mustered out with regiment; Died Aug. 6, 1907.

John Owen (John Owens)   Private; 19; Henrico County, VA; Farmer; April 11, 1865–October 28, 1866; Mustered out with regiment.

Henry Parker   Private; 19; Pitt County, NC; Farmer; September 23, 1863–June 12, 1865; Transferred from Co. B, 36th USCT; Mustered out of the service at Norfolk, VA, Jun. 12, 1865.

Quiller Parker   Private; 21; Pitt County, NC; Farmer; July 26, 1863–July 26, 1866; Mustered out on expiration of enlistment, July 26, 1866; Died Oct. 12, 1916 at Eustis, FL.

William Parker   Private; Gates County, NC; Farmer; January 5, 1864–October 28, 1866; Wounded at New Market Heights, VA, Sept, 29, 1864; Mustered out with regiment.

Gray Paton   Corporal; 27; July 15, 1863–September 29, 1864; Killed at New Market Heights, Sept. 29, 1864.

William H. Paxton   Private; 19; Elizabeth City, NC; Cook; November 16, 1863–October 28, 1866; Mustered out with regiment.

George Perkins   Private; 38; Camden County, NC; Farmer; January 12, 1864–October 28, 1866; Mustered out with regiment.

Sidney W. Phillips   Captain; c 24; Worcester, MA; Clerk; April 27, 1864–September 20, 1864; Promoted from First Lieutenant, Co. F, Apr. 27, 1864; On detached service as ordinance officer; Discharged, Sept. 20, 1864.

Charles Pierce   Private; 33; Plymouth, NC; Farmer; July 26, 1863–August 16, 1866; Mustered out on expiration of enlistment, Aug. 16, 1866.

David Pierce   Private, First Sergeant, Corporal, Sergeant; 21; Plymouth, NC; Farmer; July 15, 1863–July 15, 1866; Promoted First Sergeant, Mar. 16, 1865; Reduced to ranks for disobedience of orders, Jul. 5, 1865; Promoted Corporal, Dec. 19, 1865; Promoted Sergeant, Dec. 28, 1865; Mustered out on expiration of enlistment, July 15, 1866.

Lewis Pollard   Sergeant; 21; Jones County, NC; Farmer; August 3, 1863–January 18, 1866; Appointed Sergeant, Sept. 20, 1863; Discharged for disability at Baltimore, MD, Jan, 18, 1866.

John Pree (John Dupree)   20; Pitt County, NC; Farmer; July 26, 1863–May 1, 1866; Transferred to Co. C, May 1, 1866.

Isaac Pritchett   Private, Sergeant; 23; Elizabeth City, NC; Farmer; January 12, 1864–October 28, 1866; Promoted Sergeant, Jul. 28, 1866; Wounded at New Market Heights, VA, Sept, 29, 1864; Mustered out with regiment.

Dempsey Randall (Dempsey Fernando)   Private; 20; Pitt County, NC; Farmer; July 26, 1863–July 26, 1866; Mustered out on expiration of enlistment, July 26, 1866.

Pinckney Raspberry   Private; 20; Greene County, NC; Farmer; July 26, 1863–July 26, 1866; Mustered out on expiration of enlistment, July 26, 1866; Died Aug. 14, 1910.

Richard Richmond   Sergeant; 24; Tarboro, NC; Farmer; July 26, 1863–July 26, 1866; Promoted Sergeant, Feb. 1, 1865; Mustered out on expiration of enlistment, July 26, 1866; Died Sept. 28, 1914 at Norfolk, VA.

Reuben Reddick   Private, Corporal; 25; Hertford County, NC; Farmer; September 30, 1863–September 30, 1866; Promoted Corporal, Jul. 28, 1866; Mustered out on expiration of enlistment, Sept. 30, 1866.

Calvin Roundtree   Corporal, Sergeant, First Sergeant; 18; Greene County, NC; Farmer; July 26, 1863–July 26, 1866; Appointed Corporal; Promoted Sergeant, May 1, 1865; Promoted First Sergeant, Jul. 15, 1866; Mustered out on expiration of enlistment, July 26, 1866; Died July 16, 1930 at Hermanville, MS.

Erias Roundtree   Private; 23; Pitt County, NC; Farmer; July 26, 1863–July 26, 1866; Mustered out on expiration of enlistment, July 26, 1866.

Hardy Roundtree   Private; 21; New Bern, NC; Farmer; July 26, 1863–July 26, 1866; Mustered out on expiration of enlistment, July 26, 1866.

George L. Seagrave   First Lieutenant; 26; Uxbridge, MA; Teacher; July 24, 1863–April 19, 1864; Formerly Private, Co. A, 25th MA Inf; Appointed First Lieutenant, Jul. 24, 1863; Discharged Apr. 19, 1864.

Peter Sewell   Private, Corporal; 25; Gloucester County, VA; Farmer; January 5, 1864–August 29, 1866; Promoted Corporal, Jul. 28, 1866; Died of cholera at Brazos Santiago, TX, Aug. 29, 1866.

Henry Scott   Corporal; 20; VA; Servant; September 30, 1863–May 21, 1865; Appointed Corporal at time of Muster in of regiment; Discharged for disability at White Hall Gen. Hosp., Bristol, PA, May 21, 1865.

Martin Smith   Private, Corporal, Sergeant First, Sergeant; 24; Suffolk, Nansemond County, VA; Farmer Laborer; January 5, 1864–October 28, 1866; Promoted Corporal, Aug. 1, 1865; Promoted Sergeant, Mar. 23, 1866; Promoted First Sergeant, Jul. 28, 1866; Mustered out with regiment.

Moses C. Smith   Private; 34; Pitt County, NC; Farmer; October 15, 1863–September 13, 1866; Died of cholera at Brazos Santiago, TC, Sept.13, 1866.

William H. Tan   Private; 18; Plymouth, NC; Waiter; July 26, 186–July 26, 1866; Mustered out on expiration of enlistment, July 26, 1866.

Robert Thomas   Private; 19; Martin County, NC; Farmer; July 26, 1863–July 26, 1866; Mustered out on expiration of enlistment, July 26, 1866.

Henry N. Thorburn (Harry N. Thorburn)   First Lieutenant; c23; Orange County, NY; Book Agent, Teacher; March 6, 1865–October 28, 1866; Transferred from Co. I, Mar. 6, 1865; Mustered out with regiment.

William M. Titcomb   Second Lieutenant; 18; Dedham, MA; Student; September 8, 1863–March 1, 1864; Formerly Private, Co. I, 35th MA Inf; Appointed Second Lieutenant, Sept. 8, 1863; Promoted First Lieutenant and transferred to Co. H, Mar. 1, 1864.

Alexander E. Wakefield   Second Lieutenant; 22; New Florence, PA; August 23, 1865–October 28, 1866; Formerly Private (Artificer), Co. B, U.S. Engineer Battalion; Appointed Second Lieutenant, Aug. 23, 1865; Mustered out with the regiment.

Joshua Waller (Joseph Barnes)   Private, Corporal; 20; Greene County, NC; Waiter; July 26, 1863–July 26, 1866; Promoted Corporal, Jul. 1, 1866; Mustered out on expiration of enlistment, July 26, 1866.

George War   Private; 33; Essex County, VA; Farmer; June 21, 1864–October 28, 1866; Mustered out with regiment

Ira White   Private; 20; Elizabeth City, NC; Farmer; January 2, 1864–October 28, 1866; Mustered out with regiment.

Jacob Whitfield   Sergeant, Private, Corporal; 25; Whitehall, NC; Waiter; July 13, 1863–July 26, 1866; Promoted Sergeant — reduced to ranks, Feb. 1, 1865; Promoted Corporal, May 15, 1865; Wounded at New Market Heights, VA, Sept, 29, 1864; Mustered out on expiration of enlistment, July 26, 1866.

Spencer Whitehouse; Private; 19; Princess Anne County, VA; Farmer; November 27, 1863–September 29, 1864; Killed in action at New Market Heights, Sept. 29, 1864.

Bristow Wilson; Private; 18; Norfolk, VA; Farmer; October 6, 1863–January 31, 1865; Died of Pneumonia at Point of Rocks Hospital, VA, Jan. 31, 1865.

Allen Wiggins   Private; 22; New Bern, NC; Farmer; July 26, 1863–July 26, 1866; Wounded at New Market Heights, VA, Sept, 29, 1864; Mustered out on expiration of enlistment, July 26, 1866.

Paul Wiggns   Private; 22; Gates County, NC; Farmer; January 5, 1864–October 28, 1866; Mustered out with regiment.

David Willey (David I. Willey)   Private; 40; Gates County, NC; Farmer; January 6, 1864–August 27, 1866; Died of cholera at Brazos Santiago, TX, Aug. 27, 1866.

Duke Williams   Private, Corporal, Sergeant; 26; Tarboro, NC; Farmer; July 26, 1863–July 26, 1866; Promoted Corporal, Feb. 1, 1864; Promoted Sergeant, Jul. 15, 1866; Mustered out on expiration of enlistment, July 26, 1866.

Frederic Williams   Private; 20; Washington, NC; Farmer; July 26, 1863–July 26, 1866; Mustered out on expiration of enlistment, July 26, 1866.

Granville Williams   Private, Corporal; 25; July 26, 1863–; Promoted Corporal, Feb. 1, 1864; Absent in hospital since Oct. 26, 1864; Reduced to ranks, July 1, 1866.

Irving Williams   Private, Corporal; 19; Greenville, NC; Farmer; July 26, 1863–July 26, 1866; Promoted Corporal Dec. 28, 1865; Mustered out on expiration of enlistment, July 26, 1866.; Died Jan. 25, 1910.

Thomas Willis   Private; 18; Richmond, VA; Laborer; April 11, 1865–October 28, 1866; Mustered out with regiment.

## Company E

Thomas Adams   Private; 23; Essex County, VA; Farmer; June 21, 1864–October 28, 1866; Wounded in action at New Market Heights, VA, Sept. 29, 1864; Mustered out with regiment.

Henry N. Adkins (Henry A. Nepean)   First Sergeant, Private; 20; New York City, NY; Gardner; September 1, 1863–May 1, 1864; Appointed First Sergeant at time of Muster in of the regiment; Reduced to ranks, Feb. 10, 1864; Promoted to Sergeant Major and transferred to noncommissioned staff, May 1, 1864.

Richard Adkins   Private; 32; Isle of Wight County, VA; Farmer; October 19, 1863–November 20, 1863; Died at Portsmouth, VA, Nov. 20, 1863.

Isaac Alexander   Private; 23; June 21, 1864–June 15, 1866; Discharged June15, 1866; Died Nov. 15, 1912.

George Alfred   Private; 21; Princess Anne County, VA; Farmer; November 24, 1863–January 22, 1866; Discharged on Surgeon's certificate of disability, Jan. 22, 1866.

Hiram W. Allen   Captain; c 27; Chelsea, MA; Clerk; September 3, 1865–October 28, 1866; Promoted from First Lieutenant, Co. G, Sept. 3, 1863; Mustered out with regiment.

George Ammit   Sergeant; 21; Farmer; August 1, 1863–April 4, 1864; Died of disease at Point Lookout, MD, Apr. 4, 1864.

William Armstead   Private; 18; Gloucester County, VA; Farmer; August 13, 1863–August 13, 1866; Wounded in action at New Market Heights, VA, Sept. 29, 1864; Mustered out on expiration of enlistment, Aug. 13, 1866.

Solomon Atwood   Private; 18; Princess Anne County, VA; Farmer; November 23, 1865–August 31, 1866; Wounded in action at New Market Heights, VA, Sept. 29, 1864; Died of cholera at Brazos Santiago, TX, Aug. 31, 1866.

Paul Baxter (Paul Bray)   Private; 22; NC; Farmer; November 12, 1863–October 28, 1866; Mustered out with regiment.

Alledy Bell   Private; 20; Camden County, NC; Farmer; August 13, 1863–August 13, 1866; Mustered out on expiration of enlistment, Aug. 13, 1866.

Charles F. Bly   First Lieutenant; c 20; East Abington, MA; Cordwainer; June 13, 1866–October 28, 1866; Transferred from Second Lieutenant, Co. D, Mar. 18, 1865; Promoted First Lieutenant, Jun. 13, 1866.; Mustered out with regiment.

William Bray   Private; 28; Currituck County, NC; Farmer; August 13, 1863–August 13, 1866; Mustered out on expiration of enlistment, Aug. 13, 1866.

John Brooks   Private; 18; Norfolk, VA; Farmer; December 14, 1863–May 20, 1865; Died of disease at Field Hospital, City Point, VA, May 20, 1865.

William H. Burton   Private, Sergeant; 21; Powhatan County, VA; Shoemaker; August 15, 1863–August 15, 1866; Promoted Sergeant, Sept. 15, 1863; Mustered out on expiration of enlistment, Aug. 15, 1866; Died Mar. 24, 1924 at Norfolk, VA.

Thompson Butler   Private; 27; Norfolk, VA; Cooper; November 20, 1863–October 28, 1866; Mustered out with regiment.

Alfred Canada   Private; 22; Duplin County, NC; Farmer; July 20, 1863–July 20, 1866; Mustered out on expiration of enlistment, July 20, 1866.

James Casey (James Cason)   Private; 32; Princess Anne County, VA; Farmer; January 13, 1864–October 28, 1866; Mustered out with regiment; Died Mar. 28, 1915 at Lynnhaven, VA.

Thomas Casey   Private; 21; Princess Anne County, VA; Farmer; November 24, 1863–

October 28, 1866; Mustered out with regiment.

Edward Charnhouse  Private; 47; Pasquotank County, NC; Farmer; August 13, 1863–August 13, 1866; Mustered out on expiration of enlistment, Aug. 13, 1866.

Anthony Collins  Private; 52; Norfolk, VA; Farmer; August 13, 1863–June 1, 1865; Wounded in action at New Market Heights, VA, Sept. 29, 1864; Discharged at Willets Point, NY, Jun. 1, 1865.

George Cooper  Private; 21; Norfolk, VA; Farmer; August 13, 1863–August 13, 1866; Mustered out on expiration of enlistment, Aug. 13, 1866.

Richard Cornice  Private; 18; Princess Anne County, VA; Farmer; August 13, 1863–February 3, 1864; Died of small pox at Portsmouth, VA, Feb. 3, 1864.

Peter Cornick  Private; 22; Princess Anne County, VA; Farmer; November 22, 1863–October 28, 1866; Wounded in action at New Market Heights, VA, Sept. 29, 1864; Mustered out with regiment.

Phillip Cornick  Private; 19; Princess Anne County, VA; Farmer; November 22, 1863–October 28, 1866; Mustered out with regiment; Died Jun. 28, 1914 at Portsmouth, VA.

Richard Cornick  Private, Corporal; 24; Princess Anne County, VA; Farmer; November 24, 1863–October 28, 1866; Promoted Corporal, Aug. 21, 1866; Mustered out with regiment.

Daniel J. Courtney  First Lieutenant; c 25; Newport, Wales; Brookline, MA; Student Clerk; May 22, 1866–June 13, 1866; Promoted First Lieutenant from Second Lieutenant, Co. K, May 22, 1866; Transferred to Co. K, June 13, 1866.

Thomas Covenant (Thomas Carrington)  Private; 34; Essex County, VA; Farmer; June 21, 1864–June 10, 1866; Died of dropsy at Post Hospital, Brazos Santiago, TX, Jun. 10, 1866.

Lazarus Cross  Private; 19; Gates County, NC; Farmer; August 13, 1863–August 13, 1866; Mustered out on expiration of enlistment, Aug. 13, 1866.

John J. Dangerfield  Private; 21; Essex County, VA; Farmer; June 21, 1864–January 31, 1866; Discharged at Baltimore, MD, Jan. 31, 1866.

Nelson Davis  Private; 32; Halifax County, NC; Farmer; December 13, 1863–October 28, 1866; Mustered out with regiment; Died Jan. 12, 1896 at Montgomery, AL.

Spain Davis  Private; 33; Halifax County, NC; Farmer; August 13, 1863–March 1, 1864; Died of disease at Portsmouth, VA, Mar. 1, 1864.

Thomas Davis  Private, Sergeant; 31; Northampton County, NC; Farmer; September 11, 1863–September 25, 1865; Promoted Sergeant, Feb. 1, 1864; Died of dysentery Corps d'Afrique Hospital, New Orleans, LA, Sept. 25, 1865.

William Davis  Sergeant, First Sergeant; 27; Halifax County, NC; Farmer; August 15, 1863–August 15, 1866; Appointed Sergeant, Aug. 18, 1863; Promoted First Sergeant, Feb. 12, 1864; Mustered out on expiration of enlistment, Aug. 15, 1866.

James Dixon  Private; 24; Pitt County, NC; Farmer; August 24, 1863–March 18, 1865; Discharged before Richmond, VA, Mar. 18, 1865.

Isaac Edwards  Private; 37; Southampton County, VA; Farmer; November 20, 1863–October 28, 1863; Mustered out with regiment.

Solomon Edwards  Private; 46; Isle of White, VA; Farmer; December 25, 1863–March 4, 1865; Wounded in action at New Market Heights, VA, Sept. 29, 1864; Discharged before Richmond, VA, Mar. 4, 1865.

Miles Fentress  Private, Corporal, Sergeant, First Sergeant; 22; Norfolk, VA; Farmer; December 12, 1863–October 28, 1866; Promoted Corporal, Jan. 1, 1864; Promoted Sergeant, Aug. 21, 1866; Promoted First Sergeant, Mustered out with regiment.

George Ferebee (George Furby)  Private; 21; Currituck County, NC; Engineer; August 13, 1863–August 13, 1866; Mustered out on expiration of enlistment, Aug. 13, 1866.

March Ferebee  Private; 20; Currituck County, NC; Engineer; November 20, 1863–October 28, 1866; Mustered out with regiment.

Mark Gordon  Private; 29; Camden County, NC; Farmer; January 30, 1864–August 3, 1864; Died of disease at Point Lookout, MD, Aug. 3, 1864.

Byron Gowns  Private; 22; Greenville, NC; Farmer; August 13, 1863–August 13, 1866; Wounded in action at New Market Heights, VA, Sept. 29, 1864; Mustered out on expiration of enlistment, Aug. 13, 1866; Post-war service in Co. C, 39th U.S. Inf.; Died May 9, 1915 at Homma, LA.

Felix Grassup   Private; 19; Fount Hill, VA; Farmer; June 21, 1864–; Absent sick at Fort Monroe, VA since, July 2, 1864.

Madison Grimes (Mattison Grimes)   Private; 19; Fount Hill, VA; Farmer; June 21, 1864–April 18, 1865; Wounded in action at New Market Heights, VA, Sept. 29, 1864; Discharged for disability at Portsmouth Grove, RI, Apr. 18, 1865; Died Feb. 5, 1919 at Portsmouth, VA.

Samuel Hall   Private; 21; Duplin County, NC; Farmer; July 20, 1863–July 20, 1866; Wounded in action at New Market Heights, VA, Sept. 29, 1864; Mustered out on expiration of enlistment, July 20, 1866.

Cornelius Harris   Private; 21; Princess Anne County, VA; Farmer; November 21, 1863–September 1, 1866; Died of cholera at Brazos Santiago, TX, Sept. 1, 1866.

Joseph J. Hatlinger   Captain; 27; Funfkirchen, Hungary; New Haven, CT; Medical Student; March 4, 1864–March 19, 1865; Formerly Sergeant Major, F&S, 5th RI Inf. (5th RI Hvy Art.); Appointed First Lieutenant, Oct. 27, 1863; Promoted Captain, Co. E, Mar. 4, 1864; Discharged, Mar. 19, 1865; Died Apr. 28, 1908.

Anthony Haynes   Private; 18; Princess Anne County, VA; Farmer; November 24, 1863–October 28, 1866; Mustered out with regiment.

George Haynes   Private, Corporal; 17; Princess Anne County, VA; Farmer; January 13, 1864–October 28,1866; Promoted Corporal, Aug. 21, 1866; Mustered out with regiment.

Frederick Henry (Frederick Henley)   Private; 21; Princess Anne County, VA; Farmer; November 24, 1863–October 28, 1866; Mustered out with regiment.

William Henry (Moses McCoy)   Private, Corporal; 18; Norfolk, VA; Waiter; August 13, 1863–August 13, 1866; Promoted Corporal, Jan. 1, 1864; Mustered out on expiration of enlistment, Aug. 13, 1866; Died May 26, 1927 at Hampton, VA.

George Hinton   Private; 21; August 13, 1863–February 15, 1864; Died at Portsmouth, VA, Feb. 15, 1864.

Joseph Hone   Private, Corporal, Sergeant; 21; Edgecombe County, NC; Farmer; August 21, 1863–August 21, 1866; Promoted Corporal, Sept. 10, 1863; Promoted Sergeant, Nov. 15, 1865; Mustered out on expiration of enlistment, Aug. 21, 1866; Died Dec. 17, 1916 at Chattanooga, TN.

Alexander Hubbard (Alexander Hubert)   Private; 35; Norfolk, VA; Farmer; August 13, 1863–August 13, 1866; Mustered out on expiration of enlistment, Aug. 13, 1866.

Africa Ives (Africa Allman)   Private, Corporal; 23; Norfolk, VA; Farmer; August 13, 1863–August 13, 1866; Promoted Corporal, Feb. 1, 1864; Mustered out on expiration of enlistment, Aug. 13, 1866; Died Jan. 28, 1917 at Norfolk, VA.

John Ives   Private; 22; Currituck County, NC; Farmer; August 13, 1863–November 6, 1865; Died of diarrhea at Post Hospital, Brazos Santiago, TX, Nov. 6, 1865.

Miles Ives   Private; 19; Norfolk, VA; Farmer; August 13, 1863–August 13, 1866; Mustered out on expiration of enlistment, Aug. 13, 1866.

George James   Private; 45; Norfolk, VA; Farmer; August 13, 1863–March 4, 1865; Discharged before Richmond, VA, Mar. 4, 1865.

Peter James   Private; 18; Gloucester County, VA; Sailor; August 13, 1863–July 17, 1866; Died of heart disease in Post Hospital at Brazos Santiago, TX, Jul. 17, 1866.

Gilbert Joiner (Gilbert Joyner)   Private, Sergeant; 21; NC; Farmer; August 28, 1863–August 28, 1866; Promoted Sergeant, Feb. 29, 1864; Mustered out on expiration of enlistment, Aug. 28, 1866.

Shedrick Land (Shadrack Land)   Private, Corporal; 21; Princess Anne County, VA; Farmer; November 24, 1863–October 28, 1866; Wounded in action at New Market Heights, VA, Sept. 29, 1864; Promoted Corporal, Aug. 21, 1866; Mustered out with regiment.

Charles Lauringhouse   Private; 21; Edgecombe County, NC; Farmer; August 21, 1863–September 29, 1864; Killed in action at New Market Heights, VA, Sept. 29, 1864.

Spencer Laws   Corporal, Private; 18; Lancaster County, VA; Waiter; August 10, 1863–August 10, 1863; Appointed Corporal, Sept. 1, 1863; Reduced to ranks; Promoted Corporal, Mar. 7, 1866; Mustered out on expiration of enlistment, Aug. 10, 1866.

John Lee (Jack Lee)   Private; 18; Camden County, NC; Farmer; August 13, 1863–August 13, 1866; Mustered out on expiration of enlistment, Aug. 13, 1866; Also served in

Co. G, 22nd USCT and post war service in Co. B, 39th U.S. Inf.

George Loomis (George Lomax)  Private; 46; Gloucester County, VA; Sailor; August 13, 1863–August 13, 1866; Mustered out on expiration of enlistment, Aug. 13, 1866.

John Malone  Private; 22; December 28, 1863–June 5, 1865; Discharged at Norfolk, VA, June 5, 1865.

John S. Mansur  First Lieutenant; 31; Monroe, ME; Houlton, ME; January 3, 1865–May 22, 1866; Formerly Private (Bugler), Co. E, 1st ME Cav.; Second Lieutenant, Co. H, 9th USCT; Appointed First Lieutenant, Jan. 3, 1865; Transferred to Co. C,, May 22, 1866.

Elijah McDonald  Private; 23; Duplin County, NC; Farmer; July 20, 1863–July 20, 1866; Mustered out on expiration of enlistment, July 20, 1866.

Johnson Mitchell  Private; 36; Essex County, VA; Farmer; November 24, 1863–October 28, 1866; Mustered out with regiment; Died Apr. 14, 1908 at Washington, DC.;

Charles Moore  Private; 21; Pitt County, NC; Farmer; August 13, 1863–August 13, 1866; Mustered out on expiration of enlistment, Aug. 13, 1866.

Isaac Northern  Private; 19; Currituck County, NC; Farmer; August 13, 1863–May 12, 1866; Discharged at Brazos Santiago, TX, May 12, 1866.

Aaron Parker  First Lieutenant; 30; Marlborough, NH; Worcester, MA; Carpenter; March 4, 1864–April 19, 1864; Formerly Corporal, Co. D, 25th MA Inf.; Appointed Second Lieutenant, Jul. 17, 1863; Promoted First Lieutenant, Mar. 4, 1864; Discharged, Apr. 19, 1864.

Hezekiah Parker  Private; 23; Pitt County, NC; Farmer; August 13, 1863–August 13, 1866; Mustered out on expiration of enlistment, Aug. 13, 1866.

Samuel Paton  Private; 30; Princess Anne County, VA; Farmer; November 27, 1863–October 28, 1866; Mustered out with regiment.

Marshall Pritchett  Private; 28; Camden County, NC; Farmer; January 13, 1864–June 27, 1866; Died of disease at Post Hospital, Brazos Santiago, TX, Jun. 27, 1866.

Charles Reddick  Private; 18; Isle of Wight County, VA; Farmer; August 13, 1863–August 13, 1866; Mustered out on expiration of enlistment, Aug. 13, 1866; Post-war service Co. C, 39th U.S. Inf. and Cos. A, I, 25th U.S. Inf.; Died Oct. 13, 1923 at Bedford, VA.

Robert Redmon  Private; 22; Norfolk, VA; Mason; August 13, 1863–August 13, 1866; Mustered out on expiration of enlistment, Aug. 13, 1866.

Richard Robbs  Private; 21; Essex County, VA; Farmer; June 21, 1864–October 28, 1866; Wounded in action at New Market Heights, VA, Sept. 29, 1864; Mustered out with regiment.

José A.A. Robinson  Second Lieutenant; c 18; NY; November 4, 1864–January 1, 1866; Transferred from Co. A, Nov. 4, 1864; Promoted First Lieutenant and transferred to Co. A, Jan. 4, 1866.

Joshua Scott  Private; 23; Norfolk, VA; Farmer; November 24, 1863–November 3, 1865; Died of chronic diarrhea on board steamer *Thomas Collyer* enroute from Fort Monroe, VA to Baltimore, MD, Nov. 3, 1865.

Clinton Shorter  Private; 18; Princess Anne County, VA; Farmer; April 14, 1864–September 1, 1866; Died of cholera at Brazos Santiago, TX, Sept. 1, 1866.

Ambrose Skinner  Private; 18; Edenton, NC; Farmer; August 13, 1863–August 13, 1866; Mustered out on expiration of enlistment, Aug. 13, 1866; Post-war service Co. B, 39th U.S. Inf. and Co. B, 25th U.S. Inf.; Died Apr. 28, 1922 at Phoenix, AZ.

John Simmons  Private; 27; Princess Anne County, VA; Farmer; November 24, 1863–October 28, 1866; Mustered out with regiment.

William H. Simpson  Private; 23; August 13, 1863–October 28, 1865; Wounded in action at New Market Heights, VA, Sept. 29, 1864; Discharged at Fort Monroe, VA, Oct. 28, 1865.

Richard Singleton  Private; 17; Richmond, VA; Farmer; July 31, 1864–October 28, 1866; Mustered out with regiment.

Burgess Small  Private; December 4, 1863–February 2, 1864; Died of small pox at Portsmouth, VA, Feb. 2, 1864; Buried in Hampton National Cemetery, VA (Plot 3487 as "B. Small").

Rhone Smithedge  Private; 20; Plymouth, NC; Farmer; May 14, 1863–May 14, 1866;

Wounded in action at New Market Heights, VA, Sept. 29, 1864; Mustered out on expiration of enlistment, May 14, 1866.

David Sparrow   Private; November 24, 1863–July 17, 1864; Died of drowning at Point Lookout, MD, Jul. 17, 1864.

Samuel Stanley   Private; 22; Beaufort County, NC; Sailor; August 24, 1863–August 24, 1866; Mustered out on expiration of enlistment, Aug. 24, 1866.

Richard Still (Henry Still)   Private, Musician; 17; September 22, 1863–July 31, 1864; Died of drowning in the Appomattox River at Point of Rocks, VA, Jul. 31, 1864.

Sandy Sykes   Private, Corporal, Sergeant, First Sergeant; 37; Norfolk, VA; Farmer; November 25, 1863–September 1, 1866; Promoted Corporal; Promoted Sergeant, Aug. 21, 1866; Promoted First Sergeant; Died of cholera at Brazos Santiago, TX, Sept. 1, 1866.

William Sylvester   Private; 18; Beaufort County, NC; Farmer; August 13, 1863–August 13, 1866; Mustered out on expiration of enlistment, Aug. 13, 1866.

Robert Taylor   Private, Corporal; 38; Hanover County, VA; Carpenter; August 13, 1863–August 13, 1866; Promoted Corporal; Mustered out on expiration of enlistment, Aug. 13, 1866.

John Thomas   Private; 23; Norfolk, VA; Farmer; August 13, 1863–August 13, 1866; Mustered out on expiration of enlistment, Aug. 13, 1866.

Peter Thomas   Private; 20; Portsmouth, VA; Farmer; August 13, 1863–March 4, 1865; Wounded in action at New Market Heights, VA, Sept. 29, 1864; Discharged before Richmond, VA, Mar. 4, 1865.

William H. Thomas   Private; 20; Isle of Wight County, VA; Farmer; August 13, 1863–August 13, 1866; Mustered out on expiration of enlistment, Aug. 13, 1866.

Isaac W. Thurlow   Second Lieutenant; c 20; Methuen, MA; Farmer, Hatter; June 1, 1864–December 10, 1864; Formerly Private, Co. F, 1st MA Hvy Arty; Private, Co. H, 32nd MA Inf.; Appointed Second Lieutenant, Jun. 1, 1864; Wounded at New Market Heights, Sept. 29, 1864; Promoted First Lieutenant and transferred to 107th USCT, Dec. 10, 1864.

Peter Vaughn   Private; 40; King and Queen County, VA; Farmer; August 13, 1863–August 13, 1866; Mustered out on expiration of enlistment, Aug. 13, 1866.

John Walston   Private; 30; Portsmouth, VA; Farmer; January 13, 1864–April 30, 1865; Died of disease at Gen. Hospital, Point of Rocks, VA, Apr. 30, 1865.

George Washington (George Hooker)   Private; 16; Washington, NC; Farmer; August 10, 1863–August 10, 1866; Mustered out on expiration of enlistment, Aug. 10, 1866; Post-war service Co. G, 39th U.S. Inf.; Died Oct. 7, 1926 at New Orleans, LA.

Thomas West   Private; 19; Bertie County, NC; Farmer; August 13, 1863–August 13, 1866; Mustered out on expiration of enlistment, Aug. 13, 1866.

Turner White   Private; 19; Pasquotank County, NC; Farmer; August 13, 1863–August 13, 1866; Wounded in action at New Market Heights, VA, Sept. 29, 1864; Mustered out on expiration of enlistment, Aug. 13, 1866.

John Whitehurst (John Whitest)   Private, Corporal; 35; Norfolk, VA; Farmer; August 13, 1863–; Promoted Corporal, July 1, 1864; Absent sick in hospital at Brazos Santiago, TX, Oct. 27, 1866; Died of dysentery, Nov. 1, 1866.

Griffin Whitlin (Griffin Whitler)   Private; 27; Fount Hill, Essex County, VA; Farmer; June 21, 1864–July 10, 1864; Deserted near Point of Rocks, VA, Jul. 10, 1864.

Spencer Wiggins   Private; 22; Pitt County, NC; Farmer; August 13, 1863–August 13, 1866; Mustered out on expiration of enlistment, Aug. 13, 1866.

Walter H. Wild   Captain; 27; Brookline, MA; August 14, 1863–March 4, 1864; Formerly First Lieutenant, Co. K, 54th MA Inf.; Appointed Captain, Aug. 14, 1863; Serving on staff of Brig. Gen. Wild since May 1863; Transferred to Co. C, Mar. 4, 1864.

John Williams   Private; 19; Pasquotank County, NC; Farmer; August 13, 1863–June 7, 1865; Discharged at White Hall, PA, Jun. 7, 1865.

March Williams   Private; 23; Norfolk, VA; Farmer; December 18, 1863–September 1, 1866; Died of cholera at Post Hospital, Brazos Santiago, TX, Sept. 1, 1866.

Sandy Williams   Private, Corporal; 19; Martin County, NC; Farmer; August 13, 1863–August 13, 1866; Promoted Corporal, Nov. 27, 1865; Mustered out on expiration of enlistment, Aug. 13, 1866; Died Nov. 14, 1910.

William Williams   Private; 21; Essex County, VA; Farmer; June 21, 1864–October 28, 1866; Mustered out with regiment; Died Sept. 16, 1910 at Lloyds, VA.

Encoh Wilson   Private; 24; Chowan County, NC; Farmer; December 10, 1863–October 28, 1866; Promoted Corporal, Aug. 1864; Promoted Sergeant, Aug. 21, 1866; Mustered out with regiment.

James Wilson   Private; 34; Norfolk, VA; Farmer; December 10, 1863–October 28, 1866; Mustered out with regiment.

America Woodis   Private; 28; Norfolk, VA; Farmer; December 1, 1863–June 25, 1865; Mustered out at Fort Monroe, VA, Jun. 26, 1865; Died Jan. 18, 1913.

Oliver Young   Private, Sergeant; 23; Norfolk, VA; Farmer; August 13, 1863–August 13, 1866; Promoted Sergeant, Feb. 1, 1864; Mustered out on expiration of enlistment, Aug. 13, 1866.

Priestly Young   First Lieutenant; 44; Schenectady, NY; Worcester, MA; Merchant; April 27, 1864–October 15, 1864; Formerly Corporal, Co. D, 15th MA Inf.; Appointed Second Lieutenant, Feb. 1864; Promoted First Lieutenant, Apr. 27, 1864; Discharged for disability, Oct. 15, 1864; Died Mar. 6, 1893 at Worcester, MA.

## Company F

Edmund Allen   Private; 21; Goochland County, VA; Laborer; April 11, 1865–October 28, 1866; Mustered out with regiment.

John Allen   Private; 18; Goochland County, VA; Laborer; April 11, 1865–October 28, 1866; Mustered out with regiment.

Willis Amsey (Willis A. Mundon)   Private; 19; Princess Anne County, VA; Farmer; December 12, 1863–June 23, 1865; Mustered out at Fort Monroe, VA, June 23, 1865.

Marshall Anderson   Private; 45; Pitt County, NC; Farmer; August 23, 1863–October 8, 1863; Died of typhoid pneumonia at Regimental Hospital, October 8, 1863; Never mustered.

Lindsey Babley (Lindsey Beverly)   Private, Corporal, Sergeant, First Sergeant; 18; Essex County, VA; Farmer; June 21, 1864–October 28, 1866; Promoted Corporal, July 24, 1866; Promoted Sergeant, Sept. 22, 1866; Promoted First Sergeant, Sept. 23, 1866; Mustered out with regiment.

William Babley   Private; 22; Essex County, VA; Laborer; June 21, 1864–July 7, 1864; Deserted at Point of Rocks, VA, July 7, 1864.

James B. Backup   First Lieutenant; 20; Roxbury, MA; Clerk; May 30, 1864–July 1864; Formerly Private, Co. B, 39th MA Inf.; Appointed Second Lieutenant, Aug. 13, 1863; Transferred to Co. I, Nov. 1863; Transferred as First Lieutenant from Co. D, May 30, 1864: Transferred to Co. I, Aug. 12, 1864.

Albert Banks   Private, Corporal; 27; Southampton County, VA; Farmer; October 29, 1863–October 28, 1866; Wounded at New Market Heights, VA, Sept. 29, 1864; Promoted Corporal, Aug. 31, 1866; Mustered out with regiment; Died Nov. 16, 1915 at Suffolk, VA.

Jerry Banks   Private; 20; Pasquotank County, NC; Farmer; December 1, 1863–October 28, 1866; Mustered out with regiment.

Charles W. Barnett   Private; 23; Princess Anne County, VA; Farmer; December 1, 1863–October 28, 1866; Mustered out with regiment.

Stewart Bell   Corporal, Private; 22; Halifax County, NC; Farmer; September 11, 1863–September 11, 1866; Appointed Corporal, Sept. 3, 1863; Reduced to ranks, Sept. 12, 1865; Promoted Corporal, Dec. 21, 1865; Mustered out on expiration of enlistment, Sept. 11, 1866.

Ephraim Bember   Private; 21; Bertie County, NC; Farmer; October 27, 1863–January 27, 1864; Died of heart disease at U.S. Gen. Hospital, Portsmouth, VA, Jan. 27, 1864.

Leon Bember   Private; 20; Chowan County, NC; Farmer; August 24, 1863–August 24, 1866; Mustered out on expiration of enlistment, Aug. 24, 1866; Died June 9, 1918 at Elizabeth City, NC.

David Berry   Private; 20; Hertford, NC; Servant; December 10, 1863–May 25, 1865; Discharged at City Point, VA, May 25, 1865.

Henry Blunt   Private; 36; Chowan County, NC; Farmer; August 7, 1863–August 7, 1866; Mustered out on expiration of enlistment, Aug. 7, 1866.

George W. Bowser  Private; 25; Currituck County, NC; Farmer; August 26, 1863–August 26, 1866; Free on or before April 19, 1861; Mustered out on expiration of enlistment, Aug. 26, 1866.

Thomas Braxton  Private; 25; Richmond, VA; Farmer; June 21, 1864–June 12, 1865; Mustered out at Fort Monroe, VA, June 12, 1865 (Patient in U.S. Gen. Hospital, Fort Monroe, VA).

Isaac Brinkley  Private; Died of heart disease at Regimental Hospital; Never mustered.

James Brooks  Private; 20; Martin County, NC; Farmer; August 25, 1863–August 25, 1866; Free on or before April 19, 1861; Mustered out on expiration of enlistment, Aug. 25, 1866.

Jesse Brooks  Private; 21; Martin County, NC; Farmer; July 13, 1863–February 4, 1864; Discharged on Surgeon's certificate of disability, Feb. 4, 1864.

Charles Brown  Private; 18; Washington, DC; Drummer; August 22, 1863–May 21, 1866; Dishonorably discharged from service by order of Gen. Court Martial and sentenced to five years imprisonment at the Dry Tortugas, FL with loss of all pay and allowances, May 21, 1866.

Jonas Capps  Private; 22; Princess Anne County, VA; Farmer; September 11, 1863–October 19, 1864; Died of wounds received in action at New Market Heights (Sept. 29, 1864) at U.S. Gen. Hospital, Fort Monroe, VA, Oct.19, 1864.

Edward Carr  Private; 25; Edgecombe County, NC; Farmer; August 17, 1863–August 17, 1866; Mustered out on expiration of enlistment, Aug. 17, 1866.

David Cartwright  Private, Corporal; 18; Pasquotank County, NC; Farmer; November 24, 1863–October 28, 1866; Promoted Corporal, Aug. 31, 1866; Mustered out with regiment.

Thomas J. Cate  First Lieutenant; 34; Effingham, NH; Lawrence, MA; April 24, 1864–August 12, 1864; Formerly First Lieutenant, 16th U.S. Inf.; Serving the majority of time on detached service with the Commissary Department; Transferred to Co. I, Aug. 12, 1864.

Toby Cornick  Private; 20; Norfolk, VA; Farmer; December 5, 1863–October 28, 1866; Mustered out with regiment.

William H. Crocker  Private, Corporal; 23; Petersburg, VA; Farmer; August 13, 1863–July 8, 1866; Free on or before April 19, 1861; Promoted Corporal, Oct. 11, 1864; Reduced to ranks, Dec. 21, 1865; Promoted Principal Musician and transferred to noncommissioned staff, Jul. 8, 1866.

John Cromwell  Private, Corporal; 22; Norfolk, VA; Farmer; December 4, 1863–October 28, 1866; Free on or before April 19, 1861; Promoted Corporal, Aug. 31, 1866; Mustered out with regiment.

Lewis Curtis  Private, Corporal; 23; Greenville, NC; Farmer; August 13, 1863–January 1, 1865; Promoted Corporal, Oct. 2, 1864; Died of effects of irritative fever of gunshot wound (received Dec. 10, 1864), U.S. Gen. Hospital, Fort Monroe, VA, Jan. 1, 1865.

Edward H. Davis  Second Lieutenant; c 26; Marshfield, MA; Stitcher Shoemaker; March 28, 1865–January 1, 1866; Formerly Private, Co. K, 3rd MA Hvy Arty.; Appointed Second Lieutenant, Mar. 28, 1865; Serving on headquarters staff, 2nd Brig, 3rd Div, 25th AC, July 11, 1865; Resigned Jan 1, 1866. Died Sept. 3, 1912 at Worcester, MA.

Miles Davis  Private; 18; Chowan County, NC; Farmer; October 19, 1863–August 9, 1865; Died of scurvy at U.S. Gen. Hospital, Brazos Santiago, TX, Aug. 9, 1865.

Walter Dealt  Private; 22; Isle of Wight, VA; Farmer; September 1, 1863–September 1, 1866; Mustered out on expiration of enlistment, Sept. 1, 1866.

Thomas Dowdy  Private; 35; Currituck County, NC; Farmer; August 24, 1863–August 24, 1866; Mustered out on expiration of enlistment, Aug. 24, 1866.

James Dozier  Private; 19; Princess Anne County, VA; Farmer; August 13, 1863–August 13, 1866; Mustered out on expiration of enlistment, Aug. 13, 1866.

Valentine Dozier  Private; 45; Norfolk, VA; Farmer; August 24, 1863–February 3, 1864; Died of small pox at Pest House, Norfolk, VA, Feb. 3, 1864.

Algernon Draper  First Lieutenant; 18; Boston, MA; Laborer; April 27, 1864–May 30, 1864; Promoted from Second Lieutenant, Co. K, Apr. 27, 1864; Transferred to Co. D, May 30, 1864.

Hardy Ebon  Private; 21; Washington, NC; Farmer; August 22, 1863–August 30, 1864;

Died from wounds received by explosion of enemy's shell on company line — second line of breastworks in the trenches before Petersburg (Aug. 13, 1864) at Summit House Gen. Hospital Philadelphia, PA, Aug. 30, 1864.

Richard Etheridge   Sergeant; 21; Roanoke Island, NC; Farmer; September 2, 1863–July 20, 1866; Appointed Sergeant, Sept. 9, 1863; Promoted Commissary Sergeant and transferred to noncommissioned staff, July 20, 1866.

Henry M. Field   First Lieutenant; 23; Southwick, MA; Farmer Student; September 15, 1865–October 28, 1866; Promoted from Second Lieutenant, Co. B, Sept. 15, 1865; Mustered out with regiment; Died Dec. 17, 1907 at Brownsville, TX.

Joseph Foreman   Private; 38; Norfolk, VA; Farmer; January 4, 1864–October 28, 1866; Mustered out with regiment.

Valincourt Gaines   Private; 27; Essex County, VA; Farmer; June 21, 1864–October 28, 1866; Mustered out with regiment; Died May 12, 1909.

Joseph Gallop   Private; 18; Currituck County, NC; Farmer; August 24, 1863–August 24, 1866; Mustered out on expiration of enlistment, Aug. 24, 1866.

Simon Gaylord   Private; 23; Washington, NC; Merchant; September 18, 1863–September 29, 1864; Killed at New Market Heights, VA, Sept. 29, 1864.

Samuel Gregory, 1st   Private; 18; Perquimans County, NC; Farmer; October 19, 1863–May 17, 1865; Wounded at New Market Heights, VA, Sept. 29, 1864; Discharged from the service at Portsmouth Grove, RI (U.S. Gen. Hospital) on Surgeon's certificate of disability, May 17, 1865.

Samuel Gregory, 2nd   Private; 22; Perquimans County, NC; Farmer; December 14, 1863–September 29, 1864; Killed at New Market Heights, VA, Sept. 29, 1864.

Zachery Gregory   Private; 21; Currituck County, NC; Government Employee; August 13, 1863–August 17, 1864; Killed by a shell from the enemy in the evening in camp near Petersburg, VA, Aug. 17, 1864.

Charles Grey   Private, Corporal; 19; Onslow County, NC; Teamster; December 5, 1863–October 28, 1866; Promoted Corporal, Aug. 31, 1866; Mustered out with regiment.

Joseph Griffin   Private; 20; Pasquotank County, NC; Farmer; September 12, 1863–September 12, 1866; Free on or before April 19, 1861; Mustered out on expiration of enlistment, Sept. 1, 1866; Died Feb. 17, 1906 at South Mills, NC.

Owen Harris   Private; 28; Princess Anne County, VA; Farmer; December 4, 1863–October 28, 1866; Wounded at New Market Heights, VA, Sept. 29, 1864; Mustered out with regiment; Died Sept. 23, 1871.

William Harrison   Private; 21/18; Westmoreland County, VA; Laborer; June 21, 1864–; Absent with wounded knee-never heard from, Aug. 14, 1864.

Stephen H. Hathaway   Second Lieutenant; 29; Salem, MA, Beverly, MA; Milkman; January 20, 1865–February 27, 1865; Formerly Private, Co. C 14th MA Inf. (1st MA Hvy Arty); Appointed Second Lieutenant, Jan. 20, 1865; Transferred to Co. G, Feb. 27, 1865.

Oren A. Hendrick   Captain; c 26; Agawam, MA; East Long Meadow, MA; Jeweler/Gold China Maker; November 26, 1864–July 19, 1866; Formerly Sergeant Co. F, 19th MA Inf. and First Lieutenant, 37th USCT; Appointed Captain, Nov. 26, 1864; Promoted Major, Jul. 19, 1866.

Miles Hews (Miles Hughes)   Private; 18; Suffolk, VA; Farmer; August 27, 1863–August 27, 1866; Mustered out on expiration of enlistment, Aug. 27, 1866.

Harvey Hill   Private; 23; Camden County, NC; Farmer; November 18, 1863–October 28, 1866; Free on or before April 19, 1861; Mustered out with regiment.

Miles Holloway   Private, Corporal, Sergeant; 25; Pasquotank County, NC; Farmer; December 1, 1863–October 28, 1866; Promoted Corporal, Jan. 15, 1865; Promoted Sergeant, Aug. 31, 1866; Mustered out with regiment.

Robert Hunter   Private; 20; Princess Anne County, VA; Farmer; December 3, 1863–October 28, 1866; Mustered out with regiment.

George W. Ives   Captain; 41; Westfield, MA; Printer; July 7, 1863–November 27, 1863; Formerly, Sergeant, Co. K, 46th MA Inf.; Appointed Captain, Jul. 7, 1863; Dismissed, Nov. 27, 1863.

John James (James Minton)   Corporal, Private; 21; Norfolk, VA; Teamster; September 15, 1863–September 15, 1866; Appointed Corporal, Sept. 3, 1863; Reduced to ranks, July 1864; Mustered out on expiration of enlistment, Sept. 15, 1866; Died Oct. 4, 1914 at Atoka, OK.

Clayborn Johnson (Clairborne Johnson)   Private; 19; New Kent County, VA; Laborer; April 6, 1865–October 28, 1866; Mustered out with regiment; Died Dec. 17, 1932 at Altheimer, AK.

William H. Johnson   First Sergeant, Private; 22; Bromly, VA; Hostler; July 13, 1863–July 13, 1866; Born free; Appointed First Sergeant, Sept. 9, 1863; Reduced to ranks, Nov. 16, 1864; Mustered out on expiration of enlistment, July 13, 1866.

Henry Jones   Private; 21; Edenton, NC; Farmer; November 2, 1863–August 20, 1864; Died of wounds received (Aug. 13, 1864) by the bursting of a shell in trenches before Petersburg, VA at Summit House Hospital, Philadelphia, PA, Aug. 20, 1864.

Nixon Keaton   Private, Corporal; 25; Pasquotank County, NC; December 1, 1863–October 28, 1866; Promoted Corporal, Aug. 31, 1866; Mustered out with regiment; Died Dec. 5, 1913 at Elizabeth City, NC.

Benjamin F. Kinsley   First Lieutenant; c 22; Salem, MA; Clerk; January 18, 1864–March 4, 1864; Transferred from Co. A, Jan. 18, 1864; Transferred to Co. G, Mar. 4, 1864.

Nicholas Langley   Sergeant, Private; 20; Kempsville, VA; Farmer; August 13, 1863–August 13, 1866; Appointed Sergeant, Sept. 9, 1863; Reduced to ranks, Feb. 5, 1866; Mustered out on expiration of enlistment, Aug. 13, 1866; Died Mar. 6, 1923 at Norfolk, VA.

Moses Land   Private; 18; Princess Anne County, VA; Laborer; August 13, 1863–August 13, 1866; Mustered out on expiration of enlistment, Aug. 13, 1866; Died Aug. 30, 1919 at Lynnhaven, VA.;

John Lee   Private; 18; Plymouth, NC; Farmer; November 13, 1863–October 28, 1866; Mustered out with regiment; Died May 19, 1920 at Durant's Neck, NC.

Joseph G. Longley   First Lieutenant; 40; Hawley, MA; Westborough, MA; Teacher; September 25, 1863–January 18, 1864; Formerly Corporal, Co. C, 51st MA Inf. (9 mos.); Appointed First Lieutenant, Sept. 25, 1863; Transferred to Co. A, Jan. 18, 1864.

Henry Martin   Private, Corporal, Sergeant; 19; Tyrell County, NC; Farmer; August 24, 1863–August 24, 1866; Promoted Corporal, Oct. 1, 1864; Promoted Sergeant, Feb. 8, 1866; Mustered out on expiration of enlistment, Aug. 24, 1866; Died Feb. 24, 1921 at Elizabeth City, NC.

Ceaser McCausey   Private; Died of bilious fever at Portsmouth, VA, Oct. 27, 1863; Never mustered.

Jared McClair (Jerry McClair)   Second Lieutenant; c 35; Moscow, NY; July 25, 1863–April 19, 1864; Formerly Corporal, 24th Battery, NY Lgt Arty.; Appointed Second Lieutenant, Jul. 25, 1863; Discharged, Apr. 19, 1864.

Roderick McCoy   Private; 21; Westmoreland County, VA; Farmer; April 1, 1864–September 29, 1864; Killed at New Market Heights, VA, Sept. 29, 1864.

Andrew Messer   Private; 30; Camden County, NC; Farmer; December 24, 1863–October 28, 1866; Free on or before April 19, 1861; Mustered out with regiment; Died Dec. 29, 1915 at Belvidere, NC.

Field Midget   Corporal; 23; Currituck County, NC; Farmer; August 28, 1863–August 28, 1866; Appointed Corporal, Sept. 3, 1863; Mustered out on expiration of enlistment, Aug. 28, 1866; Died Jun. 28, 1912 at Manteo, NC.

Lawrence Midget   Corporal; 24; Currituck County, NC; Farmer; August 26, 1863–August 16, 1864; Appointed Corporal, Sept. 3, 1863; Killed on the second line in the trenches before Petersburg, VA by a bullet from enemy's sharpshooters or pickets, Aug. 16, 1864.

Riley Midget   Private; 18; Currituck County, NC; Fisherman; August 24, 1863–August 24, 1866; Wounded at New Market Heights, VA, Sept. 29, 1864; Mustered out on expiration of enlistment, Aug. 24, 1866; Died Apr. 20, 1918.

Walter Milten   Corporal, First Sergeant; 18; Suffolk, VA; Farmer; July 13, 1863–July 13, 1866; Appointed Corporal, Sept. 3, 1863; Promoted First Sergeant, Nov. 16, 1864; Mustered out on expiration of enlistment, July 13, 1866.

John H. Mines (John H. De Mines)   Private; 18; St. Mary's County, MD; Farmer; May 24, 1864–October 28, 1866; Mustered out with regiment; Died Dec. 23, 1926 at Baltimore, MD.

Aaron Mitchell  Corporal; 29; Pasquotank County, NC; Servant; September 29, 1863–October 1, 1864; Appointed Corporal, Sept. 3, 1863; Died of wounds in charge at New Market Heights, VA (Sept. 29, 1864) at Balfour Hospital, Portsmouth, VA, Oct. 1, 1864.

Cumberland Nelson  Private; 25; Fauquier County, VA; Laborer; April 11, 1865–October 28, 1866; Mustered out with regiment.

John Newby  Private; 23; Perquimans County, NC; Farmer; August 24, 1863–August 24, 1866; Mustered out on expiration of enlistment, Aug. 24, 1866.

Moses Nixon (Moses Lowe)  Private; 21; Perquimans County, NC; Farmer; October 19, 1863–October 19, 1866; Mustered out on expiration of enlistment, Oct. 19, 1866;

Edmund Overton  Private; 22; Pasquotank County, NC; Farmer; December 1, 1863–October 28, 1866; Free on or before April 19, 1861; Mustered out with regiment.

Isaac Overton  Corporal; 22; Pasquotank County, NC; Farmer; November 13, 1863–September 29, 1864; Appointed Corporal, Sept. 3, 1863; Killed at New Market Heights, VA, Sept. 29, 1864.

William H. Overton  Private, Corporal, Sergeant, First Sergeant; 24; Pasquotank County, NC; Farmer; September 19, 1863–September 19, 1866; Free on or before April 19, 1861; Promoted Corporal, Sept. 12, 1865; Promoted Sergeant, Aug. 31, 1866; Promoted First Sergeant, Sept. 10, 1866; Mustered out on expiration of enlistment, Sept. 19, 1866.

Sidney W. Phillips  First Lieutenant; c 24; Worcester, MA; Clerk; March 4, 1864–April 27, 1864; Transferred from Co. C, Mar. 4, 1864; Promoted Captain and transferred to Co. D, Apr. 27, 1864.

Single Phillips  Private; 19; Princess Anne County, VA; Farmer; September 10, 1863–May 25, 1865; Discharged at City Point, VA, May 25, 1865.

John Porter  Private; 20; Nansemond County, VA; Farmer; January 8, 1864–October 22, 1865; Died at Post Hospital, Brazos Santiago, TZ, Oct. 22, 1865.

Charles Prentiss  Private; 50; Suffolk, VA; Farmer; August 13, 1863–March 8, 1865; Discharged from service, Mar. 8, 1865.

John Preston  Private; 21; Fort Monroe, VA; Teamster; October 5, 1863–December 20, 1863; Died of wounds (at Currituck Court House, NC) received in skirmish with guerrillas at Indian Town, NC, Dec. 20. 1863.

George B. Proctor  Captain; c 23; Fitchburg, MA; March 4, 1864–April 19, 1864; Promoted Captain from First Lieutenant, Co. G, Mar. 4, 1864; Discharged, Apr. 19, 1864; Died July 24, 1932 at Brooklyn, NY.

Joseph Reed, 1st  Private, Corporal; 23; Nansemond County, VA; Farmer; December 20, 1863–September 9, 1866; Promoted Corporal, Sept. 12, 1864; Free on or before April 19, 1861; Died of cholera at Brazos Santiago, TX, Sept. 9, 1866.

Joseph Reed, 2nd  Corporal, Sergeant; 20; Perquimans County, VA; Farmer; December 10, 1863–October 28, 1866; Promoted Corporal, Feb. 8, 1866; Promoted Sergeant, Aug. 31, 1866; Mustered out with regiment; Died Nov. 1, 1921 at Berkley, VA.

Luther Robinson  Private; 18; Goochland County, VA; Laborer; April 11, 1865–October 28, 1866; Mustered out with regiment; Died Jan. 20, 1919 at Richmond, VA.

Lamb Rodgers  Private; 38; Nansemond County, VA; Farmer; December 10, 1863–October 2, 1865; Died at Corps d'Afrique U.S. Gen. Hospital, New Orleans, LA, Oct. 2, 1865.

John Sadden  Private; 18; Goochland County, VA; Farmer; April 11, 1865–October 28, 1866; Mustered out with regiment; Died Nov. 30, 1912 at Goochland County, VA.

Thomas Saunders  Private; 26; Perquimans County, NC; Farmer; December 12, 1863–August 10, 1864; Died of wounds received in the trenches near Petersburg, VA (Aug. 8, 1864) at 3rd Div., 18th Corps Hospital at Point of Rocks, VA, Aug. 10, 1864.

David Scott  Private; 24; Martin County, NC; Servant; August 28, 1863–March 8, 1864; Died of disease at Balfour Hospital, Portsmouth, VA, Mar. 8, 1864.

Swain Scott  Private; 18; Martin County, NC; Farmer; August 24, 1863–August 24, 1866; Free on or before April 19, 1861; Died Mar. 3, 1925 at Bautte, LA.

Thomas Shaw  Private; 18; Currituck County, NC; Farmer; August 25, 1863–August 25, 1866; Mustered out on expiration of enlistment, Aug. 25, 1866.

William Shaw  Private; 18; Camden County,

NC; Government Employee; August 25, 1863–August 25, 1866; Mustered out on expiration of enlistment, Aug. 25, 1866.

Pompey Simpson   Private; 21; Tyrell County, NC; Farmer; October 3, 1863–October 22, 1864; Died of wounds received at New Market Heights (Sept. 29, 1864), U.S. Gen. Hospital, Fort Monroe, VA, Oct. 22, 1864.

Jacob Skinner   Private; 18; Bertie County, NC; Farmer; November 3, 1863–October 28, 1866; Mustered out with regiment.

Luke Skinner   Private; 22; Chowan County, NC; Farmer; December 10, 1863–October 28, 1866; Mustered out with regiment.

Charles Small   Private; 45; Perquimans County, NC; Farmer; August 26, 1863–November 27, 1863; Died of typhoid pneumonia at Regimental Hospital, Nov. 27, 1863; Never mustered.

Mills Small   Private; 25; Perquimans County, NC; Farmer; August 24, 1863–August 24, 1866; Mustered out on expiration of enlistment, Aug. 24, 1866.

Landon Smith   Private; 39; Westmoreland County, VA; Farmer; April 1, 1864–October 28, 1866; Mustered out with regiment; Died in 1866 at New Orleans, LA.

Leroy Smith (Leroy Williams)   Private; 15; Mathews County, VA; Drummer; October 14, 1863–October 14, 1866; Free on or before April 19, 1861; Mustered out on expiration of enlistment, Oct. 14, 1866.

Robert Smith   Sergeant, Private; 19; Portsmouth, VA; Waiter; September 2, 1863–September 2, 1866; Appointed Sergeant, Sept. 9, 1863; Reduced to ranks, Oct. 10, 1864; Mustered out on expiration of enlistment, Sept. 2, 1866.

Jacob Spradley   Private, Corporal, Sergeant; 32; Surry County, VA; Farmer; October 3, 1863–Sept. 1, 1866; Free on or before April 19, 1861; Promoted Corporal, Nov. 16, 1864; Promoted Sergeant, Aug. 31, 1866; Promoted Sergeant Major and transferred to noncommissioned staff, Sept. 1, 1866.

Michael Sullivan   Second Lieutenant; c 22; Newton, MA; Carver; June 9, 1864–December 5, 1864; Formerly Private, Co. D, 23rd MA Inf.; Appointed Second Lieutenant, Jun. 9, 1864; Promoted First Lieutenant and transferred to 107th USCT, Dec. 5, 1864.

Charles Temple   Private; 18; Pasquotank County, NC; Farmer; August 24, 1863–August 24, 1866; Mustered out on expiration of enlistment, Aug. 24, 1866.

Benjamin Thompson   Private; 26; Richmond, VA; Farmer; April 3, 1864–October 28, 1866; Mustered out with regiment.

Isaac Tillet   Private; 18; Camden County, NC; Farmer; September 12, 1863–September 12, 1866; Mustered out on expiration of enlistment, Sept. 12, 1866; Died Jul. 4, 1928 at Moyock, NC.

John Tolliver   Private; 21; Yorktown, VA; Waiter; August 21, 1863–August 21, 1866; Mustered out on expiration of enlistment, Aug. 21, 1866.

Sampson Turner   Private; 39; Norfolk, VA; Farmer; September 7, 1863–March 20, 1866; Free on or before April 19, 1861; Discharged at Brazos Santiago, TX for physical disability, Mar. 20, 1866.

William Turner (William G. Turner)   Private; 18; Hanover County, VA; Hostler; August 20, 1863–August 20, 1866; Mustered out on expiration of enlistment, Aug. 20, 1866; Died June 13, 1901 at Moscow, TN.

Robinson Tynes   Sergeant, First Sergeant; 20; Southampton County, VA; Farmer; September 10, 1863–September 10, 1866; Appointed Sergeant, Sept. 9, 1863; Promoted First Sergeant, July 14, 1866; Mustered out on expiration of enlistment, Sept. 10, 1866.

Joseph W. Wall   Captain; 42; Dorchester, MA; Teacher; May 11, 1864–November 15, 1864; Formerly First Lieutenant, Co. A, 14th MA Inf. (1st MA Hvy Arty.); Appointed Captain May 11, 1864; Resigned Nov. 15, 1864.

Alexander Washington (Alexander Driver)   Private; 18; Nansemond County, VA; Farmer; August 13, 1863–August 13, 1866; Mustered out on expiration of enlistment, Aug. 13, 1866.

Benjamin Watkins   Private; 18; Suffolk, VA; Laborer; August 13, 1863–February 11, 1864; Discharged on Surgeon's certificate of disability, Feb. 11, 1864.

Nathaniel Watkins   Private; 21; Nansemond County, VA; Servant; October 12, 1863–October 12, 1866; Mustered out on expiration of enlistment, Oct. 12, 1866.

George Watts   Private; 20; Norfolk, VA; Fisherman; December 1, 1863–October 28, 1866; Mustered out with regiment.

Benjamin West   Private; 18; New Kent County, VA; Farmer; August 11, 1863–August 11, 1866;

Mustered out on expiration of enlistment, Aug. 11, 1866.

Hannibal Whitby  Corporal Sergeant; 22; Perquimans County, NC; Farmer; August 24, 1863–August 24, 1866; Appointed Corporal, Sept. 3, 1863; Promoted Sergeant, Oct. 11, 1865; Mustered out on expiration of enlistment, Aug. 24, 1866; Died July 14, 1912 at Durant's Neck, NC.

James Whitby  Private; 47; Perquimans County, NC; Farmer; December 14, 1863–October 28, 1866; Mustered out with regiment.

Simon Whitehead  Private; 36; Southampton County, VA; Servant; September 10, 1863–; Absent sick at Norfolk, VA since Nov. 1863.

Miles Willey  Private; 18; Norfolk, VA; Farmer; August 18, 1863–August 18, 1866; Free on or before April 19, 1861; Mustered out on expiration of enlistment, Aug. 18, 1866.

George Williams (George T. Williams)  Corporal, Sergeant; 20; Nansemond County, VA; Farmer; August 13, 1863–August 13, 1866; Appointed Corporal, Sept. 3, 1863; Promoted Sergeant, July 24, 1866; Mustered out on expiration of enlistment, Aug. 13, 1866.

Isaiah Williams  Private; 21; Norfolk, VA; Laborer; August 13, 1863–January 27, 1864; Discharged the service on Surgeon's certificate of disability, Jan. 27, 1864.

Prince Williams  Private; 19; Hardy, VA; Laborer; April 6, 1865–October 28, 1866; Mustered out with regiment.

Brewster Young (Briscoe Young)  Private; 18; Princess Anne County, VA; Government Employee; August 13, 1863–August 13, 1866; Mustered out on expiration of enlistment, Aug. 13, 1866; Died May 1, 1930 at Philadelphia, PA.

## Company G

Samuel Adams  Private; 23; Nash County, NC; Farmer; November 15, 1863–May 7, 1866; Married with 9 children; Died of heart disease at Brazos Santiago, TX, May 7, 1866.

George E. Albee  Second Lieutenant; 20; Lisbon, NH; September 18, 1865–October 23, 1865; Formerly Private, Co. G, 1st U.S. Sharpshooters; Private, 3rd WI Btty; First Lieutenant, Co. F, 36th WI Inf.; Appointed Second Lieutenant, Sept. 18, 1865; Transferred to Co. B, Oct. 23, 1865.

Hiram W. Allen  First Lieutenant; c 27; Chelsea, MA; Clerk; September 1864–September 3, 1865; Transferred from Co. K, 36th USCT, Sept. 1864; Serving on staff of General Wild since first muster into 36th USCT; Promoted Captain and transferred to Co. E, Sept. 3, 1865.

Jesse Allen  Private; 18; Warwick County, VA; Farmer; October 3, 1863–October 3, 1866; Single; Mustered out at expiration of enlistment, October 3, 1866.

Charles H. Anderson  Private; 18; Richmond, VA; Farmer; April 10, 1865–October 28, 1866; Mustered out with regiment.

Abel Archy  Private; 29; Currituck County, NC; Laborer, Boatman; October 28, 1863–October 28, 1866; Married; Mustered out with regiment.

Thomas Artis (William Chappell)  Sergeant, Private; 24; Southampton County, VA; Fisherman; September 23, 1863–September 23, 1866; Single; Appointed Sergeant; Sentenced by Gen. Court Martial (Dec. 21, 1864) to be reduced to ranks and confined one year at hard labor wearing a ball and chain.

Henry Augustus  Private; 18; Pasquotank County, NC; Farmer; December 28, 1863–August 7, 1865; Wounded at New Market Heights, VA, Sept. 29, 1864; Died of diarrhea at Post Hospital, Brazos Santiago, TX, Aug. 7, 1865.

Elijah Banks  Private; 19; Middlesex County, VA; Farmer; June 7, 1864–October 28, 1866; Mustered out with regiment; Died Dec. 18, 1925 at Harmony Village, VA.

Warren Barnes  Private, Corporal; 21; Wilson County, NC; Farmer; November 15, 1863–October 28, 1866; Promoted Corporal, Sept. 28, 1866; Mustered out with regiment.

Blunt Barnhill  Private; 47; Martin County, NC; Fisherman; September 28, 1863–June 18, 1864; Discharged the service at Point Lookout, MD for disability, June 18, 1864.

Isaac Bell  Private; 17; Currituck County, NC; Farmer; September 30, 1863–April 29, 1864; Single; Discharged the service, Apr. 29, 1864.

Francis A. Bicknell   First Lieutenant; 19; Weymouth, MA; Shoecutter; July 22, 1864–October 22, 1864; Formerly Corporal, Co. H, 35th MA In.; Appointed Second Lieutenant, May 26, 1864; Promoted First Lieutenant, July 22, 1864; Wounded at New Market Heights, Sept. 29, 1864; Promoted Captain and transferred to Co. B, Oct. 22, 1864.

John Binford   Private; 28; Henrico County, VA; Farmer; December 23, 1863–October 28, 1866; Single; Mustered out with regiment.

Joseph Blair   Private; 25; Essex County, VA; Farmer; June 18, 1864–October 28, 1866; Mustered out with regiment; Died Aug. 23, 1905 at Essex County, VA.

Morgan Blunt   Private; 20; Edenton, NC; Farmer; December 23, 1863–February 11, 1864; Single; Discharged the service at Portsmouth, VA on Surgeon's Certificate of disability, Feb. 11, 1864.

Elijah Booker   Sergeant; 23; Gloucester County, VA; Farmer; October 3, 1863–October 3, 1866; Single; Promoted Sergeant, May 1, 1864; Mustered out at expiration of enlistment, Oct. 3, 1866.

George Bradbury   Captain; 30; Newburyport, MA; Architect; July 17, 1863–July 12, 1864; Formerly Corporal, Co. A, 17th MA Inf.; Appointed Captain, Jul. 17, 1863; Discharged for disability, July 12, 1864.

Eli Britt   Private; 24; Hertford County, NC; Farmer; October 8, 1863–October 8, 1866; Single; Mustered out at expiration of enlistment, Oct. 8, 1866

James Brooks (James H. Brooks)   Private; 23; Richmond County, VA; Farmer; June 18, 1864–October 28, 1866; Mustered out with regiment.

Robert Bruce   Private; 37; NC; Farmer; September 20, 1863–February 2, 1864; Single; Discharged the service at Portsmouth, VA on Surgeon's certificate of disability, Feb. 2, 1864.

Elijah Cherry   Private; 30; Bertie County, NC; Farmer; July 15, 1863–October 27, 1864; Wounded at New Market Heights, VA, Sept. 29, 1864; Died of wounds received at New Market Heights, VA, Balfour Gen. hospital, Portsmouth, VA, Oct. 27, 1864.

George W.S. Conant   Second Lieutenant; 21; South Royalton, VT; Boston, MA; Butcher; September 25, 1863–April 29, 1864, May 11, 1864–May 17, 1864; Formerly Private, Co. A, 1st MA Inf.; Appointed Second Lieutenant, Sept 25, 1863; Transferred to Co. B, Apr. 29, 1864; Transferred from Co. B, May 11, 1864; Honorably discharged due to resignation, May 17, 1864; Died Jan. 7, 1913 at Cambridge, MA.

Solon Cooper   Private, Corporal; 34; Hertford County, NC; Farmer; January 1864–July 15, 1866; Single; Transferred from Co. H, 36th USCT; Promoted Corporal, Mar. 1, 1864; Reduced to ranks July 25, 1864; Discharged July 15, 1866.

John Corbin   Private; 30; Richmond County, VA; Farmer; June 18, 1864–October 28, 1866; Mustered out with regiment.

Charles Cornick   Private; 18; Princess Anne County, VA; Farmer; December 28, 1863–October 28, 1866; Single; Mustered out with regiment.

Miles Crickman (Miles Quickmore)   Private; 41; Norfolk County, VA; Farmer; December 24, 1863–September 29, 1864; Killed at New Market Heights, VA, Sept. 29, 1864.

Washington Darby (William W. Darby)   Private; 39; Richmond County, VA; Farmer; June 18, 1864–September 29, 1864; Deserted when company was bringing in wounded on Chaffin's Farm, VA, Sept. 29, 1864; Died Oct. 2, 1896 at Portsmouth, VA.

Frank Davenport   Private; 18; Warwick County, VA; Farmer; October 5, 1863–October 5, 1866; Single; Mustered out at expiration of enlistment, Oct. 5, 1866.

Edward Diggs   Corporal; 20; James City County, VA; Farmer; October 5, 1863–October 5, 1866; Single; Appointed Corporal; Reduced to ranks, Aug. 1864; Mustered out at expiration of enlistment, Oct. 5, 1866; Died Mar. 18, 1914 at Warwick County, VA.

Joseph Diggs   Private; 24; James City County, VA; Carpenter; October 5, 1863–June 17, 1865; Married; Wounded at New Market Heights, VA, Sept. 29, 1864; Mustered out at Norfolk, VA, June 17, 1865.

Joshua Dudley   Private, Corporal; 22; Gloucester County, VA; Farmer; June 7, 1864–October 28, 1866; Promoted Corporal, Sept. 30, 1866; Mustered out with regiment; Died July 14, 1920 at Harmony Village, VA.

Samuel Dyes   Corporal; 28; Norfolk County, VA; Farmer; December 9, 1863–October 28, 1866; Appointed Corporal; Reduced to ranks,

June 1864; Mustered out with regiment; Died July 25, 1925 at Portsmouth, VA.

Daniel Fentis (Daniel Fentress)   Private; 31; Princess Anne County, VA; Farmer; December 12, 1863–October 28, 1866; Married; Mustered out with regiment.

Anthony Floore (Anthony Flora)   Private; 45; Currituck County, NC; Farmer; October 27, 1863–April 25, 1864; Single; Discharged, Apr. 25, 1864.

Charles Floore (Charles Flora)   Corporal; 20; Currituck County, NC; Laborer; October 27, 1863–October 27, 1866; Single; Promoted Corporal, Sept. 30, 1866; Mustered out at expiration of enlistment, Oct. 27, 1866; Died May 3, 1914 at Hickory, VA.

Edward Y. Folford   Private; Single; Rejected at final muster.

Charles Foreman   Private; 19; Deep Creek, VA; Porter; December 24, 1863–April 29, 1864; Single; Discharged, Apr. 29, 1864.

Prince Flummers (John Fleming)   Private; 20; Pitt County, NC; Farmer; November 16, 1863–February 25, 1865; Single; Wounded, Aug. 21, 1864; Discharged the service on Surgeon's certificate of disability, Feb. 25, 1865; Died Feb. 11, 1921 at National Soldier's Home, VA.

William Furby (William J. Ferby)   Private; 26; Savannah, VA; Farmer; April 10, 1865–October 28, 1866; Mustered out with regiment.

James Gallop   Private, Corporal; 32; Currituck County, NC; Carpenter; September 28, 1863–September 28, 1866; Promoted Corporal, Mar. 8, 1864; Wounded at New Market Heights, VA, Sept. 29, 1864; Mustered out at expiration of enlistment, Sept. 28, 1866; A Good Soldier.

Malachi Gallop   Private; 27; Currituck County, NC; Farmer; October 1, 1863–October 1, 1866; Mustered out at expiration of enlistment, Oct. 1, 1866.

Richard Gallop   Private; 26; Currituck County, NC; Farmer; July 15, 1863–July 15, 1866; Mustered out at expiration of enlistment, July 15, 1866

Washington Gallop   Private; 19; Currituck County, NC; Farmer; October 1, 1863–September 29, 1864; Married; Died of chronic diarrhea at U.S. Gen. Hospital, Fort Monroe, VA, Sept. 29, 1864.

Theophilus Gates (Theophilus G. Young)   Private; 18; Winchester, VA; Farmer; April 10, 1865–October 28, 1866; Mustered out with regiment.

Caleb Goffigan   Private; 18; Hampton, VA; Farmer; October 18, 1863–April 26, 1864; Transferred to the Navy, Apr. 26, 1864.

Harrison Gordon   Private; 30; Richmond, VA; Carpenter; June 18, 1864–October 28, 1866; Married; Mustered out with regiment.

Uriah Griffin   Private; 50; NC; Farmer; July 13, 1863–June 18, 1864; Discharged the service on Surgeon's certificate of disability, June 18, 1864.

Wilson Griffin   Corporal; 25; Pasquotank County, NC; Shinglemaker; December 28, 1863–November 25, 1865; Single; Promoted Corporal, Sept. 30, 1864; Mustered out at Fort Monroe, VA, Nov. 25, 1865.

Peter Halston (Peter Hoskey)   Private; 23; Currituck County, NC; Farmer; December 18, 1863–October 28, 1866; Mustered out with regiment.

Moses Ham   Private; 30; Richmond County, VA; Farmer; June 18, 1864–October 28, 1866; Mustered out with regiment.

Edmund Harrison   Private; 33; Powells Point, NC; Farmer; October 1, 1863–October 1, 1866; Mustered out at expiration of enlistment, Oct. 1, 1866.

Henry Harrison   Private; 23; Yorktown, VA; Farmer; October 9, 1863–October 9, 1866; Mustered out at expiration of enlistment, Oct. 9, 1866.

John Haskett   Private; 18; Surry County, VA; Cartman; October 3, 1863–April 14, 1865; Single; Died of typhoid pneumonia at U.S. General Hospital, Apr. 14, 1865.

Stephen F. Hathaway   First Lieutenant; 30; Salem, MA; Beverly, MA; Milkman; September 4, 1865–October 28, 1866; Transferred as Second Lieutenant from Co. F, Feb. 27, 1865; Brevet Captain, USV, Mar. 13, 1865; Promoted First Lieutenant, Sept. 4, 1865; Mustered out with regiment; Assigned to Freedmen's Bureau in TX; Died June 4, 1898.

Thomas Hawkins   Private; 21; Richmond County, VA; Farmer; June 18, 1864–October 28, 1866; Wounded at New Market Heights, VA, Sept. 29, 1864; Mustered out with regiment.

Frederick Henry (Frederick Henry Harris)   Private; 28; Richmond County, VA; Farmer; June 18, 1864–October 28, 1866; Mustered out with regiment.

John Henry  Private; 22; Savannah, VA; Farmer; April 10, 1865–October 28, 1866; Mustered out with regiment.

Abner Hobson  Private; 33; York County, VA; Farmer; October 3, 1863–April 26, 1864; Single; Transferred to Navy, Apr. 26, 1864.

Silas Holly  Private; 19; Whitford, NC; Farmer; July13, 1863–April 14, 1865; Single; Wounded Nov. 24, 1864 on picket at Chaffin's Farm, VA; Discharged the service on Surgeon's certificate of disability, Apr. 14, 1865.

John Horne  Private; 20; Richmond County, VA; Farmer; June 18, 1864–June 28, 1865; Wounded at New Market Heights, VA, Sept. 29, 1864; Died of remittent fever at Post Hospital Brazos Santiago, TX, June 28, 1865.

Robert Hunter  Private; 30; Princess Anne County, VA; Farmer; October 26, 1863–April 22, 1864; Discharged Apr. 22, 1863.

Felix Jarvis  Private; 20; Currituck County, NC; Cartman; December 17, 1863–October 28, 1866; Single; Mustered out with regiment.

Isaac Kenney  Private, Corporal, Sergeant; 21; Elizabeth City, NC; Farmer; September 30, 1863–September 30, 1866; Promoted Corporal, Sept. 30, 1864; Promoted Sergeant, Dec. 1, 1864; Mustered out at expiration of enlistment, Sept. 30, 1866; Died Dec. 3, 1919 at Portsmouth, VA.

Benjamin F. Kinsley  Captain; c 23; Salem, MA; Clerk; July 22, 1864–October 28, 1866; Transferred as First Lieutenant from Co. F, Mar. 4, 1864; Promoted Captain, Jul. 22, 1864; Mustered out with regiment.

William E. Leonard  Second Lieutenant; c 27; November 22, 1864–February 25, 1865; Formerly Private, Co. F, 85th PA Inf.; Medal of Honor Recipient (Aug. 16, 1864); Appointed Second Lieutenant, Nov. 22, 1864; Honorably discharged, Feb. 25, 1865.

William Little  Private; 22; Pitt County, NC; Farmer; September 22, 1863–September 22, 1866; Mustered out at expiration of enlistment, Sept. 22, 1866; Died May 5, 1917 at Elizabeth City, NC.

Robert Lovett  Private; 25; Winchester, VA; Farmer; April 8, 1865–October 28, 1866; Mustered out with regiment.

Benjamin Mann  Corporal; 24; Tyrell County, NC; Fisherman; August 4, 1863–August 4, 1866; Married; Appointed Corporal; Reduced to ranks Sept. 30, 1864; Mustered out at expiration of enlistment, Aug. 4, 1866.

Alonzo Marshall  Private; 18; Mathews County, VA; Blacksmith; October 8, 1863–February 7, 1866; Deserted, Aug. 3, 1864; Apprehended in Camp of 38th USCT, Sept 20, 1864 and returned to company; Discharged, Feb. 7, 1866.

Sheldon F. Mekin (Sheldon F. Meekins)  Private; 45; Tyrell County, NC; Fisherman; September 26, 1863–April 29, 1864; Discharged April 29, 1864.

Henry Mitchell  Private; 26; Hertford County, NC; Farmer; January 4, 1864–October 28, 1866; Mustered out with regiment.

Peter Moore  Corporal, Sergeant; 20; Martin County, NC; Farmer; September 30, 1863–September 30, 1866; Single; Appointed Corporal; Promoted Sergeant, Sept. 30, 1864; Mustered out at expiration of enlistment, Sept. 30, 1866; Died Dec. 24, 1927 at Plymouth, NC.

Mark Morris  Corporal; 22; Elizabeth City, NC; Farmer; October 10, 1863–October 10, 1866; Promoted Corporal, June 30, 1865; Reduced to ranks, June 21, 1866; Mustered out at expiration of enlistment, Oct. 10, 1866; Served in U.S. Navy on board USS *Tennessee*.

Peter Murdin (Peter Murden)  Private; 23; NC; Farmer; September 29, 1863–February 12, 1864; Discharged the service on Surgeon's certificate of disability, Feb. 12, 1864; Died July 15, 1916.

Andrew Newbern  Private; 36; Currituck County, NC; Farmer; October 1, 1863–November 25, 1864; Killed by enemy's shell when on picket at Chaffins Farm, VA (Blown all to pieces), Nov. 25, 1864; Buried at Fort Harrison National Cemetery, VA (Section C, Grave 269 as "Andrew Newbern").

Cicero Newby (Cicero Nubie/Newbie)  Private; 18; Perquimans County, NC; Farmer; September 30, 1863–August 3, 1865; Died of diarrhea at Post Hospital, Brazos Santiago, TX, Aug. 3, 1865.

Elijah Newsome  Private; 21; Wilson County, NC; Farmer; November 15, 1863–August 2, 1865; Died of scurvy, Aug. 2, 1865 on the passage from Brazos Santiago, TX to New Orleans, LA on the steamer *Matamgasda*.

Ezekiel Nottingham (Abraham Dennis)  Corporal; 22; Norfolk County, VA; Farmer; October 18, 1863–October 18, 1866; Promoted Corporal, June 30, 1866; Mustered out at expiration of enlistment, Oct. 18, 1866; Post-war service in 40th U.S. Inf. and Co. D, 25th U.S. Inf.; Died Oct. 16, 1919 at Havelock, NC.

William Olmstead   Private; 25; Mathews County, VA; Farmer; October 9, 1863–October 9, 1866; Mustered out at expiration of enlistment, Oct. 9, 1866.

Thomas Ormthede   Private; 22; Williamsburg, VA; Oysterman; October 4, 1863–October 4, 1866; Single; Mustered out at expiration of enlistment, Oct. 4, 1866.

Warren Ormthede (Warren Armfield)   Private; 24; Yorktown, VA; Sailor; October 3, 1863–April 26, 1864; Single; Transferred to the Navy (Potomac Flotilla and *Saphronia*), Apr. 26, 1864; Died Aug. 16, 1909 at Washington, DC.

Henry Palmer   Private; 22; Richmond, VA; Farmer; June 18, 1864–October 28, 1866; Mustered out with regiment.

Israel Phillips   Private; 26; Princess Anne County, VA; Farmer; October 26, 1863–October 26, 1866; Mustered out at expiration of enlistment, Oct. 26, 1866.

Richard Piner   Sergeant; 35; Currituck County, NC; Carpenter; October 3, 1863–November 2, 1864; Appointed Sergeant; Died of disease at U.S. Gen. Hospital, Fort Monroe, VA, Nov. 2, 1864.

Anthony Pool (Anthony W. Pool)   First Sergeant; 20; Surry County, VA; Farmer; October 3, 1863–June 3, 1865; Single; Appointed First Sergeant, Oct. 3, 1863; Wounded in action near Deep Bottom (New Market Heights), VA, Sept. 29, 1864; Mustered out at Fort Monroe, VA, June 3, 1865.

Merritt Pool   Sergeant, First Sergeant; 23; Surry County, VA; Farmer; October 3, 1863–October 3, 1866; Appointed Sergeant, Oct. 3, 1863; Promoted First Sergeant, June 30, 1865; Mustered out at expiration of enlistment, Oct. 3, 1866.

Smith Pratt   Private; 19; Richmond, VA; Farmer; June 18, 1864–October 28, 1866; Mustered out with regiment; Died July 10, 1919 at Ennis, TX.

George B. Proctor   First Lieutenant; c 23; Fitchburg, MA; October 27, 1863–March 4, 1864; Formerly Corporal, Co. F, 25th MA Inf.; Promoted Captain and transferred to Co. F, Mar. 4, 1864.

Robert Rankin   Private; 34; Richmond County, VA; Farmer; June 18, 1864–August 31, 1865; Died at U.S. Gen. Hospital, New Orleans, LA, Aug. 31, 1865.

George W. Reed (George W. Reid)   Private; 33; Bertie County, NC; Farmer; September 28, 1863–September 28, 1866; Mustered out at expiration of enlistment, Sept. 28, 1866

Daniel Rich   Private; 19; Richmond County, VA; Farmer; June 18, 1864–May 31, 1865; Mustered out May 31, 1865.

William Rich   Private; 19; Middlesex County, VA; Farmer; June 7, 186–June 3, 1865; Mustered out June 3, 1865.

Benjamin Robinson (Benjamin Roberson)   Private, Corporal, Sergeant; 20; Essex County, VA; October 22, 1863–October 22, 1866; Promoted Corporal, July 15, 1866; Promoted Sergeant, Oct. 3, 1866; Mustered out at expiration of enlistment, Oct. 22, 1866; Died Oct. 15, 1914 at Adner, VA.

James H. Samuel   Private; 19; Richmond County, VA; Farmer; June 18, 1864–October 28, 1866; Mustered out with regiment.

John Saunders   Private; 22; Essex County, VA; Farmer; June 3, 1864–October 28, 1866; Mustered out with regiment; Died Oct. 24, 1912.

Kinsey Saunders (McKenzie Sanders)   Private; 19; Essex County, VA; Farmer; June 6, 1864–October 28, 1866; Mustered out with regiment; Died Nov. 1899 at Baltimore, MD.

Albert Sawyer   Corporal, Sergeant; 28; Pasquotank County, NC; Farmer; January 5, 1864–October 28, 1866; Promoted Corporal, June 30, 1865; Promoted Sergeant, Sept. 30, 1866; Mustered out with regiment.

Raddrick Sears (Roddrick Sears)   Private; 40; September 28, 1863–April 7, 1864; Died of small pox at Pest House, Portsmouth, VA, Apr. 7, 1864.

London Sheppard   Private; 23; Essex County, VA; Farmer; October 23, 1863–October 23, 1866; Single; Mustered out at expiration of enlistment, Oct. 23, 1866.

Charles Shields; Corporal; 19; Elizabeth City County, VA; Farmer; October 18, 1863–October 18, 1866; Promoted Corporal, June 30, 1865; Reduced to ranks, June 21, 1866; Mustered out at expiration of enlistment, Oct. 18, 1866.

Henry Simmons   Corporal; 20; Tyrell County,

NC; Farmer; July 13, 1863–July 13, 1866; Promoted Corporal, Sept. 30, 1864; Mustered out at expiration of enlistment, July 13, 1866.

Moses Simmons  Private; 34; Currituck County, NC; Farmer; September 28, 1863–August 1, 1866; Died of cholera at Post Hospital, Galveston, TX, Aug. 1, 1866.

Raddrick Simmons  Private; 38; Martin County, NC; Shinglemaker; September 28, 1863–August 24, 1865; Married with 2 children; Died of rheumatic fever at Post Hospital, Brownsville, TX, Aug. 24, 1865.

Frederick Smith  Private; 21; Baltimore, MD; Farmer; April 6, 1865–October 28, 1866; Mustered out with regiment.

James Smith  Private; 23; Essex County, VA; Farmer; June 18, 1864–; Sentenced per Gen. Orders #5, HdQrts. 25th Army Corps, Dec. 21, 1864

Mechlin Smith  Private, Corporal; 36; Surry County, VA; Carpenter; October 3, 1863–June 3, 1865; Promoted Corporal, Aug. 1,1864; Discharged from Balfour U.S. Gen. Hospital, VA, June 3, 1865.

Charles Spellman  Private; 18; Camden County, NC; Farmer; October 5, 1863–October 5, 1866; Mustered out at expiration of enlistment, Oct. 5, 1866; Died May 28, 1932 at Houston, TX.

Bannister Spruel  Private; 27; Alligator, Tyrrell County, NC; Farmer; September 28, 1863–September 28, 1866; Mustered out at expiration of enlistment, Sept. 28, 1866

Wilson Stogley  Private, Corporal, Sergeant, First Sergeant; 20; Pasquotank County, NC; Farmer; January 5, 1864–October 28, 1866; Promoted Corporal, May 1, 1864; Wounded at New Market Heights, VA, Sept. 29, 1864; Promoted Sergeant, Sept. 8, 1866; Promoted First Sergeant, Oct. 3, 1866; Mustered out with regiment.

George Taylor  Corporal, Sergeant; 19; Surry County, VA; Farmer; October 18, 1863–October 28, 1866; Promoted Corporal, Aug. 1, 1866; Promoted Sergeant, Oct. 3, 1866; Mustered out with regiment.

Joseph Thatch  Private; 37; Chowan County, NC; Farmer; September 23, 1863–September 23, 1866; Mustered out at expiration of enlistment, Sept. 23, 1866

Jerry Thomas  Private; 20; Hampton, VA; Farmer; October 26, 1863–October 26, 1866; Mustered out at expiration of enlistment, Oct. 26, 1866; Died Jan. 6, 1868.

Samuel Toler  Private; 30; Currituck County, NC; Farmer, Brickmaker; October 1, 1863–June 2, 1866; Married; Died of anemia at Post Hospital, Brazos Santiago, TX, June 2, 1866.

Henry Turner  Private; 25; King William County, VA; Farmer; June 7, 1864–October 28, 1866; Mustered out with regiment; Died Nov. 16, 1910 at Harmony Village, VA.

Isum Turner  Private; 19; Gloucester County, VA; Laborer; June 7, 1864–October 28, 1866; Mustered out with regiment.

George Vena  Private; 20; Richmond County, VA; Farmer; June 18, 1864–October 28, 1866; Mustered out with regiment; Died Apr. 19, 1914 at Tidewater, VA.

William Walker  Private, Corporal, Sergeant; 20; Warwick County, VA; Farmer; September 7, 1863–September 7, 1866; Promoted Corporal, Mar. 8, 1864; Promoted Sergeant, June 30, 1865; Mustered out at expiration of enlistment, Sept. 7, 1866.

Luke Warren  Private; 20; Edenton, NC; Farmer; October 3, 1863–February 2, 1864; Single; Discharged at Portsmouth, VA on Surgeon's certificate of disability, Feb. 2, 1864.

Perry Washington  Private; 20; Spotsylvania County, VA; Farmer; April 10, 1865–October 28, 1866; Mustered out with regiment.

Elisha Waters  Private; 22; Plymouth, NC; January 14, 1864–October 28, 1866; Single; Mustered out with regiment; Died Aug. 1, 1915 at Galveston, TX.

Milford Wenderley  Private; 19; Plymouth, NC; Farmer; May 12, 1864–October 28, 1866; Mustered out with regiment; Died Dec. 25, 1912 at Blantonsville, SC.

Robert White  Corporal, Sergeant; 26; Norfolk County, VA; Farmer; December 30, 1863–October 28, 1866; Promoted Corporal, July 25, 1864; Promoted Sergeant, Sept. 30, 1866; Mustered out with regiment.

Green Whitfield  Private; 19; NC; Farmer; July 13, 1863–Aug. 26, 1864; Deserted when the company was on the march from Petersburg, VA, to Deep Bottom, VA, Aug. 26, 1864.

Edmund Williams  Private; 25; Pasquotank County, NC; Farmer; January 8, 1864–October 4, 1864; Married with 3 children; Killed by a shell from the rebel gunboat while at work in a fort at Chaffin's Farm, Oct. 4, 1864.

Henry F. Willis (Henry F. Woodhouse) Drummer; 15; Norfolk, VA; Errand Boy; October 4, 1863–October 4, 1866; Single; Wounded at New Market Heights, VA, Sept. 29, 1864; Mustered out at expiration of enlistment, Oct. 4, 1866; Died Jan. 8, 1932.

George Wilson Corporal; 44; Norfolk County, VA; Woodcutter; September 22, 1863–June 3, 1865; Married with 11 children; Promoted Corporal, Dec. 1, 1864; Discharged June 3, 1865.

Randall Wilson Private; 44; Norfolk County, VA; Woodcutter; December 29, 1863–October 28, 1866; Married with 11 children; Mustered out with regiment.

Cudjoe Woodhouse Corporal; 29; Currituck County, NC; Farmer; September 29, 1863–October 6, 1864; Married; Appointed Corporal; Died of wounds received in action at Deep Bottom, VA (Sept. 29, 1864) at Base Hospital 18th Army Corps, Oct. 6, 1864.

Oscar Yerbey Private, Corporal; 24; Richmond County, NC; Farmer; June 18, 1864–October 28, 1866; Promoted Corporal, Sept. 6, 1866; Mustered out with regiment; Post-war service in Co. G, 40th U.S. Inf. and Co. H, 25th U.S. Inf.

## Company H

Isaiah Allen Private; 33; Loudoun County, VA; Blacksmith; June 24, 1863–June 24, 1866; Free on or before April 19, 1861 (born Free); Mustered out at expiration of enlistment, June 24, 1866.

Abraham Armstead Sergeant, Color Sergeant; 43; Bertie County, NC; Laborer; July 13, 1863–July 13, 1866; Appointed Sergeant, Sept. 1, 1863; Appointed Color Sergeant, June 24, 1864; Mustered out at expiration of enlistment, July 13, 1866.

George Baysmore Private, Corporal; 28; Bertie County, NC; Farmer; July 13, 1863–October 28, 1866; Promoted Corporal, May 26, 1864; Wounded at New Market Heights, VA, Sept. 29, 1864; Mustered out with regiment.

James Bell Private; 36; Hampton, VA; Waiter; July 13, 1863–July 3, 1866; Died of cerebral appoplexy, Post Hospital Brazos Santiago, TX, July 3, 1866.

Eason Berry Private; 20; Martin County, NC; Farmer; June 13, 1863–June 13, 1866; Mustered out at expiration of enlistment, June 13, 1866.

Abraham Blango Private; 38; Beaufort County, NC; Farmer; July 13, 1863–September 29, 1864; Free on or before April 19, 1861 (born Free); Killed in action near Deep Bottom (New Market Heights), VA, Sept. 29, 1864.

Elasa Blango Private; 19; Beaufort County, NC; Farmer; June 12, 1863–June 12, 1866; Free on or before April 19, 1861 (born Free); Mustered out at expiration of enlistment, June 12, 1866.

Giles Blango Private; 19; Beaufort County, NC; Farmer; June 24, 1863–June 24, 1866; Free on or before April 19, 1861 (born Free); Mustered out at expiration of enlistment, June 24, 1866; Died Aug. 7, 1922 at Craven County, NC.

Alexander Blunt Private; 19; Washington, NC; Waiter; June 20, 1863–June 20, 1866; Mustered out at expiration of enlistment, June 20, 1866.

Moses Blunt Corporal, Private; 19; Beaufort County, NC; Farmer; June 22, 1863–June 22, 1866; Appointed Corporal; Reduced to ranks Apr. 1864; Mustered out at expiration of enlistment, June 22, 1866..

Jerry Blunt Private; 19; Bertie County, NC; Farmer; July 13, 1863–March 20, 1864; Died of small pox at Regimental Hospital, Point Lookout, MD, Mar. 20, 1864.

West Bond Private; 26; Bertie County, NC; Farmer; July 13, 1863–July 13, 1866; Mustered out at expiration of enlistment, July 13, 1866.

Linnier Bonner Private; 38; Beaufort County, NC; Farmer; June 3, 1863–March 21, 1864; Discharged for disability at Point Lookout, MD, Mar. 21, 1864.

Henry Brown Private; 17; Pitt County, NC; Farmer; June 5, 1863–November 9, 1865; Died of acute pleuritis at Post Hospital Brazos Santiago, TX, Nov. 9, 1865.

**John Brown** Sergeant, Private; 21; New Bern, NC; Waiter; June 24, 1863–May 5, 1865; Appointed Sergeant, Sept. 1, 1863; Reduced to ranks, Aug. 1864; Wounded at New Market Heights, VA, Sept. 29, 1864; Discharged the service on Surgeon's certificate of disability at Balfour U.S. Gen. Hospital, Portsmouth, VA, May 5, 1865; Died Mar. 20, 1899 at New Bern, NC.

**Joseph Brown** Private; 18; Pitt County, NC; Farmer; June 26, 1863–June 26, 1866; Mustered out at expiration of enlistment, June 26, 1866; Died Feb. 15, 1922 at Norfolk, VA.

**Moses Brown** Private; 33; Martin County, NC; Fireman; July 13, 1863–October 1, 1864; Free on or before April 19, 1861 (born Free); Died of disease of the bowels at Base Hospital, Point of Rocks, VA, Oct. 1, 1864; Buried at City Point National Cemetery, VA (Grave 3713).

**Ransom Brown** Private; 24; Pitt County, NC; Farmer; June 13, 1863–June 13, 1866; Mustered out at expiration of enlistment, June 13, 1866.

**Edward Brumser** Private; 22; Currituck County, NC; Farmer; June 22, 1863–October 28, 1866; Wounded at New Market Heights, VA, Sept. 29, 1864; Mustered out with regiment.

**Riley Bryant (Riley Willis)** Private; 18; Washington, NC; Fisherman; June 24, 1863–June 24, 1866; Mustered out at expiration of enlistment, June 24, 1866.

**Alexander Bunch** Private; 31; Bertie County, NC; Farmer; July 13, 1863–July 13, 1866; Mustered out at expiration of enlistment, July 13, 1866.

**Charles Caldwell** Corporal; 27; Currituck County, NC; Fisherman; June 20, 1863–; Appointed Corporal at time of Muster in of company; Deserted at Brazos Santiago, TX, Mar. 20, 1866.

**Joseph Capehart** Private; 21; Plymouth, NC; Farmer; July 13, 1863–June 19, 1865; Mustered out at Fort Monroe, VA June 19, 1865.

**Hayward Carter** Private; 24; Beaufort County, NC; Farmer; June 12, 1863–June 12, 1866; Free on or before April 19, 1861 (born Free); Mustered out at expiration of enlistment, June 12, 1866; Died Jan. 1902.

**Daniel Cherry** Private; 25; Bertie County, NC; Blacksmith; July 13, 1863–November 9, 1865; Discharged at Corps d'Afrique U.S. Gen. Hospital, New Orleans, LA on Surgeon's certificate of disability, Nov. 9, 1865; Died Mar. 26, 1913.

**Noah Cherry** Private; 42; Bertie County, NC; Farmer; July 13, 1863–November 19, 1865; Discharged at Brazos Santiago, TX on disability, Nov. 19, 1865.

**Samuel Cherry** Private; 25; Martin County, NC; Farmer; June 5, 1863–June 5, 1866; Mustered out at expiration of enlistment, June 5, 1866.

**Henry Clay** Private; 28; Maryland County, MD; Farmer; March 1, 1864–October 28, 1866; Mustered out with regiment.

**Henry Coonce** Private; 26; Duplin County, NC; Farmer; July 4, 1863–September 6, 1865; Died of pneumonia on board steamer *St. Mary* on the passage from Brazos Santiago, TX to New Orleans, LA, Sept. 6, 1865.

**Moses Davis** Private, Corporal; 20; Hyde County, NC; Waiter; June 22, 1863–June 22, 1866; Promoted Corporal, Aug. 15, 1865; Mustered out at expiration of enlistment, June 22, 1866.

**Clayburn Demdrick** Private; 35; VA; Blacksmith; April 7, 1865–April 11, 1865; Deserted at Richmond, Apr. 11, 1865; Never mustered.

**James Edwards** Private; 36; Pitt County, NC; Carpenter; June 9, 1863–March 20, 1865; Wounded at New Market Heights, VA, Sept. 29, 1864; Discharged on Surgeon's certificate of disability, U.S. Gen. Hospital Summit House Philadelphia, PA, Mar. 20, 1865.

**Irvin Ellerson** Private; 23; Beaufort County, NC; Brickman; June 5, 1863–June 5, 1866; Mustered out at expiration of enlistment, June 5, 1866; Died Feb. 1, 1927 at Washington, DC.

**William Etheridge** Corporal, Sergeant; 24; Roanoke Island, NC; Fisherman; June 22, 1863–September 29, 1864; Appointed Corporal, Sept. 1, 1863; Promoted Sergeant, Aug. 1864; Killed in action New Market Heights, VA, Sept. 29, 1864.

**Hilliard Everett** Private; 26; Edgecombe County, NC; Farmer; July 28, 1863–July 3, 1865; Died of typhoid fever at Base Hospital, Point of Rocks, VA, July 3, 1865.

**Henry M. Field** Second Lieutenant; 21; Southwick, MA; Farmer, Student; January 27, 1864–April 19, 1864; Transferred from Co. K,

Jan. 27, 1864; Discharged Apr. 19, 1864; Restored to rank and transferred to Co. A, Mar. 26, 1865.

**Riley Galloway (Riley Guilford)** Private; 42; Beaufort County, NC; Farmer; July 2, 1863–July 2, 1866; Mustered out at expiration of enlistment, July 2, 1866.

**Edwin C. Gaskill** First Lieutenant; 20; Mendon, MA; Farmer; July 11, 1864–July 19, 1864; Transferred from Co. C, July 11, 1864; Transferred, July 19, 1864.

**David Gibbs** Private, Corporal; 21; Washington, NC; Waiter; July 1, 1863–July 1, 1866; Free on or before April 19, 1861 (born Free); Promoted Corporal, Jan. 1, 1865; Mustered out at expiration of enlistment, July 1, 1866; Died Apr. 10, 1927 at Norfolk, VA.

**Hardy Gilliard** Private; 28; Washington, NC; Lumberman; July 13, 1863–July 13, 1866; Mustered out at expiration of enlistment, July 13, 1866.

**Robert Green** Private, Corporal; 38; Washington, NC; Farmer; June 4, 1863–June 4, 1866; Promoted Corporal, Nov. 1, 1864; Reduced to ranks, May 1864; Promoted Corporal, Nov. 1, 1864; Mustered out at expiration of enlistment, June 4, 1866; Died July 17, 1901.

**Larry Griffin** Drummer, Private; 15; Martin County, NC; Farmer; July 5, 1863–January 1, 1865, July 13, 1865–July 25, 1865, October 9, 1865; Transferred to noncommissioned staff as Principal Musician, Jan. 1, 1865; Reduced to ranks, July 13, 1865; Transferred to noncommissioned staff as Principal Musician, July 25, 1865; Reduced to ranks, Oct. 9, 1865.

**William Groves** Private, Corporal; 16; Washington, NC; Waiter; June 23, 1863–June 23, 1866; Promoted Corporal, Apr. 1, 1866; Mustered out at expiration of enlistment, June 23, 1866.

**William H. Hart** Captain; 27; Lynn, MA; Shoemaker, Cordwainer; May 11, 1864–September 25, 1864; Formerly Sergeant, Co. M, 1st MA Hvy Arty; Appointed Captain May 11, 1864; Promoted Major, Sept. 25, 1864.

**John Herring** Private; 18; Duplin County, NC; Farmer; July 24, 1863–July 24, 1866; Mustered out at expiration of enlistment, July 24, 1866.

**Caesar Hodges (Caesar F. Hodges)** Private, Corporal; 23; Pitt County, NC; Farmer; June 2, 1863–June 2, 1866; Promoted Corporal, Nov. 1, 1864; Mustered out at expiration of enlistment, June 2, 1866; Died Feb. 25, 1918 near Washington, DC.

**George Hodges (George H. Hodges)** Private; 20; Washington, NC; Farmer; July 1, 1863–July 1, 1866; Promoted Corporal, May 1, 1866; Mustered out at expiration of enlistment, July 1, 1866; Died Apr. 16, 1914 at New York City, NY.

**Benjamin Holly** Private; 24; Bertie County, NC; Farmer; July 13, 1863–July 20, 1865; Died of diarrhea at Post Hospital, Brownsville, TX, July 20, 1865.

**Miles Hooket (Miles Howcott)** Private; 34; Duplin County, NC; Farmer; July 8, 1863–July 8, 1866; Mustered out at expiration of enlistment, July 8, 1866; Died May 17 at Plymouth, NC.

**Walter Jackson** Private; 18; New Bern, NC; Farmer; July 13, 1863–July 13, 1866; Mustered out at expiration of enlistment, July 13, 1866.

**William Jenkins** Private; 20; Hertford, NC; Farmer; July 13, 1863–July 13, 1866; Mustered out at expiration of enlistment, July 13, 1866; Died July 14, 1909.

**Sidney Joiner (Sidney Joyner)** Private; 26; Edgecombe County, NC; Farmer; July 1863–February 22, 1864; Free on or before April 19, 1861 (born Free); Left in camp at Portsmouth, VA, Feb. 22, 1864 since which time nothing has been heard of him — never mustered in; Deserted.

**Benjamin Keyes** Private, Corporal; 20; Washington, NC; Farmer; June 6, 1863–June 7, 1865; Free on or before April 19, 1861 (born Free); Promoted Corporal, May 1864; Mustered out at Fort Monroe, VA, June 7, 1865.

**James Keyes** Corporal, Sergeant; 22; Washington, NC; Farmer; July 1, 1863–July 1, 1866; Free on or before April 19, 1861 (born Free); Appointed Corporal, Sept. 1, 1863; Promoted Sergeant, Jan. 1, 1865; Mustered out at expiration of enlistment, July 1, 1866; Died Dec. 22, 1919 at Bonnerton, NC.

**Shadrach Keyes** Private, Corporal; 37; Martin County, NC; Carpenter; July 1, 1863–July 1, 1866; Free on or before April 19, 1861 (born Free); Promoted Corporal, July 7, 1864; Wounded at New Market Heights, VA, Sept. 29, 1864; Mustered out at expiration of enlistment, July1, 1866.

**William Keyes** Private; 26; Beaufort County,

NC; Farmer; June 24, 1863–June 24, 1866; Free on or before April 19, 1861 (born Free); Mustered out at expiration of enlistment, June 24, 1866.

Harrison Kidd   Private; 18; King and Queen County, VA; Laborer; April 7, 1865–October 28, 1866; Mustered out with regiment.

Keyresil Lamb (Careason Lamb)   Private; 19; Camden County, NC; Farmer; June 20, 1863–June 20, 1866; Mustered out at expiration of enlistment, June 20, 1866.

George H. Lamprey   Captain; 24; Lawrence, MA; Clerk; October 24, 1864–March 15, 1865; Formerly Quartermaster Sergeant, 14th MA Inf. (1st MA Hvy Art); Appointed Second Leutenant, May 11, 1864; Promoted First Lieutenant, Jul. 19, 1864; Promoted Captain, Oct. 24, 1864;Honorably discharged for disability, Mar. 15, 1865; Died in 1881 at Laconia, NH.

Perkins Linnier (Charles Williams)   Private; 19; Duplin County, NC; Farmer; June 20, 1863–July 2, 1866; Mustered out due to expiration of term of enlistment (retained due to being on detail as guard with prisoners to Corpus Christie, TX), July 2, 1866.

Jerry Little   Private; 36; Martin County, NC; Farmer; July 13, 1863–July 13, 1866; Mustered out at expiration of enlistment, July 13, 1866.

Eli Mariner   Private; 21; Martin County, NC; Farmer; June 16, 1863–June 16, 1866; Mustered out at expiration of enlistment, June 16, 1866; Died Mar. 27, 1911.

Perry Mariner   Private; 28; Bertie County, NC; Farmer; July 13, 1863–March 19, 1864; Discharged for disability at Point Lookout, MD, Mar. 19, 1864.

Willis McRae   Private; 21; Martin County, NC; Farmer; July 13, 1863–July 13, 1866; Mustered out at expiration of enlistment, July 13, 1866; Died Aug. 20, 1919 at National Soldiers Home, VA.

Jarvis Moore   Private; 40; Beaufort County, NC; Farmer; June 22, 1863–June 22, 1866; Free on or before April 19, 1861 (born Free); Mustered out at expiration of enlistment, June 22, 1866.

Riley Moore   Private; 22; Washington, NC; Farmer; July 17, 1863–July 17, 1866; Free on or before April 19, 1861 (born Free); Mustered out at expiration of enlistment, July 17, 1866; Died May 5, 1917 at Bonnerton, NC.

William Moore   Private; 25; Washington, NC; Farmer; June 20, 1863–June 20, 1866; Free on or before April 19, 1861 (born Free); Mustered out at expiration of enlistment, June 20, 1866.

Rigdon Moseley   Private; 44; Craven County, NC; Farmer; June 15, 1863–July 30, 1864; Free on or before April 19, 1861 (born Free); Discharged on Surgeon's certificate of disability at Point of Rocks, VA, July 30, 1864.

Jacob Moye (Jacob May)   Private; 35; NC; Farmer; July 8, 1863–July 8, 1866; Mustered out at expiration of enlistment, July 8, 1866.

Benjamin F. Oakes   Captain; c 21; Boston, MA; Clerk; July 8, 1863–April 19, 1864; Formerly Sergeant, Co. H, 24th MA Inf; Appointed Captain, Jul. 8, 1863; Discharged Apr. 19, 1864; Subsequent service in 4th MA Cav.

Allen Odin   First Sergeant; 24; Washington, NC; Laborer; June 16, 1863–June 16, 1866; Appointed First Sergeant, Sept. 1, 1863; Mustered out at expiration of enlistment, June 16, 1866. .

Quince Odin   Private; 21; Martin County, NC; Farmer; July 13, 1863–September 29, 1864; Killed in action at New Market Heights, VA, Sept. 29, 1864.

John Owen, Jr.   Captain; 23; Cambridge, MA; Student (Harvard); September 3, 1865–April 21, 1866; Promoted Second Lieutenant from Sergeant Major (white), Apr. 29, 1864; Promoted First Lieutenant, Oct. 24, 1864; Promoted Captain, Sept. 3, 1865; Discharged, Apr. 21, 1866; Died May 1915 at Boston, MA.

Walter Paxton   Private; 24; Edenton, NC; Farmer; June 10, 1863–June 10, 1866; Mustered out at expiration of enlistment, June 10, 1866.

Keaton Perry   Private; 26; Pasquotank County, NC; Farmer; June 1, 1863–June 1, 1866; Wounded at New Market Heights, VA, Sept. 29, 1864; Mustered out at expiration of enlistment, June 1, 1866.

Daniel Pindal (Daniel Pendall)   Private; 21; Edgecombe County, NC; Farmer; June 1, 1863–June 22, 1866; Mustered out at expiration of enlistment, June 22, 1866.

William Piner   Corporal; 31; Currituck County, NC; Laborer; June 22, 1863–June 22, 1866; Appointed Corporal, Sept. 1, 1863; Mustered out at expiration of enlistment, June 22, 1866; Died Dec. 12, 1914 at Cedar Branch, NC.

Moses Powell   Private; 22; Richmond, VA; Teamster; April 7, 1865–April 13, 1865; Deserted at Richmond, Apr. 13, 1865; Never mustered.

Richard Price   Private; 18; Hanover County, VA; Farmer; April 12, 1865–November 9, 1865; Discharged the service on Surgeon's certificate of disability at Corps d'Afrique U.S. Gen. Hospital, New Orleans, LA, Nov. 9, 1865.

Sylvester Price   Sergeant, Private; 45; Beaufort County, NC; Farmer; June 16, 1863–June 16, 1866; Appointed Sergeant, Sept. 1, 1863; Reduced to ranks, Jan. 1, 1865; Mustered out at expiration of enlistment, June 16, 1866.

Adolphus Redding (Adolphus Reddick)   Private, Musician; 21; Martin County, NC; Farmer; July 13, 1863–July 13, 1865, July 25, 1865–October 21, 1865; Transferred to noncommissioned staff as Principal Musician, July 13, 1865; Reduced to ranks, July 25, 1865; Transferred to noncommissioned staff as Principal Musician, Oct. 21, 1865; Died July 7, 1909.

William Redding (William G. Reddick)   Private; 18; Martin County, NC; Farmer; July 13, 1863–September 29, 1864; Killed in action at New Market Heights, VA, Sept. 29, 1864.

Cicero Rice   Private; 23; Craven County, NC; Farmer; June 1, 1863–July 2, 1866; Died of phthisis pulmonalis at Post Hospital, Brazos Santiago, TX, July 2, 1866.

William H. Rock   First Lieutenant; c 22; Montreal, Quebec, Canada; Hooksett, NH; November 20, 1865–October 28, 1866; Formerly Corporal, Co. K, 2nd NH Inf; Appointed Second Lieutenant, Nov. 13, 1864; Serving on staff of Bvt Brig. Gen. Draper Promoted First Lieutenant, Nov. 20, 1865; Mustered out with regiment.

David Rogers   Private, Corporal, Sergeant; 30; Martin County, NC; Farmer; July 13, 1863–June 24, 1866; Appointed Corporal, Sept. 1, 1863; Promoted Sergeant, Nov. 1, 1864; Mustered out at expiration of enlistment, June 24, 1866; Died Sept. 19, 1912 at Elizabeth City, NC.

Frank Satchell   Private; 18; Beaufort County, NC; Farmer; July 8, 1863–December 21, 1864; Died of gunshot wound received in action Sept. 29, 1864 at New Market Heights, VA, Balfour U.S. Gen. Hospital, Portsmouth, VA, Dec. 21, 1864.

William Sharpless   Private; 20; Craven County, NC; Farmer; July 10, 1863–September 29, 1864; Killed in action at New Market Heights, VA, Sept. 29, 1864.

Isaac Shellington   Private; 24; White Oak, NC; Carpenter; July 10, 1863–July 10, 1866; Mustered out at expiration of enlistment, July 10, 1866; Died Mar. 29, 1916 at Hampton, VA.

Ephraim Shirley   Private; 18; Edgecombe County, NC; Farmer; July 13, 1863–July 13, 1866; Mustered out at expiration of enlistment, July 13, 1866.

John Steward   Private; 45; Bertie County, NC; Farmer; July 13, 1863–February 21, 1864; Free on or before April 19, 1861 (born Free); Discharged at Portsmouth, VA for disability, Feb. 21, 1864.

Andrew Swan   Corporal; 33; Hamilton, Martin County, NC; Farmer; June 22, 1863–March 6, 1864; Died of disease at Regimental Hospital at Point Lookout, MD, Mar. 6, 1864.

Joseph Swan   Private; 23; Martin County, NC; Farmer; July 15, 1863–July 15, 1866; Wounded at New Market Heights, VA, Sept. 29, 1864; Mustered out at expiration of enlistment, July 15, 1866.

Gilford Swinson   Private; 39; Duplin County, NC; Farmer; July 7, 1863–July 7, 1866; Mustered out at expiration of enlistment, June 7, 1866.

March Spruel   Private; 18; Taylor, NC; Farmer; June 1, 1863–June 1, 1866; Mustered out at expiration of enlistment, June 1, 1866.

Stephen Spruel   Private; 15; Martin County, NC; Farmer; July 13, 1863–September 23, 1864; Died of wounds received in action (Aug. 11, 1864) before Petersburg, VA, Summit House Hospital, Philadelphia, PA Sept. 23, 1864.

Edward Stanley   Private; 18; Pitt County, NC; Farmer; July 13, 1863–July 13, 1866; Mustered out at expiration of enlistment, July 13, 1866.

Samuel Tamage   Private; 20; Beaufort County, NC; Farmer; July 5, 1863–March 25, 1864; Died of disease at camp, 36th USCT, Mar. 25, 1864.

James Tankhard   Private; 19; Beaufort County, NC; Farmer; July 10, 1863–July 11, 1865; Wounded at New Market Heights, VA, Sept. 29, 1864; Died of congestive fever at Corps d'Afrique U.S. Gen. Hospital, New Orleans, LA, July 11, 1865.

William M. Titcomb   First Lieutenant; c18; Dedham, MA; Student; March 1, 1864–May

17, 1864; Transferred from Co. H, Mar. 1, 1864; Transferred to Co. A, May 17, 1864.

James Tompkins  Private; 21; Amelia County, VA; Laborer; April 7, 1865–January 12, 1866; Dishonorably discharged the service per sentence of Gen. Court Martial, Brazos Santiago, TX, Jan. 12, 1866.

Allen Toodle  Private; 22; Beaufort County, NC; Farmer; July 8, 1863–July 8, 1866; Mustered out at expiration of enlistment, July 8, 1866.

Jerry Tulson (Jeremiah Tolson)  Private; 21; Beaufort County, NC; Farmer; July 18, 1863–July 9, 1866; Mustered out at expiration of enlistment, July 9, 1866.

William Turner  Sergeant; 24; Pasquotank County, NC; Farmer; June 22, 1863–June 22, 1866; Free on or before April 19, 1861 (born Free); Appointed Sergeant, Sept. 1, 1863; Mustered out at expiration of enlistment, June 22, 1866.

Joseph Walford  Private; 37; Plymouth, NC; Farmer; July 13, 1863–July 23, 1865; Wounded at New Market Heights, VA, Sept. 29, 1864; Mustered out at Fort Monroe, VA, July 23, 1865; Died Apr. 6, 1911.

March Walker  Private; 36; Roanoke Island, NC; Farmer; June 22, 1863–June 22, 1866; Mustered out at expiration of enlistment, June 22, 1866.

William Walker  Private; 24; Fredericksburg, VA; Laborer; April 8, 1865–April 16, 1865; Deserted on the march to Petersburg, VA, Apr. 16, 1865; Never mustered.

Mansury Watson (Monroe Watson)  Private; 28; Martin County, NC; Farmer; July 13, 1863–July 13, 1866; Mustered out at expiration of enlistment, July 13, 1866.

Paul Watts  Private; 33; Martin County, NC; Farmer; June 24, 1863–June 24, 1866; Mustered out at expiration of enlistment, June 24, 1866.

William Watts  Private; 35; Hampton, VA; Butcher; April 7, 1865–October 28, 1866; Mustered out with regiment.

Henry Wiggins  Corporal, Private; 29; Martin County, NC; Farmer; July 13, 1863–July 13, 1866; Free on or before April 19, 1861 (born Free); Appointed Corporal, Sept. 1, 1863; Reduced to ranks, May 26, 1864; Mustered out at expiration of enlistment, July 13, 1866.Died Apr. 18, 1904.

James Wilkins  Corporal, Private; 30; Pitt County, NC; Farmer; June 16, 1863–August 29, 1864; Free on or before April 19, 1861 (born Free); Appointed Corporal, Sept. 1, 1863; Reduced to ranks May 26, 1864/June 30, 1864; Died of gunshot wound received (Aug. 18, 1864) before Petersburg, VA, Base Hospital, Point of Rocks, VA, Aug. 29, 1864.

Charles H. Williams  Private; 18; Bermuda; Waiter; February 8, 1865–April 30, 1865; Discharged on Surgeon's certificate of disability, Apr. 30, 1865.

John Williams  Private; 20; Hanover County, VA; Farmer; April 12, 1865–October 28, 1866; Mustered out with regiment.

Toney Wilson  Drummer/Musician, Private; 15; Norfolk, VA; Waiter; December 1, 1863–August 25, 1865; Free on or before April 19, 1861 (born Free); Died of pneumonia at Post Hospital Brazos Santiago, TX, Aug. 25, 1865.

Moses Woodis  Private; 20; Currituck County, NC; Farmer; July 1, 1863 July 1, 1866, Mustered out at expiration of enlistment, July 1, 1866.

Thomas Woodis  Private; 30; Currituck County, NC; Farmer; June 22, 1863–June 22, 1866; Mustered out at expiration of enlistment, June 22, 1866.

## Company I

Livian Adams  Sergeant, First Sergeant; 23; Northampton County, VA; Laborer; September 15, 1863–September 20, 1866; Appointed Sergeant, Sept. 25, 1863; Promoted First Sergeant, Jan. 1, 1866; Mustered out at expiration of enlistment, Sept. 20, 1866.

Hiram W. Allen  First Lieutenant; c 26; Chelsea, MA; Clerk; August 13, 1863–May 2, 1864; Formerly Private, Co. H, 1st MA Inf.; Appointed First Lieutenant, Aug. 13, 1863;Transferred to Co. B, May 2, 1864; Serving on staff of General Wild since first muster into 36th USCT.

Richard F. Andrews  Captain; c 28; Lynn, MA;

Shoemaker; March 1, 1865–October 28, 1866; Transferred as Captain from Co. D, Mar. 1, 1865; Brevet Major, USV, Mar. 13, 1865; Mustered out with regiment; Assigned to Freedmen's Bureau in TX; Died Dec. 22, 1901.

Jacob Atwood   Private; 24; Princess Anne County, VA; Farmer; November 28, 1863–October 28, 1866; Mustered out with regiment.

Wesley Artise (Wesley Benn)   Sergeant; 23; Southampton County, VA; Laborer; September 21, 1863–September 20, 1866; Promoted Sergeant, May 1, 1864; Mustered out at expiration of enlistment, Sept. 21, 1866; Died Dec. 31, 1931 at Southampton County, VA.

James B. Backup   Captain; c 20; Roxbury, MA; Clerk; October 21, 1864–January 23, 1865; Transferred as Second Lieutenant from Co. F, Nov. 1863; Promoted First Lieutenant and transferred to Co. D, May 1, 1864; Transferred as First Lieutenant from Co. F, Aug. 12, 1864; Wounded in action at New Market Heights, Sept. 29, 1864; Promoted Captain, Oct. 21, 1864; Honorably discharged for physical disability from wounds received in action, Jan. 23, 1865; Died Aug. 10, 1911.

James W. Bacon   Second Lieutenant; c 22; Portsmouth, NH; Walpole, MA; Painter; December 1, 1864–March 6, 1865; Formerly First Sergeant, Co. K, 23rd MA Inf; Appointed Second Lieutenant, Dec.1, 1864; Promoted First Lieutenant and transferred to Co. B, Mar. 6, 1865.

Henry Bailey   Private; 18; Wilmington, DE; Laborer; November 21, 1863–October 28, 1866; Mustered out with regiment.

Jefferson Ballet   Private; 18; Gates County, NC; Teamster; September 18, 1863–September 12, 1864; Died of chronic bronchitis at Gen. Hospital, Alexandria, VA, Sept. 12, 1864.

Moses Barrington   Private; 26; Pasquotank County, NC; Servant; November 30, 1863–October 28, 1866; Mustered out with regiment.

Aleck (Alexander) Bell   Private; 20; Camden County, NC; Laborer; September 20, 1863–September 20, 1866; Mustered out at expiration of enlistment, Sept. 20, 1866.

Henry Bell   Private; 20; Northampton County, VA; Farmer; September 16, 1863–; Wounded at New Market Heights, Sept. 29, 1864; Absent sick at Portsmouth, VA since Sept. 19, 1864.

James Benjamin   Private; 22; Fort Monroe, VA; Farmer; October 18, 1863–December 1, 1864; Discharged at U.S. Gen. Hospital, Willets Point, New York Harbor on Surgeon's certificate of disability, Dec. 1, 1864; Died Oct. 1881 at Hampton, VA.

John Black   Private; 20; Warwick County, VA; Farmer; September 21, 1863–September 21, 1866; Mustered out at expiration of enlistment, Sept. 21, 1866.

Nelson Booker   Private, Corporal; 19; Hampton, VA; Laborer; September 16, 1863–September 20, 1866; Promoted Corporal, July 26, 1865; Mustered out at expiration of enlistment, Sept. 20, 1866; Died Sept. 11, 1928 at Washington, DC.

Richard Booker   Private; 21; King and Queen County, VA; Farmer; September 22, 1863–October 28, 1866; Mustered out with regiment; Died Nov. 9, 1912 at Hampton (Phoebus), VA.

David Boone (David W. Bow)   Private; 22; Perquimans County, NC; Laborer; September 15, 1863–September 20, 1866; Mustered out at expiration of enlistment, Sept. 20, 1866.

James Bowden   Private, Corporal; 20; Northampton County, VA; Farmer; December 1, 1863–October 28, 1866; Promoted corporal, Nov. 1, 1865; Mustered out with regiment.

Phillip Bright   Sergeant; 34; Hampton, VA; Laborer; September 15, 1863–September 20, 1866; Promoted Sergeant, Jan. 5, 1864; Mustered out at expiration of enlistment, Sept. 20, 1866.

John Brown   Private, Corporal; 38; Owensville, MD; Farmer; September 18, 1863–September 20, 1866; Promoted Corporal, Nov. 18, 1865; Mustered out at expiration of enlistment, Sept. 21, 1866.

Pompey Butt (Pompey But)   Private; 36; Norfolk, V; Farmer; December 12, 1863–October 28, 1866; Mustered out with regiment.

Thomas J. Cate   First Lieutenant; c34; Effingham, NH; Lawrence, MA; August 12, 1864–August 4, 1865; Serving the majority of time on detached service with the Commissary Department; Transferred as First Lieutenant from Co. F, Aug. 12, 1864; Brevet Major, USV, Mar. 13, 1865; Discharged for disability, Aug. 4, 1865.

William Chandler  Private; 22; Caroline County, VA; Blacksmith; June 21, 1864–October 28, 1866; Mustered out with regiment.

Joseph Cook  Private; 22; Isle of Wight County, VA; Boatman; September 15, 1863–September 20, 1866; Mustered out at expiration of enlistment, Sept. 20, 1866.

James Cornick  Private; 18; Princess Anne County, VA; Farmer; November 27, 1863–October 28, 1866; Mustered out with regiment; July 25, 1914 at Norfolk, VA.

John Cornick  Private; 28; Princess Anne County, VA; Farmer; November 27, 1863–February 2, 1866; Discharged on Surgeon's certificate of disability, Brazos Santiago, TX, Feb. 2, 1866.

James H. Curtis  Private; 18; Gloucester County, VA; Teamster; September 15, 1863–September 20, 1866; Mustered out at expiration of enlistment, Sept. 20, 1866; Died May 15, 1921 at Galveston, TX.

George Davenport  Private; 40; Edenton, NC; Servant; September 18, 1863–September 20, 1866; Mustered out at expiration of enlistment, Sept. 20, 1866.

James Downing  Second Lieutenant; c 24; Boston, MA; Mason; September 18, 1865–October 28, 1866; Formerly Private, 1st MA Hvy Arty; Captured in front of Petersburg, VA, June 22, 1864 and escaped 6 mos. later by jumping from a train car; Appointed Second Lieutenant, Sept. 18, 1865; Mustered out with regiment.

Major Dozier  Private; 20; Currituck County, NC; Farmer; September 18, 1863–October 14, 1864; Died of acute diphtheria at Military Hospital, Portsmouth Grove, RI, Oct. 14, 1864.

Robert Ellis (Robert Thompson, 1st)  Private; 20; Perquimans County, NC; Laborer; September 15, 1863–September 20, 1866; Mustered out at expiration of enlistment, Sept. 20, 1866.

Lewis Ely  Private; 36; Isle of Wight County, VA; Lumberman; September 15, 1863–; Absent sick at Fort Monroe, VA (since May 31, 1864) at Muster out of regiment.

America Fenters (America Fentress)  Private; 31; Princess Anne County, VA; Laborer; November 27, 1863–May 12, 1865; Discharged on Surgeon's certificate of disability at City Point, VA, May 12, 1865.

Max Flanagan  Private; 30; Princess Anne County, VA; Woodcutter; December 11, 1863–January 26, 1865; Died of pneumonia at Hospital, Point of Rocks, VA, Jan. 26, 1865; Buried at City Point National Cemetery (Grave 3041 under "M. Flanigan").

Anthony Fuller  Private; 20; Princess Anne County, VA; Farmer; November 27, 1863–October 28, 1866; Mustered out with regiment.

Henry Fuller  Private; 20; Princess Anne County, VA; Farmer; November 27, 1863–August 21, 1865; Died at Post Hospital, Brazos Santiago, TX, Aug. 21, 1865.

Samuel Fuller  Corporal, Sergeant; 23; Princess Anne County, VA; Farmer; November 27, 1863–October 28, 1866; Promoted Corporal, Nov. 1, 1865; Promoted Sergeant, Sept. 22, 1866; Mustered out with regiment; Died Jan. 14, 1914 at Norfolk, VA.

Charles Furby (Charles Furbee)  Private; 37; Currituck County, NC; Laborer; September 20, 1863–September 20, 1866; Mustered out at expiration of enlistment, Sept. 20, 1866.

Sandy Furby (Sandy Feraby)  Private; 30; Camden County, NC; Farmer; September 17, 1863–May 1, 1866; Died of chronic diarrhea at Post Hospital, Brazos Santiago, TX, May 1, 1866.

James Gardner (James Gardiner)  Private, Sergeant; 19; Gloucester County, VA; Oysterman; September 15, 1863–September 20, 1866; Promoted Sergeant; Medal of Honor recipient (New Market Heights, Sept. 29, 1864); Mustered out at expiration of enlistment, Sept. 20, 1866.

Humphrey Gilley  Private; 20; Yorktown, VA; Oysterman; November 18, 1863–October 28, 1866; Mustered out with regiment.

Charles Gordon  Private; 23; Yorktown, VA; Farmer; September 18, 1863–January 21, 1864; Died of confluent variola at Gen. Hospital, Norfolk, VA, Jan. 21, 1864.

John Green  Private; 19; Petersburg, VA; Hostler; September 15, 1863–April 29, 1864; Killed by an accidental discharge from his gun at Point Lookout, Maryland, Apr. 29, 1864.

Samuel Guy  Private; 18; Camden, NJ; Coachman; September 15, 1863–September 20, 1866; Mustered out at expiration of enlistment, Sept. 20, 1866.

Anthony Haines (Anthony Haynes)  Private;

24; Princess Anne County, VA; Laborer; November 24, 1863–January 23, 1864; Died of typhoid fever at Regimental Hospital, Portsmouth, VA, Jan. 23, 1864.

Charles Harrison   Private; 23; VA; Teamster; September 15, 1863–March 1, 1865; Died of disease at Field Hospital 25th Army Corps, Mar. 1, 1865.

Stephen H. Hathaway   Second Lieutenant; 29; Salem, MA, Beverly, MA; Milkman; February 27, 1865–; Transferred from Co. F, February 27, 1865; Transferred to Co. G.

Stephen Hawkins   Private; 21; St. Mary's County, MD; Farmer; May 16, 1864–October 28, 1866; Mustered out with regiment.

Pearson Henderson (Preston H. Henderson)   Private; 18; Northampton County, VA; Farmer; September 16, 1863–September 20, 1866; Mustered out at expiration of enlistment, Sept. 20, 1866; Possibly Died July 27, 1908 at Galveston, TX.

Phillip Herbert   Private; 19; Charles City County, VA; Laborer; September 16, 1863–February 26, 1865–September 20, 1866; Transferred to noncommissioned staff as Principal Musician, Feb. 26, 1865; Reduced to ranks; Mustered out at expiration of enlistment, Sept. 20, 1866.

William Holmes   Private; 22; Essex County, VA; Farmer; September 15, 1863–September 20, 1866; Mustered out at expiration of enlistment, Sept. 20, 1866.

John Hope   Private; 18; Louisa County, VA; Teamster; September 15, 1863–December 11, 1864; Died of pneumonia at Base Hospital, 18th Army Corps, Point of Rocks, VA, Dec.11, 1864; Buried at City Point National Cemetery, VA (Grave 3723 under "Jno. Hope").

George W. James   Private; 21; Princess Anne County, VA; Farmer; November 27, 1863–October 28, 1866; Mustered out with regiment.

Joseph James   Private; 18; Princess Anne County, VA; Laborer; November 27, 1863–October 28, 1866; Mustered out with regiment.

Alfred Kellum   Private; 20; Accomack County, VA; Farmer; September 16, 1863–September 20, 1866; Mustered out at expiration of enlistment, Sept. 20, 1866 (in confinement at Brownsville, TX).

Southey Kellum   Private; 26; Accomack County, VA; Farmer; November 27, 1863–October 28, 1866; Mustered out with regiment; Died Apr. 1, 1914 at Diamond, VA.

Oliver Kemp   Private; 20; Gloucester County, VA; Farmer; September 16, 1863–September 20, 1866; Mustered out at expiration of enlistment, Sept. 20, 1866; Died Apr. 29, 1910.

Frank Land   Private; 32; Norfolk, VA; Farmer; November 25, 1863–October 28, 1866; Wounded at New Market Heights, Sept. 29, 1864; Mustered out with regiment.

Lamb Lovett   Private, Corporal, Sergeant; 25; Princess Anne County, VA; Farmer; November 27, 1863–October 28, 1866; Promoted Corporal, Jan. 10, 1864; Promoted Sergeant, Sept. 22, 1866; Mustered out with regiment.

George H. Merrison   Private; 18; Hampton, VA; Farmer; September 16, 1863–September 20, 1866; Mustered out at expiration of enlistment, Sept. 20, 1866.

Charles Moore   Private; 18; Princess Anne County, VA; Farmer; November 27, 1863–October 28, 1866; Mustered out with regiment.

Solomon Moore   Private, Corporal; 22; Princess Anne County, VA; Farmer; November 27, 1863–October 28, 1866; Promoted Corporal, Sept. 22, 1866; Mustered out with regiment.

Joseph Mullen   Private; 23; Norfolk, VA; Laborer; September 22, 1863–December 18, 1863; Killed in a skirmish with guerrillas at Indiantown, NC, Dec. 18, 1863.

Isaac Nickerson (Isaac Nickson)   Private; 26; Edenton, NC; Farmer; September 15, 1863–January 27, 1864; Discharged on disability, Jan. 27, 1864; Died June 27, 1919 at National Military Home, OH.

Benjamin Olds   Private; 25; Currituck County, NC; Laborer; September 20, 1863–July 1865; Died at Post Hospital, Brazos Santiago, TX, July 1865.

Moses Outland   Private; 18; Isle of Wight County, VA; Farmer; September 16, 1863–September 20, 1866; Mustered out at expiration of enlistment, Sept. 20, 1866.

Frank Page   Private; 19; Gloucester County, VA; Farmer; September 15, 1863–September 20, 1866; Mustered out at expiration of enlistment, Sept. 20, 1866; Died Apr. 14, 1916 at Gloucester, VA.

Alexander W. Palmer   Corporal; 24; Norfolk County, VA; Laborer; January 13, 1864–October 28, 1866; Appointed Corporal, Jan. 10, 1864; Mustered out with regiment.

William H. Palmer   Private, Corporal; 18; Accomack County, VA; Laborer; October 22, 1863–May 1, 1865; Promoted Corporal, Jan. 10, 1864; Promoted Quartermaster Sergeant and transferred to noncommissioned staff, May 1, 1865.

Daniel Parker   Private; 18; Chambersburg, PA; Servant; September 15, 1863–September 20, 1866; Mustered out at expiration of enlistment, Sept. 20, 1866.

James Parker   Private; 23; Frederick County, VA; Servant; September 15, 1863–September 20, 1866; Deserted from Norfolk, VA while on detached duty in Asst. Quartermaster's Dept., 1st Division, 25th Army Corps, June 2, 1865; Apparently restored to company in good standing; Mustered out at expiration of enlistment, Sept. 20, 1866.

Frederick Phillips   Private; 23; Mathews County, VA; Farmer; September 21, 1863–September 21, 1866; Mustered out at expiration of enlistment, Sept. 21, 1866.

Warren Pierce   First Lieutenant; c24; Tyngsboro, MA; Medical Student; March 6, 1865–September 1865; Formerly Private, Co. K, Hospital Steward, 1st MA Hvy Arty; Appointed Second Lieutenant, May 11, 1864; Transferred to Co. A,, July 1864; Transferred from Co. A, Sept. 1864; Promoted First Lieutenant and appointed Adjutant, Nov. 6, 1864; Transferred back to Co. I, Mar. 6, 1865; Transferred to Co. B, Sept. 1865.

Edmund Price   Private; 35; Gates County, NC; Boatman; September 18, 1863–September 20, 1866; Wounded at New Market Heights, Sept. 29, 1864.

Jesse Reed   Private; 30; Currituck County, NC; Laborer; September 21, 1863–September 21, 1866; Mustered out at expiration of enlistment, Sept. 21, 1866.

Wilson Reed   Private; 23; Currituck County, NC; Farmer; November 10, 1863–January 27, 1866; Wounded at New Market Heights, Sept. 29, 1864; Discharged on Surgeon's certificate of disability, Brazos Santiago, TX, Jan. 27, 1866.

James Roach   Private, Corporal, Sergeant; 23; VA; Servant; September 16, 1863–September 20, 1866; Promoted Corporal, Jan. 10, 1864; Reduced to ranks, Nov. 21, 1864; Promoted Sergeant, July 13, 1865

William Roberson   Private; 20; Gloucester County, VA; Farmer; September 18, 1863–September 20, 1866; Mustered out at expiration of enlistment, Sept. 20, 1866.

Edward Sample   Private (Recruit); 22; Princess Anne County, VA; Laborer; September 1863–October 4, 1863; Died of hemorrhage of the lungs at Regimental Hospital, Portsmouth, VA, Oct. 4, 1863; Never mustered.

George Sample   Private; 22; Accomack County, VA; Farmer; November 17, 1863–October 28, 1866; Mustered out with regiment.

Shepard D. Sample   Private; 19; Northampton County, VA; Farmer; November 27, 1863–October 28, 1866; Mustered out with regiment.

Joseph Sarr   Private; 21; Hampton, VA; Farmer; September 16, 1863–March 30, 1864; Died of consumption at Balfour U.S. Gen. Hospital, Portsmouth, VA, Mar. 30, 1864.

Braxton Saunders   Private; 24; September 15, 1863–; Discharged for disability.

Miles Sheppard   First Sergeant, Sergeant; 27; Portsmouth, VA; Laborer; September 15, 1863–September 20, 1866; Appointed First Sergeant, Sept. 25, 1863; Reduced to Sergeant, Jan. 1, 1866; Mustered out at expiration of enlistment, Sept. 20, 1866.

Nat Simmons   Private; 22; Princess Anne County, VA; Laborer; September 15, 1863–September 20, 1866; Mustered out at expiration of enlistment, Sept. 20, 1866.

Gilbert Skinner   Privat; 30; Hertford, NC; Laborer; September 15, 1863 September 28, 1864; Died of disease at Gen. Hospital, Baltimore, MD, Sept. 28, 1864.

Willis Skinner (Willis Sanders)   Private, Corporal; 20; Nansemond County, VA; Waiter; September 15, 1863–March 4, 1865; Promoted Corporal, Feb. 1, 1865; Died of variola at Main Hospital, Baltimore, MD, Mar. 4, 1865.

Celius Smith   Private; 28; North, VA; Laborer; September 15, 1863–September 20, 1866; Mustered out at expiration of enlistment, Sept. 20, 1866.

John M. Smith   Captain; August 13, 1863–August 18, 1864; Formerly Sergeant, United States Marine Corps; Appointed Captain, Aug. 13, 1863; Resigned Aug. 18, 1864.

Washington Smith (Washington Griffin)   Private; 18; Nansemond County, VA; Laborer; September 15, 1863–September 20, 1866;

Mustered out at expiration of enlistment, Sept. 20, 1866.

William Smith   Private; 29; Norfolk, VA; Laborer; November 30, 1863–November 8, 1865; Wounded at New Market Heights, Sept. 29, 1864; Discharged on Surgeon's Certificate of disability, Corps d'Afrique U.S. Gen. Hospital, New Orleans, LA, Nov. 8, 1865.

Harrison Sneed   Sergeant; 20; Baltimore, MD; Baker; September 17, 1863–August 20, 1864; Appointed Sergeant; Killed in the trenches before Petersburg, VA, Aug. 20, 1864.

Peter Stone   Private; 30; Princess Anne County, VA; Farmer; November 27, 1863–January 27, 1866; Discharged for disability, Brazos Santiago, TX, Jan. 27, 1866.

Samuel Sutton   Private; 34; Hertford, NC; Laborer; September 18, 1863–January 27, 1866; Discharged for disability, Brazos Santiago, TX, Jan. 27, 1866.

James Taylor   Private; 24; Norfolk, VA; Laborer; September 20, 1863–November 9, 1865; Discharged on Surgeon's certificate of disability, Corps d'Afrique U.S. Gen. Hospital, New Orleans, LA, Nov. 9, 1865.

Zachariah Taylor   Private; 14; Blackwater, VA; Waiter; September 16, 1863–September 20, 1866; Mustered out at expiration of enlistment, Sept. 20, 1866.

Robert Thomas (Robert Thompson, 2nd)   Private, Corporal; 21; Baltimore, MD; Laborer; September 15, 1863–September 20, 1866; Promoted Corporal, Jan. 10, 1864; Mustered out at expiration of enlistment, Sept. 20, 1866.

Henry N. Thorburn (Harry N. Thorburn)   First Lieutenant; 22; Orange County, NY; Book Agent Teacher; January 3, 1865–March 7, 1865; Formerly Second Lieutenant, Co. H, 9th USCT; Appointed First Lieutenant, Jan. 3, 1865; Transferred to Co. D, Mar. 7, 1865.

Martin Van Buren   Private, Corporal; 25; Norfolk, VA; Farmer; December 12, 1863–October 28, 1866; Promoted Corporal, Sept. 22, 1866; Mustered out with regiment.

John Veal   Corporal; 18; Edenton, NC; Servant; September 18, 1863–September 21, 1866; Appointed Corporal, Sept. 15, 1863; Mustered out at expiration of enlistment, Sept. 21, 1866; Died Aug. 21, 1916 at Baltimore, MD.

Tully Walk   Private, Corporal; 25; Princess Anne County, VA; Farmer; November 27, 1863–October 23, 1865; Promoted Corporal June 6, 1864; Discharged on Surgeon's certificate of disability, Corps d'Afrique U.S. Gen. Hospital, Oct 23, 1865.

Ely Warren   Private; 19; Edenton, NC; Laborer; September 15, 1863–September 20, 1866; Mustered out at expiration of enlistment, Sept. 20, 1866.

Oscar Warren   Private; 20; Edenton, NC; Laborer; September 15, 1863–November 7, 1864; Died at Base Hospital, 18th Army Corps, Point of Rocks, VA, Nov. 7, 1864.

Miles Waters   Private; 21; Princess Anne County, VA; Farmer; November 27, 1863–June 15, 1865; Discharged at U.S. Gen. Hospital, Fort Monroe, VA, June 15, 1865.

John Wesley   Private; 21; Canal Bridge, NC; Laborer; September 15, 1863–April 13, 1866; Sentenced by Gen. Court Martial, Dec. 1864; Deserted fromNorfolk, VA while serving sentence, Apr. 13, 1866.

Elijah H. Wheeler   First Lieutenant; 20; East Abington, MA; Shoe Cutter; September 4, 1865–October 28, 1866; Transferred as Second Lieutenant from Co. K, Feb. 25, 1865; Promoted First Lieutenant, Sept. 4, 1865. Mustered out with regiment.

Jacob White   Private; 44; Princess Anne County, VA; Laborer; November 30, 1863–February 20, 1864; Died of disease at Gen. Hospital, Portsmouth, VA, Feb. 20, 1864.

John White   Private; 28; Mathews County, VA; Laborer; September 18, 1863–May 28, 1865; Discharged at Louverture Gen. Hospital, PA, May 28, 1865.

Willis Wiggins   Private; 26; Nansemond County, VA; Laborer; April 5, 1865–October 28, 1866; Mustered out with regiment.

Henry Williams   Private; 19; Lewisburg, VA; Laborer; September 15, 1863–September 20, 1866; Mustered out at expiration of enlistment, Sept. 20, 1866.

Humphrey Willis (Humphrey Ware)   Private; 19; Hampton, VA; Farmer; September 21, 1863–September 21, 1866; Mustered out at expiration of enlistment, Sept. 21, 1866; Died Mar. 12, 1926 at North, VA.

Albert Wilson (Joseph Green)   Private, Corporal; 21; Warwick County, VA; Laborer; September 11, 1863–September 20, 1866; Promoted Corporal, Sept. 1, 1864; Mustered out at expiration of enlistment, Sept. 20, 1866.

Edward Wilson (Edward Felton) Private; 18; Beaufort, NC; Servant; November 10, 1863–October 28, 1866; Mustered out with regiment.

Enoch Woodhouse Private; 20; Edenton, NC; Laborer; November 28, 1863–August 30, 1865; Died of disease at Camp Brazos Santiago, TX, Aug. 30, 1865.

Joseph Wright Private; 22; Petersburg, VA; Farmer; September 11, 1863–October 28, 1866; Wounded at New Market Heights, Sept. 29, 1864.

John Young Private; 23; Portsmouth, VA; Bricklayer; September 15, 1863–October 28, 1866; Mustered out with regiment.

## Company K

Peter Alexander Private; 20; Essex County, VA; Farmer; June 21, 1864–; Deserted near Petersburg, VA while on detached service, Aug. 1864.

Hiram W. Allen First Lieutenant; c 27; Chelsea, MA; Clerk; July 23, 1864–September 1864; Transferred from Co. B, July 23, 1864; Serving on staff of General Wild since first muster into 36th USCT; Transferred to Co. G, Sept. 1864.

Alfred Athridge Private; 20; Norfolk, VA; Farmer; October 20, 1863–January 12, 1864; Died at Balfour Hospital, Portsmouth, VA, Jan. 12, 1864.

Amory O. Balch Second Lieutenant; c 19; Roxbury, MA; Clerk; May 18, 1864–April 19, 1864 (August 15, 1864); Transferred from Co. D, May 18, 1864; Mustered out, Aug. 15, 1864.

Charles Barnett Private; 21; Norfolk County, VA; Farmer; October 25, 1863–February 19, 1866; Died of acute dysentery, Post Hospital, Brazos Santiago, TX, Feb. 19, 1866.

William Barnett Private; 39; VA; Blacksmith; April 15, 1865–October 28, 1866; Mustered out with regiment.

Isaac Barker Private; 25; Camden County, NC; Farmer; December 25, 1863–October 28, 1866; Mustered out with regiment.

David Baxter Private; 21; Norfolk County, VA; Farmer; September 25, 1863–September 25, 1866; Mustered out at expiration of enlistment, Sept. 25, 1866.

Simon Bess Private; 28; Wayne County, NC; Farmer; September 19, 1863–September 12, 1866; Died of cholera, Brazos Santiago, TX, Sept. 12, 1866.

Lewis Blue Private; 19; Hampton, VA; Farmer; September 20, 1863–May 2, 1865; Discharged for disability, May 2, 1865.

Washington Braxton Private; 21; Gloucester County, VA; Laborer; April 6, 1865–September 8, 1866; Died of cholera, Brazos Santiago, TX, Sept. 8, 1866.

Alfred Brock (Alfred Wilson) Private; 19; Norfolk, VA; December 13, 1863–October 28, 1866; Mustered out with regiment.

Jesse Brock Private; 19; Princess Anne County, VA; Farmer; December 24, 1863–September 29, 1864; Killed at New Market Heights, VA, Sept. 29, 1864.

Dagan Brocket Private; 19; Princess Anne County, VA; Farmer; November 28,1863–October 28, 1866; Mustered out with regiment.

John A. Brown Corporal; 22; New Castle, ME; Barber; September 25, 1863–September 25,1866; Mustered out at expiration of enlistment, Sept. 25, 1866.

Miles Brown Private; 25; Norfolk County, VA; Farmer; December 1, 1863–October 28, 1866; Mustered out with regiment.

Henry Burt Private; 25; Princess Anne County, VA; Laborer; October 3, 1863–October 3, 1866; Mustered out at expiration of enlistment, Oct. 3, 1866.

Dandridge Carter Private; 20; Henrico County, VA; Farmer; April 6, 1865–September 13, 1866; Died of cholera, Brazos Santiago, TX, Sept. 13, 1866.

Henry Case Corporal, Private; 22; Accomack County, VA; Farmer; October 24, 1863–October 24, 1866; Reduced to ranks, April 1864; Mustered out at expiration of enlistment, Oct. 24, 1866.

Oscar Clinton Private; 19; Point No Point, MD; Farmer; March 17, 1864–October 26, 1866; Died Aug. 31, 1911.

Sonny Collins Private; 22; Norfolk County,

VA; Farmer; September 21, 1863–March 12, 1864; Killed (accidently shot) at Point Lookout, MD, Mar. 12, 1864.

Dandridge Cooper Private; 20; Norfolk County, VA; Farmer; October 6, 1863–; Absent sick in hospital since Feb. 1865.

Daniel Cooper Private; 18; New Bern, NC; Laborer; September 4, 1863–September 4, 1866; Mustered out at expiration of enlistment, Sept. 4, 1866.

Frank Cornick Private; 21; Princess Anne County, VA; Farmer; January 3, 1864–March 27, 1866; Wounded at New Market Heights, VA, Sept. 29, 1864; Discharged Mar. 27, 1866

George Cornick Private; 18; Princess Anne County, VA; Farmer; November 30, 1863–October 28, 1866; Mustered out with regiment.

James Cornick Private; 21; Norfolk County, VA; Farmer; November 21, 1863–October 28, 1866; Mustered out with regiment.

Moses Cornick Corporal, Sergeant; 23; Norfolk, VA; Farmer; November 25, 1863–October 26, 1866; Promoted Sergeant, Oct. 1, 1865.

Norris Corporal Private; 27; Princess Anne County, VA; Farmer; October 21, 1863–June 11, 1865; Discharged U.S. Gen. Hospital, Fort Monroe, VA, June 11, 1865.

Alfred Counsel Private; 22; Bladen County, NC; Farmer; September 18, 1863–September 18, 1866; Mustered out at expiration of enlistment, Sept. 18, 1866.

Charles Counsel Private; 20; New Bern, NC; Farmer; September 18, 1863–September 18, 1866; Mustered out at expiration of enlistment, Sept. 18, 1866.

Samuel Counsel Private; 37; Bladen County, NC; Laborer; September 18, 1863–September 18, 1866; Mustered out at expiration of enlistment, Sept. 18, 1866.

Daniel J. Courtney First Lieutenant; c 25; Newport, Wales; Brookline, MA; Student Clerk; June 13, 1866–October 28, 1866; Promoted Second Lieutenant and transferred from Quartermaster Sergeant (white), Mar. 24, 1865; Promoted First Lieutenant and transferred to Co. E, May 22, 1866; Transferred from Co. E, June 13, 1866; Mustered out with regiment.

Samuel Crofts Corporal; 18; Petersburg, VA; Farmer; September 25, 1863–September 25, 1866; Wounded at New Market Heights, Sept. 29, 1864; Mustered out at expiration of enlistment, Sept. 25, 1866.

Cornelius Crowley First Sergeant; 24; Port Richmond, NY; Sailor; September 25, 1863–September 25, 1866; Mustered out at expiration of enlistment, Sept. 25, 1866.

Benjamin Davis Private; 18; Hampton, VA; Farmer; October 3, 1863–October 3, 1866; Mustered out at expiration of enlistment, Oct. 3, 1866; Post-war service in Co. B, 39th U.S. Inf. and Co. G, 25th U.S. Inf.; Died July 30, 1916 at Newark, NJ.

George Davis Private; 18; Staunton, VA; Farmer; April 15, 1865–October 26, 1866

Carey Dozier Private; 20; Norfolk, VA; Farmer; November 28, 1863–August 19, 1864; Died of wounds in action near Petersburg, VA, Aug. 19, 1864.

Wilson Dozier Private; 20; Norfolk, VA; Farmer; September 7, 1863–February 7, 1864; Discharged for disability (loss of finger on right hand), Feb. 7, 1864.

Algernon Draper Second Lieutenant; 19; Boston, MA; Laborer; March 12, 1864–April 27, 1864; Formerly Private, Co. C, 1st MA Hvy Arty; Appointed Second Lieutenant, Mar. 12, 1864; Promoted First Lieutenant and transferred to Co. F, Apr. 27, 1864.

Aleck Edwards Private; 23; Currituck County, NC; Farmer; November 30, 1863–June 14, 1865; Discharged U.S. Gen. Hospital, Fort Monroe, VA, June 14, 1865.

James Edwards Private; 22; Currituck County, NC; Farmer; November 28, 1863–October 5, 1866; Died of cholera, Brazos Santiago, TX, Oct. 5, 1866.

George Evans Private; 26; Southampton, VA; Laborer; October 6, 1863–October 6, 1866; Mustered out at expiration of enlistment, Oct. 6, 1866.

Henry M. Field Second Lieutenant; 21; Southwick, MA; Farmer Student; November 5, 1863–January 27, 1864; Formerly Private, Co. G, 34th MA Inf.; Appointed Second Lieutenant, Nov. 5, 1863; Transferred to Co. H, Jan. 27, 1864.

Denson Flory Private; 18; Norfolk County, VA; Farmer; October 25, 1863–October 25, 1866; Mustered out at expiration of enlistment, Oct. 25, 1866.

Benjamin Franklin (Benjamin B. Franklin)

Private; 21; Caraway, NC; Waiter; September 6, 1863–September 6, 1866; Mustered out at expiration of enlistment, Sept. 6, 1866; Died Feb. 9, 1915 at Halifax, NC.

Jesse Fuller   Private; 21; Princess Anne County, VA; Laborer; October 24, 1863–October 24, 1866; Mustered out at expiration of enlistment, Oct. 24, 1866; Died May 17, 1912 at Bird's Nest, VA.

Morris Furby   Private; 22; Camden County, NC; Farmer; November 30, 1863–October 4, 1865; Died of chronic diarrhea at Corps d'Afrique Hospital, New Orleans, LA, Oct. 4, 1865.

Samuel Gilchrist   Sergeant, First Sergeant; 24; Surry County, VA; Carpenter; October 3, 1863–June 17, 1865; Discharged, U.S. Gen. Hospital, Fort Monroe, VA, June 17, 1865.

Benjamin Gordon   Private; 21; Henrico County, VA; Laborer; April 6, 1865–October 28, 1866; Mustered out with regiment; Died Aug. 8, 1911.

Frank H. Graves   First Lieutenant; 19; February 24, 1865–January 3, 1866; Promoted from Second Lieutenant, Co. B, Feb. 24, 1865; Serving on staff of Gen. Paine since July 22, 1864;Brevet Lieutenant Colonel, USV, Nov. 27, 1865; Honorably discharged, Jan. 3, 1866.

Solon Green   Private; 24; Smithfield, VA; Miner; April 9, 1865–October 28, 1866; Mustered out with regiment; Died Oct. 7, 1909.

Dawson Grey (Dawson Gray)   Private; 19; Isle of Wight County, VA; Farmer; October 1, 1863–October 1, 1866; Mustered out at expiration of enlistment, Oct. 1, 1866; Died Apr. 1, 1922 at Chuckatuck, VA.

Alexander Hall   Private; 23; Southampton, VA; Laborer; September 6, 1865–October 28, 1866; Mustered out with regiment.

William Hanson (William Hancher)   Private; 21; Henrico County, VA; Laborer; April 6, 1865–October 28, 1866; Mustered out with regiment.

Charles Haskell   First Lieutenant; 24; Ipswich, MA; Tinman; October 24, 1864–January 3, 1865; Formerly Sgt. Co. A, 1st MA Hvy Arty; Appointed Second Lieutenant, Oct. 6, 1864; Promoted First Lieutenant, October 24, 1864; Transferred to Co. B, Jan. 3, 1865.

Daniel Hawley (Daniel Holly)   Private; 19; New Bern, NC; Laborer; September 9, 1863–April 17, 1865; Died of pneumonia, Balfour Hospital, Portsmouth, VA, Apr. 17, 1865.

Moses Haynes   Private; 28; Princess Anne County, VA; Not Known; November 25, 1863–October 28, 1866; Mustered out with regiment.

Joseph Hendly   Private; 22; VA County, VA; Farmer; September 25, 1863–April 12, 1864; Died of small pox at Pest House, Norfolk, VA, Apr. 12, 1864.

James Henry   Private; 18; Hampton, VA; Farmer; September 25, 1863–February 27, 1865; Discharged on certificate of disability, Feb. 27, 1865; Died Sept. 8, 1922 at National Solder's Home, VA.

Thomas Hicks   Private; 19; Gates County, NC; Laborer; September 22, 1863–September 22, 1866; Mustered out at expiration of enlistment, Sept. 22, 1866.

James Hodges   Private; 20; Norfolk County, VA; Farmer; September 25, 1863–September 25, 1866; Mustered out at expiration of enlistment, Sept. 25, 1866.

Seaborn Hodges (Seaburn Hodges)   Private; 39; Yorktown, VA; Farmer; September 22, 1863–February 7, 1864; Died of small pox, Norfolk, VA, Feb. 7, 1864.

William Jackson   Private; 19; Hanover County, VA; Farmer; September 25, 1863–September 25, 1866; Mustered out at expiration of enlistment, Sept. 25, 1866.

Charles James   Private; 24; Princess Anne County, VA; Farmer; November 25, 1863–October 28, 1866; Mustered out with regiment; Died June 1901 at Norfolk, VA

James H. Jefferson   Drummer, Private; 15; Norfolk County, VA; Laborer; October 6, 1863–October 6, 1866; Mustered out at expiration of enlistment, Oct. 6, 1866.

Thomas Jefferson   Corporal, Private; 23; Mathews County, VA; Laborer; October 1, 1863–December 12, 1865; Reduced to ranks, May 1864; Mustered out at Fort Monroe, Dec. 12, 1865.

Nelson Jenkins   Corporal; 24; Norfolk County, VA; Farmer; October 20, 1863–October 20, 1866; Mustered out at expiration of enlistment, Oct. 20, 1866.

David Johnson   Musician, Fifer, Private; 31; Nansemond County, VA; Laborer; December 26, 1863–October 28, 1866; Mustered out with regiment.

John A. Jones   Private; 27; Hanson, VA; Laborer; April 6, 1865–October 28, 1866; Mustered out with regiment.

Miles H. Jordan   Private; 18; Isle of Wight County, VA; Farmer; September 30, 1863–September 30, 1866; Mustered out at expiration of enlistment, Sept. 30, 1866; Post-war service in Co. D, 40th U.S. Inf. and Co. C, 25th U.S. Inf.

Frances Keeling   Private; 43; Charleston, SC; Laborer; December 30, 1863–June 18, 1865; Discharged for disability, U.S. Gen. Hospital, Fort Monroe, VA, June 18, 1865.

Isaac Kelling   Private; 26; Norfolk County, VA; Laborer; September 24, 1863–September 24, 1866; Wounded at New Market Heights, VA, Sept. 29, 1864; Mustered out at expiration of enlistment, Sept. 24, 1866.

Samuel Kellum   Private; 35; Accomack County, VA; Farmer; November 25, 1863–October 28, 1866; Mustered out with regiment.

George Keyes   Private; 21; Princess Anne County, VA; Farmer; October 20, 1863–October 20, 1866; Mustered out at expiration of enlistment, Oct. 20, 1866; Died Mar. 28, 1910.

Samuel Lofton   Private; 18; Jones County, NC; Teamster; September 23, 1863–September 23, 1866; Mustered out at expiration of enlistment, Sept. 23, 1866.

Toney Lovett   Private; 22; Kempsville, VA; Farmer; October 4, 1863–February 1, 1864; Died of small pox at Small Pox Hospital, Norfolk, VA, Feb. 1, 1864.

Daniel Lyons   Private; 23; Bladen County, NC; Laborer; September 18, 1863–September 18, 1866; Mustered out at expiration of enlistment, Sept. 18, 1866; Died May 5, 1916 at Wilmington, NC.

George William Mayo   Private; 19; Hanover County, VA; Laborer; April 6, 1865–October 28, 1866; Mustered out with regiment.

Cary McClellen   Private; 21; Norfolk County, VA; Farmer; December 24, 1863–February 22, 1864; Died of small pox, Norfolk, VA, Feb. 22, 1864.

Major Meekins   Private; 26; New Kent County, VA; Farmer; October 6, 1863–October 6, 1866; Died Apr. 9, 1918 at Norfolk, VA.

Gilbert Midgett   Private; 28; Norfolk County, VA; Farmer; November 25, 1863–February 12, 1864; Died of small pox at Small Pox Hospital, Norfolk, VA, Feb. 12, 1864.

Henry F.H. Miller   Captain; 29; Germany; Norton, MA; Minister (Baptist); August 13, 1863–August 13, 1866; Formerly Chaplain (Baptist), 35th MA Inf.; Appointed Captain, Aug. 13, 1863; Promoted Brevet Major, USV, Mar. 13, 1865; Mustered out due to expiration of enlistment; Died Aug. 12, 1897 at Sharon, MA.

Oscar Miller   Private; 26; Norfolk County, VA; Farmer; November 25, 1863–October 28, 1866; Mustered out with regiment.

James N. Mitchell   Sergeant, Private, Corporal; 23; Washington County, VA; Farmer; October 6, 1863–October 6, 1866; Reduced to ranks, Aug. 15, 1865; Promoted Corporal, Oct. 1, 1865; Mustered out at expiration of enlistment, Oct. 6, 1866.

Edward M. Montague   Private; 21; Gloucester County, VA; Farmer; September 22, 1863–September 29, 1864; Killed at New Market Heights, VA, Sept. 29, 1864.

Ned (Edward) Moore   Corporal; 28; Norfolk County, VA; Farmer; November 25, 1863–October 28, 1866; Mustered out with regiment.

Jerome Morris   Private; 33; Norfolk County, VA; Farmer; November 25, 1863–October 28, 1866; Mustered out with regiment; Died Sept. 1, 1913.

Thomas Morris   Private; 27; Pasquotank County, NC; Farmer; December 14, 1863–October 28, 1866; Mustered out with regiment.

Daniel Mundun (Daniel Mundin)   Private; 23; Princess Anne County, VA; Farmer; December 1, 1863–October 28, 1866; Mustered out with regiment; Died Oct. 22, 1919 at Norfolk, VA.

Milton Murray   Private, Corporal; 20; Norfolk County, VA; Farmer; September 2, 1863–September 24, 1866; Promoted Corporal, Oct. 1, 1865; Mustered out at expiration of enlistment, Sept. 24, 1866; Died Nov. 21, 1917 at South Mills, NC.

Andrew Nelson   Sergeant; 18; King William County, VA; Cook; September 20, 1863–September 20, 1866; Wounded at New Market Heights, VA, Sept. 29, 1864; Mustered out at expiration of enlistment, Sept. 20, 1866; Died Sept. 18, 1910.

William H. Nickols   Corporal; 22; Petersburg,

VA; Laborer; November 25, 1863–October 28, 1866; Mustered out with regiment.

William Norris   Private; 20; Pitt County, NC; Farmer; September 18, 1863–September 18, 1866; Mustered out at expiration of enlistment, Sept. 18, 1866.

George W. Nuby (George W. Newby)   Private; 33; Norfolk County, VA; Farmer; October 7, 1863–February 1864; Died of small pox, Hospital, Portsmouth, VA, Feb. 1864.

Thomas Parker   Private; 27; Hampton, VA; Farmer; September 20, 1863–September 20, 1866; Mustered out at expiration of enlistment, Sept. 20, 1866.

Edward Pettis   Private; 45; Norfolk County, VA; Farmer; October 6, 1863–June 11, 1865; Died of liver complaint, Gen. Hospital, David Island, NY, June 11, 1865.

Archy Philips   Private; 20; Spotsylvania County, VA; Laborer; April 9, 1865–October 28, 1866; Mustered out with regiment.

Alfred Pilden (Alfred Pilton)   Private; 22; Norfolk, VA; Farmer; October 11, 1863–October 11, 1866; Mustered out at expiration of enlistment, Oct. 11, 1866.

George E. Poole   Private; New York City, NY; Sailor; April 22, 1865; Enlisted (presumably under a false name) from CT for bounty; Sent by the Provost Marshal to the regiment and left behind to guard baggage and deserted when ordered to join the regiment, Richmond, VA, Apr. 22, 1865.

Smith Pratt   Corporal; 27; Fredericksburg, VA; Farmer; September 28, 1863–February 27, 1865; Discharged on certificate of disability, Feb. 27, 1865.

William Pressy (William Preston/Bill Williams)   Private; 18; Hampton, VA; Farmer; September 20, 1863–September 20, 1866; Died Sept. 28, 1919 at New Orleans, LA.

Orange Redmon   Sergeant, Private, Corporal; 25; King and Queen County, VA; Farmer; September 21, 1863–September 21, 1866; Promoted Sergeant; Reduced to ranks, April 1864; Promoted Corporal; Reduced to ranks, Feb. 1865; Mustered out at expiration of enlistment, Sept. 21, 1866; Died Dec. 20, 1912.

Frank W. Rhoades   First Lieutenant; 23; Roxbury, MA; Clerk; September 14, 1863–July 15, 1864; Formerly Sergeant, Co. K, 35th MA Inf.; Appointed First Lieutenant, Sept. 14, 1863; Transferred to Co. B, July 15, 1864.

James Roberts (James Booth)   Private; 20; King and Queen County, VA; Teamster; October 5, 1863–September 29, 1864; Killed at New Market Heights, VA, Sept. 29, 1864.

Edward Robinson   Private; 17; Yorktown, VA; Laborer; September 16, 1863–June 6, 1865; Discharged, Norfolk, VA, June 6, 1865.

Joseph Saunders   Private; 18; Yorktown, VA; Farmer; September 4, 1863–September 4, 1866; Mustered out at expiration of enlistment, Sept. 4, 1866.

Miles Simmons   Corporal; 25; Princess Anne County, VA; Farmer; November 25, 1863–October 28, 1866; Mustered out with regiment.

Cabal Smith (Gabriel Nelson)   Private; 23; Spotsylvania County, VA; Laborer; April 6, 1865–October 28, 1866; Mustered out with regiment.

Jacob Smith   Corporal; 20; Gates County, NC; Laborer; October 5, 1863–October 5, 1866; Mustered out at expiration of enlistment, Oct. 5, 1866.

John Smith   Private; 20; Yorktown, VA; Farmer; September 20, 1863–September 20, 1866; Mustered out at expiration of enlistment, Sept. 20, 1866.

Moses Smith   Private; 20; Norfolk County, VA; Laborer; September 24, 1863–September 24, 1866; Mustered out at expiration of enlistment, Sept. 24, 1866; Died Jan. 30, 1909.

William Smith   Private; 20; Norfolk County, VA; Laborer; December 21, 1863–October 28, 1866; Mustered out with regiment.

Whitford Staden (Whitford Staton)   Private; 22; Edgecombe County, NC; Farmer; September 2, 1863–September 2, 1866; Mustered out at expiration of enlistment, Sept. 2, 1866; Died Aug. 8, 1923 at Suffolk, VA.

Richard Triby   Private; 19; Henrico County, VA; Laborer; April 6, 1865–October 28, 1866; Mustered out with regiment.

Jefferson Valentine   Private; 19; Beaufort County, NC; Farmer; September 18, 1863–September 18, 1866; Wounded at New Market Heights, VA, Sept. 29, 1864; Mustered out at expiration of enlistment, Sept. 18, 1866; Died Mar. 19, 1930 at Sunflower, MS.

Toney Ward   Private; 18; Princess Anne County, VA; Farmer; November 30, 1863–October 28, 1866; Mustered out with regiment.

Elijah H. Wheeler   Second Lieutenant; 20; East

Abington, MA; Shoe Cutter; January 1, 1865–February 25, 1865; Formerly Sergeant Major (white), F&S, 37th USCT; Appointed Second Lieutenant, Jan. 1, 1865;Transferred to Co. I, Feb. 25, 1865.

Washington Whitish (Washington White)   Private; 18; Yorktown, VA; Farmer; September 20, 1863–June 15, 1866; Promoted Hospital Steward and transferred to noncommissioned staff, June 15, 1866; Died Aug. 19, 1919 at Method, NC.

Frank Williams   Private; 18; Princess Anne County, VA; Farmer; November 28, 1863–November 20, 1865; Died of chronic diarrhea, Post Hospital, Brazos Santiago, TX, Nov. 20, 1865.

George Williams   Private; 18; Princess Anne County, VA; Farmer; November 27, 1863–October 28, 1866; Mustered out with regiment; Died Jan. 31, 1909.

Jerome Williams   Private; 24; Currituck County, NC; Farmer; November 25, 1863–June 23, 1865; U.S. Gen. Hospital, Fort Monroe, VA, June 23, 1865.

Lemuel J. Williams   Private; 18; Norfolk County, VA; Farmer; November 27, 1863–October 28, 1866; Mustered out with regiment.

Moses Williams   Private; 18; Norfolk County, VA; Farmer; November 17, 1863–February 1864; Died of small pox at Hospital, Portsmouth, VA, Feb. 1864.

Henry Woodhouse (Henry Woodis)   Private; 25; Norfolk County, VA; Farmer; November 26, 1863–October 28, 1866; Mustered out with regiment.

# APPENDIX 1

# Composition of a Regiment of Infantry
## *Ten Companies*

### FIELD AND STAFF

**Regimental Field Officers:**
    1 Colonel
    1 Lieutenant Colonel
    1 Major

**Regimental Staff Officers:**
    1 Adjutant (with rank of First Lieutenant)
    1 Quartermaster (with rank of First Lieutenant)
    1 Surgeon (with rank equivalent to Major)
    2 Assistant Surgeons (with rank equivalent to First Lieutenant or Captain)
    1 Chaplain (with rank equivalent to Captain; later Major)

**Regimental Noncommissioned Officers:**
    1 Sergeant Major
    1 Quartermaster Sergeant
    1 Commissary Sergeant
    1 Hospital Steward
    1 Principal Musician

### INFANTRY COMPANY

**Company (Line) Officers:**
    1 Captain
    1 First Lieutenant
    1 Second Lieutenant

**Company Noncommissioned Officers:**
    1 First Sergeant
    4 Sergeants
    8 Corporals
    2 Musicians
    1 Wagoner

**Company Enlisted Personnel:**
 64 Privates — Minimum
 83 Privates — Maximum

**Sources:** "Appendix One" in James Kenneth Bryant, II, "The Model 36th Regiment: The Contribution of Black Soldiers and Their Families to the Union War Effort, 1861–1866" (Ph.D. diss. University of Rochester, 2001), 379; Hondon B. Hargrove, *Black Union Soldiers in the Civil War* (Jefferson, NC: McFarland, 1988), 125; and Fred Albert Shannon, *The Organization and Administration of the Union Army, 1861–1865*, vol. 2 (1928; reprint, Gloucester, MA: Peter Smith, 1965), 269–270.

# APPENDIX 2

# U.S. Army Ranks
## *U.S. Army Volunteers, 1861–1866*

**Enlisted Rank:**
1. Private

**Enlisted Rank (Noncommissioned Officers):**
2. Musician
3. Principal Musician
4. Hospital Steward
5. Corporal
6. Sergeant
7. First Sergeant
8. Commissary Sergeant
9. Quartermaster Sergeant
10. Sergeant Major

**Commissioned Officers Rank:**
11. Second Lieutenant
12. First Lieutenant
13. Captain
14. Major
15. Lieutenant Colonel
16. Colonel
17. Brigadier General
18. Major General
19. Lieutenant General (Reactivated March 1864)

**Sources:** "Appendix Two" in James Kenneth Bryant, II, "The Model 36th Regiment: The Contribution of Black Soldiers and Their Families to the Union War Effort, 1861–1866" (Ph.D. diss. University of Rochester, 2001), 380; U.S. War Department, *Revised Regulations for the Army of the United States, 1861* (Philadelphia, PA: J.G.L. Brown, 1861; reprint, Harrisburg, PA: The National Historical Society, 1980), 9, 524–526.

# APPENDIX 3

# Unit Organization in the Union Army

1. Section (10–11 Privates under a Corporal)[1]
2. Squad (2 Sections under a Sergeant — about 25 men)
3. Platoon (2 Squads under a Lieutenant — about 50 men)[2]
4. Company (2 Platoons under a Captain —100 men)[3]
5. Battalion (2–4 Companies)[4]
6. Regiment (10 Companies standard —1,000 men under a Colonel)
7. Brigade (2–4 Regiments under a Brigadier General)
8. Division (3–4 Brigades under a Major General)
9. Corps (3–4 Divisions under a Major General)
10. Army and/or Military Department (2–3 Corps under a Major General)[5]
11. Theater Command (2 or more Armies/Departments under a Major General)[6]
12. U.S. Army (All U.S. Theater Commands — in 1864 under a Lieutenant General)[7]

**Sources:** "Appendix Three" in James Kenneth Bryant, II, "The Model 36th Regiment: The Contribution of Black Soldiers and Their Families to the Union War Effort, 1861–1866" (Ph.D. diss. University of Rochester, 2001), 381; "Organization of the Civil War Armies," Fredericksburg Battlefield Visitor Center Files, Fredericksburg and Spotsylvania National Military Park, Fredericksburg, Virginia.

## Appendix 4

# Colonel Alonzo G. Draper's Report of Knott's Island, N.C.,
### the Arrest of Nancy White and the Altercation with Lieutenant Colonel Frederick F. Wead, 98th New York Volunteers[1]

Present-day scholars have pointed out Colonel Alonzo G. Draper's apparent silence on his controversial expedition through Knott's Island, North Carolina, and the arrest of Nancy White as a hostage. Jerry V. Witt in *Wild in North Carolina* (1993) has written that Draper never mentioned his activities on Knott's Island, and Frances H. Casstevens in *Edward A. Wild and the African Brigade in the Civil War* has asserted that "Draper made no mention of his raid on Knott's Island, the burning of several homes there, or the incident that led to his taking Miss White hostage."[2] Yet, Draper's lengthy report of December 23, 1863, found in the Regimental Letterbook for the 36th USCT (2nd North Carolina Colored Volunteers) and reproduced here, describes from his own perspective the operations on Knott's Island, the arrest of Nancy White, and the later confrontation with Lieutenant Colonel Frederick F. Wead of the 98th New York. Draper's immediate superior, Brigadier General Edward A. Wild, incorporated some elements of this particular report into his December 28, 1863, official report of his larger raid into northeastern North Carolina as well as used Draper's account as a basis to refute charges against Draper in his January 10, 1864, report to Brigadier General James Barnes, commanding the District of Virginia on the status of Nancy White and the charges Colonel Wead filed against Draper. Both the works of Witt and Casstevens through their use of unpublished primary source documents and critical analysis of these aforementioned events have elevated Wild's 1863 North Carolina Expedition from the depths of obscurity to an important chapter in the broader history of the American Civil War.

### Alonzo G. Draper to Hiram W. Allen, December 23, 1863, Regimental Letterbook, 36th USCT, RG 94, NARA

Head Quarters 2d N.C. Col$^d$ Vols.
Portsmouth Va. Dec, 23 1863

Lieut:-

In obedience to orders from Brig. General Edward A. Wild commanding an Expeditionary Force sent out from Norfolk and Portsmouth, I embarked on Monday Dec. 21, with two hundred and fifty men of the 1st and 2d. N.C., on board the steamer Three Brothers[.] [A]t Currituck Court House we landed and burnt the houses of Henry White, Lieut. [i]n Capt. Caffey's Guerilla Company, and of Caleb White, 1st Sergt. in the same company. At this point, which is about fifteen miles from the nearest picket, I arrested miss White, daughter of Henry White, as hostage for two of our men who had been captured by guerrillas.

At night, we bivouacked on Knott's Island.

The next morning, at 7½ o'clock, I received dispatches of which the following are copies:

"Post Head Qrs. Pongo Bridge
Va. Dec. 22, nd 1863.

Col. Draper, comd'g. 2d. N.C. Vols.,
Sir,-

Being informed that your command has landed on Knott's Island, I deem it not improper to inform you that, almost without exception, the people of that Island, and the County, have taken or signified their intention of taking the prescribed oath of allegiance. Over that Island, and the portion of Princess Ann County south of the Court House, I have the honor, under the orders of the Brig. Gen. Commanding the District, to exercise military jurisdiction, and in this am directed to protect private property, and especially that of persons who have taken the oath of allegiance, against violence of whatever nature. These people have complied, or are as fast as possible complying with the requirements of General Orders No. 49 of Dec. 10/63, from Hd. Qrs., 18th A.C., Dept. Va. & N.C.; and having complied with this, have become entitled to the respect and protection due to loyal citizens.

As you may require transportation, I send you this morning two army wagons, and should you need subsistence stores, I shall be glad to send them to you from your own, which were last evening unloaded at my dock. In case you desire this, Lieut. Leyden, who presents this to you, will send a messenger hither for them.

    I am sir
    Very Respectfully
    Your Obed't Servt'
    (signed) F.F. Wead
    Lieut. Col.
    Comd'g. Post."

"Post Head Qrs. Pongo Bridge
Va. Dec. 22, *nd* 4 A.M.

Col.:-

I have just rec'd. information that Col. De Forest, 81st N.Y. and Gen. Wild have been attacked near North West Landing, by a strong force of the enemy, who have come across the White Oak Spring Canal. It is my intention to move at daylight to support Col. De Forest.

I would respectfully suggest that you immediately march to this Post, and thence to join Gen. Wild.

    I am
    Sir
    Very Respectfully
    Your Obed't Servt'
    (Signed) F.F. Wead
    Lieut. Col. Comd'g Post.

Col. Draper
2*nd* N.C.C. Vols,
Knots [sic] Island N.C."

I immediately put my command in motion, to reinforce Gen. Wild, via Pongo Bridge, at which point we arrived at about noon. I went to Lt. Col. Wead's HeadQuarters for further information, and directly afterwards ordered my battalion down to the landing, to receive their rations and prepare to cross the North Landing River. Directly after, an officer of the 98th N.Y. informed Lt. [George W.S.] Conant of the 2d. N.C., who had charge of Miss White, that the Colonel desired her to come into the house. Supposing the message to come from me, Lt. Conant took her in to rest while the troops were crossing.

After some other conversation, Lt. Col. Wead informed me that the lady could not leave the house, as I had no right to arrest her within the lines. I informed him courteously that I had made the arrest by order of Gen. Wild, who had also directed me to repel force by force, if any interference were offered. I informed him that Major General Commanding the Department, had issued an order authorizing Gen. Wild to pass through Gen. Getty's lines.

I reminded him that I was superior to him in rank, and responsible for my acts, if not justified by my orders, and that Gen. Wild was responsible for the orders which he had given me, and that if any wrong had been committed, Lt. Col. Wead could obtain redress in the regular manner; but would not be justified in taking my prisoner by force. I directed Lt. Conant to go out with the prisoner, which he attempted to do, when Lt. Col. Wead resisted him by pressing him back from the door, and preventing him from passing through.

Lt. Conant then informed me that all the other doors had been locked upon him. I had laid my sword on a couch when I first entered the room, unsuspicious of any plot. Seeing preparations to rescue my prisoner by force, I had a moment before gone to the couch and drawn my sword as a precautionary measure, for my own safety. Col Wead had also procured his revolver, I think a moment later. I again ordered Lt. Conant to take the lady out and Lt. Col Wead again resisting him, I caught him by the shoulder, and drew him away from the door, when the lady was brought as far as the door. Perceiving that Lt. Col. Wead's revolver was in a horizontal position with the muzzle toward my breast, I caught it and held the muzzle up with my left hand. Either before the beginning of the struggle, or directly after[,] Col. Wead ordered his Regiment formed, and drawn upon the four sides of the house.

By this time, Lt. Col. Wead had summoned to his aid a large posse of his enlisted men, who threw themselves upon Lt. Conant and myself with considerable violence. I thrust at one man who had grappled me in front, but his belt plate probably saved him, as my sword blade was considerably bent. Directly after, my sword was wrenched from me. During the melee, I was pretty severely choked, and roughly handled. I called out to any orderly to have my battalion formed[?] they being as a distance of fifty or sixty rods from the house. As soon as I could escape, unarmed and hatless, where the 98th. N.Y. were already in line of battle to receive us, with a detachment of cavalry in rear of their left flank ready for a charge.

While marching towards the house Col. Cullen of the 96th. N.Y., met me, and urged me to wait until he could confer with Lt. Col. Wead, as he thought the difficulty could be adjusted. To this I consented, and after a reasonable delay, again moved my battalion, halting the column at about thirty yards from Lt. Col. Wead's left; here Col. Cullen and Lt. Col. Wead met me, and Col. Cullen informed me that Lt. Col. Wead would agree to either of two propositions, 1st: that I should leave the lady in his custody, subject to the orders of the Department Commander.

It may be well to remark here that on my first expedition into Princess Anne County,

Lt. Col. Wead had informed me that if he had not seen my written orders, he should have been obliged to fight me. It was in consequence of this gratuitous menace, unprovoked and unresented by me, that Gen. Wild had on this occasion given me positive orders to resist any violent interferences of Lt. Col. Wead, by force of arms. I therefore informed him that the emergency having been foreseen and provided for by my Commanding officer, I had not discretion in the matter, but must obey my orders, and leave the responsibility with the General.

He then offered to give me a certificate that he had taken the prisoner from me by force. My reply was that this would not justify me with Gen. Wild, as I could not acknowledge that he had sufficient force to take her. During the conversation, though I think not in connection with the certificate, he remarked that he had five hundred men to my two hundred and fifty and that he should have as many more in a few minutes. Irritated by the implied menace, I replied with perhaps too little courtesy, that I did not care a damn if he had ten thousand as my orders had no reference to numbers. He immediately apologized for the threat, remarking that he ought not to have spoken so.

His second proposition was that the lady should be sent under my guard to Gen. [James H.] Ledlie, his commanding officer. To this, I could not consent, as I was not subject to Gen. Ledlie's orders, but proposed to deliver her to Gen. Barnes, for his decision. Col. Cullen then proposed that she be sent in charge of my guard to Gen. Ledlie, with a note of explanation from Lt. Col. Wead, and thence taken by my guard to Gen. Barnes, the question of jurisdiction to be settled between the two generals. To this we both agreed; the note was written, and delivered to my Adjutant; we crossed the North Landing River, and hastened to North West Landing, in the belief that our forces there were in imminent danger.

Here we arrived in the evening, and found Gen. Wild, who the next morning marched our force to Great Bridge where he sought an interview with Gen. Ledlie, and not finding him, explained the case to his Assistant Adj't. Gen. [Captain A.H. Davis], who desired to retain the lady, until the affair could be adjusted. It was my desire to take the lady to Gen. Barnes but my Commanding officer, Gen. Wild, required me to deliver her to him, and brought her with him to Norfolk. In this affair, I have been governed by the simple desire to obey my orders.

I have the honor to be
Very Respectfully
Your Obed't. Serv't.
A.G. Draper, Col. 2d N.C.
Col$^d$ Vols. Comd'g.

Lt. Hiram W. Allen
A.A.A.G. Colored Troops,
Norfolk and Portsmouth

# APPENDIX 5

# Letter of Sergeant Major Henry N. Adkins, 36th USCT
## Requesting an Appointment as a Second Lieutenant, with Endorsements and Reply[1]

### A.

Camp 36th Regt U S C T
1st Brig. 1st Div. 25th Army Corps
Before Richmond Va
March 18th 1865

Capt. H.B. Scott
Asst. Adjt. Genl.
Bureau of Colored Troops
Hd. Qrs. Dept of Va.

Sir:

I have the honor to request an appointment as 2nd Lieutenant in the 36th Regt. U.S.C.T.

I also have the honor to state, that I entered the service Sept. 1st 1863. I am 20 years of age, born in New York City, and by profession a Gardener.

I am, sir,
Very respectfully your
Obedient Servant.
Henry N. Adkins
Sergt Major 36th U.S.C.T.

### B.

Headquarters 36th U.S. Colored Troops.
1st Brig. 1st Division 25th Army Corps
Before Richmond. Virginia
March 18th 1865.

Capt. H.B. Scott

Adj't. Gen'l Bureau of Colored Troops,
Head Quarters Department of Virginia

Captain,

I most respectfully recommend the appointment of Sergeant Major Henry N. Adkins (colored) 36 th U.S.C.T. to be 2nd Lieutenant in this regiment vice 2nd Lieutenant James W. Bacon promoted to 1st Lieutenant.

Serg't Major Adkins was born in New York City, has had a good education, has been with the regiment about eighteen months, has always been a faithful and good soldier, always done his duty, whether in the camp, on the march, or in Battle. I consider him well qualified for a position as line officer, and by his brave and meritorious conduct has proved himself worthy of promotion, and would, in my opinion, honorably distinguish himself as an officer in the service of the United States.

Very respectfully, your obedient servant
B.F. Pratt
Lieutenant Colonel 36th U.S.C.T. Commanding
[Endorsements]

Hd. Qrs. 1st Brig. 1st Div. 25th
AC. Before Richmond Va,
March 18, 1865

Respectfully forwarded if it be the policy to commission colored men Serg't Major Adkins has all the proper qualifications.

A.G. Draper
Bvt Brig. Gen. Comd'g

Hd. Qrs. 1st Div. 25th A.C.
In the field Va. Mch. 19/65.

Respectfully forwarded approved and earnestly recommended

Edw$^d$. A. Wild
Brig. Gen. Comdg

Hd. Qrs. 25th Army Corps
Before Richmond Va Mar. 20/65

Respectfully forwarded Disapproved

G. Weitzel
Maj. Genl
Comadg

## C.

Bureau of Colored Troops,
Head Quarters Department of Virginia,
Army of the James.
Before Richmond, Va., March 21, 1865

Major General G. Weitzel
Commanding 25th Army Corps,

General

I have the honor to acknowledge the receipt of a communication from Lieut Colonel Pratt, 36th U.S. Colored Troops recommending for a commission, Sergt. Major Henry N. Adkins, 36th U.S. Colored Troops, which was forwarded by you disapproved.

I am instructed by the Major General Commanding to inform you in reply that there is no authority under which colored men can be commissioned as officers, and that in his opinion the time has not yet come for this step. When that authority is given and it is deemed expedient to commission colored men as officers, due notification will be given, but, until that time comes, it is considered highly inexpedient to introduce dissension into the colored corps by such recommendations.

You will please acquaint General Wild and Colonel Pratt with the views of the Major General Commanding on this subject, and inform them that their application has been disapproved.

Very Respectfully,
Your Obedt. Servt.
H.B. Scott
Major, 4th Mass. Cavalry
A.A.A.G.

# Chapter Notes

## Introduction

1. "National Cemetery Fredericksburg, Va. Jan. 1, 1873," in Archival Storage, Fredericksburg and Spotsylvania National Military Park, National Park Service, Fredericksburg, Virginia. A listing of Fredericksburg interments (in particular Peter Wilson) are readily accessible in *Roll of Honor*, vol. 25 (Washington, D.C.: GPO, 1868; reprint, Baltimore, MD: Genealogical Printing Co., 1994), 128; *OR*, ser. I, vol. 37, pt. 1, 163–167.

2. William A. Gladstone, *United States Colored Troops, 1863–1867* (Gettysburg, PA: Thomas, 1990), 10–11; CMSR, Peter Wilson, Co. C, 36th USCT, RG 94. NARA.

3. Pension file of Peter Wilson, 36th USCT, RG 15, NARA; CMSR, Peter Wilson, Co. C, 36th USCT, RG 94, NARA; "Schedule 2, Bertie County, North Carolina, Turner Wilson, p. 1," *Population Schedules of the Eighth Census of the United States*, M653, roll #920, NARA; "Schedule 4, Windsor, Bertie County, North Carolina, Entry #11, Turner Wilson, p. 1," *U.S. Census Office, North Carolina: Selected Schedules*, reel #1.

4. Gerald W. Thomas, *Divided Allegiances: Bertie County During the Civil War* (Raleigh: Division of Archives and History, North Carolina Department of Cultural Resources, 1996), 91; CMSR, Peter Wilson, Co. C, 36th USCT, RG 94, NARA; Co. C, Descriptive Book, 36th USCT, RG 94, NARA.

5. *OR Supp.*, pt. 2, vol. 77, 779–790.

6. Edward A. Wild to J.B. Kinsman, December 26, 1863, Regimental Unbound Papers, 36th USCT, RG 94, NARA.

7. *OR Supp.*, pt. 2, vol. 77, 779–790.

8. Pension file of Peter Wilson, 36th USCT, RG 15, NARA.

9. Ibid.

10. Thomas Morris Chester, *Black Civil War Correspondent: His Dispatches from the Virginia Front*, ed. R.J.M. Blackett (New York: Da Capo, 1989), 96.

11. About 8 percent of casualties among African American Union soldiers were battle related. It is estimated that 20,000 African Americans served in the U.S. Navy during the war. "Report of the Provost Marshal General's Bureau, 17 March 1866, pt. IV," in *Blacks in the United States Armed Forces: Basic Documents*, vol. 2, *Civil War and Emancipation*, eds. Morris J. MacGregor and Bernard C. Nalty (Wilmington, DE: Scholarly Resources, 1977), 171; Noah Andre Trudeau, *Like Men of War: Black Troops in the Civil War, 1862–1865* (Boston: Little, Brown, 1998), 466.

12. Approximately 138,344 black soldiers were recruited from Union-occupied areas of the South. According to the Eighth U.S. Census, slaves accounted for 3,953,769 of the total black population of 4,441,830. While these statistics do not distinguish between the number of southern black soldiers who had been slaves or free persons, it is inferred from this data that the majority of these southern soldiers had been slaves at least until early 1861. "Report of the Provost Marshal General's Bureau, 17 March 1866, pt. IV," 171; U.S. Interior Department, Office of the Census, *Population of the United States in 1860; Compiled from the Original Returns of the Eighth Census, under the Direction of the Secretary of the Interior*, vol. 1, *Population* (Washington, D.C.: GPO, 1864; reprint, New York: Norman Ross, 1990), 598–599. There were 261,918 free blacks residing in the southern slave states in 1860. For a book-length study on free antebellum blacks in the South, see Ira Berlin, *Slaves Without Masters: The Free Negro in the Antebellum South* (1974; New York: New Press, 1992). Also see Russell Duncan's biographical essay on Colonel Robert G. Shaw concerning "the most amazing single statistic" on the number of free black northerners in the Union Army in Robert Gould Shaw, *Blue-Eyed Child of Fortune: The Civil War Letters of Robert Gould Shaw*, ed. Russell Duncan (Athens: University of Georgia Press, 1992), 20.

13. A growing body of scholarship within the past two decades has examined the role black southerners played in support of the Confederate war effort. Such works include Richard Rollins, ed., *Black Southerners in Gray: Essays on Afro-Americans in Confederate Armies* (Murfreesboro, TN: Southern Heritage Press, 1994); Charles Kelly Barrow et al., eds., *Forgotten Confederates: An Anthology About Black Southerners* (Atlanta, GA: Southern Heritage Press, 1995); and Ervin L. Jordan, Jr., *Black Confederates and Afro-Yankees in Civil War Virginia* (Charlottesville: University Press of Virginia, 1995), esp. pp. 216–231.

14. Bell Irvin Wiley, *Southern Negroes, 1861–1865* (1938; reprint, New Haven, CT: Yale University, 1964), ix; Peter Kolchin, "Slavery and Freedom in the Civil War South," in *Writing the Civil War: The Quest to Understand*, ed. James M. McPherson and William J. Cooper, Jr. (Columbia: University of South Carolina Press, 1998), 242.

15. Edward G. Longacre, *A Regiment of Slaves: The 4th United States Colored Infantry, 1863–1866* (Mechanicsburg, PA: Stackpole, 2003), x. Primary accounts of the 1st South Carolina Colored Volunteers recruited from among former slaves in the South include Thomas Wentworth Higginson, *Army Life in a Black Regiment* (1869; New York: W.W. Norton, 1984); and Susie King Taylor, *Reminiscences of My Life in Camp with the 33rd United States Colored Troops* (Boston: Susie King Taylor, 1902). Also see James G. Hollandsworth, Jr., *Louisiana Native Guards: The Black Military Experience During the Civil War* (Baton Rouge: Louisiana State University Press, 1995) for a secondary work on southern black soldiers fighting for the Union composed of former slaves and New Orleans' significant free black population.

16. While four companies of the 36th USCT contained an overwhelming number of North Carolinians by birth,

five companies had more soldiers born in Virginia. The breakdown from the Company Descriptive Books (A–K), 36th USCT, RG 94, NARA is as follows:

Company A: North Carolina — 84.0 percent, Virginia — 14.0 percent
Company B: North Carolina — 54.9 percent, Virginia — 44.3 percent
Company C: North Carolina — 76.7 percent, Virginia — 20.4 percent
Company D: North Carolina — 68.4 percent, Virginia — 8.4 percent
Company E: North Carolina — 35.2 percent, Virginia — 55.2 percent
Company F: North Carolina — 44.6 percent, Virginia — 49.1 percent
Company G: North Carolina — 42.2 percent, Virginia — 52.9 percent
Company H: North Carolina — 84.3 percent, Virginia — 11.1 percent
Company I: North Carolina — 23.8 percent, Virginia — 70.5 percent
Company K: North Carolina — 18.4 percent, Virginia — 76.3 percent

17. Significant works on wartime Reconstruction include Willie Lee Rose, *Rehearsal for Reconstruction: The Port Royal Experiment* (New York: Bobbs-Merrill, 1964); Louis S. Gerteis, *From Contraband to Freedman: Federal Policy Toward Southern Blacks, 1861–1865* (Westport, CT: Greenwood, 1973); and Robert F. Engs, *Freedom's First Generation: Black Hampton, Virginia, 1861–1890* (Philadelphia: University of Pennsylvania Press, 1979).

18. Introduction in *Toward A Social History of the American Civil War: Exploratory Essays*, ed. Maris A. Vinovskis (New York: Cambridge University Press, 1990), xii.

19. Two recent works examining the lives of post-war black veterans and their families are Elizabeth Regosin, *Freedom's Promise: Ex-Slave Families and Citizenship in the Age of Emancipation* (Charlottesville: University Press of Virginia, 2002), and Donald R. Shaffer, *After the Glory: The Struggles of Black Civil War Veterans* (Lawrence: University Press of Kansas, 2004). For a post-war examination of black Union veterans from North Carolina see Richard Reid, "USCT Veterans in Post–Civil War North Carolina," in *Black Soldiers in Blue: African-American Troops in the Civil War Era*, ed. John David Smith (Chapel Hill: University of North Carolina Press, 2002), 391–421, as well as his recent *Freedom for Themselves: North Carolina's Black Soldiers in the Civil War Era* (Chapel Hill: University of North Carolina Press, 2008), esp. pp. 255–322. The Civil War service and post-war career of the 36th USCT's own Richard Etheridge is treated in David Wright and David Zoby, *Fire on the Beach: Recovering the Lost Story of Richard Etheridge and the Pea Island Lifesavers* (New York: Scribner, 2000).

20. Sylvia R. Frey, *Water from the Rock: Black Resistance in a Revolutionary Age* (Princeton, NJ: Princeton University Press, 1992), 328.

21. Mary F. Berry, *Military Necessity and Civil Rights Policy: Black Citizenship and the Constitution, 1861–1868* (Port Washington, NY: Kennikat, 1977), x.

## Chapter 1

1. "The Names and ages of Negroes belonging to Stephen A. Norfleet, January 1st, 1844," in Norfleet Family Papers, 1784–1895, *Records of Ante-bellum Plantations*, ser. J, pt. 12, reel #27, frame #702; Pension File of Saunders Norfleet, 36th USCT, RG 15, NARA; "Schedule 4, Roxobel, Bertie County, North Carolina, Entry #17, Stephen A. Norfleet, p. 35," in *U.S. Census Office, North Carolina: Selected Schedules*, reel #1; "Schedule 2, Bertie County, North Carolina, Stephen A. Norfleet, pp. 82–84," in *Population Schedules of the Eighth Census of the United States*, Microfilm Publication M653, Roll #920, NARA; Gerald W. Thomas, *Divided Allegiances: Bertie County During the Civil War* (Raleigh: Division of Archives and History, North Carolina Department of Cultural Resources, 1996), 5; *Population of the United States in 1860*, vol. 2, *Agriculture*, 247.

2. Pension File of Saunders Norfleet, 36th USCT, RG 15, NARA.

3. Ibid.

4. Microfilmed pension index rolls (Microfilm Publication T289) contain the names of soldiers in Union regiments who applied for pensions or dependents filing under the soldier's name if deceased. Pension application numbers for these soldiers enabled researchers to obtain the actual records. Pension Index, 36th USCT, Microfilm Publication T289, NARA, roll #550.

5. There were 548 soldiers born in North Carolina, 479 soldiers born in Virginia, 20 soldiers born in other places, and 29 soldiers whose birthplace were not listed or unknown. Most North Carolina-born soldiers came from that state's coastal plain region that included the following counties: Beaufort, Bertie, Camden, Carteret, Chowan, Craven, Currituck, Hertford, Martin, Pasquotank, Perquimans, Pitt, and Washington. Virginia-born soldiers came from the southeastern counties of Elizabeth City, Gloucester, Norfolk, Nansemond, Princess Anne, and York. A significant minority of soldiers came from Virginia's Northern Neck counties (situated between the Potomac and Rappahannock Rivers). Many of these soldiers enlisted into the 36th USCT while it was on duty in St. Mary's County, Maryland, directly across the Chesapeake Bay from the Northern Neck. Companies A–K, Descriptive Books, 36th USCT, RG 94, NARA.

6. Among the South's 384,884 slaveholders, about 12.1 percent owned 20 or more slaves. More than 50 percent of the total southern slave population lived and worked on farms and plantations with these particular sized holdings. Approximately 25 percent of these slaves lived on holdings of 50 or more slaves. However, slightly less than 88 percent of the entire South's slaveholders owned 19 slaves or less. In North Carolina, more than 165,526 slaves lived on plantations with 20 or more slaves owned by only 12.1 percent of the state's total slaveholding population (the same percentage among the South's total slaveholders). In Virginia, over 254,432 slaves resided on slaveholding with 20 or more slaves. These particular Virginia slaveholders made up only 9.2 percent of the state's slaveholding population but owned well over 15 percent of the total slave population. U.S. Interior Department, Office of the Census, *Population of the United States in 1860; Compiled from the Original Returns of the Eighth Census, under Direction of the Secretary of the Interior*, vol. 2, *Agriculture* (Washington, D.C.: GPO, 1864; reprint, New York: Norman Ross, 1990), 247. The following counties had 30 or more soldiers of the 36th USCT claiming as their place of birth. The numbers in parenthesis are the actual number of claimants; In North Carolina: Currituck (52), Washington (47), Pitt (45), Beaufort (43), Bertie (42), Pasquotank (39), Martin (37); In Virginia: Norfolk (112), Princess Anne (92). Companies A–K, Descriptive Books, 36th USCT, RG 94, NARA. The average percentage for small to large farmers owning between 1 to 19 slaves in these nine counties was 88.1 percent. The average for small plantations employing between 20 and 49 slaves was 9.6 percent. The average percentage of medium to large size plantations employing 50 slaves or

# Notes — Chapter 1

more was 2.3 percent. These statistics concerning white slaveholders fall well within the general statistics for the South in 1860. *Population of the United States in 1860*, vol. 1, *Population*, 235–236, 244.

7. Eugene D. Genovese, *Roll, Jordan, Roll: The World the Slaves Made* (1974; reprint, New York: Vintage Books, 1976), 111; Peter Kolchin, *American Slavery, 1619–1877* (New York: Hill and Wang, 1993), 111–112. Bassett estimated that in 1860 North Carolina slaveholders held on average 9.6 slaves while Virginia slaveholders held 9.4 slaves. See John Spencer Bassett, *Slavery in the State of North Carolina* in *Johns Hopkins University Studies in Historical and Political Science*, ser. 17, no.7–8 (Baltimore: Johns Hopkins University, 1899), 78.

8. Pension files of Romulous Cooper, Allen Cooper, 36th USCT, RG 15, NARA; "Schedule 4, Murfreesboro, Hertford County, North Carolina, Entry #18, R.G. Cooper, p. 9," in *U.S. Census Office, North Carolina: Selected Schedules*, reel #1; "Schedule 2, Hertford County, North Carolina, R.G. Cooper, pp. 23–24," in *Population Schedules of the Eighth Census of the United States*, Microfilm Publication M653, roll #923, NARA.

9. Pension files of Spencer Gallop, Malachi Gallop, 36th USCT, RG 15, NARA; "Schedule 4, North Banks District, Currituck County, North Carolina, Entry #28, Hodges Gallop, p. 27," in *U.S. Census Office, North Carolina: Selected Schedules*, reel #1. Gallop held an additional five slaves in trust for minor heirs. "Schedule 2, Currituck County, North Carolina, Hodges Gallop, p. 29," in *Population Schedules of the Eighth Census of the United States*, Microfilm Publication M653, roll #922, NARA.

10. Pension file of Malachi Gallop, 36th USCT, RG 15, NARA.

11. Ann Gallop's sister-in-law, Nancy Ann Gallop Jackson, asserted that Ann's daughter, Sophia, born on June 1, 1855, was from the union with her brother Richard and not George. Ann maintained George's paternity of Sophia. There was obvious tension between Nancy and Ann. If Nancy resented the past relations Ann kept with her two brothers, Ann probably resented Nancy's efforts to be claimed as the sole heir of her deceased brothers, George and Richard, to collect their pensions. Pension files of George Gallop, Spencer Gallop, James Gallop, 36th USCT, RG 15, NARA; "Schedule 4, Powell's Point, Currituck County, North Carolina, Entry #12, C.T. Sawyer, p. 27," in *U.S. Census Office, North Carolina: Selected Schedules*, reel #1; "Schedule 2, Currituck County, North Carolina, C.T. Sawyer, p. 29," in *Population Schedules of the Eighth Census of the United States*, Microfilm Publication M653, roll #922, NARA.

12. Pension files of Frank Cornick, John Cornick, 36th USCT, RG 15, NARA; "Schedule 2, Princess Anne County, Virginia, John Gornto, p. 4," in *Population Schedules of the Eighth Census of the United States*, Microfilm Publication M653, roll #1396, NARA; "Schedule 2, Princess Anne County, Virginia, James Gornto, p. 14," in *Population Schedules of the Eighth Census of the United States*, Microfilm Publication M653, roll #1396, NARA.

13. Pension file of Samuel Kellum, 36th USCT, RG 15 NARA. Accomack County, Virginia, had several white slave owners bearing the surname of Kellum (also spelled Kellam). "Schedule 2, St. George Parish, Accomack County, Virginia," in *Population Schedules of the Eight Census of the United States*, Microfilm Publication M653, roll #1386, NARA.

14. Thomas, Sawney, and Henry apparently had the same father, but Henry had a different mother. Jonathan Jaycox may have been a son or nephew of Jesse Jaycox. Pension files of Thomas Jaycox, Henry Jaycox, Cicero Jaycox, John Buck, 36th USCT, RG 15, NARA.

15. Pension files of David H.A. Henderson, Frederick Henry Harris, John Bufort, 36th USCT, RG 15, NARA.

16. John C. Inscoe, "Carolina Slave Narratives: An Index to Acculturation," *Journal of Southern History* 49 (February 1983): 531, 541; Herbert G. Gutman, *The Black Family in Slavery and Freedom, 1750–1925* (New York: Vintage Books, 1976), 186; Kolchin, *American Slavery*, 46. White convincingly argues that slave mothers were the primary links to their children's paternal heritage and family history by providing their children with the names of male relatives, especially fathers. See Deborah Gray White, *Ar'n't I a Woman?: Female Slaves in the Plantation South* (New York: W.W. Norton, 1985, 1987), 109.

17. Pension files of Frank Cornick, James Cornick, 36th USCT, RG 15, NARA.

18. Pension Index, 36th USCT, Microfilm Publication T298, NARA, rolls #550–551. Shaffer's broader study of black Union veterans suggests that after the war they often discarded their former owners' surname in favor of their fathers' surname, even if they had not known them or if they had been white. It was the symbolic act of changing one's surname rather than its source that was important to former slaves. Donald Robert Shaffer, "Marching On: African-American Veterans in Postbellum America, 1865–1951," (Ph.D. diss., University of Maryland, 1996), 78–79.

19. Frederick Douglass, *Narrative of the Life of Frederick Douglass, An American Slave* (1845; reprint, New York: Penguin, 1986), 47; Pension files of Harrison Gordon, Moses Brown, 36th USCT, RG 15, NARA.

20. Booker T. Washington, *Up from Slavery: An Autobiography*, in *Three Negro Classics* (1901; New York: Avon Books, 1965), 29; Pension file of Noah C. Cherry, 36th USCT, RG 15, NARA.

21. Pension file of Spencer Gallop, 36th USCT, RG 15, NARA.

22. Pension file of James H. Samuel, 36th USCT, RG 15, NARA.

23. Pension file of Henry Cornick, 36th USCT, RG 15, NARA.

24. Ibid.; "Schedule 2, Charles City County, Virginia, John Tyler, p. 11," in *Population Schedules of the Eighth Census of the United States*, Microfilm Publication M653, roll #1385, NARA.

25. George Potter and Joseph Harrison, both of Company A were 51 at the time of their enlistment. Charles Prentiss (Company F) and Uriah Griffin (Company G) were 50. David H. Allen (Company A), James Grantly (Company C), James Ellison (Company C), George Washington (Company E) and William Groves (Company H) were 16. Allen initially served as a bugler. Grantly and Ellison served as drummers. Leroy Smith (Company F), Henry T. Willis (Company G), Toney Wilson (Company H), and James H. Jefferson (Company K) were 15. Smith and Griffin served as drummers. Griffin became Principal Musician (Regimental Band Leader) later in the war. Companies A–K, Descriptive Books, 36th USCT, RG 94, NARA.

26. Leslie Howard Owens, *This Species of Property: Slave Life and Culture in the Old South* (New York: Oxford University, 1976), 56.

27. Companies A–K, Descriptive Books, 36th USCT, RG 94, NARA.

28. Pension file of Miles James, 36th USCT, RG 15, NARA.

29. Pension file of Paul Wiggins, 36th USCT, RG 15, NARA.

30. Pension file of James H. Johnson, 36th USCT, RG 15, NARA. John Critcher would become a lieutenant

colonel in the 15th Virginia Cavalry. The 36th USCT would engage in skirmishes and capture several members (as well as former members) belonging to this unit while on duty in southeastern Virginia and on expeditions in Virginia's Northern Neck region. See John Fortier, *15th Virginia Cavalry* (Lynchburg, VA: H.E. Howard, 1993), 12–13.

31. Pension file of George Gallop, 36th USCT, RG 15, NARA.

32. Pension file of John Cornick, 36th USCT, RG 15, NARA.

33. Joseph T. Glatthaar, *Forged in Battle: The Civil War Alliance of Black Soldiers and White Officers* (New York: Free Press, 1990), 174.

34. Adkins would be promoted to regimental sergeant major in early 1864. Pool enlisted into the 36th USCT from Connecticut, but never served and was listed as a deserter. Companies E,H,I,K, Descriptive Books, 36th USCT, RG 94, NARA.

35. Companies C,F H, Descriptive Books, 36th USCT, RG 94, NARA. Free blacks in Nansemond County, Virginia, did particularly well economically. There were 86 free black farmers in 1860, 15 of them owned farms of 100 acres or more. See Louis S. Gerteis, *From Contraband to Freedman: Federal Policy Toward Southern Blacks, 1861–1865* (Westport, CT: Greenwood, 1973), 42.

36. Pension file of Moses Brown, 36th USCT, RG 15, NARA; Company H, Descriptive Book, 36th USCT, RG 94, NARA.

37. Pension file of Richard Etheridge, 36th USCT, RG 15, NARA. Joe A. Mobley, *Ship Ashore! The U.S. Lifesavers of Coastal North Carolina* (Raleigh: Division of Archives and History, North Carolina, 1994), 94–99. Wright and Zoby believe that the paternity of Richard Etheridge will remain a mystery—see David Wright and David Zoby, *Fire on the Beach: Recovering the Lost Story of Richard Etheridge and the Pea Island Lifesavers* (New York: Scribner, 2000), 43–47.

38. Companies A–K, Descriptive Books, 36th USCT, RG 94, NARA.

39. Ibid.

40. Ibid.

41. Pension file of Anson Farrier, 36th USCT, RG 15, NARA; Companies A–K, Descriptive Books, 36th USCT, RG 94, NARA; Alonzo G. Draper to John A. Andrew, September 19, 1863, in Executive Letters, vol. 102, no. 94, MA. Also see Richard Reid, "Raising the African Brigade: Early Black Recruitment in Civil War North Carolina," *North Carolina Historical Review* 70 (1993): 286.

42. Companies, A,B,D,F,H,K, Descriptive Books, 36th USCT, RG 94, NARA.

43. Pension files of Isaiah Dickson, John Buck, 36th USCT, RG 15, NARA.

44. *Population of the United States in 1860*, vol. 1, *Population*, 244. Goldin estimates that in 1860 the majority of slave hirers in Norfolk used 10 or more slaves mainly in commerce. Claudia Dale Goldin, *Urban Slavery in the American South, 1820–1860: A Quantitative History* (Chicago: University of Chicago Press, 1976), 21.

45. LeGrand B. Cannon, *Personal Reminiscences of the Rebellion* (New York: Burr, 1895), 108.

46. "Endorsements on Applications for return of captured horses," [January or February 1863], Regimental Letterbook, 36th USCT, RG 94, NARA; Company A,F, Descriptive Book, 36th USCT, RG 94, NARA.

47. "Endorsements on Applications for return of captured horses," [January or February 1863], Regimental Letterbook, 36th USCT, RG 94, NARA; Company A, C, Descriptive Books, 36th USCT, RG 94, NARA.

48. Donna Johanna Benson, "'Before I Be a Slave': A Social Analysis of the Black Struggle for Freedom in North Carolina, 1860–1865" (Ph.D. diss., Duke University, 1984), 107; W.E.B Du Bois, *Black Reconstruction: An Essay Toward a History of the Part Which Black Folk Played in the Attempt to Reconstruct Democracy in America, 1860–1880* (1935; reprint, New York: Touchstone, 1995), 57.

49. John Hope Franklin, and Loren Schweninger. *Runaway Slaves: Rebels on the Plantation* (New York: Oxford University Press, 1999), 210.

50. Ibid., 291; Elizabeth Curtis Wallace, *Glencoe Diary: The War-Time Journal of Elizabeth Curtis Wallace*, eds. Eleanor P. Cross and Charles B. Cross, Jr. (Chesapeake, VA: Norfolk County Historical Society, 1968), 17.

51. Wilder is quoted in Ira Berlin et al., eds., *Free at Last: A Documentary History of Slavery, Freedom, and the Civil War* (Edison, NJ: Blue and Grey Press, 1992), 107–109.

52. Pension files of Spencer Gallop, Malachi Gallop, Romulous Cooper, 36th USCT, RG 15, NARA; Companies A–K, Descriptive Books, 36th USCT, RG 94, NARA. This Soney Jaycox was a different person than Sawney Jaycox. Both were owned by the same individual. The former served in Company A and the latter in Company C. Pension file of Soney Jaycox, 36th USCT, RG 15, NARA.

53. "Names of Negroes that went to the Yankees in Washington, N.C., 1862," in Grimes Family Papers, 1713–1866, *Records of Ante-bellum Plantations*, ser. J, pt. 12, reel #48, frame #487; Companies A–K, Descriptive Books, 36th USCT, RG 94, NARA.

54. Ira Berlin, et al., eds., *Freedom: A Documentary History of Emancipation, 1861–1867*, ser. I, vol. I, *The Destruction of Slavery* (New York: Cambridge University Press, 1985), 77.

55. Pension files of Paul Wiggins, David H.A. Henderson, 36th USCT, RG 15, NARA.

56. Du Bois, *Black Reconstruction*, 59; Benson, "'Before I Be a Slave,'" 122; Tracy Whittaker Schneider, "The Institution of Slavery in North Carolina, 1860–1865" (Ph.D. diss., Duke University, 1979), 141; Ervin L. Jordan, Jr., *Black Confederates and Afro-Yankees in Civil War Virginia* (Charlottesville: University Press of Virginia, 1995), 72.

57. Emory M. Thomas, *The Confederate Nation, 1861–1865* (New York: Harper Torchbooks, 1979), 91; Wayne K. Durrill, *War of Another Kind: A Southern Community in the Great Rebellion* (New York: Oxford University Press, 1990), 157–159.

58. At least 401 soldiers of the 36th USCT claimed their place of birth in the aforementioned North Carolina and Virginia counties that made up and surrounded the Great Dismal Swamp. Companies A–K, Descriptive Books, 36th USCT, RG 94, NARA.

59. Hugo Prosper Leaming, *Hidden Americans: Maroons of Virginia and the Carolinas* (New York: Garland, 1995), 222; Herbert Aptheker, "Maroons Within the Present Limits of the United States," in *Maroon Societies: Rebel Slave Communities in the Americas*, ed. Richard Price (Baltimore, MD: Johns Hopkins University Press, 1983), 152; Bassett, *Slavery in the State of North Carolina*, 94–95; Franklin and Schweninger, *Runaway Slaves*, 291–292.

60. Redpath reprinted Charley's narrative that had been originally transcribed by a Mrs. Knox of Boston who had visited fugitive slaves residing in Canada. James Redpath, *The Roving Editor, or Talks with Slaves in the Southern States*, ed. John R. McKivigan (University Park: Pennsylvania State University Press, 1996), 241–242, 244–245.

61. Charley is quoted (via Mrs. Knox) in Redpath, *The Roving Editor*, 245.

62. Douglass, *Narrative*, 137–138. Church is quoted in Frederick Law Olmsted, *A Journey in the Seaboard Slave States, with Reports on Their Economy* (New York: Dix and Edwards, 1856), 159–160.

63. Aptheker, "Maroons Within the Present Limits of the United States," 152; Olmsted, *A Journey in the Seaboard Slave States*, 154; Bland Simpson, *The Great Dismal: A Carolinian's Swamp Memoir* (Chapel Hill: University of North Carolina Press, 1990), 46–48, 71–73, 105; Companies A–K, Descriptive Books, 36th USCT, RG 94, NARA. Also see Peter C. Stewart, "Man and the Swamp: The Historical Dimension," in *The Great Dismal Swamp*, ed. Paul W. Kirk, Jr. (Charlottesville: University Press of Virginia, 1979), 57–73.

64. Douglass, *Narrative*, 121–122.

65. Two views of thought have emerged in scholarly debate on slave emancipation. One view, the "self-emancipation thesis," argues that the slaves escaping to Union lines freed themselves. The other view supports President Lincoln's active role in shaping polices leading to the abolishment of slavery. See James M. McPherson, *Drawn with the Sword: Reflections on the American Civil War* (New York: Oxford University Press, 1996), 192–207.

## Chapter 2

1. H.S. Beals to S.S. Jocelyn, August 18, 1863, *AMA* (North Carolina), roll #150, frame #99706. Also see Joe A. Mobley, *James City: A Black Community in North Carolina* (Raleigh: North Carolina Department of Cultural Resources, Division of Archives and History, 1981), 43.

2. Beals to Jocelyn, frame #99706.

3. Beals to Jocelyn, frame #99707.

4. Ibid.

5. Beals to Jocelyn, frame #99708.

6. Beals to Jocelyn, frame #99709; Richard Reid, "Raising the African Brigade: Early Black Recruitment in Civil War North Carolina," *North Carolina Historical Review* 70 (1993): 276, 287; Edwin S. Redkey, "Black Chaplains in the Union Army," *Civil War History* 33 (December 1987): 276; William A. Gladstone, *United States Colored Troops, 1863–1867* (Gettysburg, PA: Thomas, 1990), 110.

7. Beals to Jocelyn, frame #99708.

8. Beals to Jocelyn, frames #99708–99709.

9. *OR*, ser. I, vol. 3, 466–67, 469, 477–478, 485; *OR*, ser. III, vol. 2, 42–43.

10. B.F. Butler to Thomas H. Hicks, April 23, 1861, *NMSUS*, reel #1, frame #394; *OR*, ser. II, vol. 1, 750; Hans L. Trefousse, *Ben Butler: The South Called Him Beast!* (New York: Twyane, 1957), 53, 57.

11. Tallmadge was the son of Nathaniel P. Tallmadge, a U.S. Senator from New York during the 1830s and later governor of the Wisconsin Territory. He had graduated from the United States Military Academy at West Point in 1848. A career army officer, Tallmadge, like Butler, had been a "Breckinridge Democrat." Once the war began, Lieutenant Tallmadge remained in the army reinforcing his allegiance and commitment to the Union. [Charles] D. Brigham to William F. Smith, April 18, 1892, in William Farrar Smith Papers, VTHS. Also see Francis B. Heitman, *Historical Register and Dictionary of the United States Army*, vol. 1 (Washington, D.C.: GPO, 1903), 944.

12. In Brigham's letter to General Smith 30 years later, he quotes Tallmadge as saying to Butler: "There is war: these fugitives are contrabands, they are contrabands of war as much so as Magruder's [Confederate commander at Hampton] guns or men are in my judgment. It is your duty not only to keep these men that have come in but you should go for more and take them whenever they can be found." [Charles] D. Brigham to William F. Smith, April 18, 1892, in William Farrar Smith, VHS; *New York Tribune*, October 12, 1862; *New York Tribune*, October 15, 1862.; Ervin L. Jordan, Jr., *Black Confederates and Afro-Yankees in Civil War Virginia* (Charlottesville: University Press of Virginia, 1995), 83. Tallmadge, later promoted to captain, was placed in charge of paying and supplying black laborers at Fort Monroe. According to some of the early AMA missionaries, Tallmadge conducted questionable and improper practices defrauding freedmen and pocketing funds at their expense. He would die of illness in October 1862. See Robert F. Engs, *Freedom's First Generation: Black Hampton, Virginia, 1861–1890* (Philadelphia: University of Pennsylvania Press, 1979), 31–33.

13. *OR*, ser. I, vol. 2, 649; John B. Cary to Benj. F. Butler, March 9, 1891, in Benjamin F. Butler, *Private and Official Correspondence of General Benjamin F. Butler During the Civil War*, vol. 1, ed. Jessie Ames Marshall (Norwood, MA: Plimpton, 1917), 102–103; Benjamin F. Butler, *Butler's Book: A Review of His Legal, Political, and Military Career* (Boston: A.M. Thayer, 1892), 256–258; Edward L. Pierce, "The Contrabands at Fortress Monroe," *Atlantic Monthly* 49 (November 1861): 627–628.

14. Pierce, "The Contrabands at Fortress Monroe," 628; *OR*, ser. I, vol. 2, 53, 649–650; Engs, *Freedom's First Generation*, 20.

15. Pierce, "The Contrabands at Fortress Monroe," 628.

16. Benjamin Quarles, *The Negro in the Civil War* (1953; New York: Da Capo, 1989), 94; James M. McPherson, *The Struggle for Equality: Abolitionists and the Negro in the Civil War and Reconstruction* (1964; Princeton, NJ: Princeton University Press, 1995), 165.

17. *OR*, ser. I, vol. 2, 53, 62; *OR*, ser. III, vol. 1, 243. Also see Ira Berlin et al., eds., *Free at Last: A Documentary History of Slavery, Freedom, and the Civil War* (Edison, NJ: Blue and Grey Press, 1992), 10.

18. *OR*, ser. III, vol. 1, 388, 395–396, 717; James M. McPherson, ed., *The Negro's Civil War: How American Blacks Felt and Acted During the War for the Union*, 3rd ed. (1965; reprint, New York: Ballantine, 1991), 28–29.

19. Engs, *Freedom's First Generation*, 30–31.

20. A.E. Burnside to E.M. Stanton, May 19, 1862, *NMSUS*, reel #1, frame #506 (this same report is also found in *OR*, ser. II, vol. 1, 819); John G. Barrett, *The Civil War in North Carolina* (1963; Chapel Hill: University of North Carolina Press, 1983), 66–69. Redkey suggests that the above quoted Union soldier of the 8th Connecticut Infantry may have been an African American man "passing" as a white soldier. See William H. Johnson to *Pine & Palm* (Boston, MA), March 9, 1862, in Edwin S. Redkey, ed., *A Grand Army of Black Men: Letters from African-American Soldiers in the Union Army, 1861–1865* (New York: Cambridge University Press, 1993), 19.

21. *OR*, ser. III, vol. 2, 276, 282.

22. *OR*, ser. III, vol. 2, 584–585, 892–897; John Hope Franklin, *The Emancipation Proclamation* (Garden City, NY: Doubleday, 1963), 19.

23. *OR* ser. III, vol. 3, 2–3; John W. Blassingame, "The Union Army as an Educational Institution for Negroes, 1862–1865," *Journal of Negro Education* 34 (1965): 154; Joseph T. Glatthaar, *Forged in Battle: The Civil War Alliance of Black Soldiers and White Officers* (New York: Free Press, 1990), 9.

24. The earliest black regiments were the 1st Kansas Colored Infantry (79th USCT-new), 1st South Carolina Colored Volunteers (33rd USCT), and the 1st, 2nd, 3rd Regiment Louisiana Native Guards (respectively, 73rd, 74th,

75th USCT). The 1st Kansas has the distinction of being the first black regiment to participate in combat while in Missouri in October 1862. See Gladstone, *United States Colored Troops*, 9; and Dudley Taylor Cornish, *The Sable Arm: Black Troops in the Union Army, 1861–1865* (1956; reprint, Lawrence: University Press of Kansas, 1987), 76–78. For information concerning John Brown's "Secret Six" see Stephen B. Oates, *To Purge This Land With Blood: A Biography of John Brown*, 2nd ed. (1970; Amherst: University of Massachusetts Press, 1984), esp. 229–252; Roy Morris, Jr., "A Shadowy Group of New England Abolitionists Helped John Brown Plan the Raid at Harper's Ferry," *America's Civil War* 9 (March 1996): 6; and James M. McPherson, *Battle Cry of Freedom: The Civil War Era* (1988; New York: Ballantine, 1989), 204–213. Other book-length studies on the "Secret Six" include Otto J. Scott, *The Secret Six: John Brown and the Abolitionist Movement* (New York: Times Books, 1979); and Edward J. Renehan, Jr., *The Secret Six: The True Tale of the Men Who Conspired with John Brown* (New York: Crown, 1995).

25. The best work on the Port Royal Experiment remains Willie Lee Rose, *Rehearsal for Reconstruction: The Port Royal Experiment* (New York: Bobbs-Merrill, 1964).

26. Reid, "Raising the African Brigade," 275; Richard Reid, "General Edward A. Wild and Civil War Discrimination," *Historical Journal of Massachusetts* 13 (January 1985): 15; Edward G. Longacre, "Brave Radical Wild: The Contentious Career of Brigadier Edward A. Wild," *Civil War Times Illustrated* (June 1980): 10.

27. T.M. Vincent to Edward A. Wild, April 14, 1863, *NMSUS*, reel #2, frame, #131 (this same order to Wild is also found in *OR*, ser. III, vol. 3, 122).

28. Ira Berlin et al. *Freedom: A Documentary History of Emancipation, 1861–1867*, ser. II, *The Black Military Experience* (New York: Cambridge University Press, 1982), 114; and Robert Gould Shaw, *Blue-Eyed Child of Fortune: The Civil War Letters of Colonel Robert Gould Shaw*, ed. Russell Duncan (Athens: University of Georgia Press, 1992), 35–36, 323.

29. Frederick H. Dyer, *A Compendium of the War of the Rebellion*, vol. 1 (New York: Thomas Yoseloff, 1959), 390.

30. *OR*, ser. I, vol. 27, pt. 3, 732. James Chaplin Beecher was the son of Rev. Lyman Beecher and the half-brother of Rev. Henry Ward Beecher and Harriett Beecher Stowe, author of *Uncle Tom's Cabin*. Reid, "Raising the African Brigade," 286, 288; Redkey, *A Grand Army of Black Men*, 92.

31. Joseph E. Williams to *Christian Recorder* (Philadelphia), July 4, 1863, in Redkey, *A Grand Army of Black Men*, 91. For a study on the freedman on Roanoke Island during the war, see Patricia C. Click, *Time Full of Trial: The Roanoke Island Freedmen's Colony, 1862–1867* (Chapel Hill: University of North Carolina Press, 2001).

32. Reid, "Raising the African Brigade," 290; John Sullivan to George L. Stearns, October 15, 1863, Regimental Unbound Papers, 36th USCT, RG 94, NARA; "Company H, 36th USCT," *Compiled Records Showing Service of Military Units In Volunteer Union Organization, United States Colored Troops*, Microfilm Publication M594, roll #209, NARA. These *Compiled Records* are also known as "Record of Events" for military units in the Union army during the war. The "Record of Events" for the 36th USCT are also found in *OR Supp.*, pt. 2, vol. 77, 779–790.

33. Alonzo G. Draper to J.A. Judson, August 8, 1863, Regimental Unbound Papers, 36th USCT, RG 94, NARA; Alonzo G. Draper to John A. Andrew, September 19, 1863, in Executive Letters, vol. 102, no. 94, MA.

34. Alonzo G. Draper to John A. Andrew, September 19, 1863, in Executive Letters, vol. 102, no. 94, MA.

35. Reid, "Raising the African Brigade," 291; Alonzo G. Draper to John A. Andrew, September 19, 1863, in Executive Letters, vol. 102, no. 94, MA; J.A. Judson to Alonzo G. Draper, August 29, 1863, Regimental Unbound Papers, 36th USCT, RG 94, NARA. As of August 29, 1863, the 2nd North Carolina (36th USCT) consisted of: Company A–75 men; Company B–50 men; Company C–61 men; Company D–51 men; Company E–53 men; Company F–43 men; and Company G–8 men. Companies A–K, Descriptive Books, 36th USCT, RG 94, NARA; Alonzo G. Draper to S. Hoffman, October 5, 1863, Regimental Letterbook, 36th USCT, RG 94, NARA; Alonzo G. Draper to Hiram W. Allen, December 29, 1863, folder #2159, file #2, in Edward A. Wild Papers, USMHI; "Company H, 36th USCT," *Compiled Records Showing Service of Military Units In Volunteer Union Organization, United States Colored Troops*, Microfilm Publication M594, roll #209, NARA.

36. Reid, "Raising the African Brigade," 289; Alonzo G. Draper to John A. Andrew, September 19, 1863, in Executive Letters, vol. 102, no. 94, MA.

37. Alonzo G. Draper to John A. Andrew, September 19, 1863, in Executive Letters, vol. 102, no. 94, MA.

38. Henry F.H. Miller to Alonzo G. Draper, September 11, 1863, Regimental Letterbook, 36th USCT, RG 94, NARA.

39. Henry F.H. Miller to Alonzo G. Draper, September 11, 1863, Regimental Letterbook, 36th USCT, RG 94, NARA; Alonzo G. Draper to John A. Andrew, September 19, 1863, in Executive Letters, vol. 102, no. 94, MA.

40. U.S. War Department, Adjutant General's Office, *Revised Regulations for the Army of the United States, 1861* (Philadelphia: J.G.L. Brown, 1861; reprint, Harrisburg, PA: The National Historical Society, 1980), 90.

41. James N. North to Alonzo G. Draper, September 16, 1863, Regimental Letterbook, 36th USCT, RG 94, NARA; *Revised Regulations for the Army of the United States, 1861*, 139; Alonzo G. Draper to John A. Andrew, September 19, 1863, in Executive Letters, vol. 102, no. 94, MA.

42. Alonzo G. Draper to John A. Andrew, September 19, 1863, in Executive Letters, vol. 102, no. 94, MA.

43. *OR*, ser. I, vol. 9, 369. General Ambrose E. Burnside in 1862 had set pay scales for skilled black civilians employed at New Bern higher than army pay and those paid to common black laborers. Stevedores earned $15 a month and teamsters earned $20 a month. Blacksmiths, carpenters, masons, and mechanics could be paid from $.75 to $3.00 per day. These pay scales were roughly the same by November 1863. Reid, "Raising the African Brigade," 289; Alonzo G. Draper to John A. Andrew, November 6, 1863, in Executive Letters, vol. 100, no. 47, MA.

44. Alonzo G. Draper to John A. Andrew, September 19, 1863, in Executive Letters, vol. 102, no. 94, MA; Alonzo G. Draper to John A. Andrew, November 6, 1863, in Executive Letters, vol. 100, no. 47, MA.

45. Aaron Parker to C.D. Griggs, September [?], 1863, Regimental Unbound Papers, 36th USCT, RG 94, NARA.

46. Alonzo G. Draper to John A. Andrew, September 19, 1863, in Executive Letters, vol. 102, no. 94, MA.

47. Henry F.H. Miller to Alonzo G. Draper, September 11, 1863, Regimental Letterbook, 36th USCT, RG 94, NARA.

48. Draper claimed 631 men for the entire regiment as of September 19, 1863. Additionally, he reported 125 recruits arriving on average each week with 40 or 50 coming into camp in one day. These may be exaggerations as the Company Books show fewer, but still significant enlistments came into the regiment during this time. Some of these new recruits may have been destined for the 3rd

North Carolina (37th USCT), still organizing under Draper's direction at Portsmouth. Alonzo G. Draper to John A. Andrew, September 19, 1863, in Executive Letters, vol. 102, no. 94, MA; Pension file of Paul Wiggins, Co. D, 36th USCT, RG 15, NARA. The highest month for recruitment was in July 1863 with 218 enlistments. Companies A–K, Descriptive Books, 36th USCT, RG 94, NARA.

49. Alonzo G. Draper to R.S. Davis, November 14, 1863, Regimental Unbound Papers, 36th USCT, RG 94, NARA; Alonzo G. Draper to John A. Andrew, September 19, 1863, in Executive Letters, vol. 102, no. 94, MA.

50. Alonzo G. Draper to R.S. Davis, November 14, 1863, Regimental Unbound Papers, 36th USCT, RG 94, NARA; Extract of Report of Captain Hazard Stevens, Assistant Inspector General of Colored Troops, n.d., Regimental Letterbook, 36th USCT, RG, NARA. Also see Frank H. Scudder to C.D. Griggs, November 12, 1863, Myles McSweeney to C.D. Griggs, September 14, 1863, and A.H. Clark to C.D. Griggs, November 12, 1863, Regimental Letterbook, 36th USCT, RG 94, NARA for supporting evidence of the 36th's difficulties in obtaining stockading equipment, lack of animal teams, and insufficient supplies of medicine for the regimental hospital.

51. Alonzo G. Draper to R.S. Davis, November 14, 1863, Regimental Unbound Papers, 36th USCT, RG 94, NARA.

52. Alonzo G. Draper to George H. Johnston, September 14, 1863, Regimental Letterbook, 36th USCT, RG 94, NARA; Alonzo G. Draper to John A. Andrew, September 19, 1863, in Executive Letters, vol. 102, no. 94, MA.

53. Alonzo G. Draper to John A. Andrew, September 19, 1863, in Executive Letters, vol. 102, no. 94, MA.

54. Alonzo G. Draper to S. Hoffman, October 14, 1863, Regimental Papers Unbound, 36th USCT, RG 94, NARA; Alonzo G. Draper to John A. Andrew, September 19, 1863, in Executive Letters, vol. 102, no. 94, MA.

55. Alonzo G. Draper to John A. Andrew, September 19, 1863, in Executive Letters, vol. 102, no. 94, MA; Alonzo G. Draper to John A. Andrew, November 6, 1863, in Executive Letters, vol. 100, no. 47, MA.

56. Although Barnes replaced Naglee in October 1863, Draper wrote Andrew that Barnes' authority did not extend beyond Norfolk and Portsmouth and "has no power to send a corporal's guard beyond his own lines." The rest of south eastern Virginia that included Nansemond and Princess Anne Counties where Draper wanted to recruit soldiers was under the command of Brigadier General George W. Getty who outranked Barnes, commanded more Union forces, and in Draper's words was "not our friend." Alonzo G. Draper to John A. Andrew, October 14, 1863, in Executive Letters, vol. 100, no. 44, MA; Alonzo G. Draper to John A. Andrew, November 6, 1863, in Executive Letters, vol. 100, no. 47, MA.

## Chapter 3

1. Charles H. Frye to C.D. Griggs, December 26, 1863, Regimental Letterbook, 36th USCT, RG 94, NARA; *Vital Records of Salem Massachusetts to the End of the Year 1849*, vol. 1, *Births* (Salem, MA: The Essex Institute, 1916), 328; Pension file of Charles H. Frye, 36th USCT, RG 15, NARA; *MSSMCW*, vol. 1, 393; vol. 2, 623; vol. 7, 298; William Kreutzer, *Notes and Observations Made During Four Years of Service with the Ninety-Eighth N.Y. Volunteers in the War of 1861* (Philadelphia: Grant, Faires, and Rodgers, 1878), 164–166, 170–175.

2. Butler was highly criticized for his infamous "Woman Order" (General Orders No. 28) while commanding New Orleans in 1862. His order declared that any woman in the streets of the city who made negative remarks about the U.S. Government and the Union army or chastised Union troops under his command would be promptly arrested "as a woman of the town plying her avocation." Confederate President Jefferson Davis branded Butler an "outlaw" to be executed on sight if captured by Confederate forces. Butler's New Orleans command was marred by frequent charges of corruption, extortion, and embezzlement of government funds. He would be a defendant (via proxy) in several suits filed against him throughout the war. See "General Orders No. 28, May 15, 1862," in Benjamin F. Butler, *Private and Official Correspondence of General Benjamin F. Butler*, vol. 1, ed. Jessie Ames Marshall (Norwood, MA: Plimpton, 1917), 490; and Richard S. West, Jr., *Lincoln's Scapegoat General: A Life of Benjamin F. Butler, 1818–1893* (New York: Houghton-Mifflin, 1965), 219. For information on Butler's role in raising black regiments in New Orleans see Howard C. Westwood, *Black Troops, White Commanders, and Freedmen During the Civil War* (Carbondale: Southern Illinois University Press, 1992), 37–54.

3. Dick Nolan, *Benjamin Franklin Butler: The Damnedest Yankee* (Novato, CA: Presidio Press, 1991), 241; West, *Lincoln's Scapegoat General*, 222.

4. Jerry V. Witt, *Wild in North Carolina: General Edward A. Wild's December 1863 Raid into Camden, Pasquotank, and Currituck Counties* (Springfield, VA: J.V. Witt, 1993), 4.

5. Hiram W. Allen to Alonzo G. Draper, November 17, 1863, Regimental Letterbook, 36th USCT, RG 94, NARA. This order is also reprinted in Ira Berlin et al., eds., *Freedom: A Documentary History of Emancipation, 1861–1867*, ser. I, vol. I, *The Destruction of Slavery* (New York: Cambridge University Press, 1985), 92; Alonzo G. Draper to John A. Andrew, December 10, 1863, in Executive Letters, vol. 100, no. 62, MA.

6. "Schedule 2, Princess Anne County, Virginia, Edgar Burroughs, p. 13," in *Population Schedules of the Eighth Census of the United States*, Microfilm Publication M653, roll #1396, NARA; "Schedule 2, Princess Anne County, Virginia, John T. Caffee, p. 12," in *Population Schedules of the Eighth Census of the United States*, Microfilm Publication M653, roll #1396, NARA; John Fortier, *15th Virginia Cavalry* (Lynchburg, VA: H.E. Howard, 1993), 5, 124; John S. Wise, *The End of an Era* (New York: Houghton, Mifflin, 1899), 167; William Kruetzer, *Notes and Observation Made During Four Years of Service with the Ninety-Eighth N.Y. Volunteers in the War of 1861* (Philadelphia: Grant, Faires, and Rodgers, 1878), 170–171.

7. Alonzo G. Draper to Hiram W. Allen, November 27, 1863, Regimental Letterbook, 36th USCT, RG 94, NARA; Jeffrey C. Weaver, *The Virginia Home Guards* (Lynchburg, VA: H.E. Howard, 1996), 99–100. The 68th North Carolina was organized in July 1863 as a local defense unit for northeastern North Carolina. The various companies of the regiment often acted independent of each other and operated with various guerrilla bands throughout the latter half of 1863. See John W. Moore, *Roster of North Carolina Troops in the War Between the States*, vol. 4 (Raleigh, NC: Edwards-Broughton, 1882), 148–149; Walter Clark, ed., *Histories of the Several Regiments and Battalions from North Carolina in the Great War 1861–'65*, vol. 3 (Goldsboro, NC: Nash Brothers, 1901), 713–714; and Witt, *Wild in North Carolina*, 61–68.

8. Hiram W. Allen to Alonzo G. Draper, November 17, 1863, Regimental Letterbook, 36th USCT, RG 94, NARA; Alonzo G. Draper to John A. Andrew, December 10, 1863, in Executive Letters, vol. 100, no. 62, MA;

William H. Hart to D.D. Wheeler, July 16, 1865, Regimental Letterbook, RG 94; NARA.

9. Alonzo G. Draper to Hiram W. Allen, November 27, 1863, Regimental Letterbook, 36th USCT, RG 94, NARA.

10. Ibid.

11. Ibid.

12. Ibid. Caffee and some of his men had been previously employed by Union forces as laborers hauling lumber and other materials from confiscated vessels near Currituck Sound and Knott's Island in North Carolina to Norfolk. Their pay had been supplemented with provisions and rations for their families in Princess Anne. By the summer of 1863, Caffee was suspected as a Confederate guerrilla and Union authorities sought his capture. Francis H. Pierpoint, governor of Union-held Virginia and West Virginia, argued in favor of Caffee's loyalty to the Union. Francis H. Pierpoint, *Letter of Governor Pierpoint to his Excellency the President and the Honorable Congress of the United States of the Subject of Abuse of Military Power in the Command of General Butler in Virginia and North Carolina* (Washington, D.C.: McGill & Witherow, 1864), 33, 37.

13. Alonzo G. Draper to Hiram W. Allen, November 27, 1863, Regimental Letterbook, 36th USCT, RG 94, NARA; Alonzo G. Draper to John A. Andrew, December 10, 1863, in Executive Letters, vol. 100, no. 62, MA.

14. Lucy Chase to [Anna?] Lowell, November 29, 1863 in *Dear Ones at Home: Letters from Contraband Camps*, ed. Henry L. Swint (Nashville, TN: Vanderbilt University Press, 1966), 99.

15. Alonzo G. Draper to Hiram W. Allen, November 27, 1863, Regimental Letterbook, 36th USCT, RG 94, NARA; *New York Tribune*, January 27, 1864; Fortier, *15th Virginia Cavalry*, 124; Ervin L. Jordan, Jr., *Black Confederates and Afro-Yankees in Civil War Virginia* (Charlottesville: University Press of Virginia, 1995), 282.

16. Jno. Ebbs to F.F. Wead, November 24, 1863, Regimental Letterbook, 36th USCT, RG 94, NARA; F.F. Wead to Hazard Stevens, November 27, 1863, Regimental Letterbook, 36th USCT, RG 94, NARA.

17. Alonzo G. Draper to R.S. Davis, January 4, 1864, Regimental Letterbook, 36th USCT, RG 94, NARA.

18. L.T. Gaskill to C.D. Griggs, January 4, 1864, Regimental Letterbook, 36th USCT, RG 94, NARA; Daniel Foster to A.G. Draper, n.d, Regimental Letterbook, 36th USCT, RG 94, NARA.

19. Charles H. Frye to C.D. Griggs, December 26, 1863, Regimental Letterbook, 36th USCT, RG 94, NARA; B. Frank Kinsley to [C.D.] Griggs, December 26, 1863, Regimental Letterbook, 36th USCT, RG 94, NARA.

20. Oren A. Hendrick to Alonzo G. Draper, January 2, 1864, Regimental Letterbook, 36th USCT, RG 94, NARA.

21. Ibid.

22. Ibid.

23. According to Fox-Genovese in her study of black and white women in the antebellum South, the possession of keys to the storerooms and outbuildings of plantations and farms symbolically represented the elevated status of white women within the patriarchal society when their husbands were absent or deceased. See Elizabeth Fox-Genovese, *Within the Plantation Household: Black and White Women of the Old South* (Chapel Hill: University of North Carolina Press, 1988), 110.

24. B. Frank Kinsley to [C.D.] Griggs, December 26, 1863, Regimental Letterbook, 36th USCT, RG 94, NARA.

25. Alonzo G. Draper to R.S. Davis, January 4, 1864, Regimental Letterbook, 36th USCT, RG 94, NARA. The 5th USCT (200 men) under Major Ira C. Terry and a detachment of white Union cavalry reinforced Draper's expedition on November 22, 1863. "Regimental Returns, 5th USCT," *Compiled Records Showing Service of Military Units In Volunteer Union Organizations, United States Colored Troops*, Microfilm Publication M594, roll #206, NARA; Versalle F. Washington, *Eagles on Their Buttons: A Black Infantry Regiment in the Civil War* (Columbia: University of Missouri Press, 1999), 25–26, 33.

26. *New York Tribune*, December 3, 1863.

27. *New York Times*, January 9, 1864.

28. *OR*, ser. I, vol. 29, pt. 1, 910.

29. This particular order would cover numerous aspects concerning freedmen under Butler's command including military and civilian pay for soldiers and their families as well as establish their personal rights under his military protection and guidance. "General Orders No. 46, December 5, 1863," in Butler, *Private and Official Correspondence of General Benjamin F. Butler*, vol. 3, 183–190. This order is also found in *OR*, ser. III, vol. 3, 1139–1144; and "General Orders No. 46, December 5, 1863," *NMSUS*, reel #2, frame 752–755.

30. For general accounts of Wild's raid into North Carolina, December 5–21, 1863, see *OR*, ser. I, vol. 29, pt. 1, 910–917; Richard M. Reid, *Freedom for Themselves: North Carolina's Black Soldiers in the Civil War Era* (Chapel Hill: University of North Carolina Press, 2008), 117–123; Frances H. Casstevens, *Edward A. Wild and the African Brigade in the Civil War* (Jefferson, NC: McFarland, 2003), 100–144; Noah Andre Trudeau, *Like Men of War: Black Troops in the Civil War, 1862–1865* (Boston: Little, Brown, 1998), 112–118; John G. Barrett, *The Civil War in North Carolina* (1965; Chapel Hill: University of North Carolina Press, 1983), 177–180; Witt, *Wild in North Carolina*, esp. pp. 1–30; Washington, *Eagles on Their Buttons*, 33–34; and David Wright and David Zoby, *Fire on the Beach: Recovering the Lost Story of Richard Etheridge and the Pea Island Lifesavers* (New York: Scribner, 2000), 65–77.

31. *New York Tribune*, December 3, 1863; *New York Times*, January 9, 1864; *OR*, ser. I, vol. 29, pt. 1, 911; Elizabeth Curtis Wallace, *Glencoe Diary: The War-Time Journal of Elizabeth Curtis Wallace*, ed. Eleanor P. Cross and Charles B. Cross, Jr. (Chesapeake, VA: Norfolk County Historical Society, 1968), 78. The 1st USCT was composed of black soldiers primarily from Washington, D.C., and its surrounding vicinity.

32. This supporting detachment of white troops consisted of Co. M, 5th Pennsylvania Cavalry under Captain Anderson Faith, Co. G, 11th Pennsylvania Cavalry under Captain James A. Skelley, and a section of artillery (probably two 6-pound guns) under a Lieutenant Thomas. Captain Skelley held overall command of this detachment. *OR*, ser. I, vol. 29, pt. 1, 911; "Post War Diary of Edward A. Wild," Edward A. Wild Papers, USAMHI; *New York Times*, January 8, 1864; Barrett, *The Civil War in North Carolina*, 177, West, *Lincoln's Scapegoat General*, 222–223; Witt, *Wild in North Carolina*, 8.

33. *New York Times*, Dec. 7, 1863; *OR*, ser. I, vol. 28, pt. 2, 534; *OR*, ser. I, vol. 29, pt. 1, 911.

34. *New York Times*, January 8, 1864; Witt, *Wild in North Carolina*, 8.

35. *OR*, ser. I, vol. 28, pt. 2, 562.

36. *OR*, ser. I, vol. 29, pt. 1, 912, 917; Barrett, *The Civil War in North Carolina*, 178, 180–181; Benj. F. Butler to F. Morton, December 6, 1863, in Butler, *Private and Official Correspondence of General Benjamin Butler*, vol. 3, 182.

37. *OR*, ser. I, vol. 29, pt. 1, 912; *New York Times*, January 9, 1864; Barrett, *The Civil War in North Carolina*, 178; West, *Lincoln's Scapegoat General*, 224; Witt, *Wild in North Carolina*, 12, 14, 17–18. Phoebe Munden and Elizabeth Weeks, the two women hostages, had husbands in Captain John T.

Elliot's guerrilla company officially designated as Company A, 68th North Carolina. The captured black soldier was Private Samuel Jordan, Company D, 5th USCT. See Company D, Descriptive Book, 5th USCT, RG 94, NARA; Ohio, Adjutant General, *Official Roster of the Soldiers of the State of Ohio in the War of the Rebellion, 1861–1866*, vol. 1 (Akron, OH: The Werner Company, 1893), 605.

38. Alonzo G. Draper to Hiram W. Allen, December 24, 1863, Regimental Letterbook, RG 94, NARA; *OR*, ser. I, vol. 28, pt. 1, 912; Barrett, *The Civil War in North Carolina*, 179; Witt, *Wild in North Carolina*, 16. Draper's same report of December 24, 1863, is also found in *OR Supp.*, pt. 1, vol. 5, 637–640.

39. *OR*, ser. I, vol. 29, pt. 1, 912; Alonzo G. Draper to Hiram W. Allen, December 24, 1863, Regimental Letterbook, 36th USCT, RG 94, NARA; "Company I, 36th USCT," *Compiled Records Showing Service of Military Units In Volunteer Union Organization, United States Colored Troops*, Microfilm Publication M594, roll #209, NARA; Barrett, *The Civil War in North Carolina*, 179.

40. The Confederate guerrillas who engaged Draper's men were probably elements of companies commanded by Captains Willis B. Sanderlin, Caleb B. Walston, and Cyrus W. Grandy. These units were officially designated as Companies B, C, and G of the 68th North Carolina respectively. Alonzo G. Draper to Hiram W. Allen, December 24, 1863, Regimental Letterbook, 36th USCT, RG 94, NARA. Draper's report erroneously refers to Captain Cock as "Captain Cutler." There is no Captain Cutler listed in the rosters for the 5th USCT. Captain Cock was present with Draper's detachment during the North Carolina expedition. *OR*, ser. I, vol. 51, pt. 1, 210; U.S. War Department, Adjutant General's Office, *Official Army Register of the Volunteer Force of the Unites States Army for the Year 1861, '62, '63, '64, '65*, vol. 8 (Washington, D.C.: GPO, 1867), 174; Washington, *Eagles on Their Buttons*, 34; Witt, *Wild in North Carolina*, 70.

41. Alonzo G. Draper to Hiram W. Allen, December 24, 1863, Regimental Letterbook, 36th USCT, RG 94, NARA; "List of Deceased Soldiers," Regimental Returns/Muster Rolls, 36th USCT, RG 94, NARA; *Official Roster of the Soldiers of the State of Ohio*, vol. 1, 613; Washington, *Eagles on Their Buttons*, 34; "Companies G,H, I, 5th USCT," *Compiled Records Showing Service of Military Units In Volunteer Union Organization, United States Colored Troops*, Microfilm Publication M594, roll #206; *OR*, ser. I, vol. 51, pt. 1, 210; "Company I, 36th USCT," *Compiled Records Showing Service of Military Units In Volunteer Union Organization, United States Colored Troops*, Microfilm Publication M594, roll #209; Companies F,I, Descriptive Books, 36th USCT, RG 94, NARA; *OR*, ser. I, vol. 29, pt. 1, 912–913; Barrett, *The Civil War in North Carolina*, 179; Witt, *Wild in North Carolina*, 23.

42. This was Captain Sanderlin's guerrilla camp. *OR*, ser. I, vol. 29, pt. 1, 913; Barrett, *The Civil War in North Carolina*, 179; Witt, *Wild in North Carolina*, 23–24.

43. This was Captain Grandy's guerrilla camp. Alonzo G. Draper to Hiram W. Allen, December 24, 1863, Regimental Letterbook, 36th USCT, RG 94, NARA; *OR*, ser. I, vol. 29, pt. 1, 913; Barrett, *The Civil War in North Carolina*, 179; Witt, *Wild in North Carolina*, 25. The captured (and still unidentified) soldier of the 2nd North Carolina apparently escaped and returned to the regiment. Major Gregory's first name was not a military title, but his given name.

44. *OR*, ser. I, vol. 29, pt. 1, 913; Witt, *Wild in North Carolina*, 30–31, 79; Casstevens, *Edward A. Wild and the African Brigade in the Civil War*, 133–134.

45. *OR*, ser. I, vol. 29, pt. 1, 913; Barrett, *The Civil War in North Carolina*, 179; Witt, *Wild in North Carolina*, 23–24; *New York Times*, January 9, 1864.

46. F.F. Wead to Draper, December 22, 1863, Regimental Letterbook, 36th USCT, RG 94, NARA; Alonzo G. Draper to Hiram W. Allen, December 23, 1863, Regimental Letterbook, 36th USCT, RG 94, NARA.

47. Alonzo G. Draper to Hiram W. Allen, December 23, 1863, Regimental Letterbook, 36th USCT, RG 94, NARA.

48. Ibid.

49. Ibid.; *OR*, ser. I, vol. 29, pt. 1, 913.

50. Witt, *Wild in North Carolina*, 32–33, 36, 73–75; Casstevens, *Edward A. Wild and the African Brigade in the Civil War*, 134–136, 138.

51. Casstevens, *Edward A. Wild and the African Brigade in the Civil War*, 138; Alonzo G. Draper to Hiram W. Allen, December 23, 1863, Regimental Letterbook, 36th USCT, RG 94, NARA.

52. *OR*, ser. I, vol. 28, pt. 2, 562; Richard Reid, "General Edward A. Wild and Civil War Discrimination," *Historical Journal of Massachusetts* 13 (January 1985): 14; *OR*, ser. I, vol. 28, pt. 2, 596; Nolan, *Benjamin Franklin Butler*, 242. Ward may have been upset by the fact that, William H. Johnson, possibly a black man "passing" for a white soldier in his regiment reported the regiment's activities in the newspaper. See Edwin S. Redkey, ed., *A Grand Army of Black Men: Letters from African-American Soldiers in the Union Army, 1861–1865* (1992; reprint, New York: Cambridge University Press, 1993), xi, 19.

53. White, Wild, and Wead are quoted in Casstevens, *Edward A. Wild and the African Brigade in the Civil War*, 139–140.

54. *OR*, ser. I, vol. 29, pt. 1, 913–914; "List of Deceased Soldiers," Regimental Returns/Muster Rolls, 36th USCT, RG 94, NARA; Witt, *Wild in North Carolina*, 41.

55. *OR*, ser. I, vol. 29, pt. 1, 913–914; *OR*, ser. I, vol. 28, pt. 2, 596.

56. W. Buck Yearns and John G. Barrett, eds., *North Carolina Civil War Documentary* (Chapel Hill: University of North Carolina Press, 1980), 56; Nolan, *Benjamin Franklin Butler*, 243–244. Official reports concerning the Jordan hanging can be found in *OR*, ser. II, vol. 6, 845–847.

57. Griffin is quoted in Yearns and Barrett, *North Carolina Civil War Documentary*, 56. Griffin may not have been aware that one of the prisoners had already escaped his Confederate captors during the expedition.

58. Nolan, *Benjamin Franklin Butler*, 244; *OR*, ser. II, vol. 6, 877–878.

59. *OR*, ser. I, vol. 28, pt. 2, 596.

60. D.H. Hill, Jr., *Confederate Military History*, vol. 5, *North Carolina* (1899; reprint, Wilmington, N.C.: Broadfoot, 1987), 219; Witt, *Wild in North Carolina*, 30.

61. C.S. House of Representatives, Special Committee, *Report of the Special Committee To Inquire into Certain Outrages of the Enemy* (Richmond, VA: n.d.), 1–2. This complete report is also found in *OR*, ser. II, vol. 6, 1127–1129. Portions of this report are included in *Richmond Enquirer*, February 9, 1864.

62. *New York Times*, January 9, 1864.

63. *New York Times*, January 3, 1864; *New York Tribune*, January 4, 1864; John Sullivan to George L. Stearns, October 15, 1863, Regimental Unbound Papers, 36th USCT, RG 94, NARA; West, *Lincoln's Scapegoat General*, 225.

## Chapter 4

1. Henry F.H. Miller to Edward A. Wild, February 3, 1864, Folder # 2160, File #1, in Edward A. Wild Papers,

USAMHI. Miller's report to Wild is also found in *OR Supp.*, pt. 1, vol. 6, 274–277.

2. Regimental Association, *History of the Thirty-Fifth Regiment Massachusetts Volunteers, 1862–1865* (Boston: Mills, Knight, 1884), 97; Henry W. Tisdale, "Civil War Diary of Sergeant Henry W. Tisdale, Company I, Thirty-Fifth Regt. Mass Volunteers, 1862–1865," (typed Manuscript in possession of the Fredericksburg and Spotsylvania National Military Park, Fredericksburg, Virginia), 25, 29.

3. Pension file of Henry F.H. Miller, 36th USCT, RG 15, NARA.

4. Company E, Descriptive Book, 36th USCT, RG 94, NARA; Glatthaar continues to remain the primary work concerning Civil War leadership in black Union army regiments. See Joseph T. Glatthaar, *Forged in Battle: The Civil War Alliance of Black Soldiers and White Officers* (New York: Free Press, 1990).

5. James M. McPherson, *For Cause and Comrades: Why Men Fought in the Civil War* (New York: Oxford University Press, 1997), 54; Reid Mitchell, *The Vacant Chair: The Northern Soldier Leaves Home* (New York: Oxford University Press, 1993), 19–37, 115–133.

6. Companies A–K, Descriptive Books, 36th USCT, RG 94, NARA.

7. Glatthaar, *Forged in Battle*, 111.

8. "Testimony of General B.F. Butler, Comds. Dept. of the Gulf, New Orleans, November 28th, 1862," in *Blacks in the United States Armed Forces: Basic Documents*, vol. 2, *Civil War and Emancipation*, eds. Morris J. MacGregor and Bernard C. Nalty (Wilmington, DE: Scholarly Resources, 1977), 107; "Col. T.W. Higginson's Testimony," in *Blacks in the United States Armed Forces*, vol. 2, 102.

9. Glatthaar, *Forged in Battle*, 111; Companies A–K, Descriptive Books, 36th USCT, RG 94, NARA.

10. Glatthaar, *Forged in Battle*, 108–109; William L. Van Deburg, *The Slave Driver: Black Agricultural Labor Supervisors in the Antebellum South* (Westport, CT: Greenwood, 1979), 114–116; John W. Blassingame, *The Slave Community: Plantation Life in the Antebellum South*, 2nd ed. (1972; New York: Oxford University Press, 1979), 258–260; and Eugene D. Genovese, *Roll, Jordan, Roll: The World the Slaves Made* (1974; New York: Vintage Books, 1976), 388.

11. Randall M. Miller, "The Man in the Middle: The Black Slave Driver," *American Heritage* 30 (October/November 1979): 45.

12. Edward M. Coffman, *The Old Army: A Portrait of the American Army in Peacetime, 1784–1898* (New York: Oxford University Press, 1986), 207. Noncommissioned officers were enlisted men recommended and appointed by their company and regimental officers. Noncommissioned ranks in ascending order were: corporal, sergeant, first sergeant, commissary sergeant, quartermaster sergeant, and sergeant major. The rank of private was the lowest rank held by union soldiers. Commissioned ranks of the Union army in ascending order were: second lieutenant, first lieutenant, captain, major, lieutenant colonel, colonel, brigadier general, major general, and lieutenant general. U.S. War Department, Adjutant General's Office, *Revised Regulations for the Army of the United States, 1861* (Philadelphia: J.G.L. Brown, 1861; reprint, Harrisburg, PA: The National Historical Society, 1980), 9. Also see Appendix One.

13. Companies A–K, Descriptive Books, 36th USCT, RG 94, NARA; *OR*, ser. I, vol. 42, pt. 3, 169; Leslie Suzanne Rowland, "Emancipation and the Black Military Experience During the American Civil War: A Documentary History," pt. 2 (Ph.D. diss., University of Rochester, 1991), 635–636.

14. Richard Reid, "Raising the African Brigade: Early Black Recruitment in Civil War North Carolina," *North Carolina Historical Review* 70 (1993): 286–287. There was no unified examining board approved by the War Department during the war for the commission of white officers in black units. Departmental commanders in the various Union commands held wide authority over a candidate's qualifications and composition of examining boards. Usually an applicant had to posses some military experience, general education, and satisfactory recommendations attesting to quality leadership and good moral character before appearing before a board. The findings of the various boards were forwarded to the Bureau of Colored Troops. Colonel John H. Taggart opened the Free Military School for Applicants for Command of Colored Troops in December 1863. Located in Philadelphia, Pennsylvania, Taggart's 30-day instructional program prepared applicants for commissions in black regiments. By the time the school was discontinued on September 15, 1864, 484 graduates had passed commissioning board examinations. See Glatthaar, *Forged in Battle*, 44–55.

15. Special Order, No. 302, War Department, Adjutant General's Office, July 8, 1863, Regimental Letterbook, 36th USCT, RG 94, NARA; "2nd Regt. N.C. Colored Vols, Roster Accepted, 1863," War Department Correspondence, 1863, Edward A. Wild Papers, USAMHI; Reid, "Raising the African Brigade," 287; Glatthaar, *Forged in Battle*, 100.

16. Pension files of Benjamin F. Pratt, Daniel J. Preston, 36th USCT, RG 15, NARA.

17. Reid, "Raising the African Brigade," 287; *Vital Records of Brookline, Massachusetts, to the end of the Year 1849* (Salem: The Essex Institute, 1929), 74–75.

18. Special Order, No. 302, War Department, Adjutant General's Office, July 8, 1863, Regimental Letterbook, 36th USCT, RG 94, NARA; Companies A–K, Descriptive Books, 36th USCT, RG 94, NARA; "2nd Regt. N.C. Colored Vols, Roster Accepted, 1863," War Department Correspondence, 1863, in Edward A. Wild Papers, USAMHI; Tisdale, "Civil War Diary," 65.

19. Pension file of Benjamin F. Pratt, 36th USCT, RG 15, NARA; *History of the Thirty-Fifth Regiment Massachusetts Volunteers*, 98.

20. *History of the Thirty-Fifth Regiment Massachusetts Volunteers*, 126, 124.

21. Special Order, No. 302, War Department, Adjutant General's Office, July 8, 1863, Regimental Letterbook, 36th USCT, RG 94, NARA; "2nd Regt. N.C. Colored Vols, Roster Accepted, 1863," War Department Correspondence, 1863, in Edward A. Wild Papers, USAMHI. Information on Edwin C. and Leonard T. Gaskill can be found in *MSSMCW*, vol. 7, 298 and in *Vital Records of Mendon, Massachusetts, to the Year 1850* (Boston: New England Historic Genealogical Fund, 1920), 82.

22. Thomas Waln-Morgan Draper, *The Drapers in America, Being A History and Genealogy of Those of That Name and Connection* (New York: John Polhemus, 1892), 207–208; Alonzo G. Draper to John A. Andrew, March 2, 1863, Executive Letters, vol. 14, no. 50., MA.

23. Draper, *The Drapers in America*, 208; Alonzo G. Draper to John A. Andrew, March 2, 1863, Executive Letters, vol. 14, no. 50, MA. For a recent book-length study on the Anthony Burns case and its impact on New England, see Albert J. Von Frank, *The Trials of Anthony Burns: Freedom and Slavery in Emerson's Boston* (Cambridge, MA: Harvard University Press, 1998).

24. Alonzo G. Draper to John A. Andrew, April 28, 1863, Executive Letters, vol. 102, No. 58, MA; Draper, *The Drapers in America*, 209; Pension file of Alonzo G. Draper, F&S, 36th USCT, RG 15, NARA.

25. Draper, *The Drapers in America*, 209; Alan Dawley,

*Class and Community: The Industrial Revolution in Lynn* (Cambridge, MA: Harvard University Press, 1976), 79, 191; Paul G. Faler, *Mechanics and Manufacturers in the Early Industrial Revolution: Lynn, Massachusetts, 1780–1860* (Albany: State University of New York Press, 1981), 199; Alonzo Lewis and James R. Newhall, *History of Lynn, Essex County, Massachusetts* (Boston: John L. Shorey, 1865), 456. Lause views Draper as a successful "free labor" advocate with his service in the USCT as a logical outgrowth of this ideology. See Mark A. Lause, "Turning the World Upside Down: A Portrait of Labor and Military Leader, Alonzo Granville Draper," *Labor History* 44 (2003): 189–204.

26. *Lynn* (MA) *Weekly Reporter*, September 30, 1865 quoted in Draper, *The Drapers in America*, 209; *Lynn* (MA) *Bay State*, December 13, 1860; Faler, *Mechanics and Manufacturers*, 230.

27. Alonzo G. Draper to John A. Andrew, April 28, 1863, Executive Letters, vol. 102, no. 58, MA; Alfred Seelye Roe and Charles Nutt, *History of the First Regiment of Heavy Artillery Massachusetts Volunteers Formerly the Fourteenth Regiment of Infantry, 1861–1865* (Regimental Association, 1917), 20. Draper may have exaggerated to Massachusetts Governor John A. Andrew the time required for him to train his company in order to gain a commission to command a regiment of former slaves. One source cited that it took two months for Draper's company to have enough volunteers to be accepted into federal service and that he had hired a professional drillmaster in training his company. See Draper, *The Drapers in America*, 209; Draper's occupation was listed as a teacher in a wartime roster of the 14th Massachusetts Infantry. See "Typo," *Officers and Privates, Attached to the Fourteenth Regiment Heavy Artillery, Massachusetts Volunteers* (Lawrence, MA: George S. Merrill, 1862), 3, 12.

28. Draper, *The Drapers in America*, 209.

29. Alonzo G. Draper to John A. Andrew, April 28, 1863, in Executive Letters, vol. 102, no. 58, MA.

30. Alonzo G. Draper to John A. Andrew, March 2, 1863, in Executive Letters, vol. 14, no. 50, MA; Alonzo G. Draper to John A. Andrew, April 28, 1863, in Executive Letters, vol. 102, no. 58, MA; Draper, *The Drapers in America*, 209.

31. Butler had advocated a ten-hour workday for all factory workers in the state as a Massachusetts legislator during the 1850s. He also advocated the interests of striking women employed in the factories of his hometown of Lowell, Massachusetts, in 1860. For information on Butler's interest in the growing labor movement among ethnic workers and women, see Robert S. Holzman, *Stormy Ben Butler* (New York: Macmillan, 1954), 12–14; Hans L. Trefousse, *Ben Butler: The South Called Him Beast!* (New York: Twyane, 1957), 27–33; and Richard S. West, Jr., *Lincoln's Scapegoat General: A Life of Benjamin F. Butler, 1818–1893* (New York: Houghton-Mifflin, 1965), 26–29; 30–38.

32. Alonzo G. Draper to John A. Andrew, September 19, 1863, in Executive Letters, vol. 102, no. 94, MA.

33. Regimental Descriptive Book, 36th USCT, RG 94, NARA; B.F. Pratt to I.R. Sealy, February 22, 1865, Regimental Letterbook, RG 94, NARA; Wm. H. Hart to Israel R. Sealy, November 14, 1864, Regimental Letterbook, RG 94, NARA.

34. Pension file of Henry E. Nepean [Henry N. Adkins], Co. E, F&S, 36th USCT, RG 15, NARA; Compiled Military Service Record of Henry N. Adkins, Co. E, F&S, 36th USCT, RG 94, NARA; Regimental Descriptive Book, 36th USCT, RG 94, NARA.

35. Approximately 100 black men were commissioned as officers during the war. The majority served as surgeons and chaplains. Only a small number served in line or command positions, mainly from northern black regiments, and were commissioned at the end of the war. In early 1865, a petition with at least 185 signatures, including black noncommissioned officers in black regiments, sympathetic white politicians, and white Union commanders, requested that Secretary of War Stanton raise black regiments "officered *exclusively by colored men*." However, by the time black soldiers were commissioned as officers, the war was over and the army began demobilizing its forces. See Ira Berlin et al., *Freedom: A Documentary History of Emancipation, 1861–1867*, ser. II, *The Black Military Experience* (New York: Cambridge University Press, 1982), 340–341.

36. W.H. Hart to Oliver Stephens, November 27, 1864, Regimental Letterbook, 36th USCT, RG 94, NARA.

37. Richard M. Ried, *Freedom for Themselves: North Carolina's Black Soldiers in the Civil War Era* (Chapel Hill: University of North Carolina Press, 2008), 151–152. The author had the distinct pleasure of being shown the Alonzo Gould Diary in the summer of 1995 by Dr. Richard J. Sommers, chief archivist of the U.S. Army Military History Institute.

38. Alonzo G. Draper to John A. Andrew, September 19, 1863, in Executive Letters, vol. 102, no. 94, MA; Alonzo G. Draper to John A. Andrew, October 2, 1863, in Executive Letters, vol. 14, no. 101, MA.

39. Circular, 36th U.S.C. Troops, May 21, 1864, Regimental Order Book, 36th USCT, RG 94, NARA.

40. John W. Blassingame, "Negro Chaplains in the Civil War," *Negro History Bulletin* (October, 1963): 23; *Revised Regulations for the Army of the United States*, 36; Glatthaar, *Forged in Battle*, 180.

41. Reid, "Raising the African Brigade," 276, 287. Butler is quoted in Edwin S. Redkey, "Black Chaplains in the Union Army," *Civil War History* 33 (December 1987): 276; William A. Gladstone, *United States Colored Troops, 1863–1867* (Gettysburg, PA: Thomas, 1990), 110.

42. *Revised Regulations for the Army*, 351, 353; Blassingame, "Negro Chaplains in the Civil War," 22; Glatthaar, *Forged in Battle*, 181. Johnson was a Presbyterian clergyman born in Greenville, New York, but raised and educated in Wisconsin. He served with the Christian Commission until his appointment as chaplain of the 127th USCT in November 1864. Since the 127th USCT was composed of soldiers holding one-year enlistments, Johnson transferred to the 36th USCT. Robert Norman Hartwig, "A Recollection of Chaplain Thomas Scott Johnson of the 127th United States Colored Troops and the 36th United States Colored Troops During and After the Civil War,"( M.S. Seminar Paper, Wisconsin State University at La Crosse, 1970), 11, 33.

43. Black units organized in Massachusetts, Connecticut, and some in Louisiana retained their state designations rather than a U.S. Colored Troops designation as all other units received. Glatthaar, *Forged in Battle*, 10; Gladstone, *United States Colored Troops*, 9, 11.

44. Reid, "Raising the African Brigade," 276.

45. Edwin M. Stanton to B.F. Butler, December 5, 1863, *NMSUS*, reel #2, frame #749; Glatthaar, *Forged in Battle*, 177. In February 1865, Lincoln had an interview with northern-born African American abolitionist Martin R. Delany. Delany expressed to Lincoln his idea of an "Underground Railroad in reverse." He would create a military unit of 40,000 black soldiers under the command of black officers to be sent south to organize slaves and fight as guerrillas behind Confederate lines to bring the war nearer to a close. This is essentially what Edward A. Wild had in mind in creating his North Carolina African Brigade in 1863. Delany would promptly be commissioned a major, the highest-ranking black line officer in the war, commanding

the 104th USCT. The war was over before Delany completed the regiment's organization. He served as a Freedmen's Bureau Commissioner in South Carolina after the war. See Dorothy Sterling, *The Making of an Afro-American: Martin Robison Delany, 1812–1885* (1971; New York: Da Capo, 1996), 240–251.

46. CMSR of Henry N. Adkins, Co. E, F&S, 36th USCT, RG 94, NARA.

47. H.B. Scott to G. Weitzel, March 21, 1864, Letters Sent, October 1864 to May 1865, Department of Virginia and North Carolina, RG 393, NARA.

48. General Orders No. 9, Headquarters 36th USCT Cold. Vols., August 17, 1863, Regimental Order Book, 36th USCT, RG 94, NARA; Special Orders No. 1, Headquarters 36th USCT, January 28, 1864, RG 94, NARA.

49. Bradbury cited disability, sickness in his family, and being absent from his family for more than two years without a single day of furlough or leave. George Bradbury to S. Hoffman, September 29, 1863, Regimental Unbound Papers, 36th USCT, RG 94, NARA.

50. Alonzo G. Draper to S. Hoffman, November [?], 1863, Regimental Letterbook, 36th USCT, RG 94, NARA; J.G. Longley to H.W. Allen, November 10, 1863, Regimental Letterbook, 36th USCT, RG 94, NARA.

51. Alonzo G. Draper to S. Hoffman, November [?], 1863, Regimental Letterbook, 36th USCT, RG 94, NARA; J.G. Longley to H.W. Allen, November 10, 1863, Regimental Letterbook, 36th USCT, RG 94, NARA; Company A,E, Descriptive Books, 36th USCT, RG 94, NARA.

52. *MSSMCW*, vol. 4, 556; William Gates Atkins, *History of the Town of Hawley, Franklin County, Massachusetts, from its First Settlement in 1771 to 1887* (West Cummington, MA: William Gates Atkins, 1887), 22, 96. Also see very brief references to notes concerning Longley as an AMA superintendent in Wilmington, North Carolina, in William McKee Evans, *Ballots and Fence Rails: Reconstruction on the Lower Cape Fear* (Athens: University of Georgia Press, 2004), 38, 230.

53. Alonzo G. Draper to John A. Andrew, March 2, 1863, in Executive Letters, vol. 14, no. 50, MA.

54. Thomas Morris Chester, *Black Civil War Correspondent: His Dispatches from the Virginia Front*, ed. R.J.M. Blackett (New York: Da Capo, 1989), 171; Versalle F. Washington, *Eagles on Their Buttons: A Black Infantry Regiment in the Civil War* (Columbia: University of Missouri Press, 1999), 153.

55. "Company G, 36th USCT," *Compiled Records Showing Service of Military Units in Volunteer Union Organizations, United States Colored Troops*, Microfilm Publication M594, roll #209 (this same "Record of Events" for Company G, 36th USCT is also found in *OR Supp.*, pt. 2, vol. 77, 787); Benjamin F. Butler, *Butler's Book: A Review of His Legal, Political, and Military Career* (Boston: A.M. Thayer, 1892), 742.

56. Alonzo G. Draper to John A. Andrew, March 2, 1863, in Executive Letters, vol. 14, no. 50, MA; Memorandum of the dismissal of Captain Ives for drunkenness, November 27, 1863, Regimental Unbound Papers, 36th USCT, RG 94, NARA; E.A. Wild to George W. Ives, October 15, 1863, Regimental Letterbook, 36th USCT, RG 94, NARA; George W. Ives to S. Hoffman, October 23, 1863, Regimental Letterbook, 36th USCT, RG 94, NARA; Special Order, No. 302, War Department, Adjutant General's Office, July 8, 1863, Regimental Order Book, 36th USCT, RG 94, NARA.

57. *OR*, ser. II, vol. 7, 66–68.

58. General Orders No. 46, 18th Army Corps, Department of Virginia and North Carolina, April 19, 1864, Regimental Unbound Papers, 36th USCT, RG 94, NARA. This order was different from Butler's General Orders No. 46, December 5, 1863, that concerned black soldiers' families.

59. General Orders No. 46, 18th Army Corps, Department of Virginia and North Carolina, April 19, 1864, Regimental Unbound Papers, 36th USCT, RG 94, NARA; Special Order, No. 302, War Department, Adjutant General's Office, July 8, 1863, Regimental Order Book, 36th USCT, RG 94, NARA. According to Denny, 12 officers submitted their resignations, but Draper did not forward them as they were received until nine had been collected and then the batch forwarded to Fort Monroe. J. Waldo Denny, *Wearing the Blue in the Twenty-Fifth Mass. Volunteer Infantry, with Burnside's Coast Division, 18th Army Corps, and the Army of the James* (Worcester, MA: Putnam and Davis, 1879), 257.

60. General Orders No. 46, 18th Army Corps, Department of Virginia and North Carolina, April 19, 1864, Regimental Unbound Papers, 36th USCT, RG 94, NARA; Denny, *Wearing the Blue*, 257.

61. Pension file of George F. Allen, Co. D, 36th USCT, RG 15, NARA.

62. General Orders No. 46, 18th Army Corps, Department of Virginia and North Carolina, April 19, 1864, Regimental Unbound Papers, 36th USCT, RG 94, NARA.

63. General Orders No. 46, 18th Army Corps, Department of Virginia and North Carolina, April 19, 1864, Regimental Unbound Papers, 36th USCT, RG 94, NARA.

64. General Orders No. 46, 18th Army Corps, Department of Virginia and North Carolina, April 19, 1864, Regimental Unbound Papers, 36th USCT, RG 94, NARA.

65. General Orders No. 46, 18th Army Corps, Department of Virginia and North Carolina, April 19, 1864, Regimental Unbound Papers, 36th USCT, RG 94, NARA; *American and Commercial Advertiser* (Baltimore, MD), May 10, 1864.

66. H. George Weymouth to Alonzo G. Draper, April 26, 1864, Regimental Unbound Papers, 36th USCT, RG 94, NARA; C.G. Atwood to R.S. Davis, April 28, 1864, Regimental Unbound Papers, 36th USCT, RG 94, NARA.

67. Denny, *Wearing the Blue*, 260.

68. The commander of the 25th Massachusetts is quoted in Denny, *Wearing the Blue*, 261.

69. Although he received an honorable discharge from the 36th USCT, Fletcher believed "the good of the service under the present Commander of the Regiment will be promoted" by acceptance of his resignation. Colonel Draper in his endorsement of Fletcher's resignation wrote: "I have good reason to believe that this officer [Fletcher] has been more active than my other line officers, in promoting discontent, and in creating the present combination. I believe that the acceptance of his resignation will be for the interest of the service." CMSR of John W. Fletcher, Co. A, 36th USCT, RG 94, NARA; Andrew is quoted in Denny, *Wearing the Blue*, 260–261.

70. Pratt and Preston are quoted in Denny, *Wearing the Blue*, 262.

71. Denny's history of the 25th Massachusetts devotes about half a chapter to the six dismissed officers of the 36th USCT. Portions of a heavily edited letter written by an "unidentified officer" in the 36th USCT describes the alleged part played by Draper on December 22, 1863. On the very next page is a reprinted photograph of "Captain Geo. B. Proctor." Reid cites portions of Proctor's May 3, 1864, letter to Governor John A. Andrew where Proctor writes that Draper "threatened to shoot any one of his officers who would not go in & fight the 98th ... [and] detailed 2nd Lieut ... Backup & instructed him to *kill* Lt. Col Wead by his aiming the first fire & all his company were to aim at Col. W & and kill him, this, said Col D. I think will end the trouble." Denny, *Wearing the Blue*, 257–258; Richard Reid, *Freedom for Themselves: North Carolina's*

*Black Soldiers in the Civil War Era* (Chapel Hill: University of North Carolina Press, 2008), 350 (n18).

72. Conant believed that his resignation "will be for the benefit of the service under the present Commander of the Regt," although he had ample grounds to resign due to his prior service wounding. Proctor, first lieutenant and acting commander of Company G during Wild's Expedition, had relinquished command to Conant on December 12, 1863, on the march into North Carolina due to an undisclosed disability. Therefore, Proctor may not have been present for significant events occurring for the majority of the expedition. CMSR of George W.S. Conant, Co. G, Co. B, 36th USCT, RG 94, NARA; CMSR of George B. Proctor, Co. G, Co. F, 36th USCT, RG 94, NARA; Companies F and G, Descriptive Books, 36th USCT, RG 94, NARA.

73. Lincoln is quoted in Denny, *Wearing the Blue*, 262–263.

74. *MSSMCW*, vol. 6, 462 ; Company H Descriptive Book, 36th USCT, RG 94, NARA.

75. *MSSMCW*, vol. 5, 575, 577, vol. 7, 290, 296; Companies D,I, Descriptive Books, 36th USCT, RG 94, NARA.

76. *MSSMCW*, vol. 7, 300; CSMR, William H. Hart, Co. E, F&S, 36th USCT, RG 94, NARA; "Typo," *Officers and Privates, Attached to the Fourteenth Regiment*, 30.

77. Pension file of Joseph J. Hatlinger, 36th USCT, RG 15, NARA.

78. CSMR, William H. Hart, Co. E, F&S, 36th USCT, RG 94, NARA; Joseph Wall to R.S. Davis (?), September 26, 1864, Letters Received, October to December 1864, Department of Virginia and North Carolina, RG 393, NARA.

79. Company C, Descriptive Book, 36th USCT, RG 94, NARA; *OR*, ser. I, vol. 42, pt. 1, 820; William H. Hart to R.S. Davis (?), January 5, 1865, Register of Letters Received, December 1864-March 1865, RG 393, NARA; U.S. War Department, Adjutant General's Office, *Official Army Register of the Volunteer Force of the United States Army for the Years 1861, '62, '63, '64, '65*, pt. 8 (Washington, D.C.: GPO, 1867), 208; Chester, *Black Civil War Correspondent*, 97. Simmons, born in Buffalo, New York, had enlisted as a substitute in Company C, 5th New Hampshire Infantry. He was appointed a second lieutenant in Company C, 36th USCT on July 16, 1864. See New Hampshire, Adjutant General, *Revised Register of the Soldiers and Sailors of New Hampshire in the War of the Rebellion, 1861–1866* (Concord, NH: Ira C. Evans, 1895), 267, 1024.

80. "J. O'Brien, Co. B, 14th Maine Infantry, Co. C, 14th Maine Infantry Battalion," Civil War Index File, Maine State Library, Augusta, ME; *OR*, ser. I, vol. 37, pt. 1, 164.

81. Chester, *Black Civil War Correspondent*, 96–97; Compiled Military Service Record of John O'Brien, Co. D, 36th USCT, RG 94, NARA; Regimental Descriptive Book, 36th USCT, RG 94, NARA.

82. See *New York Tribune*, December 3, 1863; *New York Times*, January 9, 1864; *American and Commercial Advertiser* (Baltimore, MD), April 18, 1864, May 17, 1864, June 23, 1864.

83. For a biographical essay on Chester, see Chester, *Black Civil War Correspondent*, 3–91.

84. Chester, *Black Civil War Correspondent*, 282.

85. Stephen F. Hathaway to Cousin Gus, May 28, 1865, in Stephen F. Hathaway Papers, DU.

86. Edward A. Wild, "Draperisms 1865," Folder #2157, in Edward A. Wild Papers, USAMHI.

87. *OR*, ser. I, vol. 42, pt. 2, 416.

88. Chester, *Black Civil War Correspondent*, 115; Company G, Descriptive Book, 36th USCT, RG 94, NARA.

89. Rowland, "Emancipation and the Black Military Experience," pt. 2, 623–624.

90. *OR*, ser. I, vol. 42, pt. 2, 417.

91. General Orders No. 5, 25th Army Corps, December 21, 1864, Regimental Unbound Papers, 36th USCT, RG 94, NARA; Companies A,G, Descriptive Books, 36th USCT, RG 94, NARA.

92. General Orders No. 5, 25th Army Corps, December 21, 1864, Regimental Unbound Papers, 36th USCT, RG 94, NARA.

93. General Orders No. 5, 25th Army Corps, December 21, 1864, Regimental Unbound Papers, 36th USCT, RG 94, NARA; Company I, Descriptive Book, 36th USCT, RG 94, NARA.

94. Glatthaar, *Forged in Battle*, 86.

95. Alonzo G. Draper to R.S. Davis, November 14, 1863, Regimental Unbound Papers, 36th USCT, RG 94, NARA; Washington, *Eagles on Their Buttons*, 94.

96. Shurtleff is quoted in Washington, *Eagles on Their Buttons*, 35–36.

97. Glatthaar, *Forged in Battle*, 174–175; Redkey, *A Grand Army of Black Men*, 231.

98. "General Orders No. 46, December 5, 1863," in Benjamin F. Butler, *Private and Official Correspondence of General Benjamin F. Butler*, vol. 3, ed. Jessie Marshall Ames (Norwood, MA: Plimpton, 1917),184.

# Chapter 5

1. Company I had been detailed for duty at Camp Henry Lighthouse, Virginia, on February 13, 1864, and would not join the regiment at Point Lookout until April 24, 1864. "Company I, 36th USCT," *Compiled Records Showing Military Units in Volunteer Union Organizations, United States Colored Troops*, Microfilm Publication, M594, Roll #209, NARA; *American and Commercial Advertiser* (Baltimore, MD), March 1, 1864; Martin A. Haynes, *A History of the Second Regiment, New Hampshire Volunteer Infantry in the War of the Rebellion* (Lakeport, NH: 1896), 211; A.W. Bartlett, *History of the Twelfth Regiment New Hampshire Volunteers in the War of the Rebellion* (Concord, NH: Ira C. Evans, 1897), 159.

2. John W. Stevens, *Reminiscences of the Civil War: A Soldier in Hood's Texas Brigade, Army of Northern Virginia* (Hillsboro, TX: Hillsboro Mirror Print, 1902), 152–153.

3. Frank J. Welcher, *The Union Army, 1861–1865: Organization and Operations*, vol. 1, *The Eastern Theater* (Bloomington: Indiana University Press, 1989), 559; Frederick W. Dyer, *A Compendium of the War of Rebellion*, vol. 1 (New York: Thomas Yoseloff, 1959), 392.

4. Names of specific former slaves guarding their former masters remain elusive. *New York Herald*, May 6, 1864; Gerald W. Thomas, *Divided Allegiances: Bertie County in the Civil War* (Raleigh: Division of Archives and History, North Carolina Department of Cultural Resources, 1996), xv; Lonnie R. Speer, *Portals to Hell: Military Prisons of the Civil War* (Mechanicsburg, PA: Stackpole, 1997), 170. A Confederate prisoner at Point Lookout, Maryland, recognized a black soldier in the 4th USCT briefly serving as a guard who he had remembered as a childhood playmate. They renewed their acquaintance after the war. See Edward G. Longacre, *A Regiment of Slaves: The 4th United States Colored Infantry, 1863–1866* (Mechanicsburg, PA: Stackpole, 2003), 66.

5. Luther W. Hopkins, *From Bull Run to Appomattox: A Boy's View* (Baltimore, MD: Fleet-McGinley, 1908), 170–171, 174; James Huffman, *Ups and Downs of a Confederate Soldier* (New York: William E. Rudge's Sons, 1940), 90–91; Berry Benson, *Berry Benson's Civil War Book: Memoirs of a Confederate Scout and Sharpshooter*, ed. Susan Williams Benson (Athens: University of Georgia Press, 1992), 90–91; Speer, *Portals to Hell*, 153.

6. [John Owen, Jr., to [?], March or April 1864, John Owen, Jr., Papers, MHS.

7. James E. Hall, *The Diary of A Confederate Soldier*, ed. Ruth Woods Dayton (Lewisburg, WV: 1961), 96.

8. Sergeant Bartlett Yancey Malone, Company H, 6th North Carolina Infantry and the register of deaths for Company I, 36th USCT reported that Green had shot himself. Private John W. Stevens, Company K, 5th Texas Infantry and news correspondent "Physic" reported that Green had been shot by a comrade while practicing the manual of arms. Bartlett Yancey Malone, *Whipt 'Em Every Time: The Diary of Bartlett Yancey Malone*, ed. William Whatley Pierson, Jr. (Jackson, TN: McCowan-Mercer, 1960), 101; Edwin W. Beitzell, *Point Lookout Prison Camp for Confederates* (Abell, MD: 1972), 56; Company I, Descriptive Book, 36th USCT, RG 94, NARA; Stevens, *Reminiscences of the Civil War*, 153; *American and Commercial Advertiser* (Baltimore, MD), May 3, 1864.

9. *American and Commercial Advertiser* (Baltimore, MD), March 29, 1864; Beitzell, *Point Lookout Prison Camp*, 29, 32. Peyton was also reported to have been a private in Company I, 2nd Kentucky Cavalry.

10. Transcribed testimony of the board as well as Canby's, Butler's, and Hoffman's correspondence are quoted in Beitzell, *Point Lookout Prison Camp*, 33–35.

11. Alonzo G. Draper to C.W. Lawrence, April 17, 1864, Regimental Letterbook, 36th USCT, RG 94, NARA; Alonzo G. Draper to C.W. Lawrence, April 20, 1864, Regimental Letterbook, 36th USCT, RG 94, NARA. The 2nd New Hampshire soldiers allegedly involved in the first incident were reported as being Private [Charles] Henry Danforth, Company B, Private Phillip C. Eastman, Company E, and Private Orsino Roberts, Company I. One of them was apparently drunk during the incident. See New Hampshire, Adjutant General, *Revised Register of the Soldiers and Sailors of New Hampshire in the War of the Rebellion, 1861–1866* (Concord, NH: Ira C. Evans, 1895), 44, 48, 80. The civilian was allegedly Mr. William Uncle.

12. *American and Commercial Advertiser* (Baltimore, MD), May 10, 1864.

13. General Orders No. 10, May 9, 1864, Regimental Unbound Papers, 36th USCT, RG 94, NARA.

14. Circular Order, May 9, 1864, Regimental Unbound Papers, 36th USCT, RG 94, NARA.

15. *OR*, ser. II, vol. 7, 385; Beitzell, *Point Lookout Prison Camp*, 38.

16. Petition of 67 Confederate Prisoners to W.A. Crafts, April 20, 1864, Regimental Unbound Papers, 36th USCT, RG 94, NARA.

17. *OR*, ser. II, vol. 7, 384.

18. *OR*, ser. I, vol. 37, pt. 1, 72.

19. Draper had 1,654 soldiers to guard 11,000 prisoners in the camp. The 36th USCT had 753 officers and men present for duty. *OR*, ser. II, vol. 7, 153–154.

20. Ibid., 154.

21. Ibid.

22. Ibid., 163.

23. Ibid., 384; Company D, Descriptive Book, 36th USCT, RG 94, NARA.

24. *OR*, ser. II, vol. 7, 163–164.

25. Ibid., 164.

26. Ibid.

27. Ibid.

28. Ibid., 164–165.

29. Company B, Descriptive Book, 36th USCT, RG 94, NARA; *OR*, ser. I, vol. 36, pt. 3, 68; *OR*, ser. II, vol. 7, 164–165; Beitzell, *Point Lookout Prison Camp*, 182.

30. *OR*, ser. II, vol. 7, 165.

31. *OR*, ser. I, vol. 36, pt. 3, 175

32. Ibid.; *OR*, ser. II, vol. 7, 165–166.

33. Five major expeditions from Point Lookout into Virginia's "Northern Neck" region were conducted by Union soldiers in 1864, including the three made by the 36th USCT. See Beitzell, *Point Lookout Prison Camp*, 26. The January raid was conducted by white soldiers of the 2nd, 5th, and 12th New Hampshire Infantry along with a section of a Rhode Island artillery battery under General Marston. See Bartlett, *History of the Twelfth New Hampshire Volunteers*, 158; and Haynes, *A History of the Second Regiment*, 211.

34. Ezra J. Warner, *Generals in Blue: Lives of the Union Commanders* (Baton Rouge: Louisiana State University Press, 1964), 229–230; Welcher, *The Union Army*, vol. 1, 559; Beitzell, *Point Lookout Prison Camp*, 181; *OR*, ser. I, vol. 33, 268; *NOR*, ser. I, vol. 5, 410–411; *American and Commercial Advertiser* (Baltimore, MD), April 12, 1864, April 18, 1864; U.S. Congress, *Report of the Secretary of the Navy, 1864* (Washington, D.C.: GPO, 1865), 603. The U.S. Navy during the Civil War had different ranks among its commissioned officers. These ranks in ascending order (with their corresponding rank in the Union army in parenthesis) were: ensign (second lieutenant), master (first lieutenant), lieutenant (captain), lieutenant commander (major), commander (lieutenant colonel), captain (colonel), commodore (brigadier general), rear admiral (major general). At the close of the war the ranks of vice admiral and admiral were used much like the resurrection of lieutenant general and general in the army. See U.S. War Department, Adjutant General's Office, *Revised United States Army Regulations of 1861, with an Appendix Containing the Changes and Laws Affecting Army Regulations and Articles of War to June 25, 1863* (Washington, D.C.: GPO, 1863), 535.

35. *OR*, ser. I, vol. 33, 268–269; *Report of the Secretary of the Navy, 1864*, 604. Jordan credits the 36th USCT for making the first combat appearance of black Union soldiers in Confederate Virginia on this April expedition. But there had been expeditions into the nominal Confederate counties of King and Queen, New Kent, Mathews, and Middlesex by the 4th and 6th USCT from their base in Yorktown during the early half of March 1864. The former regiment had a large number of free African Americans and slaves who had lived and labored in the Baltimore area. The latter regiment had been recruited from among free African Americans in Pennsylvania. The "free" status of these black Union soldiers did not escape the wrath of pro–Confederate news reporters. See Ervin L. Jordan, Jr., *Black Confederates and Afro-Yankees in Civil War Virginia* (Charlottesville: University of Press Virginia, 1995), 275; *Richmond* (VA) *Daily Enquirer*, April 12, 1864; Saml. A. Duncan to Stephen R. Reynolds, March 31, 1864, *NMSUS*, reel #2, frame #782; Longacre, *A Regiment of Slaves*, 60–62; and James M. Paradis, *Strike the Blow for Freedom: The 6th United States Colored Infantry in the Civil War* (Shippensburg, PA: White Mane, 2000), 46–47.

36. Maddox claimed that he had paid Reverdy Johnson, a former U.S. Senator and U.S. Attorney General from Maryland, the sum of $1,000 to have previous charges against him dropped. His brother, who also resided in Westmoreland County, verified Maddox's claim. *OR*, ser. I, vol. 33, 269; *NOR*, ser. I, vol. 5, 410. Reverdy Johnson's allegiance to the Union would be questioned many times throughout the war. See Noah Andre Trudeau, *Out of the Storm: The End of the Civil War, April–June 1865* (Boston: Little, Brown, 1994), 362.

37. *Richmond* (VA) *Daily Enquirer*, April 22, 1864; *American and Commercial Advertiser* (Baltimore, MD), April 18, 1864; *OR*, ser. I, vol. 33, 269.

38. *Richmond* (VA) *Daily Enquirer*, April 22, 1864.

39. Ibid., July 7, 1864.

40. *American and Commercial Advertiser* (Baltimore, MD), April 18, 1864; *OR*, ser. I, vol. 33, 269.

41. Ira Berlin et al., *Freedom: A Documentary History of Emancipation, 1861–1867*, ser. I, vol. 2, *The Wartime Genesis of Free Labor: The Upper South* (New York: Cambridge University Press, 1993), 502–503; *American and Commercial Advertiser* (Baltimore, MD), April 26, 1864

42. Berlin, *Freedom*, ser. I, vol. 2, 503–504; *American and Commercial Advertiser* (Baltimore, MD), April 26, 1864. On May 4, 1864, the U.S. Government organized the Sothoron Estate and two farms owned by Joseph B. Forrest, a Confederate enlistee, into a single project with a civilian manager and an army officer as superintendent. See Richard Paul Fuke, "A School for Freed Labor: The Maryland 'Government Farms,' 1864–1866," *Maryland Historian* 16 (1985): 12–13.

43. *OR*, ser. I, vol. 37, pt. 1, 71–72; *NOR*, ser. I, vol. 5, 422; *American and Commercial Advertiser* (Baltimore, MD), May 12, 1864.

44. *OR*, ser. I, vol. 37, pt. 1, 72; *NOR*, ser. I, vol. 5, 423; *American and Commercial Advertiser* (Baltimore, MD), May 12, 1864. Henry D. Barrick (also spelled Barrack) commanded Company I, 55th Virginia Infantry early in the war and resigned on May 17, 1862. See Richard O'Sullivan, *55th Virginia Infantry* (Lynchburg: H.E. Howard, 1989), 103.

45. *OR*, ser. I, vol. 37, pt. 1, 72; *American and Commercial Advertiser* (Baltimore, MD), May 12, 1864; Companies A, F, H, Descriptive Books, 36th USCT, RG 94, NARA; "List of Deceased Soldiers," Regimental Returns/Muster Rolls, 36th USCT, RG 94, NARA; Joseph T. Glatthaar, *Forged in Battle: The Civil War Alliance of Black Soldiers and White Officers* (New York: Free Press, 1990), 166.

46. *OR*, ser. I, vol. 37, pt. 1, 72; *NOR*, ser. I, vol. 5, 423–424; *American and Commercial Advertiser* (Baltimore, MD), May 12, 1864.

47. *OR*, ser. I, vol. 37, pt. 1, 72.

48. *American and Commercial Advertiser* (Baltimore, MD), May 12, 1864.

49. *American and Commercial Advertiser* (Baltimore, MD), July 6, 1864; *OR*, ser. I, vol. 36, pt. 3, 278. Other black regiments stationed at Point Lookout during the war were 4th USCT, 24th USCT, 28th USCT, 5th Massachusetts (Colored) Cavalry, and the 3rd and 4th Maryland (Colored) Infantry. The last two units may have been early designations of USCT regiments recruited by Brigadier General William Birney in Maryland. The 4th Maryland (Colored) Infantry may have been the early name for the 4th USCT. See Beitzell, *Point Lookout Prison Camp*, 181.

50. *OR*, ser. I, vol. 36, pt. 3, 740; Benj. F. Butler to E.M. Stanton, June 10, 1864; Benj. F. Butler to [U.S.] Grant, July 5, 1864, in Benjamin F. Butler, *Private and Official Correspondence of General Benjamin F. Butler During the Civil War*, vol. 4, ed. Jessie Ames Marshall (Norwood, MA: Plimpton, 1917), 333, 467.

51. William Glenn Robertson, *Back Door to Richmond: The Bermuda Hundred Campaign, April–June 1864* (Baton Rouge: Louisiana State University Press, 1987), 246; Noah Andre Trudeau, *The Last Citadel: Petersburg, Virginia, June 1864–April 1865* (Boston: Little, Brown, 1991), 44–45.

52. *OR*, ser. I, vol. 36, pt. 3, 174–175; Benj. F. Butler to Draper, April 26, 1864 in Butler, *Private and Official Correspondence*, vol. 4, 136.

53. *OR*, ser. I, vol. 37, pt. 1, 163; *American and Commercial Advertiser* (Baltimore, MD), June 23, 1864.

54. Ibid.; ibid.

55. Ibid.; ibid.

56. *OR*, ser. I, vol. 37, pt. 1, 163.

57. Ibid.; *American and Commercial Advertiser* (Baltimore, MD), June 23, 1864.

58. *OR*, ser. I, vol. 37, pt. 1, 164–165.

59. News correspondent "Physic" reported that the force Draper engaged on June 16 consisted of no more than 30 rebels. *OR*, ser. I, vol. 37, pt. 1, 164–165; *American and Commercial Advertiser* (Baltimore, MD), June 23, 1864.

60. *American and Commercial Advertiser* (Baltimore, MD), June 23, 1864; *OR*, ser. I, vol. 37, pt. 1, 164; Company C, Descriptive Book, 36th USCT, RG 94, NARA.

61. *OR*, ser. I, vol. 37, pt. 1, 164–165.

62. Ibid., 165; *American and Commercial Advertiser* (Baltimore, MD), June 23, 1864.

63. *OR*, ser. I, vol. 37, pt. 1, 164–165; Robert K. Krick, *9th Virginia Cavalry*, 3rd ed. (Lynchburg, VA: H.E. Howard, 1982), 37. Hart is quoted in Thomas Waln-Morgan Draper, *The Drapers in America, Being a History and Genealogy of Those of that Name and Connection* (New York: John Polhemus, 1892), 212. "Physic" reported that a portion of these troops form the 7th Virginia Cavalry and 49th Virginia had been part of an advance guard sent out by Confederate Major General Wade Hampton with the intent of capturing Draper's expedition. *American and Commercial Advertiser* (Baltimore, MD), June 23, 1864.

64. *OR*, ser. I, vol. 37, pt. 1, 165.

65. Ibid.

66. Ibid., 165–166; *American and Commercial Advertiser* (Baltimore, MD), June 23, 1864.

67. *OR*, ser. I, vol. 37, pt. 1, 166; *American and Commercial Advertiser* (Baltimore, MD), June 23, 1864.

68. Ibid.; ibid..

69. *OR*, ser. I, vol. 37, pt. 1, 166–167; *American and Commercial Advertiser* (Baltimore, MD), June 28, 1864. Peter Wilson was removed from Pierson's Farm, Richmond County, Virginia, and reinterred in the Fredericksburg (Virginia) National Cemetery (Grave #814) after the war. It is possible that the unidentified "contraband" also found with Wilson may have been Henry Lee. Private Lee might well be among the majority of unknown Union soldiers interred in the Fredericksburg National Cemetery.

70. The majority of these "Northern Neck" soldiers enlisted between June 19 and 21 after the June expedition into Richmond County. Companies A–K, Descriptive Books, 36th USCT, RG, NARA; Pension file of David Cherry, 36th USCT, RG 15, NARA.

71. Draper, *The Drapers in America*, 212; *NOR*, ser. I, vol. 5, 450, 446.

72. *OR*, ser. I, vol. 40, pt. 2, 684.

73. Ibid., 689.

74. Ibid., 704–705.

75. Ibid., 706.

76. *Richmond* (VA) *Daily Enquirer*, July 5, 1864.

77. Ibid., July 7, 1864.

78. *OR*, ser. I. vol. 40, pt. 3, 743; Robert E.L. Krick, *Staff Officers in Gray: A Biographical Register of the Staff Officers in the Army of Northern Virginia* (Chapel Hill: University of North Carolina Press, 2003), 82, 95.

79. *OR*, ser. I. vol. 40, pt. 3, 744.

80. *NOR*, ser. I, vol. 5, 451.

81. Proctor is quoted in Reid, *Freedom for Themselves*, 135; Robert I. Alotta, *Civil War Justice: Union Army Executions Under Lincoln* (Shippensburg, PA: White Mane, 1989), 187; Jordan, *Black Confederates and Afro-Yankees*, 132.

82. Jordan, *Black Confederates and Afro-Yankees*, 272.

83. White is quoted in Glatthaar, *Forged in Battle*, 86.

84. White is quoted in William R. Forstchen, "The 28th United States Colored Troops: Indiana's African-Americans Go To War, 1863–1865" (Ph.D. diss., Purdue University, 1994), 196.

85. J. Owen, Jr., to Aunt, May 6, 1864, John Owen, Jr., Papers, MHS.

## Chapter 6

1. Alonzo G. Draper to John A. Andrew, December 15, 1864, in Executive Letters, vol. 100, no. 117, MA. Draper's quote is also found in John W. Blassingame, "Negro Chaplains in the Civil War," *Negro History Bulletin* 27 (October 1963): 24.

2. Edward G. Longacre, *Army of Amateurs: General Benjamin F. Butler and the Army of the James, 1863–1865* (Mechanicsburg, PA: Stackpole, 1997), xi–xii, 45; Edward G. Longacre, "Black Troops in the Army of the James, 1863–65," *Military Affairs* 45 (February 1981): 2. Ira Berlin and his associates with the Freedmen and Southern Society Project place the number of black soldiers that served from eastern North Carolina and southeastern Virginia at 11,000. Ira Berlin et al., eds., *Freedom: A Documentary History of Emancipation, 1861–1867*, ser. II, *The Black Military Experience* (New York: Cambridge University Press, 1982), 116.

3. Longacre, *Army of Amateurs*, 45–46; Longacre, "Black Troops in the Army of the James," 1.

4. Longacre, "Black Troops in the Army of the James," 1.

5. Solon A. Carter, "Fourteen Months' Service with Colored Troops," in *Civil War Papers Read Before the Commandery of the State of Massachusetts, Military Order of the Loyal Legion of the United States*, vol. 1 (Boston: F.H. Gilson, 1900), 159–161. Also see Robertson, *Back Door to Richmond*, 60–61; Schiller, *The Bermuda Hundred Campaign*, 63; and Longacre, *Army of Amateurs*, 73.

6. Ulysses S. Grant, *The Personal Memoirs of Ulysses S. Grant*, Vol. 2 (Charles L. Webster, 1885), 148. Robertson, Schiller, and Longacre all concur that Butler believed his primary objective during the spring 1864 campaign was securing strategic bases along the James and Appomattox Rivers below Richmond until such time a junction could be made with the Army of the Potomac pursuing Lee from the north before making an assault against Richmond. See William Glenn Robertson, *Back Door to Richmond: The Bermuda Hundred Campaign April–June 1864* (Baton Rouge: Louisiana State University Press, 1987), 22; Herbert M. Schiller, *The Bermuda Hundred Campaign: "Operations on the South Side of the James River, Virginia–May, 1864"* (Dayton, OH: Morningside, 1988), 30–31; and Longacre, *Army of Amateurs*, 63–64.

7. Benjamin F. Butler, *Speech of Maj.-Gen. Benj. F. Butler, Upon the Campaign Before Richmond, 1864. Delivered at Lowell, Mass., January 29, 1865* (Boston: Wright and Potter, 1865), 11–12. Most secondary works concerning Butler's view of his orders from Grant in May 1864 (including Robertson, Schiller, and Longacre) cite his 1892 autobiography as the primary source for this view. His 1865 speech at Lowell, Massachusetts, is similar to how he perceived his mission in his autobiography 27 years later.

8. J. Wilson Shaffer to Butler, July 8, 1864, in Benjamin F. Butler, *Private and Official Correspondence of General Benjamin F. Butler During the Civil War*, vol. 4, ed. Jessie Ames Marshall (Norwood, MA: Plimpton, 1917), 475; OR, ser. I, vol. 40, pt. 2, 582, 615.

9. "Field and Staff, 36th USCT," *Compiled Records Showing Service of Military Units In Volunteer Union Organizations, United States Colored Troops*, Microfilm Publication M594, roll #209, NARA; OR, ser. I, vol. 42, pt. 2, 622; Ezra J. Warner, *Generals in Blue: Lives of the Union Commanders* (Baton Rouge: Louisiana State University Press, 1964), 354–355.

10. [John Owen, Jr.] to Mother, September 10, 1864, John Owen, Jr., Papers, MHS.

11. Companies A–K, Descriptive Books, 36th USCT, RG 94, NARA; Thomas Morris Chester, *Black Civil War Correspondent: His Dispatches from the Virginia Front*, ed., R.J.M. Blackett (New York: Da Capo, 1989), 101, 109.

12. "Company G Descriptive Book, 36th USCT, RG 94, NARA; Chester, *Black Civil War Correspondent*, 197.

13. [John Owen, Jr.] to Mother, September 10, 1864, John Owen, Jr., Papers, MHS.

14. Circular Order, Headquarters 36th U.S.C. Troops, April 7, 1864, Regimental Order Book, 36th USCT, RG 94, NARA; Circular Order, Hd. Qrts., 36th U.S.C.T., February 14, 1864, Regimental Order Book, 36th USCT, RG 94, NARA: General Orders No. 4, Hd. Qrts., 36th U.S.C.T, March 14. 1864, Regimental Order Book, 36th USCT, RG 94, NARA; General Orders No. 9, Headquarters, 36th USCT, May 8, 1864, Regimental Order Book, 36th USCT, RG 94, NARA.

15. Horace Montgomery, "A Union Officer's Recollections of the Negro as a Soldier," *Pennsylvania History* 28 (April 1961): 174.

16. Pension file of John Buck, 36th USCT, RG 15, NARA. Bray would later testify to pension examiners that Buck had not been wounded by the shell as he would claim after the war. Chester, *Black Civil War Correspondent*, 191.

17. Benjamin F. Butler, *Butler's Book: A Review of His Legal, Political, and Military Career*. (Boston: A.M. Thayer, 1892), 726–727; Carter, "Fourteen Months' Service with Colored Troops," 169; Barry Popchock, "A Shower of Stars at New Market Heights: Butler's 'Contrabands' Prove Their Mettle," *America's Civil War* 46 (August 1994): 34.

18. Butler, *Butler's Book*, 722–730.

19. Carter, a staff officer under General Paine, reported that the 2nd and 3rd Brigades totaled 3,000 men. It is more reasonable to assume that all three brigades totaled close to 3,000 men. Carter, "Fourteen Months Service with Colored Troops," 170. Captain Livermore, also of Paine's staff, reported that the 2nd and 3rd Brigades of Paine's Division actually totaled 1,978 men. Livermore points out that the 1st Brigade had been counted among the colored troops in Birney's Colored Brigade of the 10th Corps. See Thomas L. Livermore, *Numbers and Losses in the Civil War in America: 1861–1865* (Bloomington: Indiana University Press, 1957), 128. Sergeant Major Fleetwood, 4th USCT, reported that Duncan's 3rd Brigade only totaled 683 soldiers in the assault on New Market Heights. See Christian A. Fleetwood, *The Negro as a Soldier* (Washington, D.C.: Howard University Press, 1895), 17. Captain McMurray, 6th USCT, reported that his regiment only had 367 present for duty in the assault, leaving Fleetwood's 4th USCT with only 316 men present for duty. See Montgomery, "A Union Officer's Recollections of the Negro as a Soldier," 177. Therefore, Draper's 2nd brigade had about 1,295 (estimated at 1,300, according to Draper himself). The 36th USCT probably had least 450 men present in the assault on New Market Heights.

20. Butler, *Butler's Book*, 731. The Fort Pillow massacre further demonstrated that the Confederacy would not recognize black Union soldiers on equal footing with white Union soldiers. Black soldiers would fight their enemies even harder to avoid capture. See Leon Litwack, *Been in the Storm So Long: The Aftermath of Slavery* (New York: Alfred A. Knopf, 1979), 92–93. For additional works on what is known as "The Fort Pillow Massacre" see Noah Andre Trudeau, *Like Men of War: Black Troops in the Civil War, 1862–1865* (Boston: Little, Brown, 1998), 156–181; and William R. Brookshear, "Betwixt Wind and Water: A Short Account of Confederate Major General Nathan Bedford Forrest's Attack on Fort Pillow," in *The Price of Freedom: Slavery and the Civil War*, vol. 1, *The Demise of Slavery*, eds. Martin H. Greenberg and Charles G. Waugh (Nashville, TN: Cumberland House, 2000), 287–297.

21. The Confederate forces on New Market Heights were under the overall command of Brigadier General John Gregg. Gregg's "Texas Brigade," composed of the 3rd Arkansas, 1st Texas, 4th Texas, and 5th Texas Infantry Regiments, was situated on the right portion of New Market Heights. A cavalry brigade under the command of Brigadier General Martin W. Gary, made up of the Hampton Legion (cavalry component), 7th South Carolina Cavalry, and the 24th Virginia Cavalry, occupied the left portion of the New Market line. Approximately 2,000 feet behind Gary's extreme left on a hill sat four artillery cannon of the 1st Rockbridge Artillery Battery. The 25th Virginia Infantry Battalion, composed of hastily assembled volunteers from Richmond, was situated to the immediate right of Gregg's Brigade. Butler, *Butler's Book*, 723; Richard J. Sommers, *Richmond Redeemed: The Siege at Petersburg* (Garden City, NY: Doubleday, 1981), 34–35; Popchock, "A Shower of Stars at New Market Heights," 31.

22. Chester, *Black Civil War Correspondent*, 150.

23. Sommers, *Richmond Redeemed*, 34–35; *OR*, ser. I, vol. 42, pt. 1, 817.

24. Popchock, "A Shower of Stars at New Market Heights," 36; Sommers, *Richmond Redeemed*, 35.

25. Fleetwood, *The Negro as a Soldier*, 17; Popchock, "A Shower of Stars at New Market Heights," 37.

26. Popchock, "A Shower of Stars at New Market Heights," 37; Montgomery, "A Union Officer's Recollections of the Negro as a Soldier," 177–178.

27. *OR*, ser. I, vol. 42, pt. 1, 815, 819; Popchock, "A Shower of Stars at New Market Heights," 37; Sommers, *Richmond Redeemed*, 36.

28. *OR*, ser. I, vol. 42, pt. 1, 819; Sommers, *Richmond Redeemed*, 36.

29. *OR*, ser. I, vol. 42, pt. 1, 819–820; Chester, *Black Civil War Correspondent*, 150–151; Popchock, "A Shower of Stars at New Market Heights," 37.

30. *OR*, ser. I, vol. 42, pt. 1, 820; Draper, *The Drapers in America*, 212; Joseph J. Scroggs, "The Earth Shook and Quivered," ed. Sig Synnestvedt, *Civil War Times Illustrated* 11 (December 1972): 34.

31. John Owen, Jr., to Mother, September 30, 1864, John Owen, Jr., Papers, MHS; Chester, *Black Civil War Correspondent*, 151–152; *OR*, ser. I, vol. 42, pt. 1, 820; B.F. Pratt, "Report of Casualties in the 36th Regt. U.S. Cold. Troops, during an assault upon the enemy's work at New Market Heights, Va.," Sept. 29, 1864, Regimental Unbound Papers, 36th USCT, RG 94, NARA; Pension file of James Cornick, 36th USCT, RG 15, NARA.

32. Chester, *Black Civil War Correspondent*, 152; *OR*, ser. I, vol. 42, pt. 1, 820.

33. Chester, *Black Civil War Correspondent*, 151; *OR*, ser. I, vol. 42, pt. 1, 820; Pension file of Henry Cornick, 36th USCT, RG 15, NARA.

34. J.B. Polley, *Hood's Texas Brigade: Its Marches, Its Battles, Its Achievements* (Dayton, OH: Morningside, 1976), 253; D.H. Hamilton, *History of Company M: First Texas Volunteer Infantry* (1925; Waco, TX: W.M. Morrison, 1962), 61.

35. *OR*, ser. I, vol. 42, pt. 1, 820. Lieutenant Colonel Pratt later reported 22 men killed, 5 officers and 89 men wounded with one missing. B.F. "Pratt, Report of Casualties in the 36th Regt. U.S. Cold. Troops, during an assault upon the enemy's work at New Market Heights, Va.," Sept. 29, 1864, Regimental Unbound Papers, 36th USCT, RG 94, NARA. The regimental service records reported 102 men wound. "Field and Staff, 36th USCT," *Compiled Records Showing Service of Military Units in Volunteer Union Organizations, United States Colored Troops*, Microfilm Publication M594, roll #209. Butler, *Butler's Book*, 733; *OR*, ser. I, vol. 42, pt. 3, 169.

36. Pension file of Soney (Sawney) Jaycox, 36th USCT, RG 15, NARA.

37. Pension file of Wilson Burrus, Co. A, RG 15, NARA.

38. John Owen, Jr., to Mother, September 30, 1864, John Owen, Jr., Papers, MHS.

39. Butler, *Butler's Book*, 742.

40. Carter, "Fourteen Months' Service with Colored Troops," 170.

41. Trudeau, *Like Men of War*, 306–307.

42. *OR*, ser. I, vol. 42, pt. 1, 814–817; Trudeau, *Like Men of War*, 307–309; Pension file of John Burfort (Bufort), 36th USCT, RG, 15, NARA.

43. Companies A–K, Descriptive Books, 36th USCT, RG 94, NARA.

44. Ibid.

45. James M. McPherson, *Battle Cry of Freedom: The Civil War Era* (1988; New York: Ballantine, 1989), 485–486; Joseph T. Glatthaar, *Forged in Battle: The Civil War Alliance of Black Soldiers and White Officers* (New York: Free, 1990), 187–188; Berlin, *Freedom*, ser. II, 633.

46. Draper is quoted in Thomas Truxtun Moebs, *Black Soldiers—Black Sailors—Black Ink: Research Guide on African-Americans in U.S. Military History, 1526–1900* (Chesapeake Bay, MD: Moebs, 1994), 1310.

47. Peter Kolchin, *American Slavery, 1619–1877* (New York: Hill and Wang, 1993), 113–114; Berlin, *Freedom*, ser. II, 634. For further discussion on initial physical examinations of enlisting freedmen see Glatthaar, *Forged in Battle*, 76–78.

48. Pension file of Smith Pratt, 36th USCT, RG 15, NARA.

49. Pension files of Allen Cooper and Malachi Gallop, 36th USCT, RG 15, NARA.

50. Glatthaar, *Forged in Battle*, 188–189; Otto Friedrich, "'We Will Not Do Duty Any Longer for Seven Dollars per Month,'" *American Heritage* 39 (February 1988): 68.

51. Inspectors of State Alms House [Massachusetts], "Certification of H.H. Mitchell," April 19, 1861; H.H. Mitchell to E.D. Townsend, October 10, 1863, in Henry Hedge Mitchell Papers, 1861–1880, MHS.

52. General Order No.6, Headquarters 36th U.S. Cold. Troops, April 3, 1864, Regimental Order Book, 36th USCT, RG 94, NARA.

53. U.S. War Department, Adjutant General's Office, *Official Army Register of the Volunteer Force of the United States Army for the Years 1861, '62, '63, '64, '65*, pt. 8 (Washington, D.C.: GPO, 1867), 207; Pension file of John B. Fisher, F&S, 36th USCT, RG 15, NARA.

54. John Owen, Jr., to Mother, March 4, 1865, John Owen, Jr., Papers, MHS.

55. Ella Forbes, *African American Women During the Civil War* (New York: Garland Publishers, 1998), 53.

56. John Owen, Jr., to Mother, September 26, 1864, John Owen, Jr., Papers, MHS.

57. For more information concerning voting in the field see McPherson, *Battle Cry of Freedom*, 803–806. Butler and about 5,000 soldiers from the Army of the James were detailed to New York City in November 1864 to protect citizens and property from possible terrorism and sabotage from Confederate sympathizers on Election Day. A year earlier, New York City had been the scene of racist violence as a result of the mandatory draft issued by the War Department. See Longacre, *Army of Amateurs*, 238–243.

58. Frederick H. Dyer, *A Compendium of the War of Rebellion*, vol. 1 (New York: Thomas Yoseloff, 1959), 390; Robert S. Lanier, ed., *The Photographic History of the Civil War: Armies and Leaders* (New York: Fairfax, 1983), 232, 234; Longacre, "Black Troops in the Army of the James," 1.

59. Chester, *Black Civil War Correspondent*, 209.

60. Ibid., 195–196.

61. "Field and Staff, 36th USCT," *Compiled Records Showing Service of Military Units In Volunteer Union Organizations, United States Colored Troops,* Microfilm Publication M594, roll #209, NARA.
62. Chester, *Black Civil War Correspondent,* 289.
63. Ibid., 290.
64. Ibid., 290–291.
65. Ibid., 289; "Company H, Company K, 36th USCT," *Compiled Records Showing Service of Military Units in Volunteer Union Organizations, United States Colored Troops,* Microfilm Publication M594, roll #209, NARA; Edward A. Wild, "Draperisms 1865," Folder #2157, in Edward A. Wild Papers, USAMHI.
66. Alonzo G. Draper to Benjamin Perley Poore, April 29, 1865, in Miscellaneous Bound Manuscripts, MHS.
67. Ibid.
68. Hart is quoted in an unidentified Lynn, Massachusetts, newspaper, April 4, 1865, Newspaper Clipping File, vol. 17, p. 91, LPL. Pratt is quoted in Trudeau, *Like Men of War,* 422; Clippings of *Richmond Daily Whig,* April 4, 1865, in Executive Letters, vol. 100, no. 132, MA; Stephen F. Hathaway to Cousin Gus, April 19, 1865, in Stephen F. Hathaway Papers, DU.
69. Trudeau maintains that it may never be known what units actually entered Richmond "and claims for the black units' primacy have as much validity as those for the others." See Trudeau, *Like Men of War,* 422, 423–424. Witt also writes that the 36th was one of the first regiments to enter Richmond, but suggests in a footnote that the 29th Connecticut may have been the very first. See Jerry V. Witt, *Wild in North Carolina: General Edward A. Wild's December 1863 Raid into Camden, Currituck, and Pasquotank Counties* (Springfield, VA: J.V. Witt, 1993), 57. Furgerson argues that the 36th USCT was not the first unit to enter the Richmond city limits. See Ernest B. Furgerson, *Ashes of Glory: Richmond at War* (New York: Alfred A. Knopf, 1996), 331–332.
70. George Templeton Strong, *Diary of the Civil War, 1860–1865,* ed. Allan Nevins (New York: Macmillan, 1962), 575; Horace Greeley, *The American Conflict: A History of the Great Rebellion in the United States of America, 1860–'65,* Vol. 2 (Hartford, CT: O.D. Case, 1866), 737.
71. Ervin L. Jordan, Jr., *Black Confederates and Afro-Yankees in Civil War Virginia* (Charlottesville: University Press of Virginia, 1995), 292; Testimony of Major General Godfrey Weitzel before Congressional Committee on the Conduct of War, May 18, 1865, *NMSUS,* reel #4, frame #149.
72. Rembert W. Patrick, *The Fall of Richmond* (Baton Rouge: Louisiana State University Press, 1960), 120–123.
73. Patrick, *The Fall of Richmond,* 122–123.
74. Chester, *Black Civil War Correspondent,* 299.
75. Jordan, *Black Confederates and Afro-Yankees,* 289; Longacre, "Black Troops in the Army of the James," 6; Testimony of Major General Godfrey Weitzel before Congressional Committee on the Conduct of War, May 18, 1865, *NMSUS,* reel #4, frame #149.
76. "Field and Staff, 36th USCT," *Compiled Records Showing Service of Military Units In Volunteer Union Organizations, United States Colored Troops,* Microfilm Publication M594, roll #209, NARA; Jordan, *Black Confederates and Afro-Yankees,* 289; Glatthaar, *Forged in Battle,* 218; Trudeau, *Like Men of War,* 461–462.
77. Butler, *Speech of Maj-Gen. Benj. F. Butler, Upon the Campaign Before Richmond, 1864,* 4–5.
78. William Birney to Benjamin F. Butler, April 23, 1865, in Butler, *Private and Official Correspondence of General Benjamin F. Butler,* vol. 5, 600.
79. Pension file of Paul Wiggins, 36th USCT, RG 14, NARA.
80. Entry 4167, Rations Issued, Records of Persons Receiving Rations, Norfolk, Virginia, 1865, RG 105, NARA; Berlin, *Freedom,* ser. I, vol. II, 179–182.
81. Bird is quoted in Berlin, *Freedom,* ser. I, vol. II, 179–180.
82. Glatthaar, *Forged in Battle,* 174–175.
83. Adjutant General [L. Thomas] to Edwin M. Stanton, June 5, 1865 (excerpt) in Leslie Suzanne Rowland, "Emancipation and the Black Military Experience During the American Civil War: A Documentary History," pt. 3 (Ph.D. diss., University of Rochester, 1991), 986–987.
84. Geo. H. Gordon to O. Brown, June 6, 1865 in Rowland, "Emancipation and the Black Military Experience," pt. 3, 985–986.
85. The Etheridge-Benson letter is quoted from Ira Berlin and Leslie S. Rowland, eds., *Families and Freedom: A Documentary History of African-American Kinship in the Civil War Era* (New York: New Press, 1997), 125–126.
86. Berlin and Rowland, *Families and Freedom,* 125–126.
87. [Frank] James and Draper are quoted in Berlin, *Freedom,* ser. II, 730.
88. A triumvirate of conservative military leaders dominated the newly established District of Virginia, occupied by Union forces in mid-1865. Major General Henry W. Halleck, a foe of General Butler, commanded the overall district. Major General Ord continued in command of the Army of the James. Brigadier General Marsena F. Patrick, former Provost Marshal General for the Army of the Potomac, assumed similar duties in the district. All three had reputations of indifference toward the use of black soldiers. See Chester, *Black Civil War Correspondent,* 43.
89. Companies A–K, Descriptive Books, 36th USCT, RG 94, NARA.
90. Trudeau, *Like Men of War,* 456; Glatthaar, *Forged in Battle,* 218–219.
91. Oliver Willcox Norton, *Army Letters, 1861–1865* (Chicago: O.C. Deming, 1903), 259.
92. John Owen, Jr., to Mother, June 13, 1865, John Owen, Jr., Papers, MHS; "Field and Staff, 36th USCT," *Compiled Records Showing Service of Military Units In Volunteer Union Organizations, United States Colored Troops,* Microfilm Publication M594, roll #209, NARA.
93. "Field and Staff, 36th USCT," *Compiled Records Showing Service of Military Units In Volunteer Union Organizations, United States Colored Troops,* Microfilm Publication M594, roll #209, NARA.
94. Stephen F. Hathaway to Cousin Gus, July 19, 1865, in Stephen F. Hathaway Papers, DU; Companies A–K, Descriptive Books, 36th USCT, RG 94, NARA.
95. Alonzo Draper to Benj. F. Butler, May 28, 1865, in Butler, *Private and Official Correspondence of General Benjamin F. Butler,* vol. 5, 622.
96. Draper, *The Drapers in America,* 212–213; Compiled Military Service Record of Alonzo G. Draper, F&S, 36th USCT, RG 94, NARA.
97. Draper is quoted from Draper, *The Drapers in America,* 213; Special Orders No. 40, Headquarters, 3rd Div., 25th A.C., September 4, 1865, Regimental Unbound Papers, 36th USCT, RG 94, NARA.
98. *Lynn (MA) Weekly Reporter* quoted in Draper, *The Drapers in America,* 213–214.
99. Special Orders, 25th AC, September 6, 1865, Folder #2170, in Edward A. Wild Papers, USAMHI.
100. Eric Foner, *Reconstruction: America's Unfinished Revolution, 1863–1877* (New York: Harper and Row, 1988), 102–103.
101. Pension Index, 36th USCT, Microfilm Publication T289, NARA, rolls #550–551. By March 1869, black soldiers in the 38th and 41st Infantries were consolidated into the 24th Infantry while those in the 39th and 40th In-

fantries were combined into the 25th Infantry. These two units, along with the all-black 9th and 10th Cavalry, maintained a distinguished record while serving in the post-war American West and in the Spanish-American War. See Arlen L. Fowler, *The Black Infantry in the West, 1869–1891* (1971; Norman: University of Oklahoma Press, 1996), 16–17.

## Conclusion

1. Pension file of Frederick Henry, 36th USCT, RG 15, NARA.
2. Joe A. Mobley, *James City: A Black Community in North Carolina* (Raleigh: North Carolina Department of Cultural Resources, Division of Archives and History, 1981), 43–91.
3. Pension files of Frank Cornick, Miles James, 36th USCT, RG 15, NARA.
4. Pension files of David H. Allen and Henry N. Adkins, 36th USCT, RG 15, NARA.
5. The four Pinkett brothers (Sandy, Stephen, Adam, and Wilson) were slaves in Somerset County, Maryland. Stephen served in the 7th USCT and the other three brothers served in the 9th USCT. Both regiments were recruited, organized, and led by Brigadier General William Birney. Harold T. Pinkett, "A Brothers' Fight for Freedom," *Maryland Historical Magazine* 86 (Spring 1991): 49.
6. W.E.B. Du Bois, *John Brown: A Biography*, ed., John David Smith (1909; Armonk, NY: M.E. Sharpe, 1997), 191–192.
7. Among the representative works illustrating such efforts include Mobley, *James City*; David Wright and David Zoby, *Fire on the Beach: Recovering the Lost Story of Richard Etheridge and the Pea Island Lifesavers* (New York: Scribner, 2000); and Patricia C. Click, *The Time Full of Trial: The Roanoke Island Freedmen's Colony, 1862–1867* (Chapel Hill: University of North Carolina Press, 2001), particularly pp. 198–199.
8. Solon A. Carter, "Fourteen Months Service with Colored Troops," in *Civil War Papers Read Before the Commandery of the State of Massachusetts, Military Order of the Loyal Legion of the United States*, vol. 1 (Boston: F.H. Gilson, 1900), 179.
9. W.H. Hart to R.S. Oliver, October 23, 1865, Regimental Letterbook, 36th USCT, RG 94, NARA; Company G Descriptive Book, 36th USCT, RG, NARA.

## Unit Roster

1. Regimental Descriptive Book, Companies A–K, Descriptive Books, 36th USCT, RG 94, NARA; Pension Index, 36th United States Colored Infantry, Microfilm Publication T289, rolls 550–441, NARA; Miscellaneous correspondence, Regimental Letterbook and Unbound Papers, 36th USCT, RG 94, NARA. Since the late 1990s, a non-profit organization has undertaken an ambitious and worthwhile project of creating and maintaining a website titled "The NC–US Colored Troops Project," http://www.rootsweb.ancestry.com/~ncusct/usct.htm, that includes primary and secondary source articles as well as transcriptions of the regimental and company descriptive books for the 35th USCT, 36th USCT, 37th USCT, and 14th U.S. Colored Heavy Artillery. These transcriptions are direct duplications of the information originally written in the regimental and company books, including glaring and obvious mistakes. The unit roster for the 36th USCT in this present work attempts to make corrections and provide clarification where possible.
2. See *Record of Service of Connecticut Men in the Army and Navy of the United States During the War of the Rebellion* (Hartford, CT: Case, Lockwood, and Brainard, 1889);

*MSSMCW*, vols. 4, 6; *Official Roster of the Soldiers of the State of Ohio in the War of the Rebellion, 1861–1866*, vol. 1 (Akron, OH: Werner, 1893); Samuel P. Bates, *History of Pennsylvania Volunteers, 1861–5*, vol. 5 (Harrisburg, PA: B. Singerly, 1871); L. Allison Wilmer et al., *History and Roster of Maryland Volunteers, War of 1861–5*, vol. 2 (Baltimore: Guggenheimer, Weil, 1899).
3. Pension file of Alonzo G. Draper, 36th USCT, RG 15, NARA; Alonzo G. Draper to John A. Andrew, 1861–1865, Executive Letters, Massachusetts Archives, Boston, MA; Alonzo G. Draper Letters, 1862, 1865, Massachusetts Historical Society, Boston, MA; Thomas Waln-Morgan Draper, *The Drapers in America* (New York: John Polhemus, 1892), 208–214; *MSSMCW*, vol. 5, 577; vol. 7, 296; Roger D. Hunt and Jack Brown, *Brevet Brigadier Generals in Blue* (Gaithersburg, MD: Olde Soldier Books, 1990), 172; Mark A. Lause, "Turning the World Upside Down: A Portrait of Labor and Military Leader, Alonzo Granville Draper," *Labor History* 44 (May 2003): 189–204; Alonzo Lewis and James R. Newhall, *History of Lynn, Essex County, Massachusetts* (Boston: John L. Shorey, 1865), 456; Paul G. Faler, *Mechanics and Manufacturers in the Early Industrial Revolution: Lynn, Massachusetts, 1780–1860* (Albany: State University of New York Press, 1981), 199, 230; Alan Dawley, *Class and Community: The Industrial Revolution in Lynn* (Cambridge, MA: Harvard University Press, 1976), 79, 191.
4. Pension file of Benjamin F. Pratt, 36th USCT, RG 15, NARA; "Death of Gen. B.F. Pratt," *Boston Globe*, July 30, 1890; "Marriages and Deaths," *Weymouth Weekly Gazette*, August 1, 1890; *MSSMCW*, vol. 3, 693; vol. 7, 307; Hunt and Brown, *Brevet Brigadier Generals in Blue*, 490; Francis Greenleaf Pratt, comp., *The Pratt Family: A Genealogical Record of Mathew Pratt of Weymouth, Massachusetts, 1627–1885* (Boston: 1889), 214–214; *Vital Records of Weymouth, Massachusetts to the Year 1850*, vol. 1, *Births* (Boston: New England Historic Genealogical Society, 1910), 224; *Vital Records of Weymouth, Massachusetts to the Year 1850*, vol. 2, *Marriages and Deaths* (Boston: New England Historic Genealogical Society, 1910), 146, 318.
5. CMSR, William H. Hart, Co. H, F&S, 36th USCT, RG 94, NARA; *MSSMCW*, vol. 5, 650; vol. 7, 300; *Vital Records of Lynn, Massachusetts, to the End of the Year 1849*, vol. 1, *Births* (Salem, MA: Essex Institute, 1905), 178; John Clark Rand, ed., *One of a Thousand: A Series of Biographical Sketches of One Thousand Representative Men, 1888–1889* (Boston: First National Publishing, 1890), 285–286; *Journal of the Thirty-second Annual Encampment Department of Massachusetts, Grand Army of the Republic* (Boston: E.B. Stillings, 1898), 135.
6. Pension file of Daniel J. Preston, 36th USCT, RG 15, NARA; "Letter from Israel P. Proctor to Charles P. Preston, Aug. 31, 1839" in *The Historical Collections of the Danvers Historical Society*, vol. 9 (Danvers, MA: Danvers Historical Society, 1921), 102; Oliver Ayer Roberts, *History of the Military Company of the Massachusetts Now Called the Ancient and Honorable Artillery Company of Massachusetts, 1637–1888*, vol. 3 (Boston: Alfred Mudge and Sons, 1898), 286; *MSSMCW*, vol. 3, 681; vol. 7, 307; *Vital Records of Danvers, Massachusetts to the End of the Year 1849*, vol. 1, *Births* (Salem, MA: Essex Institute, 1909), 281; *Vital Records of Danvers, Massachusetts to the End of the Year 1849*, vol. 2, *Marriages and Death* (Salem, MA: Essex Institute, 1910), 227; Frank E. Moynahan, ed., *Danvers, Massachusetts: A Resume of Her Past History and Progress...* (Danvers, MA: Danvers Mirror, 1899), 28; *Report of the Committee Appointed to Revise the Soldiers' Record* (Danvers, MA: Town of Danvers, 1895), 164.
7. *MSSMCW*, vol. 1, 711; vol. 7, 300; Joseph Keith

Newell, ed., *"Ours": Annals of 10th Regiment, Massachusetts Volunteers, in the Rebellion* (Springfield, MA: C.A. Nichols, 1875), 503; *Proceedings at the Centennial Celebration of the Incorporation of the Town of Longmeadow, October 17th, 1883* (Secretary of the Centennial Committee, 1884), 278; Alfred S. Roe, *The Tenth Regiment Massachusetts Volunteer Infantry, 1861-1864: A Western Massachusetts Regiment* (Springfield, MA: Tenth Regiment Veteran Association, 1909), 436; Elizabeth Gadsby, *Lineage Book: National Society of the Daughters of the American Revolution, 1898*, vol. 25 (Washington, D.C.: National Society of the Daughters of the American Revolution, 1908), 43; Charles Theodore Hendrick, *The Hendrick Genealogy: Daniel Hendrick of Haverhill, Mass.* (Rutland, VT: Tuttle, 1923), 263.

8. Pension file of Henry F.H. Miller, 36th USCT, RG 15, NARA; *MSSMCW*, vol. 3, 647; vol. 7, 304; *Journal of the Thirty-Second Annual Encampment, Department of Massachusetts, Grant Army of the Republic* (Boston: B. Stillings, 1898), 132.

9. *Vital Records of Brookline, Massachusetts, to the End of the Year 1849* (Salem: Essex Institute, 1929), 75; Augustus Woodbury, *A Narrative of the Campaign of the First Rhode Island Regiment* (Providence, RI: Sidney R. Rider, 1862),174; "War Department Adjutant General's Office, Washington, Feb. 16, 1863, Special Orders No. 77 [Extract]," *New York Times*, February 23, 1863; *MSSMCW*, vol. 4, 710; vol. 7, 314; "From Norfolk," *New York Times*, November 19, 1863.

10. *MSSMCW*, vol. 4, 265; vol. 7, 297; George Adams, *The Massachusetts Register for the Year 1856* (Boston: Damrell and Moore, 1856), 94; Roberts, *History of the Military Company of the Massachusetts*, vol. 3, 211; *Illustrated Boston: The Metropolis of New England*, 2nd ed. (New York: American Publishing and Engraving, 1889), 110; Charles Henry James Douglas, ed., *A Collection of Family Records with Biographical Sketches, and Other Memoranda of Various Families and Individuals Bearing the Name Douglas ...* (Providence, RI: E.L. Freeman, 1879), 79; Thomas W. Baldwin, comp., *Vital Records of Chelsea, Massachusetts, to the Year 1850* (Boston: New England Historic Genealogical Society, 1916), 111.

11. Pension file of Charles H. Frye, 36th USCT, RG 15, NARA; *MSSMCW*, vol. 1, 393; vol. 2, 623; vol. 7, 298.

12. *MSSMCW*, vol. 4, 383.

13. *MSSMCW*, vol. 2, 821; vol. 6, 462; vol. 7, 305.

14. Pension file of George F. Allen, 36th USCT, RG 15, NARA; *MSSMCW*, vol. 3, 21; vol. 7, 290.

15. *Vital Records of Newburyport, Massachusetts, to the End of the Year 1849*, vol. 1, *Births* (Salem, MA: Essex Institute, 1911), 43; *MSSMCW*, vol. 2, 274; vol. 7, 291.

16. Regimental Descriptive Book, 36th USCT, RG 94, NARA.

17. Pension file of Joseph J. Hatlinger, 36th USCT, RG 15, NARA; John K. Burlingame, comp., *History of the Fifth Regiment of Rhode Island Heavy Artillery* (Providence, RI: Snow and Farnham, 1892), 198, 266; "Murder Will Out!" *The College Courant*, vol. 6 (New Haven, CT: Charles C. Chatfield, 1870), 181; *Twelfth Exhibition of the Massachusetts Charitable Mechanic Association* (Boston: Alfred Mudge and Son, 1874), 92; *Directory of the Living Non-Graduates of Yale University, 1910* (New Haven, CT: Tuttle, Morehouse, and Taylor, 1910), 57.

18. *MSSMCW*, vol. 3, 37; vol. 7, 307; *Abstract of General Orders and Proceedings of the Thirty-Second Annual Encampment, Department of New York, G.A.R.* (New York: Wynkoop Hallenbeck Crawford, 1898), 116; *The Fitchburg Directory ... for the Year Commencing January 15, 1882* (Fitchburg, MA: Price, Lee, 1882),195; U.S. Department of the Interior, *Official Register of the United States Containing a List of Officers and Employés in the Civil, Military, and Naval Service on the First of July, 1885*, vol. 2, *The Post-Office Department and the Postal Service* (Washington, D.C.: Government Printing Office, 1885), 319; William A. Emerson, *Fitchburg, Massachusetts: Past and Present* (Fitchburg, MA: Blanchard and Brown, 1887), 156, 157, 169; "Capt. George B. Proctor (1841-1932)," http://www.findagrave.com/cgi-bin/fg.cgi?page=gr&GRid=69135810.

19. *MSSMCW*, vol. 2, 740; vol. 7, 302; *The United States Army and Navy Journal and Gazette of the Regular and Volunteer Forces*, vol. 3, *1865-1866* (New York: 1865), 731.

20. CMSR, Sidney W. Phillips, Co. C,F,D,E, 36th USCT, RG 94, NARA; *MSSMCW*, vol. 3, 8; vol. 7, 307.

21. *MSSMCW*, vol. 1, 46; vol. 7, 290.

22. CMSR, Richard F. Andrews, Co. C,D,I, 36th USCT, RG 94, NARA; Pension file of Richard F. Andrews, 36th USCT, RG 15, NARA; *MSSMCW*, vol. 5, 575; vol. 7, 290; *The United States Army and Navy Journal and Gazette of the Regular and Volunteer Forces*, vol. 3, *1865-1866* (New York: 1865), 532.

23. CMSR, James B. Backup, Co. I,F, 36th USCT, RG 94, NARA; *MSSMCW*, vol. 4, 54; vol. 7, 290.

24. *MSSMCW*, vol. 3, 690; vol. 7, 291.

25. Draper, *The Drapers in America*, 208, 214-215; *MSSMCW*, vol. 5, 577; vol. 7, 296.

26. *MSSMCW*, vol. 3, 13 ; vol. 7, 298; Thomas W. Baldwin, comp., *Vital Records of Mendon, Massachusetts, to the Year 1850* (Boston: New England Historic Genealogical Society, 1920), 82; Francis B. Heitman, *Historical Register of the United States Army* (Washington, D.C.: The National Tribune, 1890), 286; Jessica Delaney, "Veterans' Observance Notes 'Cost of Freedom,'" *Town Crier*, June 3, 2005; Phil Porter, *A Desirable Station: Soldier Life at Fort Mackinac, 1867-1895* (Mackinac Island State Park Commission, 2003), 45.

27. *MSSMCW*, vol. 5, 635; vol. 7, 302; *Containing Life Sketches of Leading Citizens of Belknap and Strafford Counties, New Hampshire*, vol. 21, 26

28. Pension file of John Owen, Jr., 36th USCT, RG 15, NARA; John Owen, Jr., Papers, Massachusetts Historical Society, Boston, MA; *Vital Records of Cambridge, Massachusetts to the Year 1850*, vol. 1, *Births* (Boston: Wright and Potter, 1914), 530; *MSSMCW*, vol. 7, 306.

29. *MSSMCW*, vol. 5, 583; vol. 7, 312.

30. *MSSMCW*, vol. 1, 6; vol. 6, 256; vol. 7, 299; *New York Times*, July 8, 1862; *Memorial Service in Memory of the Dead of the First Regt. Massachusetts Volunteer Infantry, 1861-64, Faneuil Hall, Boston, Mass., May 21, 1911* (Boston, MA: First Regt. Massachusetts Volunteer Infantry, 1911?), 3.

31. Heitman, *Historical Register of the United States Army*, 578.

32. Regimental Descriptive Book, 36th USCT, RG 94, NARA.

33. *MSSMCW*, vol. 3, 706; vol. 5, 327; vol. 7, 308.

34. Pension file of George L. Seagrave, 36th USCT, RG 15, NARA; *MSSMCW*, vol. 3, 9; vol. 7, 309; Thomas W. Baldwin, comp., *Vital Records of Uxbridge, Massachusetts, to the Year 1850* (Boston: Wright and Potter, 1916), 132.

35. *MSSMCW*, vol. 3, 21; vol. 7, 312.

36. Baldwin, *Vital Records of Mendon, Massachusetts, to the Year 1850*, 82; *MSSMCW*, vol. 3, 13; vol. 7, 298.

37. *MSSMCW*, vol. 3, 26; vol. 7, 306; William H. Ward, ed. *Records of Members of the Grand Army of the Republic* (San Francisco, CA: H.S. Crocker, 1886), 183.

38. *MSSMCW*, vol. 4, 556; Charles F. Pierce, *Souvenir of Army Life, 1862-1863: Company C, 51st Massachusetts Regiment* (n.p., 1863?); William Gates Atkins, *History of the Town of Hawley, Franklin County, Massachusetts, from Its First Settlement in 1771 to 1887* (West Cummington, MA: William Gates Atkins, 1887), 22, 96.

39. *MSSMCW*, vol. 3, 700; vol. 7, 312.
40. CMSR, Henry M. Field, Co. K, H, B, A, F, 36th USCT, RG, 94, NARA; Pension file of Henry M. Field, 36th USCT, RG 15, NARA; *MSSMCW*, vol. 3, 624 ; vol. 7, 297; Frederick Clifton Pierce, *Field Genealogy*, vol. 2 (Chicago: W.B. Conkey,1901), 623.
41. *MSSMCW*, vol. 1, 383; vol. 6, 758; vol. 7, 293; "Thomas Cate, Minuteman of '61," http://freepages.genealogy.rootsweb.ancestry.com/~tneg/catethomas.html; "Thomas Jackson Cate (b. October 04, 1829, d. September 08, 1912), http://familytreemaker.genealogy.com/users/d/i/m/Donna-M-Dimartino-2/WEBSITE-0001/UHP-0082.html; J. Rodney Ball, "Feeding the Army of the Potomac," *New England Magazine*, 32 (March-August 1905), 345–352.
42. Heitman, *Historical Register of the United States Army*, 555; *MSSMCW*, vol. 7, 309.
43. *MSSMCW*, vol. 5, 562; vol. 7, 300.
44. *Annual Report of the Adjutant-General of the State of New York for the Year 1900*, serial no. 24, *Register* (Albany, NY: James B. Lyon, 1901), 676.
45. *MSSMCW*, vol. 5, 637; vol. 7, 307; *Vital Record of Tyngsboro, Massachusetts, to the end of the Year 1849* (Salem, MA: Essex Institute, 1913), 29.
46. Ezra D. Simons, *A Regimental History: The One Hundred and Twenty Fifth New York Volunteers* (New York: Ezra D. Simons, 1888), 168, 177–178, 339; *History and Roster of Maryland Volunteers, War of 1861–1865*, vol. 2 (Baltimore: Guggenheimer, Weil, 1899), 195.
47. Edward P. Tobie, *History of the First Maine Cavalry, 1861–1865* (Boston: Emery and Hughes, 1887), after 526, 531, 674; *History and Roster of Maryland Volunteers, War of 1861–1865*, vol. 2, 200. *Rowell's American Newspaper Directory* (New York: George P. Rowell, 1873), 360; U.S. Department of the Treasury, *The United States Treasury Register, 1874* (Washington, D.C.: Government Printing Office, 1874), 142; Arthur S. Boyd, *The Boyd Family* (New York: Leland E. Dorothy, 1924), 27.
48. *MSSMCW*, vol. 2, 769; vol. 7, 290; James A. Emmerton, *A Record of the Twenty-Third Regiment Mass. Vol. Infantry of the War of the Rebellion, 1861–1865* (Boston: William Ware, 1886), 259.
49. *MSSMCW*, vol. 4, 258; Edwin Atlee Barber, *Genealogical Record of the Atlee Family* (Philadelphia: William F. Fell, 1884), 50; Federal Register 1891, 123; Albert Gallatin Wheeler, *The Genealogical and Encyclopedic History of the Wheeler Family in America* (Boston: American College of Genealogy, 1914), 568.
50. Stephen F. Hathaway Papers, William R. Perkins Library, Duke University, Durham, NC; Pension file of Stephen F. Hathaway, 36th USCT, RG 15, NARA; *MSSMCW*, vol. 5; 578; vol. 7, 300.
51. *MSSMCW*, vol. 4, 468; vol. 6, 739.
52. *History of Second New Hampshire*, 96.
53. *MSSMCW*, vol. 4, 232; vol. 6, 738.
54. *MSSMCW*, vol. 1, 286; vol. 7, 294; CMSR, Daniel J. Courtney, F&S, E,K, 36th USCT, RG 94, NARA.
55. *MSSMCW*, vol. 2, 162; vol. 7, 315; "Roster and Genealogies of the 15th Massachusetts Volunteer Infantry: 1861–1864, " http://www.nextech.de/ma15mvi/ma15mvi-p/p28.htm; *Worcester* (Massachusetts) *Telegram*, March 1893, http://www.nextech.de/ma15mvi/ma15mvi-p/p28.htm.
56. J.W. Merrill, comp., *Records of the 24th Independent Battery, N.Y. Light Artillery, U.S.V.* (Perry, NY: Ladies' Cemetery Association, 1870), 91, 195; *Annual Report of the Adjutant-General of the State of New York for the Year 1898*, serial no. 15, *Registers of the Marine Artillery and First to Thirty-Fourth Batteries* (New York: Wynkoop Hallenbeck Crawford, 1899), 1061.
57. *MSSMCW*, vol. 3, 701; vol. 7, 290.
58. CMSR, George W.S. Conant, Cos. G,B,A 36th USCT, RG 94, NARA; Pension file of George W.S. Conant, 36th USCT, RG 15, NARA; *MSSMCW*, vol. 1, 5; vol.7, 294.
59. Regimental Descriptive Book, 36th USCT, RG 94, NARA.
60. *MSSMCW*, vol. 2, 741; vol. 4, 347; vol. 7, 311.
61. *MSSMCW*, vol. 3, 512; vol. 5, 607; vol. 7, 312.
62. CMSR, John O'Brien, Co. D, 36th USCT, RG 94, NARA; "J. O'Brien, Co. B, 14th Maine Infantry, Co. C, 14th Maine Infantry Battalion," Civil War Index File, Maine State Library, Augusta, ME.
63. William Child, *A History of the Fifth Regiment New Hampshire Volunteers in the American Civil War, 1861–1865* (Bristol, NH: R.W. Musgrove, 1893), 164.
64. Luther S. Dickey, *History of the Eighty-Fifth Regiment Pennsylvania Volunteer Infantry, 1861–1865* (New York: J.C. and W.E. Powers, 1915), 356, 364–365, 449.
65. *MSSMCW*, vol. 4, 251; vol. 5, 831; vol. 7, 295.
66. Regimental Descriptive Book, 36th USCT, RG 94, NARA.
67. Ibid.
68. Homer Wakefield, comp. *Wakefield Memorial: Comprising an Historical, Genealogical, and Biographical Register of the Name and Family of Wakefield* (Bloomington, IL: 1897), 237–238.
69. *MSSMCW*, vol. 5, 649; vol. 7, 296.
70. *The Story of American Heroism* (Springfield, OH: J.W. Jones, 1897), 749–750; James M. Aubery, *The Thirty-Sixth Wisconsin Volunteer Infantry* (Milwaukee: 1900), 352–356.
71. *Vital Records of East Bridgewater, Massachusetts, to the Year 1850* (Boston: New England Historic Genealogical Society, 1917),92; Henry Hedge Mitchell Papers, 1861–1880, Miscellaneous Bound Manuscripts, Massachusetts Historical Society, Boston, MA; *Annual Report of the Adjutant-General of the State of New York for the Year 1899*, register no. 18, *Registers of the Sixth, Seventh, Eighth, Ninth, Tenth, and Eleventh Regiments of Infantry* (Albany, NY: James B. Lyon, 1900), 1174; *MSSMCW*, vol. 1, 270; vol. 4, 48; vol. 7, 304; *Annual Report of the Adjutant-General of the Commonwealth of Massachusetts ... for the Year Ending December 31, 1861* (Boston: William White, 1861), 14.
72. Edward A. Wild to Thomas A. Vincent, March 26, 1864, File 2164, Edward A. Wild Papers, USAMHI; George Shrady, ed., *Medical Record*, vol. 1, March 1, 1866–February 15, 1867 (New York: William Wood, n.d.), 535.
73. Regimental Descriptive Book, 36th USCT, RG 94, NARA.
74. Pension file of Theodore Wild, 36th USCT, RG 15, NARA.
75. W.J. Maxwell, comp., *General Alumni Catalogue of the University of Pennsylvania,1917* (Philadelphia: University of Pennsylvania, 1917?), 692.
76. Edwin S. Redkey, "Black Chaplains in the Union Army," *Civil War History* 33 (December 1987): 338, 350.
77. Robert Norman Hartwig, "A Recollection of Chaplain Thomas Scott Johnson of the 127th United States Colored Troops and the 36th United States Colored Troops During and After the Civil War," (M.S. Seminar Paper, Wisconsin State University at La Crosse, 1970).

# *Appendix 3*

1. The terms "section" and "squad" were used at times to designate particular groups of infantry soldiers in the

Union Army. Section often referred to a component of artillery units consisting of two or three artillery cannon.

2. Platoons were recognized within the Union military structure, but still not fixed entities. It was assumed that both the First and Second Lieutenants each commanded one of the company's two platoons.

3. The company was the smallest administrative unit for an infantry soldier. It was through the company where pay and military equipment were issued. The soldiers' basic military education was conducted at the company level. Company noncommissioned officers (First Sergeants, Sergeants, and Corporals) exercised the most leadership at this level.

4. The battalion was a variable unit both fixed and flexible. Formal battalions, often composed of four companies, were used for special service. In a standard infantry regiment, a battalion could be composed of two to six companies. In the regimental formation, the Lieutenant Colonel commanded the "right wing" of five companies and the Major commanded the "left wing" of five companies. In the field, the Colonel, Lieutenant Colonel, Major, or a ranking Captain could command any number of companies as a battalion.

5. The 36th USCT at the time of the Battle of New Market Heights (September 29–30, 1864) was under the command of Lieutenant Colonel Benjamin F. Pratt. The regiment was in the 2nd Brigade (commanded by Colonel Alonzo G. Draper), 3rd Division (commanded by Brigadier General Charles J. Paine), 18th Army Corps (commanded by Major General Edward O.C. Ord), Army of the James (commanded by Major General Benjamin F. Butler). The Army of the James was the military field force of the Department of Virginia and North Carolina also under the command of General Butler.

6. Major General William T. Sherman in March 1864 commanded the Military Division of the Mississippi or the "Western Theater" of the war, encompassing the vast territory between the Appalachian Mountains and the Mississippi River. Sherman's command included the Armies of the Tennessee, Cumberland, and Ohio with their respective departments.

7. Ulysses S. Grant became Lieutenant General General-in-Chief of the Union Armies in March 1864. Declining to command from a desk in Washington, D.C., Grant made his field headquarters at Culpeper, Virginia, near the Army of the Potomac. As a result, Grant not only commanded the entire Union Army but was the de facto commander of the Eastern Theater, and soon an operational commander over the Army of the Potomac in spite of the fact that Major General George G. Meade retained nominal command of that particular army.

## Appendix 4

1. A.G. Draper to Hiram W. Allen, December 22, 1863, Regimental Letterbook, 36th USCT, RG 94, NARA.
2. Jerry V. Witt, *Wild in North Carolina: General Edward A. Wild's December 1863 Raid into Camden, Pasquotank, and Currituck Counties* (Springfield, VA: J.V. Witt, 1993), 46–47; Frances H. Casstevens, *Edward A. Wild and the African Brigade in the Civil War* (Jefferson, NC: McFarland, 2003), 133.

## Appendix 5

1. Henry N. Adkins to H.B. Scott, March 18, 1865, B.F. Pratt to H.B. Scott, March 18, 1865 (with endorsements), CMSR, Henry N. Adkins, Co. E, F&S, 36th USCT, RG 94, NARA; H.B. Scott to G. Weitzel, March 21, 1865 in Letters Sent (Oct. 1864–May 1865) Bureau of Colored Troops, Department of Virginia and North Carolina, RG 393, NARA.

# Bibliography

## *Unpublished Primary Sources*

ARCHIVAL AND MANUSCRIPT COLLECTIONS

Fredericksburg and Spotsylvania National Military Park, National Park Service, Fredericksburg, Virginia
  Bound Volumes
    Willis Neister, 25th Virginia Battalion, memoir (BV #325)
    Charles A. Raine, 23rd Virginia, memoir (BV# 4)
  Chancellorsville Battlefield Visitor Center Museum Special Collections
    Fredericksburg National Cemetery Registry Book, 1873
  Fredericksburg Battlefield Visitor Center Research Library
    Henry W. Tisdale, "Civil War Diary of Sergeant Henry W. Tisdale, Company I, Thirty-Fifth Regt. Mass. Volunteers. 1862–1865" (Typescript Manuscript in possession of the Fredericksburg and Spotsylvania National Military Park, Fredericksburg, Virginia)
Lynn Public Library, Lynn, Massachusetts
  Newspaper Clipping File
    "Brig. Gen. Alonzo G. Draper" in Unidentified Newspaper
Massachusetts Archives, Boston, Massachusetts
  Executive Department Letters, 1853–1899
    Series GO1 567X, vols. 19, W100
      Alonzo G. Draper to John A. Andrew, 1861–1865
Massachusetts Historical Society, Boston, Massachusetts
  Miscellaneous Bound Manuscripts
    Alonzo G. Draper Letters, 1862, 1865
    Henry Hedge Mitchell Papers, 1861–1880
    John Owen, Jr., Papers, 1863–1865
National Archives and Records Administration, Washington, D.C.
  Record Group 15: Records of the Veterans' Administration
    Selected Pension Files
      36th United States Colored Infantry
  Record Group 94: Records of the Adjutant General's Office, 1780s–1917
    5th United States Colored Infantry
      Compiled Military Service Records
      Regimental/Company Descriptive Books
      Regimental Order Book
    35th United States Colored Infantry
      Compiled Military Service Records
      Regimental Descriptive Book
    36th United States Colored Infantry
      Compiled Military Service Records
      Regimental/Company Descriptive Books
      Regimental Letter Books
      Regimental Order Books
      Regimental Returns/Muster Rolls
      Regimental Unbound Papers

Record Group 105: Records of the Bureau of Refugees, Freedmen, and Abandoned Lands
   Virginia: 1865–1867, Box #45
Record Group 393: Records of the United States Army Continental Commands, 1821–1920
   Records Created and Maintained by the Department of Virginia and North Carolina
      Bureau of Colored Troops
New Hampshire Historical Society, Concord, New Hampshire
   Duncan-Jones Papers
      Samuel A. Duncan Letters, 1864
North Carolina State Archives, Raleigh, North Carolina
   Samuel Sutton Paper, 978
United States Army Military History Institute, Carlisle, Pennsylvania
   Solon A. Carter Papers
   Edward A. Wild Papers
Vermont Historical Society, Montpelier, Vermont
   William Farrar Smith Papers
David M. Rubenstein Rare Book & Manuscript Library,
   Duke University, Durham, North Carolina
      Stephen F. Hathaway Papers, 1863–1866
      B.G. Rennolds Account Records, 1863–1867
      Jordan F. Vollavey Letter, Sept. 25, 1865
      Edward Clements Yellowley Papers, June 1863–February 1864

## Microfilm Collections

*American Missionary Association,* Manuscripts. New Orleans, LA: Amistad Research Center, Dillard University, 1983.
   North Carolina, 1861–1866, Rolls #150–151
   Virginia, 1861–1866, Rolls #206–211
National Archives and Records Administration, Washington, D.C.
   Microfilm Publication M123
      *1890 Special Census of Union Veterans and Their Widows, Disabled, Deceased*
         North Carolina, Roll #58
   Microfilm Publication M324
      *Compiled Service Records of Confederate Soldiers Who Served in Organizations from Virginia*
      15th Cavalry, Roll #139
      55th Infantry, Roll #960
   Microfilm Publication M594
      *Compiled Records Showing Service of Military Units in Volunteer Union Organizations, New York*
      7th Battery, Light Artillery, Roll #113
      *Compiled Records Showing Service of Military Units In Volunteer Union Organization, Pennsylvania*
      5th Cavalry, Roll #164
      11th Cavalry, Roll #165
      *Compiled Records Showing Service of Military Units in Volunteer Union Organization, United States Colored Troops*
      1st Infantry, Roll #205
      5th Infantry, Roll #206
      35th Infantry, Roll #209
      36th Infantry, Roll #209
   Microfilm Publication M653
      *Population Schedules of the Eighth Census of the United States*
         North Carolina [Schedule 2 — Slave Schedules], Rolls #920, #922
         Virginia [Schedule 2 — Slave Schedules], Rolls #1386–1397
Microfilm Publication T288, Pension Index, Alphabetical Name Listing, Rolls #1–544
Microfilm Publication T289, Pension Index, Union Military Units
   36th United States Colored Infantry, Rolls #550–551
*The Negro in the Military Service of the United States: A Compilation of Official Records, State Papers, Historical Abstract, Etc. Relating to His Military Status and Service.* Washington, D.C.: National Archives and Records Service, 1973. 5 Reels.

*Records of Ante-Bellum Southern Plantations: From the Revolution to the Civil War.* Bethesda, MD: University Microfilms of America.
    Series D: *Selections from the Maryland Historical Society.* 14 Reels.
    Series E: *Selections from the University of Virginia Library.*
        Part 1: *Virginia Plantations.* 39 Reels.
    Series J: *Selections from the Southern Historical Collection, Manuscripts Department, Library of the University of North Carolina at Chapel Hill.*
        Part 2: *Pettigrew Family Papers.* 29 Reels.
        Part 12: *Tidewater and Coastal Plain North Carolina.* 50 Reels.
U.S. Census Office. *North Carolina: Selected Schedules, 1860.* Raleigh: North Carolina Department of Archives and History, 1956. 3 Reels.
———. *Population Schedules of the Eighth Census of the United States, 1860: Maryland.* Washington, D.C.: National Archives and Records Service, 1967. 28 Reels.

## *Published Primary Sources*

### Autobiographies, Diaries, Memoirs, and Unit Histories

Baker, Joel C. "The Fall of Richmond." In *Vermont War Papers and Miscellaneous States Papers and Addresses for the Military Order of the Loyal Legion of the United States.* Vol. 57, 25–40. 1892. Reprint, Wilmington, NC: Broadfoot, 1994.
Barziza, Decimus et Ultimus. *The Adventures of a Prisoner of War, 1863–1864.* Edited by R. Henderson Shuffler. Austin: University of Texas Press, 1964.
Benson, Berry. *Berry Benson's Civil War Book: Memoirs of a Confederate Scout and Sharpshooter.* Edited by Susan Williams Benson. Athens: University of Georgia Press, 1992.
Butler, Benjamin F. *Butler's Book: A Review of His Legal, Political, and Military Career.* Boston: A.M. Thayer, 1892.
Cannon, LeGrand B. *Personal Reminiscences of the Rebellion.* New York: Burr, 1895.
Carter, Solon A. "Fourteen Months Service with Colored Troops." In *Civil War Papers Read Before the Commandery of the State of Massachusetts, Military Order of the Loyal Legion of the United States.* Vol. 1, 155–179. Boston: F.H. Gilson, 1900.
Clark, Walter, ed. *Histories of the Several Regiments and Battalions from North Carolina in the Great War 1861–65.* Vol. 3. Goldsboro, NC: Nash Brothers, 1901.
Committee of the Regimental Association. *History of the Thirty-Fifth Regiment Massachusetts Volunteers, 1862–1865.* Boston: Mills, Knight, 1884.
Cowden, Robert. *A Brief Sketch of the Organization and Services of the Fifty-Ninth Regiment of United States Colored Infantry.* Dayton, OH: United Brethren, 1883.
Creecy, Richard B. "Old Times in Betsy: Old Wild, the Sherman of the Civil War in North Carolina." *The Economist* (August 24, 1900).
Day, D.L. *My Diary of Rambles with the 25th Massachusetts Volunteer Infantry, with Burnside's Coast Division; and Army of the James.* Milford, MA: King and Billings, 1884.
Denny, J. Waldo. *Wearing the Blue in the Twenty-Fifth Mass. Volunteer Infantry, with Burnside's Coast Division, 18th Army Corps, and the Army of the James.* Worcester, MA: Putnam and Davis, 1879.
Douglass, Frederick. *Narrative of the Life of Frederick Douglass, an American Slave.* 1845. Reprint, New York: Penguin, 1986.
Dix, Morgan, comp. *Memoirs of John Adams Dix.* 2 vols. New York: Harper & Brothers, 1883.
Emilio, Luis F. *A Brave Black Regiment: History of the Fifty-Fourth Regiment of Massachusetts Volunteer Infantry.* 1894. Reprint, New York: Bantam Books, 1992.
Grant, Ulysses S. *The Personal Memoirs of Ulysses S. Grant.* 2 vols. New York: Charles L. Webster, 1885.
Hall, James E. *The Diary of a Confederate Soldier.* Edited by Ruth Woods Dayton, 1961.
Hamilton, D.H. *History of Company M: First Texas Volunteer Infantry.* 1925. Reprint, Waco, TX: W.M. Morrison, 1962.
Higginson, Thomas Wentworth. *Army Life in a Black Regiment.* 1869. Reprint, New York: W.W. Norton, 1984.
Hopkins, Luther W. *From Bull Run to Appomattox: A Boy's View.* Baltimore, MD: Fleet-McGinley, 1908.
Huffman, James. *Ups and Downs of a Confederate Soldier.* New York: William E. Rudge's Sons, 1940.
Hurmence, Belinda. *My Folks Don't Want Me to Talk About Slavery: Twenty-one Oral Histories of Former North Carolina Slaves.* Winston-Salem, NC: John F. Blair, 1984.

Kruetzer, William. *Notes and Observation Made During Four Years of Service with the Ninety-Eighth N.Y. Volunteers in the War of 1861.* Philadelphia: Grant, Faires, and Rodgers, 1878.

Lee, Amos William. *'61 to '65: Recollections of the Civil War.* New York: Christmas, 1913.

Lockwood, Lewis C. *Two Black Teachers During the Civil War: Mary S. Peake, The Colored Teacher at Fortress Monroe.* 1862. Reprint, New York: Arno, 1969.

Loehr, Charles T. "Point Lookout." *Southern Historical Society Papers* 18 (1890): 113–130.

Matson, Dan. "The Colored Man in the Civil War." In *War Sketches and Incidents as Related by Companions of the Iowa Commandery Military Order of the Loyal Legion of the United States.* Vol. 56, 235–254. Des Moines, IA: 1898. Reprint, Wilmington, NC: Broadfoot, 1994.

Main, Edwin M. *The Story of the Marches, Battles, and Incidents of the Third United States Colored Cavalry, a Fighting Regiment in the War of the Rebellion, 1861–5.* Louisville, KY: Globe Print, 1908.

Malone, Bartlett Yancey. *Whipt 'Em Every Time: The Diary of Bartlett Yancey Malone.* Edited by William Whatley Pierson, Jr. Jackson, TN: McCowan-Mercer, 1960.

Olmsted, Frederick Law. *A Journey in the Seaboard Slave States, with Reports on Their Economy.* New York: Dix and Edwards, 1856.

Osborne, Frederick M. *Private Osborne: Massachusetts 23rd Volunteers, Burnside Expedition, Roanoke Island, Second Front Against Richmond.* Gretna, LA: Pelican, 2002.

Polley, J.B. *Hood's Texas Brigade: Its Marches, Its Battles, Its Achievements.* Dayton, OH: Morningside, 1976.

Putnam, Samuel H. *The Story of Company A, Twenty-Fifth Regiment, Mass. Vols., in the War of the Rebellion.* Worcester, MA: Putnam, Davis, 1886.

Rawick, George P., ed. *The American Slave: A Composite Autobiography.* Vol. 14. *North Carolina Narratives,* Pt. 1. Westport, CT: Greenwood, 1972.

———. *The American Slave: A Composite Autobiography.* Vol. 15. *North Carolina Narratives,* Part 2. Westport, CT: Greenwood, 1972.

———. *The American Slave: A Composite Autobiography.* Vol. 16. *Virginia Narratives.* Westport, CT: Greenwood, 1972.

Roe, Alfred S., and Charles Nutt. *History of the First Regiment of Heavy Artillery Massachusetts Volunteers.* Regimental Association, 1917.

Scroggs, Joseph J. "The Earth Shook and Quivered." Edited by Sig Synnestvedt. *Civil War Times Illustrated* (December 1972): 30–37.

Smith, William F. *The Autobiography of Major General William F. Smith, 1861–1864.* Edited by Herbert M. Schiller. Dayton, OH: Morningside, 1990.

Stevens, John W. *Reminiscences of the Civil War.* Hillsboro, TX: Hillsboro Mirror Print, 1902.

Strong, George Templeton. *Diary of the Civil War, 1860–1865.* Edited by Allan Nevins. New York: Macmillan, 1962.

Taylor, Susie King. *Reminiscences of My Life in Camp with the 33rd United States Colored Troops.* Boston: 1902.

Thompson, S. Millett. *Thirteenth Regiment of New Hampshire Volunteer Infantry in the War of the Rebellion, 1861–1865: A Diary Covering Three Years and a Day.* Boston: Riverside, 1888.

"Typo." *Officers and Privates, Attached to the Fourteenth Regiment Heavy Artillery, Massachusetts Volunteers.* Lawrence, MA: George S. Merrill, 1862.

Wallace, Elizabeth Curtis. *Glencoe Diary: The War-Time Journal of Elizabeth Curtis Wallace.* Edited by Eleanor P. Cross and Charles B. Cross, Jr. Chesapeake, VA: Norfolk County Historical Society, 1968.

Washington, Booker T. *Up From Slavery: An Autobiography.* In *Three Negro Classics.* 1901. Reprint, New York: Avon Books, 1965.

Wells, James T. "Prison Experience, No. 2." *Southern Historical Society Papers* 7 (August 1879): 393–398.

West, George Benjamin. *When the Yankees Came: Civil War and Reconstruction on the Virginia Peninsula.* Edited by Parke Rouse, Jr. Richmond, VA: Dietz, 1977.

Wise, John S. *The End of an Era.* New York: Houghton, Mifflin, 1899.

## Confederate States of America Government Publications

*Regulations for the Army of the Confederate States, Authorized Edition, 1862.* Richmond, VA: West & Johnston, 1862.

Special Committee, House of Representatives, Confederate States of America, *Report of the Special Committee to Inquire into the Certain Outrages of the Enemy, (Relates to Expedition of Gen. Wild in the eastern part of North Carolina in December, 1863).* Richmond, VA, 1864 [Courtesy of Special Collections, Library of Virginia, Richmond, Virginia].

## Correspondence, Letters, Published Reports, and Speeches

Berlin, Ira, et al., eds. *Free At Last: A Documentary History of Slavery, Freedom, and the Civil War.* Edison, N.J.: Blue and Grey, 1992.

———. *Freedom: A Documentary History of Emancipation, 1861–1867.* Ser. I, Vol. I. *The Destruction of Slavery.* New York: Cambridge University Press, 1985.

———. *Freedom: A Documentary History of Emancipation, 1861–1867.* Ser. I, Vol. II. *The Wartime Genesis of Free Labor: The Upper South.* New York: Cambridge University Press, 1993.

———. *Freedom: A Documentary History of Emancipation, 1861–1867.* Ser. I, Vol. III. *The Wartime Genesis of Free Labor: The Lower South.* New York: Cambridge University Press, 1990.

———. *Freedom: A Documentary History of Emancipation, 1861–1867.* Ser. II. *The Black Military Experience.* New York: Cambridge University Press, 1982.

———. *Remembering Slavery: African-Americans Talk About Their Personal Experiences of Slavery and Emancipation.* New York: New Press, 1998.

Berlin, Ira, and Leslie S. Rowland, eds. *Families and Freedom: A Documentary History of African-American Kinship in the Civil War Era.* New York: New Press, 1997.

Blassingame, John W., ed. *Slave Testimony: Two Centuries of Letters, Speeches, Interviews, and Autobiographies.* Baton Rouge: Louisiana State University Press, 1977, 1999.

Butler, Benjamin F. *Private and Official Correspondence of General Benjamin F. Butler During the Civil War.* 5 vols. Edited by Jessie Marshall Ames. Norwood, MA: Plimpton, 1917.

———. *Speech of Major General Benjamin F. Butler upon the Campaign Before Richmond, 1864. Delivered at Lowell, Mass., January 29, 1865.* Boston: Wright and Potter, 1865.

———. *Speech on Emancipation. February 4, 1866.* Boston, MA, 1866.

[Chase, Lucy, and Sarah Chase]. *Dear Ones at Home: Letters from Contraband Camps.* Edited by Henry L. Swint. Nashville, TN: Vanderbilt University Press, 1966.

Chester, Thomas Morris. *Black Civil War Correspondent: His Dispatches from the Virginia Front.* Edited by R.J.M. Blackett. New York: Da Capo, 1989.

Colyer, Vincent. *Report of the Services Rendered by the Freed People to the United States Army, in North Carolina, in the Spring of 1862, After the Battle of Newbern.* New York: Vincent Colyer, 1864.

Gooding, James Henry. *On the Altar of Freedom: A Black Soldier's Civil War Letters from the Front.* Edited by Virginia Adams. 1991. Reprint, New York: Warner Books, 1992.

James, Horace. *Annual Report of the Superintendent of Negro Affairs in North Carolina, 1864. With an Appendix Containing the History and Management of Freedmen in the Department up to June 1, 1865.* Boston: W.F. Brown, 1865.

Lincoln, Abraham. *Of the People, by the People, and for the People and Other Quotations from Abraham Lincoln.* Edited by Gabor S. Boritt, et al. New York: Columbia University Press, 1996.

McPherson, James M., ed. *The Negro's Civil War: How American Blacks Felt and Acted During the War for the Union.* 3rd ed. 1965. Reprint, New York: Ballantine, 1991.

Norton, Oliver Willcox. *Army Letters, 1861–1865.* Chicago, IL: O.C. Deming, 1903.

[Omenhausser, John J.] *Sketches from Prison: A Confederate Artist's Record of Life at Point Lookout Prisoner-of-War Camp, 1863–1865.* Baltimore: Maryland State Park Foundation, Inc., 1990.

Pierce, Edward L. "The Contraband at Fortress Monroe." *Atlantic Monthly* 49 (November 1861): 626–640.

———. "The Freedmen at Port Royal." *Atlantic Monthly* 52 (September 1863): 291–315.

Pierpoint, Francis H. *Letter of Governor Pierpoint to His Excellency the President and the Honorable Congress of the United States, on the Subject of Abuse of Military Power in the Command of General Butler in Virginia and North Carolina.* Washington, D.C.: McGill and Witherow, 1864.

Redkey, Edwin S., ed. *A Grand Army of Black Men: Letters from African-American Soldiers in the Union Army, 1861–1865.* 1992. Reprint, New York: Cambridge University Press, 1993.

Redpath, James. *The Roving Editor, or Talks with Slaves in the Southern States, by James Redpath.* Edited by John R. McKivigan. University Park: Pennsylvania State University Press, 1996.

Shaw, Robert Gould. *Blue-Eyed Child of Fortune: The Civil War Letters of Colonel Robert Gould Shaw.* Edited by Russell Duncan. Athens: University of Georgia Press, 1992.

Stephens, George E. *A Voice of Thunder: The Civil War Letters of George E. Stephens.* Edited by Donald Yacovone. Chicago: University of Illinois Press, 1996.

Yearns, W. Buck, and John G. Barrett, eds. *North Carolina Civil War Documentary.* Chapel Hill: University of North Carolina Press, 1980.

## General Works

Casey, Silas. *Infantry Tactics for the Instruction, Exercise, and Manoeuvres of the Soldier, A Company, Line Skirmishers, Battalion or Corps D'Armee*. 3 vols. New York: D. Van Nostrand, 1865.
Fleetwood, Christian A. *The Negro as a Soldier*. Washington, D.C.: Howard University Press, 1895.
Johnson, Robert, and Clarence Buel, eds. *Battles and Leaders of the Civil War*. 4 vols. 1887–1888. Reprint, New York: Appleton Century Crofts, 1956.
Livermore, Thomas L. *Numbers and Losses in the Civil War in America, 1861–65*. Bloomington: Indiana University Press, 1957.
MacGregor, Morris J., and Bernard C. Nalty., eds. *Blacks in the United States Armed Forces: Basic Documents*. Vol. 2, *Civil War and Emancipation*. Wilmington, DE: Scholarly Resources, 1977.
Moore, Frank, ed. *The Rebellion Record: A Diary of American Events with Documents, Narratives, Illustrative Incidents, Poetry, etc*. 11 vols. New York: D. Van Nostrand, 1864.
Williams, George W. *History of the Negro Troops in the War of the Rebellion, 1861–1865*. New York: G.P. Putnam and Sons, 1888.
Wilson, Joseph T. *The Black Phalanx: African-American Soldiers in the War of Independence, the War of 1812, and the Civil War*. 1887. Reprint, New York: Da Capo, 1994.

## Newspapers

*Baltimore American and Commercial Advertiser*, 1864
Lynn (MA) *Bay State*, 1860
*Boston Globe*, 1891
*The Cavalier* (Williamsburg/Yorktown, VA), 1862
*New York Herald*, 1863–1864
*New York Times*, 1863–1864
*New York Tribune*, 1861–1864
Richmond (VA) *Daily Enquirer*, 1863–1864
Richmond (VA) *Whig*, 1865
*The True Southerner* (Hampton, VA), 1865
*Weekly Gazette and Eastern Virginia Advertiser* (Williamsburg, VA), 1859–1860
*Yankee Cavalier* (Yorktown, VA), 1862–1864

## State Government Publications

Massachusetts. Adjutant General. *Annual Report*. 6 vols. Boston: Wright and Potter, 1861–1865.
_____. Adjutant General. *Massachusetts Soldiers, Sailors, and Marines in the Civil War*. 6 vols. Norwood: Norwood, 1932.
New York. Adjutant General. *Annual Report of the Adjutant-General of the State of New York for the Year 1902: Registry of the ... Ninety-Eighth Regiment of Infantry*. Albany: Argus, 1903.
Ohio. Adjutant General. *Official Roster of the Soldiers of the State of Ohio in the War of the Rebellion, 1861–1866*. 2 vols. Akron: Werner, 1893.

## United States Publications

Heitman, Francis B. *Historical Register and Dictionary of the United States Army from Its Organization, September 29, 1789 to March 2, 1903*. 2 vols. Washington, D.C.: GPO, 1903.
Hewett, Janet B., et al., eds. *Supplement to the Official Records of the Union and Confederate Armies*. 95 vols. Wilmington, NC: Broadfoot, 1995–1998.
U.S. Congress. *Report of the Secretary of the Navy, 1864*. Washington, D.C.: GPO, 1865.
U.S. Interior Department. Office of the Census. *Population of the United States in 1860; Compiled from the Original Returns of the Eighth Census, Under the Direction of the Secretary of the Interior*. 4 vols. Washington, D.C.: GPO, 1864. Reprint, New York: Norman Ross, 1990.
U.S. Navy Department. *Official Records of the Union and Confederate Navies in the War of the Rebellion*. 30 vols. Washington, D.C.: GPO, 1894–1922.
U.S. War Department. Adjutant General's Office. *Official Army Register of the Volunteer Force of the United States Army for the Year 1861, '62, '63, '64, '65*. Vol. 8. Washington, D.C.: GPO, 1867.

_____. Adjutant General's Office. *War of the Rebellion: A Compilation of the Official Records of the Union and Confederate Armies.* 130 vols. Washington, D.C.: GPO, 1880–1901.

_____. Adjutant General's Office and Surgeon General's Office. *Alphabetical List of Battles and Roster of Regimental Surgeons and Assistant Surgeons During the War of Rebellion.* Compiled by J.W. Wells and N.A. Strait. Washington, D.C.: G.M. Van Buren, 1883.

_____. Quartermaster General's Office. *Roll of Honor: Names of Soldiers Who Died in Defense of the American Union, Interred in the National Cemeteries.* 27 vols. Washington, D.C.: GPO, 1868. Reprint, Baltimore, MD: Genealogical Co., 1994.

_____. *Revised Regulations for the Army of the United States, 1861.* Philadelphia, PA: J.G.L. Brown, 1861. Reprint, Harrisburg, PA: The National Historical Society, 1980.

_____. *Revised United States Army Regulations of 1861, with an Appendix Containing the Changes and Laws Affecting Army Regulations and Articles of War to June 25, 1863.* Washington, D.C.: GPO, 1863.

## VITAL RECORDS PUBLICATIONS

*Vital Records of Brookline, Massachusetts, to the End of the Year 1849.* Salem: The Essex Institute, 1929.

*Vital Record of Cambridge, Massachusetts, to the Year 1850.* Vol. 1, *Births*, Thomas W. Baldwin, comp. Boston: New England Historic Genealogical Society, 1914.

*Vital Record of Chelsea, Massachusetts, to the Year 1850*, Thomas W. Baldwin, comp. Boston: New England Historic Genealogical Society, 1916.

*Vital Record of Danvers, Massachusetts, to the Year 1849.* Vol. 1, *Births*. Salem: The Essex Institute, 1909.

*Vital Record of Danvers, Massachusetts, to the Year 1849.* Vol. 2, *Marriages and Deaths*. Salem: The Essex Institute, 1910.

*Vital Records of Mendon, Massachusetts, to the Year 1850.* Boston: New England Historic Genealogical Fund, 1920.

*Vital Records of Salem, Massachusetts, to the End of the Year 1849.* Vol. 1, *Births*. Salem: The Essex Institute, 1916.

# *Secondary Sources*

## ARTICLES

Aptheker, Herbert, "Maroons Within the Present Limits of the United States." In *Maroon Societies: Rebel Slave Communities in the Americas.* Edited by Richard Price, 2nd ed., 151–167. 1973, 1979. Reprint, Baltimore: Johns Hopkins University Press, 1983.

Berlin, Ira et al. "Family and Freedom: Black Families in the American Civil War." *History Today* 37 (January 1987): 9–15.

Blassingame, John W. "Negro Chaplains in the Civil War." *Negro History Bulletin* 28 (October 1963): 23–24.

_____. "The Union Army as an Educational Institution for Negroes, 1862–1865." *Journal of Negro Education* 34 (1965): 152–159.

_____. "Using the Testimony of Ex-Slaves: Approaches and Problems." In *The Slave's Narrative*, Charles T. Davis and Henry Louis Gates, Jr., eds., 78–98. New York: Oxford University Press, 1985.

Cullen, Jim. "'I's a Man Now': Gender and African-American Men." In *Divided Houses: Gender and the Civil War*, eds. Catherine Clinton and Nina Silber, 76–91. New York: Oxford University Press, 1992.

Foner, Eric. "Slavery and the Origins of the Civil War." *Social Education* 62 (October 1998): 333–339.

_____. "The South's Inner Civil War." *American Heritage* 40 (March 1989): 47–56.

Franklin, John Hope. "The Enslavement of Free Negroes in North Carolina." *Journal of Negro History* 29 (October 1944): 401–428.

Friedrich, Otto. "'We Will Not Do Duty Any Longer for Seven Dollars per Month.'" *American Heritage* 39 (February 1989): 64–73.

Fuke, Richard Paul. "A School for Freed Labor: The Maryland 'Government Farms,' 1864–1866." *Maryland Historian* 16 (1985): 11–23.

Gutman, Herbert G. "Mirrors of Hard, Distorted Glass: An Examination of Some Influential Historical Assumptions About the Afro-American Family and the Shaping of Public Policies, 1861–1965." In *Social History and Social Policy*, David J. Rothman and Stanton Wheeler, eds., 239–273. New York: Academic Press, 1981.

Horowitz, Murray M. "Ben Butler and the Negro: 'Miracles Are Occurring.'" *Louisiana History* 17 (Spring 1976): 159–186.
Huston, James L. "Property Rights in Slavery and the Coming of the Civil War." *Journal of Southern History* 65 (May 1999): 249–286.
Inscoe, John C. "Carolina Slave Names: An Index to Acculturation." *Journal of Southern History* 49 (February 1983): 527–554.
Kolchin, Peter. "Slavery and Freedom in the Civil War." In *Writing the Civil War: The Quest to Understand*, James M. McPherson and William J. Cooper, Jr., eds., 241–260. Columbia: University of South Carolina Press, 1998.
Lause, Mark A. "Turning the World Upside Down: A Portrait of Labor and Military Leader, Alonzo Granville Draper." *Labor History* 44 (2003): 189–204.
Longacre, Edward G. "Black Troops in the Army of the James, 1863–65." *Military Affairs* 45 (February 1981): 1–8.
_____. "Brave Radical Wild: The Contentious Career of Brigadier Edward A. Wild." *Civil War Times Illustrated* (June 1980): 8–19.
Miller, Randall. "The Man in the Middle: The Black Slave Driver." *American Heritage* 30 (October/November 1979): 40–49.
Montgomery, Horace. "A Union Officer's Recollections of the Negro as a Soldier." *Pennsylvania History* 28 (April 1961): 156–186.
Morris, Roy, Jr. "A Shadowy Group of New England Abolitionists Helped John Brown Plan the Raid at Harper's Ferry." *America's Civil War* (March 1996): 6.
Neely, Mark E., Jr. "Abraham Lincoln and Black Colonization: Benjamin Butler's Spurious Testimony." *Civil War History* 25 (September 1979): 77–83.
Pinkett, Harold T. "A Brothers' Fight for Freedom." *Maryland Historical Magazine* 86 (Spring 1991): 39–50.
Popchock, Barry. "A Shower of Stars at New Market Heights: Butler's 'Contrabands' Prove Their Mettle." *Civil War: The Magazine of the Civil War Society* (August 1994): 30–39.
Redkey, Edwin S. "Black Chaplains in the Union Army." *Civil War History* 33 (December 1987): 331–350.
Reid, Richard. "General Edward A. Wild and Civil War Discrimination." *Historical Journal of Massachusetts* 13 (January 1985): 15–29.
_____. "Raising the African Brigade: Early Black Recruitment in Civil War North Carolina." *North Carolina Historical Review* 70 (1993): 266–301.
_____. "USCT Veterans in Post–Civil War North Carolina." In *Black Soldiers in Blue: African-American Troops in the Civil War Era*, John David Smith, ed., 391–421. Chapel Hill: University of North Carolina Press, 2002.
Shaffer, Donald R. "'I Do Not Suppose that Uncle Sam Looks at the Skin': African Americans and the Civil War Pension System, 1865–1934." *Civil War History* 46 (2000): 132–147.
Sproat, John G. "Blueprint for Radical Reconstruction." *Journal of Southern History* 23 (February 1957): 25–44.
Stewart, Peter C. "Man and the Swamp: The Historical Dimension." In *The Great Dismal Swamp*, edited by Paul W. Kirk, Jr., 57–73. Charlottesville: University Press of Virginia, 1979.
Trudeau, Noah Andre. "'No Brilliant Victory to Record.'" *America's Civil War* (May 1996): 34–40, 82.
Weiss, Nathan. "General Benjamin Franklin Butler and the Negro: the Evolution of the Racial Views of a Practical Politician." *Negro History Bulletin* 29 (October 1965): 3–4, 14–16, 23.

## BOOKS

Alexander, Roberta Sue. *North Carolina Faces the Freedmen: Race Relations During Presidential Reconstruction, 1865–1867*. Durham: Duke University Press, 1985.
Alotta, Robert I. *Civil War Justice: Union Army Executions Under Lincoln*. Shippensburg, PA: White Mane, 1989.
Arnold, James R. *The Armies of U.S. Grant*. London, UK: Arms and Armour, 1995.
Ball, Edward. *Slaves in the Family*. New York: Ballantine, 1999.
Barrett, John G. *The Civil War in North Carolina*. Chapel Hill: 1965. Reprint, University of North Carolina Press, 1983.
Bassett, John Spencer. *Slavery in the State of North Carolina*. In *Johns Hopkins University Studies in Historical and Political Science*. Series 17, Number 7–8. Baltimore: Johns Hopkins University, 1899.
Beitzell, Edwin W. *Point Lookout Prison Camp for Confederates*. Abell, MD: 1972.

Berlin, Ira. *Slaves Without Masters: The Free Negro in the Antebellum South*. 1974. Reprint, New York: New Press, 1992.

Berry, Mary F. *Military Necessity and Civil Rights Policy: Black Citizenship and the Constitution, 1861–1868*. Port Washington, NY: Kennikat, 1977.

Blassingame, John W. *The Slave Community: Plantation Life in the Antebellum South*. 2nd ed. 1972. Reprint, New York: Oxford University Press, 1979.

Bogger, Tommy L. *Free Blacks in Norfolk, Virginia, 1790–1860: The Darker Side of Freedom*. Charlottesville: University Press of Virginia, 1997.

Brewer, James H. *The Confederate Negro: Virginia's Craftsmen and Military Laborers, 1861–1865*. Durham: Duke University Press, 1969.

Brown, William Wells. *The Negro in the American Rebellion, His Heroism and His Fidelity*. Boston: Lee and Shepard, 1867.

Burchard, Peter. *One Gallant Rush: Robert Gould Shaw and His Brave Black Regiment*. New York: St. Martin's Press, 1965, 1989.

Cable, Mary. *Black Odyssey: The Case of the Slave Ship Amistad*. 1971. Reprint, Penguin Books, 1997.

Carroll, John M., ed. *Register of Officers of the Confederate States Navy, 1861–1865*. J.M. Carroll, 1983.

Casstevens, Frances H. *Edward A. Wild and the African Brigade in the Civil War*. Jefferson, NC: McFarland, 2003.

Cecil-Fronsman, Bill. *Common Whites: Class and Culture in Antebellum North Carolina*. Lexington: University Press of Kentucky, 1992.

Click, Patricia C. *Time Full of Trial: The Roanoke Island Freedmen's Colony, 1862–1867*. Chapel Hill: University of North Carolina Press, 2000.

Clinton, Catherine. *The Plantation Mistress: Women's World in the Old South*. New York: Pantheon, 1982.

Coffman, Edward M. *The Old Army: A Portrait of the American Army in Peacetime, 1784–1898*. New York: Oxford University Press, 1986.

Coggins, Jack. *Arms and Equipment of the Civil War*. 1962. Reprint, Wilmington, NC: Broadfoot, 1990.

Cohen, William. *At Freedom's Edge: Black Mobility and the Southern White Quest for Racial Control, 1861–1915*. Baton Rouge: Louisiana State University Press, 1991.

Cormier, Steven A. *The Siege of Suffolk: The Forgotten Campaign, April 11–May 4, 1863*. Lynchburg, VA: H.E. Howard, 1989.

Cornish, Dudley Taylor. *The Sable Arm: Black Troops in the Union Army, 1861–1865*. 1956. Reprint, Lawrence: University Press of Kansas, 1987.

Davis, William C. *"A Government of Our Own": The Making of the Confederacy*. New York: Free Press, 1994.

Dawley, Alan. *Class and Community: The Industrial Revolution in Lynn*. Cambridge, MA: Harvard University Press, 1976.

DeBoer, Clara Merritt. *"Be Jubilant My Feet": African American Abolitionists in the American Missionary Association, 1839–1861*. New York: Garland, 1994.

_____. *"His Truth Is Marching On: African Americans Who Taught the Freedmen for the American Missionary Association, 1861–1877*. New York: Garland, 1995.

Dell, Christopher. *Lincoln and the War Democrats: The Grand Erosion of Conservative Tradition*. Rutherford, NJ: Farleigh Dickinson, 1975.

Draper, Thomas Waln-Morgan. *The Drapers in America, Being a History and Genealogy of Those of that Name and Connection*. New York: John Polhemus, 1892.

Du Bois, W.E.B. *Black Reconstruction in America: An Essay Toward a History of the Part Which Black Folk Played in the Attempt to Reconstruct Democracy in America, 1860–1880*. 1935. Reprint, Touchstone, 1995.

_____. *John Brown: A Biography*. Edited by John David Smith. 1909. Reprint, Armonk, NY: M.E. Sharpe, 1997.

Durrill, Wayne K. *War of Another Kind: A Southern Community in the Great Rebellion*. New York: Oxford University Press, 1990.

Dyer, Frederick H. *A Compendium of the War of the Rebellion*. 3 vols. New York: Thomas Yoseloff, 1959.

Engs, Robert F. *Freedom's First Generation: Black Hampton, Virginia, 1861–1890*. Philadelphia: University of Pennsylvania Press, 1979.

Escott, Paul D. *Slavery Remembered: A Record of Twentieth Century Slave Narratives*. Chapel Hill: University of North Carolina Press, 1979.

Faler, Paul G. *Mechanics and Manufacturers in the Early Industrial Revolution: Lynn, Massachusetts, 1780–1860*. Albany: State University of New York Press, 1981.

Fields, Barbara Jeanne. *Slavery and Freedom on the Middle Ground: Maryland in the Nineteenth Century.* New Haven, CT: Yale University Press, 1985.
Fogel, Robert W., and Stanley L. Engerman. *Time on the Cross: The Economics of American Negro Slavery.* Boston: Little, Brown, 1974.
Foner, Eric. *Reconstruction: America's Unfinished Revolution, 1863–1877.* New York: Harper and Row, 1988.
Forbes, Ella. *African-American Women During the Civil War.* New York: Garland, 1998.
Fortier, John. *15th Virginia Cavalry.* Lynchburg, VA: H.E. Howard, 1993.
Fowler, Arlen L. *The Black Infantry in the West, 1869–1891.* 1971. Reprint, Norman: University of Oklahoma Press, 1996.
Fox-Genovese, Elizabeth. *Within the Plantation Household: Black and White Women of the Old South.* Chapel Hill: University of North Carolina Press, 1988.
Franklin, John Hope. *The Emancipation Proclamation.* Garden City, NY: Doubleday, 1963.
———. *The Free Negro in North Carolina, 1790–1860.* Chapel Hill: University of North Carolina Press, 1943.
———. *The Militant South, 1800–1861.* Cambridge, MA: Harvard University Press, 1956.
Franklin, John Hope, and Loren Schweninger. *Runaway Slaves: Rebels on the Plantation.* New York: Oxford University Press, 1999.
Fredrickson, George M. *The Black Image in the White Mind: The Debate on Afro-American Character and Destiny, 1817–1914.* 1971. Reprint, Hanover, NH: Wesleyan University Press, 1987.
Freehling, William W. *The Reintergration of American History: Slavery and the Civil War.* New York: Oxford University Press, 1994.
Frey, Sylvia R. *Water From the Rock: Black Resistance in a Revolutionary Age.* 1991. Reprint, Princeton, NJ: Princeton University Press, 1992.
Furgerson, Ernest B. *Ashes of Glory: Richmond at War.* New York: Alfred A. Knopf, 1996.
Genovese, Eugene D. *The Political Economy of Slavery: Studies in the Economy and Society of the Slave South.* 1961. Reprint, New York: Vintage Books, 1967.
———. *Roll, Jordan, Roll: The World the Slaves Made.* 1974. Reprint, New York: Vintage Books, 1976.
Gerteis, Louis S. *From Contraband to Freedman: Federal Policy Toward Southern Blacks, 1861–1865.* Westport, CT: Greenwood, 1973.
Gladstone, William A. *Men of Color.* Gettysburg, PA: Thomas, 1991.
———. *United States Colored Troops, 1863–1867.* Gettysburg, PA: Thomas, 1990.
Glatthaar, Joseph T. *Forged in Battle: The Civil War Alliance of Black Soldiers and White Officers.* New York: Free Press, 1990.
Goldin, Claudia Dale. *Urban Slavery in the American South, 1820–1860: A Quantitative History.* Chicago: University of Chicago Press, 1976.
Greenberg, Martin H., and Charles G. Waugh, eds. *The Price of Freedom: Slavery and the Civil War.* 2 vols. Nashville, TN: Cumberland House, 2000.
Gutman, Herbert G. *The Black Family in Slavery and Freedom, 1750–1925.* New York: Vintage Books, 1976.
Harding, Vincent. *There Is a River: The Black Struggle for Freedom in America.* 1981. Reprint, New York: Vintage Books, 1983.
Hargrove, Hondon B. *Black Union Soldiers in the Civil War.* Jefferson, NC: McFarland, 1988.
Harris, William C. *North Carolina and the Coming of the Civil War.* Raleigh: Division of Archives and History, Department of Cultural Resources, 1988.
Hill, D.H., Jr. *Confederate Military History: North Carolina.* Vol. 5. 1899. Reprint, Wilmington, NC: Broadfoot, 1987.
Hollandsworth, James G., Jr. *Louisiana Native Guards: The Black Military Experience During the Civil War.* Baton Rouge: Louisiana State University Press, 1995.
Holzman, Robert S. *Stormy Ben Butler.* New York: MacMillan, 1954.
Hunt, Roger D., and Jack R. Brown. *Brevet Brigadier Generals in Blue.* Gaithersburg, MD: Olde Soldier, 1990.
Jones, Howard. *Mutiny on the Amistad: The Saga of a Slave Revolt and Its Impact on American Abolitionism, Law, and Diplomacy.* New York: Oxford University Press, 1987.
Jones, Jacqueline. *Labor of Love, Labor of Sorrow: Black Women, Work, and the Family from Slavery to the Present.* 1985. Reprint, New York: Vintage Books, 1986.
Jordan, Ervin L., Jr. *Black Confederates and Afro-Yankees in Civil War Virginia.* Charlottesville: University Press of Virginia, 1995

Kenzer, Robert C. *Enterprising Southerners: Black Economic in North Carolina, 1865–1915*. Charlottesville: University Press of Virginia, 1997.
Kingman, Bradford. *Memoir of General Edward August Wild*. Boston: 1895.
Kolchin, Peter. *American Slavery, 1619–1877*. New York: Hill and Wang, 1993.
Krick, Robert E.L. *Staff Officers in Gray: A Biographical Register of the Staff Officers in the Army of Northern Virginia*. Chapel Hill: University of North Carolina Press, 2009.
Krick, Robert K. *9th Virginia Cavalry*. 3rd ed. Lynchburg, VA: H.E. Howard, 1982.
Lanier, Robert S., ed. *The Photographic History of the Civil War: Armies & Leaders*. New York: Fairfax, 1983.
Leaming, Hugo Prosper. *Hidden Americans: Maroons of Virginia and the Carolinas*. New York: Garland, 1995.
Levine, Lawrence W. *Black Culture and Black Consciousness: Afro-American Folk Thought from Slavery to Freedom*. New York: Oxford University Press, 1977.
Lewis, Alonzo, and James R. Newhall. *History of Lynn, Essex County, Massachusetts*. Boston: John L. Shorey, 1865.
Litwack, Leon F. *Been in the Storm So Long: The Aftermath of Slavery*. New York: Alfred A. Knopf, 1979.
Longacre, Edward G. *Army of Amateurs: General Benjamin F. Butler and the Army of the James*. Mechanicsburg, PA: Stackpole, 1997.
McPherson, James M. *Battle Cry of Freedom: The Civil War Era*. 1988. Reprint, New York: Ballantine, 1989.
_____. *Drawn with the Sword: Reflections on the Civil War*. New York: Oxford University Press, 1996.
_____. *For Cause and Comrades: Why Men Fought in the Civil War*. New York: Oxford University Press, 1997.
_____. *Marching Toward Freedom: The Negro in the Civil War, 1861–1865*. New York: Alfred A. Knopf, 1967.
_____. *The Struggle for Equality: Abolitionists and the Negro in the Civil War and Reconstruction*. 1964. Reprint, Princeton, NJ: Princeton University Press, 1995.
Miller, Edward A., Jr. *The Black Civil War Soldiers of Illinois: The Story of the Twenty-Ninth U.S. Colored Infantry*. Columbia: University of South Carolina Press, 1998.
Mitchell, Reid. *The Vacant Chair: The Northern Soldier Leaves Home*. New York: Oxford University Press, 1993.
Mobley, Joe A. *James City: A Black Community in North Carolina, 1863–1900*. Raleigh: North Carolina Department of Cultural Resources, Division of Archives and History, 1981.
Moebs, Thomas Truxtun. *Black Soldiers—Black Sailors—Black Ink: Research Guide on African-Americans in U.S. Military History, 1526–1900*. Chesapeake Bay: Moebs, 1994.
Moore, John W. *Roster of North Carolina Troops in the War Between the States*. Vol. 4. Raleigh, NC: Edwards, Broughton, 1882.
Nash, Howard P., Jr. *Stormy Petrel: The Life and Times of General Benjamin F. Butler, 1818–1893*. Rutherford, NJ: Farleigh Dickinson University Press, 1969.
Neely, Mark E., Jr. *The Last Best Hope of Earth: Abraham Lincoln and the Promise of America*. Cambridge, MA: Harvard University Press, 1993.
Newman, Harry Wright. *Maryland and the Confederacy*. Annapolis: Harry Wright Newman, 1976.
Nolan, Dick. *Benjamin Franklin Butler: The Damnedest Yankee*. Novato, CA: Presidio Press, 1991.
Oakes, James. *Slavery and Freedom: An Interpretation of the Old South*. 1990. Reprint, New York: Vintage Books, 1991.
Oates, Stephen B. *To Purge This Land with Blood: A Biography of John Brown*. 2nd ed. 1970. Reprint, Amherst: University of Massachusetts Press, 1984.
_____. *With Malice Toward None: The Life of Abraham Lincoln*. New York: New American Library, 1977.
O'Sullivan, Richard. *55th Virginia Infantry*. Lynchburg, VA: H.E. Howard, 1989.
Owens, Leslie Howard. *This Species of Property: Slave Life and Culture in the Old South*. New York: Oxford University Press, 1976.
Parramore, Thomas C. *Norfolk: The First Four Centuries*. Charlottesville: University Press of Virginia, 1994
Patrick, Rembert W. *The Fall of Richmond*. Baton Rouge: Louisiana State University Press, 1960.
Powell, William H. *List of Officers in the United States Army, 1776–1900*. New York: S.R. Hammersley, 1900.
Quarles, Benjamin. *The Negro in the Civil War*. 1953. Reprint, New York: Da Capo, 1989.
Quarstein, John V. *Hampton and Newport News in the Civil War: War Comes to the Peninsula*. Lynchburg, VA: H.E. Howard, 1998.

Raboteau, Albert J. *Slave Religion: The "Invisible Institution" in the Antebellum South.* 1978. Reprint, New York: Oxford University Press, 1980.

Reed, Rowena. *Combined Operations in the Civil War.* 1979. Reprint, Lincoln: University of Nebraska, 1983.

Regosin, Elizabeth. *Freedom's Promise: Ex-Slave Families and Citizenship in the Age of Emancipation.* Charlottesville: University Press of Virginia, 2002.

Reid, Richard M. *Freedom for Themselves: North Carolina's Black Soldiers in the Civil War Era.* Chapel Hill: University of North Carolina Press, 2008.

Renehan, Edward J., Jr. *The Secret Six: The True Tale of the Men Who Conspired with John Brown.* New York: Crown, 1995.

Richardson, Joe M. *Christian Reconstruction: The American Missionary Association and Southern Blacks, 1861–1896.* Athens: University of Georgia Press, 1986.

Robertson, William Glenn. *Back Door to Richmond: The Bermuda Hundred Campaign, April–June 1864.* Baton Rouge: Louisiana State University Press, 1987.

Rose, Willie Lee. *Rehearsal for Reconstruction: The Port Royal Experiment.* New York: Bobbs-Merrill, 1964.

_____. *Slavery and Freedom.* Edited by William H. Freehling. New York: Oxford University Press, 1982.

Schiller, Herbert M. *The Bermuda Hundred Campaign: "Operations on the South Side of the James River, Virginia, May 1864."* Dayton, OH: Morningside, 1988.

Scott, Otto J. *The Secret Six: John Brown and the Abolitionist Movement.* New York: Time Books, 1979.

Shaffer, Donald R. *After the Glory: The Struggles of Black Civil War Veterans.* Lawrence: University of Kansas Press, 2004.

Sifakis, Stewart. *Compendium of the Confederate Armies: North Carolina.* New York: Facts on File, 1992.

Simpson, Bland. *The Great Dismal: A Carolinian's Swamp Memoir.* Chapel Hill: University of North Carolina Press, 1990.

Simpson, Harold B. *Hood's Texas Brigade: Lee's Grenadier Guard.* Waco: Texian, 1970.

Sommers, Richard J. *Richmond Redeemed: The Siege at Petersburg.* Garden City, NY: Doubleday, 1981.

Speer, Lonnie R. *Portals to Hell: Military Prisons of the Civil War.* Mechanicsburg, PA: Stackpole, 1997.

Sterling, Dorothy. *The Making of an Afro-American: Martin Robison Delany, 1812–1885.* 1971. Reprint, New York: Da Capo, 1996.

Stevenson, Brenda E. *Life in Black and White: Family and Community in the Slave South.* New York: Oxford University Press, 1996.

Stick, David. *The Outer Banks of North Carolina, 1584–1958.* Chapel Hill: University of North Carolina Press, 1958.

Stuckey, Sterling. *Slave Culture: Nationalist Theory and the Foundations of Black America.* New York: Oxford University Press, 1987.

Thomas, Emory M. *The Confederate Nation, 1861–1865.* New York: Harper Torchbooks, 1979.

Thomas, Gerald W. *Divided Allegiances: Bertie County During the Civil War.* Raleigh: Division of Archives and History, North Carolina Department of Cultural Resources, 1996.

Trefousse, Hans L. *Ben Butler: The South Called Him Beast!* New York: Twayne, 1957.

Trudeau, Noah Andre. *The Last Citadel: Petersburg, Virginia, June 1864–April 1865.* Boston: Little, Brown, 1991.

_____. *Like Men of War: Black Troops in the Civil War, 1862–1865.* Boston: Little, Brown, 1998.

_____. *Out of the Storm: The End of the Civil War, April–June 1865.* Boston: Little, Brown, 1994.

Van Deburg, William L. *The Slave Driver: Black Agricultural Labor Supervisors in the Antebellum South.* Westport, CT: Greenwood, 1979.

Vinovskis, Maris A., ed. *Toward a Social History of the American Civil War: Exploratory Essays.* New York: Cambridge University Press, 1990.

Von Frank, Albert J. *The Trials of Anthony Burns: Freedom and Slavery in Emerson's Boston.* Cambridge, MA: Harvard University Press, 1998.

Wade, Richard C. *Slavery in the Cities: The South, 1820–1860.* New York: Oxford University Press, 1964.

Warner, Ezra J. *Generals in Blue: Lives of the Union Commanders.* Baton Rouge: Louisiana State University Press, 1964.

Weaver, Jeffrey C. *The Virginia Home Guards.* Lynchburg, VA: H.E. Howard, 1996.

Welcher, Frank J. *The Union Army, 1861–1865: Organization and Operations.* Vol. 1, *The Eastern Theater.* Bloomington: Indiana University Press, 1989.

Wesley, Charles H. *The Collapse of the Confederacy.* Washington, D.C.: Associated Publishers, 1937.

West, Richard S., Jr. *Lincoln's Scapegoat General: A Life of Benjamin F. Butler, 1818–1893*. New York: Houghton Mifflin, 1965.
Westwood, Howard C. *Black Troops, White Commanders, and Freedmen During the Civil War*. Carbondale: Southern Illinois University Press, 1992.
White, Deborah Gray. *Ar'n't I a Woman?: Female Slaves in the Plantation South*. 1985. Reprint, New York: W.W. Norton, 1987.
Whitelaw, Ralph T. *Virginia's Eastern Shore: A History of Northampton and Accomack Counties*. 2 vols. Gloucester, MA: Peter Smith, 1968.
Wiley, Bell Irvin. *Southern Negroes, 1861–1865*. 1938. Reprint, New Haven, CT: Yale University Press, 1964.
Wilson, Keith P. *Campfires of Freedom: The Camp Life of Black Soldiers During the Civil War*. Kent, OH: Kent State University Press, 2002.
Witt, Jerry V. *Wild in North Carolina: General Edward A. Wild's December 1863 Raid into Camden, Pasquotank, and Currituck Counties*. Springfield, VA: J.V. Witt, 1993.
Workers of the Writers' Program of the WPA of Virginia, comp. *The Negro in Virginia*. 1940. Reprint, Winston-Salem, NC: John F. Blair, 1994.
Wright, David, and David Zoby. *Fire on the Beach: Recovering the Lost Story of Richard Etheridge and the Pea Island Lifesavers*. New York: Scribner, 2000.
Wyatt-Brown, Bertram. *Lewis Tappan and the Evangelical War Against Slavery*. Cleveland, OH: Press of Case Western Reserve University, 1969.

## Theses, Dissertations, Scholarly Papers

Benson, Donna Johanna. "'Before I Be a Slave': A Social Analysis of the Black Struggle for Freedom in North Carolina, 1860–1865." Ph.D. diss., Duke University, 1984.
Bryant, II, James Kenneth. "Making 'A Model Regiment': The Soldiers of the 36th U.S. Colored Infantry and Their Contributions to the Union War Effort in the Civil War." Paper Presented at the Fourth Annual Graduate Conference in Southern History, University of Mississippi, March 20, 1999.
_____. "'A Model Regiment': The 36th U.S. Colored Infantry in the Civil War." M.A. thesis, University of Vermont, 1996.
_____. "The Model 36th Regiment: The Contribution of Black Soldiers and Their Families to the Union War Effort, 1861–1866." Ph.D. diss., University of Rochester, 2001.
_____. "'They Are Most Reliable Soldiers': The 36th U.S. Colored Infantry in the American Civil War." Paper Presented a the Frederick Douglass Institute for African and African American Studies Spring 1997 Seminar Series, Rochester, New York, February 26, 1997.
_____. "The 36th United States Colored Infantry: The Transformation from Slavery to Freedom." Paper Presented at the Conference on African Americans in the Civil War, Virginia State University, Petersburg, Virginia, May 26–28, 2005.
Forstchen, William R. "The 28th United States Colored Troops: Indiana's African-Americans Go to War, 1863–1865." Ph.D. diss., Purdue University, 1994.
Hartwig, Robert Norman. "A Recollection of Chaplain Thomas Scott Johnson of the 127th United States Colored Troops and the 36th United States Colored Troops During and After the Civil War." M.S. Seminar Paper, Wisconsin State University at La Crosse, 1970.
Johnson, Clifton Herman. "The American Missionary Association: A Study of Christian Abolitionism, 1846–1861." Ph.D. diss., University of North Carolina, 1959.
Rowland, Leslie Suzanne. "Emancipation and the Black Military Experience During the American Civil War: A Documentary History." 3 parts. Ph.D. diss., University of Rochester, 1991.
Schneider, Tracy Whittaker. "The Institution of Slavery in North Carolina, 1860–1865." Ph.D. diss., Duke University, 1979.
Shaffer, Donald Robert. "Marching On: African-American Civil War Veterans in Postbellum America, 1865–1951." Ph.D. diss., University of Maryland at College Park, 1996.

# Index

Numbers in ***bold italics*** indicate pages with photographs.

Adams, FSgt. Livian 34–35
Adkins, Sgt. Maj. Henry N. 16, 65–66, 67–68, 108, 126
African Church (Richmond, VA) 118
Albemarle Sound (NC) 32
Albertson, E.W. 18
Allen, Pvt. David H. 12, 19, 126
Allen, Capt. George F. 70–72
Allen, Capt. Hiram W. 60, 108
*American and Commercial Advertiser* (Baltimore, MD) 80, 84, 88
American Freedmen's Inquiry Commission 119
American Missionary Association (AMA) 24, 25, 69, 114, 128
Ames, Col. John W. 107
USS *Anacostia* (navy gunboat) 88
Andrew, Gov. John A. 31, 32, 33, 35, 37, 38, 63, 66, 67, 69, 72, 73
Andrews, Capt. Richard F. 74, 108, 117
Antietam Sept. 17, 1862 battle 30
Appomattox, VA 118
Appomattox River, VA 92, 102
Army Corps: 9th 115; 18th 32, 66, 75, 77, 102–103; 24th 115, 116; 25th 115, 116, 118–119, 122, 124
Army of Northern Virginia 30, 102, 105, 118
Army of the James 66, 75, 76, 89, 91, 92, 101, 102, 105, ***110***, 113, 115, 121, 122, 123, 124, 128
Army of the Potomac 19, 60, 89, 91, 95, 102, 105, 115
Arthur, Dr. Joshua P. 114
Artis, Sgt. Thomas 77–78
Ashby, Charity 12
Ashby, Leon 12
Auburn, NY 69

Backup, Capt. James B. 73–74, 108
Baker, Frank 27
Baker Farm (near Norfolk, VA) 19, 36, 119

Balch, Lt. Amory O. 60
Baldwin, Rep. John D. 72
Barnes, Brig. Gen. James N. 38, 52, 53
Barrick, Henry D. 90
Bateman, Barbery *see* Wilson, Barbery
Baxter, Pvt. Thaddeus 90
Baxter Farm (Norfolk County, VA) 119
Beals, Rev. H.S. 24–25
Beasley, Sgt. Spencer 104
Beaufort, NC (town) 33
Beaufort County, NC 16
Bell, Mr. 44
Bell, Mrs. 44
Benson, William 120
Bermuda 16
Bermuda Hundred, VA 92, 102
Bermuda Hundred Campaign, VA *see* Bermuda Hundred, VA
Berry, Pvt. David 90
Bertie County, NC 3, ***6***, 8, 10, 13, ***14***, 16, 130; *see also* Windsor, NC
Bicknell, Capt. Francis A. 60, 77–78, 108, 116
Bird, Francis W. 119
Birney, Maj. Gen. David B. 105
Birney, Brig. Gen. William 89
Bishop, Billy 10
Bishop, Isaac 10
Blackwater, VA 15
Blango, Pvt. Abram (Abraham) 110
Blango, Cpl. John 11, 109
Blango, Pvt. Thomas 11, 109
Bly, Lt. Charles F. 65
Boston, MA 60, 62, 65, 74, 117
Boston Education Commission 43
*Boston Globe* 116
Bradbury, Capt. George 68
Branham, Lucy A. 97
Brattleboro, VT 61
Braxton, Capt. John S. 97–98
Bray, Pvt. Albert 105
Brazos Santiago, TX 67, 119, ***122***, 123, 124, 130

Breckinridge, John C. 26
Brigham, Charles D. (*New York Tribune* news correspondent) 27
Bright, Daniel 48, 54, 55
Brock, Sarah *see* James, Sarah
Brookline, MA 32
Brown, Ann Maria 13
Brown, John 13, 20, 22, 31, 69, 95, 117, 118, ***128***, 129
Brown, Pvt. John A. 16
Brown, Pvt. Moses 13, 16
Brown, Capt. Orlando 120
Brown, William Wells 5
Brownsville, TX ***123***
Buck, Cpl. John 12, 17, 104
Bufort, Cpl. John 111
Bufort, Mariah Ferebee 119
Bureau of Freedmen, Refugees and Abandoned Lands *see* Freedmen's Bureau
Bureau of Negro Affairs 47, 121, 125
Bureau of Pensions 4
Burley, Act. Mast. Bennett G. 91
Burnside, Maj. Gen. Ambrose E. 30, 32, 59
Burroughs, Maj. Edgar 41, 42–43, 47
Burroughs, Pvt. Wilson 110
Butler, Maj. Gen. Benjamin F. 26–29, 38, 40, 46, 47, 53–55, 56, 58, 64, 66–67, 69, 70, 71, 72, 73, 74, 75–76, 79, 81, 83, 84, 88, 89, 90, 91–92, 101–102, 104, 105, 106, 109, 110, 115, 118, 119, 120, 121, 123, 127–128

Caffee, Capt. John T. 41, 42, 43, 50
Caffrey, Solomon W. 44–45
Cambridge, MA 65, 114
Camden, NJ 16
Camden County, NC 17, 20, 42, 48, 49, ***50***, 57
Camden Courthouse, NC *see* Camden County, NC
Camp Hamilton, VA 4
Cannon, Mary 15

243

# Index

Cape Hatteras, NC 13, 29–30
Cary, Maj. John B. 27
Casey, Maj. Gen. Silas 87, 122
Chaffin's Farm, VA 105
Chambersburg, PA 16
Charley (escaped slave) 20–21
Chase, Lucy 43
Chase, Secy. Salmon P. 28
Chase, Sarah 43
Cherry, Pvt. Noah C. 13
Chesapeake Bay 4, 21, 81
Chester, Thomas Morris 5, 69, 75, 76–77, 103, 105, 106, 107–108, *110*, 115, 116, 118, 130
Chowan County, NC 20, 48
Chowan River, NC 48, 54
*Christian Recorder see* Williams, Joseph E.
Church, Joseph 21
City Point, VA 10, 12, 19, 92, 102, 122
Cock, Capt. George B. 49
Collins, Pvt. Anthony 14
USS *Commodore* (navy gunboat) 95
*Commodore Foote* (U.S. army transport) 90
Conant, Lt. George W. S. 51–52, 60, 74, 125
Confederate House of Representatives 55
Confiscation Act: Aug. 6, 1861 29, 30; July 17, 1862 30, 35
Congressional Committee on the Conduct of the War 118
Congressional Medal of Honor 7, 87, *109*, 113, 126
Conine, Col. James W. 47, 79
Connecticut Units: 8th Infantry 53; 29th Infantry 67, 117
Cooper, Pvt. Allen 11, 113
Cooper, Elizabeth 11
Cooper, Lucy 11
Cooper, Richard G. 11
Cooper, Pvt. Romulous 11
"copperhead" 53, 114, 120–121
Cornick, Betsy 13
Cornick, Pvt. Frank 11, 12–13, 125
Cornick, Pvt. Henry 13, 108
Cornick, Horatio 15
Cornick, Pvt. James 11, 13, 108, 125–126
Cornick, Pvt. John 11–12, 13, 15 I
Cornick, Mary 15, 125
Cornick, Pvt. Peter 11, 125
Cornick, Sgt. Smith 84
Cornick, Victoria Broward 13
Courtney, Lt. Daniel J. 65
Courtney, Lt. Eugene J. 65
Crab's Island, NC 49
Craven County, NC 16
Crimean War 31
Critcher, John 15
Croft, Capt. James N. 53, 54

Croft, Mrs. 53, 54
Crutchfield, Ms. 42
Cullen, Col. Edgar M. 52
Currituck County, NC 11, 12, 16, 17, 18, 19, 20, 37, 42, 48, 49, 51, 130
Currituck Court House, NC *see* Currituck County, NC

Danvers, MA 59, *62*
Davis, Confed. Pres. Jefferson 26, 56, 97, 118, 123
Davis, FSgt. William 57–58, 108
Deep Bottom. VA 10, 75, 103, 105, 110
Deep Creek Village, VA 47
DeForest *see* Simmons, Lt. Samuel S.
Denney, Lt. Jeremiah C. 92, 93
Department of Richmond *see* Richmond, VA (city)
Department of Virginia and North Carolina 32, 34, 40, 67, 72, 81, 101
Department of Washington *see* Washington, D.C.
Dickson, Pvt. Isaiah *see* Dixon, Pvt. Isaiah
Dismal Swamp 20–21, 24, 47, 55
Dismal Swamp Canal 47
District of North Carolina 33
District of St. Mary's, MD 70, 88, 90, 91, 92, 96; *see also* Point Lookout, MD
District of Virginia 34, 38, 52
Dixon, Pvt. Isaiah 17
Dough, Rachel 16
Douglass, Frederick 7, 13, 21, 22
Draper, Capt. Algernon 74, 110, 124
Draper, Col. Alonzo G. 1, 3, 24, 33–38, 40–44, 46–54, 55–56, 61–65, 66, 68, 69–71, 72–74, 75–77, 79, 81, 84, 85–86, 87–88, 90–91, 92–95, 96, 97, 98–100, 101, 102, 103, 104, 105, 106, 107, 108, 109, 110, 111, 113, 115–118, 120, 121, 123–124, 128, 132–133
*Dred: A Tale of the Dismal Swamp* 21
Du Bois, Dr. W.E.B. 18, *109*, 129
Duncan, Col. Samuel A. 102, 105, 106, 107
Duplin County, NC 16
Durettsville, VA 92, 93
Dutch Gap Canal *104*, 110
Dyer, Judith M. 45

Early, Maj. Gen. Jubal A. 96
Eastman, Lt. Cmdr. Thomas H. 88, 98
Ebbs, Capt. John 43, 44, 45
Edwards, Mrs. 39, 44

Elizabeth City, NC 12, 20, 47, 48, *50*, 53, 55
Emancipation Proclamation 30, 31, 40, 43, 47, 60, 67, 89; preliminary 30
English High School (Boston, MA) 62
Epps, Dr. 12
Essex County, VA 95, 96, 130
Etheridge, John B. 16
Etheridge, CommSgt. Richard 16, 120, 129
Ewell, Lt. Gen. Richard S. 98

Fahrion, Capt. Gustave 46
Fair Oaks: 1862 battle 60; 1864 battle 111
Farrier, Pvt. Anson 16
*Favorite* (U.S. army transport) 92
Ferebee, Pvt. George 16
Ferebee, Pvt. March 16
Field, Lt. Henry M. 72, 74
Field, Assoc. Jus. Stephen D. 72
Fisher, Hosp. Stwd. John B. 114
Fleetwood, Sgt. Maj. Christian A. 6
Fletcher, Capt. John W. 41, 72
Foreman, Sgt. Bristow 18
Forrest, Lt. Gen. Nathan Bedford 105
Fort Albany, VA 63
Fort Craig, VA 63
Fort Delaware, DE 82
Fort Monroe, VA 10, 17, 18, 19, 26, 27, *28*, *29*, 32, 33, 34, 38, 47, 49, 56, 70, 71, 80, 83, 89, 102, 113, 114, 122, 129
Fort Pillow, TN 100, 105
Fort Sumter, SC 6, 15, 26
Fortress Monroe, VA *see* Fort Monroe, VA
Foster, Capt. Daniel 44
Foster, Maj. Gen. John G. 32, 34–35, 36, 37, 38
Four Mile Creek, VA 107
Franklin, VA 54
Franklin County, NC 12
Fredericksburg, VA: Dec. 13, 1862 battle 39, 60, *61*
Fredericksburg National Cemetery 1, 2, 3, *6*, 130
Freedmen's Bureau 120
Frémont, Maj. Gen. John C. 26
Frost, Cpl. Robert 18
Frye, Capt. Charles H. 39, 44, 48, 60, 75, 90
USS *Fuchsia* (navy gunboat) 88, 90
Fugitive Slave Act of 1850 26, 27, 62
Furby, Pvt. Erastus 17
Furby, FSgt. Peter 18

G, Mrs. 97
Gallop, Ann 11, 15

# Index

Gallop, Eliza 11
Gallop, George 11, 15
Gallop, Hodges 11, 19
Gallop, Cpl. James 11, 130
Gallop, Mabel 11
Gallop, Pvt. Malachi 11, 19, 113
Gallop, Nancy 11
Gallop, Richard 11
Gallop, Spencer 11, 13, 19
Gardner, Sgt. James 108, *109*
Garland, R.C. 90
Gaskill, Capt. Edwin C. 61, 78, 86, 108
Gaskill, Lt. Leonard T. 44, 61, 72
Gates County, NC 15, 19, 20, 48, 119
Gatesville, NC 10
Gaylord, Pvt. Simon 17
General Orders No. 46 47, 119, 120, 128
George, Pvt. 98
*Georgia* (U.S. army transport) 92
Georgia Units (Confederate): 62nd Cavalry 55
Germany 57
Getty, Brig. Gen. George W. 53
Gibbs, Capt. 93
Gilchrist, Sgt. Samuel 105, 108
Glencoe Plantation *see* Wallace, Elizabeth C.
Gordon, Pvt. Harrison 13
Gornto, James 12
Gornto, John 12
Gould, Alonzo (Lorenzo) 66
Grandy, Capt. Cyrus 17
Grandy, Mrs. Patsey 17
Grant, Lt. Gen. Ulysses 91–92, 96, 102, 105, 115, 119
Gray, FSgt. Jeremiah 108
Great Bridge, VA 47, 52
Great Dismal Swamp *see* Dismal Swamp
Greeley, Horace 117
Green, Pvt. John 82–83
Green, Cpl. Solon 17
Greenville, NC 86
Gregory, Cpl. Alexander 78
Gregory, Major 49, 55
Griffin, Col. Joel R. 54–55
Griffin, Prin. Musc. Larry 84
Griggs, Lt. Charles D. 60
Gulf of Mexico 122
Guy, Pvt. Samuel 16

Halifax, NC 58
Hall, Cpl. James E. 82
Halleck, Maj. Gen. Henry W. 115, 118–119
Hamilton, NC 16
Hampton, Lt. Gen. Wade 95
Hampton, VA 17, 19, 27, 28, 33, 49, 68, 126
Hapgood, Col. Charles E. 86
Harpers Ferry, VA (now WV) 22, 31, 69, ***128***

Harris, Pvt. Frederick Henry *see* Henry, Pvt. Frederick
Harrisburg, PA 25, 66, 76
Hart, Lt. Col. William H. 66, 74–75, 86, 92, 93, 94, 108, 115, 117, 121, 130
Hathaway, Lt. Stephen F. 77, 117, 123
Hatlinger, Capt. Joseph J. 24, 75, 93–94
Hatteras Island, NC *see* Cape Hatteras, NC
Hawley, MA 68, ***128***
Healy, Mary 44
Henderson, David H.A. *see* Allen, Pvt. David H.
Henderson, Hattie Brooks 126
Hendrick, Maj. Oren A. 44–45
Henry, Pvt. Frederick 12, 125
Hertford County, NC 11
Higginson, Col. Thomas W. 31, 58, 69, ***128***
Hinks, Brig. Gen. Edward W. 70, 71, 88, 89, 124
Hinton, Col. James W. 55
Hinton's Crossroads, NC 48
Hintonsville, NC 54
Hodges, Mr. 44
Hoffman, Col. William 83, 85, 87
Holman, Col. John H. 47, 48, 105, 107, 111
Holloway, Sgt. Miles 85, 87
Holly, Pvt. Silas 77–78
Holt, JAG Joseph 74
Hooker, Lt. Edward N. 90, 92, 93, 96, 98, 99
Howarrd, Maj. Gen. Oliver O. 120
Hungary 75
Hunter, Maj. Gen. David 26
Hunter, Robert M.T. 95

Indianola, TX 124
Indiantown, NC 49
Isle of Wight County, VA 20
Ives, Capt. George W. 70

James, Ella Francis 15, 126
James, Pvt. Frank 120
James, Capt. Horace 120, 121, 125
James, John 15, 126
James, Sgt. Miles 15, 87, 108, 109, 113, 126
James, Sarah 15, 126
James City, NC 125
James River 102, ***104***, 105
Jaycox, Celia 12
Jaycox, Sgt. Cicero 12
Jaycox, Hannah 19
Jaycox, Pvt. Henry 12
Jaycox, Jesse C. 12, 19
Jaycox, Jonathan 12
Jaycox, Madison 19
Jaycox, Richard 12

Jaycox, Cpl. Sawney 12, 19
Jaycox, Sgt. Thomas 12, 109–110
Jefferson Medical College, PA ***112***, 114
"John Brown's Body" *see* Brown, John
Johnson, Pvt. James H. 15
Johnson, Pvt. James T. 17
Johnson, Jerome 34
Johnson, Susan 15
Johnson, Rev. Thomas S. 67
Johnson, Pvt. William 99–100
Johnston, Capt. George H. 34, 36
Jones, Capt. Charles A. 3–4, 47
Jones, Pvt. William 85–86, 87
Jordan, Pvt. Samuel 54
Jordan's Farm, VA 99

Kellum, Isaac 12
Kellum, Samuel 12
Kempsville, VA 47
Kennansville, NC 16
Kentucky Units (Confederate): 10th Cavalry 83
Killarney, Ireland 65
Kilpatrick, Brig. Gen. Judson H. 93
King and Queen County, VA 96
Kinsley, Capt. Benjamin F. 44, 130
Knott's Island, NC 49, 50, 51, 54

Lampson, Dr. Mortimer 77, 114
Lancaster County, VA 96
Layton's Wharf, VA 93, 95
Ledlie, Brig. Gen. James H. 52, 53
Lee, Edward 11
Lee, Pvt. Henry 93
Lee, Pvt. John 11, 19
Lee, Gen. Robert E. 5, 30, 32, 88, 91, 96–97, 102, 116
Lewis, Lt. Col. Meriwether 94, 98
Lincoln, Pres. Abraham 2, 5, 25–26, 27, 28, 29, 30, 32, 40, 60, 67, 72, 74, 83, 114, 115, 118, 128
Lipscomb, Anna *see* Wilson, Anna
Lisk, Pvt. Mark 85–87
Lloyds Landing, VA 95
*Long Branch* (U.S. army transport) 80, 88, 92
Longfellow, Henry Wadsworth *see* "The Slave in the Dismal Swamp"
Longley, Lt. Joseph G. 49, 68–69, 70, 128
Lowell, MA 102, 119
Lynn, MA ***37***, 62, 63, 64, 76, 77, 93, 117, 124
Lynn Mechanics Association 63
*Lynn Weekly Reporter* 63, 124

## Index

Mace (slave boy) 61
Maddox, Joseph H. 88, 89
Maine Units: 14th Infantry 75
Mallory, Col. Charles K. 27–28
Mallory, Shepard 27
Mansur, Lt. John S. *123*
Marston, Brig. Gen. Gilman 81, 82, 83, 88
Martin County, NC 16, 17
Massachusetts Units: 1st Infantry *31*, 60; 2nd Cavalry 60; 4th Cavalry 74, 77; 5th Cavalry 67, 102, 117, 118; 14th Infantry (1st Heavy Artillery) 63, 69, 70, 93; 24th Infantry 70; 25th Infantry 59, 61, 70–71, 72, *73*; 34th Infantry 70; 35th Infantry *31*, 32, 57, 59, 60–*61*, *62*, 72; 39th Infantry 114; 43rd Infantry *41*, 72; 51st Infantry 68, *128*; 54th Infantry 31, 32, 67; 55th Infantry 31, 32, 33, 47, *50*, 63, 67
Matamoras, Mex. 123
Mathews Court House, VA 91
Maxwell, Act. Mast. John 91
McClellan, Maj. Gen. George B. 114
McIntosh, Dr. 49
McSweeney, Dr. Miles 45–46
Meade, Maj. Gen. George G. 89, 91, 102
Mendon, MA 61
Messner, Pvt. Andrew 17
Messner, Mrs. 45–46
Middlesex County, VA 90, 96
Milford Haven, VA 91
Miller, Capt. Henry H.F. 34, 36, 57–58, 75, 86, 116
Mitchell, Dr. Henry H. 112, 114
Mobile, AL 123
Montross, VA 92
Moore, Pvt. Riley 16
Mordecai, Emma 117–118
Morgan, Brig. Gen. John Hunt 83
Mosby, Lt. Col. John S. 96, 97
Moseley, Pvt. Rigdon 16
Mosley, Pvt. Rigdon *see* Moseley, Pvt. Rigdon
Mullen, Pvt. Joseph 49
Murfreesboro, NC 11

Naglee, Brig. Gen. Henry M. 34, 35, 36, 38
Nansemond County, VA 16
Nepean, Henry E. *see* Adkins, Sgt. Maj. Henry N.
Nepean, Margaret Berry 126
New Bern, NC 1, 4, 24, 25, 30, 32, 33, 34, 35, *37*, 59, 61, 71, 125
New Castle, ME 16
*New England Mechanic* 63

New Hampshire Units 2nd Infantry 83, 84; 5th Infantry 75, 82, 86
New Market Heights (1864 battle) 5, 10, 58, 75, 105–111, 113, 114, 125
New Orleans, LA *29*, 30, 40, 58, 75, 123, 124
New York City, NY 16, 126
*New York Times see* "Tewksbury"
*New York Tribune* 27, 46, 76, 117; *see also* Brigham, Charles D.
New York Units: 3rd Cavalry 43, 46; 7th Battery 47; 17th Infantry 63; 24th Battery 70; 81st Infantry 51; 96th Infantry 52; 98th Infantry 39, 43, 46, 51, 52, 53, 73
Newberne, Pvt. Andrew 103
Newport, Wales 65
Newport News, VA 19, 28, 68
Newtown (King and Queen County, VA) 05
Norfleet, Aggie 10
Norfleet, Jennie 10
Norfleet, Pvt. Saunders 10–11, *14*
Norfleet, Stephen A. 10, *14*
Norfolk, VA 4, 10, 14, 15, 17, 19, 20, 27, 32, 33, 34, 36, 38, 39, 40, 41, 42, 43, 45, 46, 47, 48, 49, 50, 52, 53, 54, 55, 56, 69, 119, 122, 125, 126
Norfolk County, VA 11, 16, 17, 18, 20, 37, 119, 125
North, Lt. James N. 34
North Carolina Units (Confederate): 4th Cavalry 84; 8th Infantry 57; 68th Infantry 41–42, 55
North Weymouth, MA 59, *61*
Northumberland County, VA 97, 98
Northwest Landing, VA 47, 51
Northwest River, VA 51

Oakes, Capt. Benjamin F. 33, 74
Oberlin College, OH 68, *128*
O'Brien, Lt. John 75–76, 93
Occupacia Creek, VA 92
Olmsted, Frederick Law 21
Onslow County, NC 34
Ord, Maj. Gen. Edward O.C. 103, 105, 109, 115, 118
Otis High School 62
Outer Banks, NC 16, 129
Owen, Capt. John, Jr. 65, 82, 103, 110, 114, 122

Paine, Brig. Gen. Charles J. 66, 75, 76, 102, 103, 105, 107, 109, 111
Palmer, Brig. Gen. Innis N. 33

Parker, Lt. Aaron 35–36
Parker, Addie *see* Norfleet, Aggie
Parker, Pvt. Daniel 16
Parker, Cmdr. Foxhall A., Jr. 96, 98
Parker, Joseph 10
Pasquotank County, NC 16, 18, 20, 42, 48, 54, 55
Pasquotank River, NC 48
Patuxent River, MD 89, 90, 91, 92, 95
Peck, Maj. Gen. John L. 33–34
Pendergrast, Comm. Garrett J. 27
Pennsylvania Units: 5th Cavalry 47; 11th Cavalry 47
Perquimans County, NC 11, 12, 19, 20, 48
Petersburg, VA 12, 66, 69, 75, 76, 77, 79, 83, 92, 96, 99, 101, 102, 103, *110*, 113, 115, 116, 118, 128, 130
Philadelphia, PA 75, *112*, 114
*Philadelphia Press see* Chester, Thomas Morris
Phillips, Capt. Sidney W. 24
Phillips, Wendell 28
"Physic" (news correspondent) 80, 83, 84, 88, 91, 92, 93, 94; *see also American and Commercial Advertiser*
Pea Island, NC 16
Piankatank River, VA 90, 91
Pierce, Edward L. 28, 129
Pierson's Farm, VA 3, 4, 94, 95, 98, 130
Piney Point, MD 87
Pitt County, NC 19
Plymouth, NC 3, 25, 33, 100
Point Lookout, MD 4, 10, 61, 64, 66, 70, 75, 76, 77, 80–81, *82*, 83, 85, 89, 91, 92, 93, 95, 96, 98, 102, 104, 110, 113, 118, 124, 127; *see also* District of St. Mary's, MD
Point-of-Rocks, VA 113
Pool, Pvt. George E. 16
Pool, Dr. William E. 48
Poore, Benjamin Perley 116
Pope's Creek. VA 88, 92
Port Royal, SC *see* Port Royal Experiment
Port Royal Experiment 31, 129
Porter, R. Adm. David D. 115
Portsmouth, VA 4, 10, 17, 32, 33, 34, 38, 39, 40, 42, 43, 47, 49, 52, 55, 57, 68, 104, 125
Potomac Flotilla 85, 88, 90, 95, 96, 98
Pratt, Lt. Col. Benjamin F. 47, 59, 60, *61*, 62, 67–68, 72–73, 74–76, 77, 84, 103, 104, 108, 115, 117, 121
Pratt, Sgt. Smith 113

Preston, Maj. Daniel J. 59, *62*, 72–73, 74, 121
Preston, Pvt. John 49
Price, Betsey 119
Price, Sgt. Sylvester 90, 119
Princess Anne County, VA 11, 13, 15, 18, 20, 37, 39, 40, 41, 43, 46, 47, 50, 51, 53, 76, **100**
Princess Anne Court House, VA *see* Princess Anne County, VA
Proctor, Capt. George B. 72, *73*, 74, 98
Pungo Point Bridge, VA 44, 51, 52, 53, 54, 74
Pungo Rangers 41, 50

Rappahannock River, VA 90, 92, 93, 97
Red Bank, NJ 126
Redpath, James 20–21
USS *Resolute* (navy gunboat) 88
Rhoades, Lt. Frank W. 60
Rhode Island Units 4th Infantry 93; 5th Infantry 75
Rice, Dr. N.P. 36–37
Richmond, Pvt. Richard (Dick) 84
Richmond, VA (city) 5, 10, 18, 40, 58, *61*, 66, 76, 91, 92, 101, 102, *104*, 105–106, 109, *110*, 113, 115–116, 117, 118, 125, 128, 130
Richmond County, VA 3, 4, *6*, 12, 13, 92, 96, 97, 98, 127, 130
*Richmond Daily Enquirer* 55, 89, 97, 117, 127
Ripley, Brig. Gen. Edward 116, 117
Roanoke Island, NC 16, 18, 19, 25, 30, 32–33, 34, 48, 49, 54, 56, 61, 120
Robinson, Lt. José A.A. 78
Roby, Pvt. Edward 78
Rock, Lt. William H. 76, 117
Rockwell, Seth 13
"Rollin" (*Philadelphia Inquirer* news correspondent) *see* Chester, Thomas Morris

Salem, MA 39
Samuel, Pvt. James H. 13
Sanders (Saunders), Pvt. Braxton 34
Sandy Hook, NC 49
Sarr, Pvt. Joseph 49
Sawyer, Caleb T. 11
"Scout" (*Richmond Daily Enquirer* news correspondent) 89
Seagrave, Lt. George L. 72
Seddon, Secy. James A. 96, 97
Shaffer, Col. J. Wilson 55, 102
Shaw, Col. Henry M. 57
Shaw, Mrs. Henry M. 57, 58
Shaw, Col. Robert G. 32, 60
Sheppard, FSgt. Miles 49, 78, 108

Sheridan, Maj. Gen. Phillip H. 95, 119
Shiloh, NC 49
Shurtleff, Lt. Col. Giles W. 79, 108
Simmons, Edmund 18
Simmons, Lt. Samuel S. 75
"The Slave in the Dismal Swamp" 21
Smith, Andrew 44
Smith, Frank 84
Smith, Mayor Jerome Van Crowninshield 62
Smith, Capt. John M. 49
Smithfield, VA 17
Sons of Temperance 62, 70
South Mills, NC 47, 49, 54
South Mountain, MD: Sept 14, 1862 battle 32, 60, *61*
Southampton County, VA 20
Stanton, Secy. Edwin M. 30, 32, 34, 54, 67, 92, 118–119, 120
*Star* (U.S. army transport) 90
Stearns, George L. 31, 32, 33
Stevens, Rev. David 25, 66–67, 115, 118
Stevens, Pvt. John W. 80, 83
Stewart, John 16
Stingray Point, VA 90, 91
Stockton, Dr. James C. 113, 114
Stowe, Harriet Beecher *see Dred: A Tale of the Dismal Swamp*
Street, Act. Mast. William Tell 90, 92, 95, 96
Streeter, Mr. Holland 120, 121
Strong, George Templeton 117
Suffolk, VA 17
Sumner, Sen. Charles 28
Sussden, William 17

Tallmadge, Capt. Grier 27
Tannatt, Col. Thomas R. 64, 66
Tappahannock, VA 92, 95, 97
Taylor, R.C. 90
Taylor, Pvt. Zachariah 15
USS *Teaser* (navy gunboat) 88
Tennessee Units (Confederate): 60th Infantry 85
"Tewksbury" (*New York Times* news correspondent) 46, 48, 51, 56, 76
Texas Brigade 5, 105, 109, 116
Texas Units (Confederate): 1st Infantry 107, 109
Thomas, Lt. Col. C.W. 34
Thomas, Brig. Gen. Lorenzo 120
Thomas, Robert 35
Thomas Farm (Patuxent River, MD) 89
Thorburn, Lt. Henry N. *122*
Thoroughgood, Pvt. Paul 84
Thurlow, Lt. Isaac W. 108
USS *Titan* 91
Titcomb, Lt. William M. 60, 86–87

Townsend, Lt. Edward 72
Townsend, James 27
Tubman, Harriet 7
Tyler, Pres. John 14

Union Wharf, VA 93, 94, 95, 98
United States Colored Troops (USCT) 3, *104*, 119; Bureau of 67–68; 1st Cavalry 12; 1st Infantry 47, 48, 49, *50*, 105; 4th Infantry 102; 5th Infantry 46, 47, 48, 49, *50*, 54, 69, 79, 105, 108, 115; 6th Infantry 105, 107; 7th Infantry 128–129; 8th Infantry 122; 9th Infantry *122*, *123*, 128–129; 10th Infantry 38; 22nd Infantry 105, 107, 111, 116, 122; 23rd Infantry 99, *100*; 28th Infantry 99; 33rd Infantry (1st South Carolina Colored Volunteers) 31, 58, 69; 35th Infantry (1st North Carolina Colored Volunteers) 1, 3, 32, 33, 34, 38, 47, 48, *50*, 125; 37th Infantry (3rd North Carolina Colored Volunteers) 1, 32, 38, 44, 65, 105, 111, 115; 38th Infantry 79, 103, 105, 116; 127th Infantry 67
United States Units: 2nd Cavalry 92; 5th Cavalry 92; 25th Infantry 124; 39th Infantry 124; 40th Infantry 124
*Up from Slavery see* Washington, Booker T.

Virginia Units (Confederate): 2nd Cavalry 85; 9th Cavalry 94, 97, 98; 15th Cavalry 41; 15th Militia 27; 24th Cavalry 107; 31st Infantry 82

Wakefield Plantation, VA 88
Walke, Mrs. Betsey 17
Wall, Capt. Joseph 75
Wallace, Elizabeth C. 18, 47
Ward, Col. John E. 53
Warsaw, VA 12, 92, 98
*Washington* (U.S. army transport) 80
Washington, Booker T. 13
Washington, Pres. George 88
Washington, D.C. 27, 30, 36, 53, 63, 66, 72, 81, 83, 87, 91, 102, 113, 115, 116
Washington, NC (town) 16, 17, 19, 33, 56
Watts, Pvt. William 17
Wead, Lt. Col. Frederick F. 39, 43–44, 46, 51–54, 73–74
Weitzel, Maj. Gen. Godfrey 68, 111, 115, 116, 117, 118
Wesley, Pvt. John W. 78
Westborough, MA 68

# Index

*Western Metropolis* (U.S. army transport) 122
Westmoreland County, VA 88, 89, 92, 96, 97–98, *100*
Weymouth, Maj. H. George O. 86, 89
Wheadbee, H.B. 11
Wheadbee, Sgt. Hannibal *see* Whitby, Sgt. Hannibal
Whitby, Sgt. Hannibal 11, 19
White, FSgt. Caleb 50, 52
White, Lt. Henry 50, 52
White, Nancy 50, 51, 52, 53, 54, 73, 74
White, Susan 50
White Oak Swamp, VA: June 30, 1862 battle 32
Wiggins, Adeline 19
Wiggins, Pvt. Allen 84
Wiggins, Augustine 119
Wiggins, Lucy 15, 19, 36, 119

Wiggins, Mary 119
Wiggins, Pvt. Paul 15, 19, 36, 104
Wild, Brig. Gen. Edward A. 1, 7, 26, 29, *31*–33, 34, 35, 37–38, 40, 41, 46, 47, 48–*50*, 51, 52, 53–55, 57, 59, 60, 61, 64–65, 66, 67, 68, 69, 70, 71, 72, 73, 75, 77, 102, 108, 115, 116, 121, 128
Wild, Dr. Theodore 114
Wild, Capt. Walter H. 60, 75
Wilder, Capt. Charles B. 18
Williams, Betsey 119
Williams, Pvt. Charles H. 16
Williams, George Washington 6
Williams, Cpl. Granville 84
Williams, Cpl. Irving 84, 86
Williams, Joseph E. 32–33
Williams, Pvt. Thomas 119
Williamsburg, VA 28

Wilmington, NC 115, *128*
Wilson, Anna 4, 5
Wilson, Barbery 3, 4, 5
Wilson, Joseph T. 6
Wilson, Pvt. Peter 1, 2, 3–*6*, 8, 93, 94, 95, 130
Wilson, Phyllis 5
Wilson, Dr. Turner 3
Wilson's Wharf 102
Windsor, NC 3, 12
Winston, Judge Patrick Henry 3
Wise, Brig. Gen. Henry A. 41
Wistar, Brig. Gen. Isaac J. 35–36
Worcester, MA 43, 70–71

USS *Yankee* (navy gunboat) 88, 90
Yorktown, VA 28, 33, 35, 36
Young, Sgt. Edwin 83–84